A SUMMARY OF THE
LITERATURES OF
MODERN EUROPE

A SUMMARY OF THE LITERATURES OF MODERN EUROPE

(ENGLAND, FRANCE, GERMANY, ITALY, SPAIN)

FROM THE ORIGINS TO 1400

COMPILED AND ARRANGED BY

MARIAN EDWARDES

LONDON: J. M. DENT & CO.

NEW YORK: E. P. DUTTON & CO.

1907

KRAUS REPRINT CO.
Millwood, N.Y.
1977

This work was originally catalogued by the Library of
Congress as follows:

Edwardes, Marian, *comp.*
   A summary of the literatures of modern Europe (England,
France, Germany, Italy, Spain) from the origins to 1400,
comp. and arranged by Marian Edwardes. London, J.M. Dent
& co., 1907.

   xvi, 532 p. 21 cm.

   1. Literature, Medieval—Hist. & crit.

PN671.E4   7—20970

ISBN 0-527-26400-8

KRAUS REPRINT CO.
A U.S. Division of Kraus-Thomson Organization Limited

Printed in U.S.A.

INTRODUCTORY NOTE

To the wayfarer through an unfamiliar country there is no more welcome sight than a sign-post. The present work aims at nothing beyond fulfilling the office of a sign-post to the inexperienced traveller along the roads and by-ways of literature. It is intended to lighten as far as possible the preliminary labour that has to be gone through before the real business of literature may be said to begin, and to that end solely it has been prepared. It seemed possible to the compiler to save much waste of time and trouble to students by providing a serviceable outline on which to base a further study of the literatures dealt with in this volume; but, it need hardly be said, within the limits of the forthcoming pages an outline alone was possible. To glance through the table of contents of a number or two of "Romania," or any kindred journal, is sufficient to become aware how great is the mass of literature which has gathered round the vernacular writings of the west of Europe. It will be further understood that only an indication could be given of the various theories connected with the chief points of controversy. Finally, the bibliography is select rather than exhaustive, but this can be pretty fully completed with the help of the books given under the heading of "General

Authorities " and of those mentioned under the separate works. The working value and service of a book of this kind can only be tested by those who use it. If this compilation should in any measure help those who need map, or landmark, in starting their literary studies, it will have well carried out its intent. And even if it does not wholly fulfil the design with which it was arranged, it may serve to clear the way for some future work which will more fully accomplish this purpose.

M. E.

MSS. IN ENGLISH LIBRARIES, Etc.

BRITISH MUSEUM—
Additional.
Arundel.
Cotton (Jul., Cal., Vesp.,
etc.).
Egerton.
Harley.
Lansdowne.
Sloane.
Stowe.
Royal (Reg.).

BODLEIAN—
Ashmole.
Bodley.
Digby.
Douce.
Fairfax.
Junius.
Laud.
Selden.
Tanner.
Vernon.

Phillipps MSS.—At Thirlestaine House, Cheltenham.

Ashburnham MSS.—Now dispersed.

Textus Roffensis.—MSS. belonging to the Collection of Charters, Anglo-Saxon and Anglo-Norman Laws, Records of Archbishops and Bishops of England, collected by Ernulf of Beauvais, Bishop of Rochester (1040–1124) preserved at Rochester.

N.B.—Reference to injury or destruction by fire.—In 1731 the Cotton Collection was seriously damaged and in part destroyed by a fire at Ashburnham House where the MSS. were at that time lodged.

ABBREVIATIONS.

C.C.C.C.—Cambridge, Corpus Christi College.

E.E.T.S.—Early English Text Society, founded by Dr. F. J. Furnivall, 1864.

Saxon and Middle English Texts are published in the "Albion" Series, ed. by Professors Bright and Kittredge (Ginn) and in the "Belles Lettres" Series, ed. by Prof. G. M. Brown (Heath).

Dict. Nat. Bio.—Dictionary of National Biography, ed. by Leslie Stephen & Sidney Lee, 1885, etc.

Works marked * are published in the Rolls Series: "Rerum Britannicarum Medii Aevi Scriptores," or, "Chronicles and Memorials of Great Britain and Ireland."

TABLE OF CONTENTS

ENGLAND.

ix

FRANCE.

VIIITH TO XTH CENTURY.

XITH CENTURY.

XIITH CENTURY.

GERMANY.

IXTH CENTURY.

XTH CENTURY.

XITH CENTURY.

XIITH AND XIIITH CENTURY.

SPAIN.

ENGLAND

PERIODS OF LITERATURE

DIVISION ACCORDING TO KÖRTING
(*Grundrisz der Geschichte der Englischen Literatur*).

ANGLO-SAXON, OR OLD ENGLISH,
FROM THE ORIGINS TO CIR. MIDDLE 11TH CENTURY (1066).

TRANSITIONAL, OR EARLY MIDDLE ENGLISH,
FROM THE CONQUEST TO CIR. MIDDLE 13TH CENTURY.

MIDDLE ENGLISH,
CIR. MIDDLE 13TH CENTURY TO CIR. MIDDLE 14TH.

LATE MIDDLE ENGLISH,
CIR. MIDDLE 14TH TO CIR. BEGINNING OF 16TH CENTURY.

ANOTHER DIVISION
(See Hadley & Kittredge, *Introd. to Webster's Internat. Dict.*).

ANGLO-SAXON,
PERIOD OF FULL INFLEXION, 450–1150.

SEMI-SAXON,
INFLEXION IN GREAT MEASURE RETAINED, 1150–1250.

OLD ENGLISH,
INFLEXION TO A GREAT EXTENT DISCARDED, 1250–1350.

MIDDLE ENGLISH,
1350–1550.

LIST OF GENERAL AUTHORITIES.

G. Körting, "Grundrisz der Geschichte der Eng. Litteratur," 4th ed., 1905; Paul, "Grundrisz der Germanischen Philologie" (Eng. section, Ten Brink and Brandl), Bd. ii. Abth. i.; H. Morley, "First Sketch of Eng. Literature," 1886, 1901; "English Writers," 1887, 1888; Ten Brink, "Geschichte der Eng. Litteratur," 1873, 1893; 2nd. ed., vol. i., Brandl, 1899; Eng. trans., Kennedy (vol. i.); Clarke Robinson (vol. ii.), 1883, 1893; Kögel, "Geschichte der deutschen Litteratur bis zum Ausgange des Mittelalters," 1894, etc.; Wülcker, "Gesch. der Eng. Litt. von den Anfängen," 1896; R. Garnett, "English Literature," vol. i., 1903; Courthope, "History of Eng. Poetry," vol. i., 1895; Saintsbury, "A Short History of Eng. Lit.," 1903; Wright, "Biographia Britannica Literaria," 1842-9.

A.-S. PERIOD.—Earle, "A.-S. Literature," 1884; Wülcker, "Grundrisz zur Gesch. A.-S. Litt.," 1885; A. S. Brooke, "History of Eng. Lit. to King Alfred," 1892; "Eng. Lit. to the Norman Conquest," 1898; Ebert, "Allgemeine Gesch. der Litt. des Mittelalters, etc.," vol. iii., 1887; Sharon Turner, "Hist. of the Anglo-Saxons, etc.," 1799-1805.

TEXTS.—Grein, "Bibliothek der A.-S. Poesie," 4 vols., 1857-64; revised, Wülcker, 1883, etc.; "Bibl. A.-S. Prosa" (cont. by Wülcker), 6 vols., 1872-1905; Wülcker, "Kleinere A.-S. Dichtungen," 1882; Sweet, "Oldest English Texts," E.E.T.S., 1885; Morris, "Specimens of Early English," 1866; ed. Skeat, 1882, 1885; Thorpe, "Analecta Ang.-Saxonica," 1834, 1846; Conybeare, "Illustrations of A.-S. Poetry," 1826; Mätzner, "Alt-Englische Sprachproben," 1867; Selections in Readers by Sweet, Earle, Cook, Baskervill, Bright, Zupitza, and Maclean (based on Zupitza).

ROMANCES.—Ritson, "Ancient Metrical Romances," 1802; Weber, "Metrical Rom. of the 13th, 14th, and 15th Centuries," 1810; Hartshorne, "Ancient Metrical Tales," 1829; Halliwell, "Thornton Romances," 1844; Ellis, "Specimens of Early English Metrical Romances," revised Halliwell, 1847.
The above works will be referred to as *op. cit.* The collections of Grein-Wülcker being complete will not be referred to under separate A.-S. works.

BIBLIOGRAPHY.—Complete in Paul, and Körting; *see* also Chevalier, "Bio-bibliographie," 1905, etc. (for English and foreign authors).

ENGLAND

ANGLO-SAXON PERIOD

SETTLEMENT OF TEUTONIC TRIBES IN BRITAIN.

THE hordes of warlike Teutons who invaded Britain in the 5th century were composed of Angles, Saxons, Jutes, and Frisians. These four tribes established themselves in different parts of the island, and the close of the following century found the Saxons settled in the South (Essex, Sussex, Middlesex, Wessex), the Jutes and Frisians in Kent and the Isle of Wight, and the Angles in Norfolk and Suffolk, and spreading northward as far as the South East of Scotland; the West still remained in possession of the Celt.

EARLY CENTRES OF CULTURE.

A.D. 597. S. Augustine landed in England. The two great centres of culture, during the period which followed upon the introduction of Christianity into the country, were the schools of Kent and the schools of York; these flourished until the land became devastated by the inroads of the Danes.

DIALECTS.

The chief dialects of the Teutonic settlers were: the Northumbrian in the North; the Mercian in the centre; the Kentish, which was the first to be associated with a literary form; and the West Saxon, the latter being confirmed in its pre-eminence by the writings of Aelfred and Aelfric.

N.B.—Anglo-Saxon remains are extant only in Southern (Wessex) transcriptions, but it is more than probable that they originated in the North (Horstmann).

1   The two most important extant collections of A.-S. prose
and poetry are—

1 *The Exeter Book* (Codex Exoniensis).   This book
was presented to his Cathedral by Leofric, the first Bishop
of Exeter, about the middle of the 11th century.   It is
preserved in the Cathedral Library at Exeter; the first
leaves are missing, and the last leaves are injured; the
handwriting of the MS. belongs probably to the first half of
the 11th century.   *Ed.*, with trans., B. Thorpe, 1842;
I. Gollancz, Poems i. to viii., E.E.T.S., 1895.

2 *The Vercelli Book* (Codex Vercellensis).   Discovered
by Dr. Blume, at Vercelli, N. Italy, in 1822.   It is
distinguished from the Exeter Book by containing prose
(Homilies, Life of S. Guthlac) as well as verse.   The MS.
dates probably from the early 11th century, and is in two, or,
perhaps, three handwritings.   *Ed.*, Text of poems (with
trans.), J. M. Kemble, 1843–56; R. Wülcker 1894 (photo.
facsimile of verse).[1]   *See* A. S. Cook, "Cardinal Guala and
the Vercelli Book," and Introduction to his ed. of "The
Dream of the Rood," 1904.

CHARACTERISTICS OF A.-S. POETRY.

The most striking characteristics of A.-S. Poetry are:
inversion of phrase; redundance of metaphor; "parallelism,"
or repetition in synonymous terms of the same fact or idea.
Both rhyme and alliteration are found in A.-S. Poetry, but
rhyme is less generally introduced.   The structure of the
verse is trochaic; the line is divided into two halves by the
Cæsura, each half line having two stressed syllables, the
unstressed syllables varying in number; the half lines are
associated by alliteration, one stressed syllable at least in each
half line beginning with a similar consonant, or vowel.   Usually
the alliteration falls on the two stressed syllables in the first
half line and the first stressed syllable in the second.

---

[1] The editions of the Exeter and Vercelli Codices will not be
referred to under the separate poems contained in them.

2 Earliest extant A.-S. poems, of uncertain date, and still preserving pagan elements.[1]

Widsith (far-traveller), sometimes called "The Traveller's Song," or "The Scop, or Scald's Tale."

The travelling minstrel gives an account of his wanderings, and a list of kings and tribes he has visited; he tells of the presents he has received, of the honourable reception he has met with, and of the welcome that greeted him on his return. Among the kings whom he mentions as his contemporaries are Hermanric, King of the Visigoths, Attila, and Aelfwine, who is generally believed to be the Alboin who reigned in Italy in the middle of the 6th century. This chronological difficulty is explained away on the one hand by ascribing the names of later date to interpolators, and on the other by assigning the whole poem to the close of the 6th century, or even to a still later period. Again, other critics see indications of great antiquity in the geographical details that Widsith introduces, which seem to point to a time when certain tribes still lived as neighbours on the Baltic shore. A principal element of interest in the poem is the mention of persons who are connected with the chief Teutonic sagas, some of whom, if parts of the poem are as genuinely old as some believe, must have been known to Widsith personally; as Mr. Stopford Brooke writes, "the very possibility that he saw these men (Hermanric and Attila) excites us." *Ed.*, trans. by Henry Morley, in A. S. Cook and C. B. Tinker's "Select Translations from old English Poetry," 1902: Wülcker, "Kleinere Angelsächsische Dichtungen." *MS.*, Cod. Ex.

The Lament of Deor, or, *The Minstrel's Consolation*. The only surviving example of an A.-S. poem written in strophic form and with a refrain.

Mr. Stopford Brooke (*op. cit.*) has translated the Lament; the last strophe, which explains Deor's complaint, is given as follows in his version:

"Whilom was I Scôp of the Heodenings:
Dear unto my Lord! *Deor* was my name.

[1] For probable date of early poems, *see* Trautmann (*op. cit.*, under Cynewulf, pp. 121-123).

> Well my service was to me many winters through;
> Loving was my Lord; till at last Heorrenda,—
> Skilled in song the man!—seized upon my land-right,
> That the guard of earls granted erst to me.
> *That* one overwent; *this* also may I."

The Heorrenda is thought to be the Horant, known in "Gudrun," who, according to the description in this of his powers was "a northern Orpheus" (see interesting note in "Modern Language Notes," vol. x. No. 2). The poet's consolation is the thought of the heroes who have suffered and overcome; here again are allusions to sagas. Authorities differ as to whether the composition dates from before the migration, or from a later period.   *Ed.*, trans., A. S. Cook and C. B. Tinker, *op. cit.*; Wülcker, *op. cit.*   *MS.*, Cod. Ex.

3   THE EPIC IN ENGLAND.[1]

No work of the epic class is extant dealing with purely Anglo-Saxon material (Körting). The full development of the epic in England appears to have been checked by the introduction of Christianity.

Beowulf, "the oldest heroic poem in a Germanic tongue," is founded on Teutonic Myth and Saga.

1st part. Beowulf's fight with Grendel.
2nd ,,   Beowulf's fight with Grendel's dam.
3rd ,,   Beowulf's return home.
4th ,,   Beowulf's fight with dragon, and death.

A magnificent hall, called Heorot, is built by Hrothgar, King of the Danes; here his warriors sleep, but they are nightly disturbed by a monster, Grendel, who invades the hall and carries off many of their number. Hearing of Hrothgar's distress, Beowulf comes to his aid, and after a fierce combat with Grendel he mortally wounds the monster. The following day there is feasting, and the men retire to rest at night, believing all danger over, but Grendel's mother, as formidable

---

[1] The Epic is peculiar to the Aryan races. Of the nations whose literature is dealt with in this volume only the English, the French, and the Germans, had an early developed epic. *See* G. Paris, "Hist. poetique de Charlemagne," pp. 2–3.

a foe as her son, comes to avenge his death and seizes one of the chiefs of the Thegns. Beowulf pursues the enemy, even to her dwelling under the water, and there has a terrible encounter with her which ends by Beowulf slaying her with a blow from an elfin sword. Beowulf returns home, and in time becomes king. Fifty years after, he meets his own death in a combat with a dragon, the guardian of an immense treasure, his faithful Wiglaf being the only follower with him at the end.

A mass of controversial criticism has gathered round this poem; space will only allow a reference here to the main arguments.

Beowulf is not known to history, but the Hygelac, of whom Beowulf was the nephew and avenger, has been identified with King Chochilaicus, mentioned by Gregory of Tours, who was killed fighting against the Frisians at some time between 515-520. As this expedition is alluded to in Beowulf, it sets a limit to the date of the origin of the main tale, and as fifty years elapse before the final catastrophe takes place, this brings us to the closing decades of the 6th century, after which a certain time must be allowed for the formation of the original lays on which the later epic was founded. We here approach the point around which controversy has been most lively. Authorities on one side, with Müllenhoff at their head, decided that the poem is a compilation of old lays; Müllenhoff dissected the poem and separated what he considered the different lays from the main text; on the other hand, the Beowulf is believed by Grein and others to be a poem complete in itself, based on older materials, the general opinion being, that the tale had its birth on the Continent, was brought over to us " presumably by the Angles," and assumed its present form on English soil, in the 7th or 8th century. Sarrazin (" Beowulf Studien," pp. 91, 109) gives the poem to Cynewulf, " who based it on an old Danish original." Trautmann opposes him (*op. cit.*, under Cynewulf). The chief actors are Danes and Geats (Goths, of the South of Sweden; identified by some with the Jutes). The scenery described, notwithstanding an attempt made by Haigh (" A.-S. Sagas," 1861) to prove that it is English, is generally conceded to be Scandinavian. Everything is thought to point to

the poem having had its birth before the migration of the
tribes to this island, and to the Christian elements in the
poem being accretions of later growth. According to Bugge
we only received back what we gave. "It is evident," he
writes, "that the author of Beowulf was familiar with a
Christian English poem on the Creation." (*See* "The Home
of the Eddic Poems," trans. Schofield, Grimm Library, xi.)
The poet who wrought the old materials into the form of the
extant version is unknown; Professor Earle traces his name in
Hygelac, which he interprets as Higeberht, who was Archbishop of Lichfield under Offa, rejecting the identification
with Chochilaicus. Authorities differ as to the locality in
which the lays were first welded into a connected poem;
some give it a birthplace in Mercia, others in Northumbria.
According to Ten Brink the MS. is in the Wessex dialect.
The myth of Beowa, the third in genealogical descent from
Sceáf, the oldest name in the heathen pedigrees, is blended
with that of Beowulf. The idea of a nature-myth underlying the Beowulf legends is accepted by some scholars.
There have been different theories as to the origin of the name
of Beowulf. Certain placenames in England preserve the
memory of the Beowulf saga. "Whatever historians have
agreed to recognise as the distinguishing features both of the
Teutonic and Scandinavian branches of our race—all these
things appear among the incidents of a poem a little over 3000
lines" (Earle).

There are similarities with the "Beowulf" in the Icelandic
Grettis Saga (*Ed.*, trans. Magnusson and Morris).

Eds., Heyne, 1863, 67, 73, 79, 7th ed., 1903; Heyne-
Socin, 1888, 1898; Zupitza (autotypes of MS.; translitera-
tion and notes), E.E.T.S., 1882; Harrison and Sharp
(based on 4th ed., Heyne); Holthausen, 1905; Prose
trans., J. M. Kemble, 1833, 35, 37 (two first eds. include
"Traveller's Song" and "Battle of Finnes-bush"); T.
Arnold, 1876; J. Earle, 1892; J. R. C. Hall, 1901;
C. B. Tinker, 1902. Verse trans., Wackerbarth, ballad
measure, 1849; Thorpe (with "The Scop, or Gleeman's
Tale," and "Fight at Finnesburg") 1855, 1875; Lumsden
(modern rhymes), 1881; Garnett, 1885, 4th ed., 1906
(full bibliography); J. L. Hall, 1892, 1900; Morris and

Wyatt, 1895, these in imitative measures; selections in blank verse, Conybeare, "Illustrations of A.-S. Poetry," 1826. For critical notices of above, see C. B. Tinker, "The Translations of Beowulf." For summary of opinions on the various contested points, see Introduction to "Deeds of Beowulf," J. Earle, 1892; and Wülcker, "Grundrisz, etc." (*op. cit.*), 1885. For further information as regards articles in literary journals, and other works, see Trautmann, in Bonner, "Beiträge zur Anglistik," Heft ii. 62, 1899; Körting (*op. cit.*) and Chevalier, *op. cit.*; Th. Krueger, "Geschichte der B. Kritik," 1884. (See Skeat, *Academy*, x. 1876, xxi. 1877, for name of Beowulf.) *MS.*, Cott. Vitell. A. xv., apparently of 10th century, injured by fire.

Battle of Finnsburg. Fragment only. This is part of a saga to which there is a reference in Beowulf. It belongs, like the latter, to the Saga-cycle of the Scandinavian coast region. *Eds.*, Hickes, "Thesaurus." Text with trans., Thorpe, 1855; prose trans. (with "Beowulf"), J. R. Clark Hall, 1901; J. M. Garnett, 1882. Harrison and Sharp (see "Beowulf"); with "Beowulf," by F. Klaeber (Belles Lettres). *MS.*, now lost. Found on a leaf bound up with A.-S. Homilies at Lambeth Library. Known from Hickes's copy.

Waldere. Two fragments — 1st frag., Hildegunde's speech to Walther, encouraging him to fight; 2nd frag., Defiant interchange of speech between Walther and Gunther, preliminary to fight. Hildegunde and Walther are escaping from Attila's court with treasure, when they are attacked by Gunther. These fragments are remains of a song or larger work belonging to the Walther-saga (Burgundian-Hunnish cycle). The A.-S. poem is thought to be founded on a High German original, now lost, probably of first half of 8th century. The fragments agree with an extant version of the Saga, represented by the Latin poem, "Waltharius," the work of Ekkehard i., a monk of St. Gall, who died 973 (*see* Germany, § 8). *Ed.*, "Two leaves of King Waldere's Lay," text and trans., G. Stephens, 1860. *MS.*, 9th century. Found 1860 in Royal Library, Copenhagen.

4   VIITH CENTURY.

668 A.D. Theodore, a Greek of Tarsus, afterwards Arch-bishop of Canterbury ; Hadrian, an African Monk ; Biscop Baducing (Benedict Biscop) ; these three came to England and spread the knowledge of Latin and Greek, and of the Arts and Sciences.

The libraries at the chief seats of learning, in Kent, Wessex, and Northumbria, were enriched by books obtained by pilgrims to Rome.

Schools of York became famous.

Anglian period of English Literature : late 7th to early 9th century. Poetry flourished chiefly in the Anglian districts, but it has not been in all cases transmitted in Northern dialect.

PROSE.

The oldest monuments are compilations of laws. Earliest written laws appeared soon after the coming of St. Augustine.

Kentish Laws. Codes of Aethelberht (d. 616) and his successors, (cir. 601 to cir. 695). Extant in W. Saxon translation.

Laws of Ine (King of W. Saxons, 688–726). The Earliest Laws of Wessex (688-695). Re-issued by King Aelfred.   *Ed.*, B. Thorpe, "Ancient Laws and Institutes of England," text and trans., 1840 ; Liebermann, "Gesetze der Angelsächsen," text and trans. into modern German, 1898, etc., in progress.   *MSS.*, Textus Roffensis ; Cott. Nero. A. 1, and several others in Cottonian Collection ; Harl. 55, and others in Harleian Coll. ; C.C.C.C. ; Camb. Univ. Libr. ; Bodleian ; foreign Libraries. For full list of MSS. see Liebermann, *op. cit.*, vol. i. pp. 13–42.

5   Anglo-Saxon Christian poetry begins with—

Caedmon, d. cir. 680. The only information we have concerning this poet is given by Baeda in his " Ecclesiastical History " (Book 4, chap. 24). Caedmon was a lay-brother of the monastery of Streoneshalh (Whitby), under the Abbess

Hilda. He had not the gift of lighter verse, and when, at the feasts, the harp went round to the guests in turn, Caedmon was unable to add his song to the others. It was his custom therefore to retire before the harp reached him, and so, one night, retreating thus to the stable, where he was in charge of the cattle, he fell asleep, and in a vision he heard a voice commanding him to sing of the Creation. He began to sing, and on awaking next morning remembered the lines, which are those that have come down to us in his Hymn. After this he was able to turn into rhythm any portion of sacred history; the fame of his marvellously acquired gift went abroad, and the Abbess Hilda received him into the monastery, the poet taking upon himself the monastic vows.

Hymn in Praise of the Creator (long lines).   1. Version in Northumbrian dialect (8th century, Körting). 2. West Saxon version in Aelfred's translation of Baeda (based on Northumbrian).   3. Latin prose version in Baeda. There is diversity of opinion as to whether the Northumbrian Hymn is to be ascribed to Caedmon; Aelfred believed in its authenticity. For authorship see Ten Brink, *op. cit.,* Appendix; Paul-Braune, "Beiträge zur geschichte der deutschen sprache u. Litteratur," vol. iii. 351; Zupitza, "Zeitschrift f. deutsches Alterthum," xxiii.   *Ed.,* Napier, "Mod. Lang. Notes," 1889; Ten Brink, *op. cit.* (Northumbrian verse and Latin paraphrase); Zupitza, "Alt. u. Mittelengl. Uebungsbuch," 1874, p. 39.   *MS.,* Famous More MS. (Baeda's "Ecc. Hist."), Univ. Libr., Camb., k.k. 5, 16; probably written at Wearmouth shortly after Baeda's death. The Northumbrian text is given on the last page, the paraphrase in an earlier part of the work.

Poetical Paraphrase of Parts of Scripture (*Genesis, Exodus, Daniel, Christ and Satan*). These poems were all ascribed to Caedmon by their first editor, Junius; later criticism hesitates to ascribe any of them to this poet. Authorities differ as regards authorship and date; as many as seven different authors have been assigned to these works. *Eds.,* Thorpe (with Eng. trans.), 1832; Bouterwek, 1851, 1854. *See* also Götzinger, "Ueber die Dichtungen des Ags-Caedmon u. deren Verfasser"; Balg, "Der Dichter Caedmon u. seine Werke," 1882. *MS.,* Bodleian, Jun. xi. Version of

" Daniel " also found in Cod. Ex. *See,* for MS., Stoddard, "Anglia," x. ; Lawrence, "Anglia," xii.

Genesis (to Abraham's Sacrifice). The whole of this portion was at one time considered the work of a single author ; in 1875, however, Sievers published "der Heliand u. die Angelsächsische Genesis," in which for the first time was pointed out that lines 235–851 were an interpolation, being a translation from an O. Saxon original, written, according to Sievers' view at that time by the author of the "Heliand" (Sievers afterwards believed it the work of a disciple of this poet). The discovery in the Vatican Library, 1894, of three fragments of an Old Saxon "Genesis" confirmed his hypothesis, the largest fragment containing 26 lines which are in the Anglo-Saxon "Genesis." Fifty lines (371–420) of this interpolation are again thought by some, among them Sievers, to be the work of a third hand ; Kögel notices a sudden change at line 389, the difference in tone continuing to 418 ; Braune, however (*see* below), refutes the idea of any interpolation. The portion translated from the O. S. "Genesis" is known as "Genesis B " ; the remainder as "Genesis A." There is still discussion as to identity of authorship of "Heliand " and "Genesis" (*see* under Germany, § 3). *MS.* of fragments, Palatinus Latinus N. 1447. Thought to belong undoubtedly to 9th century. 1st fragment. Address of God to Adam, Fall of the Angels, The Fall ; 2nd. Cain and Abel ; 3rd. Destruction of Sodom. *Ed.* (photographic facsimiles), Zangemeister u. Braune in *Neue Heidelberger Jahrbücher,* iv. Heft 2, 1894 ; *see* Kögel, *op. cit.,* vol. i. p. 288, and also supplement to vol. i. ; Ten Brink, *op. cit.,* Appendix.

Exodus and Daniel. The composition of the "Exodus" is a matter of discussion. Strobl upheld the theory of different songs being welded into a whole ; Groth only distinguished interpolations, and Ziegler upholds this view ; Muerkens thinks it the work of a single poet. The last-named authority assigns the poem to cir. 700 at latest, and believes it to have been written in Northumbria (Sievers in Kent). He is opposed by Ebert in his conviction that certain lines composing *Fitte* 6 are a separate poem. *See* Muerkens, in Bonner, "Beiträge zur Anglistik," Heft ii. 62, 1899 ; Pfeiffer's "Germania," xx. ; and Ebert in "Anglia," v.

The "Daniel" has an introductory account of the history of Israel up to the time of Daniel. Here again there is a question as to interpolation with regard to the Song of Azariah. *See* Hofer, "Anglia," xii. (who ascribes the poem to first half of ninth century); Paul-Braune, *op. cit.* xx.; Balg, *op. cit. Eds.*, "Exodus and Daniel," in Albion and Belles-Lettres Series.

Christ and Satan. Either three different poems: The Fallen Angels; Christ's Descent into Hell and Resurrection (fragment); and the Temptation (fragment) (Ten Brink); or, parts of a single poem. The dates assigned to this work vary from a period anterior to Beowulf (Groschopp, "Anglia," vi. p. 264) to end of 9th or beginning of 10th century (Ten Brink). *See* Kühn, "Ueber die Ags. gedichte von C. u. S.," 1883; Ebert, *op. cit.*, vol. iii.

N.B.—The above poems and "Judith" are written in long lines.

The Dream of the Rood (*Vision of the Cross*). This poem has been ascribed both to Caedmon and Cynewulf (q.v). Caedmon's authorship is dependent on the age of the inscription on the Ruthwell Cross ("Archaeologia," vol. 30), which corresponds to portions of the poem.

Inscription on the Ruthwell Cross. These verses were first ascribed to Caedmon by Haigh ("Archæologia Aeliana"),[1] who thought them portions of a lost poem: by him, as also by Stephens ("Runic Monuments") the cross was thought to be the work of the 7th century, and the latter deciphered certain runes, as "Cadmon me made." Later investigation has not confirmed these hypotheses: the cross is not thought by a late authority (*see* Cook, and Müller) to date before 800, the ornamentation even pointing to a period shortly before 1000; the language has also been shown to belong to the 10th century, and the Runic scholar, Vietor, rejects the assertion that Caedmon's name is decipherable on the stone. The inference drawn, therefore, is that the inscription is drawn from the extant text of the "Dream of the Rood," (*see* Cynewulf), and not from an older and lost

[1] Pub. Society of Antiquaries, Newcastle-upon-Tyne.

poem. *Ed.*, Hickes, "Thesaurus"; Cook and Tinker, "Select Trans.," etc. *See* Dietrich, "Disputatio de Cruce Ruthwellensis," 1865; S. Müller, "Die Thierornamentik im Norden," 1881; Cook, "Notes on the Ruthwell Cross"; *Academy*, 37, 153; Publ. Mod. Lang. Assoc., vol. xvii. No. 3; also Introduction to Cook's "Dream of the Rood," 1905.

Judith (fragment). One of the finest specimens of A.-S. poetry, by an unknown author. A distance of 300 years separates the earliest and latest dates assigned to this poem, the latest being the second quarter of 11th century. *Eds.*, Cook, text and trans., 1889 (with autotype facsimiles); Trans., "An English Miscellany" (Furnivall), 1901; J. M. Garnett, 1901 (with other poems); Cook and Tinker, "Select Trans.," etc. *See* T. G. Forster, "Judith Studies in Metre, Language and Style," 1892. *MS.*, Beowulf MS., Cott. Vitell. A. xv.

6 LATIN WRITERS.

Aldhelm, b. 640 (?); d. 709. Abbot of Malmesbury and Bishop of Sherborne. Under Aldhelm, Malmesbury became a noted seat of learning. Aldhelm was the earliest Anglo-Latin poet.

PROSE WORKS.—*De Laude Virginitatis sive de Virginitate sanctorum.*
Epistola ad Acircium (Aldferth, King of Northumbria). *A Treatise on verse-making*, in which are included the *Aenigmata.*
Treatise *De Pentateucho*, and other *Letters.*

POETICAL WORKS.—*De Laudibus Virginum.*
Aenigmata. Written on the model of Symposius.[1]
De Aris S. Mariae.
De Octo principibus Vitiis.
Ed., Works, J. A. Giles, "Patres Ecclesiae," 1844.

---

[1] Nothing is known of Symposius. The riddles attributed to him date from 4th or 5th century. Other collections of riddles are by Tatwine (d. 734), Eusebius, and Boniface; they date from cir. middle 7th to cir. middle 8th century.

N.B. — Aldhelm is reported to have been noted as an
A.-S. poet, but no vernacular verse by him is extant.

Baeda, b. 673 or 674; d. 735. Baeda spent his life
at Jarrow from the time he was a child.

De Sanctis Locis. Based on the similar work by Adamnan
(7th century).

De Natura Rerum.

De Temporibus (Liber Minor). *See* under Aelfric.

De Temporum Ratione (*De Temporibus*, Liber Major), to
which is appended a chronicle of the world, *De Sex Aetatibus.*
In this work the seasons and festivals are fixed according to
the Christian era.

Historia beatorum Abbatum (of Wearmouth and Jarrow).
Ed., C. Plummer, 1896.

Historia Ecclesiastica Gentis Anglorum, B.C. 55 to A.D. 731
(see Aelfred, § 11). The oldest MS. of this work is the
More MS., Camb. Univr. Libr. k.k. 5. 16. *Ed.,* C.
Plummer, 1896 (with *Vita Abbatum* and *Epistola ad Egbertum*);
Eng. trans. (Giles), ed. L. C. Jane, Temple Classics, 1903.

Lives of S. Cuthbert (prose and verse). *Ed.* (both versions), with *Vita Abbatum, Epistola ad Egbertum,* and *Chronicon,*
by J. Stevenson, 1841.

Other works are: *Retractationes, Pœnitentiale, Letters*
(letter to Ecgberht, 734, latest extant work), and *Homilies.*—
These may be supplemented by the list given by Baeda himself
at the close of his "Hist. Eccles." They include numerous
commentaries, a Martyrology, scientific and educational treatises, a life of S. Felix, a translation of Greek Life of S.
Anastasius, epigrams, and hymns. Of many of the extant
epigrams and hymns the authenticity is doubtful. One *De Die
Judicii* is also extant in A.-Saxon, *Be Domes Dæge* (Last
Judgment) (MS., C.C.C.C.), pub. by E.E.T.S. Baeda's
translation of the *Gospel of S. John,* finished on his deathbed,
is lost. *Ed.,* Complete works, with trans., J. A. Giles,
"Patres Eccles. Anglicanæ," 1843–44; Migne, "Patrologiae, etc.," 1844–64.

Other men of note of 7th and 8th centuries were Ecgberht,

2

Archbishop of York, founder of the School of York, d. 766;
Boniface (Winfrid) Apostle of Germany, d. 755; Danihel,
Bishop of the W. Saxons, d. 745.

7   VIIITH CENTURY.

VERNACULAR WRITERS.

POETRY.

Cynewulf (8th century?).   Nothing is positively known
about this poet.   Authorities have differed as to the century
in which he lived, whether he was a Northumbrian, a West
Saxon, or a Mercian, as to which, and how many poems may
be ascribed to him (*see* Beowulf, § 3).   Kemble and Thorpe
identified him with an Abbot of Peterborough, at beginning
of 11th century; later German scholars with the Bishop of
Lindisfarne, who d. 783.   The date which has been generally assigned to Cynewulf is the 8th century, but Prof. Cook
has shown what he considers the dependence of Cynewulf
on Alcuin in his description of the Day of Judgment in
" Elene," and this would necessitate his poems being brought
down to the 9th century (*see* the answer to these views,
C. F. Brown, Publ. Mod. Lang. Assoc., vol. xi. 4), and
a later date still has been assigned to him.   For summary of
views on above points, Life, etc., *see* Wülcker, "Grundrisz,
etc.," *op. cit.*; Mather, "The Cynewulf Question from a
Metrical Point of View," Mod. Lang. Notes, vii.; Ueber
Cynewulf, "Anglia," i., and following numbers; Trautmann,
"C. der Bischof u. Dichter," 1898; Ten Brink, *op. cit.*,
Appendix.   Cynewulf's poems are extant in the W. Saxon
dialect.   Only those in which the poet introduces his own
name in runes can be positively assigned to him.   The first of
the series of " Riddles " in the Exeter Book was at one time
accounted among these, but in 1893 (Phil. Soc., Dec. 8)
Prof. Gollancz showed it to be a dramatic lyric, in which
there was nothing which could be rightly interpreted as a
transmission of the name of Cynewulf.   Again, according
to a later interpretation by Prof. Schofield and Mr. Lawrence,
this so-called "First Riddle of Cynewulf" is a translation from

a Norse original, the latter being part of a cycle of heroic poetry; this cycle Prof. Schofield asserts to be the Sigurd cycle; Prof. Gollancz, admitting the main proposition, contends that it belongs to the Theodoric cycle. *See* "Modern Language Notes," vol. xvii.; *Athenæum*, Nov. 29, 1902, and following numbers.

Juliana (long lines). Cynewulf's name in runes. This is the history of a saint martyred under Maximinian. *Ed.*, W. Strunk, Belles Lettres Series. *MS.*, Cod. Ex.

Elene (long lines). C.'s name in runes. On the finding of the Cross by Constantine's mother. Both the above legends are found in "Acta Sanctorum." *Ed.*, Zupitza, 1877; Trans., J. M. Garnett (with other poems) (Albion); A. S. Cook (with Phœnix, Panther, Whale, Partridge) (Belles Lettres); with Latin original, C. W. Kent (Albion); *MS.*, Cod. Vercell.

The Christ (*Coming of Christ, Ascension, Last Judgment*) (long lines). C.'s name in runes. The poem thought by some to be in two parts; by Trautmann to be three poems, C. being author of the second only. *Ed.*, Text and trans., I. Gollancz, 1892; A. S. Cook, 1900; Whitman, trans. into Eng. prose, 1900 (Albion); W. H. Hulme (Belles Lettres). *See* Trautmann, "Anglia," xviii., and Blackburn, "On the Christ as a single Poem or not," "Anglia," xix. *MS.*, Cod. Ex., first leaves missing.

Andreas, and *Fates of the Apostles* (long lines). C.'s name in runes in the second of these poems, leaving "Andreas" among the doubtful ones. All authorities, however, do not look upon above as separate poems. Dietrich and, now, Trautmann give Andreas to Cynewulf. *Ed.*, Andreas, W. M. Baskervill (Albion); G. P. Krapp, "Two A.-S. Poems" (full discussion of different theories), 1906; Eng. trans., P. K. Root, "Yale Studies," vii. *See* Trautmann, *op. cit.*, pp. 116–117; and "Anglia," Beiblatt, vi.; Sarrazin, "Anglia," xii., and "Beibl.," vi.; Napier, "Anglia," iv.; Sievers, "Anglia," xiii. *MS.*, Cod. Vercell.

Works of which the authorship is doubtful:—

Descent into Hell (fragment, long lines). According to one view, this is an integral part of the "Christ"; Wülcker and Körting do not agree with this.   *Ed.*, W. H. Hulme with the "Christ."   *MS.*, Cod. Ex.

Guthlac (in two parts, long lines).   Source of part of this work is "Vita S. Guthlaci," by Felix of Croyland (§ 10). Dietrich believed this to be Cynewulf's work, and Trautmann thinks it probable.   Körting says first part certainly not by C.   *See* H. Forstmann, "Zur Guthlac-Legende," 1902. *MS.*, Cod. Ex.

N.B. — Two prose versions of this life are extant in A.-Saxon, one in the Vercelli Book, the other a translation from F. of Croyland (Cott. Vesp. D. xxi.).

Phoenix (long lines).   A symbolical treatment of the old legend, the latter being taken from the Latin poem attributed to Lactantius.   Prof. Cook inclines to the belief that this poem is by Cynewulf, Dietrich assigns it to him, and Trautmann thinks the authorship probable.   *Ed.*, J. L. Hall, 1902; Brown, in "Poet Lore," 1890.   *MS.*, Cod. Ex.

Dream of the Rood, or *Vision of the Cross* (long lines). (*See* under "Inscription of the Ruthwell Cross.")   Dietrich and Rieger support the view of Cynewulf's authorship of this poem : similarity of parts of the "Rood" with "Elene," and "Christ," the position of the poem between "Andreas" and "Elene," the treatment of the Bible narrative, the manner in which he speaks of himself here as in other poems, and likeness of diction, being arguments on which their belief is founded. Trautmann, though acknowledging similarities of expression on the one hand, yet on the other finds words which are unused elsewhere by Cynewulf, Sievers places it earlier than Cynewulf on linguistic grounds, and Ebert will see nothing especially indicative of unique authorship in the fact of correspondence of expression, nor in the description of himself as old and sad, as ancient poets were fond of giving such accounts of themselves.   We come to the latest editor, Prof. Cook, who considers that the weight of evidence is decidedly in favour of Cynewulf being the poet of the "Rood"; he assigns it to him as a work "composed in the maturity of his powers."   Kemble considered this work "as in some respects the most striking of all the Anglo-Saxon remains"; Ten

Brink speaks of it as "a beautifully designed composition."
The substance of the poem is the poet's vision of the Cross,
the address of the Cross to him, and Cynewulf's after-reflec-
tions, ending with a description of the feelings of the spirits
in hell when Christ visited them, of the joy of those in
heaven, and of Christ's return to His heavenly home.
Ed. (with Bibliography, Notes, and Glossary), A. S. Cook,
Clarendon Press, 1905; Grein-Wülcker, *op. cit.*; Sweet,
"Anglo-Saxon Reader." *MS.*, Cod. Vercell.

Riddles. These are contained in the Exeter Book and have
been assigned to Cynewulf; the later views, as regards the
First Riddle (*see* pp. 18–19), makes the authorship more ques-
tionable. *Ed.*, Grein-Wülcker, *op. cit.*; Cook and Tinker,
op. cit. (trans.). *See* "Anglia," vi. (Anzg.), vii. (Anzg.),
x., xiii., xvii.; and "Englische Studien," xvi.; Cook, "The
Riddles and Cynewulf" (in ed. "Christ").

Physiologus (long lines). A symbolic poem, in which the
Panther is emblematic of Christ and the Whale of Satan—
thought to be either the fragment of a Physiologus, or a work
dealing with the three divisions of the animal world as represented by the Panther, the Whale, and the Bird. Many
works of this kind are extant, the model being apparently
a Greek work, known to the West through the medium of
the Latin. A Latin Physiologus existed in the 5th century
Körting rejects all idea of C.'s authorship. *See* Lauchert,
"Geschichte des Physiologus," 1888; E. Sokoll, 1897.
MS., Cod. Ex. Panther, complete; Whale, defective; Bird,
fragment.

Of the following lyrics and didactic poems contained in
the Exeter Book some have been ascribed to Cynewulf.

LYRICS.

The Wanderer. *See* Translation in "Mod. Lang. Notes,"
vols. v., vii., by W. Rice Sims.

The Seafarer. In the "Journal of English and Germanic
Philology," vol. iv., M. Lawrence writes on "The Wanderer"
and "The Seafarer."

Rhyme Song (Rhyme and Alliteration) has been called the
"Swan-song" of Cynewulf.

The Ruin.
The Husband's Message.
Exile's Complaint.
See for trans. of several of above poems, A. S. Cook and
C. B. Tinker, "Select Translations, etc.," 1902.

DIDACTIC.
The Gifts of Man, The Fates of Man, The Disposition of Man.

GNOMIC VERSES.
Ed., Sweet, "Anglo-Saxon Reader," 1881.   Trans.,
Conybeare, "Ill. A.-S. Poetry," 1826.   *MSS.*, Cod.
Ex. ; Cott. Tib. B. 1.

Other poems of unknown authorship and of unknown or
uncertain date are—
Falsity of Man (imperfect).
A Father's Lesson.
Wonders of Creation.
The Last Judgment (different poem to the one mentioned
under Baeda).
Pharaoh (fragment).
Alms (fragment of alliterative sermon).
Prayers.
MSS., The above are in the Exeter Book, with the
exception of "Falsity of Man," which is from the Vercelli.

8   *Address of the Soul to the Body* (long lines).   Probably
      of 10th century, and from Latin original.

1st part.   Lost Soul to its Body (Exeter and Vercelli).
2nd ,,   Pious Soul to its Body (Vercelli, defective).

There are two forms of this legend extant, one in which
the soul alone speaks (A.-S. version) and another in which a
dialogue is held between body and soul (Visio Fulberti, or
Philberti).   No other poem is known similar to the 2nd
part of the A.-S. but the double scene occurring at the death
of the just and of the sinner, where the angels address the soul
of the former, and the demons mock at the soul of the latter,
and the evil soul and its body revile one another, is found in

an Irish homily in the "Leabhar Breac." (*See* R. Atkinson, "The Passions and Homilies from the Leabhar Breac," p. 507 ff.) The address of the lost soul to, or dialogue with, the body was a favourite subject for treatment in olden times. Versions are extant in French, German, Spanish, Italian, etc. There are English versions of 12th and 13th centuries. *See* for this legend and its connection with the names of S. Paul and S. Macaire, T. Batiouchkof, "Romania," xx. *See* also "Modern Language Notes," v. No. 7; (for further grouping see France, § 12).

Other Texts, Fragments discovered among the Archives of Worcester Cathedral, 12th century, and another fragment, Bodleian 343 ("For thee was a house built, etc."). *Ed.* by R. Buchholz, 1890. "The desputisoun bitwen the bodi and the soule" 13th century. *MSS.*, Auchinleck; Laud, 108; Vernon; Digby, 102; Reg. 18 A. x. *Ed.*, W. Linow, 1889. *See* also Wright, "Latin Poems," attributed to W. Map; and E. Stengel, "Codicem Manu Scriptum Digby 86," 1871.

9 *Solomon and Saturn* (didactic poem, long lines). (*See* France, § 48; and Germany, § 14.) In two parts, with prose fragment intervening.

1st part.　Solomon instructs Saturn in the Paternoster.
2nd　„　Interchange of theological and moral remarks.

From very early times versions of this dialogue appear to have been known in England. The above dates at the earliest from the 8th century, but many authorities place it later. The germ of the tradition is possibly of Jewish origin; as early as 5th century there was a composition extant, "Contradictio Salomonis." In the A.-S. version we have the oldest European form. The dialogue as a serious composition is only known to us in the A.-S. and a considerably later French version: the characteristics in other survivals is that of rough humour, very marked in the German versions. The Saturn of A.-S. is Marcolis in Eastern version; the name is thought to be a confusion with a similar one given to the oriental Saturn; in Germany the name appears as Morolt and Markolf, where he also figures in a tale in which he is of active use to Solomon in re-capturing the latter's wife. *Ed.*, Kemble, Aelfric Soc., 1848. *MSS.*, C.C.C.C. 422, and 41. An Anglo-Saxon prose version is extant in Cott. Vitell. A. xv. (Thorpe, "Analecta"), similar to "Adrian and Ritheus," in Cott. Jul. A. 2 (Kemble, *op. cit.*). *See* "The Dialogue or Communing between the Wise King Solomon and Marcolphus," E. Gordon Duff, 1892, and "Solomon in Europe," by M. W. MacCallum, "Studies in Low German and High German Literature"; Vogt (Germany, § 14).

Translation of 50th Psalm into Kentish Dialect; placed by Ten Brink before 800 A.D. *MS.*, Cott. Vesp. D. vi.

Epinal Gloss. Earliest Latin Anglo-Saxon Glossary, "oldest extant monument of our language." This glossary is placed by its editor, H. Sweet, in the first half of 8th century; he considers it a copy of older MS. of undeterminable date. Another authority has dated it early 9th century. Allied glosses are found in MSS.: C.C.C.C.; Erfurt; and Leyden. *See* for details, etc., Sweet, "Epinal Glossary," 1883. *See* "Roman Psalter," France, § 8.

10   LATIN WRITERS.

Aeddi (Eddius Stephanus).
Vita Wilfridi Episcopi. A.-S. missionary, d. 708 or 709. Written soon after 710. (Other early lives of Wilfrid are a metrical one by Frithgode of Canterbury, and a prose by Eadmer of Canterbury.)

Tatwin. Archbishop of Canterbury, 731; d. 734.
Aenigmata. In Latin hexameters. *Ed.*, Giles, "Anecdota Baedae."

Felix. Monk of Croyland, fl. cir. 730.
Vita S. Guthlaci. (Trans. into A.-S. Cott. Vesp. D. xxi. *Ed.*, C. W. Goodwin, 1848.) (*See* § 7.)

Willibald. Bishop of Eichstadt, b. 700 (?); d. 786. A traveller to Rome, Constantinople, and Palestine.
Vita seu Hodoeporicon sancti Willibaldi scriptum a sancti-

moniali. Notices of travels, dictated to and written down by author's kinswoman, a nun of Heidenheim.   *Ed.,* " Early Travels in Palestine," Bohn, Ant. Lib., 1847.

Vita S. Bonifacii. Apostle of Germany, d. 755. Also attributed to Willibald.   *Ed.,* J. A. Giles (with Aeddi's *Wilfrid,* and other lives of Anglo-Saxons), Caxton Soc., 1854; A. Nürnberger, 1895.

Alcuin, b. 735; d. 804. Known also as Flaccus or Albinus. Became the adviser of Charlemagne, and helped in the establishment of schools in France.

PROSE WORKS.
Commentaries.
Various Books, O. and T. Test.

Treatises.
De Fide Sanctae et Individuae Trinitatis, De Virtutibus et Vitiis.

Lives of Saints.
Martin of Tours, Richarius, Vedast, Willibrord.

Educational.
De Grammatica, Orthographia, Rhetorica et Virtutibus, Dialectica, Rationa Animae, etc.

Epistles.
To Charlemagne, etc.

POETICAL WORKS.
Epigrams, Aenigmata, Elegies.
De Pontificibus et Sanctis Ecclesiae Eboracensis. In this is given an account of the destruction of Lindisfarne by the Danes.   *Ed.,* J. A. Giles, " Patres Ecclesiae," 1844. Works, Migne, " Patrologiae Cursus Completus," 1851; " Monumenta Alcuintana," W. Wattenbach and G. Dümmler, 1873.

The Lindisfarne Gospels (Durham Book).   *MS.,* Cott. Nero. D. iv. Elaborately illuminated; the written Latin text dates cir. A.D. 700; the glosses in Northumbrian dialect were added later, probably middle 10th century (perhaps 9th, Earle). Each word of the Latin text has the Old Northumbrian equivalent written above. *Ed.*, with other ancient versions of the Gospels (Anglo-Saxon, Northumbrian, Mercian), by W. W. Skeat, 1871–1887. *See* also A. S. Cook, "A Glossary of the Old Northumbrian Gospels," 1894.

11 IXth CENTURY.

During this century England was overrun by the Danes; the schools of York perished, and the centre of literary culture was transferred to the south, where English prose had its rise among the West Saxons. The earliest prose works were dedicated to the instruction and edifying of the people, and consisted in great part of translations from the Latin. In his essay on "The Earlier History of English Prose" ("Essays in Mediæval Literature," 1905), Prof. Ker speaks of Anglo-Saxon prose as comparing well with the translation work of Ulfilas and Wicklyffe, "in its successful resistance of the temptation to adopt foreign grammatical constructions." "If," he continues, "there were nothing but the translations and sermons, there would still be room for satisfaction at the literary skill and promise in them." But Anglo-Saxon prose had something more original to show: "in the narratives of the northern voyages of Ohthere and Wulfstan" (Aelfred's "Orosius") . . . in some of the varying styles employed in the Chronicles . . . one comes as near as one may in early English to natural prose. Prose such as one gets there is of the rarest near the beginnings of a literature. Anglo-Saxon prose did not always maintain so high a level; it fell at times into a kind of alliterative rhythmical prose, such as we have in Aelfric's "Lives of the Saints." Some of the poems of this century show signs of change in metrical form, the old established rules of alliteration being less strictly followed. Leonine rhymes were also frequently introduced. Examples of this metrical decline are the poems on Eadgar's death, and on King Aethelred's son. "The latter," writes Ten Brink, "owing to the complete dissolution of alliterative forms and the frequent use of rhyme, reads like a product of the transition period, and almost like a poem in short couplets."

VERNACULAR WRITERS.

PROSE.

Aelfred, born at Wantage, 849; d. 901.[1] What King Aelfred was to England is summed up in the inscription on his statue at Wantage: "Aelfred found learning dead, and he restored it; education neglected, and he revived it; the laws powerless, and he gave them force; the Church debased, and he raised it; the land ravaged by a fearful enemy, from which he delivered it." As regards his purely literary work, "It was long before the other nations were as well provided in their own languages with useful handbooks of instruction" (Ker, *op. cit.*) such as Aelfred gave to his subjects. *See* Asser, "Life of Aelfred" (§ 12); Plummer, "Life and Times of A. the Great," 1902; S. Brooke, "King A. as Educator of the People, and Man of Letters," 1901.

A.'s literary activity began in 887. The chronological order of his works is thought most probably to be as follows :—

Encheiridion, or *Handbook*. Mentioned by Asser, and quoted by William of Malmesbury. This lost volume appears to have contained extracts from favourite writers, and original notes. It is thought possible that the "Soliloquies" (*see* below) may be identical with this work.

TRANSLATIONS.

Gregory's Cura Pastoralis. This translation, and that of Orosius and Boethius (890–893) are thought to be undoubtedly the work of Aelfred's own hand. The "Cura Pastoralis" is prefaced by an interesting introduction in the form of a letter from the king to each of his bishops. *Ed.*, Text and trans., H. Sweet, E.E.T.S., 1871–1872; Preface, Sweet's "A.-S. Reader." *MSS.*, Hatton, 20; Cott. Tib. B. xi., injured by fire; Cott. Otho. B. ii., destroyed.

[1] For discussion as to precise date of Aelfred's death, see *Athenæum*, Nov. 3, 1900, and following numbers.

Baeda's Historia Ecclesiastica. Probably undertaken under the king's superintendence. *Ed.*, Miller, E.E.T.S., 1890. (*See* Introduction for discussion as to authorship and birthplace of this translation.) *MSS.*, Tanner, 10; Cott. Otho, B. xi., injured by fire; C.C.C.C. 41; and Univr. Libr. k.k. 3, 18; Oxford, Corp. Christ., 279.

Orosii Historia. A history of the world to 410. Abridged in parts by Aelfred, and also furnished with additional narratives which were gathered by word of mouth from travellers (Ohthere and Wulfstan) round the North Cape and along the Baltic. *Ed.*, with Latin original of Orosius, H. Sweet, E.E.T.S., 1883 (*see* also "A.-S. Reader"). *MSS.*, Lauderdale (Helmingham, Suffolk); Cott. Tib. B. i.

Boethius.—De Consolatione Philosophiae. The metra (Choral Odes) are both in prose and verse (alliterative) in the Cotton MS., in prose in the Bodleian: in the preface of both MSS. the verse, as well as the prose, is assigned to Aelfred, but authorities differ as to the authorship of the former. (*See* introduction to Sedgefield's edit., and "Anglia," v., vi., and vii.) *Ed.*, Text with trans., Fox, 1864; Sedgefield, 1899. *MSS.*, Cott. Otho. A. vi., injured by fire; Bodley, 180; fragment, Bodley, 86.

Augustine's Soliloquia. The authorship of this work has been disputed. The chief arguments in favour of the translation being by Aelfred are: that W. of Malmesbury gives it as one of his works; the similarity between this work and the Boethius. The version as extant in its unique MS. belongs to the early 12th century. A line in the MS. seems to ascribe the work to Aelfred. Hulme ("Englische Studien," vol. xviii., 1893) asserts Aelfred's authorship. *Ed.*, Cockayne, "The Shrine, a collection of occasional papers on dry subjects," 1864–1869; Hargrove (Text, with Notes and Glossary), "Yale Studies in English," xiii., 1902; turned into modern English, *ibid.*, xxii., 1904. *MS.*, Cott. Vitell. A. 15. (Beowulf MS.).

Laws. A compilation based on the laws of Ine, Offa, and Aethelberht. *Ed.*, "Legal Code of Alfred the Great," Milton Haight Turk, 1893; Extracts, S. Cook, 1880. *MSS.*, C.C.C.C., 384 and 173; Cott. Nero. A. 1; Text. Roffensis.

WORKS ASCRIBED TO AELFRED.

Prose Version of Psalms. William of Malmesbury mentions an unfinished version of the Psalms left by Aelfred. In the Book of Psalms, commonly known as the Paris Psalter (Paris Bibl. Nat., fds. Latin, 8824), an illustrated MS., which belonged originally to Jean, duc de Berry, brother to Charles v., the first half of the Psalms (i.–li.) are in A.-S. prose, inserted to supply the lost metrical ones of which only the later numbers remain. Parallel with the Saxon version is given a Latin text, but not the one from which either the prose or verse is directly translated. Wülcker and Wichmann ("Anglia," xi.) supported the idea of Aelfred's authorship of the prose version; Bruce (*see* below) does not consider this view can be supported, the arguments which head the Psalms, and the interpretations of the text showing a familiarity with leading commentators which seems to exclude the idea of the work being by a layman. He considers, however, that the prose version may well date from the period of the Aelfredian cycle of translations. Neither does he think the linguistic proofs brought forward by Wülcker and Wichmann can stand the test. The generally accepted date of the MS. as extant is 11th century; the Commentary by Ambrose Autpert used for the rubrics was written in the second half of the 8th century. The Metrical Psalms have been assigned to Aldhelm. Fragments of the missing Psalms are found in MSS. of an English Benedictine service of cir. middle 11th century. *Ed.*, Thorpe, 1835; *see* J. Douglas Bruce, "Anglo-Saxon Version of the Book of Psalms," 1894.

N.B.—For other early illuminated A.-S. Psalters, *see* J. O. Westwood, "Facsimiles of Miniatures and Ornaments of A.-S. MSS.," 1868.

Proverbs. See under 12th century.

A Martyrology. This also has been numbered among Aelfred's works, but proof, according to the editor, is against this; "its origin must be sought in a Mercian monastery," and it may be "considered one of the oldest monuments of Mercian dialect." The "Additional" MS. cannot, he says, be original; the latter must be therefore somewhat older than the second half of 9th century, which is the date of this fragment. *Ed.*, J. Herzfeld, E.E.T.S., 1900. *MSS.*, Additional, 23211 (fragment); Cott. Jul. A. x.; C.C.C.C. 196, and 41 (fragment).

N.B.—The *Will of King Aelfred*, as preserved in a Register of the Abbey of Newminster at Winchester, was edited with trans., into English and Latin, by O. Manning, 1788, 1828.

Werferth, or Werfrith. Bishop of Worcester.

Translation of Gregory's "Dialogus," at the request of Aelfred, containing a preface by the king. A book of the lives and miracles of the Italian Fathers, and of the immortality of the soul. *Ed.*, H. Hecht, "Bibl. Angelsächs. Prosa.," Bd. v., 1900. *MSS.*, Cott. Otho. C. i.; C.C.C.C. 322; Hatton, 76.

Anglo-Saxon Chronicle.

Oldest historical work in a Germanic language.
MSS.—

Corp. Christ. Coll. Camb. (Parker MS.). B.C. 60 to 1070, with continuations (Winchester).
Cott. Tib. A. vi. Incarnation to 977 (Canterbury).
Cott. Tib. B. i. B.C. 60 to 1066 (Abingdon).
Cott. Tib. B. iv. Incarnation to 1079 (Worcester).
Bodl. Laud. 636. Incarnation to 1154 (Peterborough).
Cott. Domit. A. viii. Incarnation to 1058 (Canterbury).
Cott. Otho. B. xi. (nearly destroyed by fire). Largely a copy of the Parker MS.

The Parker MS. is generally considered the oldest: it is thought to be a copy of older original.

It is uncertain at which centre the English language was first used for the Chronicles. The nucleus of these probably consisted in short Latin Annals. The existing Annals developed into fuller records in the time of Aethelwulf, and, cir. 855, were revised and extended; they were again expanded in Aelfred's time, cir. 892, and it is in this form that the Winchester Annals are extant. After Aelfred's death, the Annals appear to have been carried on independently at different centres, until after the middle of the 12th century.

Ed., B. Thorpe, 1861; J. Earle, with trans., 1865. *Revised ed.*, Plummer and Earle, vol. i., 1892; vol. ii., 1899.

12   LATIN WRITERS.

SCHOLASTICISM.

The philosophy of the Middle Ages was influenced by Aristotelian logic and Christian theology. It was divided into two main schools: Realists and Nominalists. The Nominalists looked upon universals as pure abstractions, merely sounds upon the air—the individual alone being real; the Realists, on the contrary, maintained that they were the only Realities, particulars being mere phantasms. Realism was the more orthodox philosophy, the Nominalists being considered Rationalists by the Church. The latter school did not become prominent before the 11th century. The most active period of Scholasticism lay between the 11th and 14th centuries, its first representative being Erigena, whose theory embraced Platonic and Christian ideas. Lanfranc and Anselm, respectively, opposed Berengarius of Tours, and Roscellinus, two famous representatives of Nominalistic tendencies. Abelard endeavoured to strike out a middle course; the term "Conceptualism" being applied to his system. Towards the close of the Scholastic period, the philosophical and theological world divided into Thomists (Thomas Aquinas) and Scotists (Duns Scotus). Nominalism was revived under Occam, with whom the Scholastic era comes to a close. *See* Rashdall, "The Universities of Europe in the Middle Ages," 1895.

John Scotus Erigena, fl. 850. Of Irish birth; spent great part of his life at the Court of Charles the Bald; said to have been murdered by his scholars at Malmesbury; but this report may have arisen from the confusion of Scotus with another John, the Old Saxon.

De Praedestinatione.

De Divisione Naturae. In form of dialogue. Author's principal work, in 5 books.

Homily on Beginning of S. John, and *Commentary on Gospel.*

Translations of Dionysius and Maximus.

Commentaries on Dionysius.
Glosses on Martianus Capella.
Life of Boethius.
Poems.

Ed., Works, Migne, "Patrologia Latina," 1853; Poems,
L. Traube, "Mon. Germ. Hist.," 1896.

Dicuil, fl. 825.

De Mensurâ Orbis Terrae.   This geography of the world
professes to be based on a book on the measurements of the
Roman Empire, drawn up for Theodosius I. or II.   *Ed.*,
G. Parthey, 1870.

Asser, d. 909 or 910.   Monk of S. David's, and Bishop of Sherborne.

Annales rerum Gestarum Aelfredi Magni, cir. 894.
In two parts—
First: Events from 849–887; drawn largely from A.-S.
Chronicle.
Second: Personal account of Aelfred.

Asser's work, writes its latest editor, "possesses unique
literary interest as the earliest biography of an English
layman." The authenticity of the work has been questioned.
The unique MS. (Cott. Otho. A. xii.) was destroyed by fire,
and, of the two editions previously published, the original was
in one largely altered and interpolated, and in the other some
of the interpolations were copied as part of the original, so
that the task of deciding what is due to Asser has been a
work of difficulty. The whole matter is dealt with exhaust-
ively in the 1904 edition. There are transcripts extant
of the old MS. Among them one (C.C.C.C. 100) was
bequeathed by Bishop Parker.   *Ed.*, W. H. Stevenson,
Clarendon Press, 1904.   Trans., "Alfred in the Chronicles,"
E. Conybeare, 1900.

With Asser's Life, Mr. Stevenson has also edited "The
Annals of S. Neots," erroneously ascribed to Asser. The
author is unknown. The story of Alfred and the cakes has
its origin in this work.

13   ## Xth CENTURY.

England shared in the general condition of literary depression which prevailed on the Continent during this period. "The Ecclesiastical bent of the 10th century," writes Dr. Garnett, "benefitted art rather than literature."

The voice of the people was heard only in the patriotic songs which are preserved in the Chronicles.

The great promoters of church reform during this century were Dunstan, Archbishop of Canterbury; Aethelwold, Bishop of Winchester; and Oswald, Archbishop of York. Aelfric was a supporter of the movement. *See* F. Tupper, "History and Text of the Benedictine Reform of 10th Century," Modern Language Notes, 1893; Mary Bateson, "Rules for Monks, etc.," *Eng. Hist. Review*, ix. 1894.

VERNACULAR WRITERS.

Prose.

Aelfric, fl. 1006.   Aelfric's identity has been much discussed; he is now generally believed to have been the Abbot of Eynsham.

The Catholic Homilies (*Homiliae Catholicae*).   Two sets of sermons for the principal Sundays and festivals throughout the year, adapted from the Latin; some written in alliterative form.   *Ed.*, with trans., B. Thorpe, Aelfric Soc., 1844-46. *MSS.*, Reg. 7, c. xii. ; Camb. Univ. Gg. iii. 28, etc.

Lives of Saints (*Passiones Sanctorum*).   Homilies in the form of metrical lives of saints, "whom not the vulgar but the monks honour by special services" (SS. Eugenia, Basil, Julian, Sebastian, etc.).   Alliterative epitomes of the books of Kings and Maccabees are also included in this work.   *Ed.*, Text (Cott. Jul. E. vii.), and trans., W. W. Skeat, E.E.T.S., 1881.

Translations, or *Epitomes of Pentateuch, Joshua, Judges, Job, Esther* (MS., Laud E. 381), *Judith* (MS., Cott. Otho. B. x.), the two latter in rhythm.

Pastoral Letter (*Canones Aelfrici*) to the priests of the diocese, written for Wulfsige, Bishop of Sherborn.

3

Pastoral Letter, for Wulfstan, Archbishop of York. These two letters, with a third on the use of the Holy Oil, are *ed.*, Thorpe, text and trans., in "Ancient Laws and Institutes of England."

Abridgement of Aethelwold's Work on Monastic Rule, *De Consuetudini Monachorum.* *Ed.*, Mary Bateson, Hampshire Record Soc., 1892. *MSS.*, C.C.C.C. k. 265, etc.

Treatise on the Old and New Testament.

Version of Baeda's *De Temporum Ratione, De Temporibus*, and *De Natura Regum*, condensed into a single work, the historical parts being omitted as King Aelfred had already given a history of the world. *Ed.*, Cockayne, "Leechdoms," etc., vol. iii.

Version of work by S. Basil ("Hexameron," Advice to a Spiritual Son).

Version of Alcuin's *Interrogationes Sigevulfi in Genesin*, A Handbook on Genesis, being answers to questions put to him by his pupil Sigewulf. *Ed.*, Lat. and A.-S. text, Maclean, "Anglia," vi. and vii.

Separate Homilies.—*On the Sevenfold Gifts of the Spirit*; *Address to Wulfgeat*; *On Chastity* (to *Sigeferth*), etc.

Educational Works.—*Grammar, Glossary.* *Ed.*, Zupitza; "Sammlung Eng. Denkmaler," 1800. In Latin, *Colloquium* (enlarged by Aelfric Bata), afterwards supplied with vernacular gloss. *Ed.*, Thorpe, "Analecta Anglo-Saxonica," 1834; Leo, "Altsachs. ü. Anglosachs. Sprachproben," 1838; Zupitza, 1880. The MS. Cott. Tib. A. 3, has Saxon interlinear version.

Life of S. Aethelwold.

For works in the vernacular, *see* Grein, "Bibl. Angelsächs. Prosa." *See* also C. L. White, "Aelfric, a new Study of his Life and Writings" (Yale Studies in English). Numerous *MSS.* of Aelfric's works are in Cottonian Coll., Bodleian, and Camb. Univ. Libr., and Corp. Christi.

Anonymous.

Blickling Homilies. Probably dating from last quarter of 10th century. *Ed.*, Text and trans., R. Morris, E.E.T.S., 1874-80. *MS.*, Blickling Hall, Norfolk.

Læce Bôc (*Leech Book*). Collection of prescriptions and recipes, which mingle magic with medicine. The work is compiled from various Latin and Greek (the latter probably known through a Latin medium) sources. The names of Oxa and Dun appear as those of two authorities, and certain recipes are said to have been given to King Alfred by the Patriarch of Jerusalem. *Ed.*, Text and trans., O. Cockayne, "Leechdoms, Wort-Cunning, and Starcraft," vol. ii., 1864-66; A.-S. text, Grein, *op. cit.* *MSS.*, Reg. 12, D. xvii., with a missing part supplied from Harl. 55.

N.B.—For other MSS. extant on similar subjects, and other works of the kind, charms, etc., *see* Cockayne, *op. cit.*

14   Poetry.

Byrthnoth's Death (*Battle of Malden*) (long lines). "One of the pearls of old English poetry" (Ten Brink). This conflict with the Danes at the river Panta, near Malden, in Essex, took place either 991 or 993. *Ed.*, trans. (with "Judith," "Elene," "Brunanburh"), Garnett, 1889; Cook and Tinker, "Select Trans.," etc.; C. L. Crow, 1897. *See* Ten Brink, *op. cit.* *MS.*, Cott. Otho. A. xii. (fragment), destroyed by fire. (The poem is given in Hearne's ed. of John of Glastonbury's Chronicle, 1726.)

Poems from Anglo-Saxon Chronicle.

Victory of Athelstan at Brunanburh, 937 or 938 (Garnett, Crow, Tinker, *op. cit.*).
Conquest of Mercia (Relief of Five Towns), 942.
Coronation of Eadgar, 972-4.
Eadgar's Death, 975.
Death of Edward the Martyr, 979.
Ed., "Battle of Malden, and short poems from A.-S. Chronicle," W. J. Sedgefield, Belles Lettres Series. *MSS.*, A.-S. Chronicle. The same poem is not always found in all MSS.

Menologium. Poetical Calendar of Saints (long lines), 940-80. There were Latin models for this work in prose and verse, as well as works in the vernacular. *Ed.*, Text and trans., S. Fox, 1830. *See* Imelmann, "Anglia," Beibl. xiv. *MS.*, Cott. Tib. B. 1.

15 LATIN WRITERS.

Aethelwold, d. 984. Bishop of Winchester.

De Consuetudine Monachorum. Rule of S. Benedict.

A treatise *On the Circle*, in the Bodleian Library, is also said to have been written by him ; it is addressed to Gerbert (Silvester II.), who was a leader of the scientific movement that had begun on the Continent.

Aethelweard, d. 998 (?).

Fabii Ethelwerdi Chronicorum Libri quatuor. Creation to 975.

Earliest Latin Chronicle, founded on the Saxon Chronicle, and thought to represent a copy of the latter no longer extant. The author also makes use of Baeda.

Byrthferth, fl. 1000. Monk of Ramsey.

A Life of S. Dunstan is usually attributed to him. *Ed.*, Stubbs, * " Memorials of S. Dunstan," Rolls Series. Four treatises are his undisputed work :
Commentaries on Baeda's—
De Natura Rerum.
De Temporum Ratione.
De Indigitatione.
De Ratione Unciarum.
A Latin scientific work (" Computus ") with A.-S. trans. n Bodleian Library, has Byrthferth's name in it.
Other works ascribed to him are not known.

Wulsftan, fl. 1000. Precentor of Winchester.

Vita S. Swithuni. Latin verse. Version of Lantferth's (Monk of Winchester, fl. late 10th century) work.

There is mention also of a verified life of S. Aethelwold ; a prose life of Aethelwold, which has been published as by Wulfstan, is not now considered to be his.

16 ## XIth CENTURY (1st Half).

A noticeable feature in the vernacular literature of this period is the introduction of romance, some of the material from which the romantic writers of the succeeding centuries were to draw their inspiration having already found its way over from the Continent.

VERNACULAR WRITERS.

Prose.

Science.

Anonymous.

Herbarium Apuleii, from a Latin original, with a continuation, chiefly from Dioskorides. *Medicina de Quadrupidibus*, associated with the name of Sextus Placidus. Both these works are thought to date from first half of century. *Ed.*, Text and trans., O. Cockayne, vol. i. "Leechdoms, Wort-cunning and Starcraft," 1864–66. *MSS.*, Cott. Vitell. C. iii., coloured illus. (injured by fire); Harl. 585; Hatton, 76.

Theology.

Wulfstan (Lupus?). Bishop of Worcester and Archbishop of York, d. 1023.

Homilies. There is no unquestionable proof that these were written by Wulfstan. Napier's verdict is that the bulk of the Homilies are compilations of others; some from the Blickling and Aelfric's having only a fresh introduction. The best known of the Homilies is the "Sermo Lupi ad Anglos quando Dani maxime persecute sunt eos," written in 1012, during the horrors of the Danish invasion. This Homily and three others are, according to the editor, undoubtedly Wulfstan's. *Ed.*, Napier, "Sammlung Engl. Denkmäler," 1880. *MSS.*, Cott. Nero. A. 1; C.C.C.C.

History.

Anglo - Saxon Chronicle. *Worcester Annals, Abingdon Annals* (§ 11).

Miscellaneous.

Anglo-Saxon version of *Epistola Alexandri ad Aristotelem*, containing marvellous tales of India.   *MSS.*, Cott. Vitell. A. xv.

Anglo-Saxon version of *De Rebus in Oriente Mirabilis.* Full of wonderful accounts of extraordinary men and animals. Both the above *ed.*, O. Cockayne, " Narratiunculae Anglice Conscriptae," 1861.   *MSS.*, Cott. Tib. B. v. ; Cott. Vitell. A. xv.

A.-S. Version of *Apollonius of Tyre.* A Greek romance, of which the oldest extant form is in Latin.

Antiochus, King of Antioch, becoming enamoured of his own daughter, keeps off her suitors by proposing a riddle to each one as he arrives ; if the wooer does not answer correctly, he is put to death. Apollonius, the Prince of Tyre, having guessed aright, Antiochus, in his alarm at his wicked secret being discovered, sets a price on his head. Apollonius, fleeing for his life, is shipwrecked, but being taken into favour by the King of the land on whose shore he is thrown, finally marries the latter's daughter. Antiochus dies, and Apollonius is elected King in his stead. On his voyage to take possession of his dominion, his wife, believed to be dead, is thrown into the sea in a chest, in which money is enclosed with a request to those who find it, to give the body burial. Being washed ashore at Ephesus, the Queen is there restored to life, and retires to live among the vestals of Diana. Meanwhile Apollonius landing at Tharsus leaves his infant daughter in charge of a family that had before befriended him ; all is well with the girl till her old nurse dies, when she is only saved from being killed, by a band of pirates, who, rushing on shore, seize her, and carry her off as a slave. Her subsequent trials are of the worst description, but finally, Apollonius, who after seeking his daughter, and being told she is dead, is mournfully return-ing home, puts into the port where she is in the hands of a cruel master. She is taken on board to entertain him, riddles being here introduced, and finally recognition takes place. Sailing home together they come to Ephesus, and the tale ends with the recovery of the wife.

The translation of this poem "disclosed a strange, new world to men who had been wont to delight in the songs of Beowulf, of Athelstan, and of Byrhtnoth, a world in which all things were softer and more full of grace, but of smaller mould than at home" (Ten Brink).   *N.B.*—The tale of Apollonius is given in the "Gesta Romanorum," in Viterbo's "Pantheon," and Gower's "Confessio Amantis."   Its relation with the "Vilkina Saga," with the poem of "King Orendel" (Germany, § 14), and the Chanson of "Jourdain de Blaivies" (France, § 22), and Solomon Markolf cycle is indicated in A. H. Smyth's work (*see* below).   *Ed.*, Text and trans., B. Thorpe, 1834; and in Belles Lettres Series, with Alexander's Letters to Aristotle.   *See* S. Singer, "Apollonius von Tyrus," etc. (chief versions of story compared).   A. H. Smyth, "Shakespeare's Pericles and Apollonius of Tyre," 1898.   Fascimile of translation by R. Copland, printed by Wynkyn de Worde, 1510 (*ed.*, Ashbee, 1870).   *See* also under Riese, W. Meyer, Thielmann.   *MS.*, C.C.C.C. 201 (imperfect).

17   Poems from A.-S. Chronicle.

Imprisonment and death of Aelfred Aetheling, son of Aethelred II., 1036.   *Death of Edward the Confessor,* 1065.

18   XIth CENTURY (2nd Half).

Transitional, or Early Middle English (Körting).

The current of English Literature was checked, although not entirely interrupted in its flow, by the introduction of the Norman tongue into England.   The Literature of the country for a considerable period subsequent to the Invasion comes chiefly under the headings of Latin and Anglo-Norman. Meanwhile the native tongue began to exhibit those changes which naturally arose from its disuse for official and literary purposes, and from its banishment from polite society.   The loss of inflexion was the chief sign of the work of degenera-

tion that was going on; retained to some extent until about
the middle of the 13th century, it then became more fully discarded. The "Peterborough Annals," with which the "A.-S.
Chronicle" concludes (first half of 12th century) already show
signs of the gradual transformation that was taking place in
the old speech of the country, and is considered one of the
last monuments of Anglo-Saxon or Old English. Henry
III.'s Proclamation, the so-called "Oxford Provision," is the
earliest document of certain date in which English again
appears in use for official purposes, side by side with French.
(*Ed.* (with French text), Matzner "Alt-Englische Sprachproben," 1867 ; Marsh, "History of the English Language."
See also Skeat, *Academy*, 521, 523, and 527.) During
these transition centuries there had been great confusion
of dialects, no leading literary work winning pre-eminence
for one over the other. The three chief dialects during this
period were the Northern, Southern, and Midland. By
degrees the Midland (derived from the old Mercian) began
to take the lead among them. "As the language of London,
and as a dialect intelligible to both Northern and Southern
Englishmen, it had great advantages, and was rapidly (latter
half 14th century) becoming in some measure the common
speech, when the Wyclifite version of the Bible, and the
works of Chaucer, both in this dialect, stamped it at once
and for all time as literary English. Thus the common
English of to-day is the direct descendant not of Alfred's
West Saxon, but of the old Mercian dialect, and the modern
dialects of Somerset and other South English shires are the
only living representatives of the West Saxons." (*See* Art.
by Kittredge, Webster's "Ency. Dict.") The incorpora-
tion of a certain percentage of French words into the English
language is its only debt to Norman-French, for in spite of
the loss of inflexion and of other modifications, it retained its
Teutonic character.

Few vernacular works have come down to us from the
period following on the Norman Conquest. To the 11th
century belongs the name of Leofric of Brun; the work on
Hereward's youth which he is reported to have written is
only known to us by the mention made of it in the Latin life
of the Saxon chieftain (§ 28.)

19   LATIN WRITERS.

Prose.

Theology, Lives of Saints.

Lanfranc, b. cir. 1005; d. 1089. An Italian. Founder of Schools of Avranches and Bec; Archbishop of Canterbury, 1070. Lanfranc left few works, and of these some are lost. Chief extant work:

Liber de Corpore et Sanguine Domini nostri (Liber Scintillarum). Addressed to Berengarius in defence of the orthodox dogma of Transubstantiation, not earlier than 1079.

Letters, chiefly on Ecclesiastical matters.

Commentaries on St. Paul's Epistles. Notes only.

Ritual of the Benedictine Use in England, and other short pieces.

Of lost works ascribed to him are, *Commentary on the Psalms, Historia Ecclesiastica sui Temporis* (mentioned by Eadmer), and *Gesta Ducis Giulielmi.* A dialogue on theological matters, *Elucidarium* is attributed, not without question, to Lanfranc.

Ed., Works, J. A. Giles, "Patres Ecclesiae," 1844.

Anselm, b. cir. 1033; d. 1109. Successor of Lanfranc as Prior of Bec, and afterwards Abbot; enthroned as Archbishop of Canterbury, 1093. Also an Italian by birth.

Monologion. On the existence and nature of God; application of Platonic ideas to Christian doctrine.

Proslogion. Argument on other grounds concerning existence of God.

Cur Deus Homo. On necessity of the Incarnation.

De Fide Trinitatis. Answer to Roscellinus.

De Processione Spiritus Sancti.

De Casu Diaboli. On origin of evil.

De Concordia praescientiae et praedestinationes.

Other treatises, dialogues, homilies, letters, prayers, and meditations.

Ed., Works, Migne, "Patrologiae," 1853, etc.

Osbern, fl. 1090. Monk of Christ Church, Canterbury.

*_Vita S. Dunstani._ (Stubbs, "Memorials of S. Dunstan.")

Vita S. Alphegi, et Translatione S. Alphegi.

Vita S. Odonis (Odo, Archbishop of Canterbury). (MS. destroyed by fire.)

Two treatises : _De Re Musicae,_ and _De Vocum Consonantis,_ known only in manuscript.

20 _N.B._—For MSS. of Historical works, _see_ "Descriptive Catalogue of MSS. relating to the History of Great Britain and Ireland," T. Duffus Hardy, Rolls Series; and Potthast, "Bibl. Hist. Medii. Aevi," 1896. _See_ also C. Gross, "The Sources and Literature of English History" (complete bibliography), 1901.

History.

Marianus Scotus, b. 1028; d. 1082 (?).

Chronicle, from Christian era to 1082, continuation to 1200. This Chronicle was the basis of Florence of Worcester's work.

William of Poitiers, fl. cir. 1087.

Gesta Willelmi ducis Normannorum et regis Angliae, 1035-67. _Ed.,_ Giles, "Scriptores," Caxton Soc., 1845.

_N.B._—The history of the Normans ("Historiæ Normannorum") by Jumièges, belongs to the second half of this century.

Turgot. Bishop of St. Andrews, d. 1115.

The _Historia Dunelmensis Ecclesiae,_ for long erroneously ascribed to Turgot, is now generally attributed to Symeon of Durham. The other extant work which is assigned to him by Fordun and others is a _Life of S. Margaret of Scotland._ Other works mentioned as his not now known.

Ingulph. Abbot of Croyland, d. 1109.

Historia Croylandensis, from the foundation to 1091, with

several continuations. This work with the continuation extant to 1117, attributed to Peter of Blois, 12th century, is now known to be a forgery; a date not earlier than 14th century is assigned to both these parts. Other continuations carry the work to end of 15th century. *Ed.*, Trans., H. T. Riley. Bohn's Antiq. Libr., 1854.

21 POETRY.

Guy of Amiens, d. cir. 1076. Accompanied Queen Matilda to England. Probable author of *De Bello Hastingensi*. *Ed.*, Petrie, "Mon. Hist. Brit.," 1848.

Godfrey of Winchester, d. 1107.
Epigrams. Short poems.

22 ## XIITH CENTURY.

(SEMI-SAXON, 1150, KITTREDGE.)

The 12th century was a period of noted mental activity and of great literary production, both in England and abroad.

The University of Oxford came into being early in this century and appears to have been modelled on the schools of Paris; by the beginning of the 13th century, it had taken rank among the most celebrated schools of Western Europe. The three earliest founded of its colleges were Balliol, Merton, and University, which date from the latter half of the 13th century.

The University of Cambridge dates from the early years of the following century; its oldest college is Peterhouse, founded cir. 1286.

VERNACULAR WRITERS.

PROSE.

History.

Anglo-Saxon Chronicle: *Peterborough Annals* (§ 11). These annals closed the A.-S. Chronicle, and are one of the last monuments of the Anglo-Saxon or Old English period. They were written after the loss of the old records in the fire which destroyed Peterborough Cathedral in 1116. The annals from other centres were used as copies, but there were also interpolations from documents of a less genuine description.

Religious, Didactic.

The Ancren Riwle (*Anchoresses' Rule*). This, one of the best of the earlier prose writings, is a work in eight books, composed at the request of three sisters who had early in life dedicated themselves to the life of the cloister. Rules are given in it for the conduct and guidance of both the outer and inner life of an ascetic. The wisdom and kindliness of the learned author breathe through many charming passages. "One part of it," to quote Prof. Ker (*op. cit.*) "the 'Wooing of the Soul,' is beyond all praise for its pathetic grace and beauty. It was not left alone in its seriousness and reserve. The theme was taken up again. . . . 'The Wooing of our Lord' (*see* 13th century) as compared with the passage in the 'Ancren Riwle' may stand as one indication of the sensibility and its accompanying rhetoric that corrupted late mediæval literature in many ways." The influence of French culture is discernible in the work, and French expressions are used.

The authorship has till recently been assigned to Richard le Poor, successively Bishop of Chichester, Salisbury, and Durham, who died in 1237, his birthplace being at Tarente, in Dorsetshire, the home of the three ladies to whom the work was dedicated, and where his heart was buried. But Kölbing points out ("Eng. Studien," ix. p. 116) that C.C.C.C. MS., which is the oldest, can scarcely date later than 1150, and if so, he adds, all hitherto accepted ideas as to author and date of work are antiquated, and it is even a question whether the work is of the South, to which it has been generally assigned. In this case the work comes before the "Poema Morale." The "Ancren Riwle" has come down to us in three languages (*see* MSS.). The editor Morton showed the English text to be the original, Bramlette supports the earlier opinion of Wanley that the Latin was the earlier text. *Ed.*, J. Morton, Camden Soc., 1853; E. Flügel and L.

Stanford, "The A. R. and Early Theological Prose,"
Belles - Lettres Series; text in preparation by Kölbing;
Extracts, R. Morris, "Specimens"; Sweet, "First Middle
English Primer." *See* Bramlette, "The original language of
the A. R.," "Anglia," xv. *MSS.*, English, Cott. Nero.
A. xiv., Titus D. xviii., Cleopatra C. vi.; C.C.C.C.
(oldest); Caius 234; the Cotton MSS. also included a
Latin and a French text, both destroyed by fire; a Norman
French text is in the Vernon MS.

23 POETRY.

Anonymous.

Poema Morale (*Moral Ode*). South-west of England.
An old man expresses his remorse for wasted life. In the
course of this poem, a penitential homily in verse, the joys
of heaven as incentives to a better life, and the pains of hell
as warnings, are vividly described. "Depth of thought,
warmth of sentiment, nobility of feeling, and a spiritual
conception of spiritual things," distinguish the author of the
"Poema Morale." (*See* Ten Brink, *op. cit.*, p. 155.) From
this same source is given the following specimen of the verse.
Beginning of poem:

"I am now older than I was, in winters and in lore,
I wield more power than I did: were but my wisdom more.
Too long have I been like a child in word and eke in deed;
Yet, though I am in winters old, too young am I in heed."

This poem is of interest and importance as showing innova-
tions in rhythm and metre which distinguish it from the older
verse; it will be seen that the rhyme occurs linking the two
long lines, not the two halves of the line, as it is found in the
"Proverbs of Alfred," which is less far removed from the
old alliterative method. And "we here for the first time
encounter a principle of accentuation which was to leave its
impress upon the entire future development of English metre"
(Ten Brink). *Ed.*, Text and trans., R. Morris, "Old
English Homilies," 1878; Zupitza, "Anglia," i. and iii.
(Digby); Furnivall, 1862, "Early English Poems"
(Egerton). *MSS.*, Lambeth 487 (oldest version);

Digby A. 4; Egerton 613 (2); Oxford, Jesus Coll.; Cambridge Trin. Coll. B. 14, 52.

The so-called *Proverbs of Alfred.* Collections of Proverbs were in circulation during the 12th century, and ascribed to Alfred, and have come down to us in later versions. "In them we find the ancient long line in the midst of its transformation into the short couplet" (Ten Brink). Both alliteration and rhyme are used, the rhyme linking the two halves of the long line, and giving the impression of a rhymed couplet. *Ed.*, Wright and Halliwell, "Reliquiae Antiquae"; R. Morris, "Old English Miscellany," E.E.T.S., 1872. *See* Dr. E. Gropp, "On the Language of the Proverbs, etc.," 1879; the author endeavours to show the resemblance which to a certain extent exists between the *Proverbs* and Alfred's *Handbook* as extant in the *Soliloquia.* *MSS.*, Camb. Trin. Coll. B. 14, 39; Oxford, Jesus, I. 29; Lincoln.

Saint Godric.

"We are not so rich in English poems of the 12th century," writes Zupitza in his article, "as to be able to neglect the smallest poetical remains of that time," and among these minor contributions are the three small poems by S. Godric. The saint came of a poor family in Norfolk, and was brought up as a merchant; when he became rich enough to own a vessel of his own, he combined religious pilgrimages with his commercial voyages. Finally, after visits to Jerusalem and Rome, he retired from the haunts of men, dwelling as a hermit in a rough hut near Whitby, and afterwards in a hole in the ground, covered with grass, near Durham, where he died 1170.

Of his three small religious poems, one was taught him direct by the Virgin, and another was sung to him by his sister after her death, and the third was to S. Nicholas. S. Godric's life was written by Reginald of Coldingham, or Durham (see under Latin Writers, 27), and the poems are in the MSS. of this life. *See* J. Zupitza, "Englische Studien," xi. 401. *MSS.*, Laud, 413; Harl. 153, 322.

A poetical rendering of the *Paternoster*, dating from the second half of this century " is especially noteworthy because it is the oldest known poem in which a short rhyming couplet is consistently and regularly employed " (Ten Brink).

24 The English language, waiting to start afresh on its literary career in the original works which appeared at the close of the 12th and beginning of the 13th century was kept from falling into disuse by the copyist, who showed no great concern as regards the integrity of his text, which he manipulated as far as was necessary to bring it into conformity with his own particular dialect. Among the works chiefly chosen for transcription were the old Homilies and the Gospels; among the versions of the latter dating from the 12th century are the famous " Hatton Gospels " (Bodleian).

25 THE CYCLES OF ROMANCE.

England waited till the following century before adding works in her own tongue to swell the rising tide of romantic literature, although before the close of the 12th it had already been represented, on the Continent, by some of the most famous poems of the Middle Ages, and by the writings of Anglo-Normans. The metrical romances, and later the prose romances, a vast body of literature extending from the 12th to the 15th and 16th centuries, of which the material was in one or more of its branches, common to all the civilised nations, may be divided into three main cycles : The Arthurian, the Carolingian, and the Alexander Cycle. The story of Troy, and that of Thebes also found a place in the early romances. The first indication of the Alexander Legends having penetrated to England was noticed in the preceding century; the " Song of Roland " was sung on English land by the invading Normans at Senlac; the Arthurian legends gather round a British hero, of whom we first find mention in the so-called Nennius,[1] but who

---

[1] There is difference of opinion as to author and date of the " Historia Britonum." It has been ascribed to Gildas, and to Mark the Hermit, an Irish Bishop. Nennius is thought by Zimmer to be the real author, and to have completed his history in 796; others think that Nennius added to a more ancient text, or that his version was preceded by another Latin version of the original by Mark the Hermit. Nennius himself is severally

remained unfamiliar to the general public, and apparently also to historians, until he leapt into fame and popularity on the appearance of Geoffrey of Monmouth's famous history (§ 28). The poems of the French poet, Chrétien de Troies (*see* France, § 26), head the long list of Arthurian Romances, and considerable controversy has been active concerning the sources of his tales, and as to the medium through which the Arthurian legends reached France. According to Gaston Paris, Welsh bards had probably, even before the Norman Conquest, passed into Anglo-Saxon territory, carrying with them their " lays." In the middle of the 12th century these " lays " were brought to France, the Arthurian legends being transmitted by these, or the recited tale, either directly by the bards, or through the medium of Anglo-Norman compositions. The Welsh form of these romances was in all probability never written down, and the earliest French form is probably lost. G. Paris is strongly opposed by W. Förster and his school. Not any of the " lays," writes Förster, had anything to do with Arthur, neither does he agree to the theory of previous Anglo-Norman romances, of which no extant MS. is preserved ; according to his theory, however, such a medium was not needed, as judging by the name forms in the French romances, apart from other details, he believes the legends to have been transmitted through Armorican " Conteurs." Zimmer supports this theory, both as regards the legends passing to the French by way of Armorica, and also as to their being carried by reciters, not by singers, " for Celtic poetry was essentially lyric not epic." Golther further insists that Chrétien's Romances were not founded on purely Celtic traditions, and that the knightly idea of honour and the conjugal tenderness which are conspicuous in them were unknown to the Celt of Britain. These arguments are dealt with by Mr. Nutt, who contends for the Celtic origin of all the Arthurian romances, and brings forward examples to controvert Golther's second statement. The Celtic origin is also strongly supported by Mr. Arthur C. L.

assigned to 8th, 9th, and 10th centuries. The work itself gives a history of Britain, and a genealogy of English kings to 796. Gildas, to whom the work has been assigned by some, wrote his " De Excidio Britanniae " in Armorica in the 6th century, this history being the only contemporary authority for the conquest of Britain by the Teutonic tribes (see Gross, *op. cit.*).

Brown, who founds his theory on a comparison with extant
Welsh and Irish tales. (For further matter as regards
Chrétien de Troie's works, see under same, France, 12th
Century.)

See G. Paris, "Hist. Litt. France," tome xxx. (*see*
France, General Authorities); "Hist. Litt. Franç., au
moyen Âge," last edition, 1905.

W. Förster, "Chrestien v. Troyes Sämmtliche Werke ";
Introductions to "Yvain " and to "Eric et Enide."

Birch-Hirschfeld, "Die Sage vom Gral," 1877.

A. Nutt, "Studies on the Legend of the Holy Grail,"
1888; "Les derniers travaux allemands sur la Légende du
Saint Graal," "Revue Celtique," xii. ; and "Folk Lore," ii.,
1891 ; W. Golther, "Sitzungsber. Philos. philol. u. Hist.
der K. Bayer. Akad. Wissensch.," 1890 ("On the Conte
del Graal in its relation to the Welsh and English Versions ");
"Zeitschr. für Vergleich. Litt. Gesch.," Neue Folge, Bd. iii.
("On the Relation between French and Celtic Literature in
the Middle Ages ") ; F. Lot, "Sur la Provenance du Cycle
Arthurien," "Romania," 1895, 1896; "Glastonbury and
Avalon," 1898; J. Loth, "Des Nouvelles Théories sur
l'origine des Romans Arthuriens " (from "Revue Celtique "),
1892; Zimmer, "Göttingische Gelehrte Anzeigen," 12
and 20, 1890; (On the work of A. Nutt and G. Paris);
"Zeitschr. für französ. Sprache u. Litt.," xii. ("On the
Breton Element in G. of Monmouth, and the names in old
French Arthur romances ") ; Vollmöller, "Kritische Jahres-
bericht, etc.," Year i., Heft 4, 1890; Arthur C. L. Brown,
"Studies and Notes in Philology and Literature," vol. viii.,
1903, ("Yvain, A Study in the Origins of Arthurian
Romance "). *See* also J. L. Weston, "The Legend of Sir
Percival," Grimm Library, 1906; and D. Kempe, "The
Legend of the Holy Grail," E.E.T.S., 1905.

Ward, "Cat. of Romances," vol. i.

For Anglo-Norman Writers : Philippe de Thaon, Beroul,
Thomas, Gaimar, Wace, Marie de France, *see* France.

26 LATIN WRITERS.

PROSE.

Science.

Aethelhard, or **Adelard of Bath,** alive 1139. Traveller; said to be versed in Greek and Arab science.

De Eodem et diverso (*Identity and Difference*). An allegory on Worldliness and Philosophy, dealing with the reconciling of the existence of the individual with that of the species.
Quæstiones Naturales. Based on the author's Arab studies.
Treatises on the Astrolabe, Abacus, and *Translation of Kharismian Tables.*
Translation of Euclid, from original or Arab version.

Roger Infans, fl. 1124.

Treatise on the Compotus. (Method of Computing the Calendar.)

Daniel de Merlai, or **Marley,** fl. 1176–90. Mathematician and Astronomer; studied in Spain.

De Naturis inferiorum et superiorum. Two books.

Alexander Neckham, b. 1157; d. 1217. (§§ 27, 30, 31.) Abbot of Cirencester; teacher at University of Paris. Nicknamed "Nequam."

**De Naturis Rerum,* a Paraphrase of his own poem.
Commentaries on Aristotle, Ovid, M. Capella.

27 *Theology, Lives of Saints.*

Eadmer, d. 1124 (?). Monk of Canterbury. (*See* § 28.)

**Vita Anselmi,* **Vita Oswaldi,* **Vita Dunstani.*
Also lives of *Odo,* and *Wilfrid,* and possibly life of *Bregwin*; and Theological Tracts and Letters.

Symeon of Durham, fl. early decades of 12th century. (§ 28.)

De Miraculis et translationibus Cuthberti. Authorship conjectural.

William of Malmesbury, d. 1143 (?) (§ 28.)

Vita S. Dunstani (**Memoirs of S. Dunstan*), *Vita S. Wulfstani, De Miraculis S. Mariae, Commentary on Lamentations.* Also ascribed to him, *Passio S. Indracti, De Miraculis S. Andreae.* Other works and lives appear to be lost: among them a life of *S. Patrick,* and life of *S. Benignus.*

Lawrence, Prior of Durham, d. 1154. (§ 31.)

Vita S. Brigidae, work ascribed to him; also *Homilies.* Chiefly known as a Latin poet.

Robert Pullen, d. 1147 (?) Mentioned as Archdeacon of Rochester; Chancellor of Rome, cir. 1144.

Sententiarum Theologicarum, 8 books. Other works, *De Contemptu Mundi, Super Doctorum Dictes, Commentary on the Apocalypse, Sermons,* etc.

Hugo of Rouen, Abbot of Reading, and Archbishop of Rouen, d. 1164.

Dialogi de Summo Bono, 7 books; *De Heresibus sui Temporis,* 3 books; *De Creatione Rerum,* or *Hexameron; Vita S. Adjatoris.*

Robert de Melun, Bishop of Hereford, d. 1167. A pupil of Abelard; teacher of high repute; taught at Melun; John of Salisbury, and Thomas à Becket were his pupils. Chief work, *Summa Sententiarum* (on God, Angels, Soul of Man, and Incarnation), 5 parts.

Ailred or Ethelred, Abbot of Rievaulx, b. 1109 (?) d. 1166. (§ 28.)

De Miraculis Hagustaldensis Ecclesiae (*Saints of the Church of Hexham*). Ed., Surtees Soc., 1864-5.

Vita S. Niniani. Also several other treatises and homilies. The " Life of Margaret of Scotland," ascribed to him, is not his work.

John of Salisbury, Bishop of Chartres, d. 1180. (*See* § 30.) *Lives of S. Anselm and Becket.*

Gilbert Foliot, Bishop of London, d. 1187. A supporter of the king in the struggle between the latter and Becket.

Commentary on Song of Songs.
Valuable Collection of Letters to the Pope, and Eminent Ecclesiastics.

Giraldus de Barri (Cambrensis), Archdeacon of Brecknock, twice appointed to See of S. David's. b. 1146 (?) ; d. 1220 (?)   (§ 28, 30.)
*Speculum Ecclesiae.
*Gemma Ecclesiastica.
*De Jure et Statu Menevensis Ecclesiae.
*Vita Galfridi (Archbishop of York).
*Vita S. Remigii (Bishop of Lincoln).
*Vita S. Hugonis (Bishop of Lincoln) ; *Vita S. Davidis* (Archbishop of Monmouth) ; *Vita S. Ethelberti.*

Henry of Saltrey, fl. 1150.
Purgatorium S. Patricii. (Several MSS. in B.M.) The first to recite the tale as it was told by the Knight Owein, who, according to the legend, had himself descended into Purgatory, to Gilbert of Louth, Abbot of Basingwerk (d. 1153 ?) a friend of the author. Two later English versions are known as "Owayne Miles" ; a Metrical translation by Marie de France, and two others, are extant in French.

Reginald of Coldingham, or Durham, fl. 1170.
Life of S. Cuthbert ; Life of S. Godric the Hermit, whom Reginald cared for at the last, taking down his life from the hermit's lips.   *Ed.,* Surtees Soc.
*Life of S. Oswald, Life of S. Ebba of Coldingham.

Jocelin of Furness, fl. 1200.
Life and Miracles of S. Patrick ; Life of Kentigern, first Bishop of Glasgow ; *Life of Waltheof of Melrose ; Life of S.*

Helen, also attributed to him. Another work mentioned by
Stow is not now known. Extracts of a *Life of King David
of Scotland* are found in Fordun's " Scotichronicon."

N.B.—For lives of Becket, *see* under History.

Some sermons and tracts are extant by Alexander of
Neckham (§§ 26, 30, 31); and Nigellus Wireker wrote his
Contra Curiales et Officiales Clericos, with a prologue in verse
(§ 31). *Ed.,* Wright, "Latin Satirical Poets."

28   *History.*

Florence, Monk of Worcester, d. 1118.

Chronicon ex Chronicis. Continuations to 1141 and 1295.
Ed., B. Thorpe, Eng. Hist. Soc., 1849. Trans., Bohn's
Hist. Libr., 1847. *See* under Marianus Scotus (§ 20).

Eadmer. (§ 27.)

**Historia Novorum,* cir. A.D., 960–1122. The most reliable
authority for this period.

Symeon of Durham. (§ 27.)

**Historia de Regibus Anglorum et Dacorum,* 2 Chrons.,
616 to 1129; continued by John of Hexham.
**Historia Dunelmensis Ecclesiae,* 635–1096. Continuations
to 1154. This work was at one time attributed to Turgot.

Ordericus Vitalis, Monk of St. Evroul, b. 1075; d. 1143 (?)

Historia Ecclesiastica, 13 books. Christian Era to 1141.
Ed., A. le Prévost, "Soc. Hist. France," 1838-55. Trans.,
Bohn's Ant. Libr., 1853-56.

William of Malmesbury. (§ 27.)

**De Gestis Regum Anglorum,* A.D. 449 to 1127–8. Trans.,
J. A. Giles, Bohn's Ant. Libr., 1847.
**Historiae Novellae.* Continuation of above to 1142.
**De Gestis Pontificum Anglorum,* from A.D. 601.
De Antiquitate Glastoniensis Coenobeii, A.D. 63 to 1126.

Richard of Hexham, fl. 1141.

De Gestis Regis Stephani et de bello de Standardo, 1135-9.
Also wrote history of the Church of Hexham.

Henry, Archdeacon of Huntingdon, b. 1084 (?); d. 1154-5.

Historia Anglorum, B.C. 55 to A.D. 1154. *Ed.*, Eng.
Trans., Forester, Bohn, 1853.
Two books added to later editions were:
De Sanctis Angliae (Miracles of nineteen saints). *De Summitatibus Rerum.*
With three further epistles:
De Contemptu Mundi.
De Serie regum potentissimorum, etc.
De Regibus Britanniae.
Other works are ascribed to him, among them eight books
of *Epigrams*.

Geoffrey of Monmouth, Bishop of St. Asaph, b. 1100 (?); d. 1154.

Historia Regum Brittaniae, or *Historia Britonum*, based, as
Geoffrey tells us, upon a very old book lent him by Archdeacon Walter (Calenius) of Oxford, probably a volume of
Breton legends. Geoffrey also drew from the older history
of Nennius, but there still remains a large portion of his
work which has not been traced beyond his own pen.
The "Historia" is looked upon as an epoch-making work,
owing to the impulse it gave to the literature of Romance.
Legends afloat among the natives of Wales and Bretagne were
now given a literary garb which rendered them sufficiently
attractive to awaken the interest of the world in general, and
the imagination of the mediæval poet was aroused by the
chivalric glamour which the historian threw over his descriptions of Arthur's Court. It was a main source, but not the
exclusive one, of Arthurian legend, for independent of the
fact that many features characteristic of the latter are not
mentioned by him, there is evidence of Welsh fables being
extant in the 12th century, which supplied material for later
romances apart from Geoffrey's history. M. Gaston Paris

says the French poets made very little use of him, drawing chiefly from recitals or songs that had not gone through a Latin version. Geoffrey's work was also, as his biographer writes ("Dict. Nat. Bio.") : of powerful influence in the unification of the people of England. "The race animosities of Breton, Teuton, and Frenchman would probably have endured much longer than they did but for the legend of an origin common to them all," namely, of the descent of the British Princes from the fugitives from Troy. The work was completed, in first edition, end of 1138 (Ward) ; completed 1147 (Gross). *See* Epilogue, S. Evans. As regards the theory of different versions, *see* R. H. Fletcher, " Pub. Mod. Lang. Assoc.," 1901.

Geoffrey's "Historia" was abridged by Alfred of Beverley ; it was put into Anglo-Norman verse by Gaimar and Wace, the latter's poem serving as a basis for Layamon's English poem of the "Brut." Robert of Gloucester also produced it in an English version. It appears besides in the form of Welsh Chronicles. Geoffrey's Latin translation of the "Prophecies of Merlin" were incorporated in his history ; his "Vita Merlini" was in verse. A reference to Merlin's prophecies in Suger's "History of Louis le Gros" fixes the latest date of these, Suger dying in 1152. *Ed.*, J. A. Giles, 1844 (Caxton Society). Trans., J. A. Giles, 1848 (Six Old English Chronicles). Trans., Sebastian Evans, (with Epilogue) the "Temple Classics." *See* Ward, "Catalogue of Romances," vol. i. 203, *seq.*

Ailred, or Ethelred of Rievaulx. (§ 27.)

Vita et Miracula S. Edwardi Regis et Confessoris. Derived principally from a former life of Edward by Osbert de Clare.

Relatio de Standardo (Battle of the Standard, 1138). *De Genealogia regum Anglorum.*

Benedict, Abbot of Peterborough, d. 1193.

The following history has been ascribed to him, but it was more probably transcribed for him :—

Gesta regis Henrici Secundi, Reigns of Henry II. and Richard I. *See* below R. Fitz-Neale.

Life of Thomas Becket. *History of the Passion of T. Becket.* (Only survives in fragments incorporated in the "Quadrilogus.")

Richard of Devizes, Monk of St. Swithin's, Winchester, fl. 1191.

De Rebus Gestus Ricardi primi. Trans., "Chronicles of the Crusaders," Bohn's Antiq. Libr.

Richard Fitz-Neale, or **Richard of Ely,** d. 1198. Treasurer of England and Bishop of London.

Dialogus de Scaccario, History, etc. of the Exchequer. *Ed.,* T. Madox, "History of the Exchequer," 1711, 1769. Trans., E. F. Henderson, 1892.

A lost Chronicle of Church, State, and Miscellaneous affairs, termed "Tricolumnis," it being divided into three columns: thought possibly to be extant in the Chronicle attributed to Benedict of Peterborough, but this view is not universally accepted.

Roger of Hoveden, d. after 1201.

Chronica, A.D. 732 to 1201. Chronicle to 1192 is taken more or less directly from extant works.

William of Newburgh, b. 1136; d. cir. 1198.

Historia Rerum Anglicarum, 1066 to 1198. Continuation to 1298.

Ralph de Diceto, Dean of St. Paul's, d. cir. 1202.

Abbreviationes Chronicorum, to 1147. Extracts from previous histories.

Ymagines Historiarum, 1148–1202. Earlier part based on R. of Torigni.

Ralph Niger, fl. 1170. Was driven into exile on account of his partizanship of Becket, and in his second chronicle makes a savage attack on Henry II. in consequence.

Chronica. (1) Creation to 1199; (2) A.D. to cir. 1161, with continuation by R. Coggeshall. *Ed.,* Caxton Soc., 1851.

Gervase, Monk of Canterbury, fl. 1188.

Chronica, 1135–99, with short account of years from 1100. Contains a description of burning and restoration of the Cathedral.

Gesta Regum.   Brutus to 1210; continuation to 1328.

Actus pontificum Cantuariensis ecclesiae, 597–1205.

Mappa Mundi (on Bishops' Sees, Monasteries, etc.), list of counties of England, etc., with ecclesiastical foundations, castles, etc.

Giraldus de Barri (Cambrensis).   (§§ 27, 30.)

Topographia Hibernica.   The result of G.'s two visits to Ireland, 1183, 1185–6.   The third vol. gives the early peoples and history of the Island.

Expugnatio Hibernica.   Conquest of Ireland.

Robert de Monte, or Torigni, d. 1186.   Prior of Bec, and Abbot of Mont S. Michel.   Chief works:

Addition to *History* by Jumièges: 8th book and part of 7th.

Addition to Chronicle of Sigebert de Gemblour.   The above works are valuable for reigns of Henry I. and Henry II. Other historical treatises, and additions; among these a list of Abbots and Bishops of France and England, and a treatise on Monastic orders and Norman Abbeys.

William Fitz-Stephen, d. 1190 (?).   (§ 30.)

Life of Thomas Becket.   The introduction to this life contains an interesting account of the London of that day, which has been separately printed.

Other lives of Becket published in Rolls Series are those by: William, a monk of Canterbury; Benedict of Peterborough; John of Salisbury; Alan of Tewkesbury; Edward Grim; Herbert of Bosham; Anonymous lives, and the "Quadrilogus," a life compiled from materials in earlier biographies.

Richard de Templo, possibly Prior of Holy Trinity, London, fl. 1190–1229.   Identified as author of

Itinerarium peregrinorum et Gesta Regis Ricardi.   An

Account of the Third Crusade. First published under the name of Geoffrey de Vinsauf. It is in great part in close correspondence with a French poem by Ambroise. (*See* France, § 15.) From the notice by Nicholas Trivet of this work, stating that it was in prose and verse, it is thought that originally some or all the chapters were followed by poetical pieces, which have been suppressed by copyists.

Anonymous Chronicles:

Gesta Stephani, 1135–47. "Chief authority for years 1142–7."

Gesta Herewardi. The author mentions Leofric of Brun as his authority (§ 18). This work is also thought to be by Richard, a monk of Ely (Gross, *op. cit.*, p. 284).

29 *Law.*

Ranulf de Glanvill, Chief Justiciar of England. Accompanied King Richard to the East, and died at Acre, 1190.

The following work is generally ascribed to him:

De Legibus et Consuetudinibus regni Angliae. "Oldest of the legal classics of England."

Vacarius, b. 1115 (?); d. 1200 (?). The first to introduce into England the study of revived Roman law.

Abridgment of the Digest and Code of Justinian, 9 books, generally known as *Summa Pauperum de legibus* or *Liber Pauperum.*

Two Tracts:

De Assumpto Homine, De Matrimonio.

30 *Miscellaneous.*

Lucian of Chester, fl. cir. 1100.

De Laudibus Cestriae. "Apparently the earliest written description of a town."

Saewulf, fl. 1102. *Account of Travels.* Nothing certain is known of S., unless he is the Saewulf mentioned by W.

of Malmesbury as a merchant, who afterwards became a monk. He took a pilgrimage to Jerusalem, and his narrative begins in July 1102, on his departure from the coast of Italy, and continues to his return to Constantinople in Oct. 1103. *Ed.*, Trans., T. Wright, "Early Travels in Palestine."

John of Salisbury, Bishop of Chartres, d. 1180. A firm supporter of Becket, to whom his chief work is dedicated, and with whom he was in the cathedral at the last. The most famous man of learning of his day. (§ 27.)

Polycraticus, Sive de nugis Curialium et vestigiis Philosophorum, or *Statesman's Book*, 8 books. On government, philosophy, learning, etc., disclosing much concerning the vices at Court and corruption of the Church. "The aptest reflection of the cultivated thought of the middle of the 12th century." A metrical introduction, styled "Entheticus," is attached to the work : another longer elegiac poem, with the same title, was apparently originally intended for this purpose.

Metalogicus, 4 books. A Defence of Logic.

Letters, 4 books. *See* also under lives of Becket, on page 57. Works, *ed.*, J. A. Giles, "Patr. Eccl.," 1848.

Gervase of Tilbury, Marshal of the kingdom of Arles, fl. late 12th and early 13th centuries.

*Otia Imperialia, 3 books (decisiones). Only extant work known ; dedicated to his patron, Otho IV. of Germany. Legends, history, natural phenomena, wonders natural and artificial, and account of Kings of England. Evidently written for the amusement of the Emperor.

A book styled "Liber Facetiorum," written for Henry II.'s son, is lost.

Walter Map, or Mapes, Welshman ; Archdeacon of Oxford, b. cir. 1140 (?) ; died in 1210, often confused with his predecessor, Walter Calenius. (§ 31.)

De Nugis Curialium. Map was one of the Clerks of the royal household under Henry II., and his work has gossiping reminiscences of his life, and is enlivened with tales and legends.　　*Ed.*, T. Wright, Camden Soc., 1850.

N.B.—For the connection of W. Map with the works of the Arthurian Cycle, *see* under France, § 55.

William Fitz-Stephen. (§ 28.) The introduction to this writer's life of Thomas Becket is a valuable account of schools, amusements, manners, etc., of London of that date. This introduction has been separately published.

Giraldus Cambrensis. (§§ 27, 28.)

Topographia Hibernica, 3 books. The first two books describe the island, the third is historical. The work was the result of two visits to Ireland, 1183 and 1185–1186.

Itinerarium Cambriae, 2 books.

Topographia Cambriae, 2 books. (1) De Laudabilibus Cambriae. (2) De Illaudabilibus Wallia.

De Instructione Principium, 3 parts.

Other works, *Invectionum libellus*, *Symbolum Electorum* (chiefly letters and poems), *De Giraldo Archidiacono Mene-vensi*, *De Invectionibus*, *De Rebus a se gestis*, *Retractationes*, etc.

Alexander of Neckham. (§§ 26, 27, 31.)

Grammatical treatises. In one of these, "De Utensilibus," a kind of vocabulary, the Latin names of articles are connected by a narrative.

31　　Poetry.

Reginald, Monk of Canterbury, fl. cir. 1112.

Long poem on S. Malchus, a Syrian hermit. Other shorter *poems*.

Lawrence, Prior of Durham, d. 1154. (§ 27.)

Hypognosticon, 8 books. Scriptural history, with moralisa-tions.

Dialogorum libri quattuor. Account of Durham, and details of his own life.

Consolatio de morte amico. Imitation of Boethius; partly prose, partly verse.

Other poems given as his are a *Rhythm on Christ and His Disciples*, a *Resurrection Psalm*. A ninth book added to the *Hypognosticon* contains miscellaneous poems.

John of Salisbury. (§ 30.)

Entheticus. Metrical introduction to "Polycraticus," and a longer metrical treatise of same name.

John de Hauteville, fl. 1184. Only known work—

Archetrenius (name of hero). A long, detailed poem; satire on vice; intercourse with Greek Philosophers; finally Nature discourses on Natural Philosophy, and gives hero a wife called Moderation.

Ed., Wright, "Ang.-Lat. Sat. Poets of 12th century."

A considerable amount of Latin verse, of a loose and satirical character, known as Goliardic verse, was composed during the 12th and 13th centuries. The *Goliards*, wandering clerks or students, a class of "educated jesters," flourished in England, and on the Continent in France and Germany. Their name appears to be derived from one Golias, who is styled *Episcopus* and *Archipoeta*. Certain poems of this class are ascribed, but on no certain evidence, to—

Walter Map, or Mapes. (§ 30.)

Apocalypsis Goliae Episcopi. An attack on the clergy.

Confessio Goliae. The well-known drinking-song "Meum est propositum in tabernâ mori" is taken from this. *Ed.*, Wright, "Latin poems attributed to W. Map," 1841. Other poems under the name of Golias are extant.

Nigellus Wireker, fl. 1190. (§ 27.)

Speculum Stultorum. Brunellus, an ass, desires a longer tail; typical of certain class of ambitious monk.

Ed., Wright, *op. cit.* Other short poems and lives in verse, and prologue to prose treatise.

Joseph of Exeter (Josephus Iscanus), fl. 1190.

Accompanied Archbishop Baldwin on his crusade, 1188. One of the chief Mediæval-Latin poets.

De Bello Trojano, 6 books. First printed under the name of Cornelius Nepos. *Ed.*, Jusserand, 1st book.

Sources. There were in existence two Latin prose versions of two original Greek works on the tale of Troy. The authors of both the latter claimed to be contemporaries of the events they recorded: the one, Dares the Phrygian, fought with the Trojans; the other, Dictys, a Cretan, with the Greeks.

The name of Cornelius Nepos is attached to the translation of Dares (" De Excidio Troiae "), and although all the trans- lator's statements with regard to the Greek original may not now be believed, it may on the other hand be noted that old writers refer to a Phrygian Iliad.

The Latin version of Dictys dates from 4th or early 5th century, the original being fabled to have been found in a tomb, inscribed in Phœnician characters on the bark of a tree. The Greek version was mentioned by writers as late as 11th century.

The shorter Latin version of Dares was the most popular, and was the source of two poems in the second half of 12th century, that by J. of Exeter and that by Benoît de S. More (*see* France, § 28), and the subject continued to be a favourite one into the 14th century. Individual characters belonging to the Troy tale were immortalised by the most noted authors of the Middle Ages, and later by Shakespeare.

Antiocheis. On third crusade. This other poem by J. of Exeter is lost as a whole, and is only extant in fragments printed in Camden's " Remains."

Other poems have also disappeared.

Geoffrey de Vinsauf (Anglicus), fl. 1200.

Nova Poetria, or *Poetria Novella*. Metrical treatise on art of poetry. An example of style given by this poet is satirised by Chaucer in his Nonne Prestes tale. Geoffrey's name is said to be due to a treatise written by him on the care of the vine and other plants, " De Vino Salvo."

Alexander Neckham. (§§ 26, 27, 30.)

De laudibus Divinae Sapientiae. *See* his prose treatise,
"De Naturis Rerum," which was a paraphrase of poem.

De Contemptu Mundi. On the monastic life. This poem
has also been printed as one of Anselm's works.

Novus Aesopus. Trans. from Æsop. Six fables are printed
in Robert's "Fables Inédites." (*See* France, § 32.)

Henry of Huntingdon. (§ 28.)
Epigrams.

Giraldus de Barri (Cambrensis). (§§ 27, 28, 30.)
Epigrams, Poems.

The *Symbolum Electorum* is chiefly composed of letters and
poems.

32 THE DRAMA.

In England, as in all Christian countries, the earliest
dramatic representations were of a religious character. The
elements of the drama existed in the representations given in
the churches on the occasion of festivals, more especially at
Christmas and Easter, at first simply as tableaux, but later
with the accompaniment of words taken from the Vulgate,
alternated with recitative in song. Of these early plays there
were those that represented scenes from Bible history, and
others representing the lives and martyrdoms of saints. The
distinction between "Mysteries" and "Miracle Plays" was not,
however, known in England, where "Miracle Play" was the
term applied to all representations of religious drama. The latter
were not so exclusively connected with the Church services;
the laity took part in their performance, and we learn from
Matthew Paris that previous to 1119 a miracle play of St.
Katherine was performed in public at Dunstable, while further
corroboration of public performances in the 12th century is
found in the introduction to the Life of Thomas Becket by
Fitz-Stephen. These plays were, however, by their moral
intention, still in connection with the Church, and formed a
transitional state of the drama. A French dramatic work
of this century, written in England, known by the name of

"Adam," comprising three distinct parts, *i.e.* The Fall, The Death of Abel, and the Prophets of Christ, is representative of this transitional drama, and appears to have been performed in the porch of the church.   The development of these plays, thus emancipated from the religious services, was accelerated by the establishment of the Corpus Christi festival, inaugurated by Pope Urban IV. in 1264, although his bull was not confirmed until 1311, and the pageants arranged in celebration of this festival are thought to have been introduced into England about four years later.

The "Moralities" were later developments of religious drama ; they have been defined as the epic allegories of the 13th and 14th centuries transferred to the stage ; they did not supersede the plays of older style, which continued to be simultaneously performed.   The "Moralities" grew into the later Tragedy and Comedy by the introduction of characters supposed to be drawn from real life, in place of the original allegorical ones.   Whether the early liturgical dramas in England arose spontaneously or under French influence seems uncertain.

Ward, "A History of English Dramatic Literature, etc.," 1875–6 ; Pollard, "English Miracle Plays, Moralities, and Interludes, etc.," 1895 ; Stoddard, "References for Students of Miracle Plays and Mysteries" (full Bibliography), Library Bulletin, California University, 8, 1887 ; Davidson, "Studies in English Mystery Plays," Yale Univ., 1892 ; Payne Collier, "The History of English Dramatic Poetry," 1879 ; E. K. Chambers, "The Mediæval Stage," 1903 ; C. S. Davidson, "Miracle Plays," Belles Lettres Series ; K. Hase, "Miracle Plays," Eng. Trans., A, W. Jackson, 1880.

33   XIIITH CENTURY.

Cir. 1250 : *Middle English* (*Körting*).   *Inflexion in great measure discarded* (*Kittredge*).

Certain works give prominence to the earlier years of this century, and before its close the range of English literature had been considerably extended. The metrical romance, the short tale, the form of poem known as "desbat" had by that time been represented in works by English poets. "The Early English romance," writes Ten Brink, "did not as a whole reach the level of its French model. . . . But we are charmed by the joy manifested in nature, in the green forests; . . . the English muse, if less delicate and dainty than her French sister, was less artificial; if more passionate, less lascivious; and in her enthusiasm for what is grandly colossal, her joy in the actual, she showed . . . many of the features that were to characterise her in the time of her full splendour." The lyric developed in the south, borrowing strophic forms from the Latin hymn and the French lyric. The rhythmic homily continued a favourite form of composition. A lighter vein runs through the works which originated under the influence of French and Anglo-Norman literature, the purely English writings being, as a rule, of graver and more religious character. Between 1221–1226 the two orders of "Begging Friars" settled in England, and soon began to bring influence to bear on the teaching of the universities, and to become important factors in the social affairs of the day.

The *Metre* used by Middle-English poets, such as we find in King Horn, was "a natural development of the Old English alliterative metre. The direction of this development (greatly accelerated in its later stages by the influence of French prosody) is from the O. E. four-stressed long line, divided by a central pause, but bound together by alliteration, with rare and casual rhyme, to a Middle English short line, with two principal stresses and one or two secondary stresses bound in pairs by more or less perfect end-rhyme, alliteration surviving either in traditional combinations or being added as an occasional ornament. . . . O. E. verse, which admits of considerable variety in the number of light syllables between the stresses, and even of their absence, gives place gradually to a stricter alternation of stressed and light syllables. . . . Layamon's *Brut* is an important landmark on the way; he shows a steady progressive change in his versification, so that the contrast between the beginning and end of the poem is marked" (J. Hall, *see* Introd. to "King Horn").

5

34 VERNACULAR WRITERS.

PROSE.

Homilies and *Homiletic Treatises*.

Anonymous.

The Sawles Warde. Homily on the allegorical interpretation of Matt. xxiv. 43. *Ed.*, Text and trans., R. Morris, "Old English Homilies," E.E.T.S. *MSS.*, Reg. 17, A. 27 ; Cott. Titus, D. xviii. ; Bodl. 34.

Wohunge of ure Lauerd (*Wooing of Christ*). Corresponding in theme with a passage in the "Ancren Riwle," and the editor thinks from internal evidence that in the original form it was written by the author of the latter work ; there is, however, no conclusive evidence to support this hypothesis (and *see* Prof. Ker, *op. cit.*, under "Ancren Riwle "). *Ed.*, Text and trans., Morris, *op. cit.* *MS.*, Cott. Titus, D. xviii.

These works belong to the southern districts ; in the same group may be placed *On ureison* (prayer) *of oure Louerde* ; *Lofsong* (song of praise) *of ure Louerde* (Morris, *ob. cit.*).

35 POETRY.

Historical.

Layamon. The son of Leovenath, as he tells us in the opening lines of his poem, and Priest of King's Arley, Worcestershire.

Brut. History of England from the destruction of Troy to A.D. 689. The poet "thrummed" three books into one in his work, namely, Wace's "Geste des Bretons" (1155), his chief source, Baeda's work in his own Latin, and Aelfred's translation of the same. His poem was the first to be based on French material, and the author has the further distinction of being the first to commemorate King Arthur in English verse. The "Brut" is assigned to the early 13th century, a mention of "Peter's Pence" has been thought to refer to an agitation for its suppression in 1205. The verse is partly alliterative, partly rhymed or assonanced ; the lines are counted

long by some and short by others; "where alliteration predominates, the verse often seems, from the division of the
sentence, to break into two short lines." Layamon's "Brut"
is one of the landmarks of English history. It is a thoroughly
English work, with but slight indication of French influence,
the dialect being that of the south or Wessex (Garnett). In
accent and rhythm he clung to the Old English form,—" of
all English poets after the Conquest, none approached the
Old English epos so closely as he," and so, "a most significant
figure, Layamon stands upon the dividing-line between two
great periods" (Ten Brink). *Ed.*, F. Madden, 1847
(both versions); Extracts, R. Morris, "Specimens." *MSS.*,
Cott. Cal. A. ix.; Otho C. xiii. (somewhat later version).

36 *Religious Verse.*

Orrm, fl. in the early century, his work being nearly contemporary with the "Brut," and next to it in importance as
regards its language and metre. The writer was possibly of
Danish descent, and an Augustinian monk.

Orrmulum. A metrical paraphrase of the daily gospels;
only part of the work has come down to us, but this runs
to over ten thousand lines, and the poem equals its length
in dulness. It is strictly neither in rhyme nor alliteration,
though both occur; the metre is that of the "Poema Morale,"
manipulated with great exactness. The dialect is a Midland
one (East Midland, Brandl; Lincolnshire, Bradley) with
"Scandinavian colouring," and shows scarcely any sign of
French influence, being the last of the poets of whom this
can be said. "The author stands chronologically on the
border-line between pure English and Latinised speech"
(Garnett). *Ed.*, R. M. White, 2nd edit., 1878. *See*
Articles by Dr. Bradley and Mr. Wilson in *Athenæum*, May
19 and July 14, 21, and 28, 1906, on the identification
of the place where the Orrmulum was written, dialect, etc.
MS., Bodl. Jun. 1 (possibly autograph).

Anonymous.

Bestiary. Cir. middle 13th century. The work follows
a Latin original by Tebaldus, and deals allegorically with

its subject. The same metrical form is not sustained throughout; the lines are short, mostly joined in couplets by rhyme or alliteration, but quatrains of crossed rhymes are also introduced. The section on the Dove is not taken from the same source as the remainder of the work; it is similar to the corresponding part in Alexander Neckham's "De Naturis Rerum." *Ed.*, E. Morris, "Old Eng. Miscellany." *MS.*, Arundel, 292.

The "Bestiary" and the following work, of about the same date, originated in the Anglian territory.

Genesis and Exodus. A poetical paraphrase in short couplets. The chief source was P. Comestor's *Historia Scholastica* (12th century). French influence is more apparent than in the "Bestiary"; "it is one of the oldest English poems in which the verse and style of the French clerical poetry were successfully imitated" (Ten Brink). Two authors were thought by Ten Brink to be responsible for the paraphrase; Fritzsche (*see* below) goes thoroughly into this question, and his verdict is that there is not sufficient evidence to support the theory of more than one author; on the contrary, the resemblances in many points between the two parts speak strong for a single poet. *Ed.*, R. Morris, E.E.T.S., 2nd ed., 1874. *See* Fritzsche, "Anglia," v. *MS.* C.C.C.C. 444.

To the south belong the four following works, in alliterative long lines, or rhythmical prose, of the first half of the century, one, *S. Katerine*, the most important, being put back to the 12th by Wülcker. The three lives of saints, in "their diction, with its touch of enthusiasm, contains much that recalls the good old times of Poetry" (Ten Brink).

Lives of Seinte Juliane, Seinte Marherete. *Ed.*, O. Cockayne, E.E.T.S.

Life of Seinte Katerine. *Ed.*, E. Einenkel, 1884. *MSS.*, Reg. 17 A. xxvii.; Cott. Titus, D. xviii.; Bodl. NE. A. 3.

Homily, *Hali Meidenhad* (*Holy Maidenhood*). *Ed.*, O. Cockayne, E.E.T.S., 1866. Authorities have differed as to the combined or separate authorship of these works. They have also been attributed with "Sawles Warde" to the author of the "Ancren Riwle." More probably, thinks Einenkel, "S. Katerine" is by one author, the other two lives by another, and "Hali Meidenhad" by a third.

Ureisun of Ure Lefti. Rhyming poem.   *Ed.*, R. Morris, "O. E. Homilies."

A beautiful contribution to the religious Lyric was the poem by—

Thomas Hales, a Franciscan, fl. 1250.

A Luve Ron (Love-song). The specimen given is from Ten Brink (*op. cit.*)

> " Paris and Helen, where are they,
>   Fairest in beauty, bright to view?
> Amadas, Tristram, Ideine, yea,
>   Isold, that loved with love so true?
> And Caesar, rich in power and sway,
>   Hector, the strong, with might to do?
> All glided from earth's realm away,
>   Like shaft that swift from bowstring flew."

Ed., R. Morris, "O. E. Miscellany."

37   Miscellaneous Verse.

The Owl and the Nightingale. "A poem which is steeped in popular proverbial wisdom," dating probably from 1218–1225 (Körting), and originating in the South-West. The poet handles his rhymed couplets with a master hand, and carries his arguments through with skill. The dispute between the birds, which represent respectively Old Age and Youth, deals in turn with their several ways of life, their singing, and general qualities. One, Nicholas of Guildford (Maister Nichole), is called in as umpire; that he should also be the poet himself is considered unlikely, on account of the laudatory manner in which he is described. This lively and interesting poem is the earliest extant specimen in English verse of the "Desbat" or "Estrif," a contest in poetical dialogue, which had for some time previously been a familiar form of French verse, originally introduced by the Troubadours.　*Ed.*, Stevenson, Roxburghe Club, 1838; R. Morris, "Specimens."　*See* under Börsch and Noelle, for Language and Metre.　*MSS.*, Cott. Calig. A. ix.; Oxford, Jesus Coll.

38　METRICAL ROMANCES.

Dealing with Teutonic Material.

King Horn. Written before the middle of the century (Brandl); 2nd quarter of century (Wissmann). Körting places it later. The dialect is Southern, but not unmixed, Midland influence being traceable (Hall). Midland (Brandl, Lumby). Horn, son of Murry, King of Suddene, his father having been killed by a party of invading Saracens, is by these sent adrift in a boat with twelve companions. Landing in Westernesse, the King of the land gives them harbour, and has Horn trained in a manner befitting his station. Rymenhild, the King's daughter, and Horn fall in love with one another; their secret is betrayed to the King, and Horn is banished. After seven years of knightly adventures he returns just in time to deliver Rymenhild from an enforced marriage. Horn and Rymenhild are married; but again separation occurs, as Horn departs to recover his father's kingdom, and a second time returns only just in time to deliver his wife from the hands of a traitor, into whose house he and his companions enter disguised as minstrels. Horn returns to his own country with Rimenhild, where they reign as King and Queen.

The poem has come down in three versions, represented by the three MSS., which are traced back through intermediate redactions to the same original. There is also extant an Anglo-Norman version, "Horn et Rimenhild" (H. R.) (*see* France, § 30), another English version (Auchinleck MS.) of later date, "Horn Childe and Rimnild" (H. C.), as well as eight fragmentary ballads (*ed.*, Child, "Eng. and Scot. Popular Ballads"). There has been considerable work on the part of scholars in the effort to determine the relationship between

K. H., H. R., and H. C.[1] It seems most generally admitted that K. H. derives direct through other English versions from popular tradition (Hall, Caro, Hartenstein), and that neither of the above is directly dependent on either of the others. Schofield, however, gives a different genealogy to King Horn; starting with an original Norse saga, he traces the tradition through a lost Anglo-Saxon version, followed by a lost Anglo-Norman, from which both K. H. and H. R. are derived. Hall and Hartenstein also agree in the elimination of all intermediate French influence for H. R. and the ballads. The Southern version of King Horn is probably the nearest in character to the original; the tale "was carried to the North, somewhere about the time when the Norsemen of the Continent combined with their allies from Ireland to harry the North country, and was strongly modified to suit the local circumstances. H. C. is the direct representative of this Northern version, while the ballads are a branch of the same stem. H. R. is founded on a lost redaction made by a man who was acquainted with both streams of tradition, and combined them" (Hall). Hartenstein decides that in H. C. the stream of direct tradition is mingled with that which is filtered through H. R. Schofield traces it along the same line as K. H., and agrees with the mingling in it of the H. R. version. Each version has motives peculiar to itself. Caro traces parallels respectively in K. H. and H. R., and H. R. and H. C.; H. C. on the whole being more faithful to H. R.; he considers H. C. the more popular version, but not drawn directly from tradition. Hall writes: "The poem ('King Horn'), as we have it, is a story of the Danish raids on the South coast of England" (the Danes having become transformed into Saracens), "events which actually occurred in the S. West during the English Conquest." Schofield writes: "Records of actual depredations in Northumberland, etc." Ten Brink thinks the germ of the saga may possibly be older even than the Danish piracies. Hall further says that there are indications of the story being originally a British tradition. There are traces showing that

---

[1] H. R., according to the latest decision of scholars, dates from the 12th century, and is therefore the oldest of the three works in question. (*See* Hartenstein and Schofield.)

the text, or part of it, was intended for musical accompaniment. The metre shows more syllabic regularity than that of Layamon's poem.   *Ed.*, Rawson Lumby, E.E.T.S., 1866; Horstmann, Herrig's *Archiv*, vol. i., 1872; Joseph Hall (with "Horn Childe"), 1901; G. A. M'Knight, Belles Lettres Series.   *See* Wissmann, "Quellen u. Forschungen zur Sprach. u. Kultur Gesch.," vol. xlv.; and "Anglia," iv. "Studien zu King Horn"; Caro, "Englische Studien," xii.; Hartenstein, "Studien zur Hornsage," 1902 (with full bibliography of editions, etc., of all versions); Schofield, "Publ. Mod. Lang. Assoc.," New Series, vol. xi., 1903; Ward, Cat. Rom., vol. i.   *MSS.*, Harl. 2253; Laud, 108; Camb. Univ. Gg. 4, 27, 2.

NOTE—"Suddene has been variously interpreted—Surrey (Michel); Sussex, or Dorsetshire (Ward); South Cornwall (Hall); Ten Brink, among other scholars, interpreted it as South Daneland, and accordingly places the scene of action in the North Sea. Schofield in his interesting treatise deals with the identification of " Suddene " with the Isle of Man, of Westernesse with Ireland, and with that of other places mentioned.

N.B.—The tale in its latest form appears in the French prose romance of "Ponthus et Sidoine," possibly by la Tour-Landry (G. Paris) (*see* France, § 65), which was followed by an English and German prose version.   *See* "Publ. Mod. Lang. Assoc.," xii.; " Romania," xxvi.

Havelok, cir. 1280 (Skeat), cir. 1300 (Brandl); cir. 1280-90, "perhaps somewhat earlier than King Horn" (Körting).

Havelok is left by his father, King Birkabeyn of Denmark, in the guardianship of Earl Godard, who treacherously endeavours to have him drowned. Grim, the fisherman, entrusted to carry out this deed, is turned from the purpose by certain miraculous appearances, namely, a flame seen to issue from the sleeping child's mouth, and a cross of gold, a "King's mark," on his shoulder. He escapes with Havelok to England, where the latter, like a good mediæval knight, wins his way by his prowess in spite of all ill-fortune, and finally marries Goldborough, daughter of King Aethelwold of England. The town of Grimsby commemorates the fisherman in its name and seals, for there he landed with the rescued prince. According to Skeat the earliest version of the tale is in the French "Lai d'Aveloc," which he assigns to first half of 12th century, although the tale is thought to have had its origin in England during the Danish invasions; "Both saga and poem may have originated in a Danish colony in Lincolnshire . . . it would be hard to decide how old it (the story) is, but it was probably not completed until after the time of Cnut the Great. At the end of the tale Denmark and England are at peace, and a Danish King rules over England" (Ten Brink). Skeat places the abridged tale as told by Gaimar next in order of time; he further (pp. 4–19) gives a list of Chronicles in which Havelok's name appears, one by Rauf de Boun, "Le Petit Bruit," 1310, having made use of the English poem, gives a limit to the hither date of the latter. Skeat's conclusion, after consideration of these various references, is that the English poem is the "general result of various narratives connected with the history of Northumberland and Lindesey at the close, or probably the beginning, of the 6th century." As regards the priority of the French Lai or Gaimar's work, Kupferschmidt reverses Skeat's order: Gaimar being cir. 1150, and the Lai *impossible* to be of earlier date than beginning of 13th century; it may be added that G. Paris dates the Lai after 1160 (troisième tiers). Kupferschmidt concludes that the similarities between these two versions is due to identity of source, namely, an eight-syllabled rhymed French poem. Both Körting and Kupferschmidt derive the English poem direct from popular tradition without intervention of French influence. Again, as regards the date of the tale, Havelok has been associated (Storm, Ward) with an Olaf (or Anlaf), the Son of Sitric, a Danish prince (defeated at the Battle of Brunanburh), resemblances existing between historical facts in connection with Olaf and the tale as given in Havelok, and Olaf having a nickname conferred on him, which is found in some versions given to Havelok, and further Olaf appearing in one old chronicle and an old ballad as Havelok. Skeat gives the original dialect of the poem, which is extant in a late stage, as that of Lincolnshire ; Hupe gives preference to Norfolk as home of poet, and locates the scribe further west, nearer Oxford. The metre has lines of sixteen distinct types (Skeat, p. xxviii. *seq.*), two, or sometimes a greater number of lines being linked by the same rhyme. The text, according to Ten Brink, was written for non-musical delivery, and the poem throughout, he adds, shows that education and manners were on a lower plane in Denmark than in England. The Celtic origin, or otherwise, of the story is discussed by Skeat, Ward, and Storm.   *Ed.*, Madden, with French version, 1828 ; Skeat, E.E.T.S., 1868 ; Clarendon Press, 1902 ; E. K. Putnam, Belles Lettres Series ; Holthausen, 1901. *See* Kupferschmidt, " Romanische Studien," iv. ; Hupe, " Anglia," xiii. ; Ward, " Cat. Rom.," vol. i. ; Storm, " H. the Dane and the Norse King Olaf Kuaran," " Engl. Studien," iii. For resemblances between tale of Havelok and that of Hamlet, *see* Gollancz, " Hamlet in Iceland," 1898.   *MS.*, Laud, 108.

39   METRICAL ROMANCES.
Arthurian Cycle.
See P. Paris, " Romans de la Table Ronde," 1868-77 ; A. Nutt, " Studies in the History of the Holy Grail," 1888 ; Birch-Hirschfeld, " Die Sage vom Gral," 1877 ; Rhys, " Studies in the Arthurian Legend," 1891 ; Sommer, " Le Morte Darthur," vol. iii., 1891 ; H. Fletcher, " Arthurian Material in Chronicles," " Studies and Notes in Philol. and Lit.," x. ; J. L. Weston, " King Arthur and his Knights," " Popular Studies in Mythology, Romance, and Folklore," vol. iv., 1899 ; A. Hunt Billings, " A Guide to Middle English Metrical Romances," " Yale Studies," etc., 1901. (Bibliography and summary of theories.) *See* also works given in introductory note (§ 25).

Arthour and Merlin.[1]   In rhyming couplets, the rhyme sometimes running over four or more lines.   Date, cir. middle

---

[1] For history of Merlin *see* Grässe, " Die Grossen Sagenkreise des Mittilalters " ; San Marte, " Die Sagen von Merlin " ; Mead, " Outlines of the Legend of Merlin," in Wheatley's ed.

or last quarter of 13th century (Körting); first quarter of 14th century (date of Auchinleck MS.), at the latest; the assonance which occurs somewhat frequently points to perhaps middle or third quarter of 13th century (Kölbing) The poem originated in the neighbourhood of Kent (Körting, Kölbing). Of the two versions extant of the poem Kölbing considers the one represented by the Auchinleck MS. as the oldest, with which Bülbring does not agree. The poem gives the history of Merlin, of whom we first hear in Nennius, of his supernatural birth, of his magic power whereby he is able to assist Uther Pendragon and Arthur both in love and war; account of Arthur's birth, of his drawing forth the great sword from the miraculous stone, his coronation, and his betrothal to Guinever. Bülbring considers that "Arthur and Merlin" is solely based on the French "Merlin" of R. de Boron (*see* France, § 55), and on the continuation of the latter. According to Kölbing the first part has for its source either a lost version of R. de Boron's work, or a work by a predecessor of this poet, which corresponded to Boron's poem; founding this theory on the presence of features in the English poem which diverge from Boron; his arguments on this point are disputed by Bülbring. Kölbing assigns the authorship of "Arthur and Merlin" to the poet of "King Alisaunder," and "Richard Coer de Lion." Later English Merlin romances are a prose version (MSS., Univ. Libr. Camb., and a fragment, Bodl. Rawl. Misc.) *Ed.*, Wheatley, E.E.T.S., 1869-99; and a metrical version of cir. 15th century by Lonelich (or Lovelich). *Ed.*, E. A. Koch, E.E.T.S., 1904. Of the relationship of these with one another and to Boron's poem, *see* Introduction to Kölbing's Edition of A. and M. *Ed.*, Turnbull, Abbotsford Club, 1838; Kölbing, "Alt. Engl. Bibliothek," 1890. *See* Bülbring, "Englische Studien," xvi. (criticism of Kölbing's ed.); Gaster, "Jewish Sources of, etc.," 1887. *MSS.*, Auchinleck;[1] Lincoln's Inn, 150; Percy Folio; Douce, 236; Harl. 6223 (first 62 verses).

Sir Tristrem. Date, probably towards end of 13th century (Körting); not later than 1330 (Bédier, *see* France, § 25).

[1] The Auchinleck MS. dates, according to G. Paris, cir. 1330.

Körting and Kölbing give the birthplace of poem as probably North England or South Scotland; Brandl, North-West Midland. The earliest extant versions of this tale are those by the Anglo-Norman writers Beroul and Thomas (*see* France), the English poem being based on the work of the last-named poet. The tale hinges on the drinking of a love-potion by Tristrem and Ysonde on the voyage to England from Ireland, whence Tristrem has fetched Ysonde, King Mark awaiting her as his bride. Their love is ever after unconquerable, and finally Tristrem has to fly Mark's Court. The MS. breaks off before the final episode, which varies in different versions (*see* France, § 25). The story of Tristan and Isolt is not thought to have been originally attached to the Arthurian Cycle, although Rhys (*op. cit.*) refers to a Welsh triad where Tristan, Mark, and Arthur appear in company. The origin of the tale is a matter of discussion, the theory of this being a purely Celtic one not receiving support from all authorities. The author tells us that the story was related to him by one Thomas, at Erceldoune, which has led to Thomas of Erceldoune being accredited with the authorship of this English poem; again, a reference in Robert of Mannyng's Chronicle leaves a doubt as to whether Thomas of Erceldoune, or Thomas of Kendale is designated as author, the possibility of the latter's rightful claim being supported by some later authorities (Körting, Brandl). By others it is thought more probable that the English poet merely romanced round the name of the Anglo-Norman Thomas.

The poem is written in eleven-lined strophes rhyming a b, a b, a b, a b, c b, c. *Ed.*, Walter Scott, 1804, and later eds.; Kölbing, "Die Nordische u. Englische Version der Tristan-Sage," 1878-82; MacNeill, Scott. Text Soc., 1886. *See* Bossert, "La Legende Chevaleresque de Tristan et Iseult," 1902 (deals with different versions, particularly with that of G. de Strasburg); Golther, "Die Sage von Tristan u. Isolde," 1887; G. Paris, "Tristan et Iseut," 1894; Arts. in "Romania," xv. and xvi. *MS.*, Auchinleck.

Sir Perceval of Galles. Date, 13th century (G. Paris); middle 14th (Kölbing, "Tristrem"); or even later. The dialect is Northern, with indications of Midland influence.

Perceval's mother, her husband having been killed in a tournament by the Red Knight, brings him up in seclusion, fearing for his safety. Perceval remains in ignorance of everything connected with the outside world. One day he meets three knights from Arthur's Court; he asks which of them is the God of whom he has heard. On learning who they are, nothing will any longer keep him from becoming a Knight; and so we hear of his arrival at the Court, of his slaying the Red Knight, and other deeds of prowess, of his reunion with his mother, and of later deeds in the Holy Land. The origin of the tale, and the position of the poem among other Perceval romances, are points of discussion. Mr. Nutt vigorously supports the theory of the Celtic origin of the story. There is an old Celtic legend known as the Great Fool,—a story, Harper writes, known in some shape or other among nearly all Aryan races—which together with others belonging to Celtic literature have features in common with the tale of Perceval's boyhood. The general outline of these allied tales is known as the Aryan Expulsion and Return Formula. Mr. Nutt is opposed by German criticism, especially by Golther, who will hear nothing of a Celtic origin. As regards the connection between the English poem, Chrétien de Troies' "Perceval," and the Welsh Mabinogi, "Peredur ab Evrawc," G. Paris considers them independent of one another. According to this same authority the English poem represents an older and purer version than that which served as a source to the other two works ("Hist. Litt.," xxx. p. 29); the English together with the French and Welsh versions he traces back to Anglo-Norman poems, based on a Celtic tale (*ibid.*, pp. 13, 261). Here again Golther is in opposition, as his view is that Chrétien's work was the source of the other Perceval versions. The dependence of the English version on the French is considered greater by some who support Golther's theory than by others. It will be seen by the outline given of the story, that the English Perceval is not connected with the Grail Legend; neither apparently is the Welsh, the only mysterious things seen by the hero of the latter version being a lance dropping blood, and a head surrounded by blood, in a dish; Chrétien himself, according to Harper, had no precise conception of the meaning of the Grail though he wove it into his romance. The metre of the English poem is a strophe of sixteen lines, tail-rhymed, a a a b, c c c b, d d d b, e e e b. *Ed.*, Halliwell, " Thornton Romances," 1884 ; " Peredur " (from " Red Book of Hergest "), ed. " Lady Guest," in " Mabinogion " ; reprint in Temple Classics, 1902. *See* G. Paris, " Hist. Litt.," xxx. ; Nutt, " Studies, etc." (*op. cit.*) ; Harper, "Legend of the Holy Grail " (on its origin), "Publ. Mod. Lang. Assoc.," viii. ; Golther, " Ursprung u. Entwickelung der Sage von Perceval u. von Graal," "Bayreuther Blatter," 1891 ; and same author, " Sitzunsber. d. Münch. Akad. phil. hist. Cl.," 1890 (Chrétien's work in its relation to the Welsh and English) ; Zimmer, *op. cit.* (§ 25) ; Loth, Edition of " Mabinogion," French trans., 1889 ; J. L. Weston (*op. cit.*, § 25) ; Ellinger (on language and metre), 1889. *MS.*, Lincoln A. 1, 17 (Thornton).

40 *Dealing with Ancient and Oriental Material.*

Floriz and Blauncheflur. Written in rhymed couplets. Date, probably cir. 1250; originating in a southern district of the East Midland (Körting) ; second half of century (Lumby). The tale of a youth and maiden who have loved since they were children ; they are separated, and Blauncheflur is taken as a slave to a seraglio. Floriz seeks till he finds her, and finally is secretly conveyed into the seraglio, hidden in a basket of roses. Their story comes to the ears of the Sultan and they are condemned to be burnt alive. At the last moment her lover urges Blauncheflur to put on a talismanic ring he possesses, which will protect her from the fire ; she refuses, preferring to die with him ; the Sultan being informed of what is going on, is so struck with the beauty of their self-sacrificing love, that he forgives them, and a happy issue to all concerned is the wind up of the story. The tale is of Eastern origin, betraying Byzantine influence ; it is uncertain through what medium it passed into the West, whether or not through a Latin version, as is the case with many old romances. The French version, of 12th century (cir. 1160, or shortly before), is its first appearance in the West, and the French is certainly not taken direct from the Greek ; it then travelled through Germany, Italy, and the North, to

England (*see* Hausknecht). In France the tale was associated with the Carolingian cycle, Blauncheflur being known
as the mother of Berthe au grand Pied, who was the mother
of Charlemagne. *Ed.*, Laing, Abbotsford Club, 1829;
Lumby, E.E.T.S., 1866; Hausknecht, "Sammlung Engl.
Denkmaler," Bd. 5 (with details in introduction of origin,
versions, and manuscripts). *MSS.*, Camb. Univ. Lib. Gg.
4, 27, 2; Cott. Vitell. D. iii.; Auchinleck; Trentham
(Duke of Sutherland).[1]

Amis and Amiloun. Probably dating from close of 13th
century, and originating in the Northern boundary of the East
Midland (*see* Kölbing). A tale of ideal friendship between
two men, whose love for one another is equal to the sublimest
self-sacrifice, and who so resemble each other that they cannot
be told apart. The tale is of Greek or Oriental derivation.
It is extant in a Chanson de Geste ("Geste de Blaive," *see*
France, § 22), and connected with Cycle du Roi (Chevalerie
Ogier), but the English version stands in closer relationship to,
if not directly derived from, an old Anglo-Norman romance.
Ed., Weber, "Metrical Romances"; Kölbing, "Alt Eng-
lische Bibliothek," i. 1884 (with Anglo-Norman poem). *See*
Schwieger, "Die Sage from A. u. A.," 1885. *MSS.*,
Auchinleck; Harl. 2386; Douce, 326; Duke of Sutherland.

Sire Degarre (*L'Egaré*). (The name in the Percy MS.
appears as "Degree"). In short rhyming couplets. Hidden
as an infant by his mother, the daughter of a King of
England, who wishes to conceal his birth, he is found and
brought up by a hermit. At twenty he starts forth in search
of his parents. He finds his mother, is on the point of
marrying her, when their relationship becomes known through
the agency of a pair of gloves. Later on he meets his father,
and the tragic episode occurs of the two fighting together
before they recognise each other (see for similar incident the
old "Hildebrandslied," Germany, § 2; and the tale of "Sohrab
and Rustum," told in Matthew Arnold's beautiful poem).

[1] For account of contents of these two last mentioned MSS., *see*
Kölbing, "Englische Studien," vii., "Vier Romanzen Handschriften"
(Chetham, and Lincoln's Inn, being the other two).

Ed., for the Abbotsford Club (Auchinleck) 1849; Selections in Ellis, "Specimens."   *MSS.*, Auchinleck; Camb. Univ. Ff. ii. 38; Percy Folio. Earliest printed copy by Wynkyn de Worde (without date).

41   THE SHORT TALE.

Side by side with the Romances, the Tale, a shorter and less complicated work—described by Ten Brink as creating a greater interest in things, while the Romance creates a greater interest in persons, the former appealing more to the intellect, the latter to the imagination—began to take its place among the literary works of the country. The French Fabliau was the model of the English Tale which seems to have made its first appearance in the South-East.

Dame Siriz. Written in tail-rhymed strophes of six lines, occasionally giving place to short couplets, and dating from second half of century, probably before 1272 (Ten Brink). Through the evil machinations of Dame Siriz, who makes her believe that she will be transformed into a dog if she refuses, a young wife is persuaded into disloyalty to her husband. The tale is of Eastern origin and became known in the West, where it subsequently appeared in different forms, through the "Disciplina Clericalis" of Petrus Alfonsus.   *Ed.*, Wright, "Anecdota Litteraria," 1844   *MS.*, Digby, 86.

The Fox and the Wolf. Second half century, written in rhymed couplets. The fox falls into a well, but with his proverbial cunning contrives to escape, leaving the wolf in his stead. The tale belongs to a branch of the Roman de Renart, the fox and wolf being substituted for the fox and goat of earlier fable. This is the first English poem connected with the animal saga.   *Ed.*, Wright and Halliwell, "Reliquiae Antiquae."   *MS.*, Digby, 86.

The Land of Cockayne (Idleness). A detailed description of this land is followed by a bitingly satirical account of monastic life. This land had been known to the French before the English version appeared.   *Ed.*, Furnivall, "Early

English Poems," 1862; Ellis, "Specimens, etc.," vol. i. (in
modernised text). *MS.*, Harl. 913.

42 *Historical Verse.*

Robert of Gloucester.

*Rhymed Chronicle, from Brutus to 1270, in Alexandrine
couplets. Written cir. 1300 (Gross). The Chronicle is
based in great part on the histories of G. of Monmouth, H.
of Huntingdon, W. of Malmesbury, and use is made of other
writings. The historian was not far distant from Evesham
when the decisive battle was fought there in 1265; his work
gains interest from details of industries and products peculiar
to certain centres, from patriotic descriptions of his country
and fellow-countrymen. *See* Ten Brink, *op. cit.*, p. 275
seq. "The earlier portion to 1135 may have been written
by another person" (Gross). Strohmeyer sees the work of
three hands in the Chronicle, R. of Gloucester being responsible only for the period from Henry i.'s death to that
of Henry iii. Nothing more is known of Robert himself,
but that he was a monk of Gloucester. *See* Strohmeyer,
"Der Styl, etc.," 1891. *MSS.*, Older edition; Cott. Cal.
A. xi.; Harl. 201 (to 7th year of Stephen); Add. 19677
(to battle of Evesham); later version (according to Strohmeyer
by a third monk), Camb. Univ. Ee. 4, 31 (the narrative
abridged after the period of the Conquest); Digby, 205;
Pepys, 2014; Mostyn Library.

43 *Religious and Didactic Verse.*

Possibly separate lives of saints may have been written by
R. of Gloucester, but he is not now accredited with the
authorship of the whole "Legendarium," the Legend cycle
of the South, for which, however, the monks of Gloucester
are thought probably to be responsible. (The Northern cycle
of legends is of somewhat later date.) The sources of the
legends were chiefly the Latin lives of saints, some of these
being translated for the first time; recourse may have been
had also to French versions. The metre is the Alexandrine
couplet; the style has "no trace of the copious diction, of

6

the impassioned tone, that we find in more ancient alliterative lives of saints." *Ed.*, Horstmann, E.E.T.S. (from Laud, 108); "Alt Englische Legenden," 1875 (from various MSS.). *MSS.*, Harl. 2277 (with additional legends of Judas and Pilate); Egerton, 1993; Add. 10301, 10626; Bodl.-Ashmole, 43; Laud, 108. Other MSS. at Cambridge, Lambeth, etc.

Purgatory of St. Patrick. English version of Henry of Saltrey (*see* § 27 and France, § 10). Last quarter of century. Three English versions are extant. The oldest in long lines; the second is of about the same date and in six-lined strophes; the third is considerably younger. *Ed.*, Horstmann (oldest version), 1875; Kölbing, "Zwei Mittelenglische Bearbeitungen der Sage von S. Patrick's Purgatorium"; L. Toulmin Smith, "Engl. Studien," ix. (Brome Hall MS.). *See* for history of Legend, T. Wright, 1841; Ward, "Cat. Romances," vol. ii.; for sources of S. Patrick's Life, etc., A. Penrose Forbes, "Calendar of Scottish Saints," p. 431, *seq.* *MSS.*, (1) Egerton, 1993; Add. 10301; Cott. Jul. D. ix.; (2) Auchinleck; (3) Cott. Cal. A. 11; Brome Hall, Suffolk.

N.B.—Other ancient legends of visions of heaven and hell are associated with the names of S. Paul, and Tundal (§ 67).

Voyage of S. Brendan (*see* France, § 10). One of the most delightful of the old legends is that of S. Brandan's Voyage, in search of the " Terra repromissionis sanctorum," the final home of the saints, of which he had heard an account from his cousin, and immediately makes preparation to start with some chosen companions, their point of departure from Aran being still known as Brandon Hill; according to another account he read the description of this island of the Blessed, and, believing it to be but lies, threw it on the fire, and cursed the book, in punishment for which he was sent to wander for seven years, that he might see all with his own eyes. Brandan was an abbot of the sixth century; the date of the Latin " Navigatio " is not settled, but there are MSS. of it belonging to the 11th century. Of its relation to other old voyages, as that of Maelduin, of the resemblances in the narrative to the

tale of Sindbad, a full account is given by Goeje. *Ed.*,
T. Wright, " Early Eng. Poetry " (Percy Soc.), vol. xiv. ;
K. Meyer, " The Voyage of Bran," Grimm Library, No.
4, etc. *See* J. de Goeje, " La légende de Saint Brandan,"
1890 ; A. Nutt, " The Voyage of Bran, with essay on the
Irish vision of the happy other-world etc.," Grimm Library,
No. 4, etc. *MSS.*, Harl. 2277 ; Camb., Trin. Coll. ; Cott.
Jul. D. ix ; Add. 10301. A prose version, Add. 11565,
is the text printed by Caxton in his " Golden Legend," 1483.

N.B.—To this century belongs the famous collection of
legends known as " Legenda Aurea," compiled by Jacobus a
Voragine, Bishop of Genoa. It was Englished by Caxton
and printed 1483.

44 *Proverbs of Hendyng.* Written in tail-rhymed strophes,
each finishing with a proverb, and followed by the
words " Quoth Hendyng." Dating from the end of the
century, the dialect being of the South showing Midland
influence (Körting) Hendyng speaks of himself in the first
strophe as the son of Marcolf, the man of ready device
and wit who opposes Solomon in the well-known dialogue
(*see* Anglo-Saxon, § 9). The name Hendyng, in its derivation, signifies the quality prominent in Marcolf, and so we
may look on this proverb-monger as " the personification of
mental adroitness," and his sayings as representative of the
proverbial wisdom current among the people of his time.
Ed., Wright and Halliwell, " Reliqiuae Antiquae," vol.
i. ; Kemble, " Salomon and Saturn " (Appendix), 1848.
MSS., Harl. 2253 ; Digby, 86 ; Camb. Univ. Gg. i. 1.

45   THE SECULAR LYRIC.

In England, as on the Continent, the lighter verse of
this period was largely fostered by the itinerant clerics.
" A tone of youthful audacity, genuine and often passionate
feeling, and fresh, sometimes coarse, sensuousness marked
their secular songs, which were almost without exception
amorous. The form betrays the influence of the Latin
strollers' songs and of French love-poetry, as well as of the

English religious lyric.   The English folk-song doubtless
also acted strongly upon the poetry of the wandering clerics "
(Ten Brink).   The secular lyric in its turn exercised a
reciprocal influence on the religious lyric.   The lyric shows
the same love of nature in its poets as in those of the romances.
Among the best-known lyrics of this period, which bears the
impress of a true folk-song, is the beginning " Sumer is icumen
in, lhude sing cuccu ! " known as the "Cuckoo Song," which
has come down to us with its accompanying music (MS.
Harl. 978).   *See* Ten Brink, *op. cit.*   *See* below for MSS.

46   A number of *Political and Satirical ballads* date from
          this period.   Among the earliest is *The Battle of
Lewes*, 1264, in which the defeated Court-party is derisively
treated.   The two latest given in Harl. 2253 are the one
on the "Traille bastons" (an ordinance of the King), 1315,
and another on the death of Edward I., 1307.   Satires are
directed against the Church, against oppressors in high places,
the vanity of women, etc.   *See* Wright, "Political Songs of
England from the Reign of John to Edward I.," 1839;
*later poems, from Edward III. to Richard III., 1859.

N.B.—The MSS. Harleian 2253, Egerton 2710, and
Digby 86, contain poems in Latin, old English, and old
French, of 13th to 14th century.   *See* E. Stengel (Digby
MS.) 1871; Boeddeker, "Altenglishe Dichtungen," 1878;
Wright and Halliwell, "Reliquiae Antiquae"; Wright,
"Anecdota Litteraria" (from MSS. in Oxford, London,
Paris, and Berne), 1844; Percy Soc. (Harl. MS.).

47   DRAMA.

The Harrowing of Hell (rhymed couplets), cir. 1258
(Brandl), 1273–1307 (Körting), East Midland dialect.
The descent of Christ into Hell, from the " Evangelium
Nicodemi ",—oldest drama extant in English.   Dr. Mall
(p. 10) dates the play not later than middle 13th, basing
his calculations on the Digby MS., which belongs to Edward
I'.s reign (1272–1307).   *Ed.*, Dr. E. Mall (Harl.),
1871; Pollard, "English Miracle Plays," 1895, 4th ed.,

1904; Collier, "Five Miracle Plays," 1836; Halliwell, 1840; Laing, "Owain Miles and other inedited Fragments of Ancient English Poetry," 1837. *See* J. H. Kirkland, "A Study of the Anglo-Saxon Poem, 'The Harrowing of Hell'" (enquiry into sources of the poem on which the later dramatic rendering is based), 1885. *MSS.*, Harl. 2253 (Edward II.'s reign); Auchinleck; Bodl. Digby, 86.

48   LATIN WRITERS.

Science.

Roger Bacon. Franciscan Friar, Philosopher, Mathematician, etc., b. 1214 (?); d. 1294.

Opus Majus.   *Ed.*, S. Jebb, 1733; J. H. Brydges, 1897.

*Opus Minus.

*Opus Tertiam.

Works on *Chemistry, Alchemy, Moral Philosophy, and Mathematics.*

Of English translations of his works there are, "Discovery of the Miracles of Art and Nature, and Magick," 1597, 1659; "The Cure of Old Age and Preservation of Youth," 1683; "The Mirror of Alchemy," 1597.

Ed., J. S. Brewer, "Inedited Works," 1859.

Michael Scot, b. 1175(?); d. 1234(?). Mathematician, Physician, and Alchemist; reputed also as a Necromancer.

Liber Physiognomiae, or *de Secretis Naturae.* Pub. 1477.

Quaestio Curiosa de Natura Solis et Lunae. (Alchemy, and Philosopher's Stone.)

Mensa Philosophica, etc. (authorship uncertain); trans., known as *The Philosopher's Banquet.*

Sphere of Sacrobosco.

Trans. into Latin of Aristotle's "De Animalibus," and other works still in manuscript.

Medical Works.

Gilbert Anglicus, cir. 1290.

Laurea Anglicana.

49 *Theology, Philosophy, Logic.*

Alexander of Hales, d. 1245. Philosopher and Theologian. Called " Doctor Irrefragabilis" ; " Theologorum Monarcha " ; " Doctor doctorum."

Summa Theologia. Printed 1475.

Robert Grosseteste. Bishop of Lincoln, d. 1253. A prolific writer.

Works on Physical Science.

Letters. Ed., H. R. Luard.

Translations of Aristotle, and Dionysius Areopagitica ; of the *Testamenta xii. Patriarcharum.* Also " The Boke of Husbondry and of Plantynge of Trees and Vynes," from the French of Robert de Henley.

An Anglo-Norman French religious allegorical poem is also by Grosseteste, *Le Chasteau d'Amours,* in octosyllabic verse. *Ed.,* J. O. Halliwell, 1849 ; Cooke, 1852 ; Old Eng. trans., R. F. Weymouth, Phil. Soc., 1864 ; " Carmina Anglo-Normanniae," Caxton Soc., 1844. For full list of works, *see* Pegge, " Life of Grosseteste," 1793.

John Duns Scotus, d. 1308. Theologian, Logician, and Metaphysician.

Among his works are—

Quaestiones. Logical Treatises.

De Modis significandi sive Grammatica Speculativa.

De Rerum principio.

Commentaries on Aristotle, and on Lombard's " Sententiae."

Ed., Works, Luke Wadding, 12 vols., 1639.

50 *History.*

In the 13th and 14th centuries, Annals were chiefly compiled in the Monasteries, and dealt sometimes with purely local matters, sometimes with general history. The chief monastic centre from which Annals were issued was S. Alban's, to which school belonged Matthew Paris, Roger Wendover, and other historians of note. *See* *"Chronica Monasterii S. Albani," 793–1488.

Walter of Coventry.

Memoriale Fratris Walteri de Coventria. A compilation (Brutus to 1225) founded on earlier historians, and copied for the later years from a Chronicle of the Monastery of Barnwell, near Cambridge.

Roger Wendover, d. 1237.

Flores Historiarum (Creation to 1235). The work up to 1188 is compiled from one by John de Cella, Abbot of S. Albans.

Matthew Paris. Monk of St. Albans, d. cir. 1259.

The chief of our mediæval historians.

Chronica Majora. The earlier part is a revision of John de Cella's previous work, and of its continuation to 1235 by Roger of Wendover. Three editions appeared in 1250, 1253, and 1259.

Historia Minor. Abridgement of above, with additions.

Abbreviatio Chronicorum Angliae. Of uncertain authorship.

Vitae Abbatum S. Albani. Compiled and in part composed by M. Paris.

For the life of Stephen, Archbishop of Canterbury, attributed among other lives to M. Paris, *see* Liebermann, "Ungedruckte Ang.-Norm. Geschichtsquellen," 1879.

Ralph, Abbot of Coggeshall, d. cir. 1227.

Chronicon Anglicanum, 1066–1223.

Bartholomew Cotton. Monk of Norwich, d. cir. 1298.

Historia Anglicana, 449–1298.

Liber de Archiepiscopis et Episcopis Angliae.

John of Oxnead, or Oxenedes. Monk of St. Benet, Holme, Norfolk.

Chronica, Hengist and Horsa to 1292.

Nicholas Trevet, or Trivet, d. 1328.

Annales Sex Regum Angliae, 1135–1307.   *Ed.*, Eng. Hist. Soc., 1845.

Thomas Wykes, fl. 1258–1293.
*Chronicon, 1066–1289.   Written at Osney.

*Annals of Margan, 1066–1232, as well as those of other monasteries are extant.

51   *Law.*

Henry of Bracton, d. 1268.
*De Legibus et Consuetudinibus Angliae.
A notebook of cases tried in the King's Court in the reign of Henry III., is also thought to be by him.   *Ed.*, F. W. Maitland, 1887.

Andrew Horne, d. 1328.   A French work, *Miroir des Justices*, is usually assigned to this writer.   *Ed.*, with trans., F. W. Maitland, Selden Soc., 1895.

52   XIVth CENTURY.

Cir. 1350 : *Late Middle English (Körting) Middle English (Kittredge).*

" It is certain," writes Ten Brink, " that in the second half of the 14th century England was no longer a truly bilingual country.   Under Edward III. French ceased to be the medium of instruction in the schools; in 1362, Parliament was opened in English, and in the same year English was ordered to be used in the courts of law for the better understanding of the people.   Edward III.'s victorious campaigns had kindled the enthusiasm of the national spirit, and simultaneous with this awakening of patriotic sentiment was a return to the use of alliteration in poetry, which for some time past had been super- seded by rhyme and newer forms of verse.   During the latter half of the century a greater number of French words are found in English writings, testifying to the closer relationship that was beginning to exist, both politically and socially, be- tween the Norman and Saxon, the warfare with France helping to tighten the bond of common nationality between the alien races.

"The intellectual and spiritual movement of the 14th century, which centred at Oxford, is headed by Northerners. This movement started with the new scholastic system of Duns Scotus, then turned to mysticism under Richard Rolle and Walter Hylton, and ended in Wycliffe's religious reform. All these men were Northerners, who studied or taught at Oxford. And the English literature of the first half of the century is almost exclusively confined to the North" (Horstmann, "R. Rolle, etc."). As regards the literary productions of this period, "The 14th century," writes Professor Ker ("Mediæval Studies," *op. cit.*), "is not in prose what it is in poetry. There is no great revolution, like that which through the agency of Chaucer brought English poetry out of its corners and by-ways and made it fit to be presented at Court." Speaking of the 14th century generally, he adds that it "has a distinct character, particularly interesting as coming between the mediæval and modern world, not merely in the hackneyed part of 'an age of transition,' but as achieving certain things which no later progress has surpassed, such as the Chronicle of Froissart, the prose of Boccaccio, the poems of Dante, Petrarch, and Chaucer."

PROSE.

Science.

53 Geoffrey Chaucer, d. 1400. In 1386 Chaucer, according to his own declaration, was 40 years of age. For the life of this author, *see* under Ward (Eng. Men of Letters), Tuckwell (Miniature Series of Great Writers), Pollard, Skeat (ed. "Works"); the "Dict. National Biography"; "Life-Records of Chaucer" *ed.*, Selby, Furnivall, Bond, Kirk, Chaucer Soc., 1900; Ames, "Chaucer Memorial Lectures," 1900; and Lounsbury, "Studies in Chaucer," 1892. Editions of works: Thynne, 1532; Tyrwhitt, 1775, etc.; Skeat, 6 vols., 1894; and "Student's Chaucer," 1 vol., 1895; Pollard, Heath, Liddell, M'Cormick, 1901. The Chaucer Society, founded in 1867 by Dr. Furnivall, has published parallel texts of Chaucer's works, and Autotype Editions of some of the chief MSS. (§§ 57, 76.)

For MSS., *see* Skeat, "Works," vol. i. p. 49 *seq.*; and Introduction to "Works" by Pollard, etc.

For Chronology of Works, *see* Skeat (*op. cit.*); Koch, "The Chronology of Chaucer's Writings," Chaucer Soc., 1890; and Ten Brink, "Zur Chronologie, etc."

For language and metre, *see* Ten Brink, trans. M. Bentinck Smith, 1901.

The dates of Chaucer's works are given according to Skeat and Koch.

For further details of life, periods of literary activity, etc., *see* under § 76.

54 *Treatise on the Astrolabe*, 1391, 1392. Originally intended to be in five parts, but the work has either been in great part lost, or was never completed, as it has come down to us imperfect. Its chief literary interest resides in the introduction to "litell Lowys my sone." The treatise is based on a work by the Arabian philosopher, Messahala, which would have been known to Chaucer through a Latin version. *Ed.*, Skeat, "Works," vol. iii.

55   PROSE.

Religious, Didactic.

Dan Michel. An Augustine Monk of Canterbury, born at Northgate, in Kent.

Ayenbite of Inwyt (Remorse of Conscience), finished "On the Vigils of the holy Apostles, Simon and Jude, by a brother of the Monastery of St. Austin of Canterbury, in the year of our Lord, 1340." This work, in the Kentish dialect, is a translation of "Sommes des Vices et des Vertus," composed in 1279 by a Dominican Monk, named Lorens (France, § 40). It was written, as the author himself tells us, for "lewd," that is, unlearned, persons, and deals in turn with the Ten Commandments, Articles of Belief, Lord's Prayer, Gifts of the Spirit, and the seven heads and ten horns of the Apocalyptic beasts, a vein of allegory running through the work. "A popular handbook of moral theology," lacking "the animated, graphic manner of the Ancren Riwle" (Ten

Brink). *Ed.*, Morris, E.E.T.S., 1866; C. Horstmann, Belles Lettres Series. Selections: Mätzner, *op. cit.*; Morris and Skeat, " Specimens." *MS.*, Arundel, 57 (autograph).

Richard Rolle (§ 67), b. about or shortly before 1300; d. 1349 (Horstmann). This writer was born at Thornton in Yorkshire; he led the life of a hermit in different places in the North of England, finally settling at Hampole, near Doncaster. All that we know of his life is contained in " Officium et Legenda de Vita Ricardi Rolle" (G. Perry, " English Prose Treatises "), which was written for the nuns of a neighbouring Cistercian Convent. Richard Rolle was held in great estimation for his sanctity; pilgrims visited his grave where miracles were reported to take place. Prof. Horstmann traces the origin and growth of the mystic School of Theology in England from its early representatives, through John Hoveden and Rolle down to Wyclif. He gives the writings of several of the hermit's followers. " No one," he writes, " can read these treatises without having an enhanced opinion of the value of mediaeval theology."

Rolle was a writer of English and Latin works, and is best known as the author of the poem, " The Pricke of Conscience." It is difficult, Horstmann says, to trace Rolle's English works, as they have become confused with those of his two followers, Hilton and Wyclif. The prose treatises which are certainly his, and given under his name, are, *The Forme of livyng, Ego dormio et cor meum vigilat, The Commaundement of God, Meditatio de passione domini.* These are contained in MSS., Camb. Univ. Dd. v. 64, Ll. i. 8; Camb. Add. 304², etc. Other prose tracts are contained in the Thornton MS. (Lincoln): *Of the Vertu of the Holy Name of Jhesu*; a tale *that Rycherde made* (account of a vision); *A dreadful tale of unperfitte contrecyone*; *Moralia di Natura Apis*; *Delyte and Zernyng of Gode*, and others on the Commandments, Gifts of the Holy Ghost, Delight in God; the greater number of these are translations. *Ed.*, G. Perry, E.E.T.S.

Another undoubted work of Rolle's is a translation and commentary of the *Psalter* and certain canticles. *Ed.* (Univ. Coll., 64), H. R. Bramley, 1884; other northern MSS.,

Newcastle; Laud, 286; the remaining eleven MSS. are southern transcripts.

Ullmann, in "Engl. Studien," vii., has edited what he thinks another work of Rolle's, "On the Sorrows of Christ," Camb. Univ. Ll. i. 8.

Many other anonymous works, which are possibly or probably by Rolle, are given by Horstmann, taken from MSS., Rawl. C. 285; Arundel, 507; Vernon; Thornton; Reg. 17, B. xvii.; Harl. 1022; Laud, 210. *Ed.* (complete prose works), Horstmann, "R. R. and his followers," "English Writers," vols. 1 and 2, 1895–6. *See* Hahn, "Quellen. untersuchungen zu R. R.'s Schriften," 1900.

Translations of Rolle's Latin Treatises, *De incendio Amoris*, and *de emendatione Vitae*, dating from the 15th century, have been edited by Harvey, E.E.T.S.

N.B.—The earliest English prose version of any book of the Bible is a translation of the Psalms, which has been ascribed—wrongfully, according to Körting and others—W. of Shoreham.

Prose.

56   *Miscellaneous.*

The Voiage and Travaile of Sir John Maundeville. This work is no longer considered genuine. It is extant in French, Latin, and English; the French version (oldest MS., Bibl. Nat. Nouv. Acq. fr. 4515) being the earliest according to the latest authority. The name of Maundeville is now thought to be a borrowed one. The Liège chronicler, Jean d'Outremeuse, tells us that Jean de Bourgogne, or Jean à la barbe, a physician, revealed to him on his deathbed that he was J. Maundeville, and there is an authentic record of a funeral inscription to a Sir J. Maundeville in a church at Liège. Jean de Bourgogne had written other works, and had been in England, where he had been implicated in the killing of a nobleman. As it happens, a genuine J. Maundeville had ten years previously been implicated in the death of the Earl of Cornwall. So the matter stands. J. d'Outremeuse is not to be relied on implicitly as an authority. The work, whosoever

the author may have been, is not, as it purports to be, the
result of personal travels, but evidently a compilation. The
first part treats of the Holy Land, the second of other parts of
Asia.   *Ed.*, Warner (Egerton MS.) Roxburghe Club,
1890 (with accompanying French). *See* for above details, E.
B. Nicholson and Sir H. Yule, "Ency. Brit.," 9th ed., 1883;
and for identity with J. de Bourgogne, art. by E. B. Nicholson,
Academy, 1884, p. 261; and Bovenschen, "Untersuchungen,
etc.," 1888.   *MSS.*, Three hundred, at least, are said
to be extant. B. M., ten French, six Latin, nine English
(Cott. Titus, C. xvi.; Egerton, 198; Harl. 3954, etc.),
three German, and one Irish.

57   *Translations.*

John de Trevisa. Vicar of Berkeley, b. near Saltash,
Cornwall, 1326; d. 1412. Chiefly known as a translator of
Latin works.   Chief work—

*Trans. of Higden's *Polychronicon*, to which he added
notes, and a continuation to 1360 (§ 83). Published in a
revised form by Caxton, 1482; and later by Wynkyn de
Worde.   *MSS.*, Add. 24194; Harl. 1900; Cott. Tib.
D. vii.; S. John's Coll. Camb.

Other translations were from, *De Proprietatibus rerum*, by
B. de Glanville; *De re Militari*, by Vegetius; *De Regimine
Principum*, by Aegidius, etc.   *A Dialogue between a Lord and
a Clerk* is ascribed to him as an original work, written as an
introduction to *Polychronicon*.

John Wyclif, or **Wycliffe,** d. 1384, as Rector of
Lutterworth.

Wyclif and his fellow-workers were the first to undertake
a translation of the *whole* BIBLE. The New Testament is
generally assigned to Wyclif. Nicholas Hereford, one of his
disciples, completed the O.T. portion to Baruch iii. 20; the
remainder of the Apocrypha (except Esdras iv.) was finished
by another writer, possibly Wyclif himself. The whole was
afterwards revised, with the help of others, by John Purvey,
who shared Wyclif's pastoral labours at Lutterworth. The

work was completed before 1400, probably cir. 1388. The translation was made from the Vulgate. *Ed.*, J. Forshall and F. Madden, 1850. This edition includes the Revised Version, by J. Purvey, and the translation of the Psalms by N. Hereford, and contains a survey of early biblical versions *MSS.*, 170 in number.

All other English works ascribed to Wyclif are found:— "Three Treatises of John Wycliffe," Todd, 1851 ; "Select English Works of Wyclif," T. Arnold, 1869-71 ; "English Works of Wyclif, hitherto unprinted," F. D. Matthew, E.E.T.S., 1880.

Wyclif's Latin works are published by the Wyclif Society, founded 1882, by Dr. Furnivall.

N.B.—For early translations of portions of the Bible, see Forshall and Madden, *op. cit.* ; and A. C. Paues, "A Fourteenth Century English Biblical Version," 1902, 1904.

Geoffrey Chaucer. (*See* §§ 53, 76.)

Boece, Translation of Boethius's "De Consolatione Philosophiae." *Ed.*, R. Morris, E.E.T.S., 1868 (Addit. MS.), and in editions of works (*see* § 53). *See* K. O. Petersen, "Chaucer and Trivet," Pub. Mod. Lang. Assoc., v., 1903. *MSS.*, Add. 10340; Camb. Univ. Ii. 3, 31 (ed. for Chaucer Soc.), etc.

58　　Poetry.

Metrical Romances—Arthurian Cycle.

Morte Arthure. Alliterative (long lines). Arthur receives a summons to Rome to do honour to the Emperor (Lucius Tiberius) ; he returns a defiant answer. Their forces meet on French soil, the Britons gaining the victory ; Lucius is finally killed ; Arthur hearing of Modred's treachery returns home ; in a battle between him and his nephew, Modred is killed, and the king mortally wounded. The latter is buried at Glastonbury, all the mystical accompaniments of his death being ignored by the poet. G. of Monmouth's history is the chief but not the only source of

the poem. Divergences in the text have led to the suggestion
that the work is composed of parts originally unconnected
(Körting). The "Morte Arthure" is one of the poems
ascribed by some authorities to Huchown. Wyntoun, in his
"Originale Cronykil" (early 15th), speaks of three poems
by this writer, of which the first mentioned is "The Gret
Geste of Arthure," and argument gathers round the question
as to the identity of this poem with the "Morte Arthure."
Trautmann and Neilson are strong supporters of Huchown's
authorship (*see* Huchown, § 60). This romance "represents
elements of Arthurian tradition, which but for it would have
been lost." The dialect of the "Morte Arthure" is of the
north of England, or, according to Trautmann, of the south
of Scotland. "Much of brilliant English history," writes
Mr. G. Neilson, "in 'Morte Arthure,' and other pieces, as
to challenge for them, in virtue of their historical realism,
a place of oddly romantic authority as secondary documents
for the French wars of Edward iii., and his galant son."
The Arthur of this poem he considers partly the Arthur
of Romance, partly Edward iii.; and he further identifies
characters and places. *Ed.*, E.E.T.S. (Perry), 1865;
(Brock), 1871; M. M. Banks, 1900. *See* Branscheid,
"Ueber die Quellen, etc.," "Anglia," viii. *MS.*, Lincoln
(Thornton). A later version in strophes (Harl. 2252), *ed.*
J. Douglas Bruce, 1903.

Ywain and Gawain. Written in rhyming couplets in the
Northern dialect. First half 14th century (Körting). The
poem is a translation of Chrétien de Troies' "Yvain," or
"Le Chevalier au Lion" (*see* France, § 26), the original
being condensed by the English poet. *Ed.*, Ritson, *op.
cit.*; G. Schleich, 1887. *MS.*, Cott. Galba E. ix.

*The Avowynge of King Arther, Sir Gawan, Sir Kaye, and
Sir Bawdewyn of Bretan.* Of the vows, and the carrying out
of the same, of Arthur and his three knights. The poem is
in tail-rhymed strophes a a b, c c b, d d b, e e b, and written in
the Northern dialect, during the second half of the century.
Ed., Robson, "Three Early English Met. Rom.," 1842.

See G. Paris, "Hist. Litt.," xxx.　　*MS.*, Ireland (Hale), with Aunters of Arthur.

Sir Gawayne and the Grene Knight. Written in the West Midland dialect, in strophes of long, alliterative lines, varying in number, closed by five short lines, rhyming a b a b a. This poem, described by G. Paris as the "best jewel of English Mediæval literature," opens with the sudden appearance in Arthur's hall, during the New Year's feast, of the mysterious Green Knight, who there challenges any knight present to give him a blow with his battle-axe, all the condition he asks being the permission to return the blow at the close of a year and a day. Gawain strikes off his head, and the strange Knight rides off with it in his hands. Gawain goes in search of the Knight, meeting with many adventures. He is guilty of a slight infraction of promised faith to the lord of the castle where he is being entertained, and he suffers consequent humiliation; then follows encounter with the Green Knight, identification of same with lord of the castle, and Gawain's return to Court. Hunting scenes and descriptions of nature add beauty and life to the poem. No direct source of the poem is known. Madden thinks it mainly derived from the "Perceval" of C. de Troies; Ten Brink, who shares this opinion, writes that the English poet borrowed "in such a way that what is merely episodical in the source becomes the centre of his work, is put into new relations, and entirely remoulded." To the author of this romance have been ascribed (Morris, Madden, Trautmann) the poems, "Pearl," "Cleanness," "Patience," all the four, according to Neilson, being part of Huchown's work; "S. Erkenwald," according to the latter, would also belong to the same writer, and it is so ascribed by Horstmann as well in his "Altengl. Legenden." The chief incident is found in other French and German poems, the hero not being invariably Gawain. *See* for these and an older Irish version, the work by Miss Weston cited below. *Ed.*, F. Madden, Bannatyne Club, 1839; Morris, E.E.T.S., 1864, 1869. *See* M. C. Thomas, "Sir G. and the Green Knight," a comparison with the French "Perceval" (with notices of all other poems in which Gawain is mentioned), 1883. For tales in connection with Gawain, *see*

"The Legend of Sir Gawain," J. L. Weston, Grimm
Library, vol. vii. ; modern prose version by the same
authoress in "Arthurian Romances unrepresented in Malory's
Morte d'Arthur," No. 1, 1898 ; and J. D. Bruce, "De
Ortu Waluuanii," Pub. Mod. Lang. Assoc., vol. vi., 1898.
MS., Cott. Nero. A. x.

Libeaus Desconus (The Fair Unknown). The poem was
written about the second quarter of the 14th century by a
native of Kent (Körting). The strophes are composed of
twelve tail-rhymed verses, a a b, a a b, c c b, d d b, e e b. The
hero is the son of Gawain, brought up in seclusion by his
mother, and in ignorance of his origin. He becomes renowned through the chivalrous deeds that he accomplishes
on behalf of a maiden Elene. Among the episodes of his
adventurous life are the sojourn with the "dame d'amour"
who holds him enchained by her magic, and the final one
of the enchanted lady, who, transformed into a serpent, but
retaining her woman's face, enters Arthur's hall and kisses
him, and so doing, regains her human form ; she and the fair
unknown are finally married. Renaud de Beaujeu deals with
this same subject in "Le Bel Inconnu" ("Guinglain," France,
§ 55), both the English and French poem, according to Kölbing,
Paris, and Schofield, being based on an older French version ;
Kaluza, on the contrary, gives "Le Bel Inconnu" as the
source of the English romance. The author himself states
that he made use of a French original. The older French
version is thought to be more exactly preserved in the Italian
"Carduino." Another version is extant in the German
romance of "Wigalois," by Wirnt v. Gravenberg (Germany,
§ 30). The connection of the tale with that of "Perceval"
has been supported by Schofield, not without opposition.
Sarrazin and Kaluza (who was at first opposed to Sarrazin's
view) assign "Libeaus Desconus," as well as "Octavian,"
to Thomas Chestre.   *Ed.*, Ritson, *op. cit.* ; Kaluza, "Altengl. Bibliothek," vol. v., 1890 ; . Furnivall and Hales, Percy
MS., 1867, etc.   *See* Kölbing, "Engl. Studien," i. ; Kaluza,
"Engl. Studien," xviii. ; Sarrazin, ed. of "Octavian" (*q.v.*) ;
G. Paris, "Romania," xv. ; Schofield, "Studies in Libeaus
Desconus," "Harvard Studies, etc.," 1895 (for relationship

7

of French and English versions, source of English, and
connection with "Perceval"); J. L. Weston, "Arthurian
Romances," No. v.   *MSS.*, Cott. Cal. A. 11; Lincoln's
Inn, 150; Lambeth, 306; Ashmole, 61; Naples, Nat. Libr.;
Percy MS.

Aunters (Adventures) of Arthur at the Tarnewathelan (see
Huchown).   Written in strophes of nine long and four short
lines; alliterative, and rhymed in Northern dialect (vicinity of
Carlisle; Körting).   Of the two chief incidents, the first is
the appearance of her mother's spectre to Queen Guinevere
while she and Gawain are together in the forest near Carlisle,
these two having become separated from the remainder of the
hunting-party.   The spectre foretells the events which close
Arthur's reign, and the death of Gawain and the other knights.
The second is the fight between Gawain and a Scottish knight
who comes to claim land which Arthur has taken from him
and given to Gawain.   This poem is thought by some scholars
(*see* Neilson and Amours) to be identical with "Awntyre of
Gawain" (*see* Huchown, § 60).   That it is another work
written by the author of "Golagrus and Gawain" is also a
supposition not necessarily dependent on the authorship of
Huchown.   Neilson has traced the contemporary events which
he finds thinly shrouded in the romance, and writes that there
are "marrow bones of true history in these two poems" (A.
and A., and G. and G.).   As with the "Morte Arthure,"
the exact date depends on the acceptance or rejection of
Huchown's authorship, but is thought generally to be about
the middle, or during second half of century, 1360–1400
(Luebke).   *Ed.*, Madden (with "Sir Gawain and the
Green Knight"), 1839; Robson, "Three English Metrical
Romances," 1842; Amours, "Scottish Alliterative Poems
in Rhyming Stanzas," Scott. Text. Soc., 27. *See*, for
authorship, Trautmann, "Anglia," i.; Luebke, "A. of
A.," 1883.   *MSS.*, Lincoln (Thornton); Douce, 324;
Ireland (Hale).

Joseph of Arimathea.   Imperfect.   In long, alliterative
lines; written in W. Midland dialect; date, cir. 1350 (Skeat,
Körting).   In this, which Ten Brink considers one of the

oldest specimens of the new alliterative poetry, we have the history of J. of A. from the time of his liberation from long imprisonment to the conversion of the heathen king Evelak's subjects. The further history of Joseph's arrival in Britain, burial at Glastonbury, etc., is given by Lonelich, a poet of the 15th century, in his "Holy Grail." The "Joseph of Arimathea" and its continuation are based on the French prose, "Grand St. Graal" (France, § 55). The "Graal Saga" was attached to the legend of J. of Arimathea by the French writers. *Ed.*, Skeat, E.E.T.S., 1871 (with early prose tales printed by Wynkyn de Worde and Pynson). *See* Nutt., *op. cit.* (for theories concerning the origin of the "Graal Saga"), and Harper, *op. cit.* (*see* under Perceval of Galles, § 39). *MS.*, Vernon.

Arthur. Rhymed couplets; in the Southern dialect, with a few Northern forms. Körting dates the MS. 1408, but considers that the poem belongs to the 14th century; second half century (Brandl). The events recorded are those which form the theme of the "Morte Arthure." The editor tells us that the poem occurs in an old Latin chronicle, the author of which breaks out into English verse, the story he tells being an abstract of the earlier version of G. of Monmouth, before the Guinevere and Lancelot episode had been introduced by French-writing English romancers. *Ed.*, Furnivall, E.E.T.S., 1864, 1869. MS. in possession of the Marquis of Bath.

59 Thomas Chestre.

Launfal (Miles). The latest date assigned to this poem is 1400; according to some authorities it was written before 1350 (*see* Kaluza). The strophes are tail-rhymed, a a b, c c b, d d b, e e b; the dialect is of the South (Midland or East). This Knight of Arthur's Court is bidden by two damsels whom he meets to come to the fairy Tryamour. The latter lavishes love and riches upon him, and confers on him immunity from harm; but her love is to be kept a secret, betrayal on his part will mean the loss of everything. Provoked one day at Court by a wrongful accusation, brought against him by the Queen, he boasts of Tryamour's love; he is condemned to death, and Tryamour and her train arrive only just in time to save him. The poem is based on the "Lai de Lanval" by Marie de France (France, § 31). Allied tales are "Guingamor," "Graelent," "Partenopeus," and "Oger le Danois" (*see* G. Paris, "Romania," p. 323, 1898). Sarrazin (*ed.* "Octavian"), and Kaluza (*see* below) ascribe "Octavian" and "Libeaus Desconus," to the author of "Launfal." *Ed.*, Ritson, *op. cit.*; Kaluza (Cott. MS.), "Englische Studien," xviii.; Kittredge (Rawlinson), "Amer. Journal Phil.," x.; Hales and Furnivall (Percy); Erling, with Marie's "Lai," 1883; Kempten, 1883. *See* Kolls, "Zur Lanval-Sage, etc.," 1886; Münster, "Untersuchungen zu T. Chestre's Launfal," 1886; Schofield, "The Lays of Graelent and Lanval," Pub. Mod. Lang. Assoc., 1900; Halliwell, "Illustrations of the Fairy Mythology of a Midsummer Night's Dream," Shaks. Soc., 1845. *MSS.*, Cott. Cal. A. 11 (Launfalus Miles); Rawlinson C. 86 (Landavall); Percy (Lambewell); Malone, 941 (fragment); Douce, ii. 95 (fragment), Camb. Kk. 5, 30 (*see* Kittredge, for relationship between, and origin of these versions).

60 Huchown "of the Awle Ryale" (King's, or Royal Hall). (§ 67.)   Andrew of Wyntoun (§ 69) in his "Chronicle" refers to three works written by Huchown, "The Gret Gest off Arthure," the "Awntyre off Gawane," and the "Pystyll off Swete Susane."

Around this "mysterious friend" of Wyntoun's, as Amours calls him, has arisen much controversy: first, as to whether he is identical or not with Sir Hew of Eglintoun, a Scotchman, who was sent to England in 1367 to make terms of peace, married the sister of King Robert II. and died cir. 1381; secondly, as to the identification of the first two works mentioned above with existing Arthurian romances (*see* under Arth. Rom., § 58), and as to what other extant works may be rightly ascribed to him. The "Pystyll off Swete Susane" (§ 67) is unanimously allowed to be his. Among the latest contributions to the discussion are the works by Mr. Neilson, who has no doubt as to Huchown being Sir Hew, and ascribes to him the following works: "Morte Arthure,"

"Destruction of Troy," "Cleanness," "Patience," "Sir
Gawayne and the Grene Knight," "Golagrus and Gawayne,"
"Awntyrs of Arthur," "Pistill of Susane," "The Pearl,"
"Wars of Alexander," "Titus and Vespasian, or the Siege
of Jerusalem" (known as Titus), "The Parlement of the
thre Ages," "Wynnere and Wastoure," "Erkenwald," basing
his argument on identity of phrase, parallelism of subject or
episode, and allegorical references to events associated with
himself and his times. He also lays great stress on rubrica-
tions in manuscripts, which he thinks belonged to the poet
himself. Among Mr. Neilson's opponents is Mr. J. T. T.
Brown who considers the former's arguments untenable as
regards the works, although the identity of the poet with Sir
Hew is reasonably probable. For one work at least, "Awntyre
of Gawane," there is a statement by Dunbar that it was written
by the Clerk of Tranent. Mr. Brown thinks "Golagrus
and Gawayne" links itself to "Rauf Coilyear" generally
believed to be a 15th century poem. Trautmann, supporting
Huchown's authorship of "Morte Arthure," sees no justifica-
tion in assigning to him the following six poems in above list,
or "The Pearl." Körting thinks "Erkenwald" may well
be by the author of "G. and the Grene Knight."

So far conjecture alone seems possible as regards any works
to be ascribed to Huchown beyond the "Pystyll of Swete
Susane." *See* G. Neilson, "Huchown of the Awle Ryale.
The Alliterative poet. A historical criticism of 14th century
poems ascribed to Sir Hew of Eglintoun," 1902. J. T. T.
Brown, "Huchown of the Awle Ryale and his poems.
Examined in the light of recent criticism," 1902. Trautmann,
"Der Dichter Huchown and Seine Werke," "Anglia," i.; G.
Neilson, "Sir Hew of Eglintown and Huchown of the Awle
Ryal" (a Calendar of events in which H. and E. were con-
cerned, compiled from original sources), "Trans. Phil. Soc.
Glasgow," 1902. Amours, "Scottish Alliterative Poems,"
Introduction. *See* also *Athenæum*, June 1, and Oct. 26,
1901 (Neilson) on "Troy," "Titus," "Morte Arthure"
(association between), and on "The Parlement of the Thre
Ages"; June 21, 1902, on "The Wars of Alexander" and
MS. used by poet-translator; April 18, 1903, and following
numbers (I. Gollancz) for controversy on date, etc., of

"Wynnere and Wastoure"; and "Phil. Soc.," Nov. 1, 1901, (Gollancz), "Recent Work and Theory on Huchown and Others."

The Parlement of the Thre Ages, Wynnere and Wastoure. The Editor thinks many points tell strongly in favour of identity of authorship for these two. *Ed.*, I. Gollancz, 1897. *MS.*, Add. 31042 (which also contains "Siege of Jerusalem" (Titus), and a religious lyric resembling the P. of S.).

Titus. Ed., Kölbing and Kaluza, in press, E.E.T.S.

Golagrus and Gawain. The incidents in this romance occur during Arthur's journey to and from the Holy Land. The chief is the combat between Gawain and Golagrus, the lord of a castle that Arthur is besieging. Gawain is the victor, but, in order to save the life of his opponent, he allows himself to follow Golagrus humbly as if his prisoner, and by his courteous conduct wins Golagrus over to be a friend and subject to Arthur. Madden thought that the romance was compiled from two episodes in "Perceval," Trautmann sees only an indirect source for the work in this French poem. The work, according to Neilson, is one of Huchown's; Trautmann gives it to the Clerk of Tranent, as perhaps identical with the "Awnteris of Gawane," mentioned by Dunbar as one of this writer's works. The 15th century is the date assigned to this romance by Trautmann and Körting. *Ed.*, Madden, "Syr Gawane," 1839; Trautmann, "Anglia," ii. Amours, "Scot-Allit. Poems," etc. There are no MSS. extant, the poem survives in an early printed edition, 1508, in Advocates' Library, Edinburgh.

61 CAROLINGIAN CYCLE.

For origin of Carolingian romances (*see* France, § 6). Nearly all the English versions of these romances bear traces of being translated from French originals; the latter have not in all cases been preserved. *Ed.*, E.E.T.S. (Herrtage, Hausknecht, Lee). *See* G. Paris, "Histoire poetique de

Charlemagne" (Meyer ed.), 1905; Gautier, "Bibl. des Chansons de Geste," 1897.

Fierabras Branch.

Sir Ferumbras, written in short alternately rhyming lines (or long lines with the corresponding half-verses rhyming), and in part in tail-rhymed strophes, a a b, a a b. The dialect is a mixture of Northern and Southern (Editor), uninfluenced by Northern, according to other authorities. The English poem is a faithful translation of the French " Fierabras " (France, § 16) which in the second part was an extended and altered version of an episode of an older French poem known as " Balan," which has only survived in an outline of it given in Mousket's Chronicle (*see* Paris, *op. cit.*, 251). The chief incidents in the romance are: the reconquest from the Saracens of the relics in honour of which the fair of Lendit was instituted, the fight between Oliver and the gigantic Saracen Ferumbras, and the imprisonment of the peers. According to G. Paris the work does not seem to belong to an earlier date than end of 14th century. (The romance appears as " The Conquest of Charlemagne" in some printed editions.) *MS.*, Ashmole, 33.

Sowdone of Babylone. (Concerning Sowdone and his son Ferumbras.) The latter part of this romance corresponds with " Sir Ferumbras "; the editor thinks the first part is based on the " Destruction de Rome " (France, § 16) "a kind of introductory poem to ' Fierabras ' " (G. Paris), and the second on a version of " Fierabras " no longer extant. (For the relation of the " Destruction de Rome " to Balan and Fierabras, *see* Hausknecht, editor). The poem is in East Midland dialect, and dates from early 15th century. *MS.*, Phillipps (Farmer).

Otinel (Otuel) Branch.

Roland and Vernagu (Ferragus, the Giant). Charlemagne journeys to Constantinople to help the Emperor Constantius; campaign in Spain; combat between Roland and the Giant. Written in tail-rhymed strophes, a a b, c c b, d d b, e e b.

Otuel (from the French " Otinel "). Otuel is a Pagan

knight, who fights with Roland; the onlooking knights pray for Roland's victory and for Otuel's conversion, whereupon a dove descends on Otuel who feels himself instantly converted; the combat ceases, Roland and Otuel embrace, and Otuel becomes a Christian. The poem is in rhyming couplets, divided into "laisses" of unequal length. Both these poems are in the Auchinleck MS., and therefore date from the first quarter of the century.

The Sege of Melayne (*Milan*). Tail-rhymed strophes, a a b, c c b, d d b, e e b, from a lost French original.

Duke Rowlande and Sir Ottuell of Spayne. Tail-rhymed, a a b, a a b, c c b, c c b, based on the same Chanson de Geste as "Otuel." Both these last two poems are in MS., Add. 31042, probable date cir. end 14th, Duke Rowland perhaps later.

N.B.—G. Paris has reconstituted a poem to which he gives the name of "Charlemagne and Roland," which gives a résumé of the Emperor's wars against the Saracens. He divides it into four parts: Journey of Charlemagne to Holy Land; beginning of wars in Spain, according to Turpin, including the Episode of Ferragus; Otuel (not the Auchinleck Version); and the end of Turpin's recital. The first two parts are represented by the above-named poem of " Roland and Vernagu "; the " Otuel " was analysed by Ellis as an independent poem, the latter parts being now only known from his description of them as contained in a lost manuscript (*op. cit.*, 156)

Roland's Song (fragment). In rhymed couplets. The author bases his poem on a version of the Chanson de Roland, making use at the same time of Turpin's Chronicle "from which he borrows an important feature." The Editor dates it 1400 (?). G. Paris places it considerably earlier (13th century). *MS.*, Lansdowne, 388.

N.B.—Including all fragments, there are extant ten English romances in connection with this cycle. Seven are in verse, the others in prose.

62 Alexander Cycle.

For origin of the Alexander saga (*see* France, § 27).
See Meyer, "Alexandre le grand dans la littérature française
du moyen Âge," 1886.

Life of Alisaunder. Probably originating in the north of
ancient Mercia (Ten Brink). A legendary biography of
Alexander, drawn from the sources of other romances of the
cycle, its more immediate one being the "Roman de toute
Chevalerie," by Eustace of Kent (*see* France, § 56). Both
subject and treatment place the poem among the best of
the romances. Each chapter is prefixed by what Brandl calls
a "lyric intermezzo," with charming descriptions of landscapes,
ending up with a wise saying. The poem is in rhymed
couplets, the Auchinleck MS. decides the latest date to
which the poem can be assigned.

> "Day spryng is jolyf tide,
> He that can his tyme abyde,
> Ofte he schal his wille bytyde."

Ed., Weber, "Metrical Romances," 1810.   *MSS.*, Laud,
622; Lincoln's Inn; Auchinleck (fragment).

Alisaunder. Youth of the Macedonian King.   *Ed.*,
Skeat, with W. of Palerne, E.E.T.S.   *MS.*, Bodl.
Greaves, 60.

Alexander and Dindimus. Letters of A. to D. King of
the Brahmans, and his replies; trans. from the Latin, cir.
1340 – 50 (Skeat).   *Ed.*, Stevenson, 1849; Skeat,
E.E.T.S., 1878.   *MS.*, Bodl. 264. The above two
poems are in West Midland dialect, and written in long
alliterative lines, and are thought by Trautmann to be by
same author, and part of a large Alexander romance. *See*
Trautmann, "Ueber Verfasser u. Entstehungszeit einiger allit.
Gedichte, etc.," 1876.

N.B.—A poem ascribed by Skeat to the first half, or middle
15th century, and edited by him, 1886, as "Wars of Alexander," following the "Historia de Proeliis," and originally
written, according to the editor, in the Northumbrian dialect,

is extant in MSS. Ashmole 44; Dublin D. 4, 12. Also *ed.*, Stevenson with "Alexander and Dindimus."

TROY CYCLE (*see* France, § 28).

The *Gest Hystoriale of the Destruction of Troy*, the *Troy Book*. In long alliterative lines, originally written in Northern dialect, the MS. being a West Midland transcript (Körting). The poem is probably founded on a French version of Guido d. Colonne. The editors assign it to the same author as that of "Morte Arthure" (*see* also under Huchown, § 60). *Ed.*, Panton and Donaldson, E.E.T.S., 1869, 1874; *see* Trautmann, *op. cit.* (§ 60). *MS.*, Glasgow, Hunter T. 4, 1.

N.B.—For other poems of the Troy Saga, *see* under Chaucer and Lydgate. There are besides: a fragment, Camb. Univ. Kk. v. 30; Bodl. Douce, 148 (*see* under Barbour); Bodl. Laud, 595 ("a Romance, cir. 1400"), *ed.*, J. E. Wülfing, 1902; *see* Miss Kempe, "Engl. Studien," 29; and "The Seege, or Batayle of Troy," in rhyming couplets, *ed.*, Herrig, *Archiv*, lxxii.

63 MISCELLANEOUS ROMANCES OF GREEK AND ORIENTAL ORIGIN.

Octavian. Both versions are taken from the Anglo-Norman. The Southern is in six-lined strophes (a a a b, c, b, the b lines shorter than the others), the Northern is in twelve-lined strophes (a a b, c c b, d d b, e e b). Sarrazin thinks "Octavian" is written by the same poet as "Libeaus Desconnus" and "Launfal" (§§ 58, 59). *Ed.*, Weber, *op. cit.* (Cott. MS.); Halliwell (Camb. MS.), 1844; Sarrazin, "Zwei Mittelengl. Vers.," "Alt. Engl. Bibl.," vol. iii. *MSS.*, Cott. Cal. A. 2, Southern version; Northern version, Univ. Libr., Camb., Ff. ii. 38; Lincoln (Thornton).

N.B.—This is one of several old romances in which certain features recur: calumniated wife, separation of family, children carried off by wild beasts which become greatly attached to them, final reunion of family. These incidents, which may be traced back also to the legend of S. Eustace,[1] are found, with more or less variation in:

Isumbras.   *Ed.*, Ellis (Halliwell), 1897; Zupitza (Schleich), "Palaestra," 15, 1901.   *MSS.*, Lincoln (Thornton).   Sarrazin (*op. cit.*) thinks "Isumbras" only an imitation of "Octavian," the latter poem, however, is more complicated.   Isumbras himself has to serve seven years as a smith before he is restored to his rightful position.

Torrent of Portyngale.   *Ed.*, Adam, E.E.T.S., 1887. *MSS.*, Manchester (Chetham Libr.).

Syr Eglamour of Artois (France, § 40).   *Ed.*, Halliwell, Camden Soc.   Both these latter poems in twelve-lined, tail-rhymed strophes, thought by Adam to be taken from an older English version now lost.   There is no trace of a French original, although probably such existed.   *MSS.*, Cott. Cal. A. ii.; Camb. Univ. Ff. ii. 38; Percy (oldest MS.).

Ipomedon.   1st version, twelve-lined, tail-rhymed strophes; 2nd version, rhyming couplets.   From the French "Hippomédon," by Huon de Rotelande (France, § 29).   *Ed.*, Both versions, with French original, Kölbing and Koschwitz, 1890.   *MSS.*, 1st version, Manchester (Chetham); 2nd version, Harl. 2252.   A prose version is also extant (MS., Marquis of Bute).

The *Parthenopeu* (France, § 29) was also put into English verse.   Two versions are extant, published for Roxburghe Club, 1864 (1st version), 1873 (2nd version).   *MSS.*, 1st Eng. version, Oxford, Bodleian (Rawlinson); Univ. Coll.; New Coll. (fragment); 2nd version, Vale Royal (Lord Delamere).

King of Tars (twelve-lined, tail-rhymed strophes).   Somewhat allied to the tale of Floriz and Blauncheflur.   The King's daughter courageously marries a pagan Sultan in order to save her father, her husband being finally converted.

---

[1] St. Eustace was a high official under Trajan, the Emperor; he sees a figure of Christ while hunting, becomes a day-labourer, has his wife and children stolen from him by wild beasts, and does not find his sons again until they are grown up (*see* France, § 4).

Ed., Krause, "Eng. Studien," xi.   *MSS.*, Vernon;
Auchinleck; Add. 22283.

64   ROMANCES DEALING WITH TEUTONIC MATERIAL.

Guy of Warwick (France, § 30). The tale is probably
founded on popular tradition; both this hero and Bevis of
Hamton are found in Anglo-Norman poems of earlier date.
G. of Warwick leaves his wife and his possessions and takes
a pilgrimage to the Holy Land. He is not recognised on
his return, even by his wife, and finally dies as a hermit.
Once only does he put on his armour again as a true knight,
to fight with the giant Colbrand on behalf of King Athelstan.
Zupitza distinguishes four English versions among the texts
that have come down. The tale is allied to the S. Eustace
and S. Alexius legends (France, § 4). The hero is commemorated in the Percy MS. in the ballad of "Guy and
Colebrande." *Ed.* (Auch. and Add.), Turnbull, Abbotsford Club, 1840; Zupitza (Camb., Auch. and Caius),
E.E.T.S., 1883–91. *See* the latter's edition of 1875 for
particulars of the different versions. *See* "Dict. Nat. Bio."
and H. Morley, "Eng. Prose Romances," 1889. *MSS.*,
Auchinleck (two versions), rhymed couplets and twelve-lined
strophes; Camb. Univ. Ff. 2, 38, rhymed couplets; Camb.,
Caius Coll., 107; Sloane, 1044; Add. 14408; Douce,
fragments only. This and the following poem belong to first
quarter of century.

Sir Beves of Hamtoun (rhymed couplets and six-lined, tail-
rhymed strophes) (*see* France, § 54). Beves endeavours to
revenge his father, who has been treacherously slain by his
mother, but the latter succeeds in selling him to heathen
merchants. Many chivalrous deeds; finally carries off Josian,
daughter of heathen king, lands in England and revenges himself, etc. The English poem stands alone as derived from the
original through a different version to that made use of for the
Continental and Welsh texts. The MSS. represent different
versions. *Ed.*, Turnbull, Maitland Club, 1838. Kölbing,
E.E.T.S., Extra Series (Auchinleck MS.), 1885–1894.
See Kölbing, "Studien zur Bevis-sage"; Paul - Braune,
"Beiträge," 19; and Stimming (*op. cit.*, France, § 54).

MSS., Auchinleck; Caius Coll., Camb., 175; Univ. Libr., Camb., Ff. 2, 38; Manchester (Chetham); Duke of Sutherland; Naples.

William of Palerne (long alliterative lines). Cir. middle century. The hero of this poem goes through many adventures, in the course of which he is assisted and rescued by a Werwolf (Castilian Prince Alfonso); the heroine is Melior, the daughter of the Roman Emperor. This is a version of the French original, by one " Wiliam," who wrote his work at the request of Sir Humphrey de Bohun, the Earl of Hereford, the nephew of Edward II. Containing Greek elements (G. Paris). A Germanic saga which passed through a Byzantine version before falling into French hands (Körting). The English romance reflects something of the democratic tone of the day. *Ed.*, Madden, Roxburghe Club, 1832. Skeat, E.E.T.S., 1867. *See* Kaluza, " Engl. Stud.," iv.; and for legend of Werwolf, Kittredge, "Latin Romance of Arthur and Gorlagon," " Studies and Notes in Phil. and Lit.," viii., 1903; and Kirby F. Smith, " Publ. Mod. Lang. Assoc.," ix.; and *Academy*, No. 1088 (Nicholson) for prose version. *MS.*, Camb., King's Coll., 13.

Sir Gowther (in tail-rhymed strophes). The dialect N.-E. Midland (Breul); Northern (Kaluza). A version of the " Legend of Robert the Devil "; written probably beginning 15th (Körting). Kaluza places it earlier. *Ed.*, Utterson, " Select pieces of early Popular Poetry," 1817; K. Breul, 1886. *See* Kaluza, " Eng. Stud.," xii. *MS.*, Reg. 17, B. xliii.; Edinburgh, Advocates'.

N.B.—For " Robert the Devil " *see* W. J. Thoms, " Early English prose Romances," 1828, 1858; and H. Morley, *op. cit.*

Note.—Other English romances of 14th and 15th centuries are—

Emare. Second half 14th (*see* " Manekine," France, § 57). *Ed.*, Gough, " Old and Middle English Texts," 1901. Text in press by E. Rickert. *See* also Gough, "The Constance Saga," Palaestra, No. 23, and M. R. Cox, "Cinderella " (345 variants), 1893. *MS.*, Cott. Cal. A. ii.

Le Bone Florence (*see* France, § 54); close 14th or beginning 15th (Körting).   *Ed.*, Ritson, *op. cit.*; W. Vietor, 1899. *See* Wenzel, "Die Fassungen der Saga v. Florence de Rome, etc.," 1890).   *MS.*, Camb. Univ. Ff. ii. 38.

Sir Degrevant.   *Ed.*, Halliwell, Thornton Romances; and *Sir Cleges*, *ed.*, Weber, *op. cit.*, both slightly connected with Arthurian cycle.

See also under Historical Verse, § 70.

65   Collections of Tales.

The tales that travelled from the East were chiefly in collections of tales bound together by a common narrative.

The Sevyn Sages (*see* "A Study of the Romance, etc." Killis Campbell, "Mod. Language Notes," xiv., 1899; for Domenico Comparetti's study, *see* Spain, § 11). Known in the East as the Book of Sindibâd. The Indian original is lost, and it is impossible to determine which of the stories found in later versions were contained in the original. The Eastern group of versions differ from one another, and are quite distinct from those of the Western group.

The original of the Western group is also apparently lost. The oldest form of Western type is the "Dolopathos," put into French verse by Herbert, 13th century, from Latin prose of Johannes de Alta Silva. "As the 'Dolopathos' is evidently based on some prevailing Western type, and dates from end 12th century, the lost original may be placed at a date not later than middle 12th."

The wide difference between the Eastern and Western versions has been explained by the assumption that the latter were based on oral accounts; when these took literary form is as yet undetermined. The "Historia Septum Sapientum," thought at one time to be the original source of Western group, has been shown to be of comparatively recent date. As many as five different groups have been distinguished among the MSS., numbering about a hundred, of the Western versions.

Eight Middle-English versions are contained in as many MSS.; they are all in octosyllabic verse. The lost original of these is thought to have been undoubtedly based on a French version. The Auchinleck MS. is the oldest, cir. 1330; there-

fore the composition may be dated earlier, but not earlier than
1300.   *Ed.*, Weber, *op. cit.* ; Wright, Percy Soc., 1846.
MSS., Auchinleck, Arundel, 140; Egerton, 1995; Balliol
Coll., 354; Univ. Libr., Camb., Ff. ii. 38; Dd. i. 17.
Cott. Galba E. ix. ; Asloan, Malahide Castle, Ireland.

66   L**AIS**.

The "lai," another French form of tale (France, Marie
de France, § 31), was imitated in England. We have two
specimens extant from this century.

Lai le Freine.   From the French of Marie de France.
(Short rhyming couplets.)   Cir. beginning of century.   Tale
of young girl, exposed as an infant in the hollow of an ash-
tree (whence the title), who in after life exercises patience
and self-denial under painful trials of love, and is finally rewarded.   *Ed.*, Weber, *op. cit.* ; Ellis, *op. cit.*   *MS.*,
Auchinleck.

Sir Orfeo (*Orfeo and Heurodis*).   (Short rhyming couplets,
with frequent alliteration.)   Undoubtedly taken from French
original, but uncertain how far the author is indebted to it.
It is probably of about same date as Lai le Freine.   "The
travesty (of Orpheus and Euridice) is throughout naïve, and is
based upon such a complete appropriation and adjustment of the
antique material and mediæval views that this charming poem
seems like a fairy tale of natural growth" (Ten Brink).
Ed., Ritson, *op. cit.*, Zielke, 1880.   *See* Halliwell ; "Illustrations of the Fairy Mythology of a Midsummer Night's
Dream," 1845.   *MSS.*, Auchinleck, Ashmole, 61 ; Harl.
3810.

67   R**ELIGIOUS** P**OETRY**.

William of Shoreham.   Vicar of Chart Sutton, by
Leeds, cir. 1320.

Poems, in the Kentish dialect: *On the Seven Sacraments* ;
The Hours of the Cross ; *Seven Deadly Sins* ; *Ten Commandments* ; *Joys of the Holy Virgin* ; *Song to the Virgin* (from a
poem by Grosseteste, as stated in MS.) ; and an unfinished
one on the fundamental doctrines of the Christian Faith.

Ed., Th. Wright, Percy Soc., 1849; M. Konrath, E.E.T.S., 1902.   *MS.*, Add. 17376.

Robert Mannyng of Brunne (§ 69), fl. 1288–1338 (cir. 1260–1340, or 1345).

Handlyng Synne, 1303. A rhythmical version in short couplets, of the "Manuel des Pechiez," by Wilham Wadington (France, § 48). The author is no slavish follower of his original; he inserts illustrative tales of his own, and leaves out some sermons and prayers. He had a great deal to say against women, and inveighed against tournaments. The whole is a lively picture of the times written by a poet of a democratic turn of mind. According to Ten Brink it is "one of the most entertaining and instructive books that old England has bequeathed us." Of the poets who preceded Chaucer, Robert of Brunne, chiefly by this work of his, was one among those who exercised most influence on the English language, serving "to spread the East Midland dialect towards the South . . . through him many new Romanic words were probably either introduced into the English literary language, or at least established there" (Ten Brink). *Ed.*, Furnivall, Roxburghe Club, 1862; for E.E.T.S. (with French original), 1901. *See* G. Hellmers, "Ueber die Sprache, R. M. of Brunne, etc.," 1885; and Boerner, "Stud. Engl. Phil.," 12 (on "R. M.'s Language in its Relation to Modern Forms").

Richard Rolle. (§ 55.)

The Pricke of Conscience (in rhyming couplets). A poem in seven parts, dealing with the wretchedness of man, instability of this world's happiness, Domesday, pains of hell and joys of heaven, etc. Rolle drew for his work from many sources, displaying considerable learning. A Latin version of this work is extant (Camb. Univ. Dd. iv. 50) but not by Rolle. *Ed.*, Morris, 1863. *See* Köhler (on Sources) "Jahrb. Röm. Eng. Lit.," vi. *MSS.*, These are numerous: Northern: Cott. Galba, E. ix.; Harl. 4196; Southern transcripts: Harl. (6); Add. (6); Lansdowne, 348; Arundel, 140; Reg. 18 A. v.; Egerton, 657.

Horstmann gives two poems under Rolle's name from

Camb. Univ. Dd. v. 64, and says some of the poems in the
Thornton MS. are possibly, or probably his. *See* Kuehn,
"Ueber die Verfassenschaft der in Horstmann's English
Writers enthaltenen lyricshen Gedichte," 1900. A psalter in
verse Horstmann thinks may be a youthful production of
Rolle's, but he rejects as Rolle's work "The Myrour of
Life" (Speculum Vitae), partly given by Ullmann in his
article on Richard Rolle in "Englische Studien," vii. ; and
also the metrical paraphrase of the Seven Penitential Psalms,
Ed., Adler and Kaluza, "Engl. Studien," x.

Huchown. (§ 60.)

Pystyl (Epistle) *of Swete Susan.* The tale of Susanna told
in alliterative and rhyming strophes of thirteen lines (a b, a b,
a b, a b, c, d d d, c), the first eight lines being long, and followed
by five short ones, the ninth line having only two syllables.
Köster discovers an historical meaning in this poem, recognising
similarities in the events described with those of the life of
Margaret, the second wife of David II. *Ed.*, Amours,
"Scottish Allit. Verse," 1897 ; H. Köster, 1895. *MSS.*,
Vernon, f. 317 ; Add. 22283 ; Cott. Cal. A. ii. ; Phillipps,
8252 ; Ingilby (Ripley Castle).

N.B.—A poem of corresponding metrical form, of somewhat later date, is edited under the title of *The Quatrefoil of
Love*, by I. Gollancz, *Furnivall Miscellany*, 1901.

ANONYMOUS RELIGIOUS POEMS.

Cursor Mundi (mostly in short-rhymed couplets, the strophic
form being employed for some of the N. T. portions), a work
of nearly 20,000 lines written in the North, probably dating
from the early part of the century, consisting of a paraphrase
of the O. and N. Testament, from the Creation to Solomon
and the Prophets ; and passing on to the birth of the Virgin and
the chief incidents in the N. T. ; a final description of the
condition of the world in its last age, with account of the
coming of Antichrist and the signs preceding the judgment.
Apocryphal Gospels, the Golden Legend, the Hist. Ecclesi-
astic, and the writings of the Homilists, and probably French

8

texts, were used by the author in collecting his material.   In the course of the work we come across mediæval legends, notably the one connected with the Cross; and a motive similar to that in the "Merchant of Venice" occurs in the tale of the Jew who guided the Empress Helena to the place where the crosses were buried.   Ten Brink writes: "The most attractive legends and traditions that occupied the age were now first blended for the English people, with the most momentous passages of Bible History."   It was indeed the author's wish to give to both nations, English and French, "their own speech," that his countrymen, who composed the masses, might have something they would understand.   The work enjoyed great popularity.   The Fairfax MS. is headed with the words—

> "This is the best boke of alle,
>   The cours of the werlde men dos hit calle."

Ed., R. Morris, E.E.T.S., 1874–91. (This includes Hämich's "Inquiry into the Sources of the C. M.," and two other studies on the text, and the dialect of the MSS.) *MSS.*, Cott. Vesp. A. iii., Galba, E. ix.; Fairfax, 14; Laud, 416; Camb. Trin. Coll.; Coll. Arms.; Edin. Coll. Phys.; Bedford Libr.

Scotch Legendarium (short-rhymed couplets). A work formerly ascribed to Barbour; later criticism generally has thrown doubt on the authorship, and the work is not given to Barbour by its editor: see, however, under Barbour, for the further view on this subject as given by Neilson. *Ed.*, Metcalfe, "Legends of the Saints in the Scottish Dialects," Scottish Text Soc., 1891. *MS.*, Camb. Univ. Gg. ii. 6.

The Legend of Tungdalus, or *Tundale* (§ 43), was put into rhyming couplets end 14th or early 15th century, founded on a Latin original. *Ed.*, A. Wagner, 1893. *MSS.*, Edin. Advocates'; Cott. Cal. A. ii.; Reg. 17 B. xliii.; Ashmole, 1491.

A cycle of Northern *Homilies*, in rhyming couplets, belongs to the early part of this century, being "the Sunday Gospels for the whole year, explained in the language of the people." As usual tales are introduced to emphasize the interpretation of the Scriptures. *Ed.*, Horstmann, "Altengl. Legenden," 1881 ; Small, "Metrical Homilies," 1862. *MSS.*, Original Collection, Camb. Univ. Gg. v. 31, Dd. i. 1 ; Ashmole, 42 ; Edin. Coll. Phys. ; Harl. 2381 ; Lambeth ; Phillipps. Later Editions: Vernon ; Add. 22283 ; Harl. 4196 ; Cott. Tib. E. vii.

A version in rhyme of the "Gospel of Nicodemus," and the "Surtees Psalter" belong to this period.

The Surtees Psalter. First quarter of century. Translation of Psalms (in short couplets). *Ed.*, Anglo-Saxon and Early English Psalter. Surtees Society, 1843–47. *MSS.*, Cott. Vesp. D. vii. ; Egerton, 614 ; Harl. 1770.

The Pearl (rhyme and alliteration). The twelve-lined strophe ends with a kind of refrain, and the last word of a strophe is frequently repeated in the first line of the following : The poet lamenting the death of his young daughter, "Pearl," has a vision of her in her transfigured state. This and the two following poems are by the author of "Sir Gawayne and the Grene Knight" (§ 58). "The Pearl" ranks among the most charming of old English poems, both in thought and delicacy of feeling. *Ed.*, R. Morris, E.E.T.S., 1869 ; and I. Gollancz, 1891 (with modern rendering) ; C. G. Osgood, Belles Lettres. *See* C. F. Brown, "Pub. Mod. Lang. Assoc.," March 1904.

Cleanness (long alliterative lines). Rhythmical version of several Bible narratives.

Patience (long alliterative lines). Rhythmical paraphrase of book of Jonas, glorifying the virtue of Patience. *Ed.*, "Cleanness and Patience," O. F. Emerson, Belles Lettres. *See* also under *eds.* of Pearl." *MS.*, the three poems are in Cott. Nero. A. x.

68 *N.B.*—The *Gesta Romanorum*, a collection of tales from various sources, written in Latin, was the storehouse of material for many famous writers of 14th and 15th centuries. It is uncertain when or by whom composed, but it dates from end 13th or early 14th century, at latest. The name of Pierre Bercheur (d. 1362) and that of Helinand, have been suggested as authors, but not on what is considered by most

authorities sufficient grounds. There exist many MSS. of the Latin version, 30 in the various Libraries of Great Britain alone. The English translation was probably made in Henry VI.'s time, and was printed by Wynkyn de Worde, cir. 1510–15. *Ed.,* "Early English Versions of G. R.";
Herrtage, E.E.T.S., 1899; Trans. by C. Swan, 1887; Latin version, *ed.,* Oesterley, 1872; revised ed., 1877. *MSS.,* Eng. Version, Harl. 7333; Add. 9066; Univ. Lib., Camb., Kk. i. 6.

69   HISTORICAL VERSE.

Robert Mannyng of Brunne. (§ 67.)

* Version of Wace's "Brut," and Peter of Langtoft's "Chronicle" (*see* France, § 73).
1st part.   Short rhymed couplets.
2nd   ,,   Twelve-lined, tail-rhymed strophes.
Finished, 1338. *Ed.,* 1st part, Furnivall, 1889; Zetsche, "Anglia" ix. (Lambeth MS.); 2nd part, Hearne, 1725. *MSS.,* Inner Temple, Lambeth; Cott. Jul. A. v.; Lincoln.

John Barbour. Archdeacon of Aberdeen, b. 1316–1330 (cir. 1320 Skeat), d. 1395.

The Bruce (rhymed couplets), 1375-6. Life and deeds of Robert Bruce, and account of the carrying of his heart to the Holy Land by James Douglas.
"A national heirloom was added to the treasury of Scotland when John Barbour, Archdeacon of Aberdeen, completed under Robert II., the first of the Stewart kings, his poem of the Bruce" (Neilson).
There are allusions in the Bruce to Guido of Colonna's "Troy," to the "Romance of Alexander," the "Brut," the "Story of Thebes," and the "Romance of Ferumbras." *Ed.,* Skeat, E.E.T.S., 1870-77, Scott. Text Soc., 1894. *See* also "John Barbour, Poet and Translator," G. Neilson, 1900; the "Wallace and the Bruce restudied," J. T. T. Brown, 1900; and discussion in *Athenæum,* Nov. 17, 1900, to Feb. 23, 1901. *MSS.,* Camb., S. John's, G. 23; Edinburgh, Advocates'.

Troy fragments. A compiler of the 15th century pieced together two renderings of the Troy tale—one by Lydgate, the other a Scottish version, and at the close of the latter he writes, " Her endis Barbour and begynnis the Monk." This Barbour, however, has been identified by some authorities (*see* " Anglia," ix., and " Engl. Stud.," x.) with a writer of the 15th century. *Ed.,* Horstmann (*see* below), 1881-82. *MSS.,* Camb. Univ. Libr. Kk. v. 30 ; Douce, 14.

Legends of Saints. Metcalfe does not give these legends to Barbour. In the case of both the two last-mentioned works, the objection to Barbour's authorship has been that the vocabulary differs from that of the " Bruce." Neilson, however, considers this merely owing to difference of subject. *Ed.,* Horstmann, 1881–2 ; Metcalfe, " Legends of the Saints in the Scottish dialect," 1891, etc. *MS.,* Camb. Univ. Libr. Gg. ii. 6.

The authorship of the " Buik of Alexander," translated from the French, still remains a matter of controversy. In metre and style, and to a great extent in material, it corresponds with the " Bruce."

Neilson gives the order of Barbour's works as follows :— " Troy," " Alexander," " Bruce " (or Bruce, Alexander) " Legends."

Andrew of Wyntoun. Prior of S. Serf's Inch, Loch Leven, b. cir. 1350 ; d. 1420-30.

Orygynale Cronykil of Scotland supposed to have been finished 1419-1424. From the Creation to 1408 (rhymed couplets).

There are several references in the Chronicle to Barbour's " Bruce," and citations from it, the MSS. of the Chronicle being older than those of Barbour. It is not known how far he modified the language. *Ed.,* Laing, " Series of Scottish Historians," 8, 1872–79 ; Eyre-Todd, Abbotsford Series of the Scottish Poets (" Early Scottish Poetry "), 1891. *MSS.,* Reg. 17, D. xx. ; Cott. Nero. D. xi. ; Wemyss ; Harl. 6909 ; Advocates', A. 7, 1 ; A. 1, 13.

N.B.—In the edition of " Bruce " by Skeat, two other poems are given, found in the St. John's MS. " How the good wife taught her daughter," probably from the French, and a "Dietary," ascribed to Lydgate, of both which there are other versions extant.

70   ANONYMOUS POEMS PARTLY HISTORICAL.

Richard Coeur de Lion (rhymed couplets). In Kentish dialect of first half of century (Körting), beginning of century (Brandl). The author tells us that he took his material from a French model (Anglo-Norman poem, G. Paris) which is now lost. In the poem we have the legend of the deed of heroism by which Richard won his name. *Ed.*, Weber, *op. cit.* ; Ellis, *op. cit.* (prose summary). *MSS.*, Auchinleck ; Harl. 4690 ; Douce ; Caius Coll., Camb. ; Add. 31042 ; Coll. of Arms.

Athelston (twelve-lined, tail-rhymed strophes), of North Midland dialect, cir. 1350. Tale of the time of King Athelston (924-940) ; a nobleman is accused of plotting to murder the King ; he and his wife and sons prove their innocence by the ordeal of fire. *Ed.*, Zupitza, "Eng. Studien," xiii. and xiv. ; Hartshorne, "Ancient Metrical Tales," 1829 ; Wright and Halliwell, "Rel. Ant.," 1845. *MS.*, Caius Coll., Camb., 175.

The Earl of Tolous (tail-rhymed), in the North-east Midland dialect. The Earl fights on behalf of the innocent wife of the Emperor Diocletian, whose life and honour are assailed. He finally becomes Emperor himself. The historical basis of the romance is the connection between the Empress Judith, wife of Ludwig der Fromme and Count Bernhard of Barcelona. The Empress had to clear herself by oath before an Assembly of the States at Aix in 831 (*see* Lüdtke). It dates from end or perhaps middle 14th century (Sarrazin) ; not earlier than beginning 15th (Lüdtke). The original French version is lost. The English tale "is one of the oldest versions of a wide-spread saga, the historical origin of which may be traced back to the 9th century." *Ed.*, Ritson, *op. cit.* ; Lüdtke, "Sammlung Engl. Denkmäler," iii. *See* Sarrazin, "Engl. Studien," vii. *MSS.*, Camb. Univ. Ff. 38 ; Ashmole, 45, 61 ; Lincoln.

POLITICAL LYRICS AND BALLAD POETRY.

71 Laurence Minot. We know nothing personally of this author; his songs were composed between 1333 and 1352.

Battle of Halidon Hill.
Battle of Bannockburn.
Sea-fight of Sluys.
Siege of Tournay.
Battle of Crécy.
Siege of Calais.
Victory of Neville's Cross.
Defeat of the Spanish Fleet.
Capture of the Castle of Guisne.

Also poems on the Expedition into Brabant, and first Invasion of France.

*Ed., "Political poems and songs relating to English History," J. Wright, 1859; J. Hall, Clarendon Press, 1887. *MSS.*, Cott. Galba. E. ix.

72 Not until the second half of the 14th century do we find distinct mention of a ballad of Robin Hood, namely, in "Piers Plowman"; there seems to be little doubt however that he had been a hero of song in the previous century. In "Robin Hood" we have one of the last reminders of heathen mythology. Somewhere about the 12th century, or a little later, the god Woden was given the name of Robin, the French form of Ruprecht, which corresponds to Henodperaht, the ancient name of the god, signifying "splendid in fame." The life of outlawry with which Robin Hood is always associated is a later form of the legend of the Wild Huntsman, connected with Woden (Ten Brink). J. Grimm associated him with a wood-sprite known as Hodeken. *Ed.*, Child, "Popular Ballads," vol. v.; "Folk-lore Society," iii.; F. B. Gummere, "Old English Ballads," 1894. *See* "Dict. Nat. Bio."; Thoms, *op. cit.*; and *Academy*, 1883, pp. 181, 231, 250, 384. *MSS.*, Seven ballads of Robin Hood (Add. 27, 879); Bishop Percy's Folio, *ed.* Furnivall and Hales, 1867.

A compilation of poems on Robin Hood, called "Lytel Geste," was printed by Wynken de Worde, cir. 1490.

N.B.—In 1388 was fought the Battle of Otterburn (or Chevy Chase), to which we owe some of our most famous ballad poetry.

73 The three great poets of the 14th century were Langland, Gower, and Chaucer.

William Langland (or **Langley**).   A native of Shropshire, b. cir. 1332; d. cir. 1400.   If Langland wrote "Richard the Redeless" (see below), he was alive in 1399.

The Book of Piers Plowman, or, *William's Vision of Pierce Plowman* (long alliterative lines).   Three versions by the author himself (Skeat) of this work are extant.   Begun about 1362, the poem was interrupted before completion; in 1377 the author completed and revised it; a third revised text was prepared in 1393, or a few years later.   One of the latest views is that the three versions are by three different authors. *See* Prof. Manly, "Modern Philology," Jan. 1906.

The whole poem is allegorical, and records the visions which came to the poet as he lay one May morning on the Malvern Hills.   He first sees a "fair field full of folk," representing all classes of men, good and bad; on a hill is a tower, which a beautiful lady tells him is the Tower of Truth; a dungeon which is also visible in a deep vale is the Castle of Care.   Among the company he sees False and Meed, who are shortly to be married; and then a large assembly gathers preparatory to the marriage, against which an appeal is made to the King, who, warned by Conscience, prevents it.   After further allegorical episodes, the scene changes back to the field, where again many folk are to be seen.   Conscience preaches to them, and full of repentance they set forth on a search after Truth.   Then the Ploughman appears to show them the way, and finally Langland is awakened by a dispute between Piers and a priest concerning a pardon that has been granted to the former, which the priest declares to be no pardon.   Pondering over this question, the poet is inspired to write of Do-well, Do-bet, and Do-best; the fundamental moral being that the Pope's pardon is of no avail unless accompanied by well-doing.   *MSS.*, 12 of 1st version, of which the Vernon is the chief; 15 of 2nd version;

23 of 3rd version. Oxford, Cambridge, London, Dublin, Lincoln's Inn, and private Libraries. The Bodl. Laud. Misc., 581, is said to be an autograph MS. Some of the above MSS. have mixed texts.

Langland's writing reflects the social and religious upheavals which were taking place in his day, and reveals the great distresses of the time. He lifted his voice in condemnation and warning, the devout earnestness of his purpose being felt throughout his work underlying its satire and humour. Although not a professed antagonist of Rome, his opinions on many points coincided with those of Wyclif, and he may be reckoned among the early reformers. His style, in Ten Brink's words, is "popular and noble, easy and restrained," and proves "the superior power of Teutonic poesy, needing neither the music of language nor the charm of image to find its way to the heart, and whose very essence is directness."   *Ed.*, Skeat, in its three forms, E.E.T.S., 1867–69–73; notes and glossary, 1877, 1885; "Three parallel texts," 1886; Prologue, and *passus*, i.–vii. Clarendon Press, 1891.

Richard the Redeless (long alliterative lines). A poem dealing with the wrong-doing and weakness of Richard II., accompanied by exhortations. The poem is ascribed by the Editor, with whom other authorities agree, to Langland. Skeat writes that as the poem was written after R.'s imprisonment, but before his deposition, the latter event stayed the execution of the work. See, however, *Academy*, Sept. 19, 1874, where the date is further discussed by Dr. C. Ziepel; and Dr. Bradley, *Athenæum*, April 21, 1906, who points out that Manly's view of divided authorship for "Piers Plowman" affects that of this poem.   *Ed.*, Skeat, E.E.T.S., 1873, and with "Piers the Plowman," Clarendon Press, 1886. *MS.*, Camb. Univ. Ll. 4, 14.

74   The popularity of Langland's poem is evidenced by his imitators.

Piers the Plowman's Crede (long alliterative lines). A satire emanating from a Wyclifite source against the degeneracy of the monastic orders, cir. 1394–1399. The author is unknown. *Ed.*, Skeat, E.E.T.S., 1867, 1906. *MSS.*, Reg. 18, B. xvii.; Trin. Coll. Camb.

A poem once erroneously ascribed to Chaucer—

The Plowman's Tale. This was ascribed by Skeat in his earlier edition of above to the author of "The Plowman's Crede," but he has since (1906) come to the same conclusion as Dr. Bradley, that there are interpolations which make it less certain. As regards the date of these, and of the remaining stanzas, see *Athenæum* of July 12, 1902 (H. Bradley), where the poem is discussed, the sum of the criticism being that there was most probably a Lollard piece of the 14th century, which underwent two successive expansions in the 16th century. *Ed.*, Wright, "Political Poems"; Skeat, "Chaucerian and other Pieces," 1897.

N.B.—Two other poems are reminiscences of Langland: the little poem, "God spede the Plough," cir. 1500, a lament over the taxation that oppressed the country people (also ed. by Skeat, E.E.T.S.), and "How the Plowman lerned his Paternoster," published in "Early English Popular Poetry of England," by Hazlitt; and Wright and Halliwell, "Rel. Ant."

75 John Gower, b. cir. 1330; d. 1408.
Works, *Ed.*, G. C. Macaulay, Clarendon Press.

Little is known of the personal life of this poet. The date of his death is on his tomb in St. Saviour's Church, Southwark, and his marriage licence is extant, from which we gather that he married late in life, whether for the second time is uncertain as it is dated 1398, and already in 1390 he had referred to himself as an old man; in 1400 he became blind. His will was proved in 1408. Chaucer was among his friends, and the two poets did not ignore one another in their writings. His three chief works were "Vox Clamantis," begun soon after 1381, "Speculum Meditantis," 1376–1379, and "Confessio Amantis," 1390. All three written "for the information and instruction of others."

Gower, according to his latest Editor, "represents the average literary taste of the time before Chaucer"; "in the history of the development of the standard literary language

Gower properly takes his place beside Chaucer, notwithstanding his inferiority of genius." Gower was a partisan of the house of Lancaster. The "Confessio Amantis" was written at the suggestion of Richard ii., and there were originally complimentary lines addressed to this monarch for which others were afterwards substituted, and finally the name of Henry iv. supplanted that of the former King as the person to whom the work was dedicated. Gower wrote in three languages, and Mr. Macaulay calls attention to his productions as illustrating the transition from the use of French to that of English in the polite literature of the 14th century, Gower's French writings being among the latest specimens of Anglo-Norman literature.

Prof. Ker ("Mediaeval Studies") speaks of Gower's talents as commonplace; "correctness," he adds, "is his poetical virtue, his title of honour," . . . "the ease of his style is in its way as truly poetical as the stronger powers of imagination or lyric passion, which Gower did not possess. . . . It may be doubted whether Pope is more of an artist than Gower."

French Works.

Speculum Hominis, or *Speculum Meditantis* (octosyllabic twelve-lined strophes) a work in ten parts of didactic character as the title indicates. It is extant in one copy only, in which it is called "Mirour de l'homme." A history of the life and death of the Virgin concludes this "allegory of the soul" which won for him from Chaucer the title of the "Moral Gower." The "Speculum" takes a high place among works of its class; the framework is necessarily a large one, but its extent "is hardly less remarkable than the thoroughness with which the scheme is worked out in detail and the familiarity with the Scriptures which the writer constantly displays." The authorship of the "Mirour de l'homme" is fully discussed by the Editor in the Introduction to his edition of Gower's works. "It is a learned work not without touches of poetry." *See* R. E. Fowler, "Une source française des poèmes de Gower," 1905. *MS.*, Camb. Univ. Libr., Add., 3035.

Cinkante Balades (fifty-four in all). Dedication to Henry iv. (2), 51 ballads of love, one to the Virgin, and the Envoy.

These are thought by Mr. Macaulay to be later com-
positions of the poet, some being written with a view to
Henry IV.'s court, the collection attaining its present shape in
1399. "But for the accident that they were written in
French, this series of balades would have taken a very distinct
place in the history of English literature."   *Ed.*, G. Stengel,
John Gower's "Minnesang u. Ehezuchtbüchlein," Anglo-
Norm. Balladen, lxxii., 1886.   Earl Gower, Roxburghe
Club, 1818.   *MS.*, Trentham.

18 *Balades* (*Traitié*) (7 lined strophes, a b a b b c c).   As
explained by the author, "un traitié selonc les auctours pour
essampler les amantz marietz," etc.   (Examples for the instruction of married lovers.)   The final stanza of the last
Balade is a general envoy—

> "Al université de tout le mende
> Johan Gower ceste Balade envoie";

he excuses his French and states that he is an Englishman,
and ends—

> ". . . Mais quoique nulls en die,
> L'amour parfit en dieu se justifie."

MSS., attached to some of the MSS. of the "Confessio
Amantis"; also in All Souls MS. of "Vox Clamantis"; and
Glasgow, Hunter, T. 2, 17.

English Works.

Confessio Amantis.   Completed 1390, revised 1393 (octosyllabic couplets).   Consisting of a prologue and eight books.
Love, as being a subject of universal interest, was chosen as
the main theme of this work, and it is illustrated under its
various aspects by a succession of tales.   There are digressions,
as in the seventh book, which deals with Aristotle and his
teaching.   "Gower was an excellent narrator of tales."   *Ed.*,
"Selections," G. C. Macaulay, 1903.   *MSS.*, representing
three versions.   Oxford, Bodl. (8), New Coll., Corp. Chris.,
Magdalen, Wadham.   Camb., Univ. Libr. (2); St. John's,
Sidney, Trinity, S. Catherine's.   Egerton (2), Harl. (4), one
selections only; Stowe (1), Add. (2), Reg. (1), Chetham
(Manchester); Wollaston Hall; Keswick Hall (Norwich);

Phillipps (2) one sold; Glasgow, Hunter (1); Stafford House; Coll. of Arms; Castle Howard. Early print by Caxton, 1483.

N.B.—The Stafford MS. is believed to have been presented to John of Gaunt or Henry IV.

Another English work is a poem in fifty-five seven-lined strophes :
In Praise of Peace. Written on the occasion of Henry IV.'s accession. *Ed.*, Wright, "Political Songs."

Latin Works.

Vox Clamantis. A poem of over 10,000 elegiac verses (seven books). An account of the Peasant's revolt, dealt with circumstantially, but in allegorical form. Here, as in his English work, the change of the poet's attitude towards Richard II. can be traced in the alterations made by him in the successive versions. *Ed.*, Coxe, Roxburghe Club, 1850. *MSS.*, Oxford, All Souls; Glasgow, Hunter, T. 2, 17; Cott. Tib. A. iv. ; Harl. 6291; Cott. Titus, A. 13 (part only); Digby, 138; Laud, 719; Dublin, Trinity, D. 4, 6; Lincoln Cath. A. 72 ; Hatfield; Ecton, Northamp.

Cronica Tripertita (leonine hexameters). "An interesting contemporary record" of the events of the last twelve years of Richard II.'s reign. *MSS.*, Four first MSS. given above of "Vox Clamantis" and Bodl., Hatton, 92.
Shorter poems are also found in some of the MSS.

76 Geoffrey Chaucer.

In 1386 Chaucer declared himself to be over forty years of age. He was the son of a vintner living in Thames Street, where the poet was probably born.

1357. Page in the household of Lionel, Duke of Clarence.

1359. Took part in Edward's expedition into France and was made prisoner. 1360. Ransomed.

1367. A special pension was added to his salary, Chaucer being now in the King's service as " valettus."

1372. Mission to Italy. Chaucer had previously been abroad on the King's service.

1374. Comptroller of Customs Duties on wools, skins, etc., in the port of London.

1376–9. Other foreign missions.

1382. Comptrollership of the petty customs in the port of London.

1386. Knight of the Shire of Kent. In the same year he was deprived of his two comptrollerships.

1389. Made clerk of the works at the Palace of Westminster and other royal houses. From this post he was discharged in 1391.

1394. Pension of £20 from Richard II. He had previously been appointed forester of an estate in Somersetshire. Henry IV. on his accession increased the pension to nearly double the amount.

For twelve years Chaucer lived in a house over Aldgate Gate, 1374–1386.

1399. He removed to a house in the garden of the Lady Chapel, Westminster; Henry VII.'s chapel stands on the old site.

The date of death on Chaucer's tomb is Oct. 25, 1400.

For Lives of Chaucer, and editions and chronology of Works, etc., *see* § 54.

Chaucer's works have been divided into three or four periods.

Three periods :

1. Before Italian journey, 1372. Period of French influence.

2. 1373–84. Period of Italian influence, more especially affected by Dante, and Boccaccio's " Il Teseide," and " Il Filostrato " ; Chaucer does not appear to have been acquainted at first hand with the " Decamerone."

3. 1385 to death. Chaucer's more original work is thought to begin with " Legend of Good Women " ; it was the first poem in which he used the " heroic " couplet.

Four periods (Koch) :

1. to 1372 ; 2. 1373–1379 ; 3. 1380–1392 ; 4. 1393–1400.

The Romaunt of the Rose.[1] Chaucer mentions his translation of the " Roman de la Rose " (France, § 58) in the Prologue to his " Legend of Good Women." Three fragments of a translation have come down to us, of which the authorship is much discussed. Some authorities, among them Koch, reject it altogether as Chaucer's work ; Lounsbury assigns the whole to him ; others think that the first 1700 or 1705 (Skeat, Kittredge) lines alone can rightly be considered his ; Kaluza, the first and third parts. Skeat places the work among Chaucer's earlier productions ; Koch, 1366, 1367 (?).   *Ed.*, Kaluza, Chaucer Soc. ; *See* Kittredge, " The Authorship of the English R. di R," " Studies and Notes in Phil. and Lit.," 1892 ; Kaluza, " Chaucer u. der Rosenroman," 1892 ; Skeat, " Why the Romaunt of the Rose is not Chaucer's " (and in " Works "). Lounsbury, " Studies in Chaucer," 1892.   *MS.*, Glasgow, Hunter (3 fragments.)

A B C. Minor poem, 1368 (?) (Koch). A hymn of praise to the Virgin ; the stanzas beginning with letters of the alphabet in order.   (Rhyme, a b a b, b c b c.) The poem is translated from an A B C poem in " Le Pèlerinage de l'âme," by Guillaume de Déguilleville (France, § 72), a French writer of this century ; this French work was translated into English prose and verse, the latter being placed among Lydgate's works.   *MSS.* (collated by Skeat for his ed.), Univr. Libr. Camb. Ff. 5, 30, and Gg. 4, 27 ; St. John's Coll. Camb., Laud, 740 ; Fairfax, 16 ; Bodley, 638 ; Glasgow, Hunter ; Sion Coll.

Dethe of Blaunche, or *Booke of the Duchesse.* Minor poem, 1369, 1370 (Koch) (octosyllabic rhymed couplets). On the death of Blanche, John of Gaunt's first wife. Reading " Ceyx and Alcione " to ease his sleeplessness, the poet falls asleep and dreams of a room where the windows are painted with old tales ; in his dream he joins a hunt, and, straying, finds a young knight in grief for the loss of his young wife.

The work is influenced by Ovid, by Machault's " Rémède de Fortune," and " Dit de Morpheus," and by " Roman de la Rose." The tale of " Ceyx and Alcion " of which there

---

[1] The following works are given in order, according to Prof. Skeat's chronological table.

appears to have been an earlier edition is given at the opening
of the poem. *See* J. L. Lowes, "The Dry Sea and the
Carrenare," "Modern Philology," June 1905; and Kittredge, "Chaucer and Froissart," "Engl. Studien," 1899.
MSS., Tanner, 346; Fairfax, 16; Bodley, 638.

Lyf of Seint Cecyle 1373 (?) (Koch).   Afterwards
adapted to "Second Nun's Tale." (Seven-lined stanzas,
a b a b, b c c).   Sources: "Legenda Aurea"; "Acta
Sanctorum."

Palamon and Arcite, 1375, 1376 (?) (Koch).   Fragments
only preserved.   One of the poems mentioned in the prologue
to "Legend of Good Women."   It has been thought that
Chaucer first wrote this tale in strophes, of which we only
have fragments remaining, while we possess the later version
in "The Knight's Tale."   The introductory strophes in
"Anclida and Arcite," portions of "Troylus and Cryseyde,"
and of "Parlement of Foules" were supposed to be from the
early version.   Later criticism has come to the belief that
"Palamon and Arcite," quoted in "Legend," is identical
with "The Knight's Tale," and the other hypotheses go
down with that of an original P. and A. in stanzas. *See*
"On the date of the Knight's Tale," *Eng. Miscellany*
(Furnivall), 1901.

The Exclamacion of the Dethe of Pite, or Compleynte to Pite.
(Minor poem; 1373 (?) (Koch), rhyme, a b a b, b c c).   The
poet mourns over the death of Pity in the heart of his beloved.
The poem is the earliest example in English of the seven-
lined stanza (rhyme royal).   *MSS.*, Tanner, 346; Fairfax, 16; Bodley, 638; Harl. 78 and 7578; Univ. Lib.,
Camb., Ff. 1, 6; Trin. Coll. Camb.

Anelida and Arcite.   Minor poem; 1383, 1384 (?)
(Koch) (seven and nine-lined strophes, with two of sixteen
lines; the rhyme occasionally varies).   The poem is unfinished.   Love of Anelida for the faithless Arcite : connect-
ing-links with "Knight's Tale" and "Palamon and Arcite."
The first part of the tale is followed by a "Compleynt of
Faire Anelyda," only one stanza being left of the story when
taken up again.   Sources, Boccaccio's "Teseide," and the
"Thebais" of Statius.   Printed by Caxton, cir. 1477.   Face
simile pub. by Cambridge University Press, 1905.   *MSS.*,

Harl. 7333; Fairfax, 16; Tanner, 346; Digby, 181; Bodley, 638; Longleat, Marquis of Bath.

Complaint of Mars. Minor poem; 1379 (Koch). Sometimes referred to as "The Broche of Thebes." (Rhyme, a b a b, b c c, and nine-lined strophes, a a b, a a b, b c c.) According to tradition, this poem is an allegory of the love-affair between Princess Isabel, wife of Duke of York, and John Holland, later Duke of Exeter. There is an idea that the astral conjunction of Mars and Venus of 1379 suggested the poem. *See* J. M. Manly, "Studies and Notes in Phil. and Lit.," v. 107 ff. *MSS.*, Fairfax, 16; Tanner, 346; Harl. 7333; Trin. Coll. Camb.; Selden, B. 24.

Troylus and Cryseyde. 1379–83 (Skeat), 1380 (Koch); (rhyme, a b a b, b c c). Sources: partly condensed from Boccaccio's "Filostrato"; the poet is also thought to have made use of the work of Benoît de S. More. The characters of Troilus and Criseyde are agreeably modified in Chaucer from their originals in Boccaccio. Printed by Caxton, 1484 (?). *Ed.*, "Three more parallel texts" (Camb., S. John; Corp. Christ.; Harl. 1239), Furnivall, with note by G. C. Macaulay (on C.'s borrowing from B. de Sainte More), 1894. *See* W. M. Rossetti's work, published by Chaucer Society, 1895, for comparison of Chaucer's and Boccaccio's work. On the language of Chaucer's "Troilus," S. L. Kittredge, Chauc. Soc., 1891. On C.'s indebtedness to Guido delle Colonne and Benôit, G. L. Hamilton, "Studies in Romance, Phil. and Lit.," 1903; G. P. Krapp, "Mod. Lang. Notes," December 1904. *MSS.*, Campsall MS., copied for Henry v. when Prince of Wales; Harl. 2280 and 3943; Univ. Lib., Camb., Gg. 4, 27; Corp. Christ.

The Parlement of Foules. Minor poem, 1382 (Koch). (Seven-lined strophes, with introduction of rondel.) The poet relates how he is led by Scipio Africanus—whose dream, as given by Cicero, he has already described—into the garden of Venus and Nature, where a parliament of birds is being held, for each bird .to choose his mate, it being Valentine's day. Among these are three male eagles, wooing one "formel," and the other birds have to decide on their merits. The formel is finally allowed to choose for herself. This allegory is interpreted as signifying the wooing by

9

Richard II. of Anne of Bohemia, who had been previously
betrothed to two other suitors. It is the first of the minor
poems to betray Italian influence. Sources, Cicero's " Som-
nium Scipionis " ; passage from Boccaccio's " Teseide " ; and
for certain characteristics of birds, etc., the work of Alain
de l'Isle.   *Ed.*, T. R. Lounsbury, 1877.   *MSS.*,
Fairfax, 16 ; Univ. Lib., Camb., Gg. 4, 27, and Ff. 1, 6 ;
Trin. Coll. Camb. ; Harl. 7333 ; S. John's, Oxford ;
Tanner, 346 ; Digby, 181, etc.

The Hous of Fame. Minor poem ; 1383, 1384 (Koch).
Unfinished (octosyllabic rhymed couplets). The poet is
carried in a vision to the Temple of Venus, and thence by
an eagle to the House of Fame ; description of both places.
Modelled on Dante's " Divina Commedia " (Skeat), but *see*
Lounsbury, " Studies in Chaucer," vol. ii. 237 ff. Sources :
Ovid's " Metamorphoses " ; reminiscences of other writers.
Printed by Caxton (undated).   *Ed.*, T. R. Lounsbury.
See A. C. Garrett (on source of main framework, etc.),
" Studies and Notes in Phil. and Lit.," v. 151 ff.   *MSS.*,
Fairfax, 16 ; Bodley, 638 ; Magd. Coll. Camb. (Pepys).

Minor poems, parallel text, F. J. Furnivall, 1871, Chauc.
Soc. The best text of each poem, also ed. in one vol., 1871.

The Legende of Good Women. 1385 (Koch). (Heroic
couplets.) A prologue, followed by the histories of Cleo-
patra, Thisbe, Dido, Hypsipyle and Medea, Lucretia, Ariadne,
Philomela, Phyllis, Hypermnestra. The poem is unfinished.
Sources : Ovid's " Metamorphoses " and " Heroides " ;
Latin works by Boccaccio : " De Claris Mulieribus," and
" De Genealogia Deorum " ; Virgil ; G. de Colonne,
" Historia Troiana." The prologue exists in two different
versions : the first is only preserved in Gg. 4, 27. *See* for
date of poem, J. S. P. Tatlock, " Modern Philology,"
Oct. 1903 ; of Prologue, G. L. Kittredge, "Chaucer and
some of his friends," " Mod. Phil.," June 1903 ; Tatlock,
" Modern Language Notes," Feb. 1906 ; J. H. Lowes,
" Pub. Mod. Lang. Assoc.," 1905 ; on relations with poems
by Froissart and others, Lowes, *ibid.*, Dec. 1904 ; with Dante,
Tatlock, " Mod. Phil.," Jan. 1906.   *MSS.*, Fairfax, 16 ;
Tanner, 346 ; Bodley, 638 ; Rawlinson, 86 ; Selden, B. 24 ;

Univ. Lib., Camb., Gg. 4, 27, and Ff. 1, 6; Add. 9832, 12524, and 28617; Camb., Trin. Coll.; Magd. Coll. (Pepys).

77   CANTERBURY TALES.

Begun 1386 (Skeat). A prologue followed by twenty-four tales, told by pilgrims to the shrine of Thomas Becket at Canterbury. The original plan was for each pilgrim to tell two tales on the way thither, and two on the return journey, which, as the pilgrims, according to different reckonings, numbered from twenty-nine upwards, would, if carried out, have given a considerably larger number of tales. From certain astronomical notices found in one of the tales, calculations have been made for the purpose of deciding in which year the pilgrimage took place: according to different authorities, it was undertaken in the month of April, 1385, 1388, 1391, or 1393. (Koch's presumable date, April 18–20, 1385.) The date of the work must necessarily depend on which of the above is correct. The Pilgrimage was, as a whole, undoubtedly the work of maturer years, although some of the narratives had certainly been sketched, if not completed, several years previously. *MSS.*, The MSS. published in six-text edition of the Chaucer Society are: Univ. Lib., Camb., Gg. 4, 27; Corp. Christ. Oxford; Lansdowne, 851; Ellesmere; Hengwrt, 154; Petworth. Many others extant. The Chaucer Soc. has also ed.; each of the above MSS. separately.

Lydgate's "Storie of Thebes," and the anonymous "Tale of Beryn," of 15th century, were two projected continuations of the "Canterbury Tales."

FOR SOURCES, *see* Skeat ("Works"); "Originals and Analogues," Chaucer Soc., 1872–88; Köppel, "Chaucer u. Albertanus Brixiensis," "Archiv f. d. Studium der Neuer Sprache," 86; and K. O. Petersen (*see* below).

The "Tales" appear in the following order in the Ellesmere MS. :—

Prologue (heroic couplets). Meeting of pilgrims at the Tabard Inn, Southwark; description of the individual characters.

Knightes Tale (heroic couplets). (*See* under "Palamon

and Arcite.") Based chiefly on Boccaccio's "Teseide." *See* for date G. L. Kittredge, "Chaucer and some of his friends," "Mod. Phil.," June 1903.

Milleres Tale (heroic couplets). No similar tale is known; traces of a tale resembling it are found in a German book of 16th century. *See* R. Köhler, "Anglia," vol. i.

Reves Tale (heroic couplets). Resemblance to this tale in two French Fabliaux, and in one of the "Decamerone." Chaucer, however, does not seem to have read the "Decamerone." *See* H. Varnhagen, "Englische Studien," vol. ix.

Cokes Tale (heroic couplets). Tale of idle London apprentice; only the first sixty lines extant.

N.B.—The "Tale of Gamelyn," ascribed by a later hand to the Coke, is not by Chaucer, although found in several MSS. of his work.

Man of Lawes Tale (Prologue, heroic couplets; Tale, seven-lined strophes, a b a b, b c c). The "Tale of Constance," taken from the Anglo-Norman Chronicle of Nicholas Trivet; both Chaucer and Gower ("Conf. Aman.") drew from this source. An analogue is found in the tale of the wife of Menelaus, the Emperor, in "Gesta Romanorum," and in the life of King Offa the First, given in Matthew Paris. *See* Gough, "The Constance Saga," "Palaestra," 23.

Wif of Bathes Tale (heroic couplets). Many analogous tales extant, one of them being connected with "Sir Gawain" (ballad, Percy MS.). A familiar version is that of "The Knight and the Loathly Lady"; also a version in Gower's "Florent"; and Maynardier mentions other resemblances in "Thomas of Erceldoune"; and in the "Wolfdietrich" poems. *See* Maynardier, "The Wife of Bath's Tale; its sources and analogues," Grimm Library, 1901. W. E. Mead, "Prologue of W. of B.," Pub. Mod. Lang. Assoc., 1901.

Freres Tale (heroic couplets). Tale of Somnour, who is carried off by the devil. From an old Collection of Latin tales.

Sompnoures Tale (heroic couplets). An analogous French tale is given among the "Fables et Romans du xii. and du. xiii. siècle," *ed.* Legrand D'Aussy. Another analogue given is a Fabliau by Jakes de Basiw.

Clerkes Tale.—Tale of Griseldis (seven and six-lined strophes). The main part is more or less a translation of Petrarch's Latin version of the story as given by Boccaccio. *See* Westenholz, " Die Griseldisage in der litt. Geschichte," 1888.

Merchantes Tale (heroic couplets). Marriage of January and May, with episode of the blind husband and the pear tree. Tale found in Boccaccio; in Caxton's trans. of Æsop, and in " Comoedia Lydiae."

Squieres Tale (heroic couplets). Tale of Cambuscan and his daughter Canace. Probably of Arabian origin. As regards the assumption that the " Travels of Marco Polo " were one of Chaucer's sources, *see* J. M. Manly, " Public. Mod. Language Association," vol. xi., New Series, 4. For supposed historical allusions, Kittredge, " Eng. Studien," xiii., and Brandl, *ibid.*, xii.

Frankeleines Tale (heroic couplets). Tale of the removal of the rocks by magic. From a Breton Lai, founded on an Eastern tale. Schofield ("Mod. Lang. Assoc.," xvi., 1901) points out that previous to Marie de France there was a charming story afloat, concerning Arviragus and his wife (*see* G. of Monmouth); he also recalls parallels to the tale in the lais of " Dous Amans " and of " Doon."

Doctoures Tale (heroic couplets). Tale of Virginia. Chaucer followed the version given in " Roman de la Rose."

Pardoneres Tale (heroic couplets). Tale of the Three Robbers. Apparently taken from a Fabliau. Analogous Eastern tales are extant, the earliest being a Buddhist story, and it is found in the " Cento Novelle Antiche," and Morlini " Novellæ." *Ed.*, Dr. Koch, with readings from 55 MSS. 1900. *See* J. J. Jusserand, " Chaucer's Pardoner and the Pope's Pardoner " (Essays on Chaucer, part 5), Chauc. Soc., and G. L. Kittredge, " Modern Language Notes," Nov. 1900.

Shipmannes Tale (heroic couplets).[1] Tale of priest who borrows money for a wife from her husband, and pretends he

---

[1] The Shipman's prologue, assigned to others among the Pilgrims in some MSS., occurs in different places according to the MS., and in some it is omitted. Prof. Skeat places both prologue and "Tale of the Shipman" after "The Man of Lawes Tale," according to Selden MS.

has paid it back to her.   Probably taken from a Fabliau; a similar tale is found in "Decamerone."

Prioresses Tale (Prologue, heroic couplets; Tale, seven-lined strophes).   The Tale of Hugh of Lincoln, the child murdered by Jews, in 1255 (Matthew Paris) is one of several tales similar to this given by Chaucer.   French analogue by Gautier de Coincy, "Paris Beggar Boy," in Vernon MS.

Rime of Sire Thopas (ballad metre).   Tale told by the poet himself in ridicule of the lengthy romances which had been so much in vogue; interrupted by the host and told to tell something in prose, he starts the

Tale of Melibee (Prose; Prologue, heroic couplets).   A translation from the French, "Le livre de Melibee et de dame Prudence," which was probably an adaptation from the Latin of Albertano of Brescia, by J. le Meun.

Monkes Tale (eight-lined strophes, a b, a b, b c, b c).   Series of tragic tales, on the model of Boccaccio's "De casibus Virorum Illustrium," taken from this work of Boccaccio and his other on illustrious women, with borrowings from biblical and other secular writings.

Nonne Prestes Tale (heroic couplets).   An earlier version of this tale is among the fables of Marie de France (*see* for translation of this, *Academy*, 23rd July 1887); it is found enlarged in the "Roman de Renart."   *See*, "On the Sources of the Nonne Preste's Tale," K. O. Petersen, Radcliffe Coll., Mongraph 10.

Second Nonnes Tale (seven-lined strophes).   Lyfe of Seynt Cecile.   Partly from a Latin version closely resembling that in the "Legenda Aurea," partly from a second Latin life.

Chanones Yemannes Tale (heroic couplets).   Satire on the alchemists.

Manciples Tale (heroic couplets).   The tale of the fox and crow, which is found among the tales in the "Seven Sages" and has been constantly related ever since.   It ends with moral advice taken from Albertano of Brescia.

Persones Tale (Prose; Prologue, heroic couplets).   A long, prose sermon, generally stated to be an adaptation from the French of Lorens, or Laurent, "La Somme des Vices et des Vertus."   Miss Petersen has shown that the general source of the "Parson's Tale" was a Latin tract by Raymond

de Pennaforte, written at least thirty-six years before Lorens'
"Somme," and that the digression on the seven deadly sins
is an adaptation from "Summa seu tractatus de Viciis" of
Guilielmus Peraldus, also written many years before the
"Somme." *See* K. O. Petersen "The Sources of the
Parson's Tale," Radcliffe Coll. Monographs, 12; Prof.
Liddell, "A New Source of the Parson's Tale," "Eng.
Misc." (Furnivall) 1901.

Prof. Skeat groups the tales as follows:

Group A. Tales by the Knight, Miller, Reeve, Cook.
  ,,   B. Man of Law, Shipman, Prioress, Tale of Sir
              Thopas and Melibeus, Monk, Nun's Priest.
  ,,   C. Physician, Pardoner.
  ,,   D. Wife of Bath, Friar, Somnour.
  ,,   E. Clerk, Merchant.
  ,,   F. Squire, Franklin.
  ,,   G. Second Nun, Canon Yeoman.
  ,,   H. Manciple.
  ,,   I. Parson.

See also Shipley, "Arrangement of the C. Tales,"
Mod. Lang. Notes, 10, and E. P. Hammond, "Modern
Philology," Oct. 1905.

For editions of "Tales," *see* under "Works," p. 84;
Skeat, "Prologue and Chief Tales," "Clarendon Press Selections"; Prof. Skeat is also bringing out the Tales with
modernised texts. G. L. Kittredge, Selections; S. H.
Carpenter, "Prologue and Knight's Tale" (Albion), and *see*
also under Pollard.

78 *Other Minor Poems.*

Compleint to his Lady (fragment) in three distinct metres.
Amorous Compleints (probably genuine).
A Ballade of Compleynt (probably genuine).
Womanly Noblesse.
Words to Adam (his scrivener).
The former age.
Fortune.

Compleint of Venus (*see* O. de Granson, France, § 86).
Lenvoy to Scogan (*see* G. L. Kittredge, "Studies and Notes, etc.," vol. i. 109 ff.).
Lenvoy to Bukton.
Envoy to Compleints to his purse, 1399.
Complaint to my mortal foe (?)
Complaint to my lode starre (?)
Merciless Beaute.
Balade to Rosemounde.
Against women unconstant (probably genuine).
Compleint to his purse (envoy separate).
Lak of Stedfastnesse.
Gentilesse.
Truth.
Proverbs of Chaucer (two quatrains).

The complaint to his purse was addressed to Henry IV. and obtained for the poet an extra pension.

79 Lost works: "Of the Wretched Engendering of Mankinde," a translation of Innocent III.'s "De Miseria conditionis Humanae," mentioned in the "Legend," is partly preserved in scraps in the "Man of Lawe's Tale" (*see* Prof. Lounsbury in the "Nation," July 1889). "Origenes upon the Maudeleyne" (On Mary Magdalene), at one time attributed to Origen; "A Book of the Lion" mentioned by Lydgate, is thought to be a translation of "Le dit au Lion," by G. Machault.

A list of all the works which have been wrongly ascribed to Chaucer, with the names of such authors of the same as are known, is given by Prof. Skeat in *Athenæum*, Oct. 28th, 1905. *See* also Nov. 4th of same year. *See* Skeat, "Works," vol. vii.; G. L. Kittredge, "Chaucer and some of his friends," *op. cit.*; W. A. Neilson, "Court of Love," "Studies and Notes, etc.," 1899.

80 DRAMA.

See Hohlfeld, "Die Kollektivmisterien," "Anglia," xi.; Ebert, "Jahrbuch f. Rom. u. Engl. Lit.," I.; Ten Brink, "Hist. Lit.," vol. ii. (*See* § 32.)

The Towneley Mysteries. A Cycle of Mysteries, thought to have been performed at the yearly fair at Woodkirk in Yorkshire by the guilds of Wakefield and other surrounding towns during the festival of Corpus Christi. The Mysteries are thirty or thirty-one in number (the Jacob and Esau may be counted as one or two), dealing with both Old Testament and New Testament history. Tradition connects the Cycle with the monks of the Abbey of Woodkirk; the MS. is of the early 15th century, and the Mysteries contained in it are representative of the development of the drama during the 14th century. The oldest Mystery of the Cycle, probably of earlier date than the others, is Jacob and Esau. *Ed.* for Surtees Society, 1836; Pollard, E.E.T.S., 1897. Three separate plays, ed. respectively — Collier, "Five Miracle Plays," 1867; Douce, 1822; and Mätzner, "Alt Eng. Sprachproben," 1867. Others by Marriott, 1838. *MS.*, in possession of the Towneley family, whence the name.

The York Mysteries. The earliest notice we have regarding the performance of these Mysteries dates from 1378, but we gather from it that the dramatic representation was then of many years' standing. Five plays of this collection are identical with five in the Towneley Cycle. The York plays as a whole have a more refined character, certain rough humour and coarse realism found in the Towneley being absent in the former. Two lists of plays found in an old book, which date from the early 15th century, give their number respectively as fifty-one and fifty-seven. The Ashburnham MS. contains forty-eight. *Ed.*, Lucy Toulmin Smith, "The plays performed by the Crafts or Mysteries of York on the day of Corpus Christi in the 14th, 15th, and 16th centuries." From the unique MS. in the library of Lord Ashburnham, 1885.

Chester Mysteries. Performed at Whitsuntide. A doubtful tradition gives as early a date as 1268 to the origin of these performances. Harl. MS., 2124, assigns to Randall Higgenett the authorship, or at least the translation, of the plays into English. There are records, however, of religious plays being performed in Chester from 1329. This dramatic cycle was developed, it is thought, at the latest about the middle of the 14th century. We have twenty-four of these plays preserved in MSS. of the late 16th and early 17th centuries; and in their present form they are wanting in the more popular tone which distinguished the Mysteries of Woodkirk and York. *Ed.*, Th. Wright, Shakespeare Society, 1843-47; Deimling, E.E.T.S.; T. H. Markland, Roxburghe Club, 1818 (two plays). One in Collier, *op. cit.* *See* H. Ungemach, "Die Quellen der fünf ersten Chester Plays," Pub. Mod. Lang. Assoc., 1904. *MSS.*, Add. 10305; Harl. 2124; Harl. 2013; Bodley, 175; Duke of Devonshire.

Coventry Mysteries. Performed at Corpus Christi. Notices of these date back to 1392, and indicate still earlier representations. Of the plays as performed by the Guilds only two have come down to us, but apparently the Minorite Friars of the town had a Cycle of their own in commemoration of Corpus Christi. The Cotton MS., containing forty-two plays, is of the 15th century, and it seems a matter of question whether the plays contained in it, designated the Coventry Mysteries, are in reality those which were performed by the Franciscans. The plays are of a mixed character, and the language in them is not always that of the neighbourhood of Coventry. In spite of the ancient date at which the Coventry plays are known to have been performed, those preserved to us in the Cotton MS. have a later character about them than the Chester plays, and are considered rather representative of the condition of the drama in the 15th than in the 14th century. In some of the plays, however, there is a distinct reminiscence of older ones, such as that of "Adam" and "The Harrowing of Hell." *Ed.*, Halliwell, Shakespeare Society, 1841; one given by Collier, *op. cit.* *See* Sharp. "Dissertation on the Coventry Mysteries." *MS.*, Cott. Vesp. D. viii.

N.B.—Both rhyme and alliteration are met with in the Mysteries, as well as variety in metre and strophic forms. The second half of the 14th century and the first of the 15th were the most productive periods as regards the Mysteries; their representation, however, was carried on in certain places into the 16th and even 17th century.

Among other centres at which plays were performed

were Beverley (only titles of plays extant), Newcastle,
Dublin (one play, Collier, *op. cit.*) ; *see* Davidson, " Mod.
Lang. Notes," vii. ; and Cornwall (E. Norris, "Ancient
Cornish Drama," 1859). The Cornish MS. dates from the
14th century ; the others are later. *See* for complete list of
these, Stoddard, *op. cit.* (§ 32).

Abraham and Isaac. East Midland play. MS. found by
Miss Toulmin Smith at Brome Hall, Suffolk. In its present
form the drama belongs to the following century, but there are
evidences of an older copy having existed. It shows progress
as compared to "The Harrowing of Hell." Miss Smith
says that this play differs from every other hitherto known, and
" as our specimens of English drama are few, and none has
hitherto been found in East Anglia, it appears worthy of being
printed." Another separate copy of this play, which is found
among the plays of all the four large Cycles, has been ed. by
R. Brotanek, from a Dublin MS., "Anglia," xxi.

The earliest Morality Play of which we have any record
is one on the "Lord's Prayer." Before 1399 a Guild of
men and women was formed for its performance. This "Paternoster in the English tongue" was referred to by Wyclif.
MS., lost.

81   LATIN WRITERS.

Prose.

Science.

John o Gaddesden. Doctor of Physic, d. after 1317.
Said to have been the first Englishman employed as Court
Physician.

Rosa Anglica. A work embracing the whole practice of
physic, compiled from Arabian sources, Gilbert Anglicus, and
others. A copy of Bernard de Gordon's work (*see* France,
§ 38).

82   *Theology, Philosophy, Logic.*

William Ockham, or **Occam** (Doctor Singularis,
Doctor Invincibilis). Franciscan. Date of death uncertain,

not before 1349 (Little). Several of O.'s chief works are directed against the temporal power of the Pope, with whom the Emperor was in hot conflict.

Super Potestate summi Pontificis.
Compendium Errorum (on certain Papal institutions).
Tractatus de sacramento altaris.
De Electione Caroli VI.
Centilogium Theologicum.

For full list of works, *see* A. G. Little, "The Grey Friars in Oxford," 1892.

Robert Holcot, d. 1349. Dominican. Teacher of Theology at Oxford.

Quaestiones. On Peter Lombard's "Sentences."
De origine, etc., peccatorum.
Moralitates historiarum.
Commentaries. On books of the O.T.
Many other works, a great number unpublished.
He is believed to be the author of the "Philobiblion" (§ 84). *See* "Dict. Nat. Bio."

Thomas Bradwardine (Doctor Profundus), d. 1349. Chancellor of the University of Oxford and Archbishop of Canterbury. His chief work, attacking the Pelagians, was—

De Causâ Die.

Ars Memorativa, and several mathematical works. Much of his work is unpublished.

Ralph Strode, fl. cir. 1370. Fellow of Merton, Oxford; opponent of Wyclif.

Consequentiae.
Obligationes.

83   *History.*

Ranulf Higden, d. 1364.

*Polichronicon (§ 57). Creation to 1352. General history and description of the world. Translated into English by Trevisa.

Thomas of Malmesbury.

Eulogium Historiarum, or *Eulogium Temporis*. Creation to 1366. Continuation to 1413. The "Polychronicon" was freely used.

Adam of Murimuth, b. 1275 (?); d. 1347. Canon of S. Paul's.

Continuatio Chronicarum, 1303–47.

Robert of Avesbury, fl. cir. 1356.

Historia de mirabilibus gestis Edwardi III.

Geoffrey le Baker, d. 1358–60.

Chronicon, 1303-1356. Partly based on Murimuth.
Chroniculum. Creation to 1336.

Thomas de la More, fl. 1340.

Vita et Mors Edwardi Regis Anglice (Edward I. and Edward II.), in great part taken from Baker's work.

Richard of Cirencester, d. 1401(?).

Speculum Historiale de gestis regum Angliae, 447-1066. For particulars of another work at one time ascribed to him, "De Situ Britanniae," a forgery of the 18th century, *see* edition of "Speculum."

Flores Historiarum. Creation to 1326. Written by different writers at various times at St. Alban's and Westminster.

Walter of Hemingburgh, or Walter of Gisburn, d. after 1313.

Chronicle from 1048. It is uncertain whether the whole work, as we have it, to 1346, is by W. of Hemingburgh. *Ed.*, H. C. Hamilton, "Eng. Hist. Soc.," 1848-49.

William Rishanger, d. after 1312.

Chronica, 1259-1307. Doubtful if part of this work, if not all, is rightly ascribed to Rishanger.
Gesta Edwardi Primi.
Chronicon de duobus bellis apud Lewes et Evesham.

John of Fordun, d. cir. 1384.

Scotichronicon, or *Chronica gentis Scotorum*. Flood to 1383. First attempt at a complete history of Scotland. *Ed.*, with trans., W. F. Skene, 1871-72.

Walter Bower, Abbot of Inchcolm, d. 1449.

Continuation of J. of Fordun to 1437.

John of Trokelowe, fl. 1330, and Henry of Blaneford.

*Annals, 1307–1324. The last year only by the latter.

84 *Miscellaneous.*

Richard Aungervyle, of Bury, d. 1345. Bishop of Durham, Lord Chancellor, and Tutor to Edward, afterwards Edward III.

Philobiblion (?). Probably only written at R. de Bury's request. Eng. trans., J. B. Inglis. Morley's Universal Library, 1832 (*see* Holcot, § 82).

FRANCE

LIST OF GENERAL AUTHORITIES.

"Histoire littéraire de la France, par des religieux bénédictins de la Congrégation de Saint Maur, etc." (referred to as "Hist. Litt.") ; Gaston Paris, "La littérature française au moyen Âge," latest edition, 1905 ; "Mediaeval French Literature," trans. by H. Lynch, Temple Primers ; Gröber, "Grundrisz der Romanischen Philologie," Band II. Abth. i. ; Provençal Litterature (Stimming), Band II. Abth. ii. ; Petit de Julleville, "Histoire de la Langue et de la Littérature française des origines, etc.," 1896 ; Faquet, "Histoire de la Littérature française depuis les origines," 2nd. ed., 1900 ; Saintsbury, "Short History of French Literature," 1897 ; Dowden, "History of French Literature," 1897 ; Brunetière, "Manual," trans. 1898.

BIBLIOGRAPHY.—Gröber, G. Paris, P. de Julleville.

N.B.—"Notices et Extraits," "Notices et Extraits des Manuscrits de la Bibliothèque Nationale et autres Bibliothèques." Now published by L'Académie des Inscriptions et Belles Lettres.

N.B.—The dates of works are given according to G. Paris, "Litt. moyen Âge," 1905, as far as they are covered by this work.

1 FRANCE

THE French language, in common with the other Romance languages—as the term Romance itself implies—was derived from the colloquial Latin, which underwent the changes to which every language is subject when brought into contact with other spoken tongues.

The differentiation of the Romance languages probably began when the linguistic ties between the nations was broken by the fall of the Empire. Roughly speaking, the gradual formation of these languages continued from the 6th to the 10th century.

There is little to assist us in fixing the epoch when Latin supplanted the indigenous tongues of Gaul; evidence is extant of Gaelic being still spoken in the 3rd and 4th centuries; Latin, however, was certainly understood at the time of the Christianising of the country, which took place in the former of these two centuries. Many Gaelic names also appear among the Latin writers of the first four centuries.

The Teutonic invasion made little impression on the existing language of the country beyond adding Frankish words to the vocabulary, and the two tongues existed side by side for some time. In the 9th century it was decreed at the Councils of Tours and Mainz that homilies were to be translated both into the Germanic and the "langue rustique romane," in order that all might understand them.

The French romance was divided into two main dialects: the Langue d'oil, and the Langue d'oc; the former the dialect of the North, where the *oui* was pronounced *oil*, and the latter that of the South, where the *oui* was pronounced *oc*. The *Français*, a sub-dialect of the Langue d'oil, finally prevailed over the others of that division. A Teutonic language was again introduced by the Northerners, but it had but a short existence, and William the Conqueror carried a dialect of the French tongue over to England. The Celtic language spoken in Brittany was re-introduced from England between the 5th and 7th centuries. *See* Petit de Julleville, "Histoire de la langue et de la littérature française," 1896, vol. i.

A decay of letters in France, as elsewhere, succeeded the barbarian invasion of the 5th century, and a state of ignorance prevailed until the time of Charlemagne, who revived letters and invited learned men to his Court, among them Alcuin, Eginhard, Luitprand, Pierre de Pisa, and Paul Warnefrid, to help in the foundation of schools and spread of culture. Charlemagne himself is reported to have composed a grammar on the tudesque language, and to have made a collection of national songs of his country. The "Ecole du Palais" and the School of S. Martin de Tours (which in 800 was given in charge of Alcuin) became renowned under Charlemagne.

2 We have no text extant of the Romance language spoken in France of the 7th or 8th centuries; that it was in use, however, we have proof first, by the appointment of a Bishop in the 7th century, who was chosen because he could speak both French and German; and, secondly, from the extant glossaries of the 8th century.

VIIIth CENTURY.

Glossaire de l'abbaye de Reichenau, in two parts. First part, an explanation of the more difficult expressions of the Vulgate; second part, alphabetical list of words, in which the Latin is in a transition stage towards French. *MS.*, Bibl. Carlsruhe, 115.

Glossaire de Cassel. End 8th or beginning of 9th century. Popular Latin with translation into German. *Ed.*, W. Grimm, 1848. *MS.*, Libr. Cassel. Theol., 24.

N.B.—For the texts of these two glosses and the following early poems, *see* Foerster and Koschwitz, "Altfranzösiches Uebungsbuch," 1884–86.

IXth CENTURY.

Serment de Louis le Germanique (Strasburg Oaths), A.D. 842. The compact between Charles the Bald and Louis the German, when the latter, with his soldiers, took the oath of allegiance in French, and the former and his soldiers in German. In this document is distinctly traceable the division that was taking place in the Romance tongue between the North and South, forms peculiar to the Northern dialect being introduced. *Ed.*, Bartsch, "La langue et la littérature française, etc.," 1887; L. Constans, text, and trans. into Modern French, "Chrestomathie de l'ancien Français," 1890. Facsimiles of the MSS. of the Strasburg Oaths and Ste. Eulalie (*see* below) in "Les plus anciens Monuments de la langue Française," G. Paris, 1875. *MS.* preserved in the MS. of Nithard's "History," Bibl. Nat. Fonds. lat. 9768. The earliest date of the MS. is end 10th century, possibly beginning 11th.

N.B.—Nithard was a grandson of Charlemagne.

Cantilenè de Sainte Eulalie (strophes of two lines linked by assonance), cir. 881. This poem was found at Valenciennes in 1837 in a MS. work of S. Gregory of Nazianzen. *Ed.*, with trans., Mod. French, L. Constans, *op. cit.*; Bartsch, *op. cit.* *MS.*, Bibl. Valenciennes, 143 (MS. also contains the "Ludwigslied").

N.B.—The School of Fleuri grew into repute in this century. Alfred of England invited men of learning to his court from France, among them Grimbald and Jean of Corbie.

3 XTH CENTURY.

Homélie sur Jonas. Mixed Latin and French. Found 1839–41 on a piece of parchment which had served as cover to a MS. This is the only example that has come down to us from the early Middle Ages of a sermon in the vernacular. *MS.*, Valenciennes, 143; facsimile, "Les plus anciens monuments," etc., *op. cit.*

La Vie de Saint Léger (strophes of six octosyllabic lines, linked two and two by assonance). Probably composed by a Burgundian, and written by a Provençal. *Ed.*, Bartsch, *op. cit.* *MS.*, Libr. Clermont, 189; facsimile, "Les plus anciens monuments, etc.," *op. cit.*

Passion (poem in octosyllabic quatrains, lines linked two and two by assonance). Mixture of Northern and Southern dialects. *MS.*, Libr. Clermont, 189; facsimile, "Les plus Anciens Monuments," etc. The above (Oaths, Eulalie, Valenciennes fragment, and Passion) are ed. by E. Stengel, "Ausg. u. Abh. Rom. Phil.," xi.

N.B.—Neither of these is representative of the Langue d'oil. French literature rightly begins next century with the "Vie de S. Alexis."

4 XIᵀʜ CENTURY.

Vie de Saint Alexis (strophes of five decasyllabic lines, with the same assonance throughout each strophe). This poem was discovered within the last century in the church of S. Godoard at Hildesheim.

Alexis leaves his wife the day of their marriage and takes up a life of poverty; returns to his father's house; is unrecognised, and leads a life of voluntary misery for seventeen years; he is not recognised until after death, and then by a letter which only the Pope can take from his hand. The legend is of Syriac origin. This and other tales have incidents in common with the old legend of S. Eustace, a high official in the service of Emperor Trajan (*see* Chrétien, "Roi Guillaume," §§ 15 and 48; Eng., §§ 63, 64). Three later versions are extant of 12th, 13th, and 14th centuries, the last written in Alexandrines. *Ed.*, G. Paris, 1885; "La Cançun de Saint Alexis," facsimile of Hildesheim MS. "Ausg. u. Abhandl. Rom. Phil.," vol. i. *MSS.*, Hildesheim; Ashburnham (Tours); Nat. Bibl. fr. 19525, and other later versions in Nat. Bibl. For extant MSS. of different versions in French, English, and German (Germany, §§ 26, 40), *see* J. Brauns, "Ueber Quelle u. Entwickelung der Altfranzösischen Cançun de Saint Alexis," 1884; and for German versions, under Massmann. For legend of S. Eustace, *see* G. H. Gerould, "Pub. Mod. Lang. Assoc.," iii., 1904.

N.B.—Tedbalt de Vernon is mentioned in an old writing as the translator of lives from the Latin, and may possibly or not be the author of above.

N.B.—Religious poetry was divided into three classes: Lives of saints, Biblical narrative, and legends of miraculous intervention of saints, especially of the Virgin. Eastern lives of saints became known through Latin versions towards the end of the 10th century; Celtic lives were not known until rather later. Many lives have come down to us, mostly written in octosyllabic verse with rhyming couplets; with these, as with the Epic, short poems probably preceded the longer narrative, and like the former they finally underwent prose versions. "The 'Vie de Saint Alexis' was the chief of these lives, and ranks among them at their head, as the 'Chanson de Roland' among the Chansons de Geste." Lives of saints, and rhymed versions of the Bible, were sung by the Jongleurs. (For Lives of Saints and bibliography, *see* "Petit de Julleville," i. pp. 47, 48.) Translations of the Gospels in their entirety were not looked upon favourably by the Church; such having been written at Metz in the following century, were ordered to be destroyed (*see* Trans. of Bible, § 39). In this century the writings of Aristotle found their way into France through Spain, and followers of the philosopher arose in the former country. *See* P. de Julleville, vol. i. p. 14, ff.

5   Historical Verse.

Before the Crusades (First Crusade, 1096) all history had been written exclusively in Latin. The first histories of the Crusades in the Vernacular were in Epic form. A song of French origin known as "Chanson d'Outrée," from its refrain, was sung throughout Europe, by the first Crusaders: "Outrée," became the Crusaders' war-cry. *See* G. Paris, "Litt. moyen Âge," § 124, 1905.

Epic Cycle of First Crusade, and Swan Saga.

The legend of the "Chevalier au Cygne" was attached by the Trouvères to the First Crusade. The tale of the children changed into swans was, it would seem, quite independent originally from the legend of the Knight who arrives and disappears mysteriously. The legend which tells of the birth of the Chevalier au Cygne is found in the "Dolopathos" (Latin) of Jean de Haute-Seille, but it is one of the five tales not taken from the original Oriental romance. Many homes have been assigned to the legend, among them Lorraine, or Lothringen, whence "Lohengrin"; but the general outline of the metamorphosed children is common to all countries. Guillaume de Tyr (fl. 1187) refers to the legend, and it is also found in Mousket's "Chronicle." The former writer first mentions the Swan Saga in connection with the hero of the Crusades.

For poems in connection with this Cycle, *see* 12th Century.

N.B.—The Latin History of Guillaume de Jumièges (fl. 1070) belongs to this century.

6   THE EPIC.

CHANSONS DE GESTE.

The French epic is German in origin and French in its development, "the Germanic spirit in a Romance form" (G. Paris). Like that of other nations it was founded on national songs, of which there is evidence of existence from the 7th century, but all previous to the 11th century have been lost. The songs composed in commemoration of Charlemagne gradually absorbed those which sang the deeds of earlier kings, and he became the central figure of the French Epic. No epic is extant in which we can trace all the stages of development, and the "Roland" is the only one we possess in its first form, as it emerged from the national songs. Ogier exists in a succession of versions, but the first poem is lost.

Latin panegyrics were written on Charlemagne even in his lifetime; one fragment has been assigned, among many other suggested names, to Alcuin; but the earliest document extant of the legendary history of Charlemagne is the work written by the Monk of St. Gall, at the request of Charles le Gros. "The chief idea which informed the French Epic was the struggle of the Christian nations, with France at their head, with the Saracens."

The three chief Cycles of the French Epic are: Cycle du roi; Cycle Garin de Montglane (the central figure in this is William of Orange); Cycle Doon de Mayence. The Epic may also be divided into two classes: the Monarchic, dating back to Charlemagne; and the Feudal, dating back to the periods closing the 9th and 10th centuries, when the royal power was at war with the great vassals.

The Chansons de Geste were written in ten- or twelve-syllabled lines, divided into "laisses," which might be of any number of lines, from five to five hundred or more; the earlier Chansons were mostly decasyllabic and assonanced; the later were written in Alexandrines and rhymed. The Chansons were sung by the Jongleurs to the *vielle*, an instrument resembling a violin, but larger. From the second half of the 12th century, the Chansons can no longer be regarded as true epics; they existed for a century or two more, with additions from all kinds of outside sources, and finally expired before the close of the 15th century, prose versions succeeding to the old rhythmical ones.

The existence of many poems extant in 11th century is attested by allusions in "Roland"; some are lost, some can be recognised in later forms.

The Cyclic period began in the 13th century; early in the century there are references found to the three "Gestes," and the division into these was completely established in the 14th century; Doon de Mayence was the latest of the three to be formed, and its composition is more arbitrary than that of the other two. *See* G. Paris, "Historic Poétique de Charle-magne," 1865; 2nd. ed. (Meyer), 1905; Nyrop, "Epopea Francese," 1886; L. Gautier, "Les Épopeés Françaises," 2nd ed., 1878–82. *See* Gautier, "Bibliographie des Chansons de Geste," 1897; "Hist. Litt.," xxii. *MSS., See* Gautier, "Epopées, etc.," vol. i. 234 ff.

Chanson de Roland. MSS., Primitive version Digby, **23**, cir. 1170 (G. Paris), Venice, S. Mark, fr. iv. G. Paris considers that this chanson assumed the form, which, by aid of existing MSS., can be reconstructed, before the First Crusade, cir. 1080.

The poem relates the Battle of Roncesvaux, fought Aug. 15, 778, when the Emperor's rear-guard under Roland was attacked and annihilated by a Saracen army, the heroism of Charlemagne's peers, and death of Roland. The date is known for a certainty since the discovery of an epitaph to Eggihard, one of the three peers mentioned by Eginhard as having perished at Roncesvaux.

It has not been possible to decide whether the name of Turoldus, which occurs in the poem (Bodl. MS.) is that of the Jongleur who sang it, the composer, or the transcriber.

The earliest form of the legend is in the Latin Chronicle by Archbishop Turpin, written before the middle of the 12th century. *Ed.*, F. Castets, 1880 ; Eng. trans. in Lockhart, "Mediaeval Tales," 1884.

The discovery of a MS. of the 10th century (La Haye, fragment) also proves the existence of the epic at an earlier date; it contains the opening lines of a Latin poem commemorating a war between Charlemagne and the Saracens; the verses are reduced to prose, but there is clear indication that the Latin poem had been a translation from one in the vernacular, the first instance of the kind extant.

It has been questioned whether the song of Roland is in the form in which it was sung at Hastings by Taillefer at the head of the advancing Normans ; "it was doubtless an earlier version than the extant Roland" (G. Paris, "Litt. moyen Âge," § 35). A Latin poem, "Carmen de proditione Ganelonis, or Guenonis," of the early 12th century is also extant, and this and the "Roland" are apparently derived from the same source.

Later versions known as "Roncesvaux" exist in several MSS.: Bibl. Nat. fr. 860; Versailles (Châteauroux); Venice, S. Mar. fr. vii. ; Trin. Coll. Camb., etc. In these rhyme takes the place of assonance. England (§ 61), Germany (§ 16), Italy, Spain, Norway, Netherlands, have also their versions. *Ed.*, W. Foerster, "Altfr. Bibl.," 6 and 7 ; E. Stengel, 1900 ; "Extraits, Histoire, etc.," Petit de Julleville, 1894. Trans., Mod. French, Clédat, 1899; extracts in G. Paris and E. Langlois, "Chrestomathie," prose trans.

and notes, last ed., 1903. *See* under Seelmann for Bibliography.

Pèlerinage de Charlemagne, cir. 1060. The oldest chanson in 12-syllabled verse. The heroic character of this chanson is mingled with comedy. In it we have the account of Charlemagne's visit to Constantinople on his way back from Jerusalem, to see the King, whom his wife, as she tells him, considers his superior in charm and good looks. We have an interesting description of a revolving palace, which is as magnificent as it is remarkable. The second part is taken up with the "gabs" or "boastings" of Charlemagne and his peers. The relics brought home by Charlemagne from this "pilgrimage" were deposited in S. Denis, and exhibited once a year at the fair of the "Endit."

A version of the 13th century formed the first part of a poem called "Galien"; of this only prose versions remain, one being known as "Galien le rhetoré" (restoré). Galien was the son of Oliver and Jacqueline. *Ed.*, Extract (with prose French trans. and notes), G. Paris and E. Langlois, "Chrestomathie du moyen Âge," and Constans, "Chrestomathie, etc.," 1890. *See* "Etude du date, caractère, etc.," H. Morf, 1884.

7   XIIth CENTURY.

This century was one of the most brilliant in the history of French literature, notwithstanding the internal troubles of the country and the prejudicial effect of the Crusades.

Translations were undertaken from Greek and Arabic into Latin, and from Latin into French. Libraries were multiplied, that of the Grande Chartreuse being one of the richest. It was one of the most prolific periods of romance; and Lais, Fables, and Fableaux were among the many diversified productions of the poets.

PROSE.

Theology.

Most of the sermons that have come down to us from the Middle Ages are in Latin, but it is an undecided question whether these were always delivered in Latin; according to

some authorities they may have been written in Latin and
preached in French, with the exception of those that were
addressed to the clergy; or, again, the text as preached was
taken down by a reporter, or written out later, in Latin
Some sermons have come down written in macaronic style,
but this also may be due to the reporter, although some
authorities think that the sermons were so preached. We
know at any rate that at the close of Charlemagne's reign
the bishops were enjoined to translate their homilies "in
rusticam romanum linguam." Popular preaching began apparently in the 13th century with the rise of the Mendicant
Orders. *See* A. Lecoy de la Marche, "La Chaire française
au moyen Âge, etc.," 1868, 1886; Petit de Julleville, *op.
cit.*, vol. ii. 218 ff.

Bernard. Abbot of Clairvaux, b. 1095; d. 1153.

Of many sermons of this great orator that are preserved, a
certain number have come down to us in a French version,
and opinion differs as to which version, Latin or French, is
the original. *Ed.*, old French trans., from MS. 24768, by
W. Foerster, 1885. *MS.*, Bibl. Nat. fr. 24768; Private
Libr. Emperor of Austria.

Maurice de Sully. Bishop of Paris, 1160 to 1196.

A collection of French sermons exists in many MSS., but
the same question is raised as regards these and the Latin
versions, as concerning those of Bernard. *MSS.*, Bibl. Nat.
187, 13314–15–17; 24838; Ashmole, 1280; Douce, 270;
Hatton, 67; Laud, 471; Oxford, Corp. Christ., 36;
Lambeth, 457; Arsenal; Geneviève; Florence, Laurent.;
Chartres, Poitiers; Pisa.

8 *Translations of the Bible.*

For following details *see* Berger, "La Bible Française au
moyen Âge," 1887.

These date back to the first year of the 12th century. No
complete translation of the Bible was made until the 13th,
and only fragments are extant of the partial translations of

the 12th, owing to the persecution of Innocent iii., who ordered these to be destroyed.

All French translations of the Middle Ages were made from the Latin, neither Greek nor Hebrew being known. St. Jerome translated certain books of the Bible; a triple version of the Psalms bears his name; these are known as Hebrew Psalter, Gallican Psalter, and Roman Psalter; the first so-named became translated direct from the Hebrew; the second on account of its finding an early access to the Gallican churches; the third because it was incorporated in the Roman liturgy. The Hebrew Psalter is accompanied by an interlinear French (Old Norman) gloss. "The vernacular version of the Gallican was the French Psalter of the Middle Ages."

The Cambridge Psalter. The MS. referred to in which Jerome's triple version and the glosses are found complete is at Trinity Coll. Cambridge (called Eadwin MS. from name of copyist); another MS. less complete is at the Bibl. Nat. of Paris (fds. Latin, 8846). Both MSS. are embellished with miniatures. An Anglo-Saxon gloss is added to the Roman Psalter (*ed.*, Harsley, E.E.T.S., 1889).

The Oxford Psalter. The chief MS. in which the French Gallican form is preserved is the "Psautier de Montebourg." *MS.*, Bodleian, Douce, 320.

Ed., both Psalters, Fr. Michel, 1860; Eadwin MS., 1876.

These Anglo-Norman versions of the Psalms, the work probably of the disciples of Lanfranc in some Abbey of the South of England, cir. 1100, became so popular, that they were not again translated before the Reformation.

In this same century the Apocalypse was translated some-where in Norman territory, and this translation was preserved through the Middle Ages, being incorporated in the whole Bible of the 13th century.

One of the finest monuments of old French is the transla-tion of the *Four Books of Kings*, cir. 1150, written in a rhythmical prose, the sentences of unequal length being linked together by assonance. *Ed.*, Leroux de Lincy, 1841. *MSS.*, Bibl. Mazarine, 70 (MS. Cordelier); Arsenal, 5211.

The Book of Maccabees is also contained in the Cordelier MS.   *Ed.*, E. Görlich (Rom. Bibl. ɪɪ.), 1888.

Samson de Nanteuil (Anglo-Norman).

Book of Proverbs.   Rhymed-version with allegorical gloss *Ed.*, Extracts, Bartsch, "Langue et Litt."   *MS.*, Harl. 4388.

9   History.

The first original work in French prose of any extent is the historical work of Villehardouin. History had been hitherto written in Latin, *i.e.*, Grégoire de Tours, whose history extends from 397 to 591 ; Frédégaire, in the 8th century ; Eginhard, 9th century ; Glaber, 11th century.

Villehardouin.   For works, *see* next Century (§ 41).

The events of the first three Crusades were written in Latin by **Guillaume de Tyr** (d. 1184). It was early translated into French, *Histoire de la Terre Outre Mer* (*see* § 41). A translation from the French was made and printed by Caxton (1481) ; *ed.*, E.E.T.S., 1893.

10   Poetry.
Religious Verse.

Wace (§ 15).   Canon of Bayeux, b. cir. 1100 ; d. probably cir. 1175.

La Vie de S. Nicolas de Myra (octosyllabic couplets). From a Latin source. Oldest extant poem by Wace (G. Paris).   *Ed.*, N. Delius, 1850.   *MSS.*, Bodl., Douce, 270 ; Digby, 86.

La Fête de la Conception (octosyllabic couplets). In several copies the "Conception" is followed by two poems which the Editor, P. Meyer, does not think belong to Wace ; one is on the Three Maries, the other on the Assumption.   *Ed.*, Mancel et Trebutien, 1842 ; P. Meyer, "Notice sur deux MSS. (La Clayette), Français, etc.," "Notices et Extraits," vol. xxxiii.   *MSS.*, Bibl. Nat. fr. (five MSS.) ; Bibl. Nat. Lat. 5002 ; Bibl. Nat., La Clayette ; B.M. Add.

15606 (largely interpolated with extracts from other religious poems); St. John's Coll. Camb.; Tours, 927.

La Vie de S. Marguerite (octosyllabic couplets). Translation of Latin text. Seven rhymed French versions of this life are extant, of which only two are known by their author's name, that of Wace, and of Fouque (MS. Clayette). One (Cott. Domit. A. xi.) is probably by Bozon. An anonymous life, of which over a hundred MSS. are extant of 14th and 15th centuries, superseded the others in popularity, after the close of the 13th century. *Ed.*, A. Joly, 1879. *MSS.*, Tours, 927 (defective); Bibl. Nat. fr. 19525.

Vie de S. Georges de Lyssa. *MS.*, Tours, 927. This same saint was commemorated by Simon de Fraisne, and other anonymous poets. *See* J. E. Matzke, "Publ. Mod. Lang. Assoc.," xvii., 1902.

Benoît (Beneit, or Beneeit). Monk. (Anglo-Norman.)

Voyage de S. Brendan, 1121 (octosyllabic couplets). Composed for Alix de Louvain, wife of Henry I. During his seven years' wanderings Brendan comes across wonders by sea and land: Republic of birds; Island of Sheep; Island of Silence, etc.; and he meets Judas who is released from Hell once a week in recompence for one good action. *Ed.*, Suchier, "Rom. Studien," 1875; F. Michel (Cott. Vesp. B. x.), 1878; Bartsch, *op. cit.* (*See* under England, § 43, for further references.) *MSS.*, Cott. Vesp. B. x. (Anglo-Norman text); Bodl. Rawl. Misc.; Ashburnham; York; Arsenal, B.L. fr. 283 (version of 13th century).

Garnier de Pont-Sainte-Maxence.

Vie de S. Thomas Becket, 1173 (rhymed Alexandrines, five monorhymic lines). One of the finest lives written in French verse, and a poem of historical value. *Ed.*, I. Bekker, 1838; C. Hippeau, 1859. *See* E. Etienne, "Etude Historique, etc."; 1883. *MSS.*, Harl. 270; Cott. Domit. xi.; Bibl. Nat. fr. Supp. 2489; Wolfenbüttel.

N.B.—Another life of Becket was written in this century by another Benoît (de S. Alban, G. Paris). *Ed.*, F. Michel (with "Chronique des Ducs de Normandie"); R. Atkinson, 1876. *MSS.*, Bibl. Nat. fr. 902; Harl. 3775.

Berol (Beros, Berot).

Purgatoire de S. Patrice (Alexandrine quatrains). A French version of H. of Saltrey's Latin work; latter part of century (*see* England, § 27). This legend was seven times put into French verse. (*See* Marie de France, Geffroi de Paris.) Several anonymous versions are found in our English libraries. None of the three English versions extant are thought to be derived from the French. *See* Meyer, "Notices et Extraits," vol. xxxiv., on MS. at Sir T. Phillipps's Libr. *MSS.*, Phillipps, 4156; Tours, 948.

Marie de France. (§§ 31, 32.)

L' Espurgatoire Saint Patrice. From Henry of Saltrey (octosyllabic couplets). Probably the first work by this poetess. *Ed.*, J. A. Jenkins, 1894. *MS.*, Bibl. Nat. fr. 25407.

Another Celtic legend known in France was that of the knight Tungdalus, who is resuscitated at the end of three days, during which interval he has witnessed and himself undergone the pains of Purgatory. French literature only possesses a prose version. (*See* England, § 67.)

Denis Pyramus. (*See* Parthénopeu, § 29.)

Vie de S. Edmund, end of century.

Clemence, or Dimence de Berkinge (Barking, Essex). An Anglo-Norman Sister.

Vie de S. Catherine d' Alexandrie (octosyllabic). Taken, according to the authoress, from an older poem, probably another A.-N. work. Seven French versions of the life of this Saint are extant. *Ed.*, Jarnick, 1894. *See* "Notices et Extraits," vol. xxxiii. *MSS.*, Bibl. Nat. fr. 23112; Ashburnham, 112.

Anonymous.

Vie de S. Grégoire (octosyllabic couplets). In ignorance of his descent, Grégoire becomes the husband of his mother, and in order to expiate his involuntary crime, undergoes a terrible penance for seventeen years. Finally he is elected

Pope, and in that capacity has the joy of absolving his
mother. "One of the most remarkable monuments of our
ancient poetry" (G. Paris). The French poem served as
a model for Hartmann v. Aue (Germany, § 19).

Vie de S. Modwenne. According to G. Paris this is a
noteworthy work.

N.B.—The "Lives of the Desert Fathers,"[1] translated
into Latin by various writers, was the great Eastern source
for the lives of saints; a French prose version with a prologue in verse was prepared for Blanche, the Countess of
Champagne (Bibl. Nat. 1038).

The favourite Apocryphal Gospels were that on the Childhood of Christ and the pseudo-Nicodemus. The former
contained many legends in connection with the Virgin Mary;
several other Latin collections of miracles associated with the
Virgin and Saints were also extant.

11 Specimens of Sermons in Verse of early date :

> "Grant mal fist Adam
> quant por le Sathan,
> entamat le fruit," etc.

This was "un simple sarmun," written for "simple gent"
(rhyme a a b, c c b). Early century. *Ed.,* H. Suchier,
"Bibl. Normannica," vol. i., 1879. *MSS.,* Bibl. Nat. fr.
19525; Caius Coll. Camb. ; Bodl. Digby, 34.

Guichard de Beaujeu, d. 1137.

"*Ci Comence le Romaunz de temtacioun de Secle*" (Alexan-
drines, up to forty or more lines on same rhyme), cir. 1135.
This sermon, we are told, won for the author the title of
"Homer of the Laity." *Ed.,* G. Stengel (Digby, 86),
1871. *MSS.,* Bibl. Nat. fr. 19525; Harl. 4388; Bodl.
Digby, 86.

---

[1] The "Lives of the Desert Fathers" were written in Greek by
Palladius, Bishop of Heliopolis, from personal knowledge, and finished
in 420 ("Lausiac History," *i.e.* written at request of Lausus); He and
Rufinus are the chief sources of our knowledge of the early ascetics.
Ed., "The Book of Paradise" (English trans. of Lives and Sayings),
E. A. W. Budge, 1904; *see* also E. Preuschen, "Palladius and Rufinus,"
1897.

Other rhymed sermons are: *Deu le Omnipotent* (Arundel, 292), *Vers du Jugement*.

12 *Didactic and Satirical Verse.*

There is little to separate the didactic and satirical from the religious verse. The most celebrated of the didactic poets of this century was—

Philippe de Thaon. Anglo-Norman.

Comput, 1119 (six-syllabled lines; rhyming couplets). A versified Calendar, in which are given divisions of time, Church festivals, the Zodaic, etc., with occasional allegorical interpretations. From a Latin original. *Ed.*, G. Mall, 1873. *See* "Jahrbuch f. Rom. u. Eng. Lit.," v. and vii. (on the Sources). *MSS.*, Cott. Nero. A. v.; Arundel, 230; Sloane, 1580; Lincoln Cath.; Vatican.

Bestiaire, cir. 1130 (six-syllabled lines; last division octosyllabic). A Physiologus from Latin original, but the exact source uncertain. Three divisions: animals, birds, accompanied with moralisations; allegory of Panther and Whale similar to that in "Exeter Book," and incident in connection with Whale, also in "Voyage of S. Brendan"; third part on stones, magic properties, etc. In the Catalogue of Cott. MSS. a Latin "Bestiarius" (Cott. Vesp. E. x.) is ascribed to P. de Thaon, but it has nothing to do with him; it differs essentially from the "Bestiaire." *See* F. Mann, "Romanische Forschungen," vol. 6. *Ed.*, with Eng. trans., Thomas Wright, "Popular Treatises of the Middle Ages," 1841. E. Walberg, 1900. *MSS.*, Cott. Nero. A. v.; Kopenhagen, 3466; Merton Coll., Oxford.

Anonymous.

Lapidaire (octosyllabic, rhyming couplets), probably a little anterior to "Bestiaire," cir. 1125. Dealing with stones and their medical and magic properties. The work is the earliest French version of the Latin poem in hexameters, by Marbode, Bishop of Rennes (d. 1123), whose verse was probably based on a Latin prose original of end of 11th century. Three other translations of Marbode's work into

French verse, date from the time of Philippe Auguste; later there were numerous prose versions, and many works inspired by his original. *Ed.*, L. Pannier, "Les Lapidaires français des XIIe, XIIIe, et XIVe Siècles," 1882. *MSS.*, Bibl. Nat. Lat. 14470, containing Marbode's Latin, each chapter followed by French version; Bibl. Nat. fr. 24870.

Étienne de Fougères. Bishop of Rennes, 1168-78.

Le Livre des Manières, cir. 1170 (octosyllabic quatrains on one rhyme). In the poem the author describes "what are and what ought to be," the manners and morals of various classes of society. The poem ends with a summing up of the vanity of earthly things, and description of torments for the damned. This is "the oldest and most interesting" (G. Paris) of a class of poems in which exhortation and satire are addressed to all classes, generally known as "États du Monde." *Ed.*, Talbert, 1877. *See* J. Kremer, 1887; and Kehr, "Sprache d. Livre des Manières," 1884. *MS.*, Bibl. Angers, 295.

Le Chastoiement (Enseignement) d'un père à son fils. Anonymous version of the "Disciplina Clericalis," compiled by the Spaniard, Petrus Alfonsus, a converted Jew (of the 11th century) towards the close of the century. Another version is extant of 13th century. *Ed.*, Soc. Bibliophiles français, 1824; P. Meyer, Ashburnham MS., "Bull. Soc. Anc. Textes," 1887. (In this MS. there is a continuation, in which the father still instructs the son, but this time as to how he is to conduct himself in affairs of love.) *MSS.*, 12th century, Bibl. Nat. fr. 12581; Reg. 16 E. viii.; Add. 10289; Pavia; Wallerstein (Mayhingen); Ashburnham. 13th century, Phillipps, 4156: Harl. 527 and 4388; Digby, 86, etc.

Débats, Battailles.

A favourite form of religious and didactic teaching. In the "Débat" or "Bataille," the allegorising was applied to various things, besides actual vices and virtues, *i.e.*, "La Bataille de Carême et de Charnage." In the following century the form was also used for other than religious purposes, as in England in "The Owl and the Nightingale." *See* "Hist. Litt.," xxiii.

The most ancient extant Debat is the

Débat du Corps et de l'âme (England, § 8). Beyond the two classes of the legend, mentioned under England, there is a further distinction between the various poems, *i.e.*, some give the legend in the form of a vision, others not. The six-syllabled French version, "Un Samedi par nuit" (early 12th), is representative of the former group of compositions. There are three French versions, of which this is the oldest (*see* MSS.). *Ed.*, Text 1, H. Varnhagen, 1890; E. Stengel (Selden, 74), "Ztsch. Rom. Phil.," iv. *See* "Romania," xiii. p. 520; and also Wright, "Latin Poems att. to W. Map." *See* generally, Kleinert, "Ueber den Streit zwischen Leib u. Seele," 1880 (G. Paris, "Romania," ix.); Batiouchkof, "Romania," xx. *MSS.* (1), Six-syllabled (rhyming couplets), Arsenal, 3516; B.M. Cott. Jul. A. 7; Harl. 5234; Brussels, Bibl. Roy.; Turin. (2) Tail-rhymed strophes, Bodl. Selden, 74; B.M. Cott. Vitell. C. 8; Phillipps, 8336; Arundel, 288 (texts i. and ii. mingled). (3) Alexandrines, monorhymic strophes of four lines; many MSS.

13   *États du Monde, Dits.*

Other short, more or less allegorical poems written for amusement or instruction were called "dits." Among these are, *Dit des quatre sœurs* (Reconciliation of Justice and Truth with Peace and Mercy) (Arundel, 292); and the *Quinze signes du Jugement*. These signs, precursors of the end of the world, were a favourite theme in old times, and a series of compositions were written upon them in French. Many of them can be referred to certain predictions of a sibyl, found in a poem of Greek origin, of which a translation in hexameters by S. Augustine was widely known throughout the Middle Ages. *See* Paris, *op. cit.*, § 154.

Besides works of general satire, such as the "États du Monde," others were written against particular classes, particularly the clergy and women; the latter being subjects of much abuse in the Middle Ages. One of the ancient satires against them is—

L'Évangile aux femmes, in which the three first lines of a quatrain extols them, to be followed by a fourth which annuls the praise. Suggestions as to authorship (Marie de France?) are discussed by Keidel, who also gives the relationship of the MSS. *Ed.*, G. C. Keidel, "Romance and Other Studies," 1895; L. Constans, "Chrestomathie, etc.," 1890. *MSS.*, Bibl. Nat. fr. 1553, 837, 1593, 25545; Arsenal, fr. 2765–2768, 3123; Dijon, Epinal, Basle, Chantilly, Berne, Clermont-Ferrand.

Others were: *Chastie-Musart*, a warning against love (Harl. 4333), *La Comparaison de la pie et de la femme*, *Le dit de Chicheface*, a monster who grows like a skeleton, .being fed only on wives who obey their husbands, in contrast to another who lives on submissive husbands and grows correspondingly stout, etc. The women were not without their defenders in the satiric replies of "Dits des femmes," "Le Bien des femmes," etc. *See* "Hist. Litt.," xxiii.

N.B.—MS. Bibl. Nat. 24432, contains a collection of *Dits* and *Fableaux*.

14   *Translations.*

Maître Élie. Uncertain who Maître Élie was; may be only the name of the copyist. Trans. into verse of Ovid's "Ars amatoria." *MS.*, Bibl. Nat. fr. 19152.

Trans. of "Disticha," known in the Middle Ages under the name of "Cato," by

Élie de Winchester. *MSS.*, St. John's Coll. Oxford; C.C.C.C.; Harl. 4388.

Everard de Kirkham. *MSS.*, Arundel, 292; Add. 22283; Bodl. Vernon; and in Bibl. Nat.

An anonymous translation of "Cato" is in MS., Harl. 4657.

Simon de Fraisne.

Roman de la Fortune, cir. 1180. Adaptation of Boethius. *MSS.*, B.M. Reg. 20, B. xiv.; Bodl. Douce, ccx.

15   *Historical Verse.*

Rhymed Chronicles held a chief place in the older literature of the Normans. Two of the chief Anglo-Norman
Chroniclers were Gaimar and Wace.

Geoffroy Gaimar.

**L'Estorie des Engles.*   From the successors of Arthur to
William Rufus, cir. 1148 (octosyllabic rhyming couplets).
A first part of Gaimar's history dealing with earlier times,
and mentioned by him, is not now known to be extant.
(The tale of Havelok, "Lai d'Aveloc" is inserted in
this history.)   *MSS.*, B.M. Reg. 13, A. xxi.; Arundel,
xiv.; Durham, C. iv. 27; Lincoln, A. 4–12; Add. 32125,
lines from the lost first part.

Wace.   Canon of Bayeux, b. cir. 1100; d. probably
cir. 1175.   (§ 10.)

Le Roman de Brut (*Geste des Bretons*) (octosyllabic rhyming couplets), 1155.   Rhythmical version of G. of Monmouth's history, to which Wace added other legends.   In
this work we find the first mention of the "Round Table."
See A. C. L. Brown, "The Round Table before Wace,"
"Studies and Notes Phil. Lit.," vii.   It served as the basis
for Layamon's work (*see* England, § 35).   *Ed.*, Le Roux
de Lincy, 1836–38.   *MSS.*, Bibl. Nat. fr. 12556, 1415,
12603 (fragment); Add. 32125; Arundel, xiv.; Durham;
Lincoln.

Le Roman de Rou (*geste des Normands*) and *Chronique
Ascendante des Ducs de Normandie*, 1160–1174.   According
to later criticism, the "Chronique Ascendante" is an introduction, or prologue (Alexandrines) to the "Roman de
Rou." It gives the history of the Dukes from Henry II.
back to Rollo, or Rou.

1st part (2nd in Andresen's). History from Rou to
Richard the Fearless (Alexandrines).

2nd part (3rd in Andresen's). Second prologue, and
narrative to 1107 (octosyllabic). This part was not complete
in its present form till 1170. The second prologue with

some additions also occurs separately, and is thought to be
the beginning of an intended fresh version of first part.
Wace broke off here, as he was told of another poet being
commissioned by Henry to write of the Normans, this other
poet being Benoît de Sainte-More (G. Paris). Sources: For
earlier part Dudo de St. Quentin and Guillaume de Jumièges;
later parts mostly original. *Ed.*, H. Andresen, 1877–79;
trans. into English, E. Taylor, 1837; A. Malet, 1860.
MSS., Nat. Bibl. fr. 718; B.M. Reg. 4, C. xi.; etc.

Jourdain Fantosme. Chancellor of the Diocese of
Winchester. Angl.-Norm., fl. latter half of century.

*Chronique de la guerre entre les Anglais et les Ecossais, 1174.
(Alexandrines, laisses of unequal length, on one rhyme.)
Ed., with trans. into English, F. Michel, Surtees Soc., 1840.
See Liebermann, *English Historical Review*, 1893. *MSS.*,
Durham, C. iv. 27; Lincoln, A. i. 8.

Benoîte de Saint-More. (*See* Roman de Troye, § 28.)

Chronique des Ducs de Normandie (octosyllabic couplets),
cir. 1172–76. Dealing with the same period as Wace, but
carried on to the death of Henry I. There was an uncertainty at one time as to the identity of the author of
this work, but G. Paris assigns it to B. de Sainte-More.
Ed., F. Michel, 1836–44. *MSS.*, Harl. 1717; Tours.
The editor has published two other poems with the
"Chronique," as uncertain if the works of this Benoît.
For one, the "Life of Becket," *see* previous notice (§ 10);
the "Chanson de Croisade," is in the Harleian MS.

Guillaume de Saint-Pair.

Le Roman du Mont Saint-Michel (octosyllabic couplets),
cir. 1170. Guillaume relates to the pilgrims who visit
Saint-Michel the legend of the foundation of the Church,
with various other tales of a miraculous character connected
with the inmates of the cloister. *Ed.*, Fr. Michel, 1836–
44 (with Ducs de Normandie); Redlich, 1894. *MSS.*,
B.M. Add. 10289, copy at Avranches; 26876; other MSS.
found mentioned not known.

Ambroise.

L'Estoire de la Guerre Sainte (3rd crusade, 1190–92) (octosyllabic couplets), cir. 1196. This is "the oldest extant French historical work on contemporary events." The author gives a very detailed account of events but does not himself appear to have been among the fighting men. He was a follower of Richard I., and probably a jongleur. His estimation of those who took part in the Crusade gives interest to the work. *Ed.*, with trans., G. Paris, 1897. *MS.*, Vatican, 1659.

N.B.—The "Itinerarium Regis Ricardi" (*see* Richard de Templo, England, § 28) is in great part a Latin translation of this French work.

Chrétien.

The identity of this author with Chrétien de Troies, remains undecided. His poem is given by Foerster in his edition of C. de T's works.

Du Roi Guillaume d'Angleterre (octosyllabic couplets). The hero of this poem is a King of England called Saint Guillaume : the tale is allied to the Eustace legend (*see* Alexis, 4). *Ed.*, F. Michel, "Chron. Ang.-Norm.," 1840 ; J. A. Giles, "Script. rerum. Gest. Will. Conquestoris," 1845. *MS.*, Bibl. Nat. fr. 375 ; Camb., St. John's Coll.

Uncertain Authorship.

Le Siège d'Antioche ovesque le conquest de Jérusalem de Godefroid de Boilion (in monorhymic laisses of unequal lengths). End century. Based in great measure on Baudri de Bourgeuil's "Historia Hierosolymitana." The work, although ascribed in the poem itself to Baudri de Bourgeuil, is not thought probably his, the language not being old enough, Baudri de Bourgeuil dying in 1130. *MSS.*, Bodl. Hatton, 77 ; Add. 34114 (Spalding).

David.

Gaimar mentions a poem, now lost, on Henry I., written by this poet for Alis de Louvain, the King's widow.

Anonymous.

La Conquête d'Irlande (Conquest of Ireland in 1172 by Henry II.), cir. 1190 (in rhymed couplets). The poem is incomplete. The author tells us that he obtained his most important details from Maurice Regan, the interpreter of Dermot, King of Leinster. *Ed.*, F. Michel, 1837. *MS.*, Lambeth, 596.

16   CHANSONS DE GESTE.

Cycle du Roi.

Le Roi Louis, or *Gormont et Isembart.* Written in laisses of unequal length, some being closed with a refrain. Only a fragment remains of the poem in which Charlemagne's son Louis kills the giant Gormont, the leader of the hostile Saracens. The original hero of the tale was Louis III., but in later versions confusion arose between that king and Charlemagne's son. Old elements are traceable in this chanson. *Ed.*, "La Mort du roi Gormont," A. Scheler, 1876; also given in Intro., vol. ii., "Chronique rimée," de P. Mousket, ed. de Reiffenberg, 1836, etc. *MSS.*, Fragment; found in an old binding by M. de Ram.

Mainet (in Alexandrines). Last third of century. It describes the youthful adventures of Charlemagne (Mainet); sojourn at Court of Galafre, Saracen king in Spain; encounter with Giant Braimant; marriage with Galafre's daughter. The original hero in this chanson, as is the case in others, was a monarch of earlier date, Charles Martel being the Mainet of the original legend. The German "Karl Meinet," and the Italian "Karleto" have versions of the subject-matter of Mainet. *See* under Girart d'Amiens (§ 50). *Ed.*, G. Paris, "Romania," iv. *MS.*, One MS. fragment found by M. Boucherie, 1894, now in Bibl. Nat.

Aspremont. One of the oldest chansons, dating originally from the 11th century. War in Italy against Saracens under Agoland and Eaumont. In this poem Roland appears at fifteen years of age, and receives, as part of the booty, his sword Durandal, and his horse Vaillantif. Considered one of the best of the second order of chansons. The first part

is superior to the second.   *Ed.*, F. Guessard and L. Gautier.
MSS., Many MSS., Bibl. Nat. fr. 2495, 25529; Reg. 15,
E. vi.; Lansdowne, 782; Ashburnham, Berlin, Vatican,
Venice, etc.

La Destruction de Rome (rhymed Alexandrines). (*See*
England, § 61.) The only remaining text is of the thirteenth
century, but there existed an older version in assonance.
Two names are given at the beginning of the song as writers
of the later version, Gautier de Douai, and "Le Rois Louis."
According to the editor, this poem was the earlier part of the
old lost romance of "Balan," but it does not coincide with
the outline given of the latter by Mousket. War in Italy,
this time against Saracens Balan and Fierabras: combat
between Oliver and Fierabras.   *Ed.*, G. Gröber, 1893.
MSS., One MS., Hanover, Bibl. Municip., 578.

Fierabras (rhymed Alexandrines). (*See* England, § 61.)
Extant version, cir. 1170, but an older version existed.
Gröber attributes it to the same author as "D. de Rome,"
but this supposition is disputed. The chanson is in two
parts, distinct from one another, the first being superior.
The second part is an enlarged and altered version of an
episode in an older poem called "Balan," now lost ("Hist.
Poét.," p. 251). It tells of the landing of Charlemagne in
Spain after the war in Italy, and of the duel of Oliver and
Fierabras. This favourite chanson was put into prose in 15th
century, and was the first romance to be printed, Geneva,
1478. The Provençal "Fierabras" was a copy of the French
version.   *Ed.*, A Kröber and G. Servois, 1860.   *MSS.*,
Bibl. Nat. fr. 12603, 1500; MS. Didot (this is the most
ancient), Reg. 15, E. 6; Vatican, Escurial.

Jehan Bodel.   Also writer of songs, drama, etc.   (§ 62.)

La Chanson des Saisnes (Alexandrines, rhyme and assonance). Last third of century. Fight with Saxons under
Wittekind (Guiteclin). Episode of Wittekind's wife, Sebille,
who marries Roland's brother, Baudouin, after her husband's
death, etc. The poem is a compilation of three earlier ones,
"Les Herupois" (People of West Frankland); "Les Saisnes,"

or "Guiteclin"; "La Mort de Baudouin," or "Baudouin et Sibile," preserved in other versions. The description of the wars with the Saxons are considered reminiscences of older Merovingian struggles with this enemy. "The poem shows signs of the decadence of the genuine epic, being more allied to the romances of adventure." *Ed.*, Fr. Michel, "Roman des douze Pairs de France," 1839. *MSS.*, Phillipps; Arsenal, Anc. B. L., 175; Bibl. Nat. fr. 368; Turin.

Chevalerie Ogier le Danois. (Also connected with Cycle Doon de Mayence.) The extant text of the 12th century is the work of a jongleur, Raimbert. The whole is in twelve parts, of which the first, "Enfances Ogier," has been often separated from the rest, and was enlarged into a separate work by Adenet le Roi, 13th century. Ogier was one of the most renowned of Frankish heroes; in this poem he demands compensation for the death of his son, killed by Charlemagne's son Charlot; being refused, there ensue long years of rebellion on his part, during which occurs the long and famous siege of Castelfort; sustained at last by Ogier alone, whose men are all dead; finally he is found asleep in a valley and taken prisoner; but Charlemagne being pursued by the Saracens, releases him that he may fight for him, which Ogier refuses to do unless Charlot is given up to him; sorrow of Emperor; encounter of Ogier and Charlot, when an angel descends to stay the combat; reconciliation. In the course of the narrative Amis and Amiles are met and killed by Ogier. *Ed.*, J. Barrois, 1842. *MSS.*, Bibl. Nat. 1583; Durham, Bibl. Cosin.; Montpellier, Tours. Versions of later date, anonymous and in Alexandrines, Arsenal, 191, 192; Reg. 15, E. vi.; Turin.

Huon de Bordeaux. Last third of century. (Gautier places it early 13th century, p. 732.) Huon, having slain Charlemagne's son in fair fight, is sent by emperor to Babylon to perform some extremely difficult tasks. Huon receives help from Auberon, the dwarf. Besides the text that has come down, there was apparently another version, differing slightly, known to the chronicler, Albéric de Trois-Fontaines (first half 13th century). In both these versions the adventures in the East are given, and the dwarf introduced. These adventures, however, are thought to have been added by the later poet, for a third version, extant in the "Geste des Lorrains," has nothing of them, and makes Huon the slayer of a Count, not of Charlemagne's son. The tale is believed to be undoubtedly based on an historical fact in connection with the young son of Charles le Chauve, whose reported character corresponds to the representation of it in the poem, and Huon's father was an historical personage, killed by the Normans in 845. This is numbered among the poems which mark the transition from earlier epic to later romance.

The prologue of the Turin MS. is the "Roman d'Auberon," of later date than "H. de B.," in which poem Auberon is first introduced into the Carolingian Cycle. The figure of Auberon himself is principally of Germanic origin—he is the Alberich of German legend—but certain Celtic features are introduced. A version of this romance is found in "Ortnit" (*see* Germany, § 29), thought by some authorities to be a direct copy of "Auberon." The "Roman d'Auberon" is an inferior work of extravagant fancy, into which such diverse characters are introduced as Judas Macchabeus, Julius Cæsar, King Arthur and his sister, the fairy Morgue, S. George (twin brother to Auberon), all, however, connected by marriage or birth.

Of the continuations to "H. de B.," one, "Huon, roi de Féerie," is in the MS. at Bibl. Nat.; the others are found in the Turin MS., and are: "Chanson d'Esclarmonde"; "C. de Clarisse et Florent"; "C. d'Ide et d'Olive"; and "C. de Godin." A later version exists in Alexandrines.

In England "H. de B." was made familiar by the translation of Lord Berners in the 16th century; the dwarf, Auberon, is better known from Shakespeare's king of the fairies, and he was also introduced by Greene into the play of "James IV. of Scotland." *Ed.*, "H. de B.," F. Guessard and C. Grandmaison, 1860; Mod. French version, G. Paris, 1898. *See* Voretzsch, "Die Composition," etc., "Epische Studien," 1900. *MSS.*, Three MSS. in decasyllabic verse: Tours; Bibl. Nat. fr. 22555 (with one continuation); Turin, Bibl. Univ. H. ii. 11 (Prologue, and four continuations). One MS. (Alexandrines) Bibl. Nat. fr. 1451.

La Reine Sibile (fragment only, in Alexandrines, of 14th century), and *Macaire* (Franco-Italian). Two versions of the same tale, in which the innocent wife of Charlemagne is falsely accused and banished. A dwarf, the traitor Macaire, the dog who watches his master's dead body, and finally kills the murderer Macaire in combat, and Varocher, the woodman, who becomes a knight, are the characters in the tale. *MS.,* "Macaire," Venice, S. Mark, fr. xiii.

Alberic des Trois Fontaines (fl. 1232–1252), writer of a Latin universal history, refers to the Queen Sibile, and to a chanson concerning her, but this earlier French poem is lost, and only known in foreign versions. The whole tale of Sibile, the innocent Queen of France, was given in a German poem of the 14th century (*see* Germany, § 45), and a similar story is associated with Hildegarde, the wife of Charlemagne, which ends with the cure of her calumniator, who is attacked with leprosy, by the Queen herself. This version does not include the dog incident. The theme of the calumniated wife is found repeated in many mediæval tales. The English romance of "Syr Tryamoure" (ed. J. O. Halliwell) is based on "Macaire," beginning with the wrongful accusation of his mother, and including the episode of the dog's fidelity and attack on the murderer.

N.B.—The dog has become known as the dog of Montargis, from the representation of the old tale on the tapestries in the castle of Montargis, which date from Charles the Eighth's time.

Berte au Grand Pied, or *Aux Grands Pieds*. (Version of 12th century lost.) Berte, the mother of Charlemagne (*see* "Floire et Blancheflor," § 29), was the subject of several poems. She was the victim of a jealous and intriguing woman about the Court, who contrived to substitute her own daughter for the lawful wife. Berte undergoes a period of great suffering, but is finally rehabilitated, Pepin having discovered that she is the real Berte. For extant version, *see* under Adenet le roi (§ 50).

Le Couronnement de Louis, cir. 1150 (Gautier, end 12th), traced back to an earlier version and to historic facts from 10th to 12th century. In four parts: the first gives

Charlemagne's farewell and last advice to his son Loeys. The poem is attached to the following cycle by the description given of Guillaume au Court Nez, his wars in Italy and fight with giant Corsolt, and the help he twice gives to the young King against traitorous vassals. The whole is a compilation of chansons originally distinct from one another. *Ed.*, E. Langlois, "Soc. Anc. Textes," 1888. *MSS.*, Bib. Nat. fr. 774, 1449 and others; Reg. 20, D. xi. ; Boulogne ; Milan.

A curious tale of Charlemagne being instructed by an angel to go at night and act the part of a robber, whereby he overhears a plot against his life, was given in "Basin," also called "Charles et Elegast," or the "Couronnement de Charles" ; the poem is lost but is known by versions extant in other countries. Basin, the robber, figures in a later poem of "Jehan de Lanson" (*see* § 50.)

In the poem of *Floovent* (Montpellier, Fac. Med., 441), there are reminiscences of a Merovingian Cycle, knowledge of which has come down through old historians. The incident of the young prince being banished by his father, on account of having insulted one of his barons by cutting his beard, is found in "Gesta Dagoberti," a monkish legend of 10th cent. ; but the primitive hero, it is thought, was Floovant, the son of Clovis, as he is represented in extant poem.

17   *Cycle Garin de Montglane.*

This cycle records the deeds of a princely family of Aquitaine. The chief hero is Guillaume Fierabrace, Guillaume au Court Nez, or Guillaume d'Orange. He was early associated with an historical personage under Charlemagne who drove back the invading Saracens, and, after other warlike deeds, died in a cloister in 812. With his exploits were mingled those of other heroes, all of whom were finally represented as the sons of one Aimeri. Another branch of the cycle unites four heroes as children of Garin de Montglane. Five of the sons of Aimeri are found together in the fragment of La Haye (*see* Roland, § 6.) Twenty-four chansons are

extant of this Geste de Guillaume.   *Ed.*, W. J. A.
Jonckbloet, "Guillaume d'Orange, Chansons de geste des
xie et xiie siècles," 1854.   *MSS.*, Twenty-six MSS.: Bibl.
Nat. (11); Arsenal (3); Boulogne (1); B.M. Reg. 20,
B. xix., D. xi.; Harl. 1321; Phillipps, 8075; Venice (3);
Rome (1); Milan (1); Berne (1); Stockholm (1).

Chevalerie, or *Covenant*, *Vivien*, cir 1150.   Earlier version
lost. Vivien, nephew of Guillaume d'Aquitaine, is defeated
by Saracens; Guillaume hastens to his help. Poem apparently
unfinished, as we do not hear of Vivien's death or Guillaume's
retreat.

Aliscans or *Rainouard.*   End of 12th century, but evidence
of older poem having existed.   "Guillaume's defeat at
Villedaigne, near Arles, 793, may be considered the historical
central fact of the cycle."   The poem deals with same subject
as above but is carried on further. It is in three parts:

(1) *Aleschans.* Account of Vivien's death, and Guillaume's
defeat; tradition associated this battle with the old tombs at
Elysii Campi (Alischans.)   The giant Rainouart is introduced.

(2) *Loquifer.* Exploits of Rainouart.

(3) *Moniage Rainouart.* Rainouart retires to a monastery
and causes disturbance there. *Renier* (grandson of Rainouart)
joins this cycle to that of Crusades, by making Tancred the
son of Renier. Jendeu de Brie, who appears to have written
in Sicily, 1170 (G. Paris, *op. cit.*, § 40), is thought possibly
to be the author of the above three poems.

The "Willehalm" of W. von Eschenbach (*see* Germany,
§ 31) is an imitation of "Aleschans."

Another continuation of "Chevalerie Vivien" is *Foulque
de Candie*, cir. 1170, attributed in some MSS. to Herbert
le Duc, à Dammartin.

Moniage Guillaume, cir. 1160. Guillaume having retired
into a monastery retains his warlike propensities; being sent
to buy fish, he is attacked by robbers; mindful of monastic
injunctions he at first makes no resistance, but finally falls on
his adversaries and slays them.

Other poems of this cycle are: *Enfances Guillaume* (extant version early 13th century, but earlier versions had existed); *Département des enfans Aimeri* (three versions, of which one is possibly of 12th century); *Mort Aimeri de Narbonne* (placed end of 12th century by Editor, § 51); *Charroi de Nîmes* (first third of century); *Prise d'Orange* (second third of century). *See* also *Coronnement de Louis* under Cycle du Roi. (*See* § 51.)

The Chiswick Press, 1903, published a transcription of an "unknown Chanson de Geste" belonging to this cycle: "La Chançun de Willame" (two facsimiles.) *See* Raymond Weeks, the newly discovered C. d. W. (This MS. was sold among the items of Sir Hope Edwardes's Library, 1901.)

N.B.—The most complete collection of the Chansons of the Geste Guillaume is found in MS., B.M. Reg. 20, B. xix.

18   *Cycle Doon de Mayence.*

This cycle is of later origin than the other two. It celebrates the deeds of heroes who originally had no connection with Doon, but are finally represented as his descendants. Most of them are Charlemagne's vassals, and wage continual war with him. Another Doon, the traitor in "Beuve de Hanstone," is to be distinguished from the hero of this cycle.

Aye d'Avignon (rhymed Alexandrines). Last third of century. In two parts, apparently by different authors. Aye d'Avignon is a niece of the Emperor, and the feud between Garnier, son of Doon de Nanteuil, and grandson of Doon de Mayence, and a treacherous rival, who abducts Aye after she is married to Garnier, forms the theme of the poem. *Ed.*, F. Guessard and P. Meyer, "Anc. Poètes France," 1861. *MSS.*, Bibl. Nat. fr. 2170.

Gui de Nanteuil (rhymed Alexandrines). End 12th century or first years of 13th at latest. Son of Garnier and Aye d'Avignon. The poem forms a continuation of above, giving death of Garnier and Aye's second marriage. The hero Gui, is the victim of the jealousy of a rival for the hand of Eglantine, but finally overcomes the latter. *Ed.*,

F. Guessard and P. Meyer, "Anc. Poètes France" 1861. *MSS.*, Montpelier, Fac. Med., H. 247; Venice, S. Mark, fr. xiv., mixed dialect of Italian and French.

Parise la Duchesse, cir. 1200. The husband of Parise is a grandson of Gui de Nanteuil. Parise, the victim of calumny, undergoes exile and suffering; finally her son, who was taken from her as an infant, rescues her and restores her to husband and kingdom. "The poem is more a romance of adventure than chanson de geste." *Ed.*, "Anc. Poètes France," *op. cit.* (Guessard and Larchey.) *MS.*, Bibl. Nat. fr. 1374.

Doon de Nanteuil was the subject of a lost poem.

19 *La Geste Bourguignonne.*

Girart de Roussillon (Girart de Rosilho). Last third of century. "One of the most noted of the epics." Girart escapes by night from his castle which is besieged by the French king (here, Charles Martel); he and his wife have to support themselves by handicraft; finally he is reconciled to the Emperor through the intervention of the Empress who had formerly loved Girart. This poem is joined to more than one cycle. Girart has three brothers, of which one is Doon de Nanteuil; another brother, Aimon de Dordogne, is the father of the "Quatre fils Aimon"; an episode in "Hervis de Metz" also associates him with the Geste Lorraine. Girart appears again under the title of Girard de Fratte, and Girard de Vienne, and it is under the latter name he is associated with the Cycle Guillaume. A poem in Alexandrines of 14th century, and two prose versions of 15th century are also extant. An older chanson is lost. *Ed.*, F. Michel, 1856; Bartsch, "Chrest. Provençale," 6th ed., 1904. "Traduite pour la première fois," P. Meyer, 1884. *See* Meyer, "Romania," vii. *MSS.*, Bodl. Can. Misc. 63; B.M. Harl. 4334; Bibl. Nat. fr. 2180; Fragment (in possession of M. Meyer). Version of 14th Bibl. Nat. fr. 15103.

N.B.—The Oxford MS. and the fragment are in mixed dialect of North and South.

20 *Geste Lorraine.* Composed of five Chansons : *Hervis de Mez* ; *Garin le Loherain* ; *Girbert de Mes* ; *Anseis, fils de Girbert* ; *Yon.*

The extant version of *Garin le Loherain* is by **Jean le Flagy.** This cycle deals with the feuds between several generations of a Lothringian and a Bordelais family. There appears to be no historic foundation for the tales.

Ed., "Mise en nouveau langage," P. Paris, 1862. *MSS.,* Arsenal, B.L., 180, 181 ; Bibl. Nat. fr. 1442, 1443, 1622, 2179, etc.

21 *La Geste Saint-Gilles.* Composed of two Chansons, which originally had no connection with one another. Last third of century.

Elie de Saint-Gilles. Aiol. Both Alexandrines and decasyllabic lines are found in these two chansons, the decasyllabic believed to be remains of the older version. *See* G. Paris (Aiol, Elie, Daurel, Raoul de Cambrai), 1887. *MS.,* Bibl. Nat. fr. 25516.

22 *La Geste de Blaives.* Composed of two Chansons. Last third of century.

Amis et Amiles (*see* Prose Romances, § 43). Tale of extraordinary friendship between two men who closely resemble one another. The tale is probably of Greek or Oriental origin, and was treated in nearly every European tongue. (*See* Chevalerie Ogier, § 16 and § 43 ; and England, § 40.) *MS.,* Bibl. Nat. fr. 860.

Jourdain de Blaives. Grandson of Amis. An adaptation from *Apollonius of Tyre,* the scene of action being partly transferred to France, and the character to the time of Charlemagne. (For A. of Tyre, *see* England, § 16.) *MS.,* Bibl. Nat. fr. 860.

Ed., K. Hofman, 1882.

23 Unattached Epics.

Raoul de Cambrai, and *Beuvon de Hanstone.* (For latter, *see* § 54.)

Raoul de Cambrai. In two parts, first rhymed, the second in assonance.

1st part. Raoul, nephew of King Louis, fights for his possessions, burning and laying waste the country; is finally killed; his opponents are the sons of a Comte Herbert de Vermandois, an historical personage who died 943. The feud is continued by Raoul's nephew, Gautier.

2nd part. Is a succession of adventures in connection with Bernier, one of the former enemies of Raoul, and his wife; Bernier finally killed by his father-in-law.

Bertolais de Laon, who gives his name as author, also speaks of being an eye-witness of what he recounts, which would make this chanson one of the oldest in its primitive form. The whole work is thought to have been originally all in assonance. Three stages of it have been traced: the first by Bertolais; the second, another version of which there is a reference in a chronicle of 11th century (Chron. Valciodorense), and thirdly the extant version. *Ed.,* P. Meyer and A. Longnon, Soc. Anc. Textes, 1882. *See* G. Paris, "Aiol, Elie, etc.," 1887. *MSS.,* Bibl. Nat. fr. 2493; other MSS. lost.

Two parodies on the Chansons de Geste are extant: *Audigier,* 12th century ("Recueil de Fabliaux et Contes," Barbazan et Méon, vol. iv. 1808); and *Prise de Neuville,* 13th century. (Scheler, "Trouvères Belges," 1879.)

24 *Cycle de la Croisade.*

For collective study of poems of this cycle, *see* "Cycle de la Croisade et de la famille de Bouillon, H. Pigeonneau, 1877. *MSS.,* The poems composing this cycle are preserved in following MSS.: Nat. Bibl. fr. 12558; 1621; 786; 795; 12569; Arsenal, B.L., 165; Brussels, 10391.

It is known from contemporary references that a writer Grégoire, surnamed Béchada, who was brother to a crusader, composed a poem, early in the 12th century, on the conquest of Palestine, but this poem is lost.

The nucleus of the cycle is the

Chanson d'Antioche (rhymed Alexandrines). Written by Richard le Pèlerin, an eye-witness of the first Crusade, but only extant in a later version by Graindor de Douay, end of 12th century. The poem ends after the victory of the Crusaders under the walls of this town. *Ed.*, G. Paris, 1848 and 1878. *See* H. Pigeonneau.

Chanson de Jérusalem (rhymed Alexandrines). Of rather later date than the above, also extant in version by G. de Douay of R. le Pèlerin's work. The poem finishes with Battle of Ascalon. "Antioche," according to H. Pigeonneau, is based on two older Latin histories, but "Jérusalem" has no historical foundation. *Ed.*, C. Hippeau, 1868.

N.B.—The hero of both the above poems is Godefroi de Bouillon.

Chevalier au Cygne, and *Chanson de Godefroi.* Two versions of these dating from this century are preserved in the MSS. mentioned, one anonymous, the other by one "Renax" or Renaud, but whether original author or not is uncertain. The anonymous version is thought to be the older of the two. The outline of tale is as follows :

Lothair, King of a region beyond Hungary, meets the maiden, Eliouse, in a wood, and finally marries her. Seven children are born, one a girl, all with gold necklaces. The mother-in-law reports to King that his wife has given birth to monsters, and tries to do away with children, who are however rescued. Hearing they are still alive, the Queen mother manages to get the necklaces away from the boys, who are immediately changed into swans ; the girl retains her form. The father learns the truth, and restores necklaces, all but one which has been melted down, and the owner of this accompanies one of his brothers (Chevalier au Cygne) wherever he goes, in his swan form. The Chevalier au Cygne marries Beatrix of Bouillon, and enjoins upon her not to ask of his birth ; she eventually does so, and the knight disappears. Their daughter, Ida, marries Eustache de Boulogne, and becomes the mother of three sons, of which one is Godefroi, etc. *Ed.*, H. A. Todd, 1889.

In the other version, Lothair becomes Oriant, Eliouse becomes Beatrix, and the Chevalier au Cygne receives the name of Elie (Elyas, Helyas).   *Ed.*, C. Hippeau, 1874.

These poems were followed by a combined version of the two (Arsenal, 3139).

In the second volume of Hippeau's edition we have the poem of *Godefroi de Bouillon*, in which are given the events preliminary to the subject of *Antioch* and *Jérusalem*.

This cycle was further developed in the poem of the "Chétifs," the five Christian knights made captive during the expedition of Peter the Hermit. One of them being put to fight two Turks, he overcomes them and obtains his own liberation and that of his fellow-captives, whereupon they rejoin Godefroi de Bouillon. Later on "Baudouin de Sebourg" and the "Bâtard de Bouillon" were joined to the cycle, the latter being the final poem of the same (§ 77). A prose version is extant (Bibl. Nat. fr. 781).

English and German versions of the Swan saga are extant.

England. "Romance of the Chevelere Assigne," an abridged translation from the French.   *Ed.*, H. H. Gibbs, E.E.T.S., 1858.   *MS.*, Reg. 15, E. vi. And a prose work, "Helyas, Knight of the Swan."   *See* also under Caxton.

Germany. W. von Eschenbach, "Parzival"; K. von Wurzburg, "Schwanenritter." Lohengrin is Parzival's son, and so the Swan saga became attached to that of the Graal. In the German poem the wife who asks after his birth, dies of grief at his disappearance (*see* Germany, § 30).

N.B.—It has been thought by one authority that a confusion of words gave rise to the association of the swan legend with G. de Bouillon; le Chevalier au Signe (Crusader's Cross), being mistaken for Chevalier au Cygne.

25

For the origin of the French Romances, *see* Introductory note, "Arthurian Cycle," England (§ 25).

The first romances were in verse (octosyllabic), and generally, although often indirectly, connected with Celtic tradition. As the French versions became more independent, they developed the tone which was representative of higher society under Louis VII. and his successors.

The later romances existed in prose as well as verse, and centred round two chief points of interest, the search for the Graal, and the loves of Guinevere and Lancelot.

The romances have been divided into two classes: Episodic, descriptive of some episode in the life of one of Arthur's knights, in which class the most prominent figure was Gauvain; Biographic, giving the life and doings of one of the knights of Arthur's court, from his first appearance there to his marriage. *Ed.*, "Les Romans de la Table Ronde, mis en nouveau langage, etc.," P. Paris, 1868–77. *See* Hist. Litt., xxx.

Tristan Branch.

The tale of Tristan was not originally attached to the Arthurian Cycle. A "Tristan," by C. de Troies, and one by a writer spoken of as "La Chèvre," are both lost. The oldest extant poems are—

Béroul. Anglo-Norman (or, according to M. Foerster, in his "Eric et Enide," a Norman).

Tristan. Fragment only extant, cir. 1150. The German by Eilhart v. Oberg (Germany, § 19), and the French prose romance are allied to the version of which we have a fragment in Béroul's work. Muret concludes that there were two poets, Béroul's successor more closely following Thomas' version. G. Paris opposes the view that Chrétien's lost poem was the common source of the corresponding parts in the three allied works. *Ed.*, E. Muret, "Soc. Anc. Textes," 1903; *see* G. Paris, "Journal des Savants," 1902. *MS.*, Bibl. Nat. fr. 2171.

Thomas. Anglo - Norman. The supposition of one authority that this Thomas is identical with the author of " Horn et Rimenhild " (§ 30) is opposed by others.

Tristan, cir. 1170. The German version of " Tristan," by G. von Strassburg (Germany, § 30), and the English " Sir Tristrem " (England, § 39), are derived from Thomas' poem. Bédier gives three other works drawn from same source, one in Bodl. d. 6.

MSS., Fragments: Cambridge; Sneyd; Turin; Strasburg. *Ed.,* F. Michel, " Recueil de ce qui reste des poèmes, etc.," 1835-39 (includes Béroul fragment); F. Vetter, 1882; J. Bédier, " Soc. Anc. Textes," 1902-5.

" Tristan " was later put into prose. Nearly all MSS. of the prose version give the same account of Tristram's death: wounded by Mark, he takes refuge in a castle whither Iseut goes, and beseeches her lover to take her with him; he embraces her so closely that both their hearts break, and they die. In Eilhard v. Oberg and Thomas, although they represent different forms of the tale, the incident of the two sails, the black and the white, is introduced, " which indicates that a common and older source of the tradition preceded the work both of Béroul and Thomas." For outline of tale, *see* England, § 39. *See N.B.* 1, p. 184.

N.B.—Bédier gives as source of all extant versions of " Tristan," an Anglo-Norman poem of the earlier twelfth century. (*See* Intro., vol. 2, *op. cit.*)

26 The most famous poet of this century was—

Chrétien de Troies. (§ 28.) Works, ed. W. Foerster, 1884-1890; and in " Roman Bibl.," vols. i., xiii. (" Cligès," " Eric and Enid "). Certain works mentioned by the poet himself in the introductory lines of " Cligès," as written by him, have been lost; namely, " Tristan," and " Translations from Ovid " ; those preserved are the following ; all of them belonging to the Arthurian Cycle :—

Erec et Enide (octosyllabic rhyming couplets). Earliest extant work, cir. 1160. Erec, having lived a life of pleasure, rouses himself and affronts the most extraordinary dangers, in order to rehabilitate himself in the eyes of his lady love, his treatment of her meanwhile is familiar to the English reader in Tennyson's version. *MSS.*, Bibl. Nat. fr. 1450, 794, 375, 1376, 24403, 1420; Aumale (Chantilly).

Free German version by Hartmann v. Aue (Germany, § 19). Welsh version (Mabinogi), "Geraint." *See* Foerster, Introd., " Erec et Enide," for discussion as to relation between Welsh and French versions, in which he is opposed to G. Paris.

Cligès (octo. rhyming couplets), 1168. In two parts, giving first the history of the hero's father, Alexander, son of the Emperor of Byzantium, who goes to Arthur's Court, etc., and is given the hand of Soredamor, sister to Gauvain. Secondly, the loves of Cligès and Fenice; the latter forced to marry the uncle of Cligès, drinks a magic potion which throws her into a swoon that counterfeits death; is buried with pomp; and, more fortunate than Juliet, recovers in time to escape with Cligès.

The tale is based on the ancient one of Solomon's wife (*see* Germany, § 14). C. de Troies states himself that he took it from a book in the Cathedral of Beauvais. *Ed.* also by W. L. Holland, 1886. *MSS.*, Bibl. Nat. fr. 1374, 794, 375, 12560, 1420, 1450; Turin L. i. 13; Tours; Bodleian (fragment); Florence, Riccard. (fragment).

Lancelot, le Chevalier de la Charrette (octo. rhyming couplets), cir. 1170. An episode in the history of Lancelot, obtained for him the above surname. In this poem we have the first mention of the loves of Lancelot and Guinevere.

The poem was finished by Godefroi de Lagny, a friend of C. de Troies. *MSS.*, Bibl. Nat. fr. 794, 12560, 1450 (fragment); Vatican; Escurial; Aumale.

Yvain, le Chevalier au Lion (octo. rhyming couplets), cir. 1172. Yvain, having killed the owner of a castle and wood, after wonderful adventures met with in the latter, marries the widow Laudine. Summoned by Arthur to a tournament; leaves his wife with promise of returning in a year's time, which promise he fails to keep. Other adventures, and help given Yvain by a lion he once succoured, and by which he finally regains favour of his wife. " Whatever discussion there may be," writes Henrici (*see* Edition of H. von Aue), "concerning the relationship between the French and Welsh versions, all agree that all other versions had their origin in C. de Troies'." There are strongly opposed views as to the original source of this tale. Förster maintains that the chief motive is derived from the theme of the "easily consoled widow" (version in " Matron of Ephesus ") ; subordinate motives he traces to the story of Gyges' ring, and of Androclus and the lion. G. Paris finds analogies in far different directions, and sees variants of the chief motive in "Guingamor," "Tannhäuser," etc. A recent and full discussion of these views is given by A. C. L. Brown, who sums up by classing it among the Celtic "other world" tales.

German version, closely following French, by Hartmann v. Aue (Germany, § 19) ; Welsh version (Mabinogi) "Owain and Lunet" ; English (England, § 58). *Ed.*, W. L. Holland, 1886. *See* G. Paris, " Romania," xvii. ; A. C. L. Brown, " Studies and Notes in Philol. and Litt.," viii., x. ; Rauch (Welsh, French, and German versions), 1869 : Axel Ahlström, " Sur l'origine, etc.," 1896. *MSS.*, Bibl. Nat. fr. 1433, 794, 1450, 12560, 12603, 1638 ; Vatican ; Aumale ; Fac. Med., Montpellier.

Perceval le Gallois, or *Le Conte du Graal* (unfinished). (England, § 39.) This unfinished poem received several continuations : (1) By anonymous author, partly extant in two versions, dealing with the adventures of Gauvain. (2) By Gaucher de Denain—the history of the Graal, but unfinished. (3) Long continuation by Mennessier ; another long one by Gerbert de Montreuil (§ 57), and an anonymous one of only a few lines. In these continuations the Graal occupies a more important position than it held in Chrétien's portion of the work.

German version—Wolfram v. Eschenbach—with continuation and introduction added (*see* Germany, § 30). Welsh version, " Peredur " (Mabinogi) ; for English version, *see* England, § 39. *MSS.*, Bibl. Nat. fr. 794, 1453, 12576, 1429, 12577, 1450 ; Mons ; Berne (2) ; Fac. Med. Montpellier ; Coll. of Arms ; Edinburgh, Advocates'. *Ed.*, Potvin, " Soc. Bibliophiles," 1866-68 ; Trans., Seb. Evans, "The High History of the Holy Grail," Temple Classics. *See* J. L. Weston, "The Legend of Sir Percival," vol. i. Chrétien de Troyes and Wauchier de Denain, 1906.

For other works in connection with Saga and Poem, *see* England, Sir P. de G. (see § 39).

N.B.—(1) In the *Athenæum* for July 11, 1903, will be found a notice by J. L. Weston of the MS. 12576 of the Bibl. Nat. ; in it the writer draws attention to a section of Gerbert's work in which incidents are related from an "unknown" Tristan text.

N.B.—(2) Lancelot was the subject of an Anglo-Norman poem now lost, but known in the extant German version by Ulrich v. Zatzighoven (Germany, § 19).

27   ALEXANDER CYCLE.

See P. Meyer, " Alexandre le Grand dans la littérature française du moyen Âge," 1886.

The Alexander romances are principally derived from two Latin versions of the Pseudo-Callisthenes (cir. 200 A.D., Gröber). One of these, by Julius Valerius, was written before A.D. 340 (*op. cit.*, p. 10), of which an abridged version was made in the 9th century, and another by the Archpriest Leon (" Historia de Proeliis "), in the 10th. Additional sources were the correspondence between Alexander and Dindimus, and Alexander's " Iter ad Paradisum," and his letter to Aristotle on the Wonders of the East.

Roman d'Alexandre (Alexandrines).

Albéric de Besançon, or Briançon, was the first to use the legend of Alexander as a theme for vernacular verse. His poem was written in octosyllabic verse, and in mono-rhymic " laisses " of varying lengths. It dates from the 12th century, but is of earlier date than the *Roman d'Alexandre.* The German poet, Lamprecht (*see* Germany, § 17), based his " Alexander " on A. de B.'s French version, and from him we learn the name of this latter poet. *MS.*, Florence, Laurenz. (fragment), discovered in 1852 or 1853.

A decasyllabic version (Venice, Mus. Civ., B. 5, 8 ; Arsenal, 3472 ; another MS. has been lost) was the next in order of production. " It is the link between the poem by Albéric and the long romance in Alexandrines."

The two chief names associated with the versions in Alexandrines (last third of century) are

Lambert le Tort.

Alexandre de Bernay, or de Paris. (*See* Romances, § 29.)

This version consists of four branches (*op. cit.*, pp. 212 ff.).

(1) *Enfances Alexandre, etc., to siege of Tyre.* Free version up to a certain point of the decasyllabic version : both this and the continuation may be by Alex. de Paris (p. 237).

(2) *Fuerre de Gadres.* Entry of Alexander into Jerusalem, defeat of Darius. " Fuerre de Gadres " was originally a poem by itself, by one Eustache. It was probably inserted into the general work and continued to third branch by A. de Paris (pp. 241–3).

(3) *Pursuit and Death of Darius.* Expedition to India ; its marvels ; episode of Candace ; taking of Babylon ; treason of Antipater and Divinuspater. There are several interpolations found in this third branch : episode of Floridas and Dauris ; Voyage of Alexander to Paradise ; Vœux du Paon ; Restor du Paon. This third branch, which is unfinished, is the oldest ; it is principally by Lambert le Tort (p. 223).

(4) *Death of Alexander.* Last testament ; grief of Peers. In two parts, which, as they correspond in places, are thought to be by different authors who applied to different sources. First part, most probably by A. de Paris ; second part, possibly by Pierre de St. Cloud (§ 32), and perhaps partly the work of A. de Paris (pp. 224 ff.).

There are extant various continuations of this Roman :

Gui de Cambrai.

La Vengeance d'Alexandre, cir. 1180.

Jean le Nevelons, or li Venelais.

La Vengeance d'Alexandre. 1288–1308 ; cir. 1180 (G. Paris).

This continuation was added in the MSS. of the Roman from one or other of the above authors.

In the 14th century :

Jacques de Longuyon.
Vœux du Paon, finished after 1315.

Brisebarre.
Restor du Paon, cir. 1330.

Jean de le Mote.
Parfait du Paon, 1340.

MSS., Bibl. Nat. (18) ; Bodley, 264 ; Hatton, 67 ; Reg. 19, D. 1 ; Add. 16, 956, etc. (For MSS., *see* "Romania," xi. p. 213 ff.)

A compilation written in England by Eustache, or Thomas de Kent, dates probably from before the middle of 13th century ; it was entitled, " Le Roman de toute Chevalerie" (§ 56.)

28 From the beginning of the 12th century translations and adaptations were made from Latin versions of Greek works. Among the first of these works is :

Roman de Thèbes (rhymed octosyllabic verse), cir. 1150. This work has been ascribed to Benoît de Sainte Maure or More, but the editor considers that differences in the language between this work and the following, which is incontestably by this author, precludes this supposition, which, however, G. Paris thinks a probable one. The versions preserved in the MSS. differ. The poem had for its source the "Thebais" of Statius, or rather a résumé of the latter work preceded by a life of Oedipus. *Ed.*, L. Constans, "Anc. Textes France," 1890. *MSS.*, Bibl. Nat. fr. 375, 60, 784 ; Phillipps, 8384 ; Add. 34114 (Spalding) ; Angers (two fragments).

Roman d'Énée (rhymed octosyllabic verse). The earliest French imitation of Virgil, or "travesty," cir. 1160 (S. de G., cir. 1150). The authorship of this poem is doubtful. S. de Grave, with whom G. Paris and P. de Julleville agree, does not think *Énée* and *Troie* by same author. He rests his date for the poem on the theory that Marie de France made use of it (but *see* "Romania," xxi.). A German translation is extant by Heinrich von Veldeke (*see* Germany, § 19). *Ed.*, Salverda de Grave, 1891; parts only, A. Pey, 1856. *See* "Romania," xxi. 283; Rottig., "Die Verfasserfrage, etc.," 1892. *MSS.*, Bibl. Nat. fr. 60, 784, 1416, 1450, 12603; B.M. Add. 14100, 34114; Montpelier, Ecole Med., 251; Florence, Laur., Plut. xli.

Benoît de Sainte-More. (§ 15.)

Roman de Troie (rhymed octosyllabic verse), cir. 1165. This poem is thought to be of earlier date than the "Roman d'Enée," an opinion based on certain linguistic details in the latter poem, and by its introductory lines, which seem to be a kind of continuation of the "Roman de Troie" (P. de Julleville). The "riche dame de riche roi" referred to in poem, was probably either Eleanor, wife of Henry ii., or Adèle of Champagne, wife of Louis vii. If the latter, it would argue against this poet being the author of the "Chronique des Ducs de Normandie," which was written at request of Henry ii., notwithstanding arguments as to language, style, etc., which speak for his authorship. The poem was put into prose in second half of 13th cent. Translated into German (1190-1216) by Herbort v. Fritzlâr. For sources of poem, *see* England, Joseph of Exeter, § 31. *Ed.*, A. Joly, 1870-71. *MSS.*, Twenty-seven complete MSS.: Bible Nat. (13), Arsenal (2), B.M. Add. 30, 863; Harl. 4482; Montpellier, Fac. Med.; Vienne; Vatican; St. Petersburg; Milan (oldest and best); Phillipps, 8384.

Chrétien de Troies. (*See* Arthurian Cycle, § 26.)

Philomèle. This poem, believed to be the one referred to by C. de Troies himself as "la muance de la hupe et de l'aronde et du rossignol" (Tereus, Progne, and Philomela) once thought to be lost, was found incorporated in the work of Chrestien Legouais' "Ovide Moralisé," in which the author expressly states that he gives the tale as written by "Crestiens." *See* "Hist. Litt.," vol. xxix.   *MSS.*, Bibl. Nat. fr. (six MSS.), B.M. Add. 10324; Geneva fr. 176; etc.   *See* "Ovide Moralisé" (§ 72).

Other favourite tales from Ovid were those of

Pyramus and Thisbe (older version preserved in "Ovide Moralisé"), and of *Narcisse.*   *MSS.*, Bibl. Nat. fr. 837, 19152; Berlin (Hamilton) and MSS. of "Ovide Moralisé."

29   ROMANCES.
Chiefly from Eastern Sources.

Gautier d'Arras.

Éracle, cir. 1165 (octosyllabic couplets).   The first part is taken from a Greek romance, of which the modern poem of "Ptocholéon"[1] is a version (G. Paris); the second part is of Eastern origin.

Éracle is born gifted with three peculiar powers—a knowledge of precious stones, of horses, and of women.   After recovering the cross from the Persian king, Cosroes, he becomes and dies Emperor of Constantinople.   *MSS.*, Bibl. Nat. fr. 1444, 24430; Turin, Bibl. Naz. L. i. 13.

The other poem by this author is of Celtic origin :

Ille et Galéron, 1170 (octo. couplets).   Another form of the tale told in the "lai d'Eliduc" (§ 31).   *Ed.*, Works, E. Löseth, "Bibl. Franç. du moyen Âge," 1890; Förster, "Rom. Bibl.," 1891.   *See* G. Paris, "Comptes Rendus. Acad. Inscr.," 1887 (on connection with "Éliduc" and "Gille de Trasignies"), and "Romania," xxi.   *MS.*, Bibl. Nat. fr. 375.

Huon de Rotelande.   Anglo-Norman.

Hippomédon.   In two parts, cir. 1185.   Part 1 : Tournament of three days; hero appears in turn in white, red, and

---

[1] For "Ptocholéon," *see* "Collection de Monuments pour servir a l'étude de la langue néo-hellinique," No. 19, 1869.

black armour, and is on all occasions victorious ; he disappears without claiming the hand of the heroine, the Duchess of Calabria, called "La Fière." Part 2 : Hippomédon reappears dressed as a fool, and rescues the heroine. In this poem the author refers to Walter Map, as another who knew "the art of lying." Three English versions extant (one prose). These are edited with French version by Kölbing and Koschwitz, 1890. *MSS.*, B.M. Cott. Vesp. A. vii. ; Egerton, 2515 ; Bodl. Rawl. Misc. 1370 (fragment).

Protésilaus, one of the sons of Hippomédon who is killed before Thebes. To escape his brother's jealousy he leaves Calabria, but finally returns and regains his patrimony ; reconciliation of brothers. *See* Ward, "Catalogue of Romances, etc.," vol. i. p. 728 seq. *MSS.*, Egerton, 2515 ; Bibl. Nat. fr. 2169 (imperfect).

Aimon de Varenne, or de Châtillon.

Florimont, 1188. A fictitious personage ; poem genealogically connected with Alexander Cycle, Florimont being grandfather of Alexander the Great. Written in honour of a lady whose personality is veiled. *See* A. Risop, "Archiv f. d. Studium d. neueren Sprachen, etc.," 1885. *MSS.*, B.M. Harl. 4487, 3983 ; Bibl. Nat. (7 MSS.), fr. 353, 792, etc. ; S. Mark, 22 ; Turin, L. ii. 16.

Alexandre de Bernay, or de Paris. (§ 27, *see* La Belle Hélène, § 82.)

Athis et Porphirias (last third of century). Two friends, of whom the former sacrifices his love for the sake of the latter ; later on Porphirias, in return, gives himself up as the pretended perpetrator of a crime to save his friend's life : both are delivered. The second part is concerned with the lives of Athis and the sister of Porphyrias. All authorities do not consider that this poem is assigned to A. de Bernay on sufficient grounds. *Ed.*, Alfred Weber, 1881 (first part, Ed. considers that second part is by another poet) ; and M. H. Borg., 1882 (Stockholm MS.). *MSS.*, Bibl. Nat. fr. 793, 794 ; B.M. Add. 16441 ; Stockholm ; S. Petersburg (different version). (Germany, § 34.)

Anonymous (by some authorities attributed to Denis Pyramus) ; G. Paris entirely refutes this idea (*see* " Romania," iv. 148).

Parthénopeu de Blois (mostly in rhymed octosyllabic couplets). This is similar to the tale of " Cupid and Psyche," with the actors reversed ; the fairy Melior loses her power of magic and sends Parthénopeu away ; finally he wins her again by his brilliant feats at a tournament. The tale has come down in two versions. Two English versions are extant (England, § 63), and a German (§ 34). *Ed.*, Kölbing, " Beiträge zur vergleichenden Geschichte der Romantischen Poesie u Prosa," 1876 ; *see* same author, " Ueber die Verschiedenen Gestaltungen der Partonopeus Sage," 1875. *MSS.*, Nat. Bibl. fr. 19152, 368, 792 (frag.) ; Arsenal, 2986 ; Tours ; Berne.

Le Comte de Poitiers. Last third of century. Among many versions of this tale may be mentioned " Guillaume de Dole," " La Violette," prose tale of " Flore et Jehane " (§§ 57, 43), and " Cymbeline." *Ed.*, Fr. Michel, 1831. *MS.*, Arsenal, B.L., 325.

Floire et Blanceflor. Last third of century. This romance is connected with the Carolingian Cycle, Blanceflor being the mother of Berte au Grand Pied, the mother of Charlemagne. (For outline of tale, *see* England, § 40.) Two versions are extant of the 12th century. *Ed.*, both versions, E. du Meril, 1850. *See* Sundmacher, " Die Altfr. u. Mhd. (Middle High German), Bearbeitungen der Sage. v. F. u. B.," 1872 ; Herzog, " Die beiden sagen Kreise. v. F. u. B.," 1884). *MSS.*, Older version, Bibl. Nat. 375, 1447, 12562 ; later version, Bibl. Nat. 19, 152 ; Arsenal, 3313 (a Cotton MS. destroyed by fire).

Aucassin et Nicolette. Last third of century, partly in prose, partly in assonanced laisses of seven syllables, whence called a *Chantefable.* Garin, Comte de Beaucaire, being opposed to his son's love for Nicolette, shuts him up in a tower ; Nicolette is likewise imprisoned, but escapes to the forest, and here

Aucassin finally meets her again. *Ed.*, G. Paris, with trans. into modern French by A. Beda, 1878; H. Suchier, 1889; facsimile, F. W. Bourdillon, Clarendon Press, 1896; trans. into English, Bourdillon, 1897; into modern French, with English trans. by A. R. Macdonough, preface by G. Paris, 1880. *MS.*, Bibl. Nat. fr. 2168.

Amadas et Idoine. Extant in Anglo-Norman and French, the A.-N. being the earlier poem. Amadas is for some time mad from the effects of love. *Ed.*, Hippeau, 1863; *see* also art. by G. Paris, "English Miscellany" (Furnival), 1901. *MSS.*, Göttingen (two fragments), A.-Norman; Bibl. Nat. fr. 375, French.

ROMANS À TIROIRS.

See G. Paris, "Hist. litt. moyen Âge," § 71.

Dolopathos and Roman des Sept Sages de Rome (*see* England, § 65). From the Indian tale of Sindibâd originated the two western versions of "Dolopathos," and the "Sept Sages." (*See* Spain, § 11.) "Dolopathos," written in Latin by Jean de Hauteseille (Oesterley, 1873), towards close of 12th century, was shortly after put into French verse by Herbert. Many versions, both Latin and French, exist of the "Sept Sages," which resemble one another to a certain extent, but of which the exact relationship one with the other has been difficult to determine. To this century belongs a version in verse, and a prose version is extant of 13th. There were evidently variants of the verse version, one of which was edited by Keller, 1836. *Ed.* (prose) Leroux de Lincy, 1838 (two versions); G. Paris (two versions), Soc. Anc. Textes, 1878; "Dolopathos," *ed.* Brunet et Montaiglon, 1856. *See* Ward, "Cat. Rom.," ii. 199. *MSS.*, Prose versions, Bibl. Nat. and Arsenal (19); Brussels (4); Univ. Libr., Camb., Gg. i. 1; Harl. 3860. Herbert's verse, Bibl. Nat. fr. 1450; 24301; Nouv. acq. 934; Montpellier.

30 *Romances of Teutonic Origin.*

Mestre Thomas (not identical with the author of "Tristan," Gröber).

Horn et Rimenhild (*see* England, King Horn, § 38).
Ed., R. Brede and E. Stengel, "Ausg. u. Abh., Rom.
Phil.," viii., 1883.   *MSS.*, Bodl. Douce, 132 ; Harl. 527 ;
Camb. Univ. Libr., Ff. vi. 17.   (None of the MSS.
complete.)

Le lai d'Aveloc (*see* England, Havelok, § 38).   *See*
Kupferschmidt, "Die Haveloksage bei Gaimar, etc.," "Rom.
Studien," iv.   *MSS.*, Phillipps ; Herald's College (MS. of
Wace's "Brut" and continuation of Gaimar to which the "lai
d'Aveloc" is attached).

Gui de Warwick.   First third of century (*see* England,
§ 64).   Inedited.   *See* Winneberger, "Frankfurter Neuphil.
Beiträge," 1887, 1889.   *MSS.*, Bibl. Nat. fr. 1476,
1669 ; B.M. Reg. 8, F. ix. ; Harl. 3775 ; Coll. of Arms ;
C.C.C.C. ; Bod. Rawl. D. 913 ; Wolfenbüttel ; Phillipps.

Waldef.   Said to be based on a lost English poem (*see*
"Romania," xv.).

Guillaume de Palerne, cir. 1205.   (*See* England, § 64.)
Ed., H. Michelant, 1876.   *MS.*, Arsenal, 6565.

31   Lais.

This name is of Celtic origin, and originally signified the
melodies the bards played on the "rote," a kind of small
harp, these musical pieces being preceded by an explanatory
narrative.   The title was adopted by the French and used
by them to signify both music and text.   About twenty
lais are extant, some of which are thought to date back
to 12th century.   These narrative lais are written in octosyllabic verse.   There was also the "lai lyrique," which,
on account of its similarity of form with the "descort,"
became confounded with it ; in each there is irregularity both
in strophe-form and in the number of syllables composing the
lines.   The music of these lais and descorts has been preserved
in more than one MS., and has helped to enable scholars to
reconstruct the old metre.   *See* "Lais et Descorts Français
du xiiie Siècle, Texte et Musique."   *Ed.*, A. Jeanroy, L.
Brandin, and P. Aubry, 1901 (with facsimiles from MSS.).

Marie de France (*see* under Fables). It was probably in the middle or second half of this century that Marie wrote or published her works in England. She is the only lai writer whom we know by name, and her works are the chief representative of this class of poem. Her lais were based on Celtic material which she moulded into the courtly form of the day. Marie was either of Norman origin or from the Ile de France; but her writings show avoidance of several peculiarities characteristic of the Anglo-Norman.

Twelve lais contained in the Harleian MS. are assigned without hesitation to Marie; of others found in various MSS., it is more difficult to fix the authorship with certainty. The Harleian MS., which also contains the Fables, is the only one in which the prologue to the lais is extant. *MSS.*, Harl. 978; Cott. Vesp. B. xiv. (only Lanval). Bibl. Nat., Nouv. Acq., 1104, fr. 2168, 24432 (only Yonec).

Guigemar. A wounded knight is borne in a magic ship to an unknown land. When he and his lady-love, who has healed him, part, they exchange a magic knot and magic belt. The principal features of this tale, at times much effaced and altered, are found in " Graelent," " Lanval," " Partenopeu," "Oger le Danois." " The lai of 'Guingamor' offers one of the best versions of the theme; the simplest and most ancient was the 'Voyage of Bran.'" *See* G. Paris, " Romania," p. 323, 1898.

Equitan. A king falls in love with his seneschal's wife; they meet their death in a hot bath, in which she had intended to kill her husband.

Le Fraisne. (*See* England, § 66.)

Bisclaveret. Transformation of a man, two or three days a week, into a Werwolf. The tale is similar to that in " Lai de Melion."

Lanval. Falls in love with fairy; forbidden to speak of her or praise her beauty to anyone; doing so, Lanval loses sight of her, and she only re-appears at Arthur's court to save him from death. The tale is similar to " Lai de Graelent." (England, " Sir Launfal," § 59), *see* Schofield, " The Lays of Graelent and Lanval," " Pub. Mod. Lang. Assoc.," xv.

Les deux Amants (*dous Amanz*). A lover may only win his lady-love by carrying her up to the top of Mont S. Michel; a magic potion is given him to help accomplish the task, but arrived at the summit he dies, and his loved one does not survive him.

Yonec. Lover in form of a bird, visits his lady-love at night.

Laustic. On pretence of listening to the nightingale, the lovers rise at night to look at one another from their respective towers. The tale is found in the "Gesta Romanorum," and a similar tale to this and to that of "Bisclaveret" is found in "Renard le Contrefait." There is also a reference to the tale in "Owl and Nightingale." (England, § 37.)

Milon. Fight between father and son. Tale familiar in all countries. (*See* "Sire Degarre," England, § 40.)

Chaitivel. Name of the survivor of four knights who fight for a lady-love.

Chevrefeuille. Incident connected with Tristan and Iseut.

Éliduc. Love of a knight for two women; one thought to be dead is restored by a magic flower, and the other, the knight's wife, resigns her husband to her.

Ed., C. Warnke, "Bibl. Norm.," vol. iii., 1885, 1900.

N.B.—G. Paris thinks Marie may be the authoress of "L'Epine" and "Tidorel," but not of "Tiolet," and also attributes "Guingamor" to her (Litt. moyen Âge, § 55).

Of other well-known lais may be mentioned: *Ignaure*, and *Guiron*, both similar in tale to *Châtelain de Couci*; *lai du Cor*, a horn out of which only husbands of faithful wives can drink; "Mantel Maltaillé," which only fits faithful wives. *See* Fr. Michel, "Lais Inédits des xiie et xiiie Siècles," 1836; G. Paris, "Lais Inédits," "Romania," viii., 1879; Schofield (on Guingamor), "Child Memorial Vol.," 1896, and review by G. Paris, "Romania," 27, 1898. E. Rickert, "Marie de France" (seven lais done into English prose); J. L. Weston, "Four Lays rendered into English prose," 1900.

Another charming lai is the *Lai d'Ombre* by Jehan Renart. *Ed.*, Bédier, 1890.　　*MS.*, Bibl. Nat. fr. 1553.

32   Fables. Contes de Renard. Fableaux.

See Petit de Julleville, vol. ii. ; " Les Fables," etc.

Fables formed a considerable branch of French literature in the Middle Ages ; they served in the schools as examples of rhetoric and style, and were also used for moral instruction.

We have no positive knowledge of the origin of the Æsopic fable ; those that were known under the name of Æsop were translated into Latin. The two most popular of these collections of fables, were those of " Avianus " and " Phaedrus." Of " Avianus," there exist two versions in Latin prose, and two abridged versions in verse ; only one French translation, however, is extant, of the 14th century, known by the name of " Avionnet " ; it only contains eighteen fables.

The fables of Phædrus were known as early as, or perhaps earlier than the 9th century, under the name of " Romulus," who until the 14th century was also named as the Latin translator. Of the many Latin collections of fables which were based on Romulus, the one by an anonymous writer, " Anonyme de Névelet," became the model for two versions in French verse :

Isopet de Lyon, 13th century.   *Ed.*, Foerster, 1882.

Isopet i. (Avionnet) (Robert), 14th century.

Alexander of Neckham's " Novus Aesopus " (England, § 31), also an outcome of Romulus, gave birth to two other French versions.

Isopet de Chartres.   *Ed.*, Duplessis, " Fables en vers du xiiime Siècle," 1834.

Isopet ii. (Robert).

Ed., Robert, " Fables inédites des xiie, xiiie, and xive centuries, etc.," 1825. *See* L. Hervieux, " Les Fabulistes Latins, etc.," 1844.

Marie de France. (*See* Lais, § 40.)

Isopet (162 Fables). Taken from an English version of a Latin original, which Marie ascribed to Aelfred the Great ; the English version is lost, but judging by Latin versions

extant of the original, it is evident that much fresh material
was found in it by Marie. Some only of the Fables are
contained in Romulus; others are thought to have been
transmitted orally, and some Oriental tales to have been
known through the Jews. The latter had rich stores of
Fables; one Berachyah made a collection in the 13th
century. *Ed.*, C. Warnke, "Bibl. Norm.," vol. 6, 1898.
MSS., Twenty-three MSS., Bibl. Nat. (14); B.M.,
Cott. Vesp. B. xiv.; Harl. 978, 4333; Bodl. Douce, 132;
Univ. Libr., Camb., Ee. 6, ii.; Arsenal, 3142; York
Minster, Brussels, Vatican.

Roman de Renard.

See Jonckbloet, "Etudes sur le R. de R.," 1863; Rothe,
"Les Romans du Renard examinés," 1845; Knorr, "Diè 20
Branche des R. de R., etc.," 1866; E. Voigt, "Isengrimus,"
1884.

The earliest extant specimen of the animal epic is "Ecbasis
Captivi," a Latin poem of early 10th century; the animal
epic then developed through the Latin "Isengrimus" (or
"Reinardus Vulpes") (11th or early 12th century), by
Magister Nivardus, which was a work of Flemish origin; the
French "Roman de Renart," composed of several branches; the
"Reinhert Fuchs," by Heinrich der Glîchesaere (*see* Germany,
§ 17); the "Roman van den Vos Reinaerde," or "Reinart de
Vos," also a Flemish work, by Willem, with a second part by
Claes van Acen, end 12th and cir. middle 13th centuries; and
low German "Reineke Vos" of late 15th century, to its treatment in later days by Goethe. The French "Roman de
Renard" probably arose in the North, but its origin is obscure,
and of its authors only three names have come down to us—
Richard de Lison, a Norman prelate, Pierre de Saint-Cloud,
and a priest of Croix-en-Brie. The tales in connection with
the Renard Cycle increased in number until the close of the
13th century; about twenty-five are extant. Only later
versions are extant of the earlier French branches, but their
chief features have been transmitted through Latin and German
imitations. The poems were written in octosyllabic rhyming
couplets. The most ancient appears to be

Le Pèlerinage Renard.—Perhaps the work of Pierre de St. Cloud (§ 27). It is thought to date back to 12th century.

Le Jugement de Renard. One of the most important branches of the Roman, of which after poems were more or less inferior reproductions. It tells with clever irony of the escape of a knight from merited punishment, by going off to the Holy Land.

"Roman de Renard," *ed.*, C. Potvin, 1891; Martin, 1882. *See* L. Sudre, "Les Sources du Roman de Renard," 1892; and G. Paris, "Le Roman de Renard," 1895 (on Sudre's work); P. de Julleville, *op cit.*, vol. ii.

33 FABLEAUX.

(G. Paris considers this a preferable form to Fabliaux.) About 150 of these are extant; they are mostly amusing tales in verse, and were written from the middle of the 12th to the beginning of the 14th century; chiefly in octosyllabic couplets.

It is difficult in all cases to draw a line between the *lais* and the *fableaux*; the lais were generally more refined in subject and of higher tone, but many so-called fableaux might in these respects be placed with them, although the generality were coarser and more cynical; the fableaux were not as long as the romans, and were distinguished from the "dits" by having no didactic intention in their tales. Their heroes were chiefly of the bourgeois class, of the lower clergy, or generally bad characters. Most of the tales contained in the fableaux are such as appear common to many nations, and still form part of the folk-lore in some countries. Like the "Roman de Renard" the fableaux appear to have had their origin in the North or North-East of France.

The most ancient fableau extant is—

Richeut (1159). Tale of a courtisane and her son.

Of others a few names may be given—

Li Fabliau du Vilain Mire. The idea was borrowed by Molière in "Le Médecin malgré lui."

Les trois Aveugles de Compiègne.   Tale of three friends who each thinks the other has received a gold piece, etc.

Le Prêtre aux mûres.   One of the simpler fableaux.

Le Convoiteux et l'envieux.   "L'envieux" is offered a gift on condition the other has double; he asks for an eye to be taken out.

Saint Pierre et le Jongleur.   The latter is left in charge of hell by the devil, but loses all the souls to S. Peter in a game of dice; thereafter the devil will have no jongleurs in his regions.   Bibl. Nat. 7218, 7615, 7989, etc.

MSS., An immense number of MSS. extant, *see* Preface to Le Grand D'aussy, "Fabliaux et Contes."   For contents of MS. 7218, *see* P. Paris, "Les Manuscrits Français."

N.B.—The greater number of fableaux were written at the close of the 12th or beginning of 13th century.   Jean de Condé, who died 1340, was the last of the writers of fableaux. The names of writers of fableaux, and prose translation of the same into modern French, are given in Legrand D'aussy, "Fabliaux et Contes, Fables et Romans du xiie et du xiiie Siècle, traduits ou extraits," 1829; Méon, "Fabliaux, Contes, et Dits," 1808, 1823; Montaiglon et Raynaud "Recueil Général des Fabliaux"; Jubinal, "Nouveau Recueil de Contes, Dits, et Fables," 1839.

84   Lyric Poetry.

For following details, *see* A. Jeanroy, "Les Origines de la Poésie lyrique au moyen Âge," 1885, 1904; G. Paris, Treatise on above work, 1892.

Nearly all the lyric poetry of the Middle Ages may be traced back to the songs which were sung in accompaniment to the dance during the festivities that were held in celebration of the revival of Spring, more particularly to those which were associated with the Kalends of May, of which class were the Reverdies (Raverdies, Renverdies). These festivities in their turn originated in still more ancient pagan customs.   These rural songs first acquired their more

chivalric tone in the middle region of France, Poitou, la
Marche, and Limousin, whence, carried into the aristocratic
circles of the North, they remained for some time unchanged
in form; while in the South, to which region they were also
transported, they soon became more or less transformed. Actual
imitation of the Troubadours by the Northern poets dates back
only to the middle of the 12th century (G. Paris, p. 58).
The dances referred to above were known as "Caroles"; they
were generally danced by women alone, the men looking on,
but under any circumstances the dancers moved round hand
and hand in a circle. One of the women started the song,
and the other dancers took up the refrain. References in old
texts make it clear that such was the custom at these rural
festivals; it was a proceeding which called forth Jacques de
Vitry's invectives, who denounces the "Carole" as a circle
of which the centre is the devil, while everybody turns to the
left because all are on their way to everlasting death. The
account given by Ordericus Vitalis of the cruel fate which
befel a knight, Luc de la Barre, because he had ventured to
compose some satirical verses on King Henry I., 1124, is
proof of the existence of songs in the earlier part of the
century, and various proofs are forthcoming that secular songs,
some of them love-songs, were sung as accompaniment to
dancing by men and women, many centuries previously; such
are the admonitions of the clergy concerning them, and decrees
of the councils of Auxerre, Châlons, Arles, and Paris; the
earliest of these dates end 6th and beginning 7th century.

The following are the chief forms represented in the early
lyric poetry:

Chansons d'Histoire or *Chansons de toile*. Written in strophes
with a refrain. So called because the subject was some brief
incident in the course of love, or tale of adventure, the second
designation signifying probably that they were sung by women at
work. This class of poem and the *Chansons à personnages*,
or *Chansons de mal-mariées*, have been sometimes classed
together under the heading of "Romances." In these
Chansons de mal-mariées, the poet himself is generally represented as being present either as audience only, or as an

interested party in the affair. The earliest form was that of
the Monologue, being the complaint of a woman over the
misery of her marriage, the ill-conduct of her husband being
occasionally emphasized by a description of her own charms.
A second character appears on the scenes in the later form,
sometimes a husband, sometimes a friend, and a dialogue
ensues, the poet himself undertaking now and then to act the
part of consoler. These chansons date from the 13th century
only.

Pastourelle. The actual meaning is "Jeune pastoure,"
and the lyric so called therefore was not a pastoral song, but
a song sung by a "jeune bergère" (young shepherdess). It
represents the wooing of a shepherdess by a man of higher
rank, generally a knight, who comes across her accidentally,
and immediately makes love to her. Although the framework
is stereotyped, there is no lack of variety in the details, and
the dénouement is not by any means always the same, an
unexpected and amusing turn being given occasionally to the
address of the last speaker. M. Paris thinks the intervention
of the knight was not an essential motive in the primitive
form, which was another example of a woman's song.
Marcabrun, whose death is conjectured to have taken place
cir. 1150, left two pastourelles, and after that the form seems
for a while to have been discarded in Provence, as the chief
troubadours have left no specimen of this class of lyric; it
reappears at the close of the century but in a garb "tout
courtois." Meanwhile the pastourelle had been flourishing in
the North, and here M. Paris and M. Jeanroy disagree, for
the former thinks the revived pastourelle of the South was an
imitation of that of the North, as the name of "Robin," which
is used by the Troubadours, must, according to him, have
been an importation from the French, the Trouvères having
previously adopted it for their country lovers; M. Jeanroy,
however, rejects the idea of imitation. The latter considers
the pastourelle to be a mingling of three elements: the *contrasto*
(of which the oldest specimen is that of Cielo dal Camo, *see*
Italy, § 12); the *oaristys* (a name borrowed from "Theo-
critus"); a *gab*, or *vanto* (boast) as the poet is generally the
hero of his own poem. M. Paris, thinks this division still

leaves certain characteristics of the poem unexplained; the rural setting of the pastourelle is not thereby accounted for.

Aube. The parting of lovers at dawn. Here also the primitive form is thought to have been a monologue of the woman. In its extant specimens the essential feature of the "aube" is the desire on the part of the lovers not to believe that the growing light, and the lark's singing, are the signs of approaching day; and their endeavour to interpret them as the accompaniments of night. The parting of Romeo and Juliet is too well known to need mention; Juliet tries to persuade herself that the hour of parting has not yet come, just in the same way as the heroines of the old French aube. In the old times it was also the watchman's cry, announcing the break of day, that gave warning to the lovers. M. Jeanroy quotes interesting parallels.

M. Jeanroy gives the chief specimen of another class of lyric, which would seem to be especially related to early spring songs : here the subject is pleasing, and instead of the usual men and women, birds, the nightingale taking the lead, are introduced as speakers; if a woman appears it is in a purely idyllic form. The chansons known as *Transformations* also gave scope for charming verse. Here the lady, to escape the solicitations of her lover, threatens to transform herself into various things, but the lover is equally ready to do the same ; if she is a hare, he will be a running dog; if she an apple, he a basket; if she a star, he a white cloud to cover her—needless to say such persistency of attachment wins the day. *See* V. Smith, "Vieilles Chansons recueillies en Velay et en Florez," "Romania," vii. 628.

M. Jeanroy particularly aims at showing in his work that the varieties of lyric of which he treats, whatever may have been their origin, are not *popular* in their extant forms, but aristocratic in tone and address.

The *Rotrouenge* (etymology unknown), a song generally accompanied by a refrain, of which Richard Coeur de Lion's poem, sent to his subjects from prison, is a specimen; under the title occur also political and satirical poems; the *serventois*, songs of a more serious nature, composed for, or by, those in the service of the nobles; or, according to another suggestion, with which M. Paris does not agree, a poem depending on another (*asservi*), that is, composed to an air already known; the precise type of this class of poem has not been determined. (*see* "Romania," vii. 626); the *motet*, for more than one voice; the *balette*, *estampie*, *rondeau*, and *virelai*, songs for dancing, are other forms found among the French lyrics.

The refrains become frequent as we approach the 14th century, whence M. Jeanroy draws the conclusion that they are not necessarily the actual remains of older popular poetry, but were imitations originating with the courtly poets.

LYRIC POETS.

END XIITH AND EARLY XIIITH CENTURY.

Conon (Quesnes) de Béthune, d. cir. 1220. Marie, Comtesse de Champagne, was the object of this poet's devotion. C. de B. was also a soldier, and played a distinguished part in the 4th Crusade. *Ed.*, Wallensköld, 1891.

Huon d'Oisi and **Alard de Caux,** were also soldiers as well as poets.

Richard, Coeur de Lion. His "Rotrouenge," written from his German prison in 1191–94, is given in Bartsch, "Langue et Litt.," p. 311, and Paris and Langlois "Chrestomathie."

Blondel de Nesle. Famous, in name at least, as the deliverer of Richard. A poem ed. in Bartsch (*op. cit.*).

Gautier d' Espinaus (Épinal), fl. 1180–90.

Gace Brulé, mentioned in the "Chroniques de S. Denis" as one of the best and most celebrated of the lyrists.

Châtelain de Couci. The name of this poet is associated with the Dame de Fayel in a poem of later date (§ 57).

MSS., containing poems by above poets, Bibl. Nat. fr. 20050, 844, 845, 846, 12615; Arsenal, B.L. fr. 63; Berne. *Ed.*, "La Poésie lyrique au moyen Âge," G. Paris; L. Clédat, "La Poésie lyrique et Satirique du moyen Âge"; G. Raynaud, "Bibliographie des Chansonniers français," 1884; Meyer u. Raynaud, "Les Chansonniers français de la Bibl. St. Germain des-Près" (Nat. Bibl. 20050); Bartsch, "Altfranzösische Volkslieder," 1882; "Romanzen u. Pastourellen," 1870.; Wackernagel, "Altfranzösische Lieder u. Leiche," 1846.

35 DRAMA.

See Petit de Julleville, "Les Mystères," 1880; and "Hist. de la Langue et Litt.," vol. ii.; Monmerque et Michel, "Théatre français du moyen Âge," 1839; Sépet, "Le Drame religieux au moyen Âge," 1903.

Le Jeu d'Adam (eight and ten-syllabled lines, rhyming in couplets), Anglo-Norman play, was written in England.
Part 1. The Fall.
  ,, 2. Death of Abel.
  ,, 3. Prophecy of the Saviour by the Prophets.
This is the most ancient "jeu" in French. Before each scene the passage from the Bible relative to it was read in Latin, and afterwards in the vernacular. It appears to have been performed outside the Church, in the porch. *Ed.*, K. Grass, "Das Adamspiel" (with the "Quinze Signes du Jugement") Rom. Bibl. vi. 1891; Bartsch, "Chrestomathie." *MSS.*, Tours, Municipal Libr., 927.

Résurrection du Sauveur (fragment). *Ed.*, Jubinal, "La Resurrection du Sauveur" (French verse, given with modern prose translation), 1834. *MS.*, Bibl. Nat. fds. fr. 902.

Hilarius, pupil of Abelard. Earlier half of 12th century.

Three scriptural dramas, written in Latin, two of which have French refrains.

Miracle of St. Nicholas.

Raising of Lazarus.

Daniel.

Ed., Champollion-Figeac ("Hilarii versus et Ludi"), pp. 34, 27, 43; 1838. Meril, "Origines Latines du Théatre Moderne," pp. 272, 225, 241; 1849. *MSS.*, Bibl. Nat., Supp. Lat., 1008.

These are, among others of the period, specimens of the "Drame Liturgique," performed within the church.

36   PROVENÇAL POETRY.

The lyric was the chief feature of Provençal poetry; the South did not apparently rival the North in epic and romance, of which only a few remains have come down to us from the Troubadours. The 12th and 13th centuries covered the golden period of Provençal poetry, which declined with the loss of political independence. The chief centres of Provençal literature in France were the court of Aliénor de Poitiers, afterwards wife of Henry II. of England, and that of her daughter Marie de Champagne. Of extant epic and narrative, the best work is "Girart de Rosilho" (*see* § 19); there are besides a Provençal version of "Fierabras"; "Daurel et Beton" (version of Beuves de Hanstone); "Blandin de Cornouailles" (Cornoalha); "Flamenca," cir. 1235; and the fragment of a "Roman d'Arles," telling of the conflict between Saracens and Christians round Arles and Orange. A poetical account of the Albigensian war, by Guillem de Tudela also remains, and a fragment of "Siege of Antioch" ("Romania," xvii.). The romance of "Jaufre" belongs to the Arthurian Cycle, the hero being a Knight of the Round Table. A Provençal "Lancelot" has been ascribed to Arnaut Daniel, thought by some to be extant in the German version of "Zatzikhoven"; and the "Perceval" of Kiot, or Guiot, mentioned by W. of Eschenbach, was probably composed on the borders of the North and South.

Other fragments include an "Alexander." The Fable is poorly represented. Of remains of Drama the best extant specimen is the "Mystère de S. Agnes." The earliest attempt at a Grammar, produced in modern Europe, was the "Razos de trobar," a guide to the art of "trouver" by Raimon Vidal, who was also a celebrated writer of tales. Specimens are also extant of religious and didactic writings.

The Songs of the Troubadors and their biographies are found in collections preserved in MSS., dating from the 13th century. The greater number are in the Nat. Bibl., Paris, and the Vatican Library; others are in the Libraries of Modena, Milan, Rome, etc., one at Oxford (Bodl. Douce, 269), and one among the Phillipps MSS.

Raynouard, "Choix des Poésies Originales des Trouba-dours"; Diez, "Die Poesie der Troubadours," 1827; "Leben u. Werke des Troubadours," 1882; Fauriel, "Histoire de la Poésie Provençale," 1847; Restori, "Lett. Prov.," 1891; Bartsch, "Grundrisz der Provenzal Litt.," 1872; A. Stimming, "Grundrisz der Rom. Phil.," Bd. 2, Abth. 2; C. Chabaneau, "Les Biographies des Trouba-dours," 1885; Meyer, "De l'influence des Troubadours sur la Poésie des Peuples Romans," "Romania," v. For the "Débat" (Tensos) as represented in Provençal poetry, *see* Selbach, "Das Streitgedicht in der Provenzalischen Lyrik," 1886. For Chrestomathies, *see* under Bartsch, and Appel.

37 XIIItH CENTURY.

Prose.

Science.

Works of Science in the Middle Ages were, for the most part, translations from the Latin. Various Encyclopedias called "Miroir" or "Image du Monde," "Lucidaire," "Trésor," "Nature des Choses," were also compiled from earlier writers, for the purpose of communicating the science of the day to the laity, who knew little or no Latin. One of the earliest Latin compilations of this kind was the "Imago

Mundi" by Honorius d'Autun (cir. 1120); two large works of similar design were written by Barthélimi l'Anglais ("De Proprietatibus rerum,") and by Thomas de Cantimpré ("Liber de Natura Rerum"). A later one of considerable scope was the "unparalleled encyclopedia," the "Speculum Universale," by Vincent de Beauvais (cir. middle of 13th century), which comprised all the different facts and ideas then current in the Christian world.

Roumans de Sydrach, 1243. This is an inferior work to "Placide et Timéo," but still of value for the history of science; it enjoyed great popularity for two centuries, and was translated into nearly every European tongue. The book is also known under the title of "La Fontaine de toutes Sciences." We learn from one of the prologues, that Sidrach, a descendant of Japhet, received a divine revelation of all mysteries and science, including the mystery of the Trinity. He was the astronomer of King Tractabat, and converted King Boctus, twelve hundred years before Christ, to the Trinitarian faith. The dialogue between Sidrach and Boctus was preserved in writing by order of the latter, and the further history of this book is given up to 1243, when Jean Pierre de Lyon transcribed it from a copy in possession of the Patriarch of Antioch, to whom it had been sent by Todre, the philosopher, the latter having obtained it by bribing the Chamberlain of Emperor Frederick II. This Emperor had sent a monk to Tunis, who had translated the work from the Arabic into Latin. The work was probably written somewhat later by Jean Pierre de Lyon. The extant Provençal version may be the original one. An English version in verse is extant of 15th century, by Hughe of Caumpedene, and also an abridgment of same, transcribed by Robert Wakefelde, 1502. *See* "Hist. Litt.," xxxi. 285–318. *MSS.*, Bibl. Nat., several MSS., fr. 1160, 1161, 24395, etc.; Univ. Libr., Camb., Gg. i. 1.; B.M. Add. (2); Harl. (4); Reg. 16, F. v.; Provençal MS., Bibl. Nat. fr. 1158; Eng. vers., Lansdowne, 793; Harl. 4294; abridged, Sloane, 2232.

Le livre des secrets aux Philosophes, or *Dialogue de Placide et Timéo*, cir. 1290. This is perhaps the most ancient book of philosophy in French. It covers a wide range of subjects : Theology, Physiology, Cosmography, etc., and ends with Advice to a Prince. The dialogue is sustained by Placide, who asks questions, and the philosopher, Timéo, who answers them. In the prologue to MS. 212, Jean Bonnet gives himself as author; nothing is known of this writer beyond his own statement that he was a doctor of theology, and a native of Paris. It is thought possible that he only made use of the work of another writer of end of 13th century. Possibly a later edition was prepared by consent, or under the supervision of the author, and joined to two other similar works, for in this conjunction it appears in the early printed text of 16th century, forming the first part of this edition, which is entitled " Le Cuer de Philosophie." (*See* below, Simon de Compiègne.) *See* " Hist. Litt.," xxx. 567–595. *MSS.*, Two known MSS., Bibl. Nat. fr. 212, and 19958.

Simon de Compiègne. Monk of St. Riquier.

Treatise on the Comput. Translated from a Latin work, setting forth the doctrine of Magister Anianus (Maître Aignan); the French and Latin, however, show few points of resemblance. This Treatise by Simon de Compiègne is found with " Placide et Timéo " in " Cuer de Philosophie," joining the third part; the second part is a kind of Cosmography, entitled " L'Espère du ciel et du Monde." *See* " Hist. Litt.," xxx. 590.

Brunet Latin, b. cir. 1220; d. 1294 or 95. A native of Florence, and an adherent of the Guelph faction. After the disaster to the Florentine Guelphs in 1260, he took refuge in France, probably in Paris. While there he translated " Cicero," composed his " Tesoretto " and perhaps " Favoletto," and wrote his great French work " Li Livres dou Trésor." (For Italian works, *see* Italy, § 26.) He was the master, or guide and adviser, of Dante, as also, according to conjecture, of Guido Cavalcanti. Villani, the historian (d. 1348), speaks of him as " Gran filosofo " and " Sommo Maestro in rettorica," and as the first to refine the tastes of the Florentines. For the position assigned to him in the " Inferno " by Dante, *see* Canto xv.

Li Livres dou Trésor, cir. 1265. "Cist livres est apelés Tresors ; car si come li sires qui vuet en petit leu amasser chose de grandisme vaillance . . . tout autressi (aussi) est li cors de cest livre compilez de sapience, si come cil qui est estrais de tous les membres de philosophie en une somme briement (brièvement)." 1st Book. Theoretical Philosophy (Theology, history, natural history, etc.). 2nd Book. Practical Philosophy (Nicomachean Ethics of Aristotle, etc.). 3rd. Book. Rhetoric and Politics. *Ed.*, "Li Livres du Trésor," J. P. Chabaille, 1863 ; "Della Vita e delle opere di Brunetto Latini," trans. from the Danish of R. Renier, by Thor. Sundby, 1884. *MSS.*, Numerous MSS. at Florence, Paris, and other foreign libraries. B.M. Reg. 17, E. 1 ; Reg. 19, C. x. ; Bodleian, Douce.

Jofroi de Watreford (Ireland), who wrote in England, was a translator of various works, among them the "Secret des Secrets," of which the original was wrongly ascribed to Aristotle. J. de Watreford collaborated with Servais Copale ; "original matter in the work renders it more interesting than other contemporary writings of this class."

38 *Medicine.*

Alebrand de Florence, or of Siena.

Le Régime du corps, 1256. Work on general medicine in four parts, compiled from extant medical treatises. *MSS.*, Bibl. Nat. fr. 2021, 2022, 1288 ; Arsenal (six MSS.) ; Brussels (1).

Henri de Mondeville. Surgeon to two kings of France, Philippe le Bel and Louis le Hutin. His name is found written in twelve different ways.

Chirurgie, divided into five treatises. The work was begun 1306 and left unfinished, being interrupted by the death of the author. "It is of interest, not only as regards its chief subject matter, but in throwing light on the estimate in which a surgeon was held in those days, the rate of his fees being very low at times." The original was in Latin, but a translation was made into French by a contemporary of the author; nothing is known of the translator, but certain errors prove that he was not himself a surgeon.   *Ed.*, Dr. A. Bos, Soc. Anc. Textes, 1897; Mod. French, E. Nicaise, 1893. *MSS.*, French trans., Bibl. Nat. fr. 2030.

N.B.—**Bernard de Gordon.** A Professor at Montpellier from 1285, and who was seemingly alive in 1318, wrote several Latin works :

Opus Lilium Medicinae, etc., *De Conservatione Vitae humanae, etc.*, and other smaller works. Published, 1617, at Frankfort. *MS.*, Bibl. Nat. fr. 1288.

39   THE BIBLE.

For following details, *see* Berger, "La Bible Française, etc.," *op. cit.*

Shortly before 1250, in the time of St. Louis, the first French translation of the whole Bible was written at the University of Paris. It became the standard French version of the Scriptures. From the early years of the 14th century it was closely connected with the " Bible Historiale." This work had such unparalleled success throughout the 14th and 15th centuries, that MSS. of it are found all over France and in neighbouring countries, generally enriched by beautiful miniatures. The Church did not, in this case, interfere as usual, when attempts were made to translate and circulate the Scriptures, probably, writes Berger, because the MSS. being of such an elaborate kind, there was no fear of the Bible in this form penetrating to the poor. After the advent of the Valois, the royal families of France began to interest themselves in the translation of the Bible. One was begun for King John, but the work was stopped by the battle of Poictiers. A new version was made under Charles v., but was mostly an imitation of the older one. Despite these efforts, the people, we read, were never in such total ignorance of the Bible as during the 14th and 15th centuries, and matters continued thus until the Reformation.

14

Bible Abrégée. This work of the early 13th century is evidence of the attempts made towards a complete translation of the Scriptures. It contains parts of Genesis, Exodus, Leviticus, Numbers, Deuteronomy, Joshua, Judges, Judith, Esther, Job, Tobias, Wisdom, Proverbs, and Ruth. There are in it quotations from the "Historia Scolastica" of Petrus Comestor (d. 1179).

Paris Bible. This text was fully established before the "Bible Historiale" began to be circulated. *MSS.*, Bibl. Nat. fr. 627 (only complete copy); fr. 899 (fragmentary).

Bible Historiale. This was a free translation of the "Historia Scolastica" of Petrus Comestor, Vice-Chancellor of the University of Paris in 12th century, by Guyart des Moulins (b. 1251, died in 1322). Within twenty years of the translation being written, three-fourths of the Paris Bible were added to it, and it is in this form that it has come down to us. The two texts became so completely allied with one another that from the time the "Bible Historiale" appeared, the first part of the Paris Bible ceased to be copied, and only exists in a few MSS. : the second part of the Paris Bible is now difficult to distinguish from the second part of the "Bible Historiale." (*See* Berger, *op. cit.*) *MSS.*, First part, Paris Bible, Arsenal, 5056; Harl. 616 (Simon d'Ewes); Univ. Libr., Camb. (More); Strasburg. Second part, innumerable MSS.

N.B. — Among other works connected with the Bible may be mentioned a collection of biblical tales and apocryphal legends, called "Bible en français," written by Roger d'Argenteuil; and a versified version of the historical books of the Old and New Testaments by Jean Malkaraume. Three similar works had been composed at an earlier or contemporaneous date, one probably in 12th century, and the example was followed in the 14th by Macé de la Charité. *See* G. Paris, "Litt. moyen Âge," § 136.

For following details, *see* Gaster, "Ilchester Lectures on Greeko-Slavonic Literature."

N.B.—P. Comestor's "Historia Scolastica" was composed cir. 1175, and was the first compilation embracing the entire contents of Old and New Testaments. Dogmatical and prophetical portions of the Bible were excluded, and the whole was rather a paraphrase than a literal translation. The origin of these legends has been a matter of research. The vernacular translations of the various continental countries show an independence in part both from Comestor's History and that given of the world in the fourth division of V. de Beauvais' work. It is evident, therefore, that another source, older than the Hist. Scol. existed. With the exception of that of the Goths, the earliest vernacular version of the Bible is the Slavonic of 9th century; and almost contemporaneously appeared the "Palæa," a Slavonic "Bible Historiale," full of legends and tales. The name denotes that it is of foreign, chiefly Greek production, but the relationship between the Greek and Slavonic is difficult to decide. In course of time the "Palæa" became amplified by the addition of material drawn from different sources, but all of Byzantine or Oriental origin; to the East, therefore, we must look for the cradle of the "Bible Historiale." Similar works exist in Jewish literature: "Book of the Jubilees," or "Book of Adam," dating at latest from the first century B.C.; in this are found most of the minor legends of the "Palæa," and "Sepher Hayashar," a later work. The Greek historical Bible, which was the original of the "Palæa," probably grew out of these. One legend, "The Legend of the Cross," which is found in all the works of this group is wanting in the Comestor group.

Of the French works which are related to the "Palæa" or "Sepher Hayashar," are first the versified Bibles.

Hermann de Valenciennes, 1190.

Versified Bible to Solomon, adorned with legends. The work is much older than that of Comestor.

Geoffroi de Paris, 1243.

"Bible des Sept estats du monde." In this work, "which is certainly independent of Comestor," the legends introduced are identical with those in Hermann's poem.

Macé de la Charité, cir. 1300.

In this versified Bible the glosses are borrowed from another source than Comestor.

Éverat in his versified *Genesis* (cir. 1198) also goes to a foreign source.

The *Mistère du Viel Testament*, a dramatised Bible (*ed.*, Baron J. de Rothschild, 1878, etc., *see* "Bull. Soc. Anc. Textes," xviii. 52) is independent of Comestor. Such a "Bible Historiale" as evidently formed the basis of above works would appear to be preserved in a MS. in the Bibl. Nat. (fr. 9563 is probably a later form of the version used for the "Mistère"). "In it nearly every legendary tale which has been used for dramatising is to be found."

Religious, Didactic.

40 *N.B.*—It was the fashion at this time for preachers to introduce tales or "exemples" from all sources, sacred or profane, into their sermons, in order to render these more attractive to their congregations. The sermons of Jacques de Vitry, Cardinal Archb. of Frascati (d. 1240), addressed to all classes of society, are full of these tales, and his collection is one of the most famous. *Ed.*, Crane, 1890.

Jean, Sire de Joinville, b. cir. 1224; d. 1317–18. (§ 41.)

Credo. A manual of faith composed when about twenty-six years of age, in 1250, and revised nearly forty years later. *MS.*, Bibl. Nat., 1445–7857.

Philippe de Novare, died cir. 1265. Chancellor of Cyprus. (§§ 41, 42.)

Des quatre tenz d'aage d'ome (*Four Ages of Man*). Work composed when author was over seventy years of age. Contains instructions for bringing up children and young people, and for the occupation of adults and the aged. As the result

of the experiences and reflections of a man of high intellectual
ability, writes G. Paris, who had been associated throughout
his life with affairs of the greatest importance, this work is one
of exceptional interest.   *Ed.*, M. de Fréville, Soc. Anc.
Textes, 1888.   *MSS.*, Bibl. Nat. (three MSS.); B.M.
Add. 28260; Metz.

Anonymous.

Vies des pères.   This collection of tales extant in prose and
verse (§§ 10, 48), compiled from the " Lives of the Desert
Fathers" and other sources, was one of the most important
anonymous works of the kind produced during the Middle
Ages.   For a collection of legends dating 1244–1280, *see*
Meyer, "Notices et extraits," xxxv. 2, 467.   *MSS.*,
Bibl. Nat., 13th century, 422, 23111, 24947, etc.

Frère Lorens (or Laurent).

Somme des Vices et des Vertus (or, *Somme Lorens*, *Somme
le roi*).   Composed or compiled 1279.   The explicit of
MSS. runs : "Ce livre compila et fist (some MSS. "parfist")
uns frères de l'ordre des prescheors, à la requeste dou roy de
France Philippe en l'an de l'incarnacion Jhesu Crist M. et
cc.lxxix," indicating that Lorens only compiled or completed
the work.

The "Somme" is not identical as once thought with a
similar work, " Miroir du Monde," of which several MSS. are
extant (*ed.* Chavannes, Soc. Hist. Suisse Rom., vol. i).
Besides this work there is also an older "Miroir" (MS. Bibl.
Nat. 1109) written cir. 1310 or shortly after, the text of
which is apparently of anterior date to the "Somme."   The
relation between these three works is uncertain; it does not
seem as yet fully decided whether the "Somme," or the
"Miroir" (Chavannes) was the earlier work.   Again the
"Somme" is composed of several treatises originally independent, and different parts of it are found in different MSS.
These parts generally succeed each other in the following
order : (1) "Les X. Commandements"; (2) "Le symbole
des Apôtres"; (3) "Les sept péchés Mortels"; (4)

"L'art de bien Mourir"; (5) "Le Pater"; (6) "Les Sept dons du Saint Esprit." The fourth and fifth parts are found extant and complete in themselves apart from the "Somme." The first three parts are not found separately, but P. Meyer (see "Romania," 1894) thinks that these three treatises are anterior to 1279, and were incorporated by Lorens in his work with very little alteration. Part 6 remains, therefore, the only part to be assigned to Lorens. The text of part 4, in a different form, is found in the older "Miroir," and, according to article quoted above, the author of this work also made use of the same treatises adopted by Lorens, in parts 1 to 3. Again, there is extant a treatise in Provençal, which has part of its framework uniting the different sections, in common with the "Somme," this connecting link being more fully developed in the Provençal treatise. The common source of both texts is Hugues de Saint Victor's (d. 1141) "De quinque Septenis." The Provençal author drew directly from it, while Lorens may well have only known it indirectly. See Boser, "Romania," 1895. P. Meyer, "Bull. Soc. Anc. Textes," xviii. 68 ff. *MSS.*, B.M. Reg. 19, C. ii.; Cott. Vesp. A. v.; Add. 24125; 28162; Bibl. Alençon, 27; Mazarine, 870; Chartres, 371; Troyes, 630; S. John, Camb., B. 9; Bibl. Nat. 409, 938, 940, 943, 1824; 13304; 22932; 22934; 22935; 24431; 24780–82. Ashburnham (Barrois).

Numerous other MSS. in Bibl. Nat., Arsenal, Geneviève; Brussels and Provincial Libraries. See Gröber, "Grundrisz Rom. Phil.," p. 1027, and "Hist. Litt.," xix. 399.

N.B.—Barrois MSS., sold June 1901.

Provençal versions of the "Somme" are extant in five MSS., representing three variations of texts, which all like-wise differ from the French. Hence the question arises, whether there was an earlier French text, from which both extant Provençal and French were derived. Boser, however, comparing the fourth part of "Somme" with the earlier "Miroir" and the Provençal, decides that the Provençal is a version of the original "Somme." We have further a French translation of the Provençal version. *MSS.*, Bibl.

Nat. fr. 1049, 1745, 2427; Florence, Laurent., Ashb., 105a, 105b; Bodl. Douce, 162; B.N. fr. 959 (French trans).

An English translation of the "Somme" was made in the 14th century (Ayenbite of Inwyt, *see* § 55); another in 15th century; and a third by Caxton ("The Book Ryal," or the "Book for a King"). *Ed.*, P. Meyer, "Bull. Soc. Anc. Textes," 1892. *See* "Romania," 1894, 1895.

N.B.—Versions of "Somme" extant in Italian, Sicilian, Catalan, and Flemish.

Anonymous.

Li Riote (bavardage) del Monde, or *Dit du jongleur de Ely et de Monseignour le roi d'Engleterre.* The first part consists of question and answer between king and jongleur, the latter giving comic replies, but later on the work grows more serious, and the jongleur becomes the wise adviser of his royal companion. *Ed.*, Ulrich (different versions), "Zeitschrift d. Rom. Phil.," 8; F. Michel (Bibl. Nat. and Harl.), 1834. *See* also "The Keepsake," 1829, for English translation by Lockhart, "The King and the Minstrel of Ely." *MSS.*, Bibl. Nat. fr. 1553; Camb., Trin. Coll., O–2–45; Bern, 113. Version in verse, Harl. 2253.

41 *History.*

Translations from Latin works preceded original historical work in French. The earliest of these were translations of "Geoffrey of Monmouth," and Turpin's "Chronicle." One of the latter, by Nicolas de Senlis, dates from the end of the 12th century. The oldest original Chronicle in French was written by a native of Saintonge in the early 13th century.

Jofroi de Villehardouin, b. cir. 1165; d. before 1213 (or b. 1150–64; d. 1212–18).

La Conquête de Constantinople. A history of the Fourth Crusade, in which he took part, 1198 to 1207. One of the oldest monuments of original French prose, "preserving

somewhat of the epic tone of the former age." The work
finishes abruptly.   *Ed.*, with trans., N. de Wailly, 1872 ;
E. Bouchet, 1891.   *MSS.*, Bibl. Nat. fr. 4972, 2137,
12204, 12203, 24210, 15100; Bodleian, similar MS. to
fr. 4972.

Henri de Valenciennes.   Probably accompanied the
Crusaders who took Constantinople in 1204.

Istoire de l'Empereur Henri (successor to Baldwin of
Flanders).   Description of the events of the Fourth Crusade
from 1208–10, forming a continuation to Villehardouin's
work.   *Ed.*, P. Paris, Soc. Hist. France, 1838 ;
N. de Wailly (with "Conquête de Constantinople"), 1892.
MSS. as above.

Robert de Clari (Clairi).   Another historian of the
Fourth Crusade.   His work is an account of the taking of Constantinople, at which he was present, " Li estoires de chiaus
qui conquisent Constantinoble."   It is interesting as given
from a different point of view to that of Villehardouin, being
written by one who was only a soldier of the ranks.   The
historian also gives us considerable information regarding the
relics preserved in the churches at Constantinople.   *Ed.*,
" Bibl. Ecole des Chartes," tome xxxiii. ; A. Rambaud,
" Robert de Clari, Guerrier et Historien de la quatrième
Croisade," 1872.   *MS.*, Copenhagen, fr. Royal, 487.

Jean, Sire de Joinville.   (§ 40.) This historian lived
to see five kings on the throne of France, Louis ix. to Philippe
le Long.   He joined King Louis in his first crusade, 1248,
and returned home after an absence of six years, 1254.

Mémoires, or *Histoire et Chronique du très Chrétien roi
Saint Louis*, 1309.   The history is completed with extracts
from the "Chroniques françaises de S. Denis," and at the
close is subjoined an ordonnance of the king's, and the latter's
instructions to his son.

The "Mémoires" were written at the instance of Jeanne
de Navarre, mother of Louis le Hutin.   In them, as he
states, Joinville gives an account of the things which he

had "oralement veues et oyes." His book deals first with
the private life of the king, which he ordered according to
God and the Church; the second tells of his deeds of arms.
Although not begun until the beginning of the 14th century,
his work is considered to be rightly placed under the 13th,
as dealing with the events of that century by one who lived
through the greater part of it.

The *Enseignements* of S. Louis to his son have been
transmitted by various chroniclers with marked differences,
although the basis of the writing remains the same. *See*
"Bibl. Ecole des Chartes," xxxv., art. by Viollet.
M. Michel in his edition of above also gives *Enseignement
de S. Louis à sa fille Isabelle.* *Ed.*, F. Michel, 1859.
MSS., Three MSS. No original MS. extant. Two copies
of an authentic text originally existed: one presented by Joinville to Louis x. (Le Hutin); the other which he kept for
personal use. A. is represented by Brussels MS., and Bibl.
Nat. fr. 13568. B. by MS. de Lacques, Bibl. Nat. fr. 10148,
and by MS. Brissart-Binet.

The remaining extant work is a letter written to Louis x.
in 1315. *Ed.*, S. Louis, Credo, and Letter, Text and
trans., N. de Wailly, 1874; Eng. trans., E. Wedgwood, 1906.

Jean Pierre de Sarrasin. The First Crusade of S.
Louis was also the subject of a series of letters from J. P. de
Sarrasin, Chamberlain of the King of France, to Nicolas
Arrodo. *Ed.*, F. Michel, with Joinville's "Mémoires,"
1859.

N.B.—Other letters are extant from the Grand Master of
the Templars and others, among them to Tibaud v., King of
Navarre, and to Henry iii. and Edward i.; letter of King of
Navarre on the death of Louis at Tunis; of the chaplain
Philippe to the Comte de Poitiers. Letters of historical
interest also survive, written by Blanche de Champagne,
Duchesse de Bretagne; by Marguerite, wife of St. Louis,
and her sister, the Queen of England. *See* G. Paris, "Litt.
moyen Âge," § 98; "Hist. Litt.," xxi.

Philippe de Novare. Jurist, Chancellor of Cyprus.
Present at the seige of Damietta, 1218; entered the service

of Henry i., King of Cyprus; d. 1270. P. de Novare
was known as a writer of law treatises (§ 42), and of
a didactic work (§ 40), as well as of several poems. Of his
historical work, all that remains is—

*Estoire de la guerre qui fu entre l'empereur Frederic et Johan
d'Ibelin.* After Syria and Palestine were finally evacuated
by the French, the French government continued for some
time to reside in Cyprus. P. de Novare's work is inserted in
a compilation of the 14th century: "Les Gestes de Chiprois,"
which contains accounts from various sources; the first part
comprises a "Chronique de Terre-Sainte," 1132-1224; P.
de Novare's work is carried to 1242; and the third part gives
continuation of events in Syria to 1291, and of events in
Cyprus to 1309. *Ed.*, G. Raynaud, Soc. l'Orient Latin,
1887. *MS.*, Raynaud's ed. is from MS. found at Piedmont,
written in Cyprus in 14th century.

N.B.—Accounts of pilgrimages, written in this century,
are also extant. For description of the Holy Land in 11th,
12th, and 13th centuries, *see* "Itinéraires à Jerusalem," *ed.*,
H. Michelant and G. Raynaud, Soc. Ori. Lat., 1882.

Ernoul, and Bernard de Corbie.

An early translation, *Histoire de la terre Outre-Mer*, had
been made of the Latin history of Guillaume de Tyr (d.
1184); several isolated writings were annexed to the French
version, forming a large compilation, Ernoul's being the most
important of these separate portions. One of the first forms
of this compilation (1229–1230) is attributed to Bernard le
Trésorier, who continued Ernoul's work, written by the latter
in 1228. *Ed*, "Chronique d'Ernoul et de Bernard le
Trésorier," L. de Mas-Latrie, 1871. *MSS.*, Brussels,
Bibl. Roy., 11142; Berne, H., 41; Bibl. Nat. fr. 781.
B. le Trésorier: Arsenal, 4797; Berne, 340; Ernoul with
cont. by B. le Trésorier: Berne, H., 113.

N.B.—Other MSS. than those mentioned are extant in
Bibl. Nat. of the French translation, and of the continuation
of G. de Tyr.

Anonymous.

Chronique de Reims, or *Récits d'un Ménestrel de Reims*, 1260. The work starts with the First Crusade, and ends abruptly after the death of Louis ixth's son and an account of the suit against the Archbishop of Reims. It is full of popular tradition, and current sayings. *Ed.*, N. de Wailly, 1870. *MSS.*, B.M. Add. 11753 and 7103; Bibl. Nat. fr. 10149, and 24430; Rouen; Brussels.

Histoires de Baudouin. Baudouin vi., Comte de Hainau et ix. de Flandre, Emperor of Constantinople. His fate is unknown, after the battle of Adrianople, 1205. A large body of works has come to us under this name. It is reported that he had an abridged version made of all histories from the Creation to his own time, to be devoted especially to the annals of his own country, and to the genealogy of his ancestors; the work seems to have been carried on by his grandson, Baudouin d'Avesnes, who died 1289, or in a compilation which was in his possession. (*See* 14th century, § 66.) *Ed.*, Kervyn v. Lettenhove, 1879; "Arch. de l'Orient Latin," i., 1881. *MSS.*, Bibl. Nat. fds. fr. 15460, 17264–65–66, 2801; Nouv. Acq. 5218; Brussels; Tournay.

Livre des Histoires, or *Le Tresor des Ystoires*, cir. 1225. Also a compilation from the Bible and various histories, undertaken under the auspices of the Châtelain of Lille Rogers. It was unfinished, leaving off with Cæsar. The prologue, and some moral intercalations, are in verse. *See* "Romania," xiv. *MSS.*, B.M. Reg. 16 g. vii.; 20, D. 1; Add. 19669; Ashburnham, Barrois; Bibl. Nat. (several); Arsenal; Brussels; Dijon; Vienna; Venice.

Les Fais des Romains, or *Livre de César*, cir. 1240. Compiled from Latin historians. Intended to cover the history of the first twelve Emperors of Rome, but ending with the death of Julius Cæsar. The work is of interest from its style, and the allusions in it to people and matters of the author's time, as well as from a certain amount of extra matter. It was written about the same time as "Livre des Histoires," and served as one source for Brunet Latin's work. *See* "Hist Litt.," xxi; "Romania," xiv. *MSS.*,

B.M. Reg. 16 g. vii., and 20 c. 1 ; Ashburnham, Barrois ; Bibl. Nat. (several) ; Brussels. In several MSS. this and preceding work are found together.

Jehan de Tuim.

Li Hystore de Jules César, cir. 1240. Trans. from Lucan and other sources. A poetical version in Alexandrines (second half, 13th century) is extant by Jacot de Forest. *Ed.*, F. Settegast, 1881. *MSS.*, Arsenal, 3344; Vatican ; Brussels ; S. Omer. J. de Forest, Bibl. Nat. 1457.

Chroniques de S. Denis. Various Latin chronicles were collected into a body of history at S. Denis in the 12th century. In 1260, an author, styling himself the "Ménestrel du Comte de Poitiers" (brother of S. Louis), translated this compilation. A later translation, the one used by Joinville (G. Paris), became the basis of the above-named work, of which the most valuable portions are the later ones of original French history. *Ed.*, P. Paris, 1832. *MSS.*, Numerous MSS. in Bibl. Nat., and some at Brussels.

Jean de Prunai.

Prose version in French of the history of Philippe Auguste, from the Latin of Guillaume le Breton. An anonymous prose version, mentioned by Guillaume Guiart in "Royaux Lignages" (14th century), had previously been made, of which only the versified prologue remains. *See* "Hist. Litt.," xxi. *MS.*, B.M. Add. 21212.

N.B.—Guillaume le Breton's works were: Latin prose chronicle of Philippe Auguste ; Latin poem, "Philippide" (P. Auguste) ; and another, "Karlotis," now lost.

L'Anonyme de Bethune.

Li estore des ducs de Normandie et des rois d'Engletierre, to 1220. First part an abridgment of Guillaume de Jumièges. The anonymous author served under Robert VII. of Bethune, whom he accompanied to the wars in Flanders 1213 and 1214, as also in the English campaigns of 1215 and 1216. It is conjectured that the same author wrote "Chronique des

rois de France" (from siege of Troy to 1217, Bibl. Nat.,
Nouv. Acq., 6295), and if so, he must be reckoned among
the first chroniclers in the vulgar tongue of Northern France.
See "Notices et Extraits," xxxiv. *Ed.*, F. Michel, Soc.
Hist. France, 1840. *MSS.*, Bibl. Nat. fr. 12203,
17203; Lille.

N.B.—The Latin historians of this period were Rigord,
who wrote on the first twenty-eight years of Philippe Auguste;
his work was continued in that of G. le Breton; Jacques de
Vitry (§ 40, *N.B.*); Vincent de Beauvais, "Speculum
Historiale," trans. by Jehan de Vignay and Guillaume de
Nangis; the latter wrote lives of Saint Louis and Philippe
le Hardi, and a universal history from the time of Adam;
he himself translated a part of his own works into French.

42   *Law.*

For outlines of French law, *see* "Précis de l'Histoire
du droit Français," P. Viollet, 1884; Tardif, "Hist. des
sources du droit Français," 1890.

Établissements de Saint Louis. Compiled 1272–1273.
Formed on an ordonnance of S. Louis, and the old "Coutume
de Touraine-Anjou," and "Usage d'Orlenois." The
"Etablissements" occupy an important place in the history
of French law; they are not thought by modern authorities
to have been promulgated by S. Louis; an idea which
originated in the presence of a prologue, found in only very
few MSS., and which is not written by the king, as once
supposed. *Ed.*, P. Viollet, 1881–87. *MSS.*, Numerous
MSS., Bibl. Nat. fr. 5278, 1075, and several others;
Vatican, Montpellier, Stockholm, and other foreign libraries;
Philipps, 810, 811.

Philippe de Novare.   (§§ 40, 41.)

Assises de Jérusalem. In the Latin colonies in the East,
among them the one at Jerusalem, there were two distinct
jurisdictions: one of the Haute Cour, for the nobles, the
other the Cour des Bourgeois. After the loss of Saint-Jean
d'Acre in 1291, the Latin colonists preserved their judicial

organisation at Nicosia, in Cyprus, and it is here that the documents were preserved of what is known as the " Assises de Jérusalem," a collection of important treatises by different writers, of whom P. de Novare was one. P. de Novare, who was a poet and a soldier, was the most ancient juris-consult of the Haute Cour.

Jean d'Ibelin. Comte de Jaffa, d. 1266. A powerful

noble in the East, referred to by Joinville. He fought with S. Louis during the King's first crusade.

Le livre des Assises et des bons usages dou roiaume de Jéru-salem. Rather later in date than the work of P. de Novare. *See,* for above authors, " Hist. Litt.," xxi. p. 441, etc. ; and " Historiens des Croisades," Beugnot, 1841–43.

N.B.—There are also extant " Assises d'Antioche " of rather earlier date than above ; not in the original text, which is lost, but in an Armenian translation which has been put into modern French.

Anonymous.

Livre de Jostice et de Plet, cir. 1260. Written after 1255, during reign of S. Louis. The author quotes many names of imaginary persons as authorities, or who, at least, are not known by their writings. It is a valuable work, and with the second part of the " Etablissements," to which it was anterior in date, forms the most ancient document of the " droit Orléanais."   *Ed.,* Rapetti, 1850.   *MS.,* Unique MS., Bibl. Nat. fr. 2844.

Pierre de Fontaines.

Conseil de P. de Fontaines, cir. 1255. The " Usages de Vermandois " is given under the form of advice to a friend. Nearly identical with this work is one called " Le Livre la Roine " (fr. 1279 ; Vatican, Christine, 1451), of which there is a question as to authorship.   *Ed.,* Marnier, 1846.   *See* " Hist. Litt.," xxi. 844–48.   *MSS.,* Bibl. Nat. fr. 1225, 20048 ; Nouv. Acq. 397 ; Troyes, 1712.

Philippe de Rémi, Sire de Beaumanoir, d. 1296. (§ 57.)

Coutume de Beauvoisis, or *du Comté de Clermont en Beauvoisis*. Begun at latest, 1279; finished, 1283. "A valuable and original work." *Ed.*, Beugnot, 1840; Am. Salmon, 1899. *MSS.*, Bibl. Nat. 11652, 4516, 5357, 24059, 24060, 18761; Berlin, Bibl. Roy., Hamilton, 193; Vatican, Christine, 1055; Vatican, Ottoboni, 1155; Carpentras, Beauvais, Orleans, Troyes.

N.B.—Translations of Roman law are extant: a prose one ("Code and Institutes of Justinian") of this century; and also two versified translations, one by a Norman, Richard d'Annebaut, of the "Institutes"; and another by Guillaume Chapu, also a Norman, of the "Coutume de Normandie"; both the latter of last third of century.

43   Miscellaneous Romances.

Prose.

Ed., Moland and d'Héricault, "Nouvelles en Prose du 13ᵉ Siècle," 1856.

Constant l'Empereur. Predestined to become Emperor, Constant, in spite of his humble origin, and all efforts of the reigning Emperor to thwart the decrees of fate, marries the latter's daughter, and rises to throne: incident of letter carried by Constant himself ordering his death, being changed for one ordering his marriage and festivities. A poem on this same subject also belongs to this century (MS., Copenhagen). *Ed.*, "Li Dis de l'Empereour Constant," A. Wesselofsky, "Romania," vi. p. 161. *MS.*, Bibl. Nat. fr. 24430.

La Comtesse de Ponthieu, or *Istoire d'outre-mer.* An incident occurring while on a pilgrimage with her husband, causes her to be put to sea in a barrel, whence being rescued, she marries the Soudan of Aumaric; her father, brother and husband, being taken prisoners by the same, she helps them to escape and flies with them: reconciliation with husband.   *Ed.*, F. Michel.   *MSS.*, Bibl. Nat. fr. 12203, 12572.

Dou Roi Flore et de la bielle Jehane.   The initial incident is similar to that of "Cymbeline." Jehane follows her husband disguised as a page, and lives beside him for years without being recognised. Final explanation and reconciliation. Similar subject is basis of "Roman de la Violette," and first part of "Du Comte de Poitiers." (*See* § 57, Guillaume le Dole.)   *MS.*, Bibl. Nat. fr. 24430.

Li Amitiez de Ami et Amile.   Two parts: First, dealing with acts of self-sacrifice on the part of the two friends; Second, their death, fighting at Morterre with Charlemagne against Didier. It is as fighting champions that they were canonised (*see* Chevalerie Ogier, § 16 and § 22; England, § 40).   *MS.*, Bibl. Nat. fr. 25438.

44   *Miscellaneous Prose.*

Villard de Honnecourt, fl. probably middle and second half century.   A great architect of 13th century.

Album.   Book of drawings and notes. The writer appears to have been a man of general education, and his drawings represent groups of figures and animals, as well as more architectural designs. "It is apparently the only extant work written by an artist of France in the Middle Ages."   *Ed.*, Facsimile of MS., Lassus and Darcel, 1858.   *MS.*, Bibl. Nat. fr. 19093.

Marco Polo.   A Venetian, d. 1323.

Travels to Tartary and China.   Dictated during his imprisonment at Geneva, 1296–98, to Rusticien de Pise, his fellow-prisoner. Another version in better French was prepared by a French knight, 1305, for Thibaut de Cépoy.   *Ed.*, G. Pauthier, 1865; H. Bellanger, 1881. Eng. trans. (Marsden), *ed.*, T. Wright, 1904.   *MSS.*, First version, Bibl. Nat. fr. 1116.   Second version, Bibl. Nat.

fr. 2810, 5631, 5649; Nouv. Acq. fr. 1880; Arsenal,
5219; B.M. Reg. 19, D. i.; Bodley, 264; Berne, 125;
Brussels, 9309; Stockholm, fr. 37.

Gautier de Biblesworth. Wrote one of the oldest
treatises on the French language, cir. 1300, composed for his
sister, Dyonise de Mountechensi; it begins, "Chere soer pur
ceo ke vous me pryastes ke jeo meyse en ecryst pur vos
enfaunz, etc." Then follows instruction in verse, arranged
in couplets. *Ed.*, P. Meyer, "Recueil d'Anciens Textes,"
1874. T. Wright, "Vocabularies," 1857. *MSS.*,
Numerous MSS., Reg. 13 A. iv.; Arundel, 220; Sloane,
513, 809; Univ. Libr., Camb., Gg. i. 1; Trin. Coll.
Camb.; Corp. Christ. Camb.; Oxford, All Souls.

Richard de Fournival, d. 1260.

Bestiaire d'Amour. This is no moral treatise like most
works of their class, for R. de F. turned his "Bestiaire"
into a treatise on love, addressed to "La dame," supporting
his solicitations by reference to peculiarities of beasts and
birds. The answer of the lady is the more amusing part of
the work, for she makes use of her lover's arguments to show
that her refusal of him is based on good grounds. It seems
uncertain whether both parts are by R. de Fournival, or first
part only; the second part is superior in style, and might
well, it is thought, be the work of a clever woman.

R. de Fournival was the son of Roger de Fournival,
physician to Philippe Auguste; he was himself a physician,
and continued to practise his profession after entering the
church. He became Chancellor of the Church of Amiens.
Ed., C. Hippeau, 1860 (from MS. which has miniatures of
men and animals). *MSS.*, Bodl. Douce, 308; Bibl. Nat.
fr. 1444, 25545, 24406, 25566, 411, 12469, 12786, 15213.
Bibl. Geneviève, 2200; Arras.

Other works: "*Chansons ; jeus partis.*"
Prose: *Li Consaus d'Amors*; *La Puissanche d'Amors*; a
Latin *Biblionomia*, a catalogue of his Library (MS., Bibl.
Sorbonne), and *De Vetula*. (*See* trans. Ovid, § 46.)

15

N.B.—R. de F. began a translation into verse of his own work, but did not carry it out; 300 to 400 lines only extant, in Bibl. Nat. 25545.

45 *Translations.*

Jean de Meun (Clopinel). (§§ 48, 58.)

Letters of *Abelard and Heloïse*; Vegetius, *De Re Militari*; Boethius, *De Cons. Phil.* Two other translations, *Topo. Hibern.*, by G. Cambrensis (England, § 30), and Ailred's *De Amicitia Spirituali* are lost.

N.B.—*L'Art de Chevalerie* ("De Re Militari"), ed. with a study on this work, and on the version in octosyllabic couplets by Jean Priorat de Besançon, by Ulysse Robert, Soc. Anc. Textes, 1897.

Jofroi de Watreford.

Eutropius; Dares; *Secret des secrets* (*see* § 37).

Jean de Flixicourt. Dares.

Mahieu le Vilain. Aristotle, *De Meteorologica.*

Drouart la Vache.

De arte honeste amandi, by André le Chapelain. "A work representative of the chivalric ideal of the 12th century."

Both prose and versified translations of Saint Gregory's "Dialogues" are extant; one in octosyllabic verse by Anger, to which was added the life of the saint, was written in England at St. Frideswide, Oxford. *Ed.*, Meyer, "Recueil, etc."; "Romania," 12.

46 Translations and Imitations of Ovid (*see* "Hist. Litt. France," xxix. 455–525.)

No poet of antiquity exercised a greater influence on the literature of the age than Ovid: tales were taken from his "Metamorphoses," and his works on love were translated and

paraphrased. The earliest to make use of the " Ars Amatoria "
was Chrétien de Troies in his lost tale of " Pelops," and
his re-found poem of " Philomela." He was followed by

Maître Élie. 12th century.

Abridged translation of " Ars Amatoria " in octosyllabic
couplets, with amplification of parts and re-adjustment of
surroundings to suit the more modern age. The MS. stops
abruptly. *MS.*, Bibl. Nat. fr. 19152.

Anonymous.

La Clef d'amours (octosyll. couplets). Of about same
date as above, and dealing with original in much the same
way. The second part is addressed to women and contains
interesting allusions to the dress of the period, and directions
for their behaviour at *tête-à-tête* meals. This and the following poem introduce us to the society of the Middle Ages
(G. Paris). *Ed.*, E. Tross, 1886 (MS. in possession of
editor).

Jacques d'Amiens.

This writer gives a more liberal translation of Ovid, adding
original specimens of conversation between lovers and details
of his own life. *MSS.*, Bibl. Nat. fr. 25545, 12478.
Dresden; Utrecht (fragment).

N.B.—A MS. at Berne contains songs, a pastourelle, and
a jeu parti under the same name; as Colin Muset is the
interlocutor in the latter, the poet must have lived early 13th
century, " but the two writers are not necessarily identical, and
the ' Ovid ' appears of a later date."

Anonymous.

Towards the end of the century, a prose translation was
made of the two first books of " Ars Amatoria," accompanied
with commentaries and interspersed with refrains of songs and
proverbs. There are curious interpretations of the original
in the work, and unexpected additions. *MSS.*, Bibl. Nat.
fr. 881; Arsenal, 2741.

Guiart.

A small poem in monorhymic quatrains, in which the "Remedia amoris" is also made use of. *MS.*, Bibl. Nat. fr. 1593.

Anonymous.

Le Confort d'Amors. End 13th or early 14th century. Poem found in the Dresden MS. at the close of the work by J. d'Amiens. In it are descriptions of different kinds of love and friendship, the title only applying to the close of the poem. *MS.*, Bibl. Nat. fr. 12478.

The "Remedia" also underwent translation or rather paraphrase by another writer of the 14th century; and a translation in verse is inserted in the "Checs Amoreux" a work of second half of 14th century (Dresden, Venice).

Chrétien Legouais de Sainte-More. Franciscan.

Ovid Moralisé, cir. 1300 (octosyllabic couplets). The first complete translation of the "Metamorphoses." The work is abridged, but the commentaries, historical, moral and theological, attached to each fable, are often longer than the text itself. "This was the last effort, characteristic of the Middle Ages, to apply Christian interpretations to the works of antiquity." The tale of "Philomela" by C. de Troies (§ 28) was found incorporated in this work, as well as the earlier tale of "Pyramus and Thisbe" (12th century). *See* "Hist. Litt.," xxix. *MS.*, 14 MSS. Bibl. Nat. fr. 373, 374, 870, 871, etc.; Arsenal, B.L. fr. 19; B.M. Add. 10324; Ashburnham (Barrois) and several foreign libraries.

Ovid's tale of "Orpheus and Eurydice" underwent a great transformation. A Breton lai on this subject is known to have existed, reference being found to it in three works of the 12th century, and an English version being also extant of the 13th or early 14th century. The earlier myth had become a fairy tale in the Breton lai.

There were two works wrongly ascribed to Ovid at this time; "Pamphilus," or "De Amore," a work of the 12th

century, translated into French verse by Jehan Bras de fer in
the first half of 13th century, and the "De Vetula" (ed. H.
Cochesis, 1861) of R. de Fournival, who pretended that the
poem had been found in Ovid's tomb; this latter work was
later put into French verse by Jean le Fèvre.

47 POETRY.

Science.

Pierre de Beauvais. Fl. first third of century. (§ 48.)

La Mappemonde (octosyllabic couplets). A compilation
somewhat similar to "L'image du Monde" and "Petite
Philosophie" (*see* below): dealing with cosmographical and
geographical subjects. The author cites Solin as his chief
authority; among other works used by him was probably
the "Imago Mundi" of Honorius d'Autun (12th century).

Pierre was author of several other works in prose and verse,
one a *Bestiaire*. For these, *see* "Notice sur deux anciens
Manuscrits français ayant appartenu au Marquis de la
Clayette"; P. Meyer, "Notices et Extraits," xxxiii.
MS., La Clayette.

Gautier de Metz.

L'Image du Monde (octosyllabic couplets). The "Image"
of Gautier de Metz was the most important of the works
which, under different names, "Nature des choses," "Lucidaire," "Miroir du Monde," "Trésor," embraced all that
was known in the Middle Ages of metaphysics, geography,
astronomy, and other sciences. The work is based on Latin
originals by H. d'Autun, Jacques de Vitry, etc.; it is also
called by the author "Livre de Clergie," and ends with the
words:

> "Ci fenist l'image du Monde;
> A Deu commence, a Deu prent fin
> Qui ses biens nos doint en la fin."

It exists in two versions; the earlier and shorter dates from 1245;
(1246, G. P.); the second only two years later. *MSS.*,

Bibl. Nat. fr. 24428, 14964, 2175, 2480, etc. (over 30 MSS. at Bibl. Nat.); Arsenal, B.L., 283, 306; Bibl. Mazarine, 602; Stockholm.

Three names of authors are given in the MSS. by the copyists: "Omons (in 3 MSS.), Gossouin (in prose version as well as versified one), Gautier de Metz (in a MS. now lost). The editor thinks that Omons cannot be taken into consideration at all; that Gossouin has more claim than Gautier to be the author; but as both have good claims it is possible that the earlier edition was Gossouin's and second Gautier's; this, however, he considers doubtful, and that it is more likely one name was a mistake. The poem was put into prose at the end of the 13th century. *Ed.*, Fant, Upsala Univ., Arsskrift, 1886. *MSS.*, Bibl. Nat. fr. 574, 25344.

An English edition dates from 1480 or 1481, and is taken from a French prose version: "Thymage or Myrrour of the Worlde, translated out of French into English by me simple person, Wyll. Caxton." Only the title of another English version is known.

Pierre de Peckham (or d'Abernun), Anglo-Norman.

La Lumière as Lais (*Lumière des Laïques*) (octosyllabic couplets), 1267. Intended, like other works of its kind, to make the science of the day accessible to the laity, who knew little or no Latin. The chief source of the poem was a résumé of theology called the "Elucidarius," a Latin work which at one time was incorrectly assigned to Honorius d'Autun and published under his name. Pierre de Peckham was possibly the author of another extant work, a translation of the "Secret des Secrets," erroneously ascribed to Aristotle. *See* "Romania," xv. *MSS.*, St. John's Coll., Camb.; Univ. Libr., Gg. i. 1; Ashburnham (Barrois); Trin. Coll. Dublin; B.M. Reg. 15, D. ii. 16, E. ix.; Harl. 4390; Bodley, 399; York Chapter.

La Petite Philosophie (octosyllabic couplets), written by an Anglo-Norman, probably from the "Imago Mundi" of

H. d'Autun. *See* "Romania," xv. *MSS.*, Univ. Libr., Camb., Gg. 6, 28; DD. 10, 31. St. John's; Douce, 210; Vatican.

La Chace dou Cerf (octosyllabic couplets). Oldest vernacular work on the Chace, written in France. Contains useful information in an abridged form. *See* "Altfransösische Jagdlehrbücher," H. Werth, 1889. *MSS.*, Nat. Bibl. fr. 1593 (56). Prose version, Arsenal, 2769 (La Palaye).

N.B.—"La cace dou Cerf," or "le Cerf Amoureux" (fds. fr. 378), another extant poem, is not rightly a book on the chace, but a satirical allegory, in which the hunter is the lover, and the stag the lady.

A prose work, the "Art de Vénerie," was written in England by Guillaume de Twici, who calls himself "Venour le Roy d'Engleterre." In the English version, his collaborator is named as Maystere Johan Gyfford. The "Art de Vénerie" was the basis of the poetical version by Juliana Berners (England, 15th century). *MS.* of Eng. trans. of G. Le Twici, Cott. Vesp. 13, xii. Michelant, in his preface to Hardouin's "Trésor de Vénerie" (late 14th century) speaks of "Art de Vénerie" as the oldest work on the Chace.
(For "Roi Modus," *see* 14th century.)

48   *Religious, Didactic, Satirical, etc.*

A large number of didactic works were classed under the titles of Bible, Chastiements, or Enseignements; some were addressed to society in general; others, and these are the more interesting, attacked individual classes of society.

Anonymous.

Discipline de Clergie. Rhymed version of "Disciplina Clericalis" by Petrus Alfonsus. (*See* "Chastiement d'un père," § 12.) *See* "Romania," i. 106. *MSS.*, B.M. Add. 10289. Another version in Harl. 4388.

Simon.

Le Roman des trois Ennemis de l'homme (Devil, World, and Flesh) (octosyllabic couplets). Early century. *See* " Romania," xvi. (Text and notes). *MSS.*, Bibl. Arsenal, 5201 ; Bibl. Orléans (fragments).

Tibaud d'Amiens (?). Probably the author (G. Paris).

Prière de Nostre Dame (strophes, a a c, b b c). Early century. *See* " Romania," xiii., xviii. *MSS.*, Bibl. Nat. (3 MSS.) ; Arsenal (2) ; Bodl. Digby, 86 ; Trin. Coll., Dublin ; Phillipps ; Dijon and Pavia.

Poème Moral (Alexandrines, quatrains of one rhyme), 1190–1210 (Cloetta), cir. 1210 (G. Paris). The poem is only preserved as a fragment. The title was given it by M. Meyer who discovered the MS., and who considers it one of the most important and beautiful of the poems that have come down to us from the Middle Ages. It is written in the north-eastern dialect of France. The poem consists of introduction on the vanity of our earthly existence. Then follows life of S. Moses of Egypt, and life of S. Thais. It is next shown how much easier and pleasanter it is to serve God than man. Avarice, riches, and extravagance are dealt with ; here fragment ends. It is conjectured from a preliminary table of contents that a third part was intended to be added ; the poet evidently left his work unfinished. *Ed.*, W. Cloetta. " Rom. Forsch.," tome iii. art. 1, 1887. *MSS.*, Bodl. Canon. Misc. 74, oldest and most complete, early 13th century. Bibl. Nat. fr. 2162, 25545, 23112, 24429, 2039 ; Arsenal, 3516, 5204.

Hélinand. Monk of Froidmont.

Vers de la Mort. Sermon in verse, cir. 1220 (octosyllabic strophes of twelve lines on two rhymes). *Ed.*, F. Wulff. *MSS.*, Bibl. Nat. (many MSS.), Arsenal, 5201 ; Brussels, Berne, Pavia, Turin.

There is also an anonymous "li vers de la mort." *Ed.*, Windahl, 1887.

Barthélemi. Reclus de Moiliens.

Li Romans de Carité, cir. 1220. Poet goes in search of Charity but finds it not in any part of the world, east or west; it was driven forth from England on the death of Becket. Various classes of society are sermonised. *Ed.* (with "Miserere"), Van Hamel, 1885.

Miserere, cir. 1220. Whence came man? what is he? what was he? what will he become?

Both poems written in octosyllabic twelve-lined strophes, on two rhymes. Van Hamel thinks that "Carité" must have been written soon after Becket's death, and that there were only a few years between the composition of the two poems. The first quarter of 13th century is assigned to them by G. Paris. *Ed.*, Meyer, 1881. *MSS.*, Twenty-five MSS. of the two poems, five of "Miserere" alone. Bibl. Nat. (20); Arsenal (4); Harl. 4354; Brussels, etc.

Guillaume le Clerc, b. cir. 1170; d. cir. 1230.

Le Bestiaire Divin, 1210–11 (octosyllabic rhyming couplets). *Ed.*, R. Reinsch, 1890. *MSS.*, Twenty MSS., Egerton, 613; Reg. 16, E. viii.; Cott. Vesp. A. vii.; Ashburnham (Barrois), Bodley, 132; Phillipps, 4156; Bibl. Nat.; Vatican, etc.

Le Besant de Dieu (Talent of God), 1227. A moral poem addressed to all classes. The reading of the parable of the "Talents" had awakened the conscience of the poet. *Ed.*, E. Martin, 1869. *MS.*, Bibl. Nat. fr. 19525.

This poet also wrote: *Les treiz Moz, Les joies Notre Dame, Vie de Tobie, Vie de Magdalene.* He tells us he had originally written contes and fableaux: of the latter *La Male Honte* et *Le prêtre et Alison* were once ascribed to him, as also the Arthurian tale of *Fergus*, but recent research assigns the religious poems, the Arthurian romance, and the fableaux, to three, if not four distinct authors.

Gervaise.

Bestiaire, cir. 1215 (octosyllabic rhyming couplets). Translation of one of the many extant versions in Latin, but apparently a different one to that followed by P. de Thaon and G. le Clerc. *Ed.*, "Romania," i. 1872. *MSS.*, B.M. Add. 28260.

Chardri. Anglo-Norman. Early 13th century.

La Vie des Set Dormans (Seven Sleepers).

Barlaam et Joasaph (see below, "Gui de Cambrai"). Tale of Buddhist origin, which passed through Greek, Syriac, and Arabic versions; became known in the West in the 11th century, or perhaps earlier; translated into Latin, and finally into different vernaculars of Europe.

Le petit Plet. Poem in form of dialogue between old man and young one on value of life. The "Distiches" of Cato as well as national proverbs are brought into service. The poems are in octosyllabic rhyming couplets.

Ed., Works, J. Koch, 1880. *MSS.*, Cott. Cal. A. ix.; Jesus Coll., Oxford; Vatican (Petit Plet only).

André de Coutances. Early century. (§ 49.)

L'Évangile de Nicodème. Metrical translation from the Latin. Besides prose versions, two other rhythmical ones are extant. Chrétien (one MS., Florence), probably first half 13th century; Anonymous (Lambeth, 522), by Anglo-Norman. *Ed.*, "Trois rédactions en vers de Evan. Nico.," G. Paris and A. Bos, 1885. *MSS.*, Add. 10289.

N.B.—From this gospel emanated the legend of Joseph of Arimathea's miraculous deliverance from prison.

Anonymous.

Salomon et Marcoul. (*See* England, § 9; Germany, § 14.)

Les Proverbes de Marcoul et de Salomon, cir. 1220 (tail-rhymed strophes of six lines), by Pierre, surnamed Mauclerc, Comte de Bretagne. *MSS.*, Bib. Nat. 1830.

A Dialogue between Salomon and Marcoulf le foole (four-lined strophes, 2nd and 3rd line rhyming). *MSS.*, Bib. Nat. 7218; fds. l'Église, 2, 1; Trin. Coll. Camb.

Another version appeared in print in 1509.

The title of the second of these versions is sufficient to indicate the change of tone undergone by this famous dialogue since the A.-S. version which still echoed the gravity of the East. This change has been traced in its beginning to Flanders, towards the end of 12th century. The first French version is free from the coarser humour which distinguishes other French versions and those of Germany, in which a popular style has supplanted the mysticism of the earlier legend. The Western form of the dialogue usually represents Solomon arguing with one Marcolf (Marcholfus, Marcoul, Marcon, Marolf, Morolf), a name of Eastern origin, which may have reference to the *Mahol*, whose sons, according to biblical history, Solomon surpassed in wisdom. The earlier form of the name was corrupted from Malchol, Moloch, or Milcom. *See* MacCallum, Vogt, and Grant Duff, *op. cit.*, under England. *Ed.*, J. M. Kemble, for the Aelfric Society, 1848.

Gui de Cambrai. (*See* Alexander Cycle, § 27.)

Barlaam et Josaphat, cir. 1225 (octosyllabic rhyming couplets). *Ed.*, P. Meyer and H. Zotenberg, 1865. *MS.*, Bibl. Nat. fr. 1553.

N.B.—A third poem is extant on this subject by anonymous author; also a fragment of prose version translated direct from the Greek. (Bibl. Nat. and Vatican.)

Anonymous.

Fragments of a *Life of S. Thomas Becket*. *Ed.*, with facsimile of MS., which is ornamented with miniature paintings by P. Meyer, 1885. *MS.*, Private Library (Goethals-Vercruysse), Courtrai.

Guiot de Provins.

Bible (decasyllabic), 1204. A satire on all classes of society. *Ed.*, Méon, "Fabliaux, etc." *MSS.*, Bibl. Nat. fr. 24405 and 25437; Arsenal, 5201; Pemb. Coll. Camb.; Turin.

Hugues, or **Huon de Berzé**. (§ 62.) Two of this name are mentioned by Villehardouin; the author was most likely the younger one, born cir. 1170.

Bible, "por faire l'arme saine," cir. 1224. *Ed.*, "Romania," vi.; xviii. *MSS.*, Bibl. Nat. fr. 378 and 837; B.M. Add. 15606; Brussels (Bourgogne), Turin.

Raoul de Houdan (*see* Arth. Rom., § 55), early century. Four poems alone can be with certainty attributed to this author.

Songe d'Enfer (octosyllabic rhyming couplets). *MSS.*, Bibl. Nat. fr. 837 and 1593; Bodl. Digby, 86.

Songe, ou Voie de Paradis (similar verse). *MSS.*, Brussels, 9411-26; Bibl. Nat. fr. 837.

Li Romans des Eles (*Ailes*) (similar verse). The "wings" are "Largesse" and "Courtoisie," each having seven feathers, the signification of which forms substance of poem. At the close there is an exposition of love, as the supreme element of courtesy. *MSS.*, Bibl. Nat. fr. 837 and 19152; Turin, Berlin.

The other certain work of this author is "Méraugis de Portlesguez" (Arthurian Cycle); "Gauvain," or "La Vengeance Raguidel" (Arthurian), also thought to be his; and the "Chevalier de l'épée," has been ascribed to him.

Ed., Works, A. Scheler, "Trouvères Belges," 1879.

Gautier de Coinci. (§ 62.)

Miracles de Notre Dame, 1218-1225. The principal extant collection of tales in verse. The legends are taken from various sources, principally from a Latin compilation of 12th century, by Hugues Farsit. *Ed.*, Poquet, 1875. *MSS.*, Numerous MSS.: B.M. Harl. 4401; Bibl. Nat.; Arsenal; S. Geneviève; Tours, Blois, Brussels, etc.

Jehan le Marchant. Prebendary of Peronne, lived in the reign of Louis ix.

Le livre des Miracles de Notre-dame de Chartres. These

tales are not of such value poetically, as those of G. de Coinci, from whom le Marchant partly borrowed; his other tales are translated from a Latin original. Several of the miracles are concerned with the burning and rebuilding of the church at Chartres; the writer of his Latin source was an eye-witness of the conflagration and miracles in connection with it. The author tells us that he finished his work in 1262. *Ed.*, Duplessis, 1855. *See* H. Fölster, "Ausg. u. Abhandl. Rom. Phil.," xliii. 43. *MS.*, Chartres, 18.

N.B.—The work in question is the only extant specimen of the early dialect of this neighbourhood.

Huon de Méri.

Tournoiement Antichrist (octosyllabic couplets), cir. 1235. Allegorical poem representing fight between Christ and Antichrist. *Ed.*, G. Wimmer, 1888. *MSS.*, Bibl. Nat. (five MSS.); Harl. 4417; Bodl. Douce, 308.

Anonymous.

Vies des pères (octosyllabic couplets), cir. 1250. (§§ 10, 40.) "A veritable Christian Epic." This collection was by degrees added to, and the number of tales finally amounted to seventy-four. Early printed ed., 1486. *Ed.* (Selections), Méon, "Nouv. Recueil"; Le Coultre, "Contes dévots," 1884; H. A. v. Keller, "Zwei Fabliaux," 1840. *See* "Romania," xiii. *MSS.*, Extant in over thirty MSS., *see* Gröber, "Grundr. d. Rom. Phil.," 914, *seq.*

Vie de S. Eustace. Among other saints the life of S. Eustace (known also as S. Placide) is extant in six versions of the 13th century, one by Pierre de Beauvais (§ 47). *MSS.* (Pierre), B.N. fr. 13502, 19530; B.M., Egerton, 745.

Baudouin de Condé.   (§ 61b.)

Henri d' Andeli.   (§§ 61a, 61b.)

Wilham de Wadington (name spelt variously in different MSS.).

Le Manuel des Pechiez (Anglo-Norman). The date of poem is probably to be fixed some few years before the appearance of the English translation by Robert of Brunne (*see* England, § 67). We know nothing of author except that he was a cleric and an Englishman. There was more than one Waddington in England; the exact one cannot be identified for certain. The poem was evidently intended to be written in octosyllabic metre, but the number of syllables vary from six to ten. The author apparently addresses the middle and lower classes of the laity. Order of work: Twelve Articles of Faith; Ten Commandments; Seven Deadly Sins; Sacrilege; Seven Sacraments; Sermon on Love and Fear as Deterrents of Sin; Book on Confession, with prologue. Many legends and anecdotes of the time are inserted.

This was the earliest manual of morals which appeared in England. The author tells us that he borrowed from many sources, but much original matter is added. The plan of the work is similar to that of a popular Latin work entitled "Floretus." Among matters which call down the reproof of the author are the dramatic representations in connection with the Office, borrowing of clothes, and wearing of masks. "It is less interesting than 'Somme le Roi,' but valuable for its picture of manners and customs in England" (G. Paris). *Ed.* (with Eng. trans.), F. G. Furnivall, Roxburghe Club, 1860; and for E.E.T.S., Orig. Series, 1901–3. *MSS.*, B.M. Harl. 273, 4657; Reg. 20. B. xiv.; Bodl. Rawl. 241.

Jehan de Journi.

La Dîme de Pénitence, cir. 1290. Written, as the author tells us, at Nicosia, in Cyprus, while recovering from an illness. The poem begins:

> " Ausi com chascuns crestiens
> Si est tenus de tous ses biens
> De rendre à Diu la droite dime,"

So, he continues, as he has received much of God,

> " Veul desormais à Dieu entendre
> Et $\begin{cases} \text{loiaument} \\ \text{joiaument} \end{cases}$ ma disme rendre."

The poem falls into two parts, the first being the actual D. de P., dealing with remission of sins, causes of sin, etc. In the second part the author expresses himself on persons and matters in the form of prayer; he prays for Cardinals, several reigning sovereigns and other princes; he is distressed at the decadence of Christian power in the East, and gives an insight into the events of the time. "Its chief interest lies in the fact that it was written by a knight and not by a cleric" (G. Paris). *Ed.*, P. Meyer, "MSS. de l'ancienne litt. France conservés dans les Bibliothèques de la grande Bretagne," 1871; Dr. H. Breymann, "Bibl. Litt. Verein.," 1874. *MS.*, Add. 10015.

Adam de Suel, second third of century.

Of the many translations of the Pseudo-Cato Distiches (*see* 12th century, § 14) that of Adam de Suel, written in octosyllabic couplets, was the most popular. The work in one MS. is given under the name of Macé de Troies. *Ed.*, Ulrich, "Roman. Forsch.," xv. *See* "Romania," xvi. 65, 156. *MSS.*, Bibl. Nat. (six MSS.); B.M. Add. 15606; Arsenal; Brussels (Bourgogne), Dijon, Tours, Berne, Madrid, Evreux.

N.B.—Two other translations of the Distiches were by Jehan Chastelet, and Lefèvre.

Alard de Cambrai, second third of century.

Dits, or *Moralités des Philosophes*. The author gives the names of twenty philosophers whose ideas and sayings he has turned into verse. *See* "Hist Litt.," xxiii. *MSS.*, Bibl. Nat. fr. 12471, 17177, 24431; Arsenal, B.L., 175.

Robert de Gretham. Anglo-Norman, second third of century.

Miroir, or, *Les Evangiles des domées* (dimanches), octo-syllabic, rhyming two or more lines. Weekly gospels, with explanations for use of the laity. A compilation taken apparently from several Latin works. *See* "Romania," xv. *MSS.*, B.M. Add. 26773; Camb. Univ. Gg. i. 1. A third MS. at Trin. Coll. Camb. was also known some years ago, but has since disappeared.

N.B.—It is uncertain to which of the places called Greetham, or Greatham, in England, the author belonged.

Corset. Treatise on theology, for use of laity. This work is dedicated to one Alain, by his chaplain, Robert. M. P. Meyer ("Rom.," xv. 296) thinks it is probable that the Robert who wrote the "Corset" is identical with the author of the "Miroir." The poems resemble one another in language and versification. There was an old custom in England and France of giving the wife her husband's name with a feminine ending, and the Aline to whom the "Miroir" is dedicated may well have been the wife of Alain. G. Paris assigns it positively to R. de Gretham. *See* "Litt. moyen Âge," § 152. *MS.*, Bodl. Douce, 210.

Robert de Blois.

Chastiement des Dames. Inserted into "Beaudous." (*See* Arth. Rom., § 55.)

Sauvage.

Doctrinal Sauvage, so called from name of author (mono-rhymic quatrains in Alexandrines). One of the "Enseigne-ments" addressed to all classes. The text varies considerably in the MSS.; three different beginnings are found in them. *Ed.*, Jubinal, "Nouveau Recueil de Contes," etc. *See* "Notices et Extraits," tome xxxiii. *MSS.*, Bibl. Nat. (seven MSS.), 834, 837, etc.; Arsenal; La Clayette; B.M. Harl. 978, 4333; Egerton, 745; Bodl. Digby, 86; Jesus Coll. 29; Phillipps, 6664, etc.; Bibl. Nat. 25408.

Robert de Ho (Anglo-Norman, England).

Enseignements Trebor (Anagram of Robert) (octosyllabic couplets). The author gives a list of classical authors from whom he has borrowed, Virgil, Ovid, etc. Proverbs of Solomon and Pseudo-Cato are also made use of. The work is addressed to the author's son; it is heavy and monotonous. Among the tales introduced is a version of the fableau of the two travellers, one envious and the other covetous, who end respectively with the loss of one eye and both eyes. *See* "Hist. Litt.," xxiii.; "Romania," xxxii. *MS.,* Bibl. Nat. 25408.

Anonymous.

Ditié d' Urbain. Anglo-Norman. (Octosyllabic couplets.) Ascribed on no good foundation to Henry I. This work, like another entitled "Doctrinal de Courtoisie," and that of R. de Houdan, gives directions regarding good breeding, thereby throwing light on the usages of society in the days in which the author lived. It is addressed by "un sage home de graunt valour," by name Urbain, to his son, called "Edward," in one of the MSS. *Ed.* (from Gg. i. 1), "Mod. Language Notes," 1889. *MSS.,* Camb. Univ. Gg. i. 1; Bodl. Douce, 210; Bodley, 9 and 425; Trin. Coll. Camb.

Anonymous.

L'ordène de Chevalerie (octosyllabic couplets). On the framework of a story in connection with the Crusades, Hue de Tabarie, who is taken prisoner, instructs Saladin in the laws of chivalry; an account is given of the ceremonies accompanying the conferring of knighthood. *Ed.,* Méon, "Fabliaux, etc." *See* "Romania," 3. *MSS.,* B.M. Harl. 4333; Add. 34114; Camb. Univ. Gg. vi. 28; Phillipps, 8336; Metz, 855.

Jean de Meun. (§§ 45, 58.)

Le Testament (monorhymic quatrains in Alexandrines, divided in most MSS. into hemistiches).

16

The author's earliest work was the " Roman de la Rose " ; when drawing near the end of his life, he again turned to writing poetry, but it was now of a more devotional kind, and the writer expresses regret for having sought in his earlier verses to please the taste of the frivolous.

The "Testament" is in two parts. It contains advice and reprimand to many classes of people—married, aged, prelates, monks, etc., but is more especially addressed to clerics. He betrays his inimical spirit towards the Dominicans and Franciscans, whom he ironically attacks. The second part is more general, and deals with Paradise and Hell, on the enemies of man, on prayer for those in Purgatory, etc. In some MSS. the "Testament" is followed by "Le Codicile" (a a a b, c c c b, octosyllabic). *Ed.*, Méon, "R. de la Rose," 1814. *MSS.*, Numerous MSS., thirty-five at least, generally found in those containing " R. de R.," or his translation of Boethius.

Rustebeuf, fl. 1255-1285. (§§ 60, 61a, 61b, 62, 63.)

La voie de Paradis (octosyllabic couplets).
Un dist de Nostre-Dame (octosyllabic couplets).
L'Ave Maria Rusteboeuf (a a b, b b c, c c d, third line of four syllables).
C'est de Nostre-Dame (same rhymes through each strophe —four long and five short lines).
Les neuf joies Nostre-Dame (eight-lined strophes of alternate rhymes).
La vie Ste. Marie l'Égyptienne (octosyllabic couplets).
La vie Sainte Elysabel (octosyllabic couplets).
De la vie dou Monde (monorhymic quatrains).
Des plaies du Monde (octosyllabic couplets).
De l'Estat du Monde (octosyllabic couplets).
Ed., "Oeuvres Complétes," A. Jubinal, 1874. *MSS.* of works, Bibl. Nat. fr. 837, 1593, 1634, 1635, 24432.

For Robert Grosseteste's poem, *Chasteau d'Amours*, see England, § 49.

49 *History.*

Calendre.

Chronique des Empereurs (octosyllabic couplets). From Latin text (abridged version of Orosius), brought from Constantinople after the Fourth Crusade. The death of a Duke of Lorraine in 1213 is mentioned. Of no literary worth.

Ed., Settegast, *Calendre et sa Chronique* (extract). " Rom. Stud.," tome iii. *MS.*, Bibl. Nat. fr. 794.

Jacot de Forest. Second third of century.

César. A versified version in Alexandrines of the prose of Jehan de Tuim (§ 41). *MS.*, Bibl. Nat. 1457.

Philippe Mousket, b. cir. 1190; d. after 1243.

Rhymed Chronicle (octosyllabic couplets), 1243. History of French kings from days of Troy to 1243. In it the author refers to certain Chansons de Geste that are now lost. *Ed.*, Reiffenberg, 1840. *See* also " Historiens des Gaules et de la France," xxii. *MS.*, Unique MS., Bibl. Nat. fr. 4963.

Anonymous.

Vie de Guillaume le Maréchal (octosyllabic couplets), cir. 1224. Earl of Pembroke and Regent of England during Henry III.'s minority, d. 1219. The poem was written by a native of one of the French provinces under the King of England, perhaps the herald, Henri le Norrois. It is of great value historically, especially for the years 1186–1219, and also as regards social life and ideas in 12th and 13th centuries. The account from which the life was versified was apparently furnished by the Maréchal's friend, Jean d'Erlée (of Early, Berks), and probably written at the request of Guillaume's son and heir. The editor places the work among the most eminent in French historiography. *Ed.*, P. Meyer, " Soc. Hist. France," 1891–1902 (with an abridged translation into modern French). *MS.*, Phillipps.

Satirical poems, touching on events of the day, are not wanting in this century; many are inspired by the mutual hatred between the English and French. *See* G. Paris, "Litt. moyen Âge," § 108; "Hist. Litt.," xxiii.

André de Coutances. (§ 48.)

Li Romanz des Français (octosyllabic monorhymed quatrains). Satire aimed at the French. One, Arflet de Nohundrelande, gives an account of the victories gained by Arthur over Frolles, the King of the French; Frolles being held up to much ridicule. *MS.*, B.M. Add. 10289.

Anonymous.

La Pais aus Englois, 1264 (octosyllabic quatrains on one rhyme). A satire on the side of the French aimed at Henry III., apparently on the occasion of Louis IX.'s mediation between the parties then distracting England. *MS.*, Bibl. Nat. fr. 837.

N.B.—In the same MS. with above is "La Chartre de la Pais aux Anglois," in prose. "Probably a parody on some public proclamation"; it is written in a jargon of Anglo-French. The Bretons were held up to ridicule in a poem, "Les Privilèges aux Bretons."

Among other smaller poems, referring to events of the day, are—

Huon de Saint-Quentin.

Complainte de Jérusalem, 1221. In which the Church is reproached for keeping the money which was raised for the Crusade. *Ed.*, Bartsch, "Langue et Lit."; E. Stengel, "Codicem, etc., Digby, 86," p. 27. *MSS.*, Berne; La Haye; Bodl. Digby, 86.

Anonymous.

Complainte de l'Église d'Angleterre. Concerning troublous affairs in England under Henry II.; probably by one of the clergy, a class upon which extra taxes had been raised. *Ed.*, Wright, "Political Songs of England." *MS.*, Cott. Jul. D. vii.

Dit de Vérité. 1295. Expression of discontent on the part of the Nobles against Philippe le Bel for preference shown by him to certain men of lower birth whom he took for advisers. *Ed.*, Jubinal, "Nouv. Recueil," ii. 82. *See* "Romania," i. 246. *MSS.*, Bibl. Nat. fr. 12483; Pavia.

Le Moine de Silli. A satirical poem in alternate Latin and French lines, directed against Edward 1. of England. *MS.*, Pavia, Univ. Bibl.

Rustebeuf, the writer of fableaux, dits, and religious poems, has also his "Complainte d'Outre-Mer," "Complainte de Constantinoble," and a few dits inspired by abuses and dissensions of the day (*see* § 61b).

50 *Chansons de Geste. Cycle du Roi.*

Anseis de Carthage. Early 13th century. Anseis has been left as ruler in Spain by Charlemagne. One of his chief barons, returning from a mission to obtain the hand of the Saracen king's daughter for Anseis, learns that the latter has dishonoured his daughter. He then joins the Saracens, and brings a large force against Anseis, to whose help Charlemagne comes, and finally defeats the enemy. The baron's daughter retires into a convent. *Ed.*, J. Alton, 1892. *MSS.*, Bibl. Nat. fr. 793, 12548, 1598, 368 (fragment); Durham, Cosin, v. 11, 17; Lyons, Bibl. Acad., 59.

N.B.—A later prose version is extant.

Gui de Bourgogne (Alexandrines), cir. 1230. (Gautier places it earlier.) Charlemagne has been absent twenty-seven years in Spain. The young nobles of France elect Gui as their king, but he is no sooner in power than he starts to his emperor's assistance, and with his "enfants" captures all the towns that are still in the hands of the enemy. *Ed.*, F. Guessard and H. Michelant, 1859. *See* "Romania," xvii.   *MSS.*, Tours (Marmontier), B.M. Harl. 527.

Gaidon.   Second third of century.   The name is derived from a jay that alighted on the hero's helmet.   The events take place subsequent to Roncesvaux.   In the first part an attempt to kill the Emperor with poisoned fruit is falsely laid to Gaidon's charge, who upholds his innocence by force of arms; the second is occupied with the warfare between him and Charlemagne, which ends in reconciliation.   *Ed.*, F. Guessard and S. Luce, "Anc. Poètes Français," 1862. *MSS.*, Bibl. Nat. fr. 860, 15182, 1475.

Adenet le Roi (*see* Cycle Monglane, §§ 51 and 57).

Berte aus grands piés (Alexandrines, in monorhymic laisses of irregular lengths), cir. 1270.   *Ed.*, A. Scheler, 1874. *MSS.*, Bibl. Nat. fr. 778, 1447, 12467, 24404; Arsenal, B.L., 175; Rouen.

Enfances Ogier (decasyllabic monorhymic laisses), cir. 1270.   The early exploits of Ogier are also found in Raimbert's poem, "Chevalerie Ogier" (*see* 12th cent., § 16), and in the "Charlemagne" (S. Mark, fr. xiii.). The versions differ; but Adenet, as a whole, follows Raimbert.   *Ed.*, A. Scheler, 1874.   *MSS.*, Arsenal, B.L., 175; Bibl. Nat. fr. 12467, 1471, 1632; La Vallière, 2729.

Jehan de Lanson (Alexandrines), extant form cir. early 13th century.   Jehan is nephew of the traitor Ganelon, and turns traitor himself.   The twelve peers are sent against him by Charlemagne.   The latter has finally to go to their help, and victory in the end is theirs.   The chief personage throughout is the Enchanter Basin (§ 16), whose magic powers are effectual in saving both peers and Charlemagne himself. These events take place before the expedition in which Roland was killed.   *MSS.*, Bibl. Nat. fr. 2495; Arsenal, 3145; Berne, 773.

Galien. Last third of century. None of the "Galien" in verse have come down to us. Three of these are thought, by evidence in later prose works, to have once existed; a French version of early 13th, another of late 13th, and a Franco-Italian version of middle 13th. Three prose versions are extant of 15th century. The tale is a continuation of the "Pèlerinage à Jerusalem," Galien being the son of Oliver and Jacqueline, daughter of the King Hugon of Constantinople. *MSS.*, Prose versions, Arsenal, 3351; Bibl. Nat. 1470; and an early printed text, from last MS. of 15th century.

Simon de Pouille (Alexandrines), early 13th. An account of the adventures, etc., of twelve of Charlemagne's Barons, whom he sends to the Emir Jonas. Simon de P. is the chief of these; by his parentage he is connected with the Cycle de Guillaume. *MSS.*, B.M. Reg. 15 E. vi.; Bibl. Nat. fr. 368.

Otinel (*see* England, § 61); cir. middle century. *Ed.*, F. Guessard et H. Michelant, "Anc. Poet. Fran.," 1859.

Girard d'Amiens. (§§ 55, 57.)

Charlemagne (Alexandrines), cir. 1295. In three books: the first a version of "Mainet," the other two based on Turpin, and Chansons de Geste, etc. It gives the history of the Emperor from childhood upwards. "A work of this kind is sufficient evidence that the genuine epic was dead." *MS.*, Bibl. Nat. 778.

51 *Cycle Garin de Montglane.*

Garin de Monglane (rhymed Alexandrine laisses, closed with an unrhymed six-syllabled line). The theme of this chanson is the pursuit of an unknown lady by the hero, who accomplishes many fine achievements and finally wins and marries Mabille. Their four sons are Hernaut, Renier, Milon, and Girart. A later versified version is extant;

prose works under this title are compilations of several poems. *MSS.*, Bibl. Nat. fr. 24403; B.M. Reg. 20, D. xi.; Vatican.

Bertrand de Bar-sur-Aube.

Girart de Viane (decasyllabic laisses, with final six-syllabled unrhymed line). In two parts. The four sons of Garin (*see* above) start in their several ways in search of adventures. Renier and Girart are insulted by Charlemagne not advancing to receive them as they near Paris, and they force themselves into his presence. Renier, whose conduct at court is exceptionally brutal, is given the dukedom of Rennes by the Emperor, Girart receives that of Viane. While the latter is paying homage to the Emperor by kissing his foot, the Empress manages to put an insult upon him, of which he himself however is unaware. His nephew Aimeri learns it, and tries to kill the Empress, and he with his uncle and the latter's brothers are soon at war with the Emperor; then follow Siege of Viane, introduction of Roland and Oliver as adversaries to one another, Roland's betrothal to Oliver's sister, Aude, and news of arrival of Saracens and preparation for the campaign in which these two heroes are killed. *Ed.*, P. Tarbé, 1850. *MSS.*, Bibl. Nat. fr. 1374, 1448; B.M. Harl. 1321; Reg. 20 B. xix.; 20 D. xi.

N.B.—An earlier version is lost. Prose versions are extant.

Bertram de Bar-sur-Aube is probably also the author of following poem, which is ascribed to him by G. Paris, who dates it and the preceding one 1210–1220.

Aimeri de Narbonne. The date is fixed for some time in first 35 years of century, mention being made of one who is evidently Andrew ii. of Hungary, who died 1235. The subject for this poem is the taking of Narbonne. After the defeat of Roncesvaux, his knights, worn out with their long warfare, are unwilling to besiege the town, till an impassioned speech of the Emperor, who feels that a Roland or an Oliver would have responded to his call, rouses Aimeri to

the deed. He is successful in his attack and is rewarded with
the gift of the town. Two versions in prose of 15th century.
Ed., Passages in "Hist. Litt.," t. xxii. *See* L. Demaison,
1887. *MSS.*, Bibl. Nat. fr. 1448, 24369 ; B.M. Reg.
20 D. xi. ; 20 B. xix. ; Harl. 1321.

N.B.—Victor Hugo in his "Légende des Siècles," took
the material for his two poems, "Le Mariage de Rolland"
and "Aymerillot," from these two last Chansons de Geste.

The deeds of the brothers Renier and Hernaut have only
been preserved to us in later prose versions.

Guillaume d'Orange was confounded with other heroes of
the North of France. This difficulty is explained away in
"Charroi de Nîmes," where Guillaume receives the investi-
ture of the South as a reward for his services ("Litt. moyen
Âge," § 39). Other poems of the Cycle are "Siège de
Narbonne," and "Enfances Vivien," whose death occurred at
Aliscans.

N.B.—Girart de Viane was not originally part of the same
cycle with Aimeri de Narbonne. G. d. V. was brother
to Arnaud, or Heraud, de Beaulande, the original hero of
the Cycle Monglane ; Aimeri de N. was next in generation
to Arnaud, and he and his thirteen children are met with in
various chansons. This branch belongs to the older
version and had its origin in Provence (*see* "Hist. poét.
Charlemagne"). Bertrand de Bar-sur-Aube brought the
two into one cycle.

Adenet le Roi. (*See* Cycle du Roi, §§ 50 and 57.)

Beuves (Bovon) de Commarchis, cir. 1270 (Alexandrine
laisses ending with one unrhymed short line). A version
of the Siège de Barbastre, originally in assonanced verse of
12th century. Aimeri's son Beuves and his two grandsons
are made prisoners by the Saracens. Clarion helps to deliver
them, and they besiege and take Barbastre. They themselves
are besieged, but finally relieved by the Emperor Louis,
Guillaume d'Orange, and Aimeri de Narbonne. An episode

in the poem is the love of Malatrie, betrothed to the Emir's
son, for Gérart de Commarchis, who has overcome her
betrothed in a duel. Adenet le Roi does not bring his
poem quite to the end of the narrative. *Ed.*, A. Scheler,
1875. *MS.*, Arsenal, B.L., 175 (MS. of A. le Roi's
other romances).

Anonymous.

Mort Aimeri de Narbonne (decasyllabic laisses, with final
unrhymed six-syllabled line), end 12th (Gautier, 13th).
Killed in battle together with some of his sons. Poem also
gives death of Aimeri's wife Hermengarde, " ci endroit
fine le livres de la fin d'Aymeri, et d'Ermengarde et de
plusieurs de leurs enfants." *Ed.*, Couraye du Parc., 1884.
MSS., Bibl. Nat. fr. 24370; B.M. Reg. 20, D. xi. ; 20,
B. xix.

52   *Cycle Doon de Mayence.*

Gui de Nanteuil. (*See* § 18.)

N.B.—The last chanson in connection with this family
was the " Tristan de Nanteuil," 14th century.

Renaus de Montauban, or *Les Quatre fils Aimon* (monorhymic laisses in Alexandrines). The poem is older than the
extant versions. The whole poem, according to the editor,
is a poetical version of various sagas. The first part, which
probably existed once as a separate chanson, tells of Beuve
d'Aigremont, who kills Charlemagne's son. The brother of
this Beuve and his four sons are later on at Charlemagne's
court ; one of them, Renaus, kills Charlemagne's nephew,
who has insulted him over a game of chess. Wars ensue ;
finally Renaus goes to the Holy Land ; on his return helps
to build Cologne Cathedral, is slain by his fellow-workers,
and in the end canonised. A wonderful horse, Bayard,
given to Renaus by the Emperor, plays a conspicuous part
in the tale. Later prose versions are extant ; nearly every
European language has commemorated this hero. *Ed.*,
H. Michelant, " Bibl. Litt. Verein.," 1862. *MSS.*,

Numerous MSS., Bibl. Nat. fr. 764, 766, 775; La Vallière, 39; Arsenal, B.L., 205; Montpelier, Metz, Venice, Brit. Mus.; Bodl. Hatton; (these cover different versions of the poem).

Doon de Mayence (Gautier, 13th century). A poem of the 14th in two parts, of which the latter contains an episode apparently of older date, and which may probably have been the subject of a separate poem ("Hist. Poet. Charl."). This episode tells how Doon passed through Paris, without paying his respects to Charlemagne, who, in his anger, strikes one of his knights; Doon, hearing of this, returns with an armed force; the Emperor and Doon meet in single combat, and fight until their hands are stayed by the intervention of an angel. A prose version was written in the 15th century, called "La Fleur des Batailles, Doolin de Maience." *Ed.*, A. Peÿ, "Anc. Poètes de la France," 1859. *MSS.*, Montpellier, Med. Fac. H. 247; Bibl. Nat. fr. 12563, 1637.

53 *Geste Bourguignon.*

Auberi le Bourguignon (decasyllabic laisses), early 13th century. History of the exploits of Auberi and his "Chevalerie," of his marriage with Guiboure, widow of the King of Bavaria, and his installation as ruler of this country. The poem also tells of his "enfances," when Auberi deals terrible revenge on those of his relatives who have ill-treated him. *Ed.*, P. Tarbé, 1849. *MSS.*, Bibl. Nat. fr. 859, 860, 24368; Berlin.

54 *Unattached Chansons.*

Bovon, or *Beuvon de Hanstone*, first third of century (*see* England, § 64). Hanstone has been generally thought to signify Southampton, but it seems there are indications in poem of the scene being laid in France, *i.e.*, it speaks of reaching Mayence from Hanstone without crossing the water. *Ed.*, A. Stimming, "Bibl. Normannica," vii.; *see* same in "Abhandl. Herrn Tobler, etc.," 1895. *MSS.*, Bibl. Nat. Nouv. Acq. 4532 (Ang.-Norm.); fr. 25516, 12548;

Bibl. Didot (Ang.-Norm.); Venice, Vienna, Vatican, Carpentras, Turin.

Orson de Beauvais (Alexandrine laisses), earliest possible date, 1185; MS. of 13th century. The treachery of Ugon, Comte de Berri, who, falling in love with Orson's wife, induces her husband to go with him on a pilgrimage, and on the way sells him into bondage. He forces Aceline to marry him, who, however, by the help of a magic herb, is enabled to remain faithful to her husband. Her son Milon finally avenges his father, and Ugon is hanged. The poem has many features in common with other romances. *Ed.*, G. Paris, 1899. *MS.*, Phillipps, 222.

Florence de Rome, last third of century. Through the jealousy of her brother-in-law, the Queen Florence becomes an outcast. She finds shelter with one Thierry; Macaire makes advances to her, and, in revenge for her rejection of them, accuses her of murdering Thierry's daughter. Cast adrift again, she is first sold to a Corsair; by her prayers she raises a storm, and in the resultant shipwreck is the only one saved. She wanders to a monastery, and there becomes renowned for her wonderful cures, and in the exercise of this art she is brought into contact again with her husband, brother-in-law, and Thierry. This legend has been associated by German writers with Charlemagne's wife, Hildegarde. The tale is similar to that of "Macaire" (§ 16). (*See* England, § 63; Spain, § 17.) *MS.*, Bibl. Nat. fr. 24384.

55   *Arthurian Cycle.*

See G. Paris, "Les Romans de la Table Ronde," 1868-97. The final version of the prose romances dates from the middle of this century.

Robert de Boron, fl. cir. 1215. This poet first definitely attached the history of the Graal to the Arthurian Cycle; he also brought the legend of Merlin, of which elements are in Geoffrey of Monmouth, into connection with the romances of the Round Table.

Joseph d'Arimathie or *Le Saint Graal.* This poem was early put into prose. The prose version, "Grand Saint Graal," was afterwards incorporated in the prose "Lancelot." *Ed.*, "Saint Graal" (verse), F. Michel, 1841; "Seynt Graal, or the Sank Ryal" (French prose and English verse by Lonelich), Furnivall, 1863; re-edited, 1874, etc.; prose, Hucher (MSS., Cangé and Didot), 1875. *MS.*, Bibl. Nat. 20047. For prose MSS. *see* Hucher, vol. i. (Preface).

Merlin. Only the beginning of this poem extant. This poem was early put into prose, and supplemented with a long continuation, and as such incorporated in the prose "Lancelot." *Ed.*, "Merlin and Continuations," G. Paris and J. Ulrich (Huth MS.), Soc. Anc. Textes, 1886; O. Sommer (B.M. Add. 10292), 1894. *MS.*, Bibl. Nat. 20047. For prose MSS. *see* Wheatley's "Merlin" (England, § 39), p. cxxxvi. ff.

Perceval. This poem is lost. Early prose version extant (Hucher, vol. i.). According to G. Paris, "Litt. moyen Âge," a prose version is extant of a poem which seems to have been written about the same time as R. de Boron's "Perceval." In this, the quest is carried out by Perceval (Perlesvaus) Gawain, and Lancelot, Percival being the chosen seer of the vision. From these earlier materials was compiled a "Quête de Saint Graal," attributed to R. le Boron, in which Galahad takes the place of Perceval as the favoured knight, but of this only a Portuguese translation is extant. Later on the "Quête" was given in another version, attributed to W. Map, and in this form was incorporated with the prose "Lancelot." (*See* "Litt. moyen Âge," § 60.) For "Perlesvaus," *see* Potvin, "Perceval le Gallois," and W. A. Nitze, "The Old French Grail Romance," 1902. *See* "Romania," xvi. 582.

Élie de Boron.

Palamède, or 1st part, *Méliadus.*
    2nd ,, *Guiron le Courtois.*
Ed., Hucher, "Le Saint Graal," i. (MS., 338). *See* Ward, "Cat. Rom.," i. 336. *Ed.*, *See* under R. de Pise. *MSS.*, Bibl. Nat. (11) fr. 338, 350, 356, etc.; Arsenal

(3); B.M. Add. 12228, 23930; Phillipps; and many foreign Libraries (*see* below, Löseth, pp. 435–6).

N.B.—"According to one of the continuations of "Merlin," this same Élie wrote a poem called "Conte du brait" (or bret) signifying the last cry uttered by Merlin before being entombed alive" (G. Paris, "Litt. moyen Âge," § 63).

Other names referred to in the old romances as having contributed to this cycle are Luce de Gast, and Gace le Blond (perhaps "Wace," G. Paris). Obscurity rests on these names, and there is doubt of their genuineness. W. Map's claim to the authorship of the prose "Lancelot" rests on a statement by Élie de Boron; and on the presence of his name on MSS. of this work. G. Paris entirely puts aside Map's claim to any of the four parts of the "Lancelot" which consisted of two parts of the "Lancelot" proper, the "Quête," and the "Morte Arthur."

Rusticien de Pise, cir. 1270. Of all the previous mass of work, this author compiled an abridged version, making use of a MS. in possession of Henry III.'s son, Edward. This version was translated into Italian. *Ed.*, E. Löseth, "Le Roman en prose de Tristan, le Roman de Palamide, et la compilation de Rusticien de Pise," 1891. *MSS.*, Bibl. Nat. fr. 340, 355, 1463.

Raoul de Houdan. Early century. (§ 48.)

Méraugis de Portlesguez (octosyllabic couplets). Méraugis, after winning the hand of Lidoine, starts with her on a year's series of adventures; leaves her in the city without a name; delays his return, and Lidoine leaves to go back to her home; seized on the way by a vassal; finally rescued by Méraugis. Raoul took Chrétien de Troies as his model. *Ed.*, H. Michelant, 1869. *MSS.*, Vienna, Rome, Turin, Berlin.

Girard d'Amiens. (§§ 50, 57.)

Escanor (octosyllabic couplets), cir. 1285. A long poem dealing with the loves of the Knight Keu and the Princess of

Northumberland (Norhomberlande); of Bel Escanor and his fight with Gauvain; and his final retirement into a hermitage where he dies; and many accessory incidents with no particular connection one with another.   *Ed.*, H. Michelant, 1886.   *MS.*, Bibl. Nat. fr. 24374.

Robert de Blois.   (§ 48.)   Works: Ed., J. Ulrich, 1889.

Beaudous (octosyllabic couplets), cir. 1250.   Tale of the Knight Beaudous, son of Gauvain, who begs permission of his mother to attend a festival at King Arthur's court.   He obtains it on condition of not making known his name, until he has won his spurs.   In the MS. in which the tale is preserved it is preceded by a prologue and dedication; when the mother is advising her son as to his conduct, the opportunity is used to introduce religious and didactic poems, which are also found in the Arsenal MS.   One of the interpolations is the "Chastiement des Dames."   The tale of "Floris and Liriope" is also inserted.   Unique *MS.*, Nat. Bibl. fr. 24301 (Beaudous); Arsenal, 5201 (other works).

Other romances of this class are:

Fergus (by a Guillaume le clerc); *Ider*; *Mériadeuc*, or the *Chevalier aux deux Épées*; *Guinglain* (by Renard de Beaujeu) (*see* "Libeaus Desconus," England, § 58); *Durmart le Gallois*, etc.   For these and similar romances, *see* "Hist. Litt.," vol. xxx.

56   ALEXANDER CYCLE (*see* 12th Century, § 27).

Jean le Nevelons, or **li Venelais,** 1288–1308.   (G. Paris, end 12th century.)

Vengeance d'Alexandre.   *MS.*, Reg. 19, D. 1.

Thomas or **Eustace de Kent** (according to different MSS.).

Roman de toute Chevalerie, cir. 1250.   Compilation based on French poems and Latin works (England, § 62).   The

English "Life of Alisaunder" is in great part founded on this work. *See* P. Meyer, "Alexandre le Grand dans le Littérature française du moyen Âge," 1886. *MSS.*, Bibl. Nat. fr. 24364; Trin. Coll. Camb.; Durham; Bodleian (fragment).

N.B.—The first French prose romance on Alexander was written in the second half of this century; two other prose romances date from the 15th century.

57 MISCELLANEOUS ROMANCES.

(Oriental, Greek, Teutonic, Celtic sources, etc.)

Anonymous.

Joufroi (octosyllabic couplets). Early century. The poem is incomplete. The author tells us that he took his tale from a Latin MS. in the cloister of St. Peter of Maguelonne, but no Latin original is known. There are possibly reminiscences in "Joufroi" of the adventures of Guillaume IX., Comte de Poitiers. The three chief episodes in it are—love between hero and dame de Tonnerre; voyage incognito into England; and adventure with the Queen Alis, wife of Henry I., who also (or perhaps Henry II.) figures in the poem. *Ed.*, K. Hofmann u. F. Muncker, 1880. *MS.*, Copenhagen, Anc. frs. roy. 3555.

Anonymous.

Octavien (octosyllabic couplets). Dealing with the usual theme of the calumniated wife, children borne away by wild beasts, etc. (*see* England, § 63). *Ed.*, K. Vollmöller, 1883. *MS.*, Bodl. Hatton, 100.

Anonymous.

Guillaume de Dole, or *Le Roman de la Rose* (octosyllabic couplets), cir. 1210. A woman's virtue is made the subject of a wager. Many variants of this leading motive (*see* "Dou roi Flore," § 43), are found in romances; it is most familiar in the tale of "Cymbeline." G. Paris tells us that it is first met with in a popular Greek song. A new feature in this romance is the introductions of "Chants," some of which are not found elsewhere. *Ed.*, Servois, "Soc. Anc. Textes," 1893; Trans. "Mod. Lang. Assoc.," vol. ii., 1886. *MS.*, Vatican, Christina, 1725.

L'Escoufle (*Falcon*) (octosyllabic couplets), cir. 1210. The leading incident, found in Eastern tales, is the theft of a ring by a bird, which causes the separation of the lovers. It is introduced into other French romances, and occurs in "Sir Isumbras" (*see* England, § 63). *Ed.*, H. Michelant and P. Meyer, 1894. *MS.*, Arsenal, 6565.

Gerbert de Montreuil.

Roman de la Violette, or *de Gérard de Nevers*, cir. 1225. A tale similar to that of Guillaume de Dole. *Ed.*, F. Michel, 1834. *MSS.*, Bibl. Nat. fr. 1374, 1553.

Renaut.

Galeran de Bretagne (octosyllabic couplets), cir. 1230. Development of subject of "Lai le Frêne" (§ 31). Frêne and Galeran are brought up together, love and are separated and lost to one another; Galeran is on the eve of marriage with Frêne's sister, when Frêne is identified by an embroidered cloak, etc. The editor thinks the author may possibly be the Renaut who wrote the charming "lai de l'ombre et de l'anneau" (fr. 1553). *Ed.*, A. Boucherie, 1888. *MS.*, Bibl. Nat. fr. 24042.

Anonymous.

Eustache le Moine (octosyllabic couplets), cir. 1230. Partly based on historic facts. The hero is knight, monk, pirate, and sorcerer. He was killed in 1217 when making a descent upon England, and an account of his death is found in MS. Harl. 636, where we learn that the people of Sandwich were saved by the intervention of S. Bartholomew. *Ed.*, W. Foerster and J. Trost, "Roman. Bibl.," iv. 1891. *MS.*, Bibl. Nat. fr. 1553.

17

Gilles de Chin. Cir. 1250. The hero was an historical personage, who became a crusader; his marriage, related in the poem, is also a matter of history. Two names are mentioned in connection with poem: Gautier de Tournai and Gautier le Cordier; G. Paris assigns the work solely to the former of these. *Ed.*, de Reiffenberg, 1847. *MS.*, Arsenal, B.L., fr. 167.

Alexandre du Pont.

Roman de Mahomet (octosyllabic couplets), 1258. A history of the prophet, who is here transformed into a mediæval character. According to the author the details of his poem were furnished by a converted Mussulman, whose account was put into Latin by a monk, and translated ftom the latter by the French poet. Some of the incidents, however, are found in a Latin poem, cir. 1100, by Hildebert, Bishop of Mans, and also in Vincent de Beauvais' work, "Speculum Historiale." *Ed.*, F. Michel, 1831. *MS.*, Bibl. Nat. fr. 1553.

Philippe de Beaumanoir, b. cir. 1250; d. 1296.
(*See* Law, § 42.)
Poetical Works, *Ed.*, H. Suchier, 1884–85.

Manekine. To escape her father's persecution, Manekine cuts off her hand; is condemned to death; flees, and marries King of Scotland. She is accused of giving birth to monsters; again flees; finally is rehabilitated in her husband's esteem, and has hand restored by the Pope's prayer. Jean Wauquelin (d. 1452) put various romances into prose, among them "Manekine." *Ed.*, F. Michel, 1840. *MS.*, P. de B.'s poetical works are contained in Bibl. Nat. fr. 1588.

N.B.—Several versions are extant of this tale, which is found attached by tradition to Offa 1. Similar tales are: "La Belle Hélène" (who appears in the history of S. Martin as his mother) (*see* § 82); "La Comtesse d'Anjou" (§ 82); "Mai und Beaflor" (Germany, 13th century, § 34); "Emare" (England, § 64, note), and it is allied in parts to the story of Constance.

Jehan de Dammartin et Blonde d'Oxford.   J. de D., in love
with B. d'O., is recalled to his father's court, and only
returns in time to escape with her on the eve of her enforced
marriage.   Jehan's horse is a remarkable feature in the tale.
A variant of the same theme occurs in a later prose romance,
"Jean de Paris," and in "King Horn" (G. Paris, "Litt.
moyen Âge," § 68).   *Ed.*, Le Roux de Lincy, Camden
Soc., 1858.

Other poetical works by P. de Beaumanoir are :
*Sala d'Amours, Conte d'Amours, Conte de folle largesse,
Fatrasie* (2), *Lai d'Amours, Ave Maria, Salut à refrains.*

Jakemon Sakesep (Saket, Saquet).

Le Châtelain de Couci.   Last third of century (*see* K. v.
Würzburg, German, § 34).   Tale of the Chatelain de Couci
and the Dame de Faïel.   The culminating incident is the
serving up of the heart of the dead lover to his wife by the
husband.   The Châtelain de Couci was not the original hero
connected with this tale.   It has been associated with the
Troubadour Guilhem de Cabestaing, and with a Minnesinger.
It is seemingly of Celtic origin, and was the subject of the
lost lai of "Guiron"; a variant of the tale is found in
"Lai d'Ignaurès," where twelve husbands serve up a single
lover's heart to their wives.   A similar tale is Boccaccio's
"Guiscardo e Gismonde."   Ritson gives an English version
in his "Metrical Romances"; and Hazlitt, "Remains of
Early Popular Poetry," ii., "The Knight of Courtesy,"
etc.   *See* "Hist. Litt.," xxviii.; and "Romania," xiii.
MS., Ashburnham.

Mestre Requis.

Richars li biaus (*le beau*) (octosyllabic couplets).   Last
third of century.   In two parts, not originally connected.
The first part gives the incident familiar from the earliest
times, of the son meeting the father after many years of
separation, and the two, not recognising one another, entering
into deadly combat (*see* Sir Degarre, England, § 40).   The
second part is similar to the tale of "Sir Amadas" (Weber,

"Met. Rom.," iii.). The hero having parted with his last money to redeem the body of a knight which had been refused burial by his creditors, the grateful dead, under condition of sharing all that Richard obtains, helps the latter to a wife and possessions. *Ed.*, W. Förster, 1874. *MS.*, Turin, Univ. Bibl., L. i. 13.

The editor thinks this poem is possibly by the same author as "Blancandin," as there are similarities in incident and technique.

Sarrazin.

Le Tournoi de Ham (octosyllabic couplets), cir. 1278. Tournament supposed to take place at Ham, in Picardy. The chief aim of the poem is to show the injury done to jongleurs, workmen, and sellers of merchandise, by the prohibition of tournaments (they were suppressed for two years by Sr. Louis, after the defeat of the Christians in the East in 1260; and this ordonnance of the King's was several times renewed by his successors). The above tournament, however, takes place, and present at it are Queen Guinevere, Yvain, and other Knights of the Round Table. *Ed.*, Fr. Michel, 1840 (with "Histoire des Ducs de Normandie"). *See* also Preface to "Manekine" by same editor. *MS.*, Bibl. Nat. fr. 1588.

Adenet le Roi. (§§ 50, 51.) A protégé of Henry III. of Brabant; accompanied the armies of the Second Crusade.

Cléomadès (octosyllabic couplets), cir. 1280. This poem and the "Méliacin" of Girard d'Amiens deal with the same subject. In each there is a King with three daughters and a son (Cléomadès, or Méliacin); wise men arrive with presents of various things possessed of magic powers; one of these is a horse of ebony, which will carry its rider through the air, being guided by means of pegs. The king's son, having aroused the ill-will of the inventor, is carried into the air by the horse, before having learnt the secret of guiding it; he finds this out by accident and descends into a castle where there is a beautiful girl; obliged to escape on his horse, on account of the father, he returns later and carries off the

girl; they descend into an orchard near his home; in an
unguarded moment he leaves her with his old enemy, who
mounts the horse and goes off with her. Finally the hero
finds her again, in the power of a foreign king; she is
feigning madness to protect herself; and the hero, pretending
to be a doctor, manages again to escape with her on the
wooden horse. (*See* Girard d'Amiens.)

"A magic horse is known in Indian tales, and the tale
probably reached France through an Arab version, possibly
brought from Spain by Blanche de Castille." *Ed.*, A.
van Hasselt, 1865. *See* "Hist. Litt.," xxiii. 182–194.
MSS., Bibl. Nat. 1456, 12561, 19165 (three others);
Arsenal, 3142; Bern, 238.

Anonymous.

La Châtelaine de Vergi (octosyllabic couplets), cir. 1280.
The exposure of the love between the châtelaine and a
knight, by the jealous Duchess of Burgundy, causes the
châtelaine's death. The knight kills himself, and the Duke,
on finding out what has happened, kills his wife and goes to the
Holy Land. The personages in this poem are not fictitious.
Ed., G. Raynaud, "Romania," xxi. p. 143; prose version
(French and English), L. Brandin, 1903. *MSS.*, Bibl.
Nat. fr. 375, 837, 25545, 1555, 2136; Nouv. Acq. 4531;
Berlin, Hamilton, 257; Bodleian, 445 (later copy).

Blancandin et l'Orgueilleuse d'Amour (octosyllabic couplets).
Extant in two versions. Orgueilleuse is so incensed at being
embraced in public by Blancandin that she vows vengeance
on him, but her anger is overcome by her admiration of his
prowess, and they are betrothed. Saracen king arrives as
a rival; Blancandin made prisoner, and placed in a vessel
from which he escapes in a shipwreck; he returns, conquers
his enemies, and marries Orgueilleuse. A few extra details
are added as a finale to the second version. Two prose
versions are extant, from one of which was taken the English
version of 15th century by Caxton. *Ed.*, H. Michelant,
1867. *MSS.*, First version, Bibl. Nat. 19152, Add.
15212; second version, fds. fr. 375; Turin. *Ed.*
(Caxton), E.E.T.S., 1890.

Thibaud.

Li Romanz de la Poire (octosyllabic couplets). Early 13th century. An allegorical love poem in the style of the "Roman de la Rose." The editor thinks the poet was familiar with the first part of the latter work, otherwise the resemblance must be due to identity of source for the two works. In this poem the poet is besieged by love, and gives in; the object of his adoration is removed from him by her high station, but love's golden dart pierces her heart also, and they are united. There are allegorical personages, such as Beauty, Courtesy, etc. *Ed.*, F. Stehlich, 1881. *MSS.*, Bibl. Nat. fr. 2186, 12786, 24431.

Jacques Bretel.

Tournois de Chauvenci (octosyllabic couplets), cir. 1285. Description of tournaments. *MSS.*, Mons; Bodl. Douce, 308.

Girard d'Amiens. (§§ 50, 55.)

Méliacin (octosyllabic couplets), cir. 1290 (*see* Cléomadès). Similar subject to "Cléomadès." Although alike in many respects, the plagiarism of which G. d'Amiens has been accused, is thought to be hardly proved by comparing the two poems; the resemblance being due more probably to the identity of source from which the authors drew their material. Girard's poem is very inferior to that of Adenet. *Ed.*, Part only, E. Stengel, "Zeitschr. Rom. Phil.," x. 460. *MSS.*, Bibl. Nat. fr. 1455, 1589, 1633; Florence, Riccard.

Anonymous.

Floriant et Florete (octosyllabic couplets), 13th (or 14th) century. The hero, a son of the King of Palermo, is brought up by the fairy Morgain. At an early age he begins to show his knightly prowess, and distinguishes himself at a tournament given by King Arthur; the latter helps him to rescue his beleaguered mother; for this purpose they sail to the harbour of London, etc. Finally, Floriant is transported by Morgain to her magic castle of Mongibel, where he and Florete lose count of time in endless content. *Ed.*, Fr. Michel, "Metrical Romance of the 14th century"; Roxburghe Club, 1873. *MSS.*, Bibl. Nat. fr. 1492; Newbattle Abbey.

Douin de Lavesnes.

Trubert (octosyllabic couplets). Early 13th century. A collection of comic tales, of which the hero, the son of a poor widow, delights in deceiving everyone with whom he comes in contact. The tales are found elsewhere, and are of Oriental origin. *Ed.*, Méon, "Nouv. Rec.," i. *MS.*, Bibl. Nat. 2188.

N.B.—Imitations of Ovid are also found among the romances; of these are "Narcisse," by an anonymous author, and "Floris and Liriope" (Arsenal, 5201), by Robert de Blois (*see* under "Beaudous," § 55).

58 ALLEGORICAL ROMANCE.

Roman de la Rose. First part, cir. 1237, in 22,000 octosyllabic lines.

> "Ci est le romant de la Rose
> Où l'art d'amors est tote enclose."

The first part of this work by **Guillaume de Lorris,** carries out the intention expressed in these two lines. Amant (personified Love), endeavours to gain possession of the Rose (Beauty); he is prevented by various personified vices, but "Bel Accueil" and others give him assistance, and at last he is allowed to kiss the Rose. The latter is then placed in closer confinement, but the end of the tale is not told us, for Lorris died in the midst of his lament over this.

Second part. About forty years later, the poem was continued by Jean de Meun (§§ 45, 48), but in a very different spirit, and the latter poet apparently addressed a different class of readers. We have the same characters, but Jean de Meun was less interested in the pursuit of love than in more general matters, and his part of the work contains discussions on irrelevant subjects, and is made the vehicle of his satire and cynicism, women coming in for a large share of abuse.

The "Roman de la Rose" was the *chef d'œuvre* of the Middle Ages; no other work equalled it in renown. We have a proof of the importance attached to its influence in the writings of Christine de Pisan, who protests against the attacks on women by J. de Meun, and by the great preacher Gerson in his treatise on the poem. The "Roman" has come down also in a French version of the 16th century from the hand of the poet Marot (*see* also England, § 76). There were several imitations of this allegory, *i.e. Panthère d'Amour*, by Nicole de Margival; *Cour d'Amour*, by Mahieu le Poriier, etc. *Ed.*, F. Michel, 1864, trans. by F. S. Ellis, "Temple Classics." *See* "Hist. Litt.," xxiii.

For sources: Petit de Julleville, "Hist. Litt.," ii.; G. Paris, "Litt. moyen Âge"; Langlois, "Origines et Sources, etc.," 1891; "Romania," 24, 277. *MSS.*, These are numerous, being found in all the chief libraries of the Continent. Paris MSS. Besides those in Bibl. Nat. are Bibl. Geneviève, 1126, 1127; Mazarine, 3872–3875; Arsenal, 2988, 2989, etc. Early printed eds. of late 15th cent.

59 *Roman de Renard.*

Anonymous.

Couronnement de Renard. Composed in Flanders, cir. 1255.

Jacquemard Gélée. Also Flemish writer.

Renard le Nouveau, cir. 1288. *See*, for both the above, Méon, "Rom. de Renart," 1826.

60 *Fableaux.*

For list of names of the writers of Fableaux in the 12th century, *see* "Hist. Litt.," xxiii. pp. 114–116. Among these are—

Gautier le Long.

La Veuve ; Valet qui d'aise à malaise se met.

Courtebarbe. *Les trois aveugles.*

Bernier. *La Housse partie.*

Henri d'Andeli. (§ 61a, b). *Le lai d'Aristote.*

Jean de Condé. (§ 61b). *Clerc caché; Le Sentier battu.*

Rustebeuf. (§§ 48, 61a, b.).

Charlot le Juif ; Frère Denise.
La Dame qui alla trois fois entour le Moutier.
Le pet au vilain.

Ed., " Recueil général et complet des Fabliaux des xiiie et xive Siècles," de Montaiglon et G. Raynaud, 1872–90. (*See* § 33.) *See* " Hist. Litt.," xxiii. pp. 69–215.

61a   Miscellaneous : Débats, Dits, Contes.

Débats, Batailles.

Henri d'Andeli. (§ 60.)

La bataille des Vins (octosyllabic couplets). After 1223. *MSS.,* Bibl. Nat. fr. 837 ; Berne, 113.

La bataille des sept Arts (octosyllabic couplets). Written after 1236. Conflict between logic and grammar, and the respective schools of Paris and Orleans. *MSS.,* Bibl. Nat. fr. 837 and 19152.

Works : *Ed.,* A. Héron, 1881.

Rustebeuf. (§§ 48, 60, 61b.)

Du Croisé et du Non Croisé.
De la Descorde de l' Université et des Jacobins.

Other poems of this class are:

De la Desputoison de la Sinagogue et de Sainte Eglise.
Disputoison entre l'Hiver et l'Été (Harleian MS.).
Du Denier et de la Brebis.
Mariage des sept Arts et des sept Vertus, by Jehan le
Teinturier.
See "Hist. Litt.," xxiii. pp. 216-234.

61b DITS ET CONTES: RELIGIOUS, DIDACTIC, SATIRICAL, ETC.

One of the chief writers of "Dits" in this century was—

Baudouin de Condé. Nothing is definitely known of
the date or place of birth of either Baudouin, or of his son,
Jean de Condé. Baudouin flourished probably 1245-1275.

Dit du Gardecors.   A piece of protective dress.
  „ „ *Pellicam.*
  „ „ *Baceler.*   Conditions and duties of a "prud'homme."
  „ „ *Dragon.*   The evil speaker.
  „ „ *Mantiel.*   Mantle of honour, symbolising virtues.
  „ „ *Preudome.*   Duties and convenances of the man of
                      position.
  „ „ *d'Envie ; d'Amours ; de la Rose ; de l'Aver* (avarice).
  „ *des Mondes et des Mondés.*
  „ „ *Fust.*   This word signifies various things: tree,
                    ship, cunning.
  „ *des Hiraus* (heralds).
  „ „ *trois Mors et des trois Vis.*
  „ *de Gentilleche* (Gentillesse).
  „ „ *la Pomme.*

Other works—

Li contes dou Pel.   On the avarice of Lords and Prelates,
in allegorical form; Pel, signifying a dry stick which breaks
when used for support.

Li contes de l'Olifant (elephant).

Li vers de la Char.

Li Ave Maria.

La Voie de Paradis. Two similar poems are extant, one by Raoul de Houdan (§ 48), and one by Rustebeuf (§ 48).

Li Prisons d'amours. Long allegorical poem on different phases of love.

Ed., "*Dits et Contes de Baudouin et Jean de Condé*," A. Scheler, 1866, etc. *MSS.*, Chief MS. containing the "Dits" of B. and J. de Condé is, Arsenal, 317. Other MSS., Bibl. Nat. fr. 1446, 1634, etc.; Arsenal, 175; Brussels, Turin, Vienna.

Jean de Condé. Son of the above. (§ 60.)

Dits et Contes. Thirty-six contes, mostly entitled "dis," some narrative and some allegorical or didactic are given in the edition of Jean de Condé's work, by A. Scheler, 1866, etc.

Henri d'Andeli. (§ 60.)

Dit du Chancelier Philippe (octosyllabic couplets), 1237. A Chancellor of Paris, active in support of the Bishop of Paris in the dispute with the university and others. According to the poem, he wrote Latin and French verse. *Ed.*, "Works," A. Héron, 1881. *MS.*, B.M. Harl. 4333.

N.B.—The "Lai d'Aristote" was probably H. d'Andeli's earliest work. The authorship of "Dit du Chancelier Philippe" has been doubted on dialectic grounds. *See* for this, and for identification of H. d'Andeli, F. Augustin, "Ausg. u. Abhandl., Rom. Phil.," xliv.

Rustebeuf. (§§ 48, 60, 61a.) Date of oldest of his known poems, 1253 or 1255; latest events alluded to, 1285. Though dealing with many subjects, Rustebeuf was more particularly a satirist.

Dit de l'herberie (partly prose). Description of medical quack at a fair.

Dit de l'université. Rustebeuf took an active part in the conflict between the University of Paris and the Mendicant orders.

Les ordres de Paris.

Dit des cordeliers.

Chanson des ordres.

Of other satirical poems by Rustebeuf we have—

Li testament de l'âne.

De l'estat du Monde.

De Sainte Eglise.

Renard le Bestourné.

Du Pharisian.

Ed., "Oeuvres complètes," A. Jubinal, 1874. For *MSS. see* § 48.

Anonymous.

Ch'est Li Dis dou vrai Aniel (du vrai anneau). A father leaves his three sons each a ring; two are counterfeit; the third possesses magic qualities of healing. "The true ring is not to be confounded with the false ones, as neither the law of the Saracens, nor of the Jews, is to be mistaken for the true law of Christianity." According to G. Paris the tale was invented by some Jews to awaken doubts among Christians as to the legitimacy of their persecution, and was later adapted to Christian interpretation. Compare Lessing's "Nathan der Weise." *Ed.,* Tobler, 1871, 1884. *MS.,* Bibl. Nat. fr. 25566.

Le Chevalier au Barii. The tale of a knight who refuses to do penance, but finally consents as such to fill a small barrel of water. But the penance is not a light one after all, for water flees before him, and not one drop can he procure; so he wanders for years, and at last returns to the priest, his task still unaccomplished. But he is a changed man now; a tear of repentance falls into the barrel and the vessel is instantly filled to overflowing. *Ed.,* Méon, "Fabliaux, etc.," i.;

Bartsch, "Chrestomathie." *See* "Hist. Litt.," xxiii., and "Notices et Extraits," xxxiv.   *MSS.*, Bibl. Nat. fr. 1807. 1553, 25438, 24300; Arsenal ; Phillipps, 3643.

La Prise de Jérusalem, or, *La vengeance du Sauveur* (Alexandrine laisses). The oldest form of this tale is thought to be an apocryphal work extant in two versions, "Vindicta Salvatoris" and "Cura Sanitatis Tiberii." The legend tells of the miraculous cure of Tiberius, who is attacked by leprosy ; in the French poem it is the Emperor Vespasian whose leprosy is healed by the cloth of Veronica. He undertakes the siege of Jerusalem in gratitude to the Saviour. A French prose versior is also extant, as well as versions in English, Provençal, and Catalan. *See* P. Meyer (on Provençal text), "Bull. Soc. Anc. Textes," 1875. English version, *see* Ward, "Cat. Rom.," vol. i.   *MSS.*, Bibl. Nat. fr. 1374, 1553, 20039, 15439; Arsenal, B.L., fr. 283; B.M. Reg. 16, E. viii.; Add. 10289; Phillipps, 3657; Eng. version, Cott. Cal. A. ii.; Vesp. E. xvi.

N.B.—This was the last poem written in the old style of the Chansons de Geste.

Of other "contes" mention may be made of *Tombeur de Notre Dame*.   *MS.*, Arsenal, B.L. fr. 28 (*ed.*, "Romania," ii. 315) and *L'enfant Juif* (*see* Germany, § 13).

Légende de la Croix, also known as *Pénitence d'Adam*. Extant in various forms.

For apocryphal legends, in connection with Biblical personages, *see* under Bible Historiale, § 39.

62   LYRIC.

Before the close of the 12th century, the forms of lyric which were to become the favourite ones of the 13th century, had already been established ; such were the pastourelle, lai, virelai, rotrouenge, motet, serventois, jeux partis. The "Chansonniers" of the 13th century number nearly two hundred. Embryo academies, called Puys, were established in various places, and here honours were awarded to the poets according to the merit of their work. One of the most noted of these assemblies was the Puy d' Arras, at which centre a more original form of poetry was developed. The greater number of lyrics continued to be mere variations, in many cases of little originality, of the one absorbing theme —the courtly intercourse between man and woman, which went in those days by the name of love. *MSS.*, Lyrics of 13th and 14th centuries: Bibl. Nat. fr. 12581, principally poems of Thibaut de Navarre; fr. 847, 1109, 25566, poems of Adam de la Halle; fr. 765, 844 (Provençal poems also), 845, 846, 1591, 12483, 12615, 20050, 24406; Nouv. Acq. 1050; fr. 22928 and eight others, G. de Coinci. Arsenal; Arras; Berne, 231, 389; Vatican, etc.; Camb., Corp-Christ., 450; B.M., Egerton, 274; Bodl. Douce, 308; Lambeth (fragment). *See* "Bibliographie des Chansonniers Français des xiii⁰ et xiv⁰ Siècles," G. Raynaud, 1884.

Audefroid le Bâtard. First third of century. A poet
of Arras. He imitated the "Chansons de toile" of the 12th century, substituting rhyme for assonance, and making use of twelve-syllabled lines; he also introduced alternate rhymes, apparently imitated from the Provençal. Five of these songs are extant.

Jean Bodel. (*See* Carl. Cycle, 12th century, § 16;
Drama, § 63.) A native of Arras.

Congé, 1202. The poet, attacked by leprosy, bade adieu to his friends at Arras, in this poem of forty-two strophes.

Baude Fastoul, another poet who fell a victim to the
same disease, imitated Bodel and also wrote a "Congé" (cir. 1265).

Thibaud IV. Comte de Champagne and King of
Navarre, b. 1201; d. 1253. About seventy poems by this celebrated lyrical writer have been preserved; among them are twelve jeux-partis, thirteen serventois, and two pastourelles. The greater number of his verses are inspired by

his passionate devotion to Blanche de Castille, the mother of St. Louis. Religious poems and Chansons de Croisade are among his works.

Colin Muset.

First half of century. Two lais, three saluts d'amours, a descort, and five chansonettes, are all that are with certainty assigned to him.

Gautier de Coinci.

Better known by his larger works (§ 48); has left some songs dedicated to the Virgin, written in imitation of the profane songs which were then the fashion. As many as twenty-nine chansons are ascribed to him in various MSS.

Adam de la Halle, fl. 1250-1270. (§ 63.)

Congé. In imitation of Bodel; Adam, however, left his native town on account of political troubles, and his farewell poem is a lively satire on the town and its inhabitants. We have besides jeux-partis, rondeaux, motets, a dit d'amour, and a Noël. His poems were especially admired for the music to which he set them, and which has, in some cases, been preserved.

Rustebeuf. (§§ 48, 60, 61a, 61b, 63.)

Poems composed on his own life, on his poverty, marriage, etc.; on personages of note and great events.

Le mariage Rustebeuf.
La complainte Rustebeuf.
La mort Rustebeuf.
La Griesche d'este.
La Griesche d'yver, etc.
MSS., Bibl. Nat. 837, 1593, 1635.

Charles D A'njou.

Brother of Saint Louis, and King of Sicily. Two poems of his remain.

Guillebert de Berneville.

Native of Arras. One of the last of the Lyric poets.

Huon, or Hugues de Berze. (§ 48.)

A poem addressed to Folquet de Romans at the time of the Fourth Crusade, urging him to take the cross.

N.B.—Names of women are found among the lyric poets of this century. The serious lyric was parodied in "Sottes Chansons."

See "Hist. Litt.," xxiii. pp. 312–831; for other works, *see* under Lyric, 12th century.

Élégie Juive. A French elegy, in monorhymic quatrains, written in Hebrew characters, is preserved in the Vatican. It is the dirge of thirteen Jews who were burnt at Troyes in 1288. A Hebrew elegy, commemorating the same event, is preserved with it. *Ed.*, "Deux Elégies du Vatican," "Romania," iii. 443.

63 DRAMA.

The "jeux" of which the "jeux d'Adam" of the 12th century was a specimen, multiplied in the 13th century, and a tragic element became more conspicuous.

Jean Bodel of Arras. (§§ 16, 62.)

Jeu de S. Nicholas. The oldest French miracle play. The play takes place during the time of the Crusades; a heathen king experiences the miraculous power of a portrait of S. Nicholas, and is converted. *Ed.*, Monmerque and Michel, "Théâtre français au moyen Âge," 1842; Heithecker, 1885. *MS.*, Bibl. Nat. fr. 25566.

Rustebeuf. (§§ 48, 60, 61a, 61b, 62.)

Miracle de Théophile. Théophile is known as the Faust of the Middle Ages, for he sells his soul to the devil; he is finally delivered by the intercession of the Virgin. *See* "Works," Kressner, 1885. For *MSS.*, *see* § 48.

Adam de la Halle, b. cir. 1235; d. probably 1286.

Li Jus Adam, or *Jeu de la Feuillée,* cir. 1262; so called on account of the scene being represented in one of the green bowers erected in celebration of the returning Spring. In this satirical play he puts himself and his father, and several of the citizens of Arras, on the stage. *MSS.,* Bibl. Nat. fr. 837, 25566; Vatican (Christina).

Robin et Marion (octosyllabic), cir. 1280; probably written for a Court festival at Naples; it continued a favourite play and was acted every Whitsuntide at Angers, till cir. 1400. The play is a pastoral or a comic opera, the author himself writing the music for it, and was the first specimen of this class of drama. *MSS.,* Bibl. Nat. fds. fr. 1569, 25566; Aix en Provence, Bibl. Méjanes.

A prologue to this play is the

Jeu de Pèlerin, 1288. In it the pilgrim announces to the audience that the renowned poet who had died at Naples was the author of the play about to be given.

Ed., "Oeuvres complètes de A. de la Halle," De Coussemaker, 1874. *See* also A. Rambeau, "On the dramas assigned to A. de la Halle," 1886. *MS.,* Bibl. Nat. 26566.

The earliest farce extant is

Du Garçon et de l'Aveugle. Played at Tournai, cir. 1297. *Ed.,* Meyer, "Jahrb. Rom. u. Eng. Lit.," vi. 163.

XIVth CENTURY.

The 14th century saw a change come over the spirit of French literature; the flow of romance was checked; the Chansons de Geste were transcribed into prose versions; efforts to revive or continue the old epics resulting in feeble imitations of the earlier heroic songs. On the other hand, didactic literature flourished, the love of learning and instruction taking the place of the former delight in tales of chivalry and adventure. Certain fixed laws were now imposed upon

18

the lyric poets, which, if tending to monotony of style, had its advantages, for the modern reader ; for, as M. Julleville writes, "after getting to the end of *Baudouin de Sebourg*, as long as an Iliad and an Odyssey combined, one is filled with joy at the thought that a chant-royal never had more than sixty lines, and a balade less." The rondeau, balade, chant-royal, and lai with twelve strophes, were among the favourite forms. The balade, from the 14th century, had three, sometimes five strophes of equal length, with the same scheme of rhyme in each, and an envoy [1] ; the chant-royal had five eleven-lined strophes and an envoi of 5, 6, or 7 lines, with the same rhyme scheme in each strophe ; the rondel was composed of two quatrains and a quintain, with rules for the repetition of certain lines ; a rondeau had a tercet between two quintains, also with rules for repetition of word or words.

For further details of these and other forms, and for specimens of each, *see* Brandin and Hartog, "Book of French Prosody," 1904.

PROSE.

64   *Science.*

Anonymous.

Cy nous dit. Early 14th century. A popular work in which the moralising holds a chief place. The tales introduced in it are taken from the usual sources : Bible, Legends of Saints, etc. They are given shortly and without much attempt at literary finish. *See* "Romania," 16, 567.   *MSS.*, Bibl. Nat. fr. 425, 436, 9576, 17050, 17051, 17059, etc. ; Geneviève, 1465 ; Brussels, 9017, 10388.

Le Livre du roy Modus (*Manière*) *et de la royne Racio* (*Reason*), *qui parle des deduis* (*sport*) *et de pestilence*, cir. 1340.

1st part.   Actual book on the Chace.
2nd   „   Allegorical "Ci devise le songe de l'acteur de la pestilence et comment les vertus en furent chacées."

[1] The envoy always begins with the word *Prince*, probably addressed, it is thought, to the umpire of a real or supposed poetical tournament, the president of one of the Puys.

The work is a kind of catechism on matters of the chace. The King answers all the questions on the chace itself, and the Queen unfolds moral and symbolical interpretations. Historical allusions are found in the work, and prophecies concerning the affairs of Charles v.'s reign, "de la prophécie pestilencielle sur le royaume de France." All the MSS. begin—

> " Au temps du riche roi modus
> Fut bien le monde en paix tenus,
> Qui avoit le gouvernement
> Sur toutes manières de gent."

Ed., E. Blaze, 1839 (part only). *See* " Romania," ix. ; for discussion of authorship, *see* V. Bouton, 1888. *MSS.*, Bibl. Nat. fr. 614, 1297, 1303, 12399, etc. Several of these are illustrated. Arsenal, 3080, 5197 ; Bodl. Rawl. 676 ; Phillipps ; Ashburnham (Barrois) ; Gray's Inn. Other foreign libraries.

Count Gaston Phoebus de Foix, d. 1391.

Les déduits de Chasse. A famous book on the Chace ; considered the best extant ; "it only requires a little modernising to become the Vade Mecum of all hunters to this day." Gaston sent a manuscript of his work to Philippe le Hardi, son of King John. This MS. was carried to Spain, and disappeared from the Escurial in 1809. The editor Lavallée gives an interesting description of Gaston's life as an introduction to his work. *Ed.*, Lavallée, 1854. *MS.*, Bibl. Nat. 7098.

A version contained in a 16th century MS. of the Arsenal, was also edited by E. Jullien and P. Lacroix, 1881, under the title "Le bon varlet de chiens," taken from the last line of the work.

The science of war was not neglected, it was treated towards the close of the century by Honoré Bonet in *L'Arbre des Batailles.* *Ed.*, E. Nys, 1883. *MSS.*, fr. 9690, 9691, etc.

Part of Christine de Pisan's "Livre des faits d'Armes et de Chevalerie" is composed of a lively dialogue between herself and this author on questions of war.

65　　　　*Religious, Didactic, etc.*

Nicole Bozon.　　A Franciscan who lived in England.

Contes Moralisés, cir. 1330. This work is covered by three headings: Facts in Natural History; Examples; and Fables, properly so called, drawn from various sources.

N.B. — The Phillipps MS. also contains poems by Bozon.

Le Char d'orgueil (other MSS., Camb. Univ. Gg. 6, 28; B.M. Reg. 8, E. xvii.; Bodley, 425).
De la Bonté des femmes,
La femme comparée à la Pie (also Harl. 2253),
Poème allégorique sur la Passion (also Cott. Jul., A. v.),
Sermons en vers,
Prière à la Vierge,
Hymn on the Annunciation,
Paraphrase of the Ave Maria,
Traité de " denaturesce" (want of natural affection),
and others not given under Bozon's name but probably also his.　　*Ed.,* L. Toulmin Smith and P. Meyer, "Soc. Anc. Texts," 1889.　　*MSS.,* Gray's Inn; Phillipps, 8336.

Christine de Pisan.　　(§§ 67, 72, 73, 86.)

La Vision de Christine. In this we have her own life, as well as a history of the country and an account of different systems of philosophy.　　*MSS.,* Bibl. Nat. fr. 1176; Brussels, 10309.

La Cité des Dames. Fables and tales from both ancient and modern sources, showing forth the heroism and loyalty of women.　　*MSS.,* Bibl. Nat. fr. 607, 608, 609, 1177, 1178, 1179, etc.; Brussels, 9235, 9393.

N.B.—An old Eng. translation was published 1521.

Trésor de la Cité des Dames, or *Livre des trois Vertus.* A treatise on the duties of women addressed to all classes. Many interesting details of domestic life are given in it. *MS.,* Bibl. Nat. fr. 452, 1177, 1180.

Livre de Prudence. A paraphrase of Seneca. *MSS.,*
Bibl. Nat. fr. 605, 2240 ; Brussels, 11072, 11076.

Epistles on the Roman de la Rose. Christine's opinion of
this romance is summed up in two lines of one of her poems.

> "Se bien veult et chastement vivre,
> De la rose ne liz le livre."

MSS., Bibl. Nat. fr. 604, 835 ; Brussels, 9561.

Eustace Morel, surnamed Deschamps. (§§ 72, 86, 87.)

L'Art de dictier et de fere Chançons, etc., 1392.
Complainte de l'Eglise.
Démonstracions contre Sortilege.

Geoffroi, Chevalier de la Tour-Landry.

Le Livre du Chevalier de la Tour Landry. Gröber,
1371–72 ; G. Paris, cir. 1425. Book of instructions written
by the Chevalier for his three motherless daughters. It is a
collection of illustrative tales and examples, taken from
Scripture and the lives of saints, from fableaux and popular
tales. The prologue was originally written in verse, of which
we can detect traces in the extant prose, but the Chevalier
finally decided to write his work in prose, "pour l'abrégier et
mieulx entendre," to shorten it and make it easier to understand. He refers several times to a similar work prepared
for his sons, but this is not known to be extant. The work was
early translated into English and German. The first printed
English translation was the one by Caxton, printed 1483–84.
An earlier unprinted one by anonymous author is extant in
Harl. 1764. *Ed.,* de Montaiglon, 1854 ; T. Wright,
E.E.T.S., 1868, from early unprinted translation, the parts
wanting in this being supplied from Caxton's text. *MSS.,*
Bibl. Nat., several, 1458, 1459, 1483, 1631, etc. ; B.M.
Reg. 19, C. vii. ; Arsenal ; Brussels.

Jean des Preis. (*See* § 66.)

Three noted theologians of this period are—

Pierre d'Ailly, "L'Aigle de France," "Le Marteau des Hérétiques," b. 1350; d. cir. 1420 or 1425. An adherent of the Nominalist doctrines, as formulated by William of Ockham. D'Ailly holds a high rank among the scholastic philosophers of this later period.

Jean Gerson (Doctor Christianissimus), b. 1363; d. 1429. Born of peasant parents, and a pupil of Pierre d'Ailly.

Mathieu-Nicolas de Claminges (or Clémanges), b. cir. 1360; d. cir. 1434. A pupil of Pierre d'Ailly.

Pierre Bersuire (Berchorius), d. 1362. A friend of Petrarch.

"His translation of Titus Livius is indicative of the movement which was beginning towards the revival of classical literature."

66 *History.*

Joinville. (*See* 13th century, § 41.)

Jehan le Bel, b. last years of 13th century; d. cir. 1370.

Les Vrayes Chroniques, cir. 1355. "Histoire vraye et notable des nouvelles guerres et choses avenues l'an mil cccxxvi., jusques l'an lxi., en France, en Angleterre, en Escoce, en Bretaigne et ailleurs, et principalement des haults faitz du roy Edouart d'Angleterre et des deux roys Philippe et Jehan de France." The author accompanied the expedition into Scotland under Edward III., 1327. The earlier part of Froissart's work was based on that of Jehan le Bel. *Ed.*, L. Polain, 1863. *MS.*, Unique MS., Châlons-sur-Marne.

Jean Froissart, b. at Valenciennes cir. 1333–1337
(later date now generally thought to be the correct one);
d. cir. 1410. (§§ 78, 85, 86.)

Chroniques. Divided into four books, which constitute
four distinct works.

1st book, 1307–1377.	*Ed.,* K. de Lettenhove, 1863.
2nd „ 1377–1385.	
3rd „ 1386–1388.	
4th „ 1389–1400.	

The Chronicles have come down to us in several forms,
all equally authentic. Froissart himself prepared three versions of his first book; only the last book remained untouched,
probably because the author died before he had time for
alterations. Froissart had seen the splendour and decadence of
chivalry. Luce writes that the chronicler of Valenciennes represents nearly a whole century, and that one of transition, in his
own person, equally from the romantic and poetical point of
view, as from a historical, literary, and philological one.
Froissart does not confine himself to the history of his own
country, but enters into that of England, Spain, Portugal and
Italy, and his work is of interest to all nations who played
any considerable part in the history of the time in which he
lived. Froissart paid two visits to England, 1361 and 1395.
Queen Philippa was a native of his own home province of
Hainault, and one of his "lais" laments her death. *Ed.,*
Luce et Raynaud, 1869–99; "Works," K. de Letten-
hove, 1870–1873. *See* M. Darmesteter, "Froissart," 1894.
MSS., Immense number: Bibl. Nat. (62), and in all the
chief libraries of Europe. B.M., Arundel, 67; Harl. 4379,
4380; Reg. 14, D. ii.–vi.; 18, E. i. ii.; Hunter Museum,
Glasgow; Bodl. Laud Misc. 745 (fragment); Phillipps, 131,
1277, 24258; Ashburnham; Mostyn Hall; Clumber Park;
Stoneyhurst.

N.B.—Froissart's work was, in the 15th century, continued by Monstrelet to 1444. A further continuation to 1467,
is by Mathieu d'Escouchy. Translated into English in the
16th century (two books, 1523, 1525) by John Bourchier,

Lord Berners, and printed by Richard Pynson.   *Ed.*,
W. E. Henley, Tudor translations, 1901.

Les Grandes Chroniques de Flandre.   The original text
ends 1342 ; the remainder is chiefly borrowed from the
"Chroniques Abrégées," de Baudouin d'Avesnes.   *MSS.*,
Bibl. Nat. 5611, 20363, 2799 ; Brussels ; Lille, etc. ;
B.M. Reg. 16, F. iii. ; Cott. Nero. E. iii. ; Ashburnham.

Chroniques Abrégées, de Baudouin d'Avesnes.   (§ 41.)
Neither the author, nor the sources of this vast body of
history, are authentically known.   The Chronicles pass under
the name of Baudouin d'Avesnes, who died 1289.   *MSS.*,
Bibl. Nat. 5614, ˙7266; Arsenal, Hist., 148 ; Brussels ;
Leyde ; Berne.   Many MSS. of the principal continuation.
    Ed., "Chron. de Flandres, et Chroniques Abrégées,"
"Istore et Croniques de Flandres," K. de Lettenhove,
1879–1880.

Jean des Preis, dit d'Outremeuse, b. 1338; d. cir. 1400.   (§§ 65, 80.)

Ly Myreur des Histors.   This work, like many others
produced by the historians of this period, as the *Chronique
Liégoise* (possibly by Guillaume de Vottem), embraced the
annals of the world from the origins.   Of the four books
into which it was divided, the last is lost.   Most of the
events given in the "Geste de Liège" are repeated in the
prose history, which was carried up to 1399.   *Ed.*, A.
Borgnet, "Chroniques Belges inédites," 1864–1887.   *MSS.*,
Brussels, Bibl. Roy., three MSS.   Others in possession of
private individuals.

N.B.—Another prose work of this author's is *Trésorier
de Philosophie Naturelle*, consisting of a preface and four
books ; the second is a Lapidaire, and the fourth is interesting
as dealing with such technical matters as the colouring and
cutting of glass, etc.   *MSS.*, Bibl. Nat. fr. 12326 ; Ashburnham (Barrois).

67 Christine de Pisan. Poet, historian, and moralist, b. cir. 1363 ; d. before 1440. (§§ 65, 72, 73, 86.) An Italian by birth, and daughter of Charles v.'s astrologer. We have particulars of Christine's life from her own pen, the "Vision de Christine," "Mutation de Fortune," and "Chemin de Long Estude," being autobiographical. Left a widow when young, with a mother and three children, to provide for, she had many years of struggle. Finding her ballads successful, she took up literature as a profession. She was an ardent champion of her fellow-women, and fought against the attacks upon them by didactic writers and " contre ceulx qui dient que n'est pas bon que femmes apregnent lettres "; she was particularly incensed againt Jean de Meun, and collected her correspondence on the "Roman de la Rose," dedicating the collection to Isabeau of Bavaria. She took a lively interest in all public affairs. She wrote her last important work, " Livre du Paix," when peace was restored, after a period of silence which covered the troublous period during which the French were defeated at Agincourt. She later retired to a convent, thought probably to be at Poissy, where her daughter was a nun. Her old enthusiasm was reawakened by the reports of Joan of Arc, and her poem upon her was her farewell to the world. There is no account of her death. Her writings are in prose and verse.

Livre des faits et bonnes meurs du sage roi Charles v., 1404. A work with a moral purpose, eulogistic of the king. There are long digressions in it from Aristotle and Vegetius, and others with whom her diligent study had made her acquainted. Although she was so well read, we know from her own showing that she did not begin a methodical course of study until she was thirty-six years of age. *MSS.*, Bibl. Nat. fr. 2862, 5025, 10153, etc.

Le Corps de Pollicie. In this later work Christine addresses all classes, and touches on the evils of the times. It is largely borrowed from Aristotle and Plutarch. *MSS.*, Bibl. Nat. fr. 1197, 1198, 1199, etc. ; Brussels, 10440.

Livre des faits d'armes et de Chevalerie. Chiefly a translation from Vegetius and Frontin, and including a code of

feudal laws, of which Henry II. had a translation made.
This, and the above, are special treatises on matters already
dealt with in "Faits et Meurs." *MSS.*, Bibl. Nat. fr.
603, 586, 1183 ; Brussels, 9010, 10476.

Lamentation sur les maux de la guerre Civile, 1410.
MS., Bibl. Nat. fr. 24864.

Livre de Paix, 1412–1413. Her last work before retiring
into the cloister. Each division begins with a Latin phrase
from the Bible, or a classic writer. It begins with exhortations to the maintenance of peace, but finally becomes didactic,
and deals with one of her favourite subjects, the right
government of princes. *MSS.*, Bibl. Nat. fr. 1182 ;
Brussels, 10366.

N.B.—Most of Christine's prose works have remained in
manuscript.

68 The following histories deal with Oriental matters—

Anonymous.

Chronique de Morée, or *Livre de la Conqueste*, 1325. There
is difference of opinion as to the relation between the Greek
form and the French form of this work. By some it is
thought that they both proceed from a common source.

Hayton.   Armenian Prince.

Fleur des Histoires d'Orient. Written first in French, from
the dictation of author, 1307. Immediately translated into
Latin, and again put into French towards the middle of the
century, by Jean Lelong d'Yres. *Ed.*, L. Pannier, "Bibl.
Ecole Chartes," xxxv. 93. *MSS.*, First French text,
fr. 2810, 12201 ; Nouv. Acq. 886 ; Lat. 14737 ; Latin,
Five MSS. ; later French, fr. 1380, 12202.

Other French and Latin Chronicles.

Jean de Saint-Victor, d. 1351.

Memoriale historiarum, 1289–1322, continued to 1328.

Gilles li Muisis, b. 1272; d. 1353.

Latin Chronicle, in two parts, from the Creation to 1352;
French verse is found in one part. Valuable for history of
Northern Provinces of France in 14th century.

Jacques de Henricourt, d. 1403.

Le Miroir des Nobles de Hasbaye (heraldic and genealogical),
1398.

Aymerie de Peyrat. Abbé de Moissac.

Chronique. In three parts. On Popes, Kings of France
(from Clovis), and on the Abbots of Moissac. *See* " Notices
et Extraits," vi., vii.

Jean de Montreuil. Bishop of Beauvais, killed 1418.

De Gestis et factis Memorabilibus Francorum, in Latin and
French. Written against the English pretensions to the
French crown.

69   ROMANCES.

Arthurian Cycle.

Perceforest. Cir. 1330 (G. Paris), 1337–1390 (Gröber).
" The longest prose romance in existence." In this work
there is a mingling of the Alexander and Arthurian cycles.
After his war in India, Alexander comes to England, where he
gives the kingdom to one of his companions named Perceforest,
who establishes the knights of the Franc Palais. The Graal
is brought to England by Perceforest's grandson. One of
the episodes in the work is a variant of the tale of the
Sleeping Beauty, and another of the theme of Adam of
Cobsam's " The Wright's Chaste Wife." This tale of the
magic rose, which the husband carries with him and which
remains for ever fresh as long as his wife is faithful, but
withers otherwise, is given in " Perceforest " both in prose
and poetry. In other extant versions of the tale, by Bandello,

A. de Musset, and Massinger, there are considerable variations, a portrait taking the place of the rose in the Italian and English variants. The first part of the poem is based on the "Voeux du Paon" (*see* Alexander Cycle, § 27). *MSS.*, Arsenal, 3483–3494; complete copy of six volumes. First three vols., B.M. Reg. 15, E. v.; 19, E. ii.; 19, E. iii. Four first vols., Bibl. Nat. fr. 106–109. Three first vols. and vol. v. fr. 345–348. Vol. ii., Berlin. *See* "Romania," xxiii. 78 ff.; "Jahrb. Rom. u. Eng. Lit.," 1867, viii. 44 ff.

70   *Miscellaneous Romances.*

Jean d'Arras.

Melusine, 1382–1394 (Gröber). Tale of the serpent fairy and Raimondin of Lusignan. The latter, hunting one day in the forest, came to a beautiful fountain, and, approaching to drink, heard melodious singing. Then Melusine appears to Raimondin, and becomes betrothed to him, on condition that he never visits her on a certain day (Saturday) in the week; which so doing, he sees Melusine half serpent, half woman; whereupon she leaves him, etc. A similar motive is found in an Indian tale. A certain Coudrette put this tale into verse, in early 15th century (Add. 6796). An English version in prose is of cir. 1500 (Reg. 18, B. ii.). (A. K. Donald, E.E.T.S., 1895.) *See* M. Nowack, "Die Melusinen-Sage," 1886; and notice of same, "Litt. Blatt. Germ. Rom. Phil.," No. 8, 1887; Desaivre, "La Légende de M.," 1885; Baudot, "Les Princesses Yolande, etc.," 1900. *MSS.*, Bibl. Nat. fr. 1482–84–85, 24383; Arsenal, 3353, 3475; Harl. 4418; Brussels, 10390. Early printed edition of 1478, of which copies are at Bibl. Nat., Paris, and at Wolfenbüttel.

L'Histoire du Chevalier Bérinus (early 14th century). Composed of two distinct tales. 1st part. Berinus, son of a wealthy Roman, leaves home; comes to land of Blandic; here he is beset by swindlers, but finally delivered from them by a man named Geoffrey, who pretends to lowly station to protect himself. Berinus vanquishes his rival for the hand of

Cleopatra, daughter of King Esope, and marries her. 2nd part. His rival, Sogres, returns, and Berinus is betrayed into his hands. The latter is sent off in a vessel with his family and possessions. They come upon a magnetic rock and Berinus has to leave his son and all his riches in order to effect his release. Berinus arriving in Rome in poverty is tempted to steal into the King's treasure-house, where a trap has been set in the shape of a tub filled with glutinous matter, into which Berinus unfortunately falls. His son arrives in time to save the family honour by cutting off his father's head before he has been discovered. The son marries the Emperor's daughter and succeeds to the throne. *MSS.*, Nat. Bibl. fr. 777; Vienna; early printed edition, 1521.

N.B.—The English "Tale of Beryn" is identical with the first part of this old French romance. It has been edited by the Chaucer Society: "Supplementary Canterbury Tales." *Ed.*, F. J. Furnivall and W. G. Stone, 1876, 1887. Unique MS., Duke of Northumberland. In the edition of the English tale are given Persian and other Asiatic versions of the story by W. A. Clouston.

Gilles de Trasignies. Early 14th century. Only prose version known. A version of tale found in *Éliduc, Ille et Galéron* (§§ 29, 31). Being made a prisoner in the Holy Land, he marries Graciane, daughter of the Soudan, to save his life. Returning home with her, he explains to his first wife whom he had left behind, on going on Crusade, that it is owing to Graciane that he has the happiness of seeing her again. The two women retire together to a convent, and die the same year. Gilles puts up two monuments, leaving a space between for one for himself—returns to Holy Land, and dies of wound. *Ed.*, A. Dinaux, "Trouvères, Jongleurs et Ménéstrels," 1857–63. *MS.*, Jena.

Assenath. The tale of Potiphar's daughter, who was married to Joseph. It was first known in the West through the "Speculum Historiale" of V. de Beauvais. It was translated into French in the early 14th century, with the remainder of the S. H. by Jean de Vignay. Later on it was abridged and published separately, and appears as "Ystoire

Assenath " in the " Nouvelles Françaises du xive Siecle " (Roland et Héricault). A German version is contained in MS. Harl. 1252. For origin, symbolical interpretation, etc., *see* introduction, " Studia Patristica," fasc. 1, P. Batiffol, 1889.

POETRY.

71   *Science.*

Hardouin, Seigneur de Fontaines-Guérin.

Trésor de Vénerie (for former works on the Chace, *see* §§ 47, 64). This is more or less a versification of the earlier work by Gaston de Foix. The author was prisoner for a short time, having taken part in the strife between his feudal lord, the Duc d'Anjou and the Vicomte de Turenne—and he wrote the poem to console the loneliness of his evenings. A speciality of his work is the account he gives of different manners of " Corner," blowing the horn, as " Cornure de Chemin, Cornure d'esemble, de queste," etc.

> " Vous deves de certaine savoir
> Qui doit en une chasse avoir
> Pluseurs manières de corner,
> Qu'à chascun faut change donner,
> Comme vous poures cy aprendre
> Par ces figures et entendre."

Ed., H Michelant, 1856.   *MS.*, Bibl. Nat. fr. 25547.

72   *Religious, Didactic, etc.*

Watriquet de Couvin, fl. 1319–1329. (§ 85.)

Li Mireoirs as Dames (octosyllabic couplets). Long allegorical poem setting forth in what Beauty, in the highest acceptation of the word, consists. Beauty holds her court in a castle on the height, the thirteen stages of ascent to which are guarded by as many Virtues. The poet, in descending from the Castle, meets a company of ladies at the head of whom is one, who, from the description given of her, is

thought undoubtedly to be Jeanne d'Evreux, third wife of
Charles le Bel and niece of Philippe le Bel.   *Ed.*,
"Works," A. Scheler.   For MSS., *see* § 85.

Guillaume de Deguileville, d. cir. 1360.

Le Pèlerinage de la Vie Humaine (octosyllabic couplets),
1330–1332.   The text of this first version was revised by the
author twenty-five years later (G. Paris, revised cir. 1355).
An English verse translation of this second version is ascribed
to Lydgate.   *Ed.*, J. J. Stürzinger, Roxburghe Club,
1893.   Eng. version, *ed.*, F. G. Furnivall, E.E.T.S.,
1890–1901 ; Roxburghe Club, 1905.

Le Pèlerinage de l'âme (octosyllabic couplets), 1355 (G.
Paris), or after.   *Ed.*, J. J. Stürzinger, 1895.

Le Pèlerinage de Jhesucrist (octosyllabic couplets), 1358.
Ed., J. J. Stürzinger, 1897.
MSS., First part.   French text printed from Bibl. Nat.
fr. 1818 (illuminated MS.) ; Eng. version, Cott. Vitell. C.
13 ; Cott. Tib. A. 7 ; Ashburnham (Stowe), 952.   Second
part, Text from fr. 12466 (illustrated MS.)   Third part,
Text printed from fr. 14976 (illuminated MS.).   Innumer-
able MSS. of whole work, and part in foreign libraries ; B.M.
Add. 22937, 25594 ; Harl. 4399 ; Ashburnham (Barrois),
Phillipps, and other private libraries.

The "A B C" poem to the Virgin, by Deguileville
("Pèl. de l'âme") was Englished by Chaucer.   Deguileville's work has been thought to have possibly suggested the
"Pilgrim's Progress" to Bunyan.   *See* "The ancient poem
of G. de G. compared with the Pilgrim's Progress," I. Cust,
1858 ; J. B. Wharey, "Sources of Bunyan's Allegories,"
1904.

Eustace Deschamp.   (§§ 65, 86, 87.)
Miroir de Mariage.

Le Lay des douze estats du Monde. A picture of society under Charles VI. *Ed.*, Tarbé, 1870.

François de Rues, and Chaillou de Pesstain.

Fauvel. In two books, 1310 and 1314. Owing possibly to some play on words, the adjective " fauve " was early used in an unfavourable sense. As early as the 12th century an " Ânesse fauve " is met with as figuring deceit; Fauve and Fauvain are also terms used to signify a similar personification. In the poem under consideration " Fauvel " is a horse, the etymology of the name being explained as follows :

> " *Flaterie* si s'en derive . . .
> Et puis en descent *Avarice*
> *Vilenie* et *variété*
> Et puis *Envie* et *Lascheté* . . .
> Pren un mot de chacune lettre."

Everyone from Pope, Cardinals, and King down to the peasant, to whom only the tail is left, "torchent, peignent, or étrillent" Fauvel. "To curry Fauvel" (to deceive) passed into English and became corrupted into the expression, "to curry favour." The first part is extant in two versions, the older having a long piece in six-lined strophes, introduced into octosyllabic couplets ; this first part was interpolated and subjected to revision. A continuation was written four years later, 1314, in which Fauvel ceases to be only an allegorical expression, and becomes a living being. The writer of this gives his name enigmatically as Gerues, or Gervais du Bus ; according to the authority quoted below, he is not the author of the first part. Further amplifications are due to Chaillou de Pesstain, and either he or some other compiler joined the two parts in a volume, richly illustrated, introducing at the same time lais, motets, chansons, and rondeaux, which are interesting as representing the transition from the lyric of the 13th century to that which developed later, under new forms, by G. de Marchant and his followers. *Ed., See* " Hist. Litt.," xxxii. *MSS.*, Bibl. Nat. fr. 146 (compilation, introducing songs, illustrated MS.); fr. 580, 2139 (original version); 2140, 2195, 12460, 24375, 24436; Nouv. acq. 4579, Tours; Dijon; St. Petersburg.

Christine de Pisan.   (§§ 65, 67, 73, 86.)

Othéa à Hector, or *Cent Histoires de Troie* (printed under latter title in 15th century).   *MSS.*, Bibl. Nat. fr. 848, 1644, 1185, etc.; Brussels, 4374, 9392, etc.   Trans. by J. Fastolf, *ed.*, G. F. Warner, 1904.

Épître à Eustache Morel (Deschamps).   A criticism of contemporary morals and customs in octosyllabic couplets, to which Eustace Deschamps replied in a complimentary ballad.   *MSS.*, fr. 605.

Chemin de Long Estude, 1402.   A description of heaven and earth, and dealing with the duties of nobles and kings. *Ed.*, R. Püschel, 1887.   *MSS.*, Bibl. Nat. fr. 1643, 836, 1188, 604; Brussels, Bourgogne, 10982, 10983; Bibl. Roy. 133.

Mutation de Fortune, 1403.   *MSS.*, Bibl. Nat. fr. 603, 604; Brussels, 9508.

Enseignement et Proverbes.   Written for her son.   Each proverb written in four lines, rhyming two and two.   *MSS.*, Bibl. Nat. 1551, 1623, 2239, 825.

These proverbs were translated into English by Lord Rivers in the second half of 15th century, and printed by Caxton, 1478.   *Ed.*, Blades, 1859.

Of purely religious poems are—

Les douleurs de Notre Sauveur.
Les xv. joies de Notre-Dame.
Oraison de Notre-Sauveur.
Oraison de Notre-Dame.
Les Sept Pseaumes.

Chrétien Legouais, cir. 1300.   (§ 46.)

19

73   *History.*

Godefroi, or Geffroi de Paris.   (§ 85.)

Chronique Rimée (octosyllabic couplets), 1300–1316.   An
unfinished work ; it treats more especially of Parisian affairs,
and reflects the tone of the Bourgeoisie.   *Ed.*, " Recueil
des Historiens des Gaules et de la France," vol. xxii.
MS., Bibl. Nat. fr. 146.

Guillaume Guiart.

La Branche des Royaus Lingnages, 1306 (leonine verse).
History of reign of St. Louis, and further events to 1306 ;
the narrative deals principally with the wars of Philippe iv. ;
the author took part himself in the war in Flanders.   The
work gives valuable technical information as regards the
appliances, etc., of war.   *Ed.*, " Recueil Hist. Gaules,
etc." (Bouquet), vol. xxii.   *MS.*, Bibl. Nat. Anc. fds.
fr. 10298. 3.

Chandos le Herauld.

Le Prince Noir (octosyllabic couplets), cir. 1386.   " Cy
comence une partie de la vie et des faites d'armes d'une très
noble prince de gales, etc."   Recording three great expedi-
tions of this prince, but principally the Spanish expedition.
The poet, who is frequently mentioned by Froissart, was the
Herald of Sir John Chandos, Constable of Aquitaine.   *Ed.*,
with trans., H. D. Coxe, Roxburghe Club, 1842 ; F.
Michel, 1883.   *MS.*, Worcester College.

*Pierre de Langtoft.   Canon of Bridlington, York-
shire, d. 1307 (?).

Chronique, Brutus to 1307.   (*See* R. of Brunne, England,
§ 69.)

Christine de Pisan.   (§§ 65, 67, 72, 86.)

Jeanne d'Arc (octosyllabic, eight-lined strophes), 1429.
Last poem by authoress.   Said to be the only French verses
extant, written on Jeanne d'Arc during her lifetime.   *MS.*,
Berne.

Anonymous.

Chronique rimée Parisienne, 1214–1409. Said to contain some interesting facts.

74 Chansons de Geste.

The chief prose versions of the Chansons de Geste belong to the 14th and 15th centuries, few only dating from the 13th century.

For list of Prose Romances and MSS., *see* Gautier, " Epopées Françaises," vol. ii. pp. 544 ff., 1892.

The poetry of the age was popular and satirical, it had lost the old seriousness of the early epic.

Cycle du Roi.

Hugues Capet, cir. 1330. The decadence of the Epic is apparent in this poem which only in form is a Chanson de Geste. The mingling of the classes, which we find in it, is sufficient to show the change that had come over society. The tone of the poem, which in places borders on the comic, corresponds to that of the Bourgeois class, for which it was written. The hero is the grandson of a butcher, is deeply in debt, and pursued by creditors. There is no historical foundation for the tale, which tells us how Hugues—he arrived in Paris at a critical moment—defends the Queen-Mother, Blanchefleur (sister to Guillaume au Court-nez), against a treacherous noble, performs many feats of valour on her behalf, and finally marries the Princess Marie and is elected King.

" The poem is not without originality, and is superior to the average productions of this period. The true mediocre style of the day is more conspicuous in a poem entitled *Charles le Chauve*." *Ed.*, M. le Mis. de la Grange, 1864. Prose translation into German, " Hug Schapler," pub. Strasburg, 1500. *MS.*, Bibl. Nat. fr. 786 ; Arsenal, B.L., 186.

Two Franco - Italian Epics of the 14th century were " Entrée de Spagne " and " Prise de Pampelune."

Franco-Italian Poems (see Italy, § 8).

Entrée de Spagne. In this chanson there are considerable portions dating from the preceding century, which were transcribed from French MSS. by the Italian compiler who was a native of Padua. The whole compilation is based on French poems now lost ("Roland et Ferragus," "Prise de Nobles," "Roland en Perse," etc.). *See* Thomas, "Recherches sur l'Entrée de Spagne," and "Hist. Litt.," xxvi. *MS.*, Venice, St. Mark, fr. xxi.

Nicolas de Verona.

Prise de Pampelune, or *La Guerre en Espagne.* A continuation of the above. Nicolas de Verona is thought the composer of a poem on the Passion, in Alexandrine laisses. *Ed.*, Mussafia, "Alt. französische Gedichte," i. 1864. *MSS.*, St. Mark fr. v. Other MSS. of this epic are at Padua, Turin, and Berlin (Hamilton).

75   Cycle Garin de Monglane.

Enfances Garin de Monglane. First half 14th century (both earlier and later dates are, however, assigned to this chanson), rhymed Alexandrines, with six-syllabled line at close of laisse. *MS.*, Bibl. Nat. fr. 1460.

Renier de Gennes (fragment), rhymed Alexandrines.

Hernaut de Beaulande (fragment), rhymed Alexandrines.

These have come down in prose versions of 15th century, but in both there is preserved a laisse belonging apparently to 14th century. *MS.*, Prose versions, Arsenal, 3351.

76   Cycle Doon de Mayence.

Gaufrei. First half century. The eldest son of Doon; he becomes King of Denmark, and is the father of Ogier the Dane. He is not the only hero of the poem, for he is accompanied by many knights of equal valiance. *Ed.*, F.

Guessard and P. Chabaille, 1859. *See* also "Hist. Litt.,"
xxvi.   *MS.*, Unique MS., Montpellier.

Tristan de Nanteuil. First half century. The last poem
of the Geste de Nanteuil. "The work marks a falling off
from the plainer narrative of the older epic." *See* "Hist.
Litt.," xxvi.   *MS.*, Bibl. Nat. fr. 1478.

77   *Cycle de Croisade.*

Baudouin de Sebourg (comic-heroic poem in Alexandrines).
There is uncertainty as to date as well as to the trouvère who
wrote this poem.

Son of Rose, who was daughter of Helias, le Chevalier au
Cygne. All that is told of Baudouin, King of Jerusalem, is
fabulous. Use is made of the old legends of the Middle
Ages, and the satire directed against monks and women
betrays the sentiments of the age.   *MS.*, Bibl. Nat. fr.
12552, 12553, one apparently dating from first half of 14th
century.

Bastart de Bouillon. Continuation of "B. de Sebourg."
With this poem is closed the Cycle de la Croisade. The
historical basis of the earlier poems of the cycle had now
been entirely superseded by fable. *Ed.*, "Le Cycle de
la Croisade et la famille de Bouillon," A. Pigeonneau, 1897.
MS., Contained in MS. of B. de S. of 14th century. *See*
under "Cycle de la Croisade," 13th century.

N.B.—Of the poems of this cycle the greatest historical
interest is attached to the first of the series, "Chanson
d'Antioche"; later ones were chiefly of literary interest as
imitations of the epics of the first period.

78   Arthurian Cycle.

Jean Froissart. (§§ 66, 85, 86.)

Méliador, or *le Chevalier au soleil d'or* (octosyllabic
couplets). Froissart alludes to this romance of his in his
chronicle and in his poem of "Dit du Florin." It was

written at the request of Wenceslas of Bohemia, Duke
of Luxembourg and Brabant (d. 1383). Froissart published
two versions. Kittredge and Longnon do not agree as to
the relative date of these. Into one of them were introduced
Wenceslas de Luxembourg's lyric poems (MS. 12557). In
this immense romance, "probably the latest of the Arthurian
Cycle," we have the tale of Hermondine, daughter of the
King of Scotland, who, in order to escape the solicitations
of an over-presumptuous knight, publishes a declaration to
marry the knight who, after five years of trial, shall be
pronounced the most valiant. Then follow the usual series
of adventures. Méliador is finally the chosen one, after
slaying Camel, the original wooer, whose somnambulism (*see*
Kittredge) had been considered an obstacle to his suit.
Ed., A. Longnon, 1895. *See* Kittredge, "Engl. Studien,"
26, 1899. *MSS.*, Bibl. Nat., Nouv. Acq. Lat. 2374,
four fragments; fr. 12557 found in 1891.

79   UNATTACHED ROMANCES.

Florent et Octavien (Alexandrines). Version of *Octavien.*
Early 14th century (Octavien, § 57, and England, § 63).
These are Octavien's two sons, both of whom are carried off
by wild beasts, and have adventurous and successful careers,
etc. The narrative of the poem is complicated to a degree;
the material is taken from older works. *See* Streve, "Die
Octaviansage," 1884. Another version is extant of 15th
century. *MSS.*, Bibl. Nat. fr. 24384, 12564, 1452.

Guillaume de Machaut, b. cir. 1300–1315; d. 1377.
(For life, *see* § 86.)

Prise d'Alexandrie (octosyllabic couplets), cir. 1370. A
history of the King of Cyprus, Pierre I. de Lusignan. After
a mythological prologue we read—

> " Or est nez nostres jouvenciaus,
>   A qui li dieux qui est en ciaus
>   Doint grace, honneur et bonne vie
>   Mais il est drois que je vous die
>   L'année et le jour qu'il fu nez "

which was the fête of St. Denis, 1329.   *MSS.*, Bibl.
Nat. 1585; and three MSS. at Bibl. Nat. which contain
Machaut's complete works, 1584, 9221, 22546.

80   An attempt to revive the National epic was made in
the following poems :—

Cuvelier.

Bertrand du Guesclin (Alexandrine laisses), second half
century. This versified biography, with the "Prise
d'Alexandrie," close the cycle of Chansons de Geste. As
a genuninely historical work, it is not without interest. It
was translated into prose, and this latter version was the
starting-point of many histories and romances.   *Ed.*, E.
Charrière, "Doc. inéd. Hist. France," 1839.   *MSS.*,
B.N. fr. 850; Arsenal; Mons, etc.

N.B.—The editor, at the close of "B. du Guesclin,"
publishes another poem which is a commentary on the
former, and supplies material for filling up a gap in the history
of du Guesclin. It is entitled, "Le Libvre du bon Jehan, duc
de Bretaigne" (octosyllabic couplets) and is by Guillaume
de Saint André, who flourished at the close of the 14th
century; being written for the instruction of his son; the work
has a moral purpose, and in one MS. is found subjoined a
moral dissertation on the game of chess.   *MSS.*, Bibl.
Nat. (2 MSS.).

Jean des Preis, dit d'Outremeuse.   (§§ 65, 66.)

Geste de Liège (monorhymed laisses), second half of century.
In three books, of which 2nd and 3rd are imperfect as extant.
This immense work was written at some time anterior to the
author's Chronicle; it starts with the founding of towns after
the Trojan War. "The Geste is wearisome and chiefly of
interest to the philologist."   *Ed.*, A. Borgnet, "Chron. Belges.
inéd.," 1864-1887.   *See* also "Glossaire Philologique," A.
Scheler, 1882.   *MSS.*, Gerlache; Bibl. Roy., Brussels,
10989, and others; Ashburnham (Barrois); other MSS. in
private possession. *See* Borgnet, last vol., p. lxxii. ff.

N.B.—Other smaller poems found in a MS. of the Geste are ascribed to this author. He himself refers to a "Geste Ogier le Danois," which seems to be lost.

Anonymous.

Le Combat de Trente Bretons contre trente Anglais (mono-rhymed laisses of twelve-syllabled lines), second half of century.

"Cy cōmence la Bataille de trente Englois et de trente Bretons, qui fu faite en Bretaigne lan de Grace mil trois cens cinquante, le sammedi devant letare Jherusalem." Thirty Bretons under Beaumanoir fought and overcame thirty English under Bembrough. The encounter took place in the road between Ploërmel and Josselin. In 1819 a monument was erected on the spot to the thirty Bretons ; it took the place of an older monument, which according to tradition arose on the spot where originally stood the oak-tree which was the pre-arranged point of rendezvous for the combatants. The names and armorial bearings of the thirty Bretons are given by Crapelet. An account of the combat is found in a few MSS. of Froissart. *Ed.*, G. A. Crapelet, 1827. *MS.*, Bibl. Nat. fr. 1555.

N.B.—The last attempt made to write in monorhymic laisses was in the "Geste des Bourguignons" of the 15th century (*ed.*, K. de Lettenhove, "Chroniques relatives à l'Histoire de la Belgique, etc.," tome ii.). The decay of poetic powers is shown in all these later poems ; "prose was now to supersede verse, but in this new garb the old tales lost the charm and vitality of the old rhythmic versions."

81   ALEXANDER CYCLE.

Jacques de Longuyon.

Voeux du Paon.
1st *version*, 1310.
2nd   „   1315.
or shortly before and shortly after 1313.

Jean Brisebarre.

Restor du Paon, cir. 1330.

Jean de la Mote.

Parfait du Paon, 1340.

See P. Meyer, *op cit.* (§ 27).

82   *Miscellaneous Romances.*

Anonymous.   It has, however, been attributed to A. de Bernay (§ 29).

La Belle Hélène (*see* Manekine, 13th century, § 57), early century.

Jehan Maillard.

La Comtesse (or *Le Comte*) *d'Anjou*, cir. 1316 (octosyllabic couplets). Version of tale of "Manekine." The last of the romances in verse. *See* G. Paris, "Romania," 19. *MS.*, Bibl. Nat., Nouv. acq. fr. 4531; fr. 765. ·

83   Roman de Renard.

Anonymous.

Renard Le Contrefait (octosyllabic couplets).
1st and 2nd versions, 1322, 1328.

84   Fableaux.

The latest fableaux extant are those of Jean de Condé (§ 60), and of Watriquet de Couvin (*see* below).

85

Watriquet de Couvin. (§ 72.)

Li Dis du Connestable de France (Gaucher de Châtillon, Comte de Crecy et de Porceau, d. 1329).   A poetical eulogy in allegorical form.

Li Dis de la Nois.   Simile applied to education of children, relation of soul to body, etc.

L'Iraigne et li Crapos.   Spider, counsellor of princes; Toad, the common people; Plantain, which cures bite of spider; the Seigneurs, the natural protectors of the people.

Li Tournois des Dames.   Religious and moral parables, beginning with the tournament, signifying struggle between body and soul.

Li dis du Roy.   Exhortations addressed to Philippe de Valois, on his accession.

Li dis de la Cigogne.   Parable addressed to impenitents.

Ave Maria.   Rhymes formed on elements of the word Marie.

Fastrasie.

Dis des huit conteurs.   Venus distributes colours to eight knights, with initial letter of a woman's name, to be borne by them in fight.

Feste du Comte de Flandre.   Marriage with Marguerite, daughter of Philippe le Long.

Dit des trois vertus.

L'escole d'amours.

De Raison et de Mesure.

Du fol ménéstrel.   One who uses his art for base purposes.

Des trois Chanoinesses de Cologne. } Fableaux.
Des trois Dames de Paris. }

Dis de Faus et Faucille.   On the falsity of the world.

Li dis de l'Escharbote.   Vision of the city of the world; man compared to beetle, preferring ruin (the dunghill) to happiness (flowers).

Many "dis" on various subjects, in one of which, "Dis de l'arbre Royale," he speaks of the deaths of Philippe le Bel and his sons which so quickly succeeded one another.

The poems are mostly in octosyllabic couplets.   *Ed.,*

A. Scheler, 1868.   *MSS.*, MSS. of W. de Couvin's works, Bibl. Nat. fr. 14968, fr. 2183; Arsenal; Belles Lettres, fr. 318; Brussels, Bibl. Roy.

Geoffroi de Paris (*see* Hist., § 73).

"Plusieurs diz de Mestre Geoffroi de Paris":—

Premier Avisemens pour le Roy Louis.
Du Roy Phillippe que ore regne.
Un Songe.
Des Alliez (Latin and French).
De la Comete et de l'eclipse, et de la lune et du soleil.
La Desputaison de l'Église de Romme et de l'église de France pour le Siege du Pape.
Le Martyre de S. Bacchus.
Diz des Paternostres.

See, for some of the above, Jubinal, "Nouv. Recueil"; "Hist. Litt.," xxiii.   *MS.*, Bibl. Nat. fr. 146.

Jean Froissart.   (§§ 66, 78, 86.)

Dit dou Bleu Chevalier (3, 10, and 4-syllabled lines). In which the poet comforts a friend in love trouble. English version by Lydgate, *see* Ten Brink, *op. cit.*, vol. ii.

Débat dou Cheval et dou Levrier. In which his dog and horse exchange laments, and rejoice when they see a town where they will have food.

Dit dou Florin. The only piece of money left in his purse by thieves; we have some account of Froissart's life given in this poem.

Plaiderie de la Rose et de la Violette. The three last poems are in octosyllabic verse.

86   *Lyric.*

Guillaume de Machaut, b. 1300 or cir. 1315; d. 1377. (§ 79.)

For more than thirty years the poet was Secretary to the King of Bohemia, who was killed at the Battle of Crécy. Afterwards secretary to King Jean le bon, a celebrated poem of his being written on the latter's death. G. de Machaut was a musician as well as poet, and in one of his poems, "Le tems pastour," he enumerates the musical instruments of the day. He wrote several Dits: *de Lion, du Cheval, de l'Alerion, du Cerf blanc, de la Marguerite, de la Rose, du Vergier, de la Harpe, de la Fontaine Amoureuse.* Lais: *De Plour, Mortel, des Dames.* Other poems: *Jugement du Roi de Navarre, Complainte au Roi, le Remède de Fortune, Complainte à Henri,* etc. Ballades, Chants Royaux, and Sotes Chansons, are among his works. His *Confort d'Ami* was addressed to Charles le Mauvais, King of Navarre, when the latter was thrown into prison; in the *Jugement de Roi de Navarre* (the same monarch) to whom he pays homage, he gives a description of the plague in France, and we hear in it of the Flagellants. His most interesting work is—

Voir Dit (Histoire vraie). In which the poet tells the tale of the love awakened for the poet in the heart of a girl who had never seen him, and with whom he has an interchange of poems and letters. They finally meet on the pretext of starting for a pilgrimage. *Ed.*, P. Paris, 1875. Selections from works by Tarbé, 1849. *MSS.*, Bibl. Nat. 1584, 9221, 22546 (each of these three MSS. contains Machaut's complete works).

Philippe de Vitry. The poet addressed by Petrarch as "Tu poeta nunc unicus galliarum." His poems as a whole are lost.

Dits de Franc Gonthier. Written in praise of the life of the peasant. It was in answer to this poem that Villon wrote his "Contredits de Franc Gonthier," in which he denies that there can be happiness where there is poverty. *See* "Hist. Litt.," xxix.

N.B.—The "Ovid Moralisé," by Chrétien Legouais, was for a long time attributed to P. de Vitry.

Eustace Morel, surnamed Deschamps, b. cir. 1345; d. probably cir. 1410. (§§ 65, 72, 87.) Of lowly birth, he entered the service of the King as a royal messenger.

His work comprises love, historical, moral, and indeed every kind of poem, from which we can gather particulars of his conjugal troubles, journeys, and other personal matters. Over 1500 of his poems are extant, and also an unfinished allegorical work, begun in old age, called

Miroir de Mariage. In it the poet gives satirical portraits of women, his outlook on life as a whole being pessimistic, and marriage being forsworn by him for several reasons, while he thought it was better to have his name carried on by his writings than by children. *Ed.*, Oeuvres, Tarbé, 1865; Le Marquis de Queux de S. Hilaire et Raynaud, 11 vols., 1878. *MS.*, Bibl. Nat. 840 (Ballades, Rondeaux, Virelais, Lais, Farces, etc.).

Jean Froissart. (§§ 66, 78, 85.) Froissart, with Machaut and Morel, represented the newer style of lyric. Many of his poems are scattered throughout his longer works. Extant are pastourelles, lais, chansons roiaus amoureuses, balades amoureuses, virelais, and rondeaux. His larger works, mostly written in octosyllabic verse, are—

Le Paradis d'Amours, interspersed with a complainte, lai, virelai, two rondeaux, and a balade, written before 1369.

Li Orloge Amoureux (ten-syllable). In which he shows how, like a clock, his heart is regulated by love.

Espinette Amoureuse (a complainte, a lai, virelais, balades, and rondeaux introduced), written after 1369. In this we are given the account of his childhood and early days, of a youthful love, whose name lies hidden in one part of the text, and may be deciphered as Marguerite, of a treasured souvenir, etc.

Traitié de la prison amoureuse (complainte, balades, lais, and virelais introduced), 1372–73. In this Froissart holds a correspondence in verse with an imprisoned friend, probably Wenceslas of Brabant; they name themselves respectively Flos and Rose.

"One of F.'s most important works."

Trettié Amoureux le joli buisson de Jonèce (*Jeunesse*) (balades, rondeaux, lais, virelais, and souhaits introduced).

Allegorical poem on love, in the form of a dream, in which the poet again sees his early love beside the thorn bush where they had first met.

Temple d'onnour (octosyllabic verse). An allegorical poem composed in honour of the conferring of knighthood on the son of one of his patrons.

Loenge dou joli Mois de May. A youthful poem, in twelve-lined strophes; with two balades and virelai introduced, as also a complaint to the nightingale.

Dittié de la flour de la Margherite (in sixteen-lined strophes). *Ed.*, Poems, by Scheler, 1872; Bartsch, "Romanzen u. Pastourellen." *See* Leleu, "Les Poésies de F.," "Mem. Acad. Amiens," 1889. *MSS.*, Poetry of Froissart, with two exceptions, is contained in two MSS., Bibl. Nat. 830 and 831 (the latter thought possibly to be the MS. which Froissart gave to Richard II. of England). "La Cour de May," Brussels Bourgogne, 10492; "Trésor Amoureux," Bourgogne, 11140. For the authenticity of "La Cour de May" and "Trésor Amoureux," *see* Scheler, "Intro.," pp. livff.

Christine de Pisan.   (§§ 65, 67, 72, 73.)

Les Cent Balades. Virelais, lais, rondeaux, jeux à vendre (four or six-lined strophes), complaintes amoureuses, balades d'estrange façon.

Epître au Dieu d'Amours. The beginning of the new literature in defence of women. Translated by Occleve, 1402.

Le dit de la Rose. Crowning work of the polemic on "Roman de la Rose."

Le Débat de deux Amants.

Le livre des trois jugements. Three cases of love and loyalty.

Le Dit de Poissy. Pastoral love tale, with description of journey to Poissy, and life in the convent.

Le Dit de la Pastoure.

Le livre du duc des grais amants. Love and adventures of an anonymous Duke.

Les Cent Balades d'Amant et de Dame (only contained in Harl. 4431). *Ed.*, "Christine de Pisan," M. Roy, Soc.

Anc. Textes, 1886–1896 (with "Épître à Eustache Morel," "Enseignement et proverbes moraux, and oraisons "). *MSS.*, Bibl. Nat. 835, 606, 836, 605, 604, 12779, 1740, 2184; Brussels, Bibl. Roy., 11034; B.M. Harl. 4431.

Livre des Cent Ballades, cir. 1387. The author, according to G. Paris, was probably Jean le Seneschal. The poet, wishing for certain information concerning love, about which he has received so much contradictory advice, writes to consult some of the nobles of his time, the answers returned being in the form of balades. *Ed.*, De Queux de S. Hilaire, 1868. *MSS.*, Bibl. Nat. fr. 2360, 2201, 826; Nouv. acq. 1664, 759; Brussels, Bourg., 11218; copy at La Haye.

Oton de Granson. Killed in a duel.

Chaucer refers to this poet at the close of the "Complaint of Venus," which is taken from G.'s French, as the flower of poets. For interesting life and particulars of poetical remains that have come down to us, *see* "Romania," xix. 237 ff, 403 ff.

Alain Chartier, b. cir. 1392. The chief master of poetry in the 15th century.

Charles D'Orleans, b. 1391; d. 1465. His *Poème de la Prison* was written during his twenty-five years' captivity in England. The English translation, partly by the poet himself, was edited by G. W. Taylor, 1827.

87   *Drama.*

To this century belongs the collection of the *Miracles de Notre Dame par personnages*, of which forty are extant, probably written for one of the Puys. *Ed.*, G. Paris and Robert, 1870–83; Jubinal, "Mystères inédits," i. 1837. *MSS.*, Bibl. Nat. fr. 819, 820.

The only serious non-religious drama, although with a certain moral intention, that has come down to us from this period, is the one dealing with the history of Griseldis.

Livre de l'estoire de la Marquise de Saluce miz par personnages et rigmé, 1395. The earliest version of this tale is given by Boccaccio ; the author of the drama, according to its editor, founded his work on the version given by Petrarch in a Latin letter. *Ed.*, Groeneveld, 1888 ; Modernised version, A. Silvestre and G. Morand (given at the Comédie Française, 1891). *MS.*, Bibl. Nat. fds. fr. 2203.

N.B.—The word "mystère," applied to dramatic representations, does not occur until the 15th century. The old liturgical dramas were known as "Ludi," "Repraesentationes" ; Adam de la Halle and Rustebeuf called their pieces "Jeux," and in the 14th century we have "Miracles."

Eustace Morel wrote a farce, "Maître Trubert," and there is also a dialogue of his, in which certain offices pertaining to the King's household are personified (Cuisine, Paneterie, etc.), early examples of the profane drama, and "of interest as regards the personification which became the dominant feature in the 'Moralities.'"

GERMANY

LIST OF GENERAL AUTHORITIES.

Paul, "Grundrisz der Germanischen Philologie" (German sect. Kögel, Vogt), Bd. ii. Abth. 1; Kögel, "Geschichte der deutschen Literatur bis zum Ausgange des Mittelalters," 1894, etc. ; Wackernagel, "Geschichte der deutschen Literatur," 2nd. ed., 1879–94; Goedeke, "Grundrisz zur Geschichte der deutschen Dichtung," vol. i., 1884; Gervinus, "Gesch. der poetischen Nat. litt. der Deutschen," 5th ed., 1871; Golther, "Geschichte der Deutschen Litteratur," vol. i. 1896; Scherer, "Geschichte der d. Lit.," 1880–3; Eng. trans., 1886; Geschichte der d. Dichtung im 11ten u. 12ten Jhh., "Quell. u. Forsch. Sprach. Culturgesch.," xii.; Piper, "Die Sprache u. Litteratur Deutschlands bis zum 12ten Jahrh.," 1880; Hagen u. Büsching, "Literarische Grundrisz z. Gesch. der d. Poesie," 1812; Gostick and Harrison, "Outline of German Literature," 1883; M. E. Phillips, "Handbook of German Literature," 1895.

TEXTS.—Hagen u. Büsching, "Deutsche Gedichte des Mittelalters," 1808, etc. ; Goedeke, "Deutsche Dichtung im Mittelalter," 1871; Müllenhoff u. Scherer, "Denkmäler deutscher Prosa u. Poesie" (8th to 12th century), 3rd. ed. (Steinmeyer), 1892; Wackernagel, "Deutsches Lesebuch," 1873; Braune, "Althochdeutsches Lesebuch," 4th ed., 1897; Bartsch, "Deutsche Liederdichter," 1864; Piper, *op. cit.*; "Bibliothek der Gesammten deutscher Nat. Lit. von der ältesten bis auf die neuere Zeit.," 1835, etc.

For works on the Heroic Sagas, *see* under Raszmann, Uhland, Lange, Müllenhoff, Grimm, Mone, Grässe.

For facsimile specimens of MSS., *see* Könnecke, "Bilderatlas."

BIBLIOGRAPHY.—Paul, Wackernagel, Goedeke, Piper.

N.B.—"Zeitschrift für deutsches Alterthum," *ed.* by Haupt, vols. i.–xvi. ; Steinmeyer and others, vol. xvii., etc. ; "Germania" (Hagen's), Berlin ; (Pfeiffer's), Stuttgart.

GERMANY

The dialectical separation between the North and South German had been accomplished previous to the date of any extant literary remains. High German gained the supremacy as a literary language; it continued to develop down to the 11th century, and is known as Old High German.

No remains of German poetry have come down to us from the first seven centuries; but there are references to the existence of such.

The Goths were the first among the German tribes to embrace Christianity. From them we have one of the earliest monuments of interest as regards its bearing on the history of the German language.

1 Wulfila (Ulfilas, etc.**).** Bishop of the West Goths, b. cir. 310–11; d. 380–81. Wrote in Greek, Latin, and Gothic. His chief work was the Translation of the Bible, which he is said to have translated throughout, with the exception of the Books of Kings, which he feared would be too exciting to the warlike spirit of his people. All that now remains of the Gothic Bible consists of fragments of the O.T., Gospels, and Epistles, and these only in later copies. The N.T. remains are thought in all probability to have had Wulfila's work as original, but the O.T. fragments (only a leaf or two) give proofs of later writing. Two of his pupils are known to have been engaged with translations of the O.T., and it is possible that the master himself was unable to finish the work. *Ed.,* Bernhardt, Heyne, and others. *MSS.,* Upsala (Silver Codex); Wolfenbüttel; Milan (Ambrose).

The new religionists being persecuted by the pagan Athanarich, King of the Visigoths, Ulfilas led his people over the Danube to Moesia, where the Emperor Constantine allowed them to settle, and where, some centuries later, their descendants were still leading a pastoral life.

Another relic of Gothic prose is from an exposition of S. John's Gospel, eight leaves of which, a rescript only, are preserved, partly in the Ambrosian, partly in the Vatican Library.

Among the earliest forms of verse were the hymnic songs sung at religious festivals and at feasts, incantations or charms (remains of the earliest of these are known as the *Merseburger Sprüche*), riddles and gnomic verses, of which there is evidence in a few remains extant, and in the references to them by Tacitus and other writers; whether the love lyric existed in early times is a matter of divided opinion.

"Leich" is a word common to all the German languages, and thereby proves the antiquity of what it represents, *i.e.*, conjunction of song, melody, and action, whether of dancing or marching.

As early as the 7th century an animal saga began to develop among the Franks; it spread to the Netherlands, and was there first given to literature in Latin versions.

To the period of their migration may be traced the development of epic poetry among the German tribes. The old heroic songs were partly mythical, partly historical, the latter a younger form written in strophes, and possibly accompanied by dancing. The later epic proper was a mingling of mythical and historical elements. The earlier heroic songs are lost; a collection of native songs made by Charlemagne has disappeared; but the epic of the 12th century drew material from the popular song in which were still retained the remains of old heroic legend.

Versions of tales in Latin histories, occurrence of names of individuals evidently taken from popular heroes, Anglo-Saxon and Scandinavian saga and song, as well as internal evidence gathered from the later epic, are all thought to support the supposition of a widely spread epos in the older times.

Different tribes had their own particular heroes; so we

have the Gothic Dietrich of Bern, the "incomparable" Siegfried of the Franks, King Gunther of the Burgundians, Etzel (Attila) of the Huns.

The heroic age, with the fierceness of its untempered passion, its grandeur and mystery, passed away. An age of culture and of Christianity succeeded, in which the whole tone of literature was revolutionised by the introduction of new ideas and ideals.

2   OLD HIGH GERMAN PERIOD.

(Pepin to cir. 1150.)

Remains of alliterative (Stabreim) verse, undivided by strophes.

Hildebrandslied. Hildebrand, returning to his own country after long exile among the Huns, is met and opposed by his son, who does not recognise him; account of fight between the two; the end is lost. This tale of a fatal combat between father and son is of ancient origin, and found among many peoples (*see* England, § 40). (*See* Murray Anthony Potter, "Sohrab and Rustum, the epic theme of a combat between father and son. A study of its genesis and use in literature and popular tradition," 1902.)

The language is a mixture of High and Low German forms. It is thought, therefore, on the one hand, that the writer put into his own High German dialect a song originating in Low German (Müllenhoff, Kögel), and, on the other, that it was originally a High German poem (Möller). *Ed.*, Müllenhoff, "Denkmäler"; A. Sievers (with "Zaubersprüche," etc.), 1872; Braune, *op. cit.* *See* H. Möller, "Zur althochd. Allit. poesie," 1888; F. H. Wilkens, on MS., "Pub. Mod. Lang. Assoc.," xii., 1897. *MS.*, Cassel, 54.

The form of this early epic verse was a long line of eight beats, divided into two half lines bound to one another by alliteration, or Stabreim, *i.e.* Similarity of initial letter of words; generally two similar initials in first half, and one, or frequently two, in the second.

Other extant remains of poetry are found mixed with the prose of ancient laws; there are also specimens of incantations, etc., of later date than the *Merseburger Sprüche*. The more developed form of epic which had grown out of the earlier strophic songs was checked in its growth by two main causes: (1) Opposition of the Church to the poetry which dealt with pagan themes; so, under the Frankish kings, the singing of heathen songs was frequently forbidden, and much early poetry was consequently lost; in England the form was carried over to the Christian epic, but in Germany both form and material were superseded. (2) The smaller courts, where the trained poets had been maintained, were incorporated into the wide-spreading Frankish kingdom, and these earlier minstrels were obliged to join the ranks of the wandering gleemen (who had probably existed side by side with them), and adapt their verse to popular taste; they preserved much of the epic material, but from expediency or from inability to handle the epic poem the latter was abandoned. (*See* Koegel, "Gesch. Deutsch. Litt.," vol. i. p. 145, *seq.*)

We find beginnings of poetry from the hands of the clergy dating from Charlemagne's time. The two great centres of culture in early Christian times were the Monastery of S. Fulda, founded by Boniface, and of which Hrabanus Maurus was abbot in 9th century; and the Monastery of S. Gall in Switzerland, dating from 7th century.

The oldest monument extant of Christian poetry is the

Wessobrunner Gebet, end of 8th century. An alliterative poem, in form of native hymnic song. Fragment of a cosmogony, ending with a prayer in prose, in which rhyme and alliteration occur. *Ed.*, Müllenhoff, *op. cit.* *MS.*, Roy. Lib., Munich, Cm. 20. The MS. was found at Wessobrunn. It is a copy of older Saxon original by a monk of Bavaria. For the connection of this work with the Voluspa, and on the older Christian German poem to which these two point, *see* Bugge, *op. cit.*, under "Beowulf."

3 IXth CENTURY.

As we draw towards the close of the 9th century, the clerical tone in literature becomes more marked; it is detected in the "Ludwigslied," although a song of war.

Two old Saxon works by the same author (Kögel) are—

Heliand (*Saviour*), 825 at earliest, chiefly based on Tatian's Harmony of the Gospels. The poem is allied both in style and technique to the old epic. The writer was a monk, who had formerly been renowned as a scop. This old writer, in spite of his cowl, is a true warrior at heart. The Saviour is described as a mediæval king and hero, surrounded by high-born vassals. Peter's act in the garden is told with evident satisfaction, and the desertion of the disciples is explained as a necessary fulfilment of Scripture, for the poet knew in what detestation such an act would be held by his countrymen, who, if unconverted, were at least unwaveringly loyal. This is the last of the more important alliterative works. *Ed.*, A. Sievers (Munich and Cott. MSS.), 1878. *MSS.*, Munich, Cg. 25 (9th century); B.M. Cott., Calig., A. vii.; fragments at Prague and Vatican.

Genesis (*see* England, Caedmon, § 5). This text gives evidence of being a later work than the "Heliand."
The discovery of these fragments proved that part of the A.-S. Genesis is a translation, with very slight alteration, of this work by the author of the "Heliand."
Other poems on the O.T. probably existed by this same author, but they are now lost. *See* for ed. and MSS. under Caedmon.

Muspilli (destruction of earth by fire). Older than Otfrid's work, as he quotes a line. After description of fight for man's soul after death by good and evil powers, there is a fight between Elias and Antichrist; when the blood of Elias touches the earth, the general conflagration ensues; then follows the last judgment. Written in Bavarian dialect, in all probability from memory.

The decay of the old art of alliteration is evidenced in this work, of which parts might be taken for prose. *Ed.*, Müllenhoff, *op. cit.* *See* Bugge, *op. cit.*, for origin of title. *MS.*, Munich, Cm. 21. Found written on odd spaces and blank leaves of a book belonging to King Ludwig, to whom by some it is attributed.

4   RHYMED POETRY IN STROPHIC FORM.

Otfried, fl. second half of century. Introducer of rhyming verse.

Evangelienbuch. Founded on the Gospels of the year. Strophes of two lines; the two halves of the long lines connected by rhymes. The technique and style of alliterative verse are still seen in the older parts of the work. Written in the Frankish dialect of the South Rhine. Otfried wished to give his fellow-countrymen a national poem, such as other nations, even the Greeks and Romans, had; the Franks were so renowned in all ways, why should they alone not sing praises to God in their Frankish dialect? The poet also desired to supplant the scandalous popular songs of the time, and he counted on his rhymed verses being sung; musical notes are found here and there in the MSS. The "Christ" of Otfried, with its more reflective and emotional tone as compared with the "Heliand" is indicative of the change that had come over the spirit of literature. Coleridge translated a specimen of Otfried's verse in which he found "a flow of tender enthusiasm." *Ed.*, O. Erdmann, 1882; J. Kelle, 1870; P. Piper, 1878. Trans. into Mod. Germ., G. Rapp, 1858. *MSS.*, Vienna, 2687; Heidelberg; Munich (Freisingen), Cg. 14, Cm. iii. 4 d; Fragments (Berlin, Wolfenbüttel, Bonn).

N.B.—For Strassburg Oaths (*see* France, § 2).

Ludwigslied. Written shortly after the victory of Ludwig over the Normans at Saucourt 881, in Frankish dialect.

Strophes of two or three long rhymed lines.   *Ed.*, Braune,
op. cit.   *MS.*, Found at Valenciennes, 1837.

Other smaller poems (end 9th or early 10th century) which
show the influence of Otfried and are written in rhymed
strophes are : "Georgslied," "Petruslied" ("oldest specimen of a religious national song "); two "Gebete" : "Christus
u. die Samariterin."

5   VERNACULAR PROSE.

The earliest efforts in vernacular prose were devoted to
Glosses, of which the earliest, a gloss of the Salic law
(Marlberg), in Frankish dialect, dates back to 6th century.
An interlinear version of a Latin dictionary (Kero Gloss) is
also of great antiquity (cir. first half of 8th century) ; it is
extant in rather later MSS. (Paris, Reichenau, S. Gall), and
in a version wrongly ascribed to Hrabanus Maurus.   Early
remains are also extant of baptismal vows, prayers, forms of
belief and confession ; interlinear version of psalms and hymns,
and of the rule of S. Benedict, as well as a translation of
Isidor, much of which work was undertaken at the Monastery
of Fulda, by one or more hands, probably under the supervision of Hrabanus Maurus.   We come to no work of greater
importance before the first half of 9th century, when a Latin
work based on the Greek of Tatian's "Harmony of the
Gospels" ("Diatessaron," 2nd century) was translated into
German.   *Ed.*, Sievers, 1892.   *MS.*, St. Gall.   Others
once known are apparently lost.

For Life and Works of Maurus, *see* W. Burger, "Der
Katholik," vol. ii., 1902.

6 TALES (MÄRCHEN, NOVELLE, SCHWÄNKE) AND LEGENDS.

In the second half of the 9th century we become aware
of miscellaneous material, partly of native origin, partly of
foreign, having been absorbed by the literature of Germany.
The comic element now finds a place in literature ; the epic

had been essentially tragic. The Monk of S. Gall, who has such fine tales to tell of Charlemagne, enlivens his readers with others of the above kind. In the 10th century many of these tales were put into Latin verse; valuable specimens of this work are in MSS. at Cambridge (Univ. Libr., Gg. 5, 35) and Wolfenbüttel. Text of some given in Müllenhoff, "Denkmäler," and in "Lateinische Gedichte des 10 u. 11 Jahrh.," J. Grimm, 1838.

Xth CENTURY.

7   VERNACULAR PROSE.

Notker Labeo of S. Gall. Nephew of Ekkehard 1. (*see* below), b. cir. 952; d. 1022. According to his own account he translated eleven works, but only five have come down.

Trans. of Boethius, "De Con. Phil."; Aristotle, "Categories" u. "Hermeneutik"; Marcianus Capella, "De Nupt. Phil. et Merc." His most noted work was a "Translation of the Psalms." *MSS.*, St. Gall, Vienna, Basle.

His "Book of Job" is lost with other works. Extant of his Latin works are those on *Rhetoric, Computus,* and *De partibus logica.*

8   LATIN WORKS.

Waltherius (hexameters) (*see* England, § 3). Written by Ekkehard 1., Monk of St. Gall, d. 973. In this poem the chief actors are: Walther, Gunther, Hagen, Attila, Hildegunde, and Ospirin, Attila's wife. Walther retiring from Attila's court is attacked by Gunther on his way home; combats between Walther and Gunther, Walther and Hagen, etc. This poem is the last specimen of the epic poetry of the old heroic age; the next epic "Ruodlieb" begins the romance literature of the Middle Ages. A later version of

Waltherius was prepared by Ekkehard IV. of St. Gall, d. 1036. How far we have the work of Ekkehard I. in extant MSS. is a matter on which authorities differ. *Ed.*, with German trans., J. V. Scheffel and A. Holder, 1874. (The A.-S. fragments are also given.) H. Althof, 1896. *MSS.*, Brussels, Engelberg, Vienna.

To the early part of this century belongs the *Ecbasis*, a Latin poem in connection with the animal saga. No work in the vernacular is extant of this early date. *Ed.*, E. Voigt, 1875. (*See* France, § 32.)

Hrotsuith (Roswitha). A nun of Gandersheim, wrote, among other works, Latin plays which she thought more suitable for her nuns than those of Terence, whose style she copies.

Her six plays are: "Abraham," "Callimachus," "Dulcitius," "Fides et Spes," "Gallicanus," and "Paphnutius." *Ed.*, "Works," Barack, 1858. *MS.*, Munich. Copy at Pommersfeld.

XITH CENTURY.

9   VERNACULAR PROSE.

To the first half of the 11th century belongs the "diu rede umbe diu tier," a "Physiologus," translated from the Latin version of the "dicta chrysostomi." Both a prose and a metrical version were produced in the following century from the same source. *Ed.*, Hagen, "Denkmale, etc.," 1824. *MS.*, Vienna, 223; later prose, 2721.

Willeram, d. 1085. Abbot of Ebersberg.

Paraphrase of the *Song of Solomon*. A mixture of Latin and German. *Ed.*, J. Seemüller, 1878. *MSS.*, Leyden, Breslau, Ebersberg (Munich), Lambach (Berlin), Hohenems, B.M. Harl. 3014, and others.

10 Poetry.

Ezzo. A noted scholar of Bamberg.

A Song on the Miracles of Christ (Ezzolied). This poem is said to have been composed at the request of Bishop Gunther, as he and Ezzo were on their way to the Holy Land in 1065. It begins with the creation (*Anegenge*) and fall of man. The poem has come down to us in two versions. Facsimile of Strassburg text, *ed.*, K. A. Barack, 1879. *MSS.*, Strassburg; Vorau.

Ava. The earliest poetess of whom we know. In all probability a recluse of Austria who died 1127. In the Vorauer MS. she speaks of two sons, one who had helped her in her work being dead.

Leben Jesu.

Antichrist.

Das Jüngste Gericht. (Called from the Görlitz MS. the "Görlitzer Evangelienharmonie.") *See* A. Langguth, 1880. *MSS.*, Vorau, Görlitz.

Genesis and *Exodus.* *MSS.*, Vienna: This *Genesis* is the oldest, and is written in the style of the national epic; Millstatt: later version; Vorau: a later rhymed version of the books of Moses, of 12th century. *Ed.*, Hoffmann (Vienna), "Fundgruben f. Gesch. Sprache, etc.," 1837; Diemer (Millstatt), 1862.

N.B.—The Vorau MS. contains other religious poems, "Lob des Salomons," "Judith," "Drei Junglinge im Feurofen." *Ed.*, Müllenhoff, *op. cit.*

Merigarto. Fragment of a description of the world, found at Prague in 1834. In it there is an irregularity of measure, which became common in the following period. *Ed.*, H. Hoffmann, 1834.

See for above generally, "Geistliche Poeten der Deutschen Kaiserzeit," W. Scherer, 1894–95.

11   LATIN WORKS.

Ruodlieb. Leonine hexameters, cir. 1030. Written by a monk of Tegernsee (the first fragments found were in a MS. from Tegernsee), thought once to be Froumond v. Tegernsee.

Ruodlieb seeks shelter at a foreign court; rises to eminence; is recalled to his native land by his mother and some of his countrymen. His protector, the King, gives him on leaving twelve golden precepts. In the course of the adventures which follow, the truth of these precepts is proved. There is a combination in the poem of knightly adventure and popular tale, with reminiscences of heroic saga. The hero is already developing towards the type in later Courtly epic. "As the first of this kind of composition, it is noticeable, as showing the existence of this species before German literature was affected by French influence." *Ed.*, E. F. Seiler, 1882. *MSS.*, Fragments found at Munich, St. Florian, and Dachau.

The growing taste for realism is marked in "Ruodlieb" and in the "Dorfgesänge" (*see* Lyric), and it is seen that popular material was also chosen by the clergy for their works though writing in Latin. ·When after the pause succeeding Otfrid's "Christ," vernacular literature was revived, two strongly contrasting styles appear in the works written in the native tongue: some of these were full of the rejoicing in life, others breathed the spirit of mediaeval asceticism, which in its unflinching surrender to the demands of its own ideal has not been surpassed by any later manifestation of the highest in man.

XIIth CENTURY.

12   MIDDLE HIGH GERMAN PERIOD.

(Cir. MIDDLE 12TH to the REFORMATION.)

A mixture of High and Low German elements is found in the writings of the 12th century, but in the 13th a greater separation is noticeable in the two dialects. The Swabian dialect, the language of the Court poets, finally predominated and became the link between the older and the more modern High German. The renewed epic dealt at first with religious subjects, as in the "Annolied"; the later secular epic was represented by two distinct branches—
The National ("Nibelungenlied,") and the Courtly.

The works of the second half of the 12th century may be considered as more or less transitional. The clergy themselves prepared the way for Court epics with the "Alexanderlied" and "Rolandslied," and towards the close of the 12th century literature passed into the hands of the laity.

As regards the form of poetry, certain rules gradually became more general, and assonance was by degrees superseded by rhyme.

The most usual forms were—

(1) The Nibelungen strophe (four long lines, the first half line of four, and the second of three beats, except the second half of the fourth line, which has four; the close of the first half line is feminine, of the second half masculine).

(2) Lines rhyming two and two, undivided into strophes, the lines having three or four beats, according to whether the rhyme was feminine or masculine; the sense generally ended with the first rhyme of the couplet. In this measure were composed most of the Courtly epics and larger didactic works.

13   Religious and Didactic Poetry.

Heinrich, cir. 1160. It is known from his own statement that Heinrich belonged to the laity; he was probably lay-brother at the Cloister of Melk. Diemer thought Ava's son.

Von des Todes Gehügede (*Erinnerung an den Tod*). Two parts—

(1) Description of vices of the time.
(2) Exhortation to think upon death.
Ed., R. Heinzel, 1867.   *MS.*, Vienna, 2690.

Anonymous.

König Tyrol (of Scotland). Seven-lined strophes, a a b b, c d c. Fragments only.

A didactic poem, in which the King proposes riddles which his son Vridebrant solves. *Ed.*, E. Wilken, 1873.   *MS.*, Manesse.

Anegenge. Creation, Fall, and Redemption.   *Ed.*, Hahn, "Gedichte d. 12 u. 13 Jahrh.," 1840. *See* E. Schroeder, "Quelle. u. Forsch. Sprache, etc.," 44.   *MS.*, Vienna, 2696.

Priester Wernher.   Bavarian Secular Priest.

Marienleben, cir. 1172. In three parts or songs. (Driu Liet von der Maget.)   *Ed.*, J. Feifalik, 1860.   *MSS.*, Fragments, Munich, Vienna, Berlin, Karlsruhe, and others.

In this century begins the long line of poems dedicated to the Virgin or saints, both narrative and lyric. *See* Goedeke, "Deutsche Dichtung im Mittelalter," 1871. Among the earliest are—

Das Jüdel. Tale of a Jewish child who, having eaten of the sacramental bread, is thrown by his angry father into an oven, but is miraculously saved from injury by the Virgin. *See* G. Wolter, for legends of Jewish children, "Legende von Judenknaben," 1879.

Bonus. A pious priest who is visited at night by the Virgin and apostles, and transported into the Church, there to read Mass; the Virgin gives him a rich vestment without seam.

The *Historical Poems* of this period are little more than romances.

Annolied. (Anno, Archb. of Cologne, d. 1075, canonised 1183.) The poem starts with the Creation, gives short history of the five monarchies of the world, and that of the most famous towns, till Cologne is reached; it ends with account and eulogy of Anno.

There is a difference of opinion as to date of poem, or parts of it. It cannot it is thought be placed earlier than 1077; many authorities place it beginning 12th century; others assign still later date. *See* Piper, *op. cit.*, pp. 145, 146. *Ed.*, Dr. K. Roth, 1847. *MS.*, MS. from which M. Opitz edited poem, shortly before 1639, has been since destroyed.

Die Kaiserchronik (cir. 1150). History of Roman and German Emperors from the time of Romulus to Lothair, with continuations by later hands. The work has been attributed to the author of the " Rolandslied " (§ 16) owing to certain similarities. The writer was a strong upholder of the papal power. There are three texts extant. The second version, carried to 1250, was by a poet who endeavoured to better the rhyme and verse. The third was by the hand of a later writer who took the old version, and framed it anew in the style of R. v. Ems, while yet another, who took W. v. Eschenbach as his model, carried this work on to 1274 (Zeil MS.). *Ed.*, H. F. Massmann, 1849-54, with " Enquiry into Sources, Legends," etc. E. Schroeder, 1892 (facsimile page of MS.). *MSS.*, Old Text: Vorau (oldest MS.), Munich, Wolfenbüttel, Heidelberg, Strassburg (burnt), Pommersfeld, Copenhagen, and fragments. Second text: Vienna (2), Prague, and fragments. Third text: Vienna (2), Karlsruhe, Castle of Zeil, Munich.

The Legend of " Tundalus," of Irish origin, who was one of the fabled visitants to the other worlds of Heaven and Hell, is found in two fragments, dating from the later 12th century. *Ed.*, K. Lachmann. At the request of three nuns it was again put into verse by a priest, Alberus, a Bavarian, in 12th or beginning of the 13th century. An English version, in octosyllabic verse, is extant (*see* England, § 67). *Ed.*, A. Wagner, "Visio Tnugdali," Latin and Old German, 1882. *See* also A. Mussafia, "Sulla visione di Tundalo," "Akad. Wiss. Sitzb. Phil. Hist.," 67, and Ward, "Cat. Romances," ii. 416.

Pilatus. Birth and life of Pilate. The German fragment breaks off before the arrival of Pilate in Judea. The legend of his death and of his spirit haunting various places is found in Latin versions. *MS.*, Strassburg (fragment).

14 PopuLAR Epic of the GLeemen.

König Rother. Composed in Bavaria by a Rhenish gleeman. Not extant in original form. King Rother carries off daughter of Constantine by aid of a party of giants, of whom the most formidable is Widolt; he gains possession of her a second time, after she has been taken from him by stratagem. Mixture of Eastern elements with German theme, of which the essential features are found in the history of Osantrix (Vilkinasaga). Rother becomes the father of Pepin, whereby the tale is connected with the Carolingian cycle. *Ed.*, H. Rückert, 1872; Bahder, 1884. *See* (for Saga) Bührig, 1889. *MSS.*, Heidelberg, 390 (only complete MS.); Baden, Hanover, Munich.

Orendel. Legend of the Holy Coat, of which Orendel gains possession, and carries home to Trier (Trèves). Date of original poem uncertain. Soon after 1190 (Meyer), end 12th (Vogt), later date (Heinzel). *Ed.*, v. Hagen, 1844; Berger, 1888 (dates poem cir. 1160). Trans. into Mod. German, Simrock, 1845. *See* E. H. Meyer, Haupt's "Zeitschrift," 12; "Zeitsch. Deutsch. Phil.," xxii., xxvi.; for saga, Paul-Braune, "Beiträge," 13. *MS.*, Strassburg; (Heidelberg MS. lost).

21

König Oswalt. Extant in two versions. Oswald, King of England, having, with the help of a raven, gained the daughter of Aaron, a heathen King, gives up his bride on the very day of their marriage, at the command of Christ, who appears at the wedding feast; hence his title of saint. *Ed.*, Ettmüller (Schaffhausen), 1835; later version, F. Pfeiffer, "Zeitschrift f. d. Alterthum," 2. *MSS.*, Schaffhausen; Vienna, 3007; later version differing in many respects from the older one.

Salman and Morolf (see England, § 9; France, § 48) (strophe a a b c b; c line known as the "Waise" (Orphan)). Only extant in 14th century version. Pharaoh carries off Salman's wife, but she is restored to her husband by the help of the latter's brother, Morolf. A second abduction takes place with repetition of recovery through the wit of Morolf, who this time succeeds in persuading his brother to put his wife to death. Salman then marries Pharaoh's sister, who is baptized as Afra. The tale is possibly founded on a German legend, as a Frankish king, Salman, occurs in two Northern sagas, but *see* "Solomon in Europe" by M. W. MacCallum, *op. cit.*, and E. Gordon Duff, *op. cit.* *Ed.*, F. Vogt, "Die deutschen Dichtungen v. Salomon u Markolf," 1880. *MSS.*, Eschenburg (now missing); Stuttgart; Strassburg (burnt). (*See* § 40.)

15   Epic of the Clergy.

Herzog Ernst (fragment only). Written in Bavaria by a Rhenish poet. In the person of the hero there is a confusion of two or more historical characters. After a description of his youth and his quarrels with his step-father, we hear of his journey to the East, and the marvels he comes across. The contents of the original poem are known through two later versions: one of the 12th and another of the 13th century. Latin versions in prose and verse also exist. *Ed.*, Original fragments, Bartsch, 1869. *See* Jänicke (for dates), Haupt's "Zeitsch.," xv. *MSS.*, Prague, Vienna, Nürnberg, Gotha, Marburg (different versions, *see* Bartsch).

Graf Rudolf (fragment only) (*see* B. v. Holle, § 34).
Young knight of Flanders who goes to the East; imprisonment, escape, etc. *Ed.*, Grimm, 2nd ed., 1844.

16 CAROLINGIAN CYCLE.

Pfaffe Konrad.

Ruolandesliet (*Song of Roland*). From a French text.
Written first in Latin, then in German. This is the oldest
German imitation of a Chanson de Geste. The editor places
this poem between 1171–1177, but G. Paris puts back the
date to cir. middle century. The matter depends on whether
the work was written for Henry the Lion or his father.
Ed., Grimm (Heidelberg, with miniatures), 1838; K.
Bartsch, 1874. *MSS.*, Heidelberg (thirty-nine miniatures),
Strassburg; and other fragments (*see* Stricker, § 31).

Some of the compositions from which the Karl Meinet
of 14th century was compiled, date from this century
(*see* § 31).

17 ALEXANDER CYCLE.

Lamprecht.

Alexanderlied, cir. 1130. Not extant in original. From
the French of Albéric de Besançon (*see* France, § 27).
Ed., Kinzel, 1884. *MSS.*, Vorau, Strassburg, Basle.

18 ANIMAL SAGA (*see* France, § 32).

Heinrich der Glichezaere.

Isengrînes Nôt (fragments only). The greater part of
the poem has been preserved in a later version, "Reinhart
Fuchs." *Ed.*, Fragments, Grimm, 1840. *MSS.*,
Fragments found in Melsungen, in Hesse (now at Cassel).

19 COURTLY EPIC.

The material of the Courtly epic was chiefly taken from
French sources; old German material, however, was also
handled. With few exceptions, it was written in short
rhyming couplets, the sentence ending with the rhyme.

Late XIIth and Early XIIIth Century.

The four chief names of this period are—

Heinrick v. Veldeke,
Hartmann v. Aue,
Wolfram v. Eschenbach,
Gotfried v. Strassburg.

All four also noted as lyric poets.

Gotfried and Hartmann served as models for succeeding epic writers of 13th and 14th centuries; later on, Wolfram became the chief model.

Heinrich v. Veldeke. "The father of Courtly poetry." "If not actually first in time, he was the first to cultivate purity of rhyme, and to apply stricter metrical rules."

Eneide (finished 1189). From the French "Roman d'Enée" (*see* France, § 28). *Ed.*, H. Behaghel, 1882. *MSS.*, Berlin (with miniatures), Munich, Vienna, Eybach, Gotha, Heidelberg, and fragments.

H. v. Veldeke's other works were *Lieder* and a *Life of S. Servatius.* (*See* Braune, "Zeitsch. Deutsch. Philol.," iv., for dialect of works.)

Arthurian Cycle.

(E. v. Oberg, U. v. Zatzikhoven, H. v. Aue, W. v. Eschenbach, and G. v. Strassburg.)

Eilhard v. Oberg, fl. 1189–1209.

Tristant u. Isolde. Fragments of original only (Magdeburg, Heidelberg). Two later versions exist in verse and a later version still in prose, and according to editor there was possibly an early one in German verse (p. cxvii.). Eilhard's work is placed rather before Veldeke's "Eneide" by some authorities, but Behaghel (*see* above) thinks Eilhart borrowed from Veldeke. (*See* England, § 39; France, § 25). For relationship with the A.-N. poems of Thomas and Beroul, *see* Editor, and works under France, § 25. *Ed.*, F. Lichenstein, "Forschungen zur sprach u. Culturgeshichte, etc.," xix., 1898. *MSS.*, Later version in verse, Heidelberg, Dresden, Berlin.

Ulrich v. Zatzikhoven.

Lanzelet. From the birth to death of Lancelot. The poem is taken from an Anglo-Norman original lent to the author by Gui de Morville, who had been left in Germany as a hostage by Richard 1. (R.'s imprisonment ended in 1194.) *Ed.*, J. Baechtold, 1870. *MSS.*, Vienna, Berlin, Heidelberg, Strassburg (destroyed).

Hartmann v. Aue. Took part in Crusade of 1189 or 1197, or in both. Dead in 1220 (§ 20). Works, *Ed.*, F. Bech, 1867-69. There is a diversity of opinion as to the order in which the following poems should be dated.

Erec. Not complete as extant. From Chrétien de Troies (*see* France, § 26). *Ed.*, M. Haupt, 1871. Trans., Mod. German, S. O. Fistes, 1851. *MS.*, One MS., Vienna (Ambras).

Gregorius, or *der guote Sündaere (the Good Sinner).* A legend of Aquitaine. Of his innocent sinning, penance, and elevation to the Papacy (*see* France, § 10). The editor writes that the French poem extant in MSS. at Tours, Arsenal, and B.M. do not give the original text, nor the one used by H. v. A. *Ed.*, H. Paul, 1873, 1882 ; Bech, "Deutsche Klassiker, etc.," Bd. v. 1867. *MSS.*, Vatican, Spiez, Berne, etc.

Iwein, or *der Ritter mit dem Löwen (Knight of the Lion).* From Chrétien de Troies. *Ed.*, Benecke u. Lachmann, 1868, 1877 ; E. Henrici, "Germanistische Handbibl.," viii. 1891. Trans. into Mod. German, F. Koch, 1848. *MSS.*, Twenty-five in number—Heidelberg, Munich, Berlin, Dresden, Florence, Paris, B.M. Add. 19554.

Der Arme Heinrich. Knight attacked by leprosy, and told

the only cure is the blood of a pure maiden; one is ready to die for him, but he will not accept the sacrifice; recovers and marries her. *Ed.*, H. Paul, 1883; Wackernagel-Toischer, 1885. Trans., Mod. German, H. v. Wolzosen, 1880. *MSS.*, Strassburg, Vatican, Weingarten, Kolocza.

20   Lyric.

The lyric was not as much affected by French models as the Epic. The tone of the Minnesong was more serious than that of the love song of France. The subjects of the lyric were love, politics, religion, or a description of lower class life (Dorfgesänge).

It is a vexed question whether love lyrics existed before the middle of the 12th century, but it seems certain that priests were forbidden to sing love songs, even in Carolingian times, and that under Charlemagne there was a decree prohibiting the nuns writing or sending "Winileodes," or love songs. A love greeting in German rhymes is found in "Ruodlieb," and the following is from a maiden's Latin love letter, found among the letters of Wernher v. Tegernsee in the Munich MS.

> " Dû bist mîn, ich bin dîn:
>   des solt dû gewis sîn.
>   dû bist beslozzen
>   in mînem herzen:
>   verlorn ist daz slûzzelîn:
>   dû muost immer drinne sîn."

The three chief forms were Lied, Leich, and Spruch.

The *Lied* was composed of at least three strophes, and each strophe had three divisions, of which the first two were alike, followed by one consisting generally of more lines.

Leich. Strophes of two divisions, or undivided strophes.

Spruch. Religious and political; generally of one strophe in three divisions.

The Minnepoesie was intended to be sung, and was accompanied by a stringed instrument.

The earliest Minnelieder had no distinctive lyric form. They were in rhymed couplets (Dietmar v. Aist), or in heroic strophe (Kürenberg) ; rhyme was often only a matter of assonance. The songs of the Minnesingers were collected at the close of the 13th century.

The chief MSS. containing collections of lyrics are—

Paris, or Manesse. *See* Apfelstedt, " Germania," 26.
Heidelberg. *Ed.*, F. Pfeiffer, " Bibl. Litt. Verein.," 1844.
Weingarten. *Ed.*, F. Pfeiffer and F. Fellner, *ibid.*, 1843.

The Paris and Weingarten MSS. contain miniatures of the Minnesingers.

Other MSS., Heidelberg, Jena (ed. Saran, 1901), and Colmar.

See F. H. v. d. Hagen, " Deutsche Liederdichter des 12, 13, and 14 Jahrh., etc.," 1838 ; Lachmann u. Haupt, " Des Minnesangs Frühling," 1888 ; R. Bartsch, " Deutsche Liederdichte," 12-14 Jhh. (selection), 1893 ; W. Storck, " Lieder aus der Minneseit " (trans.) 1872 ; A. Börckel, " Die fürstlichen Minnesinger der Manesse. Hsch.," 1881 ; and a charming volume of selections by Pannier, in Modern German.

Minnesingers (12th and 13th Centuries).

The chief subject of the poets of the Court was Minne, the ideal love, the spiritualised longing of the heart, sometimes personified as Frau Minne. The beginnings of knightly lyric are found in Austria and Bavaria ; towards the latter part of the 12th century it became influenced by French poetry. The period styled the " Minnesangsfrühling " (Spring) lasted to about 1290 ; the lyrics belonging to it were simple and natural, popular in tune, and more narrative than subjective. With the poet Veldeke began an interval of greater artificiality of form, French ideas and style being taken as models. The lyric again became more independent of foreign influence, richer, more melodious, more truly lyric, and then began the Golden Age (" Blütezeit ") of the Minnesong, the true period of " Minnedienst." Before its close the growing tendency to realism had begun to show itself in the work of the poets, the

chief representative of the early realistic school being Neidhart
v. Reuenthal, in his "Dorfpoesie." The "Blutezeit" was
short, and succeeded by a period of rapid decadence. "All
the more attractive features of the Minnesong, its idealism, its
refined sensibility, and delicate intuitions gave place to qualities
entirely of the opposite character, and the form itself grew
artificial and rougher." *See* F. H. v. d. Hagen ("Works,
Lives, *op. cit.*, etc."), Paul-Braune, "Beiträge," vol. ii.
p. 406 ff.

N.B.—The Courts of Leopold VI. of Austria and his
successors, and of the Landgraves of Thuringia, were chief
centres of culture.

Among the immense number of Minnesingers only a few
can be mentioned. The following belong to the 12th century:—

Der v. Kürenberg. (*See* "Nibelungen," § 28.) Love
songs of early part of century ascribed to him ; written in
assonance and rhyme. *See* Hurch, 1889.

Meinloh v. Sevelingen.

Dietmar v. Aist.

Burggrafen v. Regensburg.

Spervogel. The oldest known writer of religious lyric.
(MSS. speak of an elder and younger Spervogel.)

Friedrich v. Hausen, d. 1190. One of the early
representatives of the artistic Minnesong.

Emperor Henry VI., d. 1197. Two songs.

END XIITH AND BEGINNING XIIITH CENTURY.

The four Epic writers—

H. v. Veldeke. (§ 19.)

H. v. Aue. (§ 19.)

W. v. Eschenbach. (§ 30.)

Gotfried v. Strassburg. (§ 30.)

Heinrich v. Morungen, fl. cir. 1200. One of the finest of the Minnesingers.

This poet and Reinmar were followers of Veldeke.

Reinmar der Alte, d. cir. 1206.

" The nightingale of Hagenau," as G. v. Strassburg entitles him. *See* E. Schmidt, " Quell. Forsch. Sprach., etc.," iv.

Walther v. der Vogelweide. Date of death uncertain.

" All the gracefulness and art of the Minnesong is concentrated in W. v. d. V." (K. Francke). The most many-sided of the old lyrists. He appears to have wandered as a " fahrender Sänger " over best part of the middle of Europe, and to have taken part in the crusade of Friedrich II. In the struggle between Pope and Emperor he was a partisan of the latter. His lyrics deal with love, politics, and religion, and he employs various forms of strophe from the simplest to the most complicated.

Walther lived for some time at the Court of Hermann v. Thüringen, the patron of Veldeke and Eschenbach. In the Manesse MS. of the " Sängerstreit auf der Wartburg," said to have taken place 1206, the Landgraf and his wife are represented presiding at the contest. Among the singers are W. v. Eschenbach, R. der Alte, and W. v. der Vogelweide; the poem is of late 13th century.

For the connection of the writings of the Minnesingers with the political events of their times, *see* " Studien zur Poesie der Minnedichter," H. Drees, 1889.

21 Chivalric culture was at its height at the beginning of the 13th century, and the ideal of mediæval life still found expression in the romances, epics, and lyrics of the poets. Before its close, a new order of social things had arisen, which by degrees wrought a complete change in the tone of literature. The power of the German Empire had received its death-blow on the fall of the Hohenstaufen dynasty; the supreme temporal power of the Pope, and the infallibility of the Church as a spiritual guide, had begun to be questioned; the initiatory stage in the transition from mediæval to modern life had been reached, and the rise of the middle classes in this century helped forward the work of dissolution and re-construction. Hints of the coming revolution in the spirit of literature had not been wanting in the writings of the three great masters of romance—Hartmann v. Aue, Wolfram v. Eschenbach, and Gotfried v. Strassburg; but it was not until poetry had passed out of the hands of the aristocracy into that of the Burgher class, that the conventionality and artificiality that had marked the style and sentiment of the works of the preceding century wholly disappeared. The fight for liberty of thought had by that time begun, and in this embryo stage of individualism, the widened sympathies of all classes, and the deepening of personal feeling, could only find adequate expression in a realism opposed to the former idealism, and in a subjectivity of style which contrasted with the detailed description of externals in which the romance writers so freely indulged.

This period of transition, however, was not favourable to the production of poetry, and for three ensuing centuries there flourished no poet of great repute.

Prose, on the other hand, gradually took a high place in literature, and in this form were written the chief literary works of these centuries.

From the close of the 13th century, a historical prose began; translations were made from many and various classical works; and old romances were put into prose. The art of preaching also rose into eminence in this century; a more popular style was adopted in the pulpit by the Dominicans and Franciscans, who made use of the vernacular for the instruction of their hearers. *See* K. Francke, "Social Forces in German Literature," chapters iii. and iv., 1901.

22 PROSE.

Religious, etc.

Among the most noted preachers of the newer style were the two Franciscans: David v. Augsburg, d. 1271 or 72, in whose writings are indications of the first awakening of the spirit of mysticism, which prevailed in the following century; Berthold v. Regensburg, a pupil of David's, who died 1272; and the Dominican, Eckhart, d. 1327, the first of the three great Mystic preachers (Suso, d. 1366, Tauler, d. 1361) of the 14th century. The writings of these three have been published. *See* also F. Pfeiffer, W. Preger, and J. H. S. Denifle, on German mystics and mysticism.

At the close of the 13th century, literature begins to show the effect of mysticism, the realisation of the intimate connection of the soul with God independent of material agency, a phase of the struggle between religious individuality and dogma which culminated in the Reformation. The nation had turned another corner of the road which was gradually leading it farther and farther away from mediævalism.

23 *History.*

The German language, used occasionally from the twenties, became towards the close of the 13th century a frequent medium for both historical and legal records. The first German prose Chronicle originated in Lower Saxony.

Sächsische Weltchronik. Oldest prose history of the world. Probably 1237: before 1251, and after 1230. It is extant in three versions. *Ed.*, L. Weiland, "Mod. Germ. Hist.," tome xi. *MSS.*, *Shortest version :* Wolfenbüttel, Munich, Vienna, Heidelberg, Frankfort, Leipzig, Berlin,

Hamburg. *Middle version*: Petersburg, Kopenhagen, Leipzig, Bremen, Berlin. *With continuations*: Dresden Hanover, Pommersfeld, Kopenhagen, Wolfenbüttel, Strassburg (destroyed).

Law.

Eike von Repkowe, fl. 1209–1233.

Sachsenspiegel. Written first in Latin. The oldest German law book. First quarter of century. It records Saxon laws of land and feofs. The author introduces his work in a rhymed preface. *Ed.*, Homeyer, 1835–44. *MSS.*, For numerous MSS. of "Sachsenspiegel," *see* "Die deutschen Rechtsbücher des Mittelalters, etc.," G. Homeyer, 1856.

From this model was prepared in South Germany a *Spiegel aller Deutschen Leute*, and on this was based the better known

Schwabenspiegel. Last quarter of 13th century. *MS.*, For MSS. *see* above, Homeyer.

The authorship of this last-named work has been assigned both to David von Augsburg and Berthold von Regensburg.

24 POETRY.

Religious, Didactic, and Narrative : Lives of Saints, etc.

Konrad v. Fuszesbrunn. Notices, thought to relate to this author, are found 1182–86; he is mentioned by R. v. Ems in "Wilhelm" between W. v. Gravenberg and K. Fleck (cir. 1230).

Die Kindheit Jesu (rhymed couplets). The descriptions of domestic life are essentially German, and interesting on that account. The author tells us that he took his material from a Latin book; he also refers to the "Anegenge" and another German poem. *Ed.*, Kochendörffer, 1881, "Quell. u. Forsch. Sprach Cult. Gesch.," viii. *MSS.*, Vienna, Laszberg (Donaueschingen), Leipzig.

Konrad v. Heimesfurt. Mentioned by R. v. Ems in "Alexander," between G. v. Strassburg and W. v. Gravenberg (cir. 1220).

Marien himmelfahrt (*Von unser Vrouwen hinfahrt*) (rhymed couplets). Death and ascension of the Virgin. *Ed.*, F. Pfeiffer, Haupt's "Zeitsch.," 8. *MSS.*, Laszberg (Donaueschingen), Berlin, Gratz.

Urstende (Resurrection) (rhymed couplets). K. v. H. gives his name in an acrostic. *Ed.*, Hahn, "Gedichte des 12th and 13th Jahrb." *MS.*, Vienna.

Hugo v. Langenstein. In 1282 this poet with his father and brothers entered the German Order, dedicated to the Virgin, founded by Duke Friedrich of Swabia in 1190.

Der heilige Martina (rhymed couplets). *Ed.*, D. v. Keller, 1856, "Bibl. Litt. Ver.," xxxviii. *MS.*, Basle.

Bruder Philipp.

Marienleben (13th or early 14th century) (rhymed couplets). *Ed.*, H. Rückert, 1853. *MSS.*, Many MSS.: Jena, Heidelberg, Gotha, Vienna, Strassburg, etc.

Anonymous.

Passional. In three books (rhymed couplets). Collection of legends of the Virgin, Apostles, and Saints, containing 100,000 lines. Written after 1250. From the "Legenda Aurea" and other sources. *Ed.*, K. A. Hahn, 1845 (first and second parts). F. K. Köpke, 1852 (third part only). *MSS.*, First and second parts: Heidelberg, Vienna, Strassburg, etc. Third part: Strassburg, Königsberg, etc.

Das Veterbuch (*Lives of the Fathers*) (rhymed couplets). From the "Vitas patrum." This is by the same compiler as the "Passional," but of earlier date.   *Ed.*, K. G. Franke, 1879.   *MSS.*, Leipzig, Hildesheim, Königsberg, etc.

N.B.—Other collections of legends are of contemporary and later date : *Buch der Maertirer* was written about the same time as *Passional* and *Veterbuch*; to later ones belongs *Der maget Krône,* 14th century.

25 A didactic tendency had been noticeable in the Minnesingers, among them W. v. d. Vogelweide, and this tendency increased as the lyrical impulse gradually died out.   Narrative poetry became more general as the national and courtly epic began to decay, cir. middle 13th century, and the short tale was now preferred to the longer romance.   The people, Stricker tells us, had grown curious and liked to be entertained, and preferred what was just long enough for an evening's amusement.

Der Winsbeke, or *des vater lêre* (ten - lined strophes, a b a b b c b d e d).   The name, according to Haupt, is that of the poet, derived from the place-name, Winsbach, given in the Paris MS. ; there are, however, differences of opinion on the matter.   A didactic poem, being the advice of a father to his son.   The poet flourished about same time as T. v. Zirclaria.

Die Winsbekin, or *der muoter lêre.*   Advice of a mother to her daughter, in imitation of above.   *Ed.*, M. Haupt, 1845. "Early German Courtesy Books," E. Oswald, E.E.T.S., Ex. Ser., viii. 1869.   *MSS.*, Weingarten, Paris, Berlin, Basle, Gotha, Vienna.

Thomasin v. Zirclaria, b. cir. 1185.

Der Wälsche Gast (the Italian or North-French Guest) (rhymed couplets), 1215 or 1216.   In books (ten) and chapters, with prose introduction.   A comprehensive work, dealing with virtue, courtesy, good-breeding, riches and poverty, soul and body, arts, theology, things good and evil, etc. Interesting as throwing light on the science, morals, and manners of the age; beside more serious matters, instruction is given for behaviour at meals and for the manner in which a lady should sit a horse. *Ed.*, H. Rückert, 1852 (the prose introduction is given at the end under "Lesarten"). *See* also for life, discussion as to interpretation of "Walsch," etc., "Early German Courtesy Books." *MSS.*, Heidelberg, Erbach, Gotha, Stuttgart, Dresden, Wolfenbüttel, Munich, etc.

The author himself mentions a former work of his, and there were probably others by him. In what language the earlier work was written is uncertain, as the "Welhische" (Wälsch) he says he wrote in, is a term used to designate romance speech generally; it is thought probable that in this instance it signified the "langue d'oil."

Freidank, fl. first half 13th century. The supposition advanced by Grimm, and supported by Wackernagel, that this author was identical with W. v. d. Vogelweide, has not been generally accepted.

Bescheidenheit (*Discretion, Discernment*) (rhymed couplets). "The chief didactic work of this period." After four lines, in which the author introduces himself and the subject of his poem, as the crown of all virtues, a variety of matters are dealt with, chiefly through the medium of fables, proverbs, and riddles. Men and women of all classes, Heaven and Hell, God, Soul, Jews, Age, Hunger, Animals, the Tongue, End of the World, are among the subjects treated by Freidank; the work ends with a prayer. Freidank took part in the crusade under Frederick II., and a part of the work may have been written in Syria. Grimm thinks the division of "Rome," and another, may be parts of a separate poem on the crusade, now lost: the author gives a lively picture of the state of things in the Holy Land. *Ed.*, W. Grimm, second edition, 1860; F. Sandvoss, 1877; Mod. Germ., Simrock, Bacmeister and K. Pannier. *MSS.*, Some MSS. only contain part : Heidelberg, Gotha, Salzburg, Bremen, Munich, Würzburg, Vienna, Dresden, Strassburg, Berlin, Memmingen, etc.

N.B.—Sebastian Brandt's version of Freidank's poem with additions, was first printed, 1508. Extracts from Freidank are also found in "Lieder Saal," edited 1820, by Freiherr v. Laszberg, from unpublished sources; also in the "Liederbuch der Clara Hätzlerin," ed. C. Haltaus, 1840, from the MS. written by C. H., a nun of Augsburg, in 1470; this MS. (Prague) contains lyrics, narrative, and didactic pieces.

26   *Novellen*, or *Maere* (short tales of various kinds) ; *Bîspel* (examples, parables) ; *Fables, Proverbs*, and *Schwänke* (merry tales), were used for didactic purposes. The most famous name of this period, as a writer of tales, was Der Stricker. The later and larger romances of this period were written in rhymed couplets.

N.B.—Collections of tales are found in MSS. at Vienna, Strassburg, Munich, Heidelberg, Kolocza, Innsbruck, Erlangen, Vatican, Weimar, etc. ; for Melk MS. *see* Leitzmann, 1904.

Der Stricker, fl. first half and middle 13th century. Mentioned by R. von Ems as a contemporary in his "Wilhelm" and "Alexander," so alive, cir. 1240 (*see* § 30). This craftsman's name may have been an assumed one, but it is traceable as a family name in Austria, from the 12th century.

Der Pfaffe Amis. An account of the roguery and tricks of an English priest. These "Schwänke" are twelve in number ; they are part of the folk-lore of the country, and reappear in later collections. "Stricker's work is the oldest specimen of tales linked together in a connected poem." *Ed.,* "Gesammtabenteuer," F. H. v. d. Hagen, 1850. (A hundred tales in verse, from 12th to 14th century, mostly in Middle High German.) "Erzaehlungen u. Schwänke,"

H. Lambel, 1872.   *MSS.*, Reidegger, Ambras (Vienna), Munich, Gotha, Strassburg MS. burnt 1870.

Frauenlob, or *Frauenehre*. In praise of good women, not without a touch of satire. He chooses the subject as "one which will for ever remain of interest, though an odd one, it will be said, for him to choose, a horse or an old cloak being more suitable. But many praise God whom they have not seen, and he has seen a good many women, and heard a great deal about their virtues." *See* Haupt's "Zeitsch.," 7 and 25. *MSS.*, Heidelberg, Vienna, Kolocza, Ambras (Vienna).

Stricker also wrote many separate tales, fables, and satirical poems; among the latter are, *Die Klage*, *Edelsteine*, *das Alter*, *Drei Dinge*. Smaller poems by Stricker, *ed.*, R. A. Hahn, 1839. *MS.*, B.M. Add. 24946, contains poems by S.

Ulrich v. Lichtenstein, of Styria, d. 1275 or 1276.

Mention of this writer is found as early as 1239; his poetical activity dates from 1223. He spent his life in attending tournaments and fulfilling other chivalric duties. At one time he rode dressed as Venus, and accompanied by a large following from Venice to Bohemia, challenging every knight he met, in his lady's name. Some years later he undertook a similar progress, this time representing King Arthur returned from Paradise, to re-establish the Round Table. For thirty-three years he was the slave of knightly love and devotion to an unknown lady, who made him a very inadequate return for his fidelity. *See* Knorr, "Quell. Forsch. Sprach., etc.," ix.

Frauendienst (*Vrouwendienest*), 1255. In this strophic poem, "the oldest German autobiographical work extant," we have an outline of the poet's life from the time he was twelve years old; it gives full details of the love affair, etc., stated above. The poem, which was finished in 1255, is interspersed with lyrics. From it we learn the height to which knightly folly attained in this century; on the other hand, the work is perfectly genuine, many things being recorded which are

22

not entirely to the poet's credit; and if everything did not entirely occur as he describes, he was evidently, as one of his editors writes, one of those men of that dual nature, who believe in what they persuade themselves to be true. *Ed.*, J. Bergmann, 1840, 1841 ("Wiener Jahrb."); R. Bechstein, 1888. Mod. Germ. Prose, L. Tieck, 1812. *MSS.*, Munich; Lyrics in Paris MS. of Minnelieder.

Frauenbuch (*der Vrouwenbuoch*) (rhymed couplets), 1257. Dialogue between poet and lady, who cast reproaches at one another concerning their respective failings. Both poems, ed. K. Lachmann, 1841. *MS.*, Ambras (Vienna).

N.B.—MS. from the Castle of Ambras, prepared for the Emperor Maximilian, 1502–15, now at Vienna.

U. v. Lichtenstein was also a lyric poet, a representative of the conventional form of "Minnesang." *See* Pannier, "Die Minnesinger," 1881.

N.B.—For description of Tournaments *see* Niedner, "Das Deutsche Turnier, in 12th and 13th Jahrh.," 1881.

Wernher der Gartenäre (Gärtner). It is a question whether or not this poet is identical with the lyric poet Bruder Wernher. *See* R. Schroeder, "Zeitsch. f. d. Phil.," 2.

Meier Helmbrecht (rhymed couplets), cir. 1250. The history of a young man, ambitious beyond his station, and unfilial in conduct, who finally becomes a highwayman, and is hanged. *Ed.*, Haupt's "Zeitsch.," 4; Mod. Germ., K. Pannier, 1876; M. Oberbreyer, 1879. *MS.*, Ambras (Vienna), Berlin.

N.B.—"Helmbrecht" and "Pfaffe Amis" are representatives of the realistic tendency of the narrative and didactic poetry of this period, which existed side by side with the courtly and artificial style of "Frauendienst" and the knightly epic.

Herrand v. Wildonie, fl. middle and second half century. A writer of tales and believed to be identical with the Minnesinger of that name. Native of Styria.

Die treue Hausfrau (diu getriu Kone).
Der getäuschte Ehemann (der verkérte Wirt).
Der Nackte Kaiser (von dem blôzen Keiser).
Die Katze (von der Katzen).

Ed., "Vier Erzaehlungen," Bergmann, 1841; "Gesammta-benteur," v. d. Hagen; "Erzaehlungen u. Schwänke," Lambel; H. R. Kummer, 1880 (with addition of poems by Suoneck, Scharfenberg, and Stadeck, as representatives with H. v. Wildonie of the knightly poetry produced in Inner Austria in the second half of the 13th century). *MS.,* Ambras (Vienna).

Konrad v. Würzburg, d. 1287, pupil of G. of Strassburg (§§ 30, 33, 34). This voluminous writer of songs, tales and epics, was of the Burgher class. He stands midway between two periods, for his poems, both in subject and treatment, belong partly to the courtly style of poetry of the earlier period, and by their erudition and tendency to didacticism are linked to the works of the following one. "Though charming in form, an over-elaboration and straining after effect in his lyric work, show signs of the decadence of poetry."

Didactic, Allegorical, and Legendary Works.

Die Goldene Schmiede (rhymed couplets). A poem in praise of the Virgin, into which the author introduces all he has gathered concerning her, from literature and tradition. The work, one of the last written by the author, enjoyed a wide-spread popularity. *Ed.,* W. Grimm, 1840. *MSS.,* Gotha, Kolocza, Heidelberg, Göttingen, Vienna, Munich, Hamburg, Breslau.

Der Welt Lohn (rhymed couplets). Allegorical tale of the knight Wirnt v. Gravenberg (author of *Wigalois,* § 30) who is converted by a vision of the world, personified in a beautiful woman, who appears finely dressed as she faces him, and when she turns shows her back covered with reptiles. A prose version of this tale exists in a MS. of the 14th century. *Ed.*, F. Roth, 1843; F. Sachse, 1857; Modern German, K. Pannier, "Kleinere Dichtungen," 1879. *MSS.*, Munich, Heidelberg, Kolocza, Vienna, Laszberg.

Silvester (rhymed couplets). Conversion of the Emperor Constantine and his mother. *Ed.*, W. Grimm, 1841. *MS.*, Unique MS., Trier.

Alexius (rhymed couplets). (*See* § 40.) One of the favourite legends of the Middle Ages (*see* France, § 4). Seven other versions exist in German. *Ed.*, Haupt, "Zeitschrift," 3; H. F. Massmann (eight versions), 1843; R. Henczynski, "Acta. Germ.," Bd. vi. Heft 1, 1898. *MSS.*, Strassburg, Innsbruck, Sarnen.

Pantaleon (rhymed couplets). Conversion and martyrdom. *Ed.*, Haupt, "Zeitsch.," vi. p. 193. *MS.*, Vienna.

Klage der Kunst (strophes of eight lines, linked by two alternate rhymes). An allegorical poem, being the complaint of Art concerning the false generosity lavished on inferior poets. "It belongs to a series of poems, which became more and more frequent from the close of the 13th century, and are proof of the lessening taste for poetry among the class to which at one time it owed its excellence and chief support." *Ed.*, E. Joseph, "Quell. u. Forsch. Sprach. Cult. Gesch.," vol. liv., 1885. *MS.*, Unique MS., Würzburg.

N.B.—A fragment of a life of S. Nicolaus is ascribed to K. v. Würzburg by Bartsch, and edited with "Partonopier."

27 Among didactic works of the 13th century was the translation of Cato's "Sententiæ" (distiches). For particulars *see* § 40.

Volmar, cir. 1252–5. (Vogt).

Das Steinbuch (rhymed couplets). On the wonderful properties of stones, and of the places where the same are to be found.

Volmar does not add religious and moral interpretations, such as are found in some works of this class.   *Ed.*, H. Lambel, 1877 (with addition of other writings on stones, verses by H. v. Mügeln, etc.).   *MSS.*, Vienna, Hamburg, Dresden, S. Gall; B.M., Sloane, 448; etc.

Der Tanhäuser, fl. middle and second half 13th cent. (§ 36.) To this author has been ascribed a lyrical work of instruction regarding manners at table, entitled, *Hofzucht,* but it is not generally accepted as his. In its present form it appears to be a version of an older work.   *Ed.,* "Altdeutsche Tischzuchten," M. Geyer, 1882.

N.B.—The wandering life led by this poet, his "Buszlied" (song of repentance), and the character of his songs generally, are accountable, it is thought, for the tale in connection with the Venusberg, which is attached to his name. For account of "Saga," allied tales, life, *see* "Der Tanhäuser u. der Ewige Jude," J. G. Th. Graesse, 1861. A. Oehlke, 1890; Siebert, 1894.

Seigfried Helbling, cir. 1230 to close of century. Pseudonym of writer, who was a knight. The chief satirical writer of this century. It is uncertain how long he lived after 1299.

Fifteen *Büechel,* or *Büchlein.* Several in dialogue form, and one called "Der Kleine Lucidarius," from an earlier prose work in this form, called "Lucidarius," or "Elucidarius," or "Aurea Gemma." These didactic poems deal with dress, food, bathing, decay of the Minnesong, introduction of foreign customs, etc.   *Ed.,* J. Seemüller, 1886; Th. Karajan, Haupt, "Zeitsch.," iv.   *MS.,* Vienna, 2887.

N.B.—Certain didactic poems received the title of Buoch, Büechel, or Büechlin; of Rede, and of Liet.

Hugo v. Trimberg. Schoolmaster at Theuerstadt, a suburb of Bamberg, 1260–1309. He wrote, as he himself tells us, both in German and Latin. Cir. 1266 he wrote a poem, now lost, called the *Samner* (Sammler); its contents were much the same as those of the poem which is preserved.

Der Renner (rhymed couplets), 1300. A long work of nearly 25,000 lines; "a castigatory sermon, enlivened with maxims and fables." It was the most highly esteemed didactic work after that of Freidank; it was imitated by later writers, and printed as early as 1549. The work is without plan; in it he bitterly attacks the higher classes, and the whole provides an interesting mirror of the times. Some MSS. bear the title of "Centiloquium," which has been interpreted as signifying the way in which thoughts follow one another as they arise in the author's mind. The above is the more usual title, which may be variously explained. The author likens himself to a rider with whom his horse is running away; again, in referring to his two books, he writes, "jenz loufet vor, ditz rennet nâch" (that one ran before, this one runs after), and an old superscription reads, "Renner ist ditz buoch genannt, wan ez Sol rennen durch diu lant," so called, because it should run through the world. *MSS.*, For the numerous MSS. of the "Renner," *see* "Zeitsch. f. deutsches Alterthum," xxviii. p. 175 *seq.*; and "Germania," xxx. p. 129.

A list of Latin authors in Latin verse, *Registrum Multorum Auctorum*, 1280, is by this author.

N.B.—The spirit which animated the realistic works of this century did not quickly die out; we meet it still in the 16th century: "a spirit of naïve fearlessness and truthfulness; a childlike delight in direct and unconventional, and even coarse, utterance; a loving tenderness for the apparently small and common; and a grim hatred of all pretence and usurpation . . . ideal figures . . . had lost their force; what people wanted to see in literature was their own life. . . ." *See* K. Francke, *op. cit.*, pp. 127–128.

28   NATIONAL EPIC.

XIITH TO XIIITH CENTURY.

The national epic of the 12th and 13th centuries deals
with the Frankish, Gothic, Longobardic, and Norman sagas;
those of other divisions of the German race being either lost,
or appearing in conjunction with that of other races. Siegfried,
of the "Nibelungen," belongs to the Frankish cycle; Dietrich v. Bern, to the East Gothic; Gunther, to the Burgundian. The sagas connected with the migration of the
nations were the basis of the Teutonic epic; to this historical
material was added Pagan myth; the mythic gods in their
turn became in time godlike heroes and knights; of such
descent was Siegfried.

Das Nibelungenlied, or *Der Nibelunge Nôt.* Written in
Middle High German; divided into thirty-nine Âventiure.
The Nibelungen strophe is composed of four lines, rhyming two and two; the first three lines have seven stressed
syllables in each line; the fourth line has four in the first
half, and four in the second.

The history of the "Nibelungenlied" cannot be traced further
back than the 12th century. Numerous writings have appeared
concerning the question as to whether or not the work is a
single and independent one, or a collection of separate songs.
The latter idea was supported by Lachmann, who distinguished
twenty ancient songs, which he thought were put together
about 1210, being connected by strophes of the poet's own.
He considered the Munich MS. to be the oldest. According
to Bartsch's later criticism, the folk-songs were brought into
a whole by an Austrian poet, about the middle of the
12th century; this earlier version being written in assonanced
lines. A later version followed in 1170, introducing rhyme;
between 1190 and 1200 two other poets undertook a new
version in stricter rhyme, leaving an assonance here and there.
These two versions are extant in numerous MSS.; the one
represented by the Laszberg MS., the other by the S. Gall
(the Munich being an abbreviated form of the latter). The

S. Gall (Nibelunge Nôt) is the one which, according to Bartsch, represents most closely the work of the original poet. For discussion of B.'s views, *see* Paul-Braune, "Beiträge," 3, p. 373 ff. The "Nôt" MS. group is generally acknowledged to represent the older version. (For later views regarding relationship of MSS. *see* Braune, "Beiträge," 25.) The oldest version of the tale is found in the songs of the "Edda"; a later version in the prose "Edda" and the "Wölsunga saga." The Norse version has Sigurd for Siegfried, and Gudrun for Kriemhild; from it we learn the history of the Nibelungen horde, and the former relation between Brunhild and Siegfried.

The first part of the "Nibelungenlied" is "Siegfried's Tod"; the second, "Kriemhild's Rache." In this later version the mythological features have nearly entirely disappeared, and the ethical element has become more conspicuous. The annihilation of a Burgundian king by Attila is the historical basis of the final catastrophe.

The outline of tale as we have it is as follows: The wooing of Kriemhild by Siegfried; Siegfried treacherously killed by Hagen, at the instigation of Brunhild, the wife of Gunther, King of the Burgundians, Kriemhild's brother; Kriemhild, Siegfried's wife, to forward her revenge, marries Etzel (Attila), King of the Huns, who invites the Burgundians to his court. Then follows the terrible scene of bloodshed, when the Burgundians are slain. The stealing of the Nibelungen hoard, which had been left by Siegfried to his wife, is a secondary cause of anger on Kriemhild's part; Hagen and Gunther had obtained possession of it and sunk it in the Rhine, and they and the King's brother agree not to divulge where the treasure is as long as either lives. It is to recover it that Kriemhild commits her final act of revenge; she herself being finally killed by Hildebrand. The dwarf, Alberich, familiar in other legends, has charge of the treasure before it is removed by the Burgundians.

For formation of poem, *see* under Lachmann, W. Grimm, v. d. Hagen, W. Müller, A. Holtzmann, Fı. Zarncke, K. Bartsch, W. Wilmanns, Kettner. *Ed.,* "Das Nibelungenlied," K. Bartsch, 1866. "Der Nibelunge Nôt," K. Bartsch, 1870, etc. Mod. German, Simrock and Bartsch.

Eng. trans., M. Armour, 1897; A. Horton, 1898, Bohn
Library. *See* for Saga, Boer, "Zeitsch. f. d. Phil.," 37, 3;
38, 1; Müllenhoff, "Zeitsch. f. d. A.," 10, 12 and 15.
MSS., Twenty-eight, some only fragmentary; three chief
MSS., S. Gall; Munich (Hohenems); Donaueschingen
(Laszberg). The two latter were originally at Hohenems.
The above MSS. represent three different versions.

N.B.—The name of the poet of the Nibelungenlied has
been a matter of research. Heinrick v. Ofterdingen, W.
v. d. Vogelweide, R. v. Ems, have all three been brought
forward as possible authors; another authority has suggested
Kürenberg, on account of the similarity of his strophe with
that of the "Nibelungen." (*See* K. Simrock, "K. u. die
Nibelungen.") Whoever the poet may have been, it is
generally conceded that he was of Austrian origin.

Die Klage (rhymed couplets), probably version of older
poem (Vogt). After a short summary of the events which
led to the death of the heroes in the "Nibelungen," the poet
describes the subsequent scenes of lament, and the carrying of
the terrible news to the relatives of the slain. The author did
not evidently know the "Nibelungen" poem as a whole, as he
is ignorant of events recorded in it; he refers to a German
source and also to the Bishop of Passau's book. According
to report, Bishop Pilgrim of Passau, received news of the
destruction of the Burgundians, from one of the messenger's
sent, named Schwemmel; from his description he had an
account of their fall written down in Latin by one Konrad.
As Bishop Pilgrim died 981, it is impossible he could have
known an eye-witness of these events; it is thought more
likely that he had old sagas written down; at any rate, the
author of the "Klage" knew his book, if not at first hand,
and was acquainted with other versions of the "Nibelungen"
saga to that which is preserved to us. "The influence of
courtly poetry is unmistakable." *Ed.*, K. Bartsch, 1875.
Mod. German, v. d. Hagen and Ostfeller. *MSS.*, *see* under
"Nibelungenlied."

N.B.—The name of the poet of the "Klage" is unknown.

Some authorities also ascribe to him the "Biterolf und Dietlieb" (*see* Dietrich Saga). They were both written by one of the school of wandering gleemen.

Gudrun (North German Sea-coast Saga). The second great national epic of the Middle High German period. Traces of the saga date back to the 8th century, and it had spread to South Germany before the middle of the 12th century. It is a more idyllic and emotional work than the "Nibelungen," and has been described as standing in relation to the latter as the "Odyssey" to the "Iliad." Authorities differ as to the evolution of the poem; the older songs probably developed into the epic soon after 1210; it is only extants in a MS. of the early 16th century. It is not written in the pure, heroic form of the "Nibelungen" strophe, the third and fourth lines ending with feminine rhymes, with lengthening of second clause of last line.

In three parts—

1st part.   Birth of Hagen, son of a King of Ireland; carried off by dragon; escape and betrothal.

2nd part.   Abduction of Hagen's daughter, Hilde.

3rd „   Abduction of Gudrun, daughter of Hilde and Hettel; her cruel treatment at the Court of Hartmut, King of Normanie; her final deliverance after fourteen years' captivity, by her brother and her betrothed.

Ed., K. Bartsch, fourth ed., 1880; E. Martin, 1883. *MS.*, Ambras (Vienna). *See* for Saga, San Marte, 1839; Müllenhoff, 1845, Wilmanns, 1873; Fécamp, 1892.

29   Dietrich Saga.

In the saga of Dietrich of Bern history and myth are mingled, and there is confusion of historical tradition. Dietrich of Bern, represented as contemporary of Attila, and even of Ermanric, King of the Goths, was the historical Theodoric, the Ostrogoth; to him are ascribed certain attributes which belonged to the old god of thunder.

Many of the songs written in connection with this saga are in thirteen-lined strophes, hence known as the " Berner Ton." All the songs of this saga are edited in " Deutsches Helden-buch," O. Jänicke, E. Martin, J. Zupitza, A. Amelung, 1866, etc. Mod. Germ., Simrock, in " Kleines Heldenbuch," and " Amelungenlied."

Biterolf und Dietlieb, cir. 1225, but placed by some authorities at close of 12th, by others later in 13th, century. In this poem we meet with Etzel and Gunther, and other Burgundian heroes. The hero, Dietlieb, leaves home when young in search of his father, Biterolf, King of Spain, who is at Attila's court, and performs prodigies of valour. The editor of this poem in " Heldenbuch " is opposed to the view of this work being by the same author as " Die Klage." *MS.*, Ambras (Vienna).

Laurin, Luarin, or *Der Kleine Rosengarten.* Earliest date of oldest extant version, end or second half of 13th century ; the poem itself must have had an earlier origin. The name of Heinrich v. Ofterdingen given in one MS. as writer. Dietrich of Bern and his followers attack the dwarf Laurin's rose-garden, into which no one may enter on pain of death without his permission. Description of combat. Part of the dwarf's accoutrements consists in a magic ring, girdle, and cap. *MSS.*, Old text, Copenhagen, Munich, Berlin, Regensburg, Vienna, Pommersfeld, Zeiz, Frankfurt. Later text, Vienna, Strassburg.

Walberan. Continuation of above, cir. 1300. Not extant in earliest version. *MS.*, complete only in Copenhagen MS.

The above three poems are in rhymed couplets. *Ed.*, O. Jänicke, 1st part, H. B.

Alpharts Tod. " Nibelungen " strophe. Original dates back to 12th century, but is extant in a MS. of fifteenth century. It is difficult to decide from this what the earliest text was like. Older parts are distinguishable, and the poem may be placed in the years immediately preceding or follow-ing 1200. Alphart is a young hero of Dietrich's army, who fights with two of the enemy and is killed.　*MS.*, Berlin (Hundeshagen).

Dietrichs Flucht. Rhyming couplets, cir. 1290, or earlier date according to some authorities. Founded chiefly on popular legend; apparently no original of written song. Dietrich, at war with his uncle Ermanrich, gives his land and possessions to redeem his followers whom the latter has taken prisoners; repairs to the court of the Huns, with whose help he finally overcomes and kills Ermanrich. The author calls himself Heinrich der Vogelaere, and was probably a wandering gleeman. *MSS.*, Castle Riedegg, Vienna (Windhagen), Heidelberg; Ambras (Vienna).

Rabenschlacht (strophes, rhyming a b a, b c c). Dietrich and his uncle at war; Attila's two sons accompany Dietrich, in spite of a dream which warns their mother of danger; they are left in safety in a town, but they escape; are parted from their guardian, Ilsans, in a fog; wander to Ravenna and are killed. Later on Dietrich and Siegfried fight together; Siegfried is overcome, and gives his sword to Dietrich; burial of children, lament of Attila and his wife, and final reconciliation with Dietrich. In both these poems Wittich, the traitor, plays a chief part. The poem is thought by some authorities to be scarcely older than 14th century. It has also been ascribed to the same author as "Dietrichs Flucht." Above poems *ed.*, G. Martin, 2nd part, H. B.　*MSS.*, Castle Riedegg, Vienna (Windhagen), Heidelberg, Ambras (Vienna).

Ortnit. Cir. 1226 (Editor), rather later (Vogt). Written in a four-lined strophe, derived from the "Nibelungen" strophe, and known as Hildebrandston; in this strophe the last line has the same measure as the three others. This King of the Longobards, with the help of the dwarf Elberich, carries off the daughter of a heathen king from Syria. The latter in revenge has two dragon's eggs taken to Ortnit's country; the dragons when full grown devastate the country, carry Ortnit off when asleep and kill him. There was probably an older version, not now extant.　*MSS.*, Original text, Vienna

(Ambras and Windhagen); Heidelberg, Strassburg, Berlin, Dresden, Frankfurt, etc.

Hug-dietrich (Hildebrandston). Dressed as a woman Hug-dietrich, King of Constantinople, gains entrance to the daughter of the King of Thessalonica; their child is carried away by a wolf and grows up with the cubs, hence his name Wolf-dietrich.

Wolf-dietrich (Hildebrandston). The adventures of the hero. We hear again of Ornit and dragon, but the MS. ends before his death. Only in a later continuation (C. v. der Roen, 15th century) do we learn that Wolf-dietrich slays dragon and marries the widow.

Wolf-dietrich has come down in four versions. A, a continuation of "Ortnit" (earlier part), original portion of B, and fragment C, contemporary with "Ortnit"; D (mingling of B and C), second half century (Editor, H. B.). Above poems: *ed.*, A. Amelung, and O. Jänicke, 3rd and 4th parts, H. B. ("Hug-dietrich" given as part of "Wolfdietrich B"). Holtzmann, 1865. *MSS., see* under *Ortnit*; later continuation of "Wolf-dietrich," in Dresden MS.

The following poems are written in thirteen-lined strophes (Bernerton, or Bernerweise):—

Virginal (or *Dietrich's Drachenkämpfe, Dietrich und seine Gesellen*, or *Dietrich's erste Ausfahrt*). *MS.*, Only extant as a whole in Heidelberg.

Sigenot. A giant with whom Dietrich fights. This and the following poem are connected in matter. *See* Steinmeyer, "Altd. Studien.," 1871. *MSS.*, Oldest form, Laszberg MS.; Strassburg, Heidelberg, Dresden.

Eckenliet. Knight who starts with the intention of bringing back Dietrich a prisoner to his Queen (in the Tyrol), but loses his own life. *See* Wilmanns, "Altd. Studien," 1871. *MSS.*, Oldest form, fragment only, Laszberg MS.; Munich, Dresden.

Goldemar. Only the beginning extant. A dwarf King, with whom Dietrich fights for a beautiful woman.   *MS.*, Nüremberg.

The above four poems are attributed to **Albrecht v. Kemenaten,** who gives his name in "Goldemar." It is thought uncertain, however, whether "Virginal" is one of his.

These poems are of first half, or middle 13th century, according to editor; another authority thinks them hardly older than 14th century.   Above poems, *ed.*, J. Zupitza, Fifth part, H. B.

Only a fragment is extant of *Dietrich und Wenezlan,* which describes a duel between Dietrich and the Polish King. It is edited with above, and dated first half of 13th century (close of century by other authority).

Der Rosen Garten (Der Grosse Rosengarten) (Hilde-brandston). The earliest version is not extant; the forms preserved are hardly older than 14th century. The rough humour in it is thought to indicate a later date than early 13th, and it was probably in the second half that the original of the extant forms was written.

In this poem the Hunnish-Gothic heroes again enter into conflict with the Burgundians and Siegfried, the latter being discomfited. Kriemhild, the Burgundian Princess, owns a rose-garden, guarded by twelve heroes, several of whom are familiar in the "Nibelungenlied." She dares Dietrich to come and try his prowess, promising a kiss and a rose-crown to the victors. A comic element is introduced in the person of Ilsan, who takes up arms again, after being for some years in a convent; "an element which betrays the growing influence of the middle classes." *Ed.*, W. Grimm, 1836. *MSS.*, Strassburg, Heidelberg, Frankfurt, Munich, Dresden, and fragments.

N.B.—For full list of the MSS. containing collections of the above heroic poems, and of the earlier and later printed editions ("Altes Heldenbuch, etc."), *see* "Geschichte der Deutschen Dichtung," Goedeke, 1884, pp. 174, 175.

30 COURTLY EPIC.

Arthurian Cycle.

Wolfram von Eschenbach. A Bavarian, b. cir. 1170
(§§ 20, 31.) The most renowned German poet of the Middle
Ages. Little is known of his life: he was at the Court of the
Landgraf, Hermann v. Thüringen, from 1203, till the latter's
death in 1217. Some time later he returned, it would seem,
to his home, and there died, for he is buried at Eschenbach.
According to his own account he could neither read nor
write. He was a contemporary of W. v. d. Vogelweide,
with whom he became acquainted at the Landgraf's Court.
An important place is assigned to him in the "Wartburgkrieg," and he is mentioned admiringly by R. v. Ems in his
"Alexander" and in his "Wilhelm." Many later poets
adopted his speech and style, and his influence is noticeable
even in the pupils and copiers of Hartmann and Gottfried.

Parzival (rhymed couplets), probably written before death
of H. v. Thüringen.

Wolfram's poem has been called "Das Hohelied von
Rittertum" (the "Knightly Song of Songs"). The poet
refers to Chrétien's work, with which parts of W.'s "Parzival"
agree, but he names as his principal source the work of one
Kyot, a Provençal; until quite recently this last-named poet
had remained unidentified, but the mystery which hung over
his name has been apparently solved by Dr. Hagen in an
article which he has lately published. In this, after bringing
forward proofs of Wolfram's close adherence to his source,
he goes on to show that this source was the work of
"Magister Philippus," a native of Poitou, one of Richard I.'s
followers, and finally Bishop of Durham. This Philippus was
captured with others of R.'s followers by Frederick of Pettau,
the king himself escaping. His captivity was passed near the
spots the description of which has been a difficulty, W.'s
personal acquaintance with them being out of the question.
All this is cleared up by identifying Trevrizent's exploits
with those of R.'s follower. Further, Dr. Hagen notes the
identity of places where Trevrizent lands and through which

he passes, with those traversed by Richard and his knights on his return from the Holy Land, Trevrizent's progress, as that of Philippus, ending at Pettau. *See* Hagen, "Zeitschrift für deutsche Philologie," vol. xxxviii. 1 and 2; and *Athenæum* (Nutt) April 7th, (Priebsch) April 14th, 1906. *MSS.*, St. Gall, oldest and best. Sixteen MSS. of this class, others of a later handled text. One fragment is at Mayer Museum, Liverpool. At the close of "Parzival," we have mention of his son Lohengrin, the Swan saga being here associated with the Gral saga (*see* France, § 24).

Titurel, or *Schionatulander* (four-lined strophes). The love of two children, brought up together, Schionatulander and Sigune. Titurel was the Gral King, Sigune his great-granddaughter. This is apparently from similar source as "Parzival"; whether these fragments are part of a continuation to "Parzival," or of an unfinished poem is uncertain. *MSS.*, Fragments only: Munich, Vienna (Ambras).

Before 1272, a continuation of this poem was written in seven-lined strophes, by Albrecht v. Scharffenberg, called *Der jungere Titurel.* The poet made use of Wolfram's two poems, and in prolix style gives us again everything he has learnt from them of the Gral, Parzival, and Schionatulander. The poem was largely read, and the strophe became known as the Titurel strophe. *MSS.*, Add. 30984, Heidelberg, Vienna, Berlin, Regensburg, Carlsruhe; old printed ed., 1477.

Ed., "Works," Lachmann, 1879; A. Leitzmann, "Altdeutsches Text Bibl.," 12, 13, and 14, 1902, 1903; "Parzival u. Titurel," Bartsch, 1875–7; E. Martin, "German. Handbibl.," i. and ii., 1900–03 (with life and many interesting particulars). Trans., Mod. Germ., Simrock, 1876; English, J. Weston, 1894, etc. *See* (for "Titurel") Ward, "Cat. Rom.," i. 932; "Der Tempel des heiligen Gral" (A. v. Scharffenberg), E. Droysen, 1872.

Gottfried von Strassburg. (§ 20.) A contemporary of Hartmann, Walther, and Wolfram. He was a lover and follower of Hartmann, and was not one of the many who

extolled Wolfram, whom he spoke of as an inventor of wild tales. He was taken as a model by writers, either consciously or unconsciously, for another century.

Tristan (rhymed couplets), cir. 1210. Unfinished work. Gottfried worked from a French model, either by, or a copy of the work by, Thomas (*see* France, § 25). Gottfried's "Tristan" stands as a whole more closely related to the English poem, than any other extant; as the close of the English version agrees in general with Thomas, it is possible that the first part of Thomas which is lost, agreed with that of Gottfried. *Ed.*, R. Bechstein, 1869. *MSS.*, Munich, Blankenheim, Rennes (private), Heidelberg, Vienna, Florence. The three first MSS. are illustrated.

About 1240 Ulrich von Türheim wrote a continuation to Gottfried's "Tristan." He follows the version used by E. v. Oberge (*see* § 19), but does not name his source. *MSS.*, Munich, Heidelberg, Blankenheim (with G.'s "Tristan").

Later still, end 13th or beginning 14th century, another continuation was written by Heinrich von Freiberg (§ 40), who on the whole covers the same ground as U. v. Türheim and follows the same tradition, although he states otherwise. His work is superior to that of his predecessor. *MS.*, Florence (with G.'s *Tristan*). Between these two writers, an unknown one also wrote a continuation.

N.B.—U. von Türheim also wrote a continuation to W. v. Eschenbach's *Willehalm*, and another work of his, *Clîes*, is mentioned by R. v. Ems, but is not now known. H. v. Freiberg also wrote two shorter poems, inferior to his "Tristan": *Ritterfahrt des Johann von Michelsperg* and *Gedicht von heiligen Kreuz.*

N.B.—Frescoes of the Tristan saga (15th century) are preserved at Castle Runkelstein, in the Tyrol. A carpet of 14th century, and another piece of work of 15th century, are also preserved respectively in the convent of Wienhausen and

23

at Erfurt Cathedral, in both of which the tale is followed as told by E. v. Oberg.

Wirnt von Gravenberg. A follower of Hartmann.

Wigalois (rhymed couplets). Beginning, or first quarter 13th century. The poet deals with the tale of "Le Bel Inconnu" (*see* France, § 55, England, § 58), not direct from any source, but from the tale as related to him by word of mouth. *Ed.*, F. Pfeiffer, 1847. *See*, for sources, etc., F. Saran, "Beitr. Gesch., etc.," 1896, Bd. xxi. Heft 2. Bethge, "Eng. Studien," i. 1881. *MSS.*, Cologne, Leiden, Stuttgart, Hamburg, Vienna, Einsiedeln, Leipzig.

Anonymous.

Wigamur (rhymed couplets). The earliest mention of "Wigamur" is by Tannhäuser, cir. 1250; it is also mentioned in "der Jungere Titurel," but the poem preserved to us is of later date. The outlines of this tale are similar to those of Wigalois. The poet refers to a book as his authority, but this was customary with the poets, to give their work an appearance of authenticity. The material of the poem was apparently drawn from several knightly romances. Wigamur's youth resembles that of Lancelot; he is carried away and brought up by a mermaid, and stolen from her by a hobgoblin; finally marries Dulciflur, who is stolen from him and won back again; and has a son Dulciwigar. The poem is not considered of much literary worth, but is the only example of a copy of Arthurian romance by an uncultivated poet, and testifies to the spread of courtly poetry among the uneducated classes. The author was not thoroughly acquainted with courtly etiquette, but is scarcely to be placed in the burgher class: he was probably a wandering gleeman of lower standing. *Ed.*, Hagen u. Büsching, *op. cit.*, Bd. i. No. 4. *See* G. Sarrazin, "Quell. Forsch. Sprach, etc.," Bd. xxxv. *MS.*, One MS., Wolfenbüttel, and fragments.

Heinrich von dem Türlin.

Diu Crône (rhymed couplets), cir. 1215 or 1220. The poem deals with King Arthur, his Court, and much that

happened there.   The author gives C. de Troies as his
authority; the source of his poem, however, remains unknown.   He says himself that he suppressed much that he
found; he adds original matter in his reflections and references
to other poets.   *Ed.*, G. H. F. Scholl, 1852, " Bibl. Litt.
Verein.," 27.   *MSS.*, Vienna (incomplete), Heidelberg.

Der Stricker.   (§§ 26, 31.)

Daniel von Blumenthal (rhymed couplets).   This poem
and " Karl der Grosse " belong to the second decade of the
13th century, being earlier works of Stricker than his didactic
ones.   The author claims A. de Besançon as his authority.
The poem differs from other Arthurian romances in keeping
the love matters in the background; the poet delights in the
description of heroic deeds of arms.   Daniel overcomes some
of the chief knights of Arthur's court.   *Ed.*, G. Rosen-
hagen, 1894, "Germ. Abhandl.," Heft ix.   *MSS.*, Heu-
bach, Copenhagen, Munich, Dresden.

Konrad v. Würzburg.   (§§ 26, 33, 34.)

Der Schwanenritter (rhymed couplets).   The saga of
Lohengrin.   Roth considers this one of Konrad's best poems.
Ed., F. Roth, 1861.   *See* "Le Chevalier au Cygne,"
Reiffenberg, 1846.   *MS.*, One MS., Frankfurt.

Anonymous.

Lohengrin, 1276–1290.   The introduction of this poem
is composed of strophes from the *Wartburgkrieg* (§ 37).
Then is told the tale of Lohengrin and Elsa; and in this
version Elsa dies of grief, after Lohengrin has been forced to
leave, owing to her having put to him the fatal question concerning his descent.   The history of the German Emperor
Heinrich 1. is interwoven with it.   It is written in the ten-
lined strophes (Schwarzerton) of the "Wartburgkrieg."
Ed., H. Rückert, 1858.   *See* Elster, Paul - Braune,
"Beiträge," 10 (on two authors).   *MSS.*, Heidelberg (two
MSS.), Coblentz (two fragments), Munich, Cg. 4871.

Der Pleier. Wrote rather after than before 1260 (*see Mai u. Beaflor*, § 34).

Gârel von dem blühenden Thal. Ed., M. Walz, 1892. *MS.*, Linz (on the Danube).

Meleranz. Ed., K. Bartsch, 1861, "Bibl. Litt. Verein.," lx. *MS.*, Donaueschingen.

Tandarois. *MSS.*, Munich, Heidelberg, Hamburg.

Three Arthurian romances, in rhymed couplets, full of adventures; taken, according to the author, from French sources. Gârel and Meleranz are both nephews of King Arthur. "Gârel" is the best of the three poems.

N.B.—Besides the "Tristan-saal" at Runkelstein, there is also the "Gârel-saal." Walz in his edition gives an account of the Gârel frescoes, which he states are of 14th century.

Konrad von Stoffel. Shows influence of Stricker and Pleier.

Gauriel von Montabel, or *Der Ritter mit dem Bocke.* The poem is an inferior work, dealing with the usual adventures. The goat is killed by Iwein, having previously killed the latter's lion. A knight with a goat is mentioned in "Diu Crône." *MSS.*, Donaueschingen, Innsbruck.

31 *Carolingian Cycle.*

Wolfram von Eschenbach. (§§ 20, 30.)

Willehalm (rhymed couplets), cir. 1215. History of William of Orange, the contemporary of Charlemagne, from a French model. It gives a short account of the abduction by William of Arabele, daughter of the heathen King Tybalt, which gave rise to the battle of Aliscans (*see* France, § 17). Wolfram died before the poem was finished. It was continued by Ulrich von Türheim (*see* under Tristan, § 30), with

whom the principal personage is the giant Rennewart, Arabele's brother. Another poet wrote a long introduction,
giving in detail the history of Arabele's abduction. Both
these additions date from the 13th century. *Ed.*, Lachmann, 1833. *See* Paul-Braune, "Beiträge," ii. 318 ff. For
connection with source, *see* San Marte, 1871. *MSS.*,
S. Gall, Munich, Heidelberg, Vienna (Ambras, etc.), Cassel,
Wolfenbüttel, Zürich, etc.

Der Stricker. (§§ 26, 30.)

Karl der Grosse (rhymed couplets). Second decade of
13th century. Version of Pfaffe Konrad's "Rolandsliet."
(§ 16.) *Ed.*, K. Bartsch, 1857, "Bibl. Nat. Litt.,"
Bd. xxxv. *MSS.*, S. Gall, Vienna, Vatican, Strassburg,
Munich, Donaueschingen, and several others.

Konrad Fleck.

Flore und Blanschflur (rhymed couplets), cir. 1220 (*see*
England, § 40). The tale is taken from a French original.
Ed., E. Sommer, 1846. *MSS.*, Heidelberg, Berlin.

Anonymous. The poet shows influence of Hartmann
and Gottfried.

Die Gute Frau. Husband and wife renounce all earthly
possessions, and wander in poverty; two children are born;
the man, with his wife's consent, sells her; he loses the
children who are left with him; finally the family is reunited,
the wife having become possessed of riches and lands. The
man is Carloman, the two children Charles and Pepin.
Ed., E. Sommer, Haupt's "Zeitsch.," ii. *MS.*, Vienna
(Ambras).

Karlmainet. Concerning the youth of Charlemagne. The
compilation known under this title belongs to the 14th century;
among the poems incorporated in it are two dating from
cir. 1200, originating on the Lower Rhine, which have been

looked upon as a single work, and as such received the above name. *See* "Ueber Karl Meinet," Keller, 1858; Bartsch, 1861.

82   *Alexander Cycle.*

Rudolf von Ems, d. 1250–54.   Follower of G. von Strassburg.   (§§ 34, 35.)

Alexander, 1230–41 or 43.   From Latin sources.   *See* "Die Quellen von Alexander," O. Zingerle, 1885 (with Latin text of "Historia de Preliis").   *MS.*, Munich.

N.B.—Rudolf, in his "Alexander," mentions the poets, Veldeke, Hartmann, Wolfram, Gottfried, K. v. Heimesfurt, Wirnt, Zozikhoven, Blicker, H. v. d. Türlin, Freidank, Fleck, A. von Kemenat, Linouw, Stricker, Wetzel, Türheimer.

Ulrich von Eschenbach, fl. end 13th century.   (§ 34.)

Alexander.   From similar sources as poem by R. v. Ems. "The writings of U. v. Eschenbach show the increasing decay of poetic art."   *MSS.*, Wolfenbüttel, Stuttgart, Basle, Heidelberg.

33   Troy Cycle.

Herbort von Fritzlar.   "One of the first to follow in the footsteps of Veldeke, who had drawn attention to the rich stores of foreign material."

Liet von Troye.   Probably before 1210.   From a French version of "Dares and Dictys," probably Benoît de S. More's poem (*see* France, § 28).   The author mingles modern ideas with the ancient material of his subject.   *Ed.*, G. K. Frommann, 1837.   *See* (for relation of H. v. Fritzlar, and R. v. Wurzburg to B. de S. More), C. Fisher, "Neuphilolog. Studien," Heft ii., 1883.   *MSS.*, Heidelberg, Berlin.

Konrad von Würzburg.   (§§ 26, 30, 34.)

Der Trojanische Krieg (rhymed couplets).   The poet died

1287, before this work was completed; it is the largest and most important of his poems. The poem begins before the birth of Helen, gives the voyage to the Argonauts, and Trojan war, at which are present heroes of German nationality. *Ed.*, A. v. Keller, "Bibl. Litt. Ver.," xliv. 1858. *See* also Bartsch, *ibid.*, cxxxiii. For relation to B. de S. More, *see* C. Fisher, under Fritzlar. *MSS.*, Strasburg, St. Gau, Nürnberg, Vienna (Ambras, etc.), Berlin, Würzburg, Zeil, Linz, and other fragments.

34 Miscellaneous Epics.

Konrad v. Würzburg. (§§ 26, 30, 33.)

Otte mit dem Barte (rhymed couplets). According to the poet, the tale is from a Latin source. The hero of the poem, Heinrich von Kempten, having lost the favour of the Emperor, regains it by rushing out from his bath and saving the latter's life from an attack on him by the populace. *Ed.*, K. A. Hahn, 1838. Hagen, "Gesammtabenteuer," and Lambel, "Schwänke, etc."; Mod. Germ., "Kleinere Dichtungen," Pannier, 1879. *MSS.*, Heidelberg, Vienna, Kolocza, Innsbruck.

Engelhart und Engeltrut, or *Von hôher triuwe* (rhymed couplets). The tale of Amis and Amile, taken from a Latin source. *Ed.*, M. Haupt, 1844; E. Joseph, 1890. *MS.*, none extant. Early printed ed., 1573 (*see* England, § 40).

Partenopier und Meliur (rhymed couplets) (*see* France, § 29). *Ed.*, K. Bartsch (with Turnei v. Nantheiz, S. Nicolaus, Lieder u Sprüche). *MSS.*, Reidegg (only complete MS.) Jena, and other fragments.

Daz Maere von der Minne, or, *Daz Herz Maere*. Tale of the Châtelain de Couci (*see* France, § 57). Thought to be undoubtedly from a French model. The tale is found in German popular song. Similar tale in " Lai d'Ignaures," and Boccaccio's "Guiscardo and Gismonde," also told in connec-

tion with the troubadour, G. de Cabestaing.   *Ed.*, F. Roth,
1846; also in Hagen, and Lambel; "Mod. Germ.," Pannier,
1879.   *See* Haupt, in "Engelhart."   *MSS.*, Strassburg,
Heidelberg, Vienna, Munich, C. Hätzlerin.

Das Turnei von Nantheiz (rhymed couplets).   This and the
Schwanenritter are youthful productions; not all authorities,
however, are agreed as to authorship.   The chief hero in the
poem is Richard, Cœur de Lion.   It is a specimen of a new
class of epic of this period, called *Heroldsdichtung*, of which
there were more partial indications in other poems by Konrad,
in which the art of jousting and the figures and colourings of
heraldry are given in prolonged descriptions.   *Ed.*, K.
Bartsch (*see* under Partenopier).   *See* as to authorship,
E. Joseph, preface to "Engelhart."   *MS.*, Munich
(Würzburger MS.).

Rudolf von Ems.   (§§ 32, 35.)

Barlaam und Josaphat (rhymed couplets).   Rudolf's chief
but not his earliest work, taken from a Latin source (*see*
France, § 48).   Other German versions are extant.   Rudolf
introduces "Beispiele" which are found separately in collections of tales.   *Ed.*, F. Pfeiffer, 1843.   *MSS.*, Munich
(Hohenems, etc.), Strassburg, Königsberg, Berlin, Heidelberg,
etc., fragment B.M. Add. 10288.

Der Gute Gerhard (rhymed couplets).   This work was
written at the request of Rudolf v. Steinach, of whom there
are authentic notices from 1209--1221.   The tale is taken
from the Latin, and is of a legendary character.   Gerhard is a
Cologne merchant, of noble and self-sacrificing character.
An account of the Emperor Otto forms a framework to the
tale.   Otto is here called the Red Emperor, there being a
similar confusion of persons as in "Otte mit dem Barte."
Ed., M. Haupt, 1840.   *MS.*, Vienna (Ambras).

Wilhelm von Orlens (rhymed couplets).   From a French
original, brought from France by Johannes von Ravenspurg.
In it the poet bewails the death of Konrad v. Oettingen, who
died before 1238, and the work was undertaken for Konrad
von Winterstetten, who died 1243.   It was written after his

"Alexander." Of the love of two children; the hero is son of a King of France; the lady, Amelie, daughter of King of England. Similarity with tale of *Jehan et Blonde* by P. de Beaumanoir (*see* France, § 57). *Ed.*, V. Junk, 1905. For sources, etc., *see* "Die Quellen v. W. v. Orlens," V. Zeidler, 1894. *MSS.*, Munich, Haag, Donaueschingen, Vienna, Bonn, Tambach, Stuttgart, etc. (17 MSS. and fragments).

Of Rudolf's poem on St. Eustachius we only know the name and a few lines, and his poem on the Trojan War is only known from his mention of it in his "Weltchronik."

N.B. — Rudolf mentions the following poets in his "Wilhelm": Veldeke, Hartmann, Wolfram, Gotfried, Blicker, Zatzikhoven, Wirnt, Freidank, Konrad von Fuszes-brunnen, Fleck, Linouw, Stricker, Gotfried von Hohenloch, A. von Kemenat, U. v. Türheim, Meister Hesse, Vasolt. Little more than the name is known of some of these poets.

Meister Otte.

Eraclius (rhymed couplets). Early 13th cent. From the French of Gautier d'Arras (*see* France, § 29). *Ed.*, H. F. Massmann (French and German poem), 1842. *MSS.*, Munich, Vienna.

Reinbot von Dürn.

Der Heilige Georg (rhymed couplets). Probably from a French source. Account of tortures and death inflicted on the saints, from which he arises uninjured. Reinbot wrote for Herzog Otto of Bavaria, who governed from 1231–1253. *Ed.*, v. d. Hagen, "Deutsche Gedichten des Mittelalters," 1808. *MSS.*, Vienna, Zürich, Möser MS., and other fragments.

Ulrich von Eschenbach. (§ 32.)

Wilhelm von Wenden (rhymed couplets). 1289–97.

The poet made use of the French poem *Guillaume d'Angleterre* (France, § 15). The details of the tale are, however, very dissimilar. Inferior work, showing, like his "Alexander," signs of the decadence in poetry.   *Ed.*, W. Toischer, 1876.   *MS.*, Hanover.

Berthold von Holle, fl. middle 13th century and onwards.

Of this writer's three poems, only fragments remain. They were written from tales told him from word of mouth. The *Crane* is based on the romance of *Graf Rudolf* (12th century). All three have certain connection with one another as regards historical places and personages.   *Ed.*, Bartsch, 1858; and "Bibl. Litt. Ver.," 123.   *MSS., Demantin*, Magdeburg, Rostock; *Crane*, Minden, Göttingen, Pommersfeld; *Darifant*, Magdeburg.

Anonymous.

Athis und Prophilias. Fragments only. From French model (*see* Alexandre de Bernay, France, § 29). The tale is of two friends, similar to that of "Amis and Amile." *Ed.* W. Grimm, 1846.

Mai und Beaflor (rhymed couplets). Thought possibly to be a younger work of Pleier. Similar to *Manekine.* (*See* France, § 57.)   *Ed.*, F. Pfeiffer, 1848.   *MSS.*, Munich, Fulda.

35   Historical Verse.

Jans der Enenkel (Enikel).

Fürstenbuch von Oesterreich u. Steieriana, to 1246. Full of anecdotes.   *Ed.*, Rauch, "Rer. Aust. Scrip.," i.   *MSS.*, Vienna (three MSS.); Prague.

Weltchronik (rhymed couplets). End 13th century, Bible history to Samson; and secular history to Frederick II. Much was taken from the "Kaiserchronik" (§ 13), and tales of various kinds are introduced. Begins "Got, aller ding ein überkraft."   *Ed.*, P. Strauch, "Mon. Germ. Hist.," tome iii. pt. i.   *MSS.*, Munich, Regensburg, Oberbayer, Innsbruck, Darmstadt, Weimar, Wolfenbüttel, Leipzig, Berlin, Heidelberg, Vienna (Ambras), etc.

Rudolf von Ems. (§§ 32, 34.)

Weltchronik 1250–54. The last work of this poet; it was left unfinished. The chief source of the poem, after the Bible, was P. Comestor's "Historia Scolastica." It begins, "Rihter got herre über alle kraft." This was the first work to give the uneducated classes a connected history of the Old Testament, and the knowledge of the Bible among the laity during the two following centuries is due to Rudolf. The numerous prose versions of this period are merely variations of the poem. "With Freidank's work, and the 'Renner,' it enjoyed greater popularity than any other work of the 13th century." *Ed.,* "Zwei Recensionen," A. F. C. Vilmar, 1839. *MSS.,* Oldest and purest version: Heidelberg, Munich, Wallerstein. Many other MSS. with additions, or of later or mingled versions.

Gottfried Hagen. Recorder of Cologne.

Reimchronik, 1270 (rhymed couplets). Account of affairs in his native town. *Ed.,* H. Lempertz, 1847.

Anonymous.

Chronik von Liefland, 1290–96. Concerning the warlike and colonising activity of the German order (*see* H. V. Langenstein, § 24).

Ottaker von Steiermark, or Horneck.

Reimchronik. Historical account of chief events at home and abroad from 1250–1309. Of historical value, and interesting as regards old customs and legends. *Ed.,* Pertz, "Script. rer. Aust.," tome iii. *See* T. Schacht, 1821. *MS.,* Vienna.

N.B.—The first rhymed chronicle of any historical value originated in Lower Germany, where a priest Eberhard wrote, in 1216, a history of the foundation of Gandersheim; other chronicles from this region are the *Holsteiner* and the *Braunschweiger.* The date of writing of the Holstein lies between 1381–1433; an earlier Holstein "Reimchronik"

existed, covering the years 1199–1261. The *Braunschweiger*
was finished 1279, but there are additions 1291 and 1298.
These are edited with " Sächsische Weltchronik," L. Weiland,
" Mon. Germ. Hist.," tome ii. *MSS.*, *Gandersheim*,
Wolfenbüttel, Kolocza ; *Braunschweig*, Hansburg, Wolfen-
büttel ; *Holstein*, Copenhagen, Hamburg, Hanover.

36   Lyric.

It was in the courtly circles where " Frauendienst " had
been cultivated that the reaction against idealism began. The
lyric was still flourishing at its best when Neidhart v. Reuenthal,
the chief founder of the realistic school, composed his
" höfische Dorfpoesie." A Bavarian of noble birth, who
flourished in the earlier part of the century, he chose for his
subjects the loves and festivities of the peasant class, in the
latter of which he himself took part. He gives comic
descriptions of their rough merriment and of their dress, and
expends much mockery and laughter on their aping of the
higher class. " The last epoch-making lyric poet." *Ed.*,
Heinz, 1889.

More than a hundred poets belong to the 13th century.
Among them were—

Reinmar von Zweter. A writer of Sprüchgedichte.
The chief metre in which he wrote was known as Frau
Ehren Ton, his moral ideal being personified in Frau Ehre.
He was the pupil of W. v. d. Vogelweide, as the latter had
been of Reinmar der Alte. *Ed.*, Roethe, 1887.

Gottfried v. Neifen. Mingling in his poems of courtly
Minnesang and Dorfpoesie. The same is found in the
poems of

Tannhäuser (§ 27), Burkhart v. Hohenfels, and
Ulrich v. Winterstetten.

Rudolf v. Rothenburg, renowned as a Leichdichter.

Steinmar. A parodist of the Minnesang.

Hadlaub. Dorfpoesie, parodies of Minnesang, with lyrics of older fashion, and pretty autumn songs.

Der Marner. Spruchdichter. *See* Rauch, " Quell. Forsch. Sprach, etc.," xiv.

Boppe. Spruchdichter.

Songs are extant by the unfortunate young Konradin, and among other princely names are those of Wenzel II. King of Bohemia, Otto IV., Margrave of Brandenburg, Duke Henry IV. of Breslau, etc., showing that the lyric had not as yet entirely passed into the hands of the burgher class, though this class was already represented among the poets.

37 DRAMA.

XIIth AND XIIIth CENTURY.

During these two centuries the drama continued in its primitive stage : dramatic representations were confined to religious subjects (Ludi), were written in Latin, with the occasional introduction of German songs, generally put into the mouth of Mary Magdalene. The drama waited for the following period for its full development.

We find in the literature of this period, however, several examples of " Streitgedichte " (Jeu parti), and we have, dating from the close of 13th or beginning of 14th century, the first attempt at a secular composition in dramatic form, in the *Wartburgkrieg.* This contest was said to have taken place in 1206 or 1207. Among the poets present were W. v. d. Vogelweide, W. v. Eschenbach, Bitterolt (of whose works there is nothing left), Reinmar der Alte, and Heinrich v. Ofterdingen ; another chief actor in the contest was Clinsor, a magician and astrologer.

The poets are first each called upon to prove, on pain of death, that the reigning prince whom he upholds is the worthiest of renown; then there follows an interchange of riddles between Clinsor and W. v. Eschenbach, followed further by interchange of ideas on various subjects, and introduction of tales. The work is entirely wanting in unity. It is written in two forms of verse—The Thuringer Ton and the Schwarzer Ton.

Different MSS. give different names of poets as author: those mentioned as such are Clinsor, Ofterdingen for the first part; Wolfram for the second. It has also been ascribed to Frauenlob, on account of his making use of both forms of verse.

The different parts are of different dates. According to Simrock, the two strophes of the seventh part, if written by W. v. d. Vogelweide, are the oldest; the other parts, ranging in date from 1231 to 1287. *Ed.*, with trans in Mod. Germ., K. Simrock, 1858. *See* A. Strack, "Zur geschichte des Gedichtes vom Wartburgkrieg," 1883. *MSS.*, Not complete in any MSS. Paris (Manesse), Jena (Liederhds.), Heidelberg, Vienna (Ambras), Munich, Kolmar, Büdingen.

N.B.—The castle at Wartburg was the abode of the Landgraf, Hermann v. Thüringen, the great patron of literature, at whose court the chief poets were hospitably received, and found a home.

XIVth CENTURY.

During the 14th and 15th centuries literature passed into the hands of the burgher class. In the writings of this new class of poets are reflected the changed conditions of life and the accompanying change in the spirit of the age. Crusades and tournaments were over, an expedition against the heathens in Prussia being the only undertaking of the former kind. Nations no longer rose to the call of enthusiasts, and rushed to recover the sacred places of the East. Knights were too busy fighting with each other, and too much engaged in political turmoils, to attend to the cultivation of poetry, and their castles ceased to be homes for the poets and centres of culture.

Their place was taken by the towns, where luxury and culture increased as the burgher class became more prosperous. Opportunities of education became more general, the laity were engaged as teachers, and literature was influenced by the seriousness of spirit that characterised the middle classes, on whom the preaching of the mystics, and the horrors of the black death produced a powerful impression. Didactic poetry flourished during this period, and the tale was popular whether written for amusement or for instruction. Prose became a far more universal medium of literary expression, and, although no noticeable works remain, the language was being moulded by its adaptation to prose for noble use in the future. Literature as a whole "was more typical than individual"; little of originality was produced. (*See* Franke, *op cit.*)

From the outset the burgher class were lacking in such tastes and qualities as would enable them to carry on poetry in the old courtly style. With the later poets expression was coarser and the subjects chosen less poetical; poetry passed from the apotheoses of Minne to scholasticism, from lyric elegance and ease to inharmonious verse, from idealism to realism or coarse naturalism. The period "was a struggle between old and new, a mixture of beginnings and remains, a wandering along old paths but with worn-out powers, a striving towards high aims but with as yet insufficient strength to reach them." (*See* Wackernagel, *op cit.*, p. 153.)

Prose.

38 *Science.*

Konrad v. Magenburg, b. cir. 1309; d. 1374. Besides works in connection with ecclesiastical matters, he compiled the first popular handbook of physics and astronomy. His work represents the general knowledge of his day.

Die deutsche Sphäre, based on a Latin work by Johann Holywood. His other work

Buch der Natur, 1349–50, was based on Thomas of Cantimpré's "De Naturis Rerum," and dealt with every

kind of subject—men, animals, planets, plants, monsters, etc.
—mingled with original observations and moral reflections.
Ed., Pfeiffer, 1861.

A chronicle has also been assigned to this author, and
may possibly be extant in a continuation of "Flores Temporum," "Mon. Germ. Script.," xxiv.

39   *History.*

Heinrich von Mügeln, fl. middle 14th century. (§ 40.)

Ungarische Chronik, to 1333. In great part a translation from
Simon Kéza. Dedicated to the Archduke Rudolf iv.   *Ed.*,
M. G. Kovachich, "Sammlung kleiner Stücke," 1805,
with other contemporary writings on Hungarian history.
MSS., Munich, Wolfenbüttel, Vienna, Heidelberg, Breslau.

Heinrich von München (Munich).

Weltchronik. Written after 1347. Continuation to Ludwig
der Fromne (*see* Rudolf von Ems, § 35.) The histories of
Rudolf and Enenkel, Konrad's *Trojanerkrieg*, and Stricker's
Karl, are made use of by the writer.   *MSS.*, Munich,
Krems, Vienna, Wolfenbüttel, etc.

Christian Kuchimeister.

Casus monasterii S. Galli (1228–1329). A continuation
of the "Annals of S. Gall," which had been carried on
from the 9th to the 13th century, by Ratpert, Ekkehart iv.,
and their successors up to 1228. Kuchimeister tells us that
he started writing after an interval of a hundred years from
this date, namely in 1335. Kuchimeister's work is considered
one of the most trustworthy of mediæval chronicles; although
a local history it gives an insight into the general history of
the kingdom. "This work and the 'Life of S. Ludwig,'
by Friedrick Koeditz, are the earliest monuments of historical
prose in High German."   *Ed.*, "Mitth. zur. Vaterl. Gesch.

S. Gall," vol. xviii. 1881–1885. *See* Bächtold, "Litt.
Gesch.," p. 220. *MSS.*, Zurich, S. Gall (Vadiana).

Fritsche Closener, d. cir. 1384. A native of Strassburg.

Chronik to 1362. One of the oldest histories to be written
in German, "the first attempt to associate the history of a
particular town with a general history." The heading of the
first chapter states that the work is a Chronicle of Popes and
Emperors, but the history of the Bishops of Strassburg and of
the events connected with the town finally occupied the larger
half of it. The author, although he does not, with one
exception, mention his authorities, made use of older annals
of Strassburg, of the chronicle known under the name of
Ellenhard, and that ascribed to Eike von Repkow. Of the
original parts, the most interesting is the detailed account of
the Flagellants; several of their devotional songs are given,
with a description of the prostrations, etc., of the Flagellants
at certain intervals, and also one of their sermons. *Ed.*,
"Die Chroniken der deutschen Städte" (14th to 16th
century), vol. viii. *See* A. Schulte, "Strassburger Studien,"
i. p. 277 ff., 1883. *MSS.*, Paris, Bibl. Nat.; 91 in
Germany.

F. Closener is also said to have compiled a Latin-German
vocabulary, and a work on the usages of the Strassburg
Church.

Jakob Twinger von Königshofen.

Chronik. Extant in three versions, arranged by the author
himself, who was a countryman of Closener's and made use of
the latter's chronicle, continuing it in the latest version of his
work to 1415. Twinger is looked upon less as an historian
than as a story-teller. His work is full of fables and legends,
his tales of ancient times being clothed in the romanticism of
the Middle Ages. As the first German prose history of the
world in Upper Germany, it was highly popular, and welcome
to the laity who were ignorant of Latin. The later historians
of Alsace and Strassburg up to the 16th century, contented

themselves with adding to Twinger's chronicle.   *Ed.*,
"Chron. Deutsch. Städte," vol. viii. *See* A. Schulte,
" Strassburger Studien," i. 277 ff., 1883.   *MSS.*, Numerous
MSS. : Augsburg, Berlin, Donaueschingen, Giessen, Görlitz,
Cologne, Strassburg, Paris, München, Vienna, Wolfenbüttel,
etc.

Several other local histories were written in the course of
the 14th and 15th centuries. Limburg had its chronicler,
who among other matters notices from time to time the
changes in the fashion of dress, and the songs which were
popular ; also Bern, Augsburg, Nuremberg, and Breslau.
The history of Cologne was printed at the close of the 15th
century ; during this and the following century Austria,
Swabia, Silesia, Prussia, and Switzerland had their histories.
See Wackernagel, " Litt. Gesch.," p. 444 ff.

POETRY.

40   *Religious, Didactic, etc*

Monk of Heilsbronn.

Four works are ascribed to this unknown author   *Ed.*,
(four works) Merzdorf, 1870.

Das puch von den vi *namen des fronleichnams* (or *Goldene
Zunge,* or *liber de corde et sanguine domini*).   Being a poem on
the six names given to the body of Christ. The prologue is
in verse, but the work itself in prose.   *MSS.*, Munich.
All four works in Heidelberg MS.

Das puch der siben grâde (short rhyming couplets). Of the
seven steps of prayer, corresponding to the seven steps of
Solomon's temple, which lead the soul to heaven.

Von der tochter Syon (short-rhyming couplets) (*see* below,
Bruder Lamprecht). The soul, longing to become united to
God, is personified in the daughter of Sion, who, when the
union has taken place, is called " Virgo Israhel." The soul
that is attached to the world is the daughter of Babylon.

Ed., Schade, 1849; Modern Germ., Simrock, 1851. *MSS.*, Kloster Neuburg, Strassburg.

Von Sant Alexius (*see* France, § 4, and England, §§ 63, 64). Eight rhymed versions (seven in rhymed couplets) are extant; one by Konrad v. Würzburg (*see* § 26); the latest in date being the one written in the "Regenbogen langem Ton," by Jörg Breininc, 1488. *Ed.*, H. F. Massmann, 1843. For other German versions, as well as French and English ones, with note of MSS., *see* J. Brauns, "Ueber Quelle u. Entwicklung der altfranzösischen Cançun de Saint Alexius," 1884. Charles Joret, eight versified and three prose versions, 1881. *MSS.*, (1) Grätz and Prague; (2) Vienna; (3) Munich, Neuburg, Heidelberg; (4) Strassburg, Innsbruck (by K. v. Würzburg, § 26); (5) Hamburg; (6) Westphalia; (7) Munich (by Jörg Zobel); (8) Heidelberg (by Jörg Breininc).

Lamprecht von Regensburg.

Leben des heiligen Franciscus (rhymed couplets), 1240. Taken from the earliest life of S. Francis, which was written at the command of Pope Gregory by Thomas of Celano, from the latter's personal knowledge, and trustworthy communications, between 1228–1230. *MSS.*, Würzburg.

Diu tohter von Syon (rhymed couplets). The author tells us that he had his material communicated to him by word of mouth by Brother Gerard, the indirect source was a pure Latin work "Filia Syon." *Ed.*, K. Weinhold, 1880. *MSS.*, Lobris (Silesia), Prague, Giessen.

N.B.—The editor considers that the poem on the same subject mentioned above is wrongly ascribed to the Monk of Heilsbronn. In considering the relations between the two poems, he gives it as his opinion, in accordance with that of Preger ("Deutsch. Mystik.") that they are independent works, both founded on "Filia Syon," and that they are contemporary.

Johannes von Frankenstein. Priest of the Johanniter order.

Der Chreuziger (rhyming couplets). A poem on the Passion, finished 1300. *Ed.*, F. Khull, "Bibl. Lit. Verein.," 160. *MS.*, Vienna.

Heinrich von Neuenstadt, or Neuwenstat. (*See* Misc. Rom., "Apollonius v. Tyrland," § 45.) The author names himself in both his works.

Von Gotes Zuokunft (*Coming of our Lord*). From the "Anticlaudianus," by Alanus ab Insulis, 12th century. *Ed.*, Strobl, 1875. *MSS.*, Gotha, Heidelberg, Munich.

Heinrich von Freiberg. (*See* G. v. Strassburg, § 30.)

Von den heiligen Kreuz (rhyming couplets). *Ed.*, F. Pfeiffer, "Altdeutsches Uebungsbuch," 1866. *MS.*, Vienna.

The other minor poem by H. v. Freiberg is the *Ritterfahrt Johanns von Michelsperg* (rhymed couplets), cir. 1300, which may be placed under the heading of "Heroldsdichtung" (*see* Turnei v. N., § 34). Description of a knightly ride through France. *See* "Germania," ii. 261–264. *MS.*, Heidelberg.

N.B.—Both these poems are inferior to the "Tristan." H. v. Freiberg, as far as style and ease of language are concerned, was one of the later writers who successfully took Gottfried for his model.

Lutwin. Nothing is known of this writer beyond his name which is inserted in poem.

Adam und Eva (rhymed couplets). The poem is nearly 4000 lines long. A legend concerning Adam and Eve, independent of the Bible tale, was widely known in Europe in early times. It apparently originated with a Hebrew writer B.C., and is preserved in Greek and Latin versions; of the latter, extant in MSS. dating from the 9th century, but probably originating in 3rd or 4th century, one served as a model for Lutwin. At the close of the poem the legend of the wood of the cross is introduced.   *Ed.*, K. Hoffmann u. W. Meyer, " Bibl. Lit. Ver.," cliii.   *MSS.*, Vienna (Ambras).

Thilo von Kulm.

Von den Sieben Siegeln (rhyming couplets), finished 1331. Written for Luder (Lothar) Hezog v. Braunschweig who was himself, according to report, an author, as well as a patron of letters ; among his works was a life of " St. Barbara " in verse.   *See* " Zeitschrift fur deutsches Alterthum," xiii. 516–18 ; Strehlke, " Script. Rer. Pruss.," vol. i. *MSS.*, Königsberg (autograph MS.)

At the request of this same Duke of Brunswick was written the German paraphrase of the book of Daniel.   *MS.*, Königsberg.

Heinrich von Hesler ("Heinrich ist min rechter name, Hesler ist min hus genant").

Paraphrase of the Apocalypse (rhymed couplets) in 23,000 lines.   *See* Hagen's " Germania," 10, 81–102 ; Pfeiffer's " Uebungsbuch," p. 23.

Translation of Evangelium Nicodemi (rhymed couplets). Pfeiffer, " Uebungsbuch," p. i.   *MSS.*, Königsberg, Danzig.

Anonymous.

Der Maget Krône (rhyming couplets).   The work is composed of a preface, a translation of " Salve Regina," paraphrases from the " Song of Solomon," with applications to the Virgin and the loving soul (*Minnende Seele*), a life of the Virgin, followed by that of the most honoured saints of the day : Saints Barbara, Dorothêâ, Margarete, Ursala, Agnes, Lûcia, Cecilia, Cristin, Anastasia, Juliana, and an Epilogue.   The work is intended for the edification of younger women who have not retired from the world.   Nothing is known of the author.   *Ed.*, T. V. Zingerle, 1864. *MSS.*, Schwerin, Görlitz, Stuttgart, Berlin, Karlsruhe. Innsbruck (in possession of L. Ettel).

Among many lives of saints dating from this period (*see* Wackernagel, "Gesch. Deutsch. Lit.," § 55; and Goedeke, "Ged. Deutsch Lit.," 231 ff.) may be mentioned one of *Saint Christophorus*, as being the oldest extant poem on the life of this saint.   There are traces in it of an earlier one on which the extant one is based.   *Ed.*, A. Schönbach, "Zeitsch. f. d. Alterth.," xvii.   *MSS.*, S. Florian (Upper Austria), Canon's Library; Vienna.

Hartwig von dem Hage.

Sieben Tagzeiten (*horae*).   The author gives his name in an acrostic at the beginning of the poem; then follow the Seven Stages of the Cross.   *See* A. Schönbach, "Zeitsch. f. d. Alterthum," 1881 (other extant "Tagzeiten" are given on pp. 252-255).   *MSS.*, Munich, Nürnberg.

A life of *Saint Margareta* is also by Hartwig v. d. Hage.

Sanct Brandan (*see* France, 12th century).   The three German versions of this legend are noticeable as differing from the Latin and French versions as regards the initial incident which gave rise to S. Brandan's voyage.   As a penance for not believing the wonders of God which he had read in a book, he is commanded to wander till he finds the promised land.   Only when he has found it and written out his experiences, thus, in a way, restoring the book which he had burnt, is he absolved and allowed to return.   The reference to the legend of S. Brandan in the "Wartburgkrieg" again differs, for in that S. Brandan, directed by an angel, finds the lost book on the tongue of an ox.   The Middle German version is only extant in one MS. of the 14th century, but both subject and treatment point to an original of earlier date, probably of the close of 12th century.   There exists, besides, a version in Low German (Schroeder, p. xv., xvi.), and a prose version of end 15th century, which became extremely popular and was put into print not less than thirteen times before the close of the first quarter of the 16th century. *Ed.*, Carl Schroeder (a Latin and three German texts), 1871.   *See*, for life of S. Brandan, versions of legend in the vernacular, from 12th to 19th century; relationship between,

and variations in, Latin and Irish versions, etc.; "Zur
Brendanus Legendi," G. Schirmer, 1888. *MS.*, Berlin.

A legend cycle in verse, *Buch der Martyrer*, was compiled from the "Legenda Aurea" during the first half of the
14th century for a Gräfin von Rosenberg. *MSS.*,
Heidelberg, Klosterneuburg.

A *Leben der Maria* is extant in versions of 13th (probably
as early) and 14th century, the earlier by Walther von Rheinau,
the later by Bruder Philipp, and a Swiss, by name Werner.

These legendary lives as a whole show the same decadence
of poetic taste and power as other works of the century.

A legend of a different kind is the tale of *Littauer*, a
heathen king who is converted to Christianity by a miraculous
vision in connection with the consecrated wafer. The author
gives his name as Schondoch, and is otherwise unknown; to
him is also ascribed a version of Mai u. Beaflor, called
"Die Königin v. Frankreich" (*see* below, § 45).

Konrad von Ammenhausen, b. 1280–90. Monk
and Parish Priest of Stein on the Rhine.

Das Schachzabelbuch (*Book of the Chess-board*, 1337). From
the work of Jacobus de Cessolis. Konrad has added much
original matter to his translation, and gives his opinions on
the condition of the country, and that of many classes of
people, as well as particulars as to the manner of life of these
same, as to what was read and what changes had taken place
in raiment. The symbolic use of the game of chess is found
as early as in Alexander of Neckham's work, "De Naturis
rerum," 1180; in the 13th century J. Gallensis used it in his
"Summa Collacionum, or Communiloquium" as a symbol of
human life, and later in the same century appeared the 'more
famous work of J. de Cessolis (chief MS. Wolfenbüttel).
Cessolis' work was translated into verse in various German
dialects and was put into German prose in the 15th century.
The imitation of this moral adaptation of chess was carried
over to games of cards, of which several specimens are extant.
Ed., F. Vetter, 1892. *See* (Hist. and Bibliography) Schmid,

1847 ; Linde, 1874. *MSS.*, Paris (Nat. Bibl.), Zofingen, Heidelberg, Vienna, Wolfenbüttel, Berlin, Munich, Stuttgart, and other foreign libraries; B.M. Add. 11616.

Hadamar von Laber, b. cir. 1300 ; d. 1350–60.

Jagd, 1335–40 (in the strophe form of the younger Titurel). Innumerable poems were written treating Minne in an allegorical form, frequently symbolizing some particular virtue. "Nowhere is the didactic tendency of the age more apparent than in this change of attitude towards the old ideal which had become a subject of reflection and doctrine." At the head of these allegorical poems stands the composition of Hadamar. Here the lover is the hunter, accompanied by his hounds : Happiness, Love, Faith, etc., the beloved one the game. The tale is intermingled with maxims and dialogues. Hadamar's poem found many imitations, his own work being held in high esteem.   *Ed.*, Karl Stejskal, 1880.   *MSS.*, Vienna, Munich, Karlsburg, Heidelberg, Erlangen, etc.

N.B.—A great influence was exercised on this class of poetry by Ovid's "Ars Amandi" and "Remedia Amoris" ; and the "Roman de la Rose" was the standing model for the application of allegory to Minne.

Boner, fl. 1324–49. A Dominican, and native of Berne.

Edelstein. A didactic work, containing 100 tales, taken from Latin sources, written in clear and simple style, not without humour ; proverbs are intermingled, and the whole has a popular tone, though the clerical outlook is not ignored. It became a general favourite and was one of the first German works to be printed (1461).   *Ed.*, Benecke, 1816 ; Pfeiffer, 1844 ; *see* also under Gottschick (order of fables), 1879 ; Mod. Germ., M. Oberbreyer, 1881.   *MSS.*, Zürich, Strassburg, Heidelberg, Basle, Stuttgart, Vienna, Munich.

Der König von Odenwalde.

The works of this poet are representative of the class of poetry which arose in direct opposition to the Minnesong.

He would have nothing to do with the flowers of spring or the song birds of the woods; he chose rather for subjects, the cow, the hen, the goose, the sheep, and has left a poem to each of these. Thirteen poems of this class are extant, one being on beards (in dialogue form), another on the bath, and two being fables. He supplies a good deal of information as regards the manners and customs of the times. The poet gives his name as above in nearly all the poems. As he describes himself as a poor man, the "König" it is thought, more probably signifies a chief of the wandering minstrels of the East Frankish district, in the dialect of which he wrote, than a King of the Heralds, which was a post of great importance only assigned to those who belonged to the nobility, and in which he would not have known want. *See* Pfeiffer, "Germania," vol. xxiii. *MSS.*, Munich (Würzburg MS.), Gotha.

N.B.—König von Odenwalde belonged to the "Reimsprecher." Beside longer didactic poems, fables, and "Beispiele," shorter poems, didactic, satirical, and entertaining, dealing with every variety of subject, were written in rhyming couplets, and called *Reimrede*; among the rhymers were those who were by calling Reimsprecher, writers of *Reimreden*, and among these was König von Odenwalde, Heinrich der Teichner, and Suchenwirt. The earliest representative of the Reimsprecher was Stricker (§ 26).

Heinrich der Teichner (for possible interpretation of surname, *see* Karajan), fl. 1350–1377.

Over 700 poems of this author are extant. He writes against the moral conditions of the age; condemns useless tournaments, deprecates campaigns against the heathen while there are so many unbelievers at home to be converted, and widows and poor people requiring protection. He was a friend of Suchenwirt's, who mourned him in a poem when he died, but unlike the latter found more cause for complaint than rejoicing. Both allegory and fable are used by Teichner for his didactic purposes. He was at first a wandering singer, and "for an unlettered man shows more depth of thought than might have been expected." *Ed.*, Docen "Miscellaneen z. Gesch d. Lit.," 1807; poems also in Laszberg and C. Hätzlerin. *See* Karajan, "Denkschrift Kais. Akad. Wissens." (Phil. Hist. Classe), 1855; Pfeiffer, "Germania," 1866, 375–381; Primisser, "Suchenwirt," p. xii. *MSS.*, Vienna, Munich, Gotha, Morsburg, Heidelberg, Berlin, Prague, Leipzig, Petersburg; B.M. Add. 24946.

Heinrich von Mügeln, fl. 1345–70. (§ 39.)

Der Meide Krantz, or, *Buoch der Meide*. Dedicated to the Emperor Karl IV., who plays an important part in the poem as umpire, between the various sciences and arts which are personified by maidens. The work represents the philosophy of the age. *See* H. J. Schröer, "Akad. Wiss. Sitzungsberichte," Vienna, lv. pp. 451–520.

Das Lobgedicht auf Maria (twelve-lined strophes).

We have, besides, *Lieder* and *Fabeln* by this poet. "The fables are noticeable as a transition from the detailed form of Stricker and Boner to the shorter one"; they are given in a single strophe of long lines. *Ed.*, "Fabeln u. Minnelieder," W. Müller, 1848. *MSS.*, Mügeln's poems are contained in MSS., Göttingen, Heidelberg, Weimar, Colmar, Wilten.

A Latin poem of this poet's is also extant. His prose works are a translation of the Psalms, a translation of Valerius Maximus, and his historical work.

Peter Suchenwirt, d. after 1395.

A writer of historical, biographical, allegorical, and didactic poems. He is a richer and more lively poet than Teichner. His verse was not confined to rhyming couplets, but he may be reckoned nevertheless among the "Reimsprecher." He attacks gambling, and lets us know how general dice-playing was in his day; one of his poems celebrates the battle of Sempach, but among the variety of his productions those that come under the heading of "Heroldsdichtung" procured him the greatest notoriety. These poems commemorated the deaths of princes and nobles, and joined with the lament was a description of their coats-of-arms beside that of their deeds. These "Ehrenrede" were probably recited at assemblies of the nobles. *Ed.*, Primisser, 1827; G. E. Friess, 1878. *See* F. Kratochwil, "P. Suchenwirt, Sein Leben u. seine Werke," "Scriptores rer. Pruss.," ii. 155, for poems referring to German order. Also a few in Clara Hätzlerin's "Lieder-buch." *MSS.*, *See* Kratochwil, "Germania," xxxiv. pp. 203, 303, 431 (twenty-one MSS); B.M. Add. 24946.

Suchensinn. A wandering singer like Suchenwirt and Teichner, who flourished end 14th and early 15th centuries. He does not hold so prominent a place among the Meister-singers as Suchenwirt; "he was unable to separate the didactic from the lyric." *MSS.*, Vienna, Kolmar, and in C. Hätzlerin.

Anonymous.

Disticha de Moribus ad Filium (Pseudo-Cato). There was probably a version of these in German, in the 11th century, for it seems from an extant letter of Notker III.'s that the latter translated them, probably into prose. The oldest extant translation only contains about two-thirds of the original, but was the basis of later and fuller ones. It is however of later date than Freidank (§ 25), for passages in the latter are found in Cato. A parody on the "Distiches" was written at some time not earlier than beginning of fifteenth century. *Ed.*, Fr. Zarncke, "Der Deutsche Cato," 1852. *MSS.*, Oldest extant translation; Melk (cir. end 13th century), Vatican, Heidelberg, Kolocza, Munich, Wolfenbüttel, etc. Later fuller translations: Stuttgart, Vienna, Munich, Berlin, etc.

Salomon u. Markolf. Written in the district of the Lower Rhine (§ 14). This is the earliest German translation of the dialogue; an early version of the epic (*see* § 14) is given at the end as an appendix. Of the dialogue two versions are extant, the later being by Gregor Haydn, middle 15th century; the earlier version is extant in a text of second half 14th century. It has all the coarse humour which developed round the early and serious form in most of the later versions. The dialogue is of earlier origin than the epic (*see* W. Schaumburg, Paul-Braune, "Beiträge, etc.," ii.). *Ed.*, Hagen u. Büsching, "Deutsche Gedichte des Mittelalters," vol. i. (Eschenburg MS.), Bobertag, "Narrenbuch" (Gregor Haydn's version). *MSS.*, Eschenburg (containing epic and dialogue), now lost; Darmstadt, Heidelberg.

Sibyllen Weissagung. Written in the time of Karl IV. In these rhymes the legend of the Cross is brought into conjunction with the account of the meeting of Solomon and the Queen of Sheba, the latter (the Sybil) prophesying of the events of the world till the end of things. The work in its complete form is in three parts—(1) Story of the wood of the cross up till the time of Solomon; (2) Sibylline prophecies; (3) the further history of the cross until the time of Christ. In it the incident occurs of the Queen of Sheba accidentally slipping on the wood of the cross whereby her web-foot was cured. Most of the complete texts correspond as regards the two first parts.

First lines:

> " Got was ie und ist immer
> und zergat sin wesen nimer,
> aller gewalt stat in siner hende,
> er ist an anfang und an ende."

Ed., Paul-Braune, "Beiträge zur Geschichte der d. Sprache und Literatur," Bd. iv. p. 48. *See* also Simrock, "Zwölf Sibyllen Weissagung," for the prose Volksbuch. *MSS.*, Aarau, Basle, Berne, Dresden, Donaueschingen, S. Gall, Munich, Nürnberg, Stuttgart, Mayhingen (Wallerstein MS.), Vienna. Early printed editions of late 15th and 16th centuries.

41 *History.*

Nikolaus von Jeroschin. Chaplain to the Grand Master of the German Order in Prussia.

Die Deutschordens Chronik (in rhymed couplets; the rhyme in many cases carried over four or more lines). A translation, in parts almost literal, of the Latin Chronicle of Peter von Dusburg, 1326. It is not held of value as an historical source, but on account of its linguistic interest a great number of unusual words and forms of speech occurring in it. *Ed.*, F. Pfeiffer, 1854; E. Strelke, " Script. rer. Pruss.," vol. i. *MSS.*, Königsberg, Stuttgart (Roy. Private Libr.), Heidelberg.

N.B. — N. v. Jeroschin also wrote *Leben des heiligen Adalbert*, in rhymed couplets, based on the life of the saint, by Johannes Canaparius. *Ed.*, " Script. rer. Pruss.," vol. ii. *MS.*, Königsberg (fragment).

Dalimil.

Chronik von Böhmen. Trans. from the Tschech. History of dukes and kings of Bohemia. *Ed.*, V. Hanka, 1859. *MS.*, Prague (Cath. Libr.).

Wigand von Marburg.

Chronik der Kriegsthaten des Deutschordens (*Wars in Prussia and Littau during the 14th century*). Finished 1394. The original work must have been 25,000 lines long. Only fragments of it are extant, but a Latin translation (Königsberg) and references to it in later works give an idea of Wigand's chronicle. An abstract of it, chronologically arranged, by Bornbach, the historian, is also extant. *See* " Script. rer. Prus.," ii. p. 429 ff. *MSS.*, Eleven fragments extant.

Anonymous.

Kreuzfahrt des Landgrafen Ludwig, 1189. 1302–1305 (rhymed couplets). As being the chief account extant of this nobleman the work is interesting, but it is of no especial poetical worth. *Ed.* Extracts, Wilken, " Gesch. d. Kreuzzüge," iv., Beilagen, 7–69. *MS.*, Vienna.

42

Arthurian Cycle.

Claus Wisse, and Philipp Colin ("Pfilippez Colin der Goltsmit").

Parzifal (rhymed couplets), 1331–1336. A continuation of W. v. Eschenbach's poem. The work of these two Strassburg poets is based on the continuations of C. de Troie's poem (Manessier, Denain, Anonymous). Some of the interpolations are the work of the two poets. The Donaues-chingen MS. contains Wolfram text, subjected to certain alterations and insertions, including the prologue of 500 lines in the second book by C. Wisse. The work was undertaken for Herr Ulrich von Rappolstein; the name given as inter-preter of the French text is that of a Jew, Samson Pine. *Ed.*, K. Schorbach, 1888. *MSS.*, Two: Donaueschingen, Fürstenberg Bibl. (original MS.); Rome, Bibl. Casanatensis.

43 *Alexander Cycle.*

Seifrid.

The history of Alexander in short rhyming couplets, 1352; the work is scarcely more than a paraphrase of the "Historia de Proeliis," and seldom reaches any pitch of excellence either in rhythm or poetic feeling. All trace in it is lost of the influence of the older epic. *See* "Zeitsch. f. Alterth.," iv. p. 248; "Jahrbücher der Literatur," 1832. *MSS.*, Heidelberg, Rome (Corsini), Vienna, Munich.

N.B.—The *Alexandries* of Quilichinus of Spoleto written in Latin distiches (1236), was also put into German rhyme between 1389 and 1397 (MS. Wernigerode, Stolberg Bibl.), (short rhyming couplets). *See* "Beiträge zur Gesch. Deutsch. Sprache, etc.," vol. x. p. 315.

44 *Troy Cycle.*

German versions of Guido de C.'s work are extant, dating from the 14th century. Hans Mair (or Yair) von Nördlingen wrote in prose, 1392; Heinrich v. Braunschweig also gave a prose account of the Trojan War, taking K. v. Würzburg as well as Guido for the basis of his work. An unknown poet, who knew certain versions of the saga, and who composed from memory, adding matter of his own invention, wrote under the assumed name of W. v. Eschenbach. *See* "Die Sage vom trojanischen Krieg," H. Dunger, 1867. *MS.*, Gottwieh Kloster.

45 *Miscellaneous Romances, from Byzantine and other Sources.*

Heinrich von Neuenstadt. (§ 40.)

Apollonius von Tyrland, after 1312 (*see* England, § 16). H. v. d. N. expressly states that before his time the Latin work had not been translated into German. "The author, in spite of the learned element he introduces, may be considered the latest representative of the traditions of the older school of courtly epic." *Ed.,* with two prose German versions (Leipzig, Donaueschingen), C. Schröder, "Mitth. Deutsch. Gesellsch. Erforsch. vaterländisch. Sprache u. Alterth.," Bd. v. Heft 2, 1873; G. Singer, "Deutsche Texte des Mittelalters," Bd. vii. *MSS.,* Vienna, Gotha.

Johann von Würzburg.

Wilhelm von Oesterreich, cir. 1314. A long poem, of which the initial incident is the pilgrimage of the hero's father to the shrine of S. John of Ephesus, to pray for an heir. Wilhelm is born. When grown up, he goes in search of Aglie, of whose beauty he has heard, the daughter of King Agrant of Zizia, who was born in the same hour as himself. During the voyage he lands on a whale's back, on which a forest has grown, taking it for an island; the whale swims towards Zizia. Wilhelm is taken on shore, and finally betrothed to Aglie, etc. *Ed.,* E. Regel, "D. T. des Mittelalters," Bd. iii. *See* "Zeitschrift f. d. Alterthum," i. 214; xxvii. 94. *MSS.,* Haag, Heidelberg, Stuttgart, Gotha, Vienna, Kleinheubach, Munich, Cassel (fragments).

Anonymous.

Reinfrid von Braunschweig, end of 13th or beginning of 14th century; 27,627 lines. The name of the author, who was an Alemannian, or perhaps a Swiss, is unknown. He gives us some details concerning himself, and we know that he was poor, and that one "Else" encouraged him in his work. While others sit at the feast—

Line 2866 :

" ich siut bî strôwes fiure,	he sits by his straw fire,
und brâte wol mîn spîse.	and cooks his morsel of food.
des muoz ich werden grîse	so he grows grey
ê zît bî junger jâren."	while he is still young.

The poem is unfinished; it is a free version of the saga of Heinrich der Löwe. Reinfrid goes to the East to help recover the Holy Sepulchre, the greater part of the poem is a relation of his adventures; before leaving, he gives the half of a ring to his wife, telling her not to believe that he is dead unless the other half is brought her. A literary interest is attached to the work from the frequent references in it to different sagas. *Ed.*, K. Bartsch, 1871, "Bibl. Litt. Verein.," cix. *MS.*, Gotha.

Die Heidinn (rhymed couplets). The abduction of a heathen wife from her husband by a Christian knight; the incident occurs in other tales (*see* "Willehalm," § 31). *MSS.*, Heidelberg, Kolocza, Vienna, Pommersfeld.

Another version of "Die Heidinn" is "Die Wittich von Jordan." *MSS.*, Gotha, Heidelberg, Innsbruck.

The Innsbruck and the Vienna MSS. probably give the oldest text. *Ed.*, v. d. Hagen, "Gesammtabenteuer" (xviii.). *See* "Hauptschrift. f. d. Alterthum," vi. 51.

Schondoch. (*See* § 40.)

Königin von Frankreich (und der ungetrene Marschall) (octo-couplets). Calumniated wife, betrayal of the traitor's murder of his master by the behaviour of the latter's dog; combat between the Marshal and dog; death of Marshal. These incidents are familiar in many other tales (*see* France,

"Macaire," § 16). *Ed.*, v. d. Hagen, "Gesammtaben-teuer," viii. ; N. Meyer and Mooyer, "Altd. Dicht.," 1833. *MSS.*, Vienna, Heidelberg, Basle, Berlin, Herzogenburg.

Hans von Bühel, or der Büheler.

Königstochter v. Frankreich (octo-couplets)   Tale of daughter of the King of France, who escapes from the perse-cution of her father, and gives herself up to the mercy of the sea ; is carried to England ; lives with peasants ; her beautiful needlework taken to London for sale, attracts attention to herself ; she is taken into household of the Marshal, and being seen by King of England, is finally married to him. Then follows the well-known episode of absence of husband when child is born ; the falsifying by mother-in-law of the messages to and from the King ; wife condemned, but saved by the Marshal ; reunion of all parties at Rome after long years of separation.   The King of France leaves his kingdom to daughter, but the same is usurped upon the daughter's death, during her husband's absence.   This is stated by author to be the origin of the pretensions of England to the French crown, and of the warfare between the two nations.

This poem and "Mai and Beaflor" (§ 34) are representa-tives of one type of the Helena saga, in which the heroine does not disfigure herself, and in which we hear nothing of the consent of the Pope to the marriage between father and daughter.   (For other allied tales, *see* under P. de Beaumanoir, France, § 57.)   Suchier (*see* below) gives four chief types of the tale.   The difference between these two poems does not prevent the probability of a common original, but shows that H. v. B. had no knowledge of the earlier German poem.   As he does not mention his source, and as no other version of the Helena saga exactly corresponds to his, there is no certitude on the matter.

We know nothing of the author beyond his name and what he tells us in his poems ; from these we learn that he was in the service of the Archbishop of Cologne, and in the early 15th century was established at Boppelsdorf, near Bonn. There is no trace of the style of the older courtly epic in his work.   *Ed.*, Merzdorf, 1867.   *See* "Strasburger Studien,"

25

iii. 243 ff., and Suchier, Introduction to Beaumanoir, "Oeuvres."
MSS., No known MS. Early printed text (Strassburg, 1500
and 1508), of which copies are at Berlin, Wolfenbüttel,
1500; Dresden, Schleusingen, 1508.

His other work was

Diocletianus' Leben, 1412. 17,500 lines. The author tells
us that a companion of his, who had put the "Seven Wise
Masters" into German prose, induced him to versify the same.
Two prose translations are extant (Heidelberg, Stuttgart),
which are later versions of a German original that probably
served H. v. B. as his source. *Ed.*, Keller, 1841. *See*
F. Seeling, "Strassburger Studien," iii. 243 ff., 1888.
MS., One MS., Basle.

Anonymous.

Friedrich von Schwaben. Recounting the adventures of an
imaginary hero, with fanciful descriptions of people and lands.
The chief interest of the poem arises from reminiscences in
it of the Scandinavian Wieland saga, which nowhere else has
found a place in Old German poetry. When Friedrich is
asked his name, he answers, "Ich bin genant Wieland."
The hero having been separated from Angelburg, through
an act of indiscretion on his part, regains her by the help of
Prangnat, whom he releases from the magic spell that has
transformed her into a stag; the latter gives him a root
whereby he can make himself invisible, and he thus accomplishes his purpose. The poem opens with a praise of Friedrich's father, who, dying, gives advice to his sons—

> "Hant lieb vor allen dingen got;
> Daz ist mein Y̌epot.
> Ir sült euch erbarmen
> Yber die armen; etc."

Ed., M. H. Jellinck, 1904. *See* Hagen, "Germania,"
Bd. vii. p. 95 ff., 1846. *MSS.*, Wolfenbüttel, Stuttgart,
Donaueschingen, Heidelberg, Munich, Vienna.

Priester Johann. This is a rhymed version of a letter said
to have been written, cir. 1165, by this legendary monarch

of the East to different Christian magnates, more especially to Manuel of Constantinople and the Emperor Friedrich. Similar letters are said to have been received by Pope Alexander III., Louis VII. of France, and the King of Portugal. The letter in question is referred to in a chronicle of 12th century ("Chronicon Alberici"), and there is mention made of it in poetical writings of the time. For a translation into Modern German prose of this letter, *see* G. Oppert, "Der Presbyter Johannes," p. 26 ff. In this letter John the Presbyter describes himself as follows: "I, Presbyter John, the Lord of Lords, excel all men under heaven in virtue, riches, and power. Seventy-two Kings pay tribute to us."

German poem, line 4—

> "Ich heize prister Johan
> Unde bin ein recht geloubic man
> Uñ pflege der cristen allen
> Die mit armute sin bevallen, etc."

Among the wonderful things mentioned in the letter are the herb which, carried about the person, keeps away evil spirits, and the stones which render a man invisible, the waterless sea from which varieties of fish are obtained, etc. There are similarities of description with that of marvels in Sindbad's voyages in the "Arabian Nights." *Ed.*, Haupt u. Hoffmann, "Altd. Blätter," p. 308 ff., 1836. *MS.*, Berlin.

N.B.—As regards the legendary monarch himself, it seems that a report was spread in the 12th century that a Christian sovereign was reigning over vast lands in Central Asia, and was prepared to march to the relief of the Crusaders. The origin of this report is thought probably to rest on the defeat of the Sultan Sindjar by the Chinese Kuchan, 1141.[1] For details of the legend and its spread, see under Oppert, Zarncke, and Brunet.

46   NOVELLEN, SCHWÄNKE, ETC.

(Tales are sometimes designated as "Sprüche.)

Diocletianus' Leben. (*See* above, Büheler, § 45.)

---

[1] In later centuries legend and name were passed on to a king of Abyssinia.

Der Staufenberger, or, *Der Ritter von Staufenberg.* Similar to the French romance of "Melusine" (*see* France, § 70). The poem has been assigned by different editors to H. v. Aue, Eckenholt, and Erckenbold.

Line 47.

> "Uns seit diu âventiure daz,
> als ich hie vor geschriben las,
> von einem werden ritter hêr,
> hiez Peterman der Diemringaer, etc."

This Peter der Diemringer was of Staufenberg; notices of a Peter von Staufenberg are extant in 1274 and 1287. *Ed.,* Jänicke, "Altd. Studien," 1871. *MSS.,* Strassburg. Several other MSS. have been known to exist. *See* edition of work. Old printed edition, probably 1480–82, of which two copies are extant, at Wolfenbüttel and Stuttgart.

Der Busant (rhymed couplets). Tale of the son of a King of England and the daughter of a King of France. Separation of the lovers through the theft of a jewel by a bird (Busant); long wanderings apart, and final reunion. Similar incident to that in *L'Escoufle* (*see* France, § 57); *see* also *Die Gute Frau,* § 31. *Ed.,* Hagen, "Gesammt. Abent.," xvi.; N. Meyer and Mooyer, "Altd. Dicht.," 1833.

Der Kaufringer. Second half of century. A wandering Spruchdichter (Spruch, tale).

Seventeen tales in verse are extant by this poet, who gives his name at the close of three of them. He tells his tale well.

Last four lines of seventeenth tale: ("The Priest and the Miller's Wife").

> "Es mochten wol zwen engel sein,
> Von got gesant in menschenschein
> Zuo der müllerin oun gevär.
> Also sprach Hainrich Kaufringer."

Ed., Euling, "Bibl. Lit. Verein.," 1888. *MSS.,* two at Munich.

Philipp Frankfurter. End 14th century.

Der Pfaff von Kalenberg. A collection of Schwänke, similar to *Der Pfaffe Amis* (*see* § 26). *Ed.*, Bobertag, " Narrenbuch." *See* "Jahrbuch f. niederd. Sprachforschung," 1875–76, and 1887. Only preserved in printed editions of 16th and 17th centuries.

47 MEISTERSINGERS.

The Meistersingers were the chief representatives of poetic art in Germany from the 13th century after the decline of the Minnesingers. Though the lyric of the 13th century was continued in form, the spirit was changed; "when the frost of winter strips the leaves from the trees," writes Uhland, referring to the Meistersang, "we find little pleasure in the bare branches and twigs, and yet they were not less there before, but then covered with the green beauty of the rustling foliage." The legend goes that twelve old masters were the founders of their art. Many facts have led to the supposition that the oldest seat of the Meistergesang was at Mainz. Not until the 15th century were regular guilds established. The most flourishing period of the Meistergesang was during the century and a half from 1400. The singers were restricted to the metrical methods of the older school, no new " Ton " being introduced until the more progressive spirit of the fifteenth century allowed of such. The rules as regards metres, and the regulations of the guilds are known to us by the " Tabulatur," the oldest of which extant is that of Nuremberg, 1540. Though strictly adhering to old rules as regards form, the spirit which informed the Meistergesang was very different to the earlier lyric. Speculations in doctrine and scholastic problems served at times for subject.

The four chief " Töne " of the Meistersingers were called " Gekrönte Töne " (crowned metres), and had been invented by Mueglin, Frauenlob, Marner, and Regenbogen. The last society of Meistersingers survived till 1839 at Ulm. *See* Grimm, " Ueber den Altdeutschen Meistergesang," 1811 ; Bartsch, " Meisterlieder der Kolmar Hds.," 1862 ; Martin,

"Die Meistersinger von Strassburg," 1882; Schnorr v. Carolsfeld, "Zur Geschichte des Meistergesanges," 1872.

Heinrich von Meissen, surnamed Frauenlob, d. 1318.

The first of the Meistersingers. His surname arose from the honour in which he held women; one of his poems is a long *Leich* in honour of the Virgin, and he held a famous controversy (*Streitgedicht*) with his rival Regenbogen, a smith, who had given up his trade to become a wandering gleeman, as to the preference of the title "Frau" to that of "Weib," and according to report he was borne to his grave by women. His "Lieder" and "Sprüche" served as models in the schools of the Meistersingers.

The two last representatives of the older style of poetry were—

Hugo VIII., Count of Montfort, b. 1357; d. 1423.

Poems: *Reden, Lieder, Briefe* (letters). In rhyming couplets, or in strophes of four to twenty-eight lines. *Ed.,* Bartsch, "Bibl. Litt. Verein.," 1899; Wackernagel, 1881.

Oswald von Wolkenstein, b. cir. 1367; d. 1445.

Escaping from home as a boy with a few pence in his pocket, he earned his living by running on foot after the knights and doing menial service. He travelled as an ordinary soldier through nearly every European country from Russia to England, and was familiar with most aspects of fortune. In 1388 he served under James Douglas against the English. Later adventures took him to the East. Shortly before his death he made a collection of his lyrics. Oswald and Hugo both belonged to the nobility, and played no inconsiderable part in political affairs. They strove to imitate the older and more ornate style of the Minnesong, but were unable to escape the tendency of the age to realism. Love songs and didactic verse are among their works, and Oswald, who shows more distinctly the influence of popular poetry, took pleasure in imitating the old "Dorfpoesie." Of the two Oswald was the poet of greater power and originality. "His life was not fuller of adventurous activity than his work of variety." *Ed.*, Beda Weber, 1847. *See* Zeitschr. f. Deutsches Alterthum," 24, 27. *MSS.*, Innsbruck; Wolkenstein (Innsbruck); Vienna; B.M. Add. 24946.

48 DRAMA.

XIIIth AND XIVth CENTURY.

As in other countries, the sacred drama in Germany was a development of the religious offices held in celebration of the chief Church festivals, and was originally written in Latin; not until the 13th century do we find German introduced into the liturgical plays. One of the finest specimens of the Latin plays was the "Tegernsee Ludus," which dealt with the legend of Antichrist (cir. 1160), and possibly performed in the presence of Frederick 1. before starting on his crusade, for with the legend is mingled the idea of an imperial dominion of the whole world.

The oldest German play, the Easter play preserved at Muri (*ed.*, Acad. Zürich, 1890), belongs to the beginning of the 13th century, and the oldest extant Passion play— Munich (Benediktbeuren [1])—belongs to its close; in this "Ludus Paschalis sive de Passione Domini," German songs are put into the mouth of Mary Magdalene. With the introduction of the vernacular, there also crept in by degrees a popular, or what may be more truly termed a comic element into the liturgical plays. In an Easter play, connected with Innsbrück, the buying of the ointment by the holy women becomes a veritable farce, by reason of the quack doctor, his wife, and the rascally manservant; Peter and John race for the grave; while the taste of the Middle Ages for realistic representations of hell found a wide field for enjoyment; and when Christ has emptied hell, it is soon repeopled, the devils carrying off the souls of people of all classes and professions from bishop to baker. The Ten

---

[1] This famous MS. was at one time preserved in the Convent at Benediktbeuren; it contains the "Carmina Burana," "Wandering Students' Songs."

Virgins was also a favourite subject, and it is reported that at a representation of a play dealing with the same, given at Eisenach in 1322, in the presence of the Landgrave of Thuringia, the latter took it so much to heart—that even the supplications of the Virgin should be unable to obtain grace from the Redeemer —that a fatal illness with which he was attacked shortly after was traced to his violent emotion ("De decem Virginibus," R. Bechstein, 1872).

Among the Passion plays known to us, the most important are the Donaueschingen, Augsburg, Frankfurt, Heidelberg, and Tyrol plays. The Christmas plays, of which the oldest in Latin, the Freising play, dates from the 11th or 12th century, did not develop in the same way as the Easter plays; among the more considerable of the former is the Christmas play preserved in the Bendiktbeuren MS. Germany also had its Corpus Christi plays (Freiburg and Künzelsau). An independent play was the Innsbrück one on the Assumption of the Virgin, cir. 1391. The Fastnacht (Carnival) plays, with their unlicensed coarseness, were in striking contrast to the deep seriousness, which in spite of the addition of secular material, characterised the religious drama. These plays were mummers' shows, performed by merry companies, who went from house to house, and who delighted their audience with mimicking scenes of daily life of the less edifying kind. *Ed.*, F. G. Mone, "Altteutsche Schauspiele," 1841; "Schauspiele des Mittelalters," 1847; Meyer, "Das geistliche Schauspiel des Mittelalters," 1879; W. R. Hoffmann, "Entwickelung des d. Schauspieles," 1879; B. Froning, "Gesch. d. geistl. Schausp. des Mittelalters"; A. Keller, "Fastnachtspiele aus dem 15th century"; K. F. Kummer, "Erlauer spiele" (Lat. and Ger.), 1882; W. Creizenach, "Mittelalter u. Frührenaissance," 1893; Wilken, "Geschichte der geistlichen Spiele in Deutschland," 1872.

ITALY

LIST OF GENERAL AUTHORITIES.

Gröber, "Grundrisz der Romanischen Philologie" (Italian Section, T. Casini), Bd. ii. 3; Gaspary, "History of Early Italian Literature to the death of Dante," Eng. trans., Oelsner, 1901; Bartoli, "Storia della Lett. Ital.," 1878, etc.; "I primi due secoli della Lett. Ital."("Storia Lett. d'Italia," vol. ii.), 1876; T. Casini, "Manuale di Lett. Ital.," 1891; D'Ancona and Bacci, "Manuale della Lett. Ital.," vol. i., 1904; Garnett, "Italian Literature," 1898; Turri, "Dizionario Storico Manuale" (1000–1900), 1900; A. D'Ancona, "Studi sulla Lett. Ital. de' primi secoli," 1884; "Studi di critica, etc.," 1880; "La Poesia Popolare Italiana" (with texts), 1878, 1906; G. Carducci, "Studi e Documenti di antica Lett. Ital.," 1900, etc.; Tiraboschi, "Storia della Lett. Ital.," 1805-13.

TEXTS.—Monaci, "Crestomazia italiana dei primi secoli," 1889; P. Savj-Lopez e M. Bartoli, "Altitalienische Chrestomathie" (with Grammar and Glossary), 1903; G. Carducci, "Primavera e Fiore della Lirica italiana," vol. i., 1903.

BIBLIOGRAPHY.—Gröber, Gaspary, Turri, Casini.

LIBRARIES.—Florence: Biblioteca Nazionale (here are collections Magliabechiana, and Palatina); Bibl. Mediceo-Laurenziana; Bibl. Riccardiana; Bibl. Marucelliana. Rome: Vatican; Bibl. Nazionale; Bibl. Casanatense; Bibl. Corsiniana; Bibl. Chigiana.

ITALY

ITALIAN was the latest developed of the Romance languages, and there is no work extant to indicate that it was used for literary puiposes before the beginning of the 13th century (cir. 1220). Latin, naturally, took deeper root in Italy than in the countries to which it was transported as an alien language by the Roman conquerors, and whereas in France, as early as 813, an order went forth from the Council of Tours that homilies were to be read in *rustica romana lingua*, so as to be understood by the people, the natives of Italy continued in general to understand Latin throughout the 13th century. For many centuries, before Italian appears in written works, its various dialects were slowly developing in the different parts of the country, but it is noticeable that the final emergence of Italian as a literary language was simultaneous all over Italy. Words in Italian dialect occur here and there in very early documents; but the first known specimen of what may rightly be termed a sentence, is found in one belonging to the Archives of Monte Cassino, dated 960. Among other sparse indications of an extant vernacular in the 11th and 12th centuries, we have a form of confession, the facsimile of an inscription formerly on an arch of the choir of the Cathedral at Ferrara,[1] and several pages of a banker's book of the early 13th century (1211) (*see* for early monuments of Italian, Monaci, "Crestomazia italiana dei primi Secoli," 1889). Nor are we without traces also of ancient popular songs in dialect, for fragments of such are given by Salimbene (13th century), in his "Chronicle," in Italian, as well as in Latin and French, and the song of a Tuscan minstrel, preserved in the Bibl. Laurenziana at

---

[1] The early date of this monument has not been unquestioned.

Florence, is possibly of the 12th century. One of the most, if not the most, ancient monuments of Italian dialect, which has come down to us in a literary setting, is the "Contrasto" of the troubadour Rambaldo di Vaquieras, who went to Italy in 1189 or 1190. In this versified dialogue, between himself and an Italian lady, he puts into her mouth words of a mixed dialect of Genoese and Provençal. Italian was also used by this troubadour in another of his poems. *See* Bartoli, "Stor. Lett.," ii. p. 4.

There has been much discussion as to the date of another early specimen of Italian—the "Ritmo Cassinese." At one time assigned to the 11th century (to which period the Codex in which it is written belongs) it has since been placed in the 13th; the writing it is in does not serve as more exact guide, as this underwent no change from the middle of the 12th to the end 13th or beginning 14th century. The poem, which is composed in Apulian dialect, is obscure; it is a dialogue between a man of the East and a man of the West, both apparently monks belonging to different orders; it has been interpreted as allegorically representing the life of this world and that of the next. *Ed.*, "Riv. Fil. Rom.," ii. 91; "Romanische Studien," Bd. iii. 143. *See* also Novati, "Studi critici," 1889.

The "Carta Arborea," published in 1845 as an ancient work, is now universally recognised as a forgery.

The beginnings of Italian literature were not contemporary, as were those of France and Germany, with the struggles of a rising nation. The voice of an already mature race, practised in the art of expression in other tongues, sounds through the verse of the first Italian poets, and this it is which explains the apparently marvellous rapidity of development in Italian literature which took place during the short time which elapsed between its rise and the renowned period of the Trecento.

Italy, at the outset of her literary career, contributed little of her own either in the way of form or subject; for both these she drew from the fully developed literatures of her neighbour France. Thus we find her earliest poets writing in Provençal or in Italianised French, in imitation of troubadours and trouvères, copying the lyric of the one and borrowing the heroes and style of the other.   For Italy had no national epic of her own, due possibly to the fact, that the Italians, with ages of culture behind them, were without the impulse to this form of verse, which the recollection of the heroic traditions and mysterious myths, associated with the days of their wild and warlike wanderings, gave to the younger nations. *See* Gaspary, "Die Sicilianische Dichterschule," 1878.

2   LATIN WORKS.

Meanwhile Latin was still the chosen medium of expression for the learned, in whose writings the growing corruption of the language was increasingly noticeable.   All the usual forms of mediæval Latin literature are represented in the works of Italian authors.   The Chronicle was the most important of these.   In the 12th and 13th centuries the historical writings began to be of interest and value.

LATIN CHRONICLES.

XTH AND XITH TO XIIITH CENTURY.

To the 10th and 11th century belong the *Annales Casinates* (914–1042) a meagre record of monastic life, in which five to twelve years are passed over in silence, to be broken only by the mention of some trifling incident, such as the renovation of an altar, or an eclipse, the sight of which filled its beholders with fear and horror.   (Pertz, "Monum. Germ.," iii.)

Chronicon Novalicense.   In this Chronicle, written by a monk of the 11th century, at Novalese, a monastery at the foot of Mt. Cenis, the introduction of legend and tradition adds more vivacity to the record of events.   We have tales of Charlemagne, of his wife Berta's death, of the minstrel who led the way into the enemy's country, of the Walter of Aquitaine known in German romance,[1] here represented as

---

[1] *See* Ekkehart, Germany, 10th century; the Waldere fragments, England, 8th century.

aged and acting as gardener to the convent, but roused to deeds of valour, equal to those of his youth, when the monastery is attacked. (Pertz, "Mon. Germ.," vii.)

N.B.—The Abbey of Monte Cassino, founded in the early 6th century by S. Benedict, was, for many centuries, a chief seat of culture. Here Paulus Diaconus wrote his "History of the Lombards"; it was visited by Charlemagne and Louis le Debonnaire, and was the refuge of the Arabian scholar, Afer of Carthage; works in prose and verse were composed within its walls, and manuscripts carefully transcribed. Twice destroyed by invaders in 6th and 9th centuries, it was twice restored, and acquired renewed renown under the Abbot, Desiderius, afterwards Pope Victor III. (second half 11th century).

Two other monastic Chronicles of the 11th to 12th century, the *Cassinese* (Pertz, vii.) and the *Farfense* (Muratori, "Rer. Ital. Script.," ii.) are more documentary in character and historically reliable. Leo Marsicanus, the writer of the former, cites several old authors, and in both works there is an advance on those of the same class that had gone before. After the close of the 11th century the Chronicles begin to cover a less limited field of matter. In the south, Malaterra ("Rer. Ital. Script.," v. and viii.) and others deal with the history of Sicily and the Norman dynasty; in the north, Sire Raul and Ottone Morena ("R. I. S.," vi.), with the wars of Barbarossa, and their attendant horrors, and with the fierce struggle between the Milanese and the people of Lodi, "the one dispassionately and impartially detailing atrocities with a calmness that lends additional terror to the account, the other with all the warmth of an ardent partisan and eye-witness." By this time all the leading towns had their annals; Milan had Arnolfo and Landolfo (Pertz, viii.) for its chroniclers, but they were of less repute than Caffaro, whose "Annales Genuenses" ("R. I. S.," vi.) are accounted among the best of these local histories; the annals were carried on after his death to 1293. (Bartoli, "Stor. Lett." i.) *See* Balzani, "Le Cronache. ital. nel medioevo," 1884.

Before passing to the 13th century, there is another style of

Chronicle to mention, which dealt with the history of the world from the beginning of time. Of these universal histories, which appeared in the 12th and 13th centuries, the most famous was the

Pantheon, by **Godefroi di Viterbo,** in which verse is mingled with prose. The author deals with the Divine essence, with the elements and angels, etc. before beginning his account of Emperors and Kings. The verse repeats what has been written in prose, as a further means of attracting readers. The nationality of Godefroi is doubtful, but certain references, and certain tales made use of, are thought to point to a German, rather than to an Italian origin. *Ed.*, " R. I. S.," vii. By this same author is a long poem, *Gesta Frederici.*

3 Fra Salimbene. Native of Parma, b. 1221 ; alive till cir. middle year 1288.

The most noted historian of this epoch, his *Chronica* being the most characteristic work of this class. While still young, he entered the order of the Franciscans, changing his name from Ognibene to Salimbene, a fellow-monk having advised it as God alone was " Ognibene." His Chronicle is more or less a general history from 1167 to 1287, but the account of events contemporary with his lifetime is given in greater detail and is the part of most historical importance. Though thoroughly mediæval in his asceticism and superstition, the more modern touch in his work, as well as the Italianised Latin in which it is written, are signs of transition in style and language. Starting with the statement that he intends to write in plain and simple language, giving impartially the facts of history, he has nevertheless, with some garrulity and a good deal of vivacity, imbued his work with lively personality, describing the chief historical figures of the day, and giving a picture of the times in easy and animated language, with considerable acuteness of observation, and entering into interesting details of minor matters, such as the dinner given the monks by Ludwig ix., etc. He dedicated his work to his niece, Agnes, a nun ; it was written when he was at an advanced age-

Ed., "Mon. hist. ad. prov. Parmensem et Placentinam pertinentia," iii. 1857. *See* for interesting life of Salimbene, E. Michael, 1809 ("Salimbene u. seine Chronik"). *MS.*, Vat xiii. 7268.

Among other Chronicles of the 13th century are: *Gesta Florentinorum*, by Sanzanome; *De obsidione Anconae Liber*, by Boncompagno (*see* below); *Historia rerum Sicularum*, by Saba Malaspina; *De rebus Gestis Frederici II.*, by Niccolò da Jamsilla. The works of Sanzanome and Boncompagno are the earliest examples of historical writing in which an advance is made on the barren style of the earlier chronicles.

XIITH TO XIIITH CENTURY.

4   DIDACTIC WORKS, ETC., PROSE AND VERSE.
Philosophy, Legend and Rhetoric.

Arrigo da Settimello, also known as **Henricus Pauper.** Flourished second half of 12th century.

Elegia de diversitate fortunae et philosophiae consolatione. A poem in four books. To the writing of this work the author, similarly with Boethius, was urged by his misfortunes, in which he sought the comfort of philosophy. It was a favourite book of the Middle Ages, and was translated later into Italian. Taking Boethius as a model for the general idea of the poem, he falls short of the older writer in the work itself; "metaphysics degenerate at the close into a commonplace morality, but where the author refers to events of his own time, or to his own experience, he is not wanting in power and genuine feeling." *Ed.*, Leyser, "Hist. poetarum et poematum Medii aevi," 1721.

Albertano of Brescia, d. 1246.
De Amore et Dilectione Dei.
De Arte Loquendi et Tacendi.
Liber Consolationis et Consilii.

These three prose treatises were translated into Italian (*see* under Translations, § 21).

Among the most celebrated of the grammarians of this period was Boncompagno da Signa, who flourished in the early 13th century. His chief work, a treatise on the art of writing, was named after himself, and has in it some interesting information and anecdotes. Further instruction was given on the same subject in other works on rhetoric, and an historical work (*see* above) is also extant by this author.

The famous "Legenda Aurea," a collection of legends of saints, was composed in this century by Jacopo da Voragine, who died Bishop of Genoa, 1298. *Ed.*, Brunet, 1843.

5   HISTORICAL VERSE.

From as far back as the 8th century, comes a song in honour of Verona; to the 9th century belongs a poem written in stanzas of three lines, each stanza beginning with a letter of the alphabet, on the imprisonment of Ludwig II., possibly the composition of one of the soldiers; in the same century, a monk, Abbone, gave an account in verse of the siege of Paris by the Normans, *De Bello Parisiaco*; in the next century we have a song exhorting the defenders of Modena to be on their guard when besieged by the Hungarians. Longer poems are a panegyric on Berengar, of the 10th century, and in the 11th and 12th centuries, *Gesta Roberti Wiscardi*, by Guglielmo of Apulia; a poem on the town of Bergamo, with legendary account of its foundation; a life of Mathilda, Countess of Tuscany. A poem, in seven books, on the conquest of the Balearic Isles, and another of a victory in Africa, gained by the Pisans, have many classical and legendary allusions in them, and are evidence of the familiarity of the Italians with the tale of Troy. A poem on Frederick Barbarossa, and another by Pietro da Eboli, on the conquest of Sicily by Henry VI., are also productions of the 12th century. *See* Bartoli, "I primi due Secoli," cap vii.; Gaspary, *op. cit.*

26

The Alexander legends are represented in a Latin poem of the 13th century, by Qualichino di Spoleto. (For " Roman d'Alexandre," *see* France, § 27.)

Latin literature flourished from the 11th to the middle of the 13th century. Universities were founded in 13th and 14th centuries; among the most famous were those of Bologna, Naples, Padua, Vercelli, Ferrara, etc. Bologna was the centre for the teaching of civil and canon law; it was brought into repute at the close of the 11th century by the lectures at that time delivered there by Irnerius (Warnerius, Garnerius); Salerno was renowned as a school of medicine, and won especial fame from the teaching of Constantius Afer, the Carthaginian refugee. With the 13th century are associated the names of the two great theologians, Bonaventura and Thomas Aquinas.

6   PROVENÇAL POETRY IN ITALY.

From the close of the 12th century, the troubadours had found their way into Italy, whither they went in search of love and adventure; later on they sought refuge at its friendly courts from the persecution which drove them from their homes. They wandered from centre to centre, and were everywhere received with affection and treated with favour. The Lords of Monferrato, of Malaspina, and of Este were their patrons and protectors, and the poets were free to exercise their *gaia scienza* at one or other of these splendid courts of Italy.

Among the earlier troubadours who visited Italy are found the names of Pier Vidal, Rambaldo di Vaquieiras, Gaucelmo Faidit; Bernard de Ventadour was, it is thought, also probably one of their number, for his fame was great in Italy. The many refugees who fled later from the south of France are too numerous to mention; the advent in Italy of the troubadours is chiefly of importance in the history of this country's literature on account of their influence on the Italian poets, who, at first, in preference to their own, chose the language of the strangers for their songs.

Troubadours in Italy, Aimerico de Pegulhan, Alberto de Gapençois, Peirol, Ugo de Bersie, Elia Cairels, Folchetto de Romans, Pietro Villems, Ugo de Saint Cyr, Guglielmo Figuierias, etc.

7   Italian Writers of Provençal Lyrics.

Alberto Malaspini was himself a poet as well as a protector of the troubadours; a Tenzone is extant between him and Rambaldo da Vaqueiras, and another with Gaucelmo Faidit, the former occasioned by a love-raid " such as only the Middle Ages could have known"; and the second being an argument as to which are greater, the pleasures or the ills of love. A third poem was a love dialogue with a lady.

Rambertino Buvallello, fl. 1209–12. The earliest of the more important poets. *See* Propugnatore, ii. 282.

Lanfranco Cigala. One Serventese of his is a violent invective against the Italian nobles who had forsaken the Ghibelline cause.

Bonifazio Calvo, and **Bartolommeo Zorzi,** the one a Genoese and the other a Venetian, from each of whom is extant a patriotic song inspired by the enmity between their native towns, the latter from his Genoese prison.

Ferrari di Ferrara, who according to his biographer understood " Meill de trobar proensal che negus om che fos mai en Lombardia," and who besides writing verse also made a collection of the works of the chief troubadours; and we also learn that when his fellow-poets visited the court of Este, which was his home, he conversed with them in improvised verse.

Simon Doria,

Guglielmo di Rosieri,

Nicoletto da Torino,

Jacopo Grillo, and many others ; and finally,

Sordello of Mantua, who died cir. 1270, doubly noted as a poet and as being immortalised by Dante. A celebrated poem of his is a *Compianto* on the death of Ser Blacas, a satire in which the poet grieves not only for the loss of a friend, but because all noble actions have died with him ; there is no likelihood of these reappearing, he continues, unless the heart of the dead man should be divided and eaten by those in power, whereby their own hearts might become less corrupt. He then enumerates the potentates, whom he thinks would do well to partake of it, stating the reasons for his advice, beginning with the Emperor, and running through the chief monarchs of the West, including the King of England.

See Bartoli, " Stor. Lett.," vol. ii. ; for biographical notices of above poets, *see* O. Schultz, " Zeitschrift Rom. Fil.," Bd. vii.

8   FRANCO-ITALIAN POETRY IN THE NORTH OF ITALY.

French literature was also well known to the Italians at this early period. *Trouvères*, as well as *trovatori*, passed over into Italy, carrying their epic poems with them, and the first Italian romances were imitations, and in some cases tran-scriptions of French originals. It was chiefly through the Venetian district that this class of poetry was spread, and it was here that the Italian romance originated. The most noticeable thing about these early Italian chivalric romances is the language, an Italianised French, in which they were written. The chief of these works are preserved at Venice in a manuscript (S. Mark, xiii.) which contains : " Buova d'Antona," " Berta," " Carleto " (youthful adventures of Charlemagne), " Berta e Milone," " Uggeri il Danese," and " Macaire."

Among others to be found in Venetian MSS. (Aspremonte, Roncisvalle, Aliscans, Gui de Nanteuil, Folco di Candia) are the " Entrée de Spagne " (S. Mark, fr. xxi.), by a Paduan (*see* A. Thomas, 1882); and the "Prise de Pampelune" (fr. v.), a continuation of the same, by Niccolò da Verona (ed. Mussafia, "Altfranzösische Gedichte aus venez. Hss.," 1864). No extant French original is known for the last two of above works, which deal with the conquest of Spain before the disaster of Roncesvalles. It may be noticed that in the Italian versions the traitors are connected with one another as members of the same family Maganzesi (from Mayence, the traitor in "B. of Hanstone" having been confused with the other "Doon of Mayence"); a further development was the connecting of the loyal heroes under the family name of Chiaramonte.

This style of verse began about the second half of the 13th century, the exact dates of the poems being undetermined; late specimens of these romances extend into the early 15th century. They were mostly written, like their models, in laisses of ten or twelve-syllabled lines.

The Italian element in this mixed dialect gradually became more pronounced, and it predominates in a version of "Bovo d'Antona," known as the Venetian "B. d'A." *Ed.*, P. Rajna, "I reali di Francia," 1863. *MS.*, Bibl. Laurenz., Med. Pal., xciii.

And also in the

Rainardo e Lesengrino, a fragment of the animal saga, which gives a version of two branches of the "Roman de Renart," only one of which exists in French. *Ed.*, E. Martin, "Le Roman de Renard," 1882. *MSS.*, Bodleian, Can., Ital., xlviii.; Udine, Bibl. Archiepis., xiii.

Another Franco-Italian poem was the *Roman d'Hector*, or *Roman d'Hercules* (*see* Prose, under Troy, § 20); it differs from the others of this class in its metrical form, being written in rhyming couplets of eight-syllabled lines. *MS.*, Paris, Bibl. Nat., 821.

A Franco-Italian poem on the *Passion* is by a Niccolò da Verona, thought to be identical with the author of "Prise de Pampelune."

9　　

In the course of the 13th and 14th centuries several Italian authors wrote their prose works in French.

Rusticiano da Pisa. (*See* France, 13th century, § 44.)

A translation into French of Marco Polo's "Travels," and a cycle of tales of the "Round Table."

Martino da Canale.

Cronique des Véniciens.

Brunetto Latini. (*See* France, 13th century, § 37.)

Li livre dou Trésor.

Aldobrando of Siena, or perhaps Florence.

Le Régime du Corps (*de Santé*). Advice and directions as to food and drink, clothing and sleep; sleeping in the day-time is said to be undesirable, as many illnesses arise from it. One chapter is devoted to physiognomy. Two tracts on the preservation of the hair and teeth, which were translated into Italian in the 14th century by Bencivenni, were edited for the first time by Zambrini, 1876. *MS.*, The oldest MS., Bibl. Nat. fr. 2021.

Egidio Romano.

De regimine Principum. A work translated into French, probably by the author himself, from the original Latin.

Both Martino da Canale and Brunetto Latini give the same reason for the use of French in their works. The former writes, "lengue franceise cort parmi le monde, et est la plus delitable a lire et a oir que nule autre."

10 The development of national literature was hindered, and the use of the national tongue for literary purposes was delayed, by the adoption by the Italians of foreign forms, subjects, and language for their earliest written non-Latin works. But the Italian dialects at length prevailed, and finally triumphed simultaneously in the various parts of Italy.

The history of Italian literature is generally divided into six or seven periods, of which the two earliest cover respectively the years dating from 1220 (when Italian began to be used as a literary language) to 1283, and those which date onward from this period to 1375, the close of the career of Petrarch and Boccaccio.

11   The Sicilian School.

Dante, in his "De Vulgari Eloquentia," divides Italian poetry into two periods, that of the *Scuola Siciliana*, and that of the *Stil Nuovo*; under the former heading may be understood the poetry which was more or less affected by Provençal influence, and which had its rise in Sicily, thence spreading into Central and Upper Italy, and carried on to the close of the 13th century.

The earliest school of Italian poetry was at Palermo [1] in the time of Frederick ii., the great encourager of letters. At his Court poets from Sicily and the Italian provinces first began to make use of the vulgar tongue. The earliest Italian canzone to which any probable date has been assigned is one by Giacomo da Lentino, a Sicilian, which is thought to refer to events which took place in 1205. There seems little doubt, however, that the Sicilian dialect had been used for poetry before the time of Frederick ii. (*see* Cesareo, "La poesia Siciliana sotto gli Svevi," 1894). This same authority considers that Provençal influence must be sought for

---

[1] This statement is not undisputed : there are authorities who think that Italian poetry sprang from Central Italy and Bologna. *See* Morandi, " Da Bologna à Palermo," "Antologia d. nostra critica litt. Mod.," 1893.

outside Sicily, to which more distant Court the troubadours would not so easily have travelled as to those of the mainland. Monaci also suggests that it was from Bologna, the centre whither the representatives of culture from all nations repaired, that this influence irradiated, and whence the Sicilian poets carried back to their homes the idea of cultivating their own vernacular, and of using it in imitation of the Provençal lyric. As Cesareo sets forth, both French and Provençal being understood in the north of Italy, there had been less inducement to make use of Italian, but matters were different in Apulia and Sicily, where neither of these languages was familiar, and where their poets had no choice but to write their lyrics in the home tongue if they wished to be understood. The poems of the Sicilian school are extant in Tuscan dialect, but it is thought most probable that they were written in Sicilian dialect (*see* below), which has become Tuscanised in the hands of the copyists (*see* Bartoli, "Stor. Lett.," vol. ii.).

The works of this early school of imitative poetry are wanting as a whole in freshness and originality. The Provençal literature which served as a model was itself by this time nearing its decline, and the lyrics of Italian writers were, if anything, more artificial than those they copied; the defects of the latter were exaggerated, and the conditions of life in Sicily prevented that correspondence with its actual surroundings which gave a measure of vitality to the Provençal lyric in its own home, and this want of correspondence was even more fatal to it when transplanted to the North, where social life was in still greater contrast with that of Provence. Thoughts and similes, with rare exceptions, as well as form, were borrowed from the Provençal; the all-absorbing theme was love, treated in the conventional way, which as yet had not been superseded among the poets of the court. Little of personal detail is known concerning these early poets, in many cases only their names survive. There is, as a rule, nothing in their poetry which gives any clue to their individual personalities, as is exemplified by what is extant of the verses of the Emperor, whose character and tastes are well known from other sources. *See* A. Gaspary, "Die Sicilianische Dichterschule," 1878; G. A. Cesareo, *op. cit.*

N.B.—There has been considerable controversy regarding the language in which the earliest poets of the Sicilian school wrote their lyrics. Cesareo sums up with saying that it cannot be affirmed that the poets, up to the time of Guittone, wrote in pure dialect, nor that they wrote in a vernacular composed of dialectic forms from all parts of Italy. Each poet endeavoured, with the help of Latin, with certain borrowings from the French and Provençal tongues, and even from allied dialects, to elevate the form of language in which he wrote, to a certain literary level, whereby to some extent a common literary language was attained, while, at the same time, the dialects retained their individuality, but not so as to render them unintelligible to the cultivated of other parts of Italy. To one fact he draws particular attention, namely, that among the Sicilian poets, and generally among the poets of the South, there is no trace of the influence of the dialects of Central or Northern Italy, whereas in these latter divisions of the country, the poetry bears strong traces of Sicilian dialect, thus proving that Italian poetry was born at the Court of Palermo.

12   POETS OF SICILIAN SCHOOL.

From Sicily and the South—

Friedrich II., King of Sicily and Holy Roman Emperor, b. 1194, d. 1250; Enzo, his son, b. 1225, died a prisoner at Bologna 1272; Pietro della Vigna, b. after 1180, entered the Emperor's service 1220; fell into disgrace for reasons imperfectly known, and committed suicide 1249. (He left some valuable letters written in Latin, as well as Italian verse.) Giacomo da Lentini, in the official service of the Emperor; spoken of by Dante as the most perfect representative among the poets of the Provençal lyric. Ruggiero d'Amici; Rinaldo d'Aquino; Jacopo d'Aquino; Folco Ruffo; Inghilfredi; Compagnetto da Prato; Raniero da Palermo; Percivalle d'Oria; Stefano di Pronto, notary of Messina; Mazzeo di Rico, of Messina; Filippo and Tommaso di Sasso; Rugieri Apugliese; Ruggerone da Palermo; Giacomino Pugliese.

From Central Italy—

Arrigo Testa d'Arezzo; Odo delle Colonne; Jacopo Mostacci da Pisa; Guido delle Colonne, Judge at Messina; Paganino da Serezano; L'Abate di Tivoli; Folcacchiero de' Folcacchieri da Siena; Tiberto Galliziani da Pisa, and others.

The above poets flourished in the first half of the 13th century. *MSS.*, Chief MSS. containing poems of the 13th century: Vat. 3793; Laurenz. rediano. 9; Palatina, 418; Chigiana, L. viii. 305; Vat. 3214; for other MSS. *see* T. Casini, "Giornale Storico," vol. iii., 1884; also for full account of all MSS. *see* Casini, "Rime dei Poeti Bolognesi," 1883.

The poetry of the Sicilian School was monotonous in idea, and artificial in style, but now and then among the earlier lyrics there are instances of a less conservative art and touches of more genuine emotion. Three poets have left works which differ distinctly in tone from the generality of the poetic productions of this period.

Giacomino Pugliese, " whose freshness and naturalness suggest the inspiration of the folk-song."

Compagnetto da Prato.

The poems by these two are fresher, more realistic and more popular in tone. The latter has the angry altercation between a husband and wife as the subject of one of his; in another, in place of the usual courtly and distant wooing of the love-poem, a maiden sends for her lover who unhesitatingly obeys her call.

Over the *Contrasto* (in thirty-two strophes) of **Ciullo,** or **Cielo, dal Camo,** beginning " Rosa fresca aulentissima, etc.," there has been prolonged controversy; opinions have differed as to date of poem, as to which class one or both the speakers of the diaolgue belong, and as to the language of the poem. (*See* d'Ancona, " Studi sulla lett. Ital. dei primi

Secoli," 1884.) The date of the poem has been settled by d'Ancona from internal evidence to be 1231 at the earliest, probably shortly after this date, and not later than 1250, the Emperor being referred to as alive, and he considers it an example of old popular Sicilian poetry. It is a lively, not over-courtly dialogue between a woman and her lover; there is an unmistakably plebeian element in the poem; but the speech has borrowed some expressions from the love poetry of the court. *Ed.*, Facsimile of Contrasto (Vat. 3793); E. Monaci, "Archivio Paleografico," vol. i. fasc. i., 1882.

13 All written works, it has been said, presuppose previous ones. Thus, the remains of popular poetry, and of the lyrics of the courtly poets in which the influence of popular poetry is apparent, which have come down to us from Sicily and the various parts of Italy, are considered undoubtedly to bespeak the existence of ancient folk-songs before the poets of the court made use of the familiar home tongue for their own more cultured and elaborate verses.

The folk-songs of Sicily have been collected by G. Pitrè, "Canti Popolari Siciliani," 1891, and a selection from these, and from the popular songs of other parts of Italy, have been published with an English translation by R. H. Bush ("Folk Songs of Italy").

14 The chief metrical form of the Italian lyric was the *Canzone*, a poem of several stanzas, which was frequently closed with one of fewer lines, called *Commiato* or *Congedo*, and in which was sometimes summed up the intention of the poem, or more clearly stated to whom it was addressed. The stanzas of the canzone were generally divided into three parts, of which two were similar. Lines of eleven or seven syllables were the most frequently used.

The *Sonnet* became more generally used by Tuscan poets; few specimens of this class are extant among remains of the Sicilian poets. The form and number of syllables was irregular among the earlier poets.

15 RELIGIOUS POETRY IN UMBRIA.

Umbria was the centre of the great religious revival of the 13th century; the spiritual enthusiasm awakened at that time among all classes of people being represented in its most highly-strung and ascetic form by the Flagellants, a sect which arose after the preaching of Raineri Fasani, in 1258. With this movement is associated the development of religious poetry in the vernacular; "laude spirituali" were sung by the grief-stricken penitents as they walked the streets or gathered for their devotional services, and their hymns of sorrow and supplication were poured forth in the language of their daily life—simple and passionate appeals for mercy and forgiveness from the troubled hearts of the suppliants, which supplanted the older Latin hymns.

Francesco d'Assisi, the "Poverel di Dio," the "Serafico d'Amore," b. 1182; d. 1226. Born of well-to-do parents, S. Francis voluntarily espoused poverty, and became the founder of the mendicant order which bears his name. His life was written by his contemporary, Tommaso da Celano; other sources of information are "Speculum Vitae" of uncertain authorship; Bonaventura's "Legenda"; "Legenda Trium Socorum," not thought by a late authority to be the work of the "three Companions," and the "Speculum Perfectionis," attributed to Brother Leo. Further details of his life are given in "The Little Flowers of S. Francis" (trans. by J. W. Arnold); the original is an exquisite specimen of Italian literature. *See* for trans. of above works, under "Temple Classics." Sabatier's "Vie de S. F. d'Assise" appeared in 1899.

Il Cantico del Sole, or *Laudes Creaturarum*. It is considered doubtful if we possess the original form of this poem. According to one of his biographers, the saint composed this work during an interval of religious ecstacy during his sojourn in the convent of San Damiano, 1224. In it God is praised through His creations, the sun and stars, etc., and through death. The question has been raised as to whether this composition is in prose or verse, the divisions of the lines being very irregular; it has seemed best to place it among such compositions as are known by the name of *prosa numerosa*, owing to the frequent rhymes, and more frequent assonances, which occur in it.   *Ed.*, A. Rossi (four different versions), 1882; Monaci, "Crestomazia." *MSS.*, Paris, Bibl. Mazarine, 1350; Assisi, L. ii. M. 6; Convents of Cortemaggiore and Buffeto; Chigiano, C. viii. 219, etc. ; first printed ed., Milan, 1510.   The works of S. Francis in prose and verse were published by J. F. H. Schlosser, 1849. Father Lemmens, 1904; Prof. Boehmer, 1904.

Jacopo dei Benedetti, or **Jacopone da Todi,** b. cir. 1230; d. 1306.   Rich, gay, and cultivated, this man, whose religious enthusiasm later on was carried almost beyond the bounds of sanity, lived an ordinary life, until nearly forty years of age.   He married a young wife, and shortly after their union, she, being one of the guests, was killed by the falling of a part of the building where a wedding festivity was being held.   Added to the poignancy of his grief for her loss, was his profound emotion on discovering that she had been wearing a hair shirt under her gay costume.   His whole life altered: he gave away his possessions, left his home, and entered the Franciscan order.   No discipline was too severe for him, no humiliation or suffering too great; he rejoiced in all that brought pain or ridicule upon him, and even went so far as to go about on all-fours with a bridle in his mouth and a saddle on his back, that he might provoke the derision of the multitude.   His angry satires aimed at Boniface viii., who was opposed to the extreme spiritualistic party, caused him to be imprisoned for life.   In one of his poems he describes the horrors of his dungeon, not in murmuring but in jubilation, such misery was what he had desired as a test of his soul. He was released by Benedict xi. and died three years later. It is said that his heart broke from overmuch love of Christ. His *Laude* are both religious and satirical.   *MSS.*, Bodl., Canon. Ital., 240; Harl. 3355; Arundel, 214, 301; Add. 14100; Paris, Nat. Bibl. Ital., 559, 607, 1037; Cambridge, and other foreign libraries.

The celebrated hymn, the *Stabat Mater*, has been

assigned to him, but there are doubts as to its authenticity. Innocent III. has also been named as the writer.

A few prose writings (Bibl. Nat. ital. 1037, 606) are also extant: How Man may soonest arrive at a Knowledge of Virtue and possess perfect Peace; on Charity and Humility, on Patience; on the three states of the Soul, and the four battles of the Soul. *See* Boehmer, "Romanische Studien," vol. i. 123. d'Ancona, "Studi sulla lett. Ital. dei primi secoli," 1881. *See* for "Laude," Monaci, "Riv. Fil. Rom.," i. ii.

Drama.

The national Drama had its origin in the Laude Spirituali, for which the dialogue form became more and more frequently adopted. Spreading from Umbria to other parts of Italy, to the Abruzzi, to the Venetian district, the Laude by degrees assumed a new form and became known as Devozione, and further developed into the Rappresentazione. Any monuments, however, that should serve as a link between the earlier forms and the Florentine Sacra Rappresentazione of the 15th century are lost, and there is nothing to show how the gradual development took place. The oldest of the Sacra Rappresentazione that as yet is known dates from 1449, namely the *Abramo ed Isaaco* of Feo Belcari. *See* d'Ancona, "Origini del teatro in Italia," 1877, and "Sacre Rappresentazione," 1872.

16　Sicilian School and Transition School of Poetry in Tuscany.

For following division, *see* Bartoli, "Stor. Lett. Ital.," vols. i. and ii. It is in the towns of Tuscany that the secular lyric is next found flourishing. The influence of Provençal poetry was as unchecked in the North as in Sicily, and so similar were the productions of the poets who wrote in imitation of the troubadours of Tuscany, Apulia, or Sicily, that it is impossible to decide by their verses to what part of the country they belonged. The Tuscan poets understood and spoke Provençal, a poem or two in Provençal has been preserved among their verse, and a Provençal Grammar was written in Italy for the Italian poets about the time when they were flourishing. But by degrees the Tuscan poets broke away from the old traditional style of poetry, and to them is due the inauguration of a less conventional school of writing, and the inclusion of other subjects than love as the themes of their verse. It was in regard to the subject matter that the poets of the North were stikingly in advance of those of the South. The latter, with but an exception or two, treated solely of love, but the Tuscans dealt with matters of the day, and morals, and have left both political and didactic poems. Between 1260 and 1280 arose the Transition School of Poetry; those who belonged to it have been classed by Trucchi ("Poesie Italiane inedite," 1846–8) as *Trovatori della Transizione*, standing midway between the *Trovatori* and the *Poeti*.

The pre-eminence of the Tuscan dialect seems to have been established by the close of the 13th century. A native of Padua, writing about that time, says: "lingua tusca magis apta est ad literam sive literaturam quam aliæ linguæ, et idea magis est communis et intelligibilis." Remains of old verse in Tuscan dialect are extant, indicating that here, as elsewhere in Italy, the people had their songs in Italian before the language was put to more elaborate purposes.

Tuscan poets—

Arezzo: Guittone del Riva, Maestro Bandino, Giovanni dell' Orto; *Siena*: Folcacchiero de' Folcacchieri; *Florence*: Chiaro Davanzati, Rustico Filippo, Monte Andrea, Cione Notajo, Orlandino Orafo, Dante da Majano[1]; *Pistoja*: Meo Abbracciavacca; *Pisa*: Gallo d'Agnello, Pucciandone Martelli, Betto Mettefuoco, Pannuccio dal Bagno, Bacciarone di Messer Bacone, Lotto di Ser Dato; *Lucca*: Dotto Reale, Buonagiunta Orbiciani; *Bologna*: Paolo Zoppo da Castello, Fabruzzo Lambertazzi; and from the *Romagna*, Tommaso, of Faenza, Ugolino Bazzuola; etc.

[1] For the questioned existence of D. d. M., *see* G. Bertacchi, "Bibl. Stor. Lett. Ital.," vol. i.

Guittone del Riva, or Guittone d'Arezzo, b. 1220; d. 1294.   (§ 22.)

The Italian troubadours of the North followed the artificial forms of their Provençal models even more closely than those of the South.   They delighted in verbal artifices, such as the repetition of a word, or similar root, throughout a whole stanza, or even a whole poem; in the repetition of rhymes, and in the play on words (Bisticci).   The obscurity naturally engendered by these poetical contrivances became greater when, under the influence of Latin, the poets began to imitate the order of words proper to this language.   Guittone is a representative of the oldest style of Tuscan poetry; his contemporaries looked up to him as a master, but that which was lacking in these poets of the older school is expressed by Dante ("Purg.," xxiv. 52 ff.) in words which he addresses to Buonagiunta; the latter, in answer, ranks himself with the Notary of Lentino and with Guittone, as poets who had not attained to the "dolce stil nuovo."   Guittone's poetry falls into two periods: during the first he wrote under Provençal influence, and considered no subject worthy of his verse but love; the second period dates from his enrolment in the order of the Cavalieri di St*. Maria, (known as the *frati godenti*, on account of the laxity with which its members kept their vows).   He was then about thirty-five years of age, and his subsequent poems indicate an entire change of feeling.   He now chose theological subjects, and many poems are little more than treatises in verse; of his political verse, two specimens are among his best work: a poem addressed in reproach to the Florentines after the battle of Monteaperti, and a *canzone* in which he admonishes his fellow-citizens. That Guittone allowed himself in later life a wider range of subject, and that he admitted Latin influence, are signs that poetry was striving to throw off its shackles, and that poets were no longer satisfied with producing a succession of stereotyped love lyrics.   Guittone therefore takes his place at the head of the transition poets of the learned school. Dante was not an admirer of Guittone; Petrarch, on the contrary, places him on a level with Dante and Cino da Pistoia, and almost seems to think he should be reckoned the first of the three. *Ed.*, "Le Rime de G. d'Arezzo," F. Pelligrini, 1901; Valeriani, 1828. *See* P. Vigo, "Giorn. Fil. Rom.," ii. 19. *MSS.*, Laur. Red. ix.; Palatino, 418; Vat. 3793, Magliabech. ii., iii., 492; Riccard. 2533; single poems in Riccard. 2846; Barberino, xlv. 47.

Political poems, inspired by the events which followed on Charles d'Anjou's victory in 1266, have come down under the names of Monte Andrea, Orlandino Orafa, Beroardo Notajo, Ser Cione Notajo, and others.

Chiaro Davanzati. Probably b. cir. 1230, fought at Monteaperti, 1260; died not later than 1280. The poets of the Transition School were mostly Florentines, among them C. Davanzati is considered one of the most original. He also began as a disciple of the Sicilian poets, and following in Guittone's footsteps he dealt like the latter with abstruse theological questions, and in a learned manner with love; but the more natural turn of phrase, a freshness, and a superior elegance of language, which characterise his writings, mark the advancing revolution in poetic style. He became an avowed opponent of the mannerisms of the older school, and, in one of his sonnets (also attributed to Rinuccini), he upbraids Buonagiunta for his imitation of the Sicilian poets, likening him to the crow of the fable dressed up in borrowed feathers. *MSS.* of poems, Laur. Red. ix.; Vat. 3793 3214. *See* Anthologies, and "A Sonnet ascribed to C. D. and its place in Fable Literature," C. D. K. MacKenzie, 1898; Casini, "Riv. Crit.," i. 71–8.

Rustico di Filippo, b. cir. 1230; d. cir. 1280. Also a representative of both schools. The sonnet was the only form in which this poet wrote (perhaps a *Sessantino*) some of his work being entirely under Provençal influence. "When he sings of the sorrows of love his voice is that of the true poet." This poet is more particularly noticeable as being the first writer of humorous verse among the Italian poets. He was "the earliest representative of the popular and realistic style which was developed during the 14th century by Pucci, Sacchetti, and others." *Ed.*, "Le Rime, etc.," Federici,

27

1898.   *See* Casini, "Un poeta umorista del secolo xiii.,"
"Nuov. Antol.," Ser. 3, xxv., 1890.   *MSS.*, Vatican,
Lat., 3793, 3214; Vatican, Urb., 697; Magliabech. vii.;
Chigi. L. viii.

Anthologies.

Vatican 3793 . .   *Ed.*,   D'Ancona and Comparetti,
        1875–78.
Vatican 3214, and ⎫
     Casanatense . .⎬   "   Mario Pelaez, 1895.
Laur. Red. ix. . .   "   Casini, 1883.
Palatino . . . .   "   Bartoli and Casini, 1877.

Valeriani . .   "Poeti del Primo Secolo," 1816.
Villarosa . .   "Raccolta di Rime Antiche," 1817.
F. Trucchi. .   "Poesie Ital. ined.," 1846.
E. Monaci . .   "Crestomazia italiana dei primi secoli,"
        1889.

English Translation of Italian Poets.

D. G. Rossetti, "Early Italian Poets from C. d'Alcamo
to D. Alighieri," with Dante's "Vita Nuova," 1861;
Edition in "Temple Classics," "Dante and his Circle
(with the Italian poets preceding him)," 1874, 1892.

17   School of the *Dolce Stil Nuovo.*

Guido Guinicelli (Guido di Guinizello de'
Principi), b. cir. 1240 at Bologna; d. cir. 1276.
Guinicelli was a partisan of the Ghibelline party, and was
banished from Bologna in 1274, probably dying in exile.
A follower at first of the Sicilian School, he finally became
the founder of the new School of the *dolce stil nuovo*, to which
Dante belonged.   The latter refers to him as "il padre Mio
e degli altri miei miglior, che mai Rime d'amore usâr dolci e
leggiadre" ("Purg.," xxvi. 97 ff.).

The chief characteristic of this school was its learned and philosophical treatment of subject. Love was explained by the subtlest methods (*casuistica amorosa*), and the writings of this school are not without their obscurity and conventionality. But in spite of drawbacks "the poetry lives"—a greater individuality and depth of feeling, a freer play of imagination, a freshness of poetic images, separate it from what went before. The attitude of adoration towards the beloved one is altered; she is still a distant object of worship, but has become an angelic being, more than woman, whose mere salutation overcomes the worshipper; and the feelings aroused by her are of the most exalted kind. Because the one loved was like an angel, there was no wrong in loving her, says Guinicelli in a famous canzone of his. It was this altered conception of love which lead to the introduction of allegory. All the emotions of the soul, even sighs, were personified as *spiriti* or *spiritelli*.

The *Ballata* was first used in Italy as a literary form by the poets of the transition school, and largely by those of the later school. It was originally a form of popular song. In the *ballata*, the stanzas were divided into three parts, with certain regulations of rhyme, while the *ripresa*, which began the poem, was repeated as a refrain at the close of each stanza. *Ed.*, Casini, "Rime dei poeti Bolognesi del sec., xiii.," 1883; Borgognoni, "G. G. e il dolce stil nuovo," "Nuovo Antologia," 1886. *MSS.*, Some chief MSS. of the poets of this school are: Chigi. L. viii. 305; Laurenz. xc. inf. 37; Palatino, E. 5, 5, 43; Vatican, 3213, 3214; Paris, Bibl. Nat. Ital., 554; Rome, Casanatense, d. v. 5.

The genius of the nation was now out of leading-strings; all the ideas and feelings of the period were seeking expression in one or other form of verse; ere long they were to find voice in the immortal harmonies of the "Swan-song of the Middle Ages."

18 Guinicelli had few disciples in Bologna; of these Onesto di Bonacorso is the only one who left any considerable body of verse. The chief followers of Guinicelli were Florentines. For precursors and contemporaries of Dante, *see* A. d'Ancona, "I precursori di Dante," 1874; Bartoli, "Stor. Lett. Ital.," 4; and "I primi due Secoli, etc." For MSS. containing poems of the 13th century, *see* Casini, "Giornale Stor. Lett. Ital.," iii. p. 161 ff.

Lapo Gianni and **Dino Frescobaldi** were both friends of Dante; the former is still allied in part to the older school, the latter is almost entirely free from its manner, and is more modern in the subjectivity of his tone; he is further characterised by "a new note of sorrow, of longing for death." *Ed.* (L. Gianni), G. Lamma, 1895; (D. Frescobaldi) Valeriani, "Poeti del primo Secolo," 1816.

Guido Orlando. An inferior poet to the two former in thought and feeling; allied to the new school by his casuistical treatment of love. His sonnet beginning "Onde si muove, e donde nasce amore?" is a characteristic specimen of his work, and is said to have called forth Cavalcanti's famous canzone, "Donna mi prega, etc." Orlando having undertaken to reprove the latter poet and to offer him instruction a lively controversy took place between them in verse; another of his sonnets, also conveying a warning, was addressed to Dante. *Ed.*, Lamma, "G. Orlandi e la Scuola del dolce stil nuovo," 1895.

Gianni Alfani. In his representation of his lady love, and in his note of personal sorrow, he is entirely one of the new school. *Ed.*, Valeriani, *op. cit.*, 1816.

A poet of greater importance than the above is—

Guido Cavalcanti, b. cir. 1255; d. 1301. As one of the Bianchi, Cavalcanti was banished in 1300; his friend Dante, one of the Priorate, being among those who had to sentence him. He was sent to Sarzana, but shortly after allowed to return, dying in August of the same year. Dino Compagni, in his "Chronicle" (Bk. i. chap. xx.) describes him as a "nobile cavalieri," and further describes him as courteous but haughty, fond of solitude, and deeply attached to study; Giovanni Villani speaks of him as "sensitive and

violent." All that his philosophic studies had taught him
about love he set forth in his canzone, "Donna mi prega,"
which has given work to many commentators; in it he
carried scholasticism to an even higher pitch than Guinicelli.
His work, however, in spite of certain abstruseness, was of
a poetic excellence sufficient to call forth Dante's praise
("Purg.," xi. 97–98), and to serve to place him among the
best poets of his period. *Ed.*, Salvadore, "La Poesia
Giovanile de G. C.," 1894; Arnone, 1881; Ercole, 1885.

N.B.—Shelley has given a translation of Dante's sonnet to
Cavalcanti—

"Guido, I would that Lapo, thou and I
  Led by some strong enchantment, might ascend
  A magic ship whose charmed sails should fly
  With winds at will, where'er our thoughts might wend," etc.

Cino Sigisbuldi of Pistoia, b. cir. 1270; d. cir.
1336. This poet, also a man of law, stands between the
first and second generation of the new school. An adherent
of the Bianchi, he also suffered exile. He studied juris-
prudence in Bologna, and taught in various places; his
commentary on Justinian held a high place for a long time.
He left love poems and some political verse. One of his
sonnets was addressed to Dante on the death of Beatrice;
in another he laments the death of Dante himself. He sang
chiefly of a donna named Selvaggia Vergiolesi. His death
was mourned by Petrarch, and Dante ("De. Vulg. Eloquio")
speaks of him as among those who sang most sweetly and
subtly. *Ed.*, G. Carducci, 1862. (His legal works are
edited by Chiappelli.) For MSS., *see* Bartoli, "Stor.
Lett.," vol. iv. p. 41 ff.

To the new school belong two humorous poets—

Cecco Angioleri, b. after 1250; alive in 1319. A
native of Siena. His poems deal with the three things which
gave him pleasure—"la donna, la taverna, e 'l dado" (women
the tavern, and dice). He commemorates a certain Becchina,

the daughter of a shoemaker; and he makes us thoroughly aware of the hatred which he bore towards his parents, his three enemies being unhappiness, and his father and mother. Dante having reproached him with living on other people, Cecco took his revenge in a sonnet when Dante was in exile eating the bread of others, and this was probably the end of their friendship. A strong vein of melancholy underlies Cecco's satire and humour. The most striking of his sonnets is the one beginning "S'io fossi fuoco, io arderei lo mondo" ("If I were fire, I would burn the world"), in which passion, satire, hatred, and laughter are each in turn uppermost. *Ed.*, Monaci e Molteni, "Il Canz. Chigi. L. viii.," 1877. *See* d'Ancona, "Studi di critica," 1880; P. Bilancioni, "Propugnatore," N.S. ii. (first lines of poems); Massera, "Studj. Romanzi," 1904.

Folgore da San Gemignano.

Scarcely anything is known of this poet. He loves to dwell on the pleasures of life, and only three of his sonnets deal with other matters, these being political, one of them referring to the battle of Montecatini, 1315. One cycle of sonnets written for the *brigata spendereccia* (*see* " Inferno," xxix. 130), or some similar society, expatiates on the joys of each month in succession; the other on those of the several days of the week. Parodies of these sonnets were written by **Cene dalla Chitarra**. Folgore will give his friends in the month of January pleasant rooms with fire, warm beds and clothing, and sugar plums to eat, and all that can soften the rigours of winter and defy its storms. Cene has only smoky fires, hammock beds, winds, poverty, and hunger to bequeath, and so on, with amusing contrast throughout the months. *Ed.*, G. Navone, 1888. *See* d'Ancona, " Studi de Critica," 1880.

19 Religious and Didactic Poetry of the North of Italy.

See Bartsch, " Stor. Litt. Ital.," i. ii.

Many poems in dialect, belonging to the North of Italy, are extant dating from the 13th century. These are mostly

of a religious or didactic character. Among the oldest
remains are some *Laudi*, a *Decalogo* (a rhymed Decalogue) in
the dialect of Bergamo, and a *Salve Regina* from the same
region.

The following poets have left longer works :—

Gherardo Patecchio of Cremona (Gerardus Patecclus, in Salimbene).

The only meagre notices of this poet are to be found in
Salimbene's "Cronaca" (Vat. 7260). A signature of his,
found in an old document (*see* "Giorn. Storico lett. Ital.," xxi.)
is proof of his having flourished at the beginning of the 13th
century ; he was a contemporary of Salimbene, who records
the incident of a joke played on the poet by the uncle of the
chronicler. Salimbene mentions a work of his as *liber
taediorum* or *de taediis* which is now lost, but from which
he gives a few extracts. "It was probably similar to the
Provençal *enueg*, in which class of poem the author enumerated
all the things that were disagreeable to him." Patecchio's
other didactic work was an explanation of the Proverbs of
Solomon.

Lo Splanamento dei Proverbi di Salomone, in the vulgar tongue
(*e'n volgar lo vol metre*), and they taught :

> " Com a le done coven boni costumi aver,
>   Com un amig a l'autro dé andar dretamente
>   E con povri e riqi dé star entre la çente."

Ed., A. Tobler, "Abhandl. Akad. Wiss.," Berlin, 1886 ;
E. Monaci, "Crest. Ital.," p. 101.   *MSS.*, Berlin, 390 ;
Bodleian, Can. Ital., 48.

Uguccione da Lodi (Uguçon da Laodho).

This poet appears to have turned penitent in later life,
having previously been a man of arms. His work, probably
compiled about the middle of the century, is also a *Splanamento*, dealing with the doctrines of Christianity, Heaven and

Hell, Coming of Antichrist, etc. It displays no particular originality, and is not well compiled, but is not without a certain realistic power. *Ed.*, A. Tobler, "Abhandl. Akad. Wiss.," Berlin, 1884; E. Monaci, "Crest Ital.," p. 110. *MS.*, Berlin, 390.

Pietro da Barsegapè (or Bascapè) of Milan.

Sermone, being the spiritual history of man from the Fall to the Day of Judgment. "A christian epic, interrupted at intervals by moral reflexions." The language is simple and direct. *Ed.*, B. Biondelli, "Poesie Lombarde inedite, etc.," 1856. E. Keller, 1901. *MS.*, Milan, Bibl. Naz.

Giacomino da Verona, fl. second half of 13th century.

A Franciscan monk, known only by his name, which is found at the close of his two works, poems which foreran a greater work in their description of the future state, described with some rough humour on the one hand for the sinner, on the other more pleasingly for the saint, according to the ideas and beliefs of the Middle Ages. *Ed.*, Ozanam, "Documents inédits pour servir à l'histoire littéraire de l'Italie," 1850. *MSS.*, S. Mark, Ital., xiii.; Udine, Archepis, i. 2° xiii. i. 26; Seville, Colombina, 7, i. 52; Copy, Bodl. Canon, xlviii.

Some other religious poems contained in the Venetian MS. have been assigned to G. da Verona; *see*, however, Gröber ("Grundrisz Phil. Roman," 2, iii. p. 33 note) who considers them merely poems of the same family.

Bonvesin da Riva, of Milan.

A will left by this poet, which has been published, shows that he was alive in 1313. His poems were, it is thought, probably written when a younger man, as they are characterised by the thought and style of an earlier period of literature, but he was more cultured than G. da Verona, and his poems are varied and interesting.

Dialogue between Satan and Mary,
On almsgiving,

On the Last Judgment (De die Judich),
On Behaviour at Table (De Quinquaginta curialitatibus ad
mensam),
Sorrows of Job (De Passione S. Job),
Life of S. Alexius,
Dialogue between Body and Soul,
The Rose and the Violet (Disputatio Rosae cum viola),
The Ant and the Fly (Disputatio muscae cum formica),
Laudes de Virgine Maria,
A Dialogue between Father and Son in Hell,
The Months (i dodici Mesi),

and other tales of saints. The didactic purpose of the poet is
most grimly carried out in the dialogue between father and son.
It has inspired a more interesting poem in that between the
Virgin and Satan. Satan's arguments, which the poet answers
to his own satisfaction through the mouth of the Virgin, touch
on highly interesting and difficult problems: Should not Mary
owe him her good services, since it was his sin that brought
the Saviour to earth, and so through him she has become the
mother of the Creator? Is it not unjust of God to punish him
for a single sin, when He was ready to give His Son for many
who had more grievously offended? And had he been made
incapable of sinning he would not have fallen. "On behaviour
at Table" gives a good insight into the manners of the time.
Some Latin works were also written by this poet, namely, a
Chronicle, a Treatise, partly in verse, on the "Vita Scolastica,"
and others. *Ed.*, T. Bekker, "Berlin Berichte Akad d.
Wissenschaft," 1850, 1851. *MSS.*, Berlin, Ital., 26;
Milan, Ambrosiana, T. 10.

20   EARLY PROSE WRITINGS.

A register of household expenses, written down by
Matasala di Spinello, of the Sienese family of the
Lambertine (*see* "Arch. Stor. Ital.," vol. v. 23), some
letters of a commercial or other character, are interesting as
extant specimens of dialect in the 13th century, but cannot be
classed under the heading of literature. The letters of

Guittone d'Arezzo are the earliest surviving monument of literary prose. All official correspondence continued during this period to be written in Latin (*see* letters by Pietro della Vigna, § 12). Translations from the French and Latin preceded original work in Italian prose.

Works from the French.

Dodici Conti Morali, by an anonymous writer of Siena. These twelve tales are didactic in character, each ending with a moral, being stories taken from the "Vie des Anciens Pères," and other French religious sources. Corresponding tales are to be found in French fableaux (*see* Bartoli, "Stor. Lett. Ital.," vol. iii.) *Ed.*, F. Zambrini, 1862. *MSS.*, Bologna, Libr. S. Salvatore, 395.

Fatti di Cesare. Two Italian versions of the *Faits des Romains* (*see* France, § 41), in which ancient history is transformed into a mediæval romance. The Italian versions date from late 13th or early 14th century: one MS. (2418) is dated 1313. *Ed.*, L. Banchi (from Sienese MS.), 1863. *See* G. Parodi, "Studi di Fil. Roman," 1889, 322 ff. *MSS.*, Siena, Bibl. Comunale, i. vii. 6; Riccardiana, 1538, 2418.

Istorietta Troiana. The Trojan legend was represented in Italy both in prose and verse. The earliest work in connection with it was the Latin prose of Guido delle Colonne. (Whether identical with the poet who has left six canzones is a question which remains undecided: he was still alive in 1287, as we have from his own words, and this date does not coincide with what is generally thought to be the period during which the early Sicilian school was flourishing.) The Italian version named above was founded on the French of Benoît de S. More, in some parts reproducing pretty closely the original, in others condensing, differing in arrangement, or omitting. *Ed.*, E. Gorra, "Storia Troiana," with introductory study of the Trojan legend in Italy, 1887. *See* G. di Marzo, "Storia di Troia," 1863. *MSS.*, Laurenz. Gadd. lxxi.; Magliabechiano, ii. iv. 4, 9. (*See Fiore de Italia*, § 32.)

N.B.—The legends of Troy reappear in the "Tesoro," "Conti di Antichi Cavalieri," "Novellino," and in the histories of Villani and Malespini. Poetic versions: "The Romance of Eltore" ("Roman d'Hector" or "Roman d'Hercules," *see* Franco-Ital. Poetry, § 8); section of "Intelligenza"; and the "Il Filostrato" of Boccaccio.

The legends in connection with the Arthurian cycle were also popularised in two works:

Tristano.　　*Ed.*, E. G. Parodi, 1896.　　*MSS.*, Riccardiano, 2543, 1729; Panciatichiano, 33.

Tavola Ritonda, or *l'istoria di Tristano,* which tells the tale of "missere Tristano e di missere Lancilotto e di molte altri cavalieri." Written about the same time as the compilation in French of Rusticien de Pise.　　*Ed.*, L. Polidori, 1864. *MSS.*, Three chief MSS., Mediceo-Laurenz. Plut., xliv. 27. Magliabech. Strozz. 68. Siena, Bibl. Comun.

Bono Giamboni. (§§ 21, 23.)

Translation of B. Latini's *Tresor.* There are numerous MSS. of the Italian version which is generally ascribed to this author.　　*Ed.*, L. Gaiter, 1878–82. First printed ed., 1474.

There were also Italian translations of Seven Sages ("Libro dei Setti Savi,") of the *Disciplina Clericale,* and of Egidio Romano's *De Regimine Principum* (§ 9), from French texts.

21　　WORKS FROM THE LATIN.

The name of **Bono Giambone** (*see* Original Prose) has come down to us as one of the chief translators of this period. To him belong the Italian versions of Orosius, and of Vegetius, "Art of War," and possibly of Innocent III.'s *De Contemptu Mundi* ("Miseria dell uomo"), and of the *Viridarium Consolationes* ("Giardino di Consolazione").

The treatises of Albertano da Brescia (§ 4) were translated

into Italian in 1268 by **Andrea da Grosseto**, and shortly after by **Soffredi del Grazia**; and Cicero, Sallust, and Titus Livius, by **B. Latini**. Cato's *Disticha* and Aesop's *Fables* were among other works put into Italian.

Among the earliest of the translations was the—

Storie de Troia et de Roma. "The oldest compilation of ancient history in Italian." It apparently dates from 1252–58, when Brancaleone degli Andalo was Senator of Rome. Many of the *Conti di Antiche Cavalieri* were taken from this work. Monaci, "Crestomazia," 118. *MSS.*, Laurenz. Gadd. rel. 148. Amburgo, Libr. Civica. Latin text: Laurenz. Strozz. 85.

22   Original Prose.

Guittone d'Arezzo.   (§ 16.)

Letters. In the MS. quoted are preserved twenty-two letters in prose and eight in verse. As previously stated his letters may be considered the earliest specimens of Italian literary prose. The letters are addressed to brothers and sisters of his order, and to other friends; they are mainly exhortations to righteousness of life, similar in subject to many of his later poems. His letter to the Florentines after the battle of Monteaperti, when he also addressed them in verse, is, however, an exception. *Ed.*, Bottari, 1745; F. Torraca and M. Menghini (lately published). *MSS.*, Laurenz. Rediano, 9.

N.B.—Other letters dating from this century have been edited by Piccolomini, 1871.

23   *Didactic.*

Frate Guidotto of Bologna.

Fiore de retorica, or *Retorica Nova*. Written 1254–1266, and dedicated to King Manfred. The work is derived from the "Rhetorica Ad Herennium," formerly ascribed to Cicero,

and was intended for the instruction of the laity. It under-
went considerable alterations in course of time, and in one
MS. (Riccard. 2338) is ascribed to Bono Giamboni. *Ed.*,
Monaci, "Crestomazia," 154 (extracts from Bibl. Naz., II.
iv. 127). *See* A. Gazzani, 1885. *MSS.*, Florence, Bibl.
Riccardiana, five MSS. and a fragment; Bibl. Naz., two
MSS.; S. Marco, one MS.

Collections of sayings, "flowers of wisdom," selected from
favourite authors, were known as "Fiore."

Anonymous Writer of Pisa, 1260–1290.

Fiore e vita di filosofi ed altri savi ed imperadori. These
tales of philosophers and other wise men and emperors are
taken nearly word for word from the "Speculum Historiale"
of Vincent de Beauvais. The editor gives the Latin and
Italian text side by side. Several tales in the *Novellino*
he traces to the *Fiore*, and he also treats of the connection
of Dante with this work. *Ed.*, H. Varnhagen, 1893.
MSS., Several MSS., Florence, Bibl. Laurenz. 2; Bibl.
Naz. Magliabech. 2; Palatino, E. 5, 6, 13; Modena, Cod.
Estense, vii. B. 8.

Ristoro d'Arezzo.

Della Composizione del Mondo, 1282. A popular work,
dealing with scientific subjects, according to the knowledge
of the day. *Ed.*, Narducci, 1864. *MSS.*, Riccardiana,
2164, possibly autograph; Chigiana.

Tommaso Gazzadini.

Fiore di Virtù (*Flor de Vertù*), second half of 13th century. This work consists of a prologue, of sayings of philosophers on different kinds of love, and on various vices and
virtues, exemplified by narratives taken from Old Testament,
Roman History, the Fathers, etc., and by anecdotes of birds
and beasts. It retained its popularity for centuries; a Tuscan
version of the 14th century is extant. *Ed.*, G. Ulrich,
1890, from Laurenz. Gadd. 115, and in 1895 from MSS,

at Vicenza, Siena, Modena, Florence and Venice.   *See* C.
Frati, "Studi di fil. rom.," vi.   *MSS.*, Numerous MSS.
at Florence (Riccardiana, Laurenziana, Magliabechiana,
Laurenz - Gaddiano, Laurenz - Rediano, Rome, Venice,
Siena, etc.

Bono Giamboni.   (§§ 20, 21.)

Introduzione alle virtù.   The author finding himself, like
Job, brought to low estate, bemoans his condition, but subsequently finds consolation in philosophy.   He sees the victory
of Virtue over Vice, and he listens to the admonitions of
Prudence, Justice, Temperance, etc.   *Ed.*, Rosini, 1800;
Tassi, 1836.   *MSS.*, Venice, S. Mark; Florence, Riccardiana.

N.B.—Research as to the origin of the *Bible* in Italian
has lead to no exact result, but it is thought that a "collective
work of the middle 13th century was the source of most of
the extant versions."   The two earliest printed versions date
from 1471.   *See* Berger, "Romania," xxiii. 358 ff., full
bibliography; G. Mazzoni, "Esercitazione sulla Lett. Rel.
nei sec. xiii. e xiv.," 1905.

24   *Historical.*

Cronichetta Pisana (1005–1276).   This is the oldest Italian
chronicle, which authorities now date back to this early period.
The *Diurnale* of Matteo Spinello is no longer considered
a genuine document, and Malespini's Chronicle, at one time
thought to be the source whence Villani drew, is now proved
on the contrary to be a copy of the latter's work.   *Ed.*,
E. Piccolomini, 1877.   *MSS.*, Library of Pisan Merchant.

Cronichetta Lucchese.   Two versions of this chronicle are
extant, one of them carried to 1260.   *Ed.*, S. Bongi, 1892.

Cronaca Fiorentina.   A chronicle of the closing years of
the 13th century.   It comprises the oldest and most complete
list extant of Florentine Consuls and Podestà, from 1180.

The work has been wrongly attributed to B. Latini. *Ed.*,
P. Villari, "I primi due secoli della storia di Firenze," 1894;
Eng. Trans., L. Villari. *MSS.*, Magliabech. Strozzi.
(autograph); Gaddiano, 15th century.

Domenico Aldobrandino.

La Sconfitta di Montaperto. Only known in MS. of the
15th century. The author was surnamed Ghinuccio, but it
is uncertain whether D. Aldobrandino or Stefano Ghinuccio
wrote the chronicle. *Ed.*, G. Porri, 1844, from MS. in
possession, collated with two others at Siena, Bibl. Comun.,
1. 1. 2, and 2. 1. 2; the former ends 1358, the two latter
1478.

Another prose account of this battle, so disastrous to the
Guelphs, "Che fece l'Arbia colorata in rosso" ("Inf.,"
x. 86), is edited by A. Ceruti ("Il Propugnatore," vi. 27)
from a MS. in the Ambrosiana, a copy of an older one.

25   Novelle.

Conti di Antichi Cavalieri. A collection of twenty short
tales or anecdotes, by an anonymous Tuscan writer, of the
second half of the 13th century. The tales are taken from
ancient and mediæval history and legend. As far as the
sources of the tales have been traced, these are French
or Latin; one, *Conto del re Tebaldo*, is taken from the
French *Foulque de Candie* (*see* Bartoli, "Lett. Ital.,"
vol. iii. p. 77). Some of the tales are found again in the
"Novellino," *i.e.* legends of Saladin and the youthful King,
son of Henry ii. of England, referred to by English chroniclers. *Ed.*, P. Papa, "Giorn. Stor. Lett. Ital.," vol. iii.
p. 192 ff.; P. Fanfari, 1851 (from Cod. in Casa Martelli).
See also "Giorn. Stor.," viii. 487. *See* Bartoli, *op. cit.*, vol.
iii. cap. iv. *MSS.*, Bibl. Casa Martelli; Florence, Bibl.
Naz., II. iv. 196.

Il Novellino, or *Le ciento novelle antike.* Probably dating from
second half or close of century. These stories cover a wide

field of legend, in which we are transported to such different periods of the world's history as are represented by Solomon and Saladin, Alexander and Tristan, Seneca and Frederick II., etc. In some cases the tales are told briefly, with little colouring; in others there is a considerable amount of detail, and "in them are traceable the beginnings of the art of story-telling, which flourished in the 14th century." Many of the tales are known in other versions; those dealing with personages of Italian origin are thought probably to be from oral tradition. The compiler states that he wishes to bring together "alquanti fiori di parlare, di belle cortesie, e di belli risposi e di belle valentie, di belli donari e di belli amori, secondo che per lo tempo passato hanno fatto già molti." The writer, judging from the language, is thought to have been a Florentine. It has been suggested that the tales are the work of more than one author (*see* Bartoli, "Stor. Lett.," cap. x.). *Ed.*, G. Biagi, 1880. *See* d'Ancona, "Studii di Critica," 1880. Bartoli, "I primi due etc.," 288 ff. Earliest printed text, C. Gualteruzzi, 1525. The MSS., eight altogether, are, with the exception of the Panciatichiano, more or less in correspondence with the G. text. Vat. 3214 (Gualteruzzi text); Florence, Panciatichiano-Palat. 138; Laurenz. Gadd. 193; Palat. (2); Magliabech. (2); Venice, Marc. (1).

26   POETRY.

Didactic.

Ser Brunetto Latini, b. cir. 1220; d. 1294–5. (*See* § 9; France, 13th century, § 37.)

Tesoretto. In this poem, sometimes called by the author "Tesoro," to distinguish it from the "Gran Tesoro," to which it is a key, we have an early specimen of the allegorical-didactic verse which was so highly developed in the 14th century. It is written in rhyming couplets of seven syllables, interspersed with prose, and is incomplete. The poet, after his return from his unsuccessful embassy to Alfonso of Castile, wanders full of grief at hearing of the exile of his fellow-Guelphs, meets a matron personifying Nature; there follows a long dialogue on matters spiritual and material, and he then goes into a wood in search of philosophy. He then comes across Virtue and her four royal daughters, and from her realm passes to that of Love. After a period of penitence and sermonising, he finally reaches the summit of Olympus, where he meets the astronomer, Tolomeo; and here the poem breaks off. Prose is introduced where the author felt it a better mode of expression—

> "Quando vorrò trattare
> Di cose, che rimare
> Tenesse oscuritate,
> Con bella brevitate
> Ti parlerò per prosa,
> E disporrò la cosa
> Parlandoti in volgare
> Che tu intende e appare."

Ed., L. Gaiter, 1878–82. *See* "Giorn. Stor. Lett. Ital.," iv. (article by Th. Cart). *MSS.*, Brescia, Bibl. Quiriniana, A. vii. 11; Florence, Riccard., 2908; Laurenz. Pl. (3); Laurenz. Strozzi. 146; Bibl. Naz. (2); Rome, Chigi. L. v. 166; L. vii. 249; Venice, Marc. C. ii. 7; Vatican, 3220, and others.

N.B.—The title of Ser denotes the profession of notary.

Allegorical poetry, of which Latini's "Tesoretto" was the earliest specimen, flourished during this period, more especially in Tuscany. The "Roman de la Rose" exercised as great an influence in Italy as elsewhere, and the earliest Italian imitation of it was a poem, of which part only remains, called

Detto d'Amore, written in seven-syllabled, rhyming couplets, or rather couplets ending with the same word (parli, parli, detto, detto, etc.), in praise of Love, the first part only of the "R. de R." serving as model. *Ed.*, S. Morpurgo, "Propugnatore," N.S., I. i. 18. *MS.*, Laurenz., Ashburnham, 1234.

The author of another version of the "R. de R." is uncertain; a Ser Durante is named in the course of the work, who probably lived at the close of 13th and beginning of 14th century. The work is known as

Fiore, a paraphrase of both parts of the "R. de R.," composed of two hundred and thirty-two sonnets. *Ed.*, G. Mazzatinti, "Invent. MSS. Ital. di Francia," iii. 611–730. *MS.*, Montpellier, H. 438.

Another anonymous work was

Intelligenza, about which there has been considerable controversy, the possible author and the date varying according to different authorities. It has been assigned both to Dino Compagni and to some Arabian writer. It is written in strophes of nine lines, and begins with a description of spring; the donna of the poet is Intelligenza, whose palace is decorated with paintings illustrating the tales of Caesar, Alexander, Troy, and Arthur, while the jewels in her crown give rise to a succession of strophes on various precious stones. "It is a work of the Middle Ages, and like others of its class exercised no influence on literature beyond the age in which it arose, and during which it held a high rank." It opens with some pleasing lines on spring.

First strophe—

> " Al novel tempo e gaio del pascore
> Che fa le verdi foglie e fior venire,
> Quando li augelli fan versi d'amore
> E l'aria fresca comincia a schiarire
> Le pratora son piene di verdore
> E li verzer cominciano ad aulire;
> Quando son dilettose le fiumane,
> È son chiare surgenti le fontane,
> E la gente comincia a risbaldire."

Ed., P. Gellrich, 1883. *MSS.*, Bibl. Naz. Magliabech. vii. 1035 (only complete copy); Medicea. Laurenz. Gadd. 71.

Francesco da Barberino. Notary of Florence; a

voluntary exile for some years on account of his political opinions; b. 1264; died of the plague, 1348.

Documenti d'amore. In this the poet gives instruction on behaviour at table, suitable conversation, etc., to which he is urged by Love, who dictates to Eloquence, and Eloquence to the twelve handmaids of Love—Docility, Industry, Constancy, etc. *Ed.,* A copy of ed. of 1640, pub. 1846. *MS.,* Barberino, xlvi. 18 (with miniatures).

Del Reggimento e costumi di donna. Finished, 1318–20. Here again certain personified virtues instruct woman, at all ages, and of all classes, married, widowed, or single, as to their duties and behaviour. Among other things he discusses whether it is good for them to learn to read and write. *Ed.,* C. Baudi di Vesme, 1875; Life, by Filippo Villani, "De origine civitatis Florentiae, et ejusdem famosis civibus." *MS.,* Barberino, xlv. 95 (copy in Vatican).

These didactic works are chiefly of interest from the pictures of social life which they afford.

27 Dante Alighieri, b. 1265; d. 1321. Dante was born of a noble family in Florence; of his parents but little is known, and only meagre details are extant concerning the early years of the poet himself. We gather, from his own words, that he was fond of drawing and singing, that he studied Latin and Provençal poets, and that he numbered some of the chief poets of the day among his friends, as also Giotto the painter. The circumstances connected with his love for Beatrice are not entirely known to us; he saw her first as a child, and again nine years later; not long after this latter meeting she was married to Simone de' Bardi, and died while still young in 1290, at which time Dante was twenty-five years of age. Some few years later he himself was married to Gemma Donati.

As regards his more active life, he served his native city both as a soldier and a statesman: he took part in the battle of Campaldino in 1289, and possibly in the siege of Caprona, and later, having become engaged in political affairs, he was, in 1300, elected one of the Priorate. It was during this term of office that Dante seconded the motion for the banishment of the chief members of the two hostile factions in Florence, whereby he was forced to consent to the exiling of his friend Cavalcanti. When, in 1302, the Neri were again in power, Dante was included among the Bianchi who were banished as a body from Florence, and was further accused of malpractices and condemned to pay a heavy fine or to the confiscation of his property. A yet harsher decree condemned him to be burnt alive, should he come at any time within reach of the power of the Commune.

The remainder of Dante's life was spent in exile; the hopes in which he indulged when the Emperor Henry VII. made his descent into Italy were doomed to bitter disappointment; this second Moses, who was to accomplish the deliverance of Italy, died with his task unfulfilled; and Dante who had endeavoured to assist his cause by addressing letters of exhortation to the princes and peoples of Italy, and equally fiery invectives against the Florentines, left a final record of his partisanship by placing his " Alto Arrigo " in the Empyrean (Par. Cant. xxx.), and the Popes Boniface and Clement in the " Inferno." In 1316 he was given the opportunity of returning to Florence, under certain conditions, but he refused to submit to the ignominy of the proposed terms.

His great work, in which he uttered the bitter cry of his exile, and that bitter exile itself, were ended in Ravenna, where, in September of 1321, he died at the age of fifty-seven, and where he was also buried. Florence commemorates the greatest of her citizens by a cenotaph in Santa Croce. Dante's earliest biographers were Boccaccio, Filippo Villani, and Leonardo Bruni. (For Biographies, see under E. Moore, P. H. Wicksteed, A. Butler, E. G. Gardner.) Trans. into Eng., " Earliest Lives of Dante " (Boccaccio and L. Bruni), J. R. Smith, " Yale Studies in English," 1898; Wicksteed, 1904; G. R. Carpenter (Boccaccio's), 1900.

Works: Italian.

N.B.—The exact chronology of Dante's works is undetermined.

Vita Nuova. Dedicated to Guido Cavalcanti; cir. 1294, or 1295; or 1294–1300. This work, consisting of twenty-five sonnets, four canzoni, a ballata, and one stanza, with intermediate prose, gives the history of Dante's love for Beatrice from his first meeting with her in 1274 to the time, when having for a while, with the idea of consoling himself for her death, transferred his allegiance to another woman, he returns to his first love, and to the worship of that spiritualised being about whom he hopes, according to his final words to say,—"quello che non fu detto d'alcuna." In the first part it is the physical beauty of Beatrice he describes; in the second, her intellectual beauty; in the third, her death; in the fourth, his love for a 'donna gentile'; and the fifth, the struggle between the new love and the remembrance of the old, and the triumph of the latter. The prose is the first artistic specimen of the kind in Italian literature. *Ed.*, Witte, 1876; Giuliani, 1883; with "Canzoniere," 1885; T. Casini, 1885, 1891. First printed as a whole, 1576.

Convivio, or *Convito*. Written in exile, 1308–1310, or perhaps somewhat earlier. A treatise, comprising prose commentaries on his allegorical and philosophical poems. It was to have consisted of fifteen parts, but only four of these were finished. The first part is an introduction and exposition of the aim of the work, in which he defends his use of the vernacular. Each of the other parts deals respectively with a single canzone, which he explains verbally and allegorically. First printed ed. 1490.

Divina Commedia :

    Inferno,   34 cantos.
    Purgatorio, 33   „
    Paradiso,   33   „

The visionary journey through these regions took place in 1300; Dante ascended from the terrestrial paradise to the highest heaven at the vernal Equinox, having passed twenty-four to twenty-five hours in the Inferno, and four to five days in Purgatory (Tozer). (*See* below for Editions, etc.)

Canzoniere, (Sonetti, Canzoni, Ballate, and Sestine). A collection of poems dating from 1283, among which are love songs, philosophical poems, and others of various kinds; some of the latter being addressed to Guido Cavalcanti ("Guido, vorrei che tu e Lapo ed io, etc.") to Cino da Pistoia, and Forese Donati. Chief MS., Rome, Chigi., lviii. 305.

Editions of minor works: Soc. Dant. Ital., 1896, etc.; A Torri, Fraticelli, Giuliani, Passerini.

WORKS: LATIN.[1]

De Vulgari Eloquentia. Written wholly or in part cir. 1305; thought by some authorities to be finished at a later date. *Ed.*, Prof. Rajna, 1896, 1897.

De Monarchia. Authorities differ as to date, which remains uncertain. *Ed.*, C. Witte, 1874.

Eclogæ. Two addressed to Giovanni del Virgilio. *Ed.*, J. E. G. Gardner and P. H. Wicksteed, 1902.

Epistolæ. Letters to the princes and people of Italy on the arrival of Henry vii., and to the "scelleratissime fiorentine"; to Henry vii., to Can Grande, and to a Florentine friend. These five letters are authentic. *Ed.*, Torri, 1842.

Edition of Latin works: G. B. Giuliani, 1878–82; Eng. trans., H. P. Wicksteed, "Temple Classics," 1904.

Bibliographies and Manuscripts:

Bibliografia Dantesca (Soc. Dant. Ital.), 1892; Dante e i codici Danteschi, etc.; Scartazzini, "Zur Dante Bibliographie, etc.," 1871; S. W. Koch, Cornell Dante Collection, 1900; Dante Colls. at Harvard and Boston Libraries, 1890; G. Acquaticci, Cat. of Coll., 1900; Zambrini, "Opere volgari a stampa dei secoli xiii. e xiv.," 1884; and other works on the MSS. of different libraries.

[1] A Latin work, *Quaestio de Aqua et Terra*, published in 1508, and stated to be a lecture given by Dante in 1320, has been generally looked upon as a forgery, but its possible genuineness has been supported by Dr. Moore ("Studies, etc.") Eng. trans. is given by Wicksteed (Latin Works), "Temple Classics."

MSS., "Commedia" (500 to 600 in number). MSS. in England, collated by E. Moore: Bodleian, Canon. Ital., several; Camb. Univ. Libr. (3); Sudbury Hall (Lord Vernon); Eton Coll. Libr.; Glasgow, Hunter; Ashburnham (several); Hockham Hall; Phillipps; Oxford, Taylor Inst.; St. Edmund Hall (Principal); B.M., MS. from Thenford House; Egerton, Harl., Lansdowne, Add.; one in possession of Dr. Moore himself. *See* E. Moore, "Contributions to the textual criticism of the D. C.," 1889.

Editions, "Commedia," First three eds., 1472; fourth, 1477 (Naples); reprinted, Lord Vernon and Panizzi, 1858; Venice, 1477; Florence, 1481.

Works. E. Moore, "The Oxford Dante," 1894, 1897, 1904.
Commedia. Moore, 1900, 1902; A. J. Butler, 1885, 1890; G. A. Scartazzini, 1874-1890 (Leipzig Commentary), 1896, 1899, 1900, 1903; *ibid.*, smaller ed., 1893; Casini, 1895, 1903; Ricci, 1896; "Il testo Wittiano," *ed.*, Paget Toynbee, 1900.

English Trans. (*Commedia*). Longfellow; Cary, 1874, etc.; Reissued, P. Toynbee, 1900; Popular ed., 1903; Ed. with Rossetti's "New Life," 1897 (N. Y.); C. E. Norton, 1891, 1892, 1902; *Prose trans.*, H. F. Tozer, 1904; *Prose trans.* (*and Ital. text*), Carlyle, Okey, Wicksteed, *ed.*, Oelsner, "Temple Classics," 1899-1901; A. J. Butler (*with Ital. text*), "Purgatory," 1880; "Paradise," 1885; "Inferno," 1892.

Trans. (*Minor works*), "Vita Nuova," D. G. Rossetti, 1861, etc.; C. E. Norton, 1893; "Convivio," K. Hillard, 1889; P. H. Wicksteed, "Temple Classics," 1903; "De Monarchia," F. J. Church, 1878; P. H. Wicksteed, 1896; "Letters," C. S. Latham, 1891; "Canzoniere," C. Lyell, 1845; D. G. Rossetti (*see* page 418); "Canzoniere and Eclogues," Plumptre, 1892; "De Vulgari Eloquentia," A. G. F. Howell, 1890.

For works in connection with Dante and his works, *see*

under Witte ("Dante-Forschungen"); E. Moore, Paget
Toynbee ("Dictionary of Proper Names and Notable Matters in
the Works of Dante," etc.), Church, M. F. Rossetti, J. A.
Symonds, Wicksteed, W. Vernon, E. Gardner (among other
works a useful primer), H. F. Tozer (commentary). (*See*
also under Bibliographies.)

Among the earliest commentators of the "Commedia"
were Graziolo Bambagliuoli and Jacopo Alighieri, Dante's
son; the former wrote in Latin on the "Inferno," the latter
in Italian, but only on the first canto. Before the century
had closed many other commentators had contributed Latin
or Italian works, among them being Giovanni Boccaccio,
who gave lectures on Dante, which he afterwards published,
and in which the literal and the allegorical sense were
separately explained: his commentary did not extend beyond
the 17th canto of the "Inferno." For the Latin commentary of Benvenuto da Imola, *see* P. Toynbee, "Eng. Miscell."
(Furnivall), 1901.

28 The didactic writers who succeeded Dante did not
take him as their model, but carried on the traditions
of the older style. Among these were—

Bindo Bonichi of Siena, b. 1260; d. 1338, who wrote
sonetti and canzoni chiefly of an allegorical and didactic
character; only one love sonnet has come down to us
"Amor, perchè m'hai tu lasciato vivo." He is occasionally
humorous and satirical. *Ed.*, P. Bilancioni, 1867. *See*
also G. Carducci, "Rime di Cino da Pistoia ed. altri,"
1862; L. Sanesi, "Giorn. Stor. Lett. Ital.," xviii.
MSS., Many MSS., Florence: Laurenziana, Magliabechiana,
Riccardiana; Bodl. Can. Ital. 263, 57; Paris, Vatican, Chisi,
Siena.

Graziolo Bambagliuoli (*see* above) of Bologna who
flourished in the first half of the 14th century.

Trattato delle volgari sentenze sopra le virtù morali. This
treatise was at one time wrongly ascribed to Robert of Anjou,

King of Jerusalem. The strophes of this work, each versifying a proverb, are of different lengths. The following one, " Who gives quickly gives twice," is a specimen :

> " Lo presto e'l bel piacer raddoppia il bene,
> E dal tardar avviene
> Che renda il dono amaro
> E mostra il suo fattor vile et avaro."

A Latin commentary was added by the author. *Ed.*, C. Cavedoni, 1821, 1865. *See* also L. Frati, "Giorn. Stor. Lett. Ital.," xvii. 367; G. Carducci, "Rime di Cino da Pistoia ed. altri."

Francesco degli Stabili (Cecco d'Ascoli), born in 1269, was a notable figure of this century ; he had relations with Dante and Petrarch, and was himself a man of advanced views and liberty of thought ; he looked upon doubt as the foundation of science, and considered the penalty of death for so-called heretics, unjust ; unfortunately the Inquisitioners did not agree with him, and Cecco was burnt alive for his heretical views in 1327.

Acerba. This work, of which the meaning of the title remains obscure, " is not a mere compilation, on a par with the ' Tesoretto,' ' Intelligenza,' and similar works, but an original disquisition on matters which the poet himself had studied." The four books deal in turn with cosmography, moral philosophy, animals and stones, love and virtue ; and other various subjects. The work is rhymed a b a, c d c, etc.

> " Oh bel paese co li dolci colli !
> Perchè no'l conoscete, o genta acerba,
> Con gli atti avari invidiosi e folli ?
> Io te pur plango, dolce mio paese ;
> Chè non so chi nel mondo ti conserba
> Facendo contro Dio cotante offese."

Cecco, in more than one place, expresses contempt for Dante's "Commedia." *Ed.*, G. Castelli, "La vita e le opera di Cecco d'Ascoli," 1892. *MSS.*, Florence: Mediceo. Laurenz. Strozziana; Bologna: Universitaria; Lucca: Governativa; Milan: Trivulziana, Ambrosiana; Modena: Estense; Rome: Vatican, Casanatense; Paris: Bibl. Nat.; Montpellier, Padua, Parma, Ravenna; B.M. Add. 21163, 10320; Harl. 3577.

Jacopo Alighieri (*see* Commentaries on Dante). Jacopo followed his father into exile, but finally returned to his native town, and died probably in 1348.

Dottrinale. A popular encyclopædia of science. Written in rhyming couplets of seven-syllabled lines, six of which form a strophe, and ten strophes a chapter. *Ed.*, Crocione, 1895. *MSS.*, Palatino, 225; Riccardiano, 2169.

Stoppa di Bostichi. A Monk of Florence, who writes as if living in the first half of the century, but in his verses, which attack political affairs, he refers apparently to later events. He addresses the various reigning monarchs of Europe in terms of reproach, not omitting Edward of England.

> " Or, Odoardo re dell' Inghiterra,
> Che per ragion dimandi il gran reame.
> E vuoi pigliarlo per forza di guerra,
> Pere' hai d'aver grandezza una gran fame.
> Con intenzion di far alcuna terra
> Rimaner molte genti triste e grame :
> Cosi suggelli con reame doppio
> E fai ogn'inimico pien di loppio."

Ed., Carducci, " Rime di C. da P.," *op. cit.*

29   *Religious.*

A considerable number of *Laude* belong to this period, originating in various districts of Italy. For Laude, *see* Monaci, " Riv. Fil. Rom.," i.; ii. ; G. Mazzoni, " Laudi Cortonesi," " Propugnatore," N.S. ii., iii. ; G. Mazzatinti,

"Poesie Religiosi del Secolo xiv." (from MS. Eugubino), 1881.

In this latter work is a long dramatic poem on the Passion, in octosyllabic couplets. It appears that it is still the custom among the Umbrian peasantry, on Good Friday evening, for the head of the family to recite the narrative portion, the others of the household taking part when the dialogue occurs : the work recited is similar to the poem here given. Another poem is a "Contrasto" between the Virgin and the Cross, and a third a sonnet in Umbrian dialect, *Memoriale de la Morte.*

30   *Historical.*

I reali di Napoli nella rotta di Montecatini. A ballata, written about 1315, in which the widow of Charles II. of Anjou asks news of her son from one who has returned from the battle. It begins—

> " Deh avrestè veduto Messer Piero
> Poi che fu'l nostro campo sbarattato ?
> Tuo viso mostra pur che vi sie stato."

Ed., Carducci, " Rime di C. da P.," *op. cit.*   *MS.*, Laurenz. Gadd. 193.

A similar Ballata was on the death of Andrew of Hungary who, when as yet not nineteen years old, was strangled in 1345 by his wife Jeanne, the successor to the throne of Robert, King of Naples. The poem was written in 1347. It begins—

> " Come'l sangue d'Abello
> Gridò vendetta isparto da Caino
> Così ciascuno latino
> Pianga la morte del buo're novello."

Ed., A. Medin, " Propugnatore," N.S. i.   *MS.*, Riccardiana, 2786.

La Resa di Treviso e la Morte di Cangrande della Scala.

A Ghibelline poem by an anonymous author. It relates the surrender of Treviso to Can Grande, his illness and death in 1329, with lamentation over it. "It is a 'cantare' full of energy and breathing the spirit of the time," distinguished by its metrical form, strophes of six lines, of which one, two, three, five, are endecasyllabic, and four and six seven-syllabled. *Ed.*, A. Medin, 1884. *See* S. Morpurgo, "Rivista Critica," iv.

A fragment of a *Serventese* of the 14th century deals with the same subject. *See*, for other similar poems, "Lamenti Storici del Secoli xiv., xv., xvi.," A Medin and L Frati, 1883.

31 PROSE.

A considerable amount of translation work was carried on during this period, both from Latin and French originals; original prose was more freely cultivated, the historians ranking foremost among its representatives. Some of the old favourite writers furnished material for the former: Boethius, Sallust, Ovid, Ægidio Colonna, Marco Polo, Septimello.

Didactic.

Bartolommeo di San Concordio, b. 1262; d. 1347.

Ammaestramenti degli Antichi. In Latin and Italian. These instructive sayings are mostly culled from old writings, but in some instances are original. It is a long work, divided under forty headings, called "Distinzione"; under each heading are quotations from several authors. Bartolommeo wrote other Latin works, and was also a translator. *Ed.*, V. Nannucci, 1840. *MSS.*, Riccardiana (3 MSS.); Laurenziana (1); Marucelliana (1).

Domenico Cavalca, b. cir. 1270 at Vico Pisano; d. 1342. A poet, translator, and original prose writer, belonging to the Dominican order, who has been called "the father of Italian prose." He wrote several religious treatises, some sonnets of an ascetic nature on the "Cavaliere di Dio," and translated, among other works, some of the lives of the Fathers. (*Ed.*, Sorio, 1858.)   *See* F. Falco, "D. C. Moralista," 1892.

Treatises—
Specchio de Croce.   *Ed.*, G. Bottari, 1738 ; B. Sorio, 1840.
Disciplina degli Spirituali.
Delle Trente Stoltizie.
Medicina del Cuore (on Patience).
Pungilingua.
Frutti della Lingua.

Ed., by G. Bottari, 1738–63. *See* "Tradizionalisti e concordisti in una questione letteraria del secolo xiv.," by L. Franceschini, discussing authorship of works which are ascribed to Cavalca. (The controversy is round the names of Cavalca, Fra Simone da Cascia, and Giovanni da Salerno.) *MSS.*, Library of PP. di s. Pantaleo in Rome ; Corsiniana ; S. Maria Novella (Florence) ; Rome, Barberina ; Florence— Magliabech. ; Riccard. ; PP. d'Ognisanti.

N.B.—The Italian version of the Bible (Venice, 1471) has been, but on insufficient grounds, it is thought, ascribed to Cavalca (*see N.B.*, § 23).

Giordano da Rivalto, b. cir. 1260; d. 1311. A Dominican and eloquent preacher ; sermons preached at Pisa, Florence, and in other places are extant.   *Ed.*, E. Narducci, 1867.   *MSS.*, Many MSS. in Florence, Bibl. Naz. ; Magliabech. Palatina ; Riccardiana, several MSS. ; Mediceo. Laurenz., 3 MSS. ; Bibl. Nat., Paris, Ancien fds. Latin, 7707.

The three authors last named are ranked with Passavanti (*see Novelle*, § 37) as the best prose writers of this period.

32   *Narrative.*

N.B.—Compilations known as *Fiore* still continued to be produced.

Guido del Carmine, of Pisa. (One of Dante's commentators.)

Fiore, or *Fiorità, de Italia*. Composed of a book on Moses, another on mythological personages, a third on Job, and a fourth on Aeneas (Fatti d'Enea). These have been published separately. The fourth book belongs to the story of Troy, and it has appeared under the title of "Fatti d'Enea" (ed. by D. Carbone, 1867). *Ed.*, L. Muzzi, 1824. Earliest printed edition, 1490.

Armannino da Bologna, fl. first half 14th century.

Fiorita, 1325. A collection of tales from the foundation of the world, gathered from classical and mediæval sources. The work is modelled on that of Boethius, verse being introduced at the close of the tales containing moral reflections on what has just been narrated. Inedited. *See* G. Mazzatinti, "Giorn Fil. Rom.," iii. 1–55. *MSS.*, Florence: Laurenz. Plut. lxii., lxxxix.; Bibl. Naz. Gadd. 136; Strozzi. 139, 138; Magliabech. 137; Bibl. Naz. Cod. 135; Venice, Cod. Marc., 15th cent.; Gubbio, Cod. Sperelliano.

Uncertain Authorship.

Fortunatus Siculus ossi L'Avventuroso Ciciliano di Busone da Gubbio. An historical romance written in 1311. Five Barons leave Sicily on account of the Sicilian Vespers, and travel to Tunis, la Rascia, Armenia, and England : tales of various kinds, speeches and descriptions of persons and customs are introduced. The work is assigned to Busone da Gubbio, a friend of Dante's, to whom Armannino's work was dedicated, but the authorship is not on that account beyond question. *Ed.*, C. F. Nott, 1832, 1833. *MS.*, Florence, Laurenz. Plut., lxxxix., Cod. 60.

33 *Historical.*

The two chief historians of this period were Dino Compagni and Giovanni Villani. (*See* for historians generally, Balzani, "Le Cronache Ital. del Medioevo," 1884.)

Dino Compagni, a Florentine, b. cir. 1257, or 1260; d. 1324. Compagni took an active part in the affairs of his native city, and was twice elected to the Priorate; exiled for a while during the ascendency of the Neri faction, he returned shortly from banishment, and subsequently led a retired life occupied in composing his Chronicle. He is spoken of as "the Sallust of the Florentine Republic."

Cronica delle cose occorrenti al tempo suo. The history covers the period between 1280 and 1312; and gives an account of the political divisions which brought such misery on Florence; "it is a work of historical and literary value, composed by a contemporary of the events recorded, in which he had taken an interested share, with the animation of an eloquent writer whose heart had throbbed in sympathy with the troubles and aspirations, hopes and disappointments of those disastrous years." *Ed.,* I. del Lungo, 1879–87. The editor discusses fully the question raised by Fanfani, and carried on by other authorities, as to the authorship of this work. Smaller ed., 1890. Eng. trans., A. G. Ferrers Howell, "Temple Classics," 1906. *MSS.,* Del Lungo's edition, based on twenty MSS.: Florence, Bibl. Naz., Magliabechiana (7); Palatina (2); Bibl. Moreniana (1); Venice, Marciana (2); Rome, Chigiana (2); Arch. Signori Compagni (Florence) (2); Riccardiana (1); Private Libraries (2). When this edition was published there were also MSS. in the Ashburnham and Phillipps collections.

Giovanni Villani, b. cir. 1275; d. of plague, 1348. "The Herodotus of the Florentine Republic." A follower of the Guelph party, and three times elected to the Priorate; a merchant, and as such a traveller into France and Flanders.

Cronica. Divided into twelve books. The work embraces a wider field than that of Compagni; it was during his visit to Rome in the Jubilee year, 1300, that Villani devised his scheme for writing the history of his native city. His history, however, also deals with the affairs of other places and countries with which Florence had connection in the way of politics or commerce. Starting from the destruction of Troy, and the traditional foundation of Florence, it almost comes under the head of a universal history. Beyond the more important historical events recorded, there are notices of floods and fires, of buildings, and lesser affairs in connection with the lives of the citizens. "The longest and most instructive historical Italian work." The work was continued after his death by his brother Matteo, and finally brought up to 1364 by the latter's son Filippo, the author of a Latin work on the lives of illustrious Florentines.

Giovanni Villani drew materials for his work from various sources; but also gives information gathered by him from people of various occupations whom he had met, adding at times his own personal view of the matters he recounts. As a history it is considered one of the most important works of its class, and equally one of the most interesting as a record of the life and manners of the Italy known to Compagni. *Ed.*, F. Gherardi Dragomanni, 1844. Ed. stated to be in preparation by S. Morpurgo.

Selections from the first nine books of the "Croniche Fiorentine" of Giovanni Villani, trans. for use of students of Dante and others by Rose E. Selfe, *ed.*, P. H. Wicksteed, 1896. *MSS.*, Magliabech., Palatino, Laurenziano, Riccardiano, Marucelliano, Ambrosiano.

N.B.—For notices of Dante in Villani, *see* "Propugnatore," II. i. 324; 2, 54.

XIVth CENTURY.

The two great writers of the 14th century were Boccaccio and Petrarch. (*See* for this period, Körting, "Geschichte der Literatur Italiens," 3 vols. (Petrarch; Boccaccio; Die Anfänge der Renaissance), 1878-84.)

34 Giovanni Boccaccio, b. in Paris, 1313; d. 1375.

The son of a Florentine merchant, who desired to train him in mercantile pursuits; his tastes, however, were in every way opposed to such a career; and, finally, he was allowed to take up more congenial work. He began attending courses on Canon Law, but these were also abandoned, and finally he was given an introduction to the court at Naples, where his personal beauty, his culture, and amiability of character made him a general favourite. Here he fell in love with an illegitimate daughter of King Robert, married to a court dignitary, who became his Fiammetta. In 1348 the plague ravaged Italy and other parts of Europe, and to this period belongs Boccaccio's masterpiece, the "Decameron." The chief solace of his older years was his warm friendship with Petrarch, with whom he exchanged frequent correspondence till the latter's death; their first meeting had been in 1350, when Petrarch was passing through Florence on his way to Rome for the Jubilee. Boccaccio occupied several important official posts, and was employed on missions of trust; and in 1373 he was appointed to the post of public reader of the "Commedia." These lectures he had carried as far as the 17th Canto only, when he was overtaken by death, dying at Certaldo, a Latin epitaph of his own being placed over his tomb. For some years before his death he had given up profane studies, having been induced to prepare for death by a change of life, by the message brought to him from a holy man who had just died in a Carthusian monastery at Siena. Boccaccio received material assistance and comfort from his friend Petrarch, who paid him a last visit in 1368. Boccaccio "endowed his country with a classic prose"; to him also is due the promotion of the study of Greek in his native country; he collected Greek manuscripts, among them being a complete copy of Homer. He and Petrarch knew little of Greek, but it became a usual study among the Italians after Chrysoloras began his lectures on Greek, in Florence, in 1396. Works, *ed.*, F. S. Zambrini and Bacchi della Lega, 1875.

WORKS: ITALIAN.

Prose.

Decameron, begun 1348, finished 1353. One hundred tales, told in the course of ten days by a company of seven ladies and three men who had fled from the plague to the hills of

Fiesole. The tales are taken from various old sources, but reappear in all freshness and liveliness of spirit and colour under the reanimating touch of Boccaccio's genius. Not only is the work a picture of the society of the author's own day, "it is the *human comedy* in all its manifold manifestations." *Ed.*, P. dal Rio, P. Fanfani, Lemonnier, Fornaciari, Finzi, Cappelletti, Donini, Fumagalli, etc. Eng. Translation, T. Wright, 1874; J. M. Rigg, 1903; J. Payne, 1886, 1893; H. M. Thomson, 1896; Selections, J. Jacobs, 1899; Tales (40), with Introduction by H. Morley, "Morley's Universal Library," and "Cassell's National Library." Earliest printed ed., 1470. *MSS.*, Oldest, Laurenziana; Berlin (Hamilton). (B.M. Harl.; Addit.)

MINOR ITALIAN WORKS.

Prose.

Filocolo. Tale of Florio and Biancofiore, cir. 1339. (*See* England, § 40.)

Ameto. An allegorical work and pastoral romance, interspersed with poems in terza rima. The whole work aims at showing how man may attain to the love of God. Ameta falls in love with the nymph Lia, who is attended by seven other nymphs symbolising different virtues, etc.

Fiammetta. A pyschological romance in which Fiammetta tells of her love for Panfilo (Boccaccio), of all that she has suffered in connection with it, and relates tales of other old unhappy loves.

Corbaccio, or *Labirinto d'Amore*. A satire in form of a vision, written against women, to revenge himself on a widow who had ridiculed him.
Ed., Minor Works, Moutier, 1827–34.

Vita di Dante.
Ed., Trans. P. H. Wicksteed, 1898; G. R. Carpenter, 1900 (Grolier Club, N. Y.). *See* also under Dante.
Commentary of the Inferno, to 17th Canto.

Poetry.

Amorosa Visione. Allegorical poem in fifty cantos, in which the poet describes how, under the guidance of a beautiful woman, he is led to the attainment of true happiness. *See* Traversi, "Studi di Fil. Roman.," vol. i., 1885.

Teseide. The Tale of "Palemon and Arcite," in twelve cantos.

Filostrato, in nine cantos. Tale of "Troilus and Cressida" ("Troilo e Griseida"). *See* Kissner ("Chaucer and Ital. Lit."), 1867.

Ninfale fiesolano. Pastoral poem in seven cantos (loves of Affrico and the nymph Mensola). *See* Zumbini, "Nuovo Antologia," xliv., 1884.

The above poems are in ottava rima.[1] "To B. belongs the honour, if not of inventing, of first using this form artistically."

Rime (Sonetti, Canzoni, and Ballate). The poems are mostly love lyrics. *See* F. Mango, "Delle Rime, etc.," 1883.

LATIN PROSE.

De genealogiis deorum gentilium. Encyclopædia of mythology.

De Claris Mulieribus. Biographies of different women, from the time of Eve.

De Casis virorum illustrium. Celebrated men from the time of Adam tell their histories.

De Montibus, Sylvis, Fluminibus, etc. A dictionary of classical geography.

Epistolæ. Letters to friends (Latin and Italian). *Ed.,* Corazzini, 1877.

---

[1] Ottava rima = strophes of eight lines, of alternate rhymes throughout the first six lines, with a third rhyme linking the last two lines.

POETRY.

Sixteen *Eclogues*. Biographical facts given in allegorical form.

See A. Hortis, "Studi sulle opp. lat. del B.," 1879.

N.B.—For other works assigned to B., *see* Casini, "Grundr. Rom. Phil.," *op. cit.*, p. 112.

35　Francesco Petrarca, b. 1304; d. 1374.

The poet was born at Arezzo, whither his father had retired on being banished from Florence as one of the Bianchi. Francesco studied at Prato, Montpellier, and Bologna, and in 1326 entered the Church, which step did not in any way prove a hindrance to the enjoyment of life or to his travels. It was in church at Avignon, on Good Friday, 1327, that he first saw Madonna Laura. In 1340 he received the joint invitation of Paris and Rome to accept a public coronation, and this function accordingly took place in the latter city in the following year. "He was," writes Garnett, "the first modern literary dictator, the first author to receive the unanimous homage of a world of culture, and may be said to be both the cause and effect of this world of culture." In 1347 Petrarch was again on his way to Rome, to rejoice with Rienzi who had just been made Tribune, but he was met at Genoa by the news of the fall of the great man whose cause he had seconded with all the enthusiasm of a friend and partisan. A letter is extant from the poet to Rienzi in which he proclaims the latter as the founder of peace, and it is generally believed that the sonnet "Spirto Gentil" was dedicated to the republican leader. Petrarch now turned his steps to Parma, where he received the news of Laura's death ; reaching Florence he was there entertained by Boccaccio whose warm friendship he retained and returned to the end ; later on he was at Rome for the Great Jubilee. Honours, ecclesiastical and civil, were showered on Petrarch during the last years of his life ; two embassies were undertaken by him for the Visconti ; the Venetian Republic gave him a palace to live in. His last days of all were spent at Arquà di Monte, on the Euganean Hills, and there one day he was found dead, with his head fallen forward on a volume of Virgil.

Petrarch, unlike Dante, was not an encourager of vernacular literature ; he was an ardent admirer of classic culture, and he and Boccaccio were two of the most prominent forerunners of the *Rinascimento*, during which period (1375–1494) the vernacular was for a while discarded as the language of higher-class literature, after which interval Italian poetry was re-vived, although it continued for some time to turn for its inspiration and for its models of form and style to the classics.

The originality of Petrarch's verse consists chiefly in the breaking away from all models; so "whereas the great re-presentatives of the *Dolce Nuovo* had dealt with love as an idea, a symbol, Petrarch treated it as a passionate reality." "Petrarch borrowed his metrical forms from his predecessors, but handled them with greater ease and brought them to perfection . . . Side by side with the Petrarch of beautiful verse rises at times the Petrarch of mannerism, the mannerism which his imitators found the easier part of his lyric models to copy, and which gave rise to the style known as *Petrarchismo*, which in its turn caused a revolt among the poets" (*see* Turri, "Diz. Stor.," *op. cit.*).

Works: Italian.

Petrarch's fame rests chiefly on his *Canzoniere*. These comprise lyrics of various forms, the sonnets forming the greater number. The poet himself was for many years engaged in the revision and arrangement of his poems. His love verses commemorate his passion for Laura ; songs of her grace and beauty, etc. (In vita di Madonna Laura); laments at her loss, etc. (In morte di Madonna Laura). Other poems touch on morals and politics; of the latter the "Spirto Gentil," already mentioned, is one of the three which have become most famous ("O aspettata in ciel beata e bella," and "Italia mia, benchè 'l parlar sia indarno "). *Ed.*, Carducci and Ferrari, 1899; Mestica, 1896; E. Modigliani, 1904. Trans. Eng., 1859 (with preface by the poet Campbell); "A Hundred Sonnets," S. Wollaston, 1844, 1855; "One Hundred Sonnets, with Hymn to the Virgin" (with Ital. text), A.

Crompton, 1898. Selections, Cyfaill, 1891; "Odes of Petrarch," R. G. Macgregor, 1851; "Nine Sonnets and a Canzone," A. Tobin (Preface by Mrs. Meynell), 1905. Trans. from Dante, Petrarch, and Camoens, R. Garnett, 1896. *MSS.*, Autograph MSS., Vat. Lat. 3195, 3196. Earliest printed ed., 1470; Aldine, 1501. (*Ed.*, Vat. Lat. 3195, E. Modigliani, 1904.)

Trionfi (terza rima), 1357–1373. The triumphs are those of the six allegorical figures of Love, Chastity, Death, Fame, Divinity. In the "Trionfo della Morta" the poet describes Laura's death. *Ed.*, Pasqualigo, 1874; Mestica, 1896 (from Vat. 3196; Palatino N. 195, and Aldine ed.). Eng. trans., Macgregor, *op. cit.*: H. Boyd, 1807. Reprint of trans., 1565, by Roxburghe Club, 1887. *MS.*, Auto. MS., Vat. 3196.

Works: Latin.

Prose.

Segretum, or De Contemptu Mundi.

De Vita Solitaria.

De Otio Religiosorum.

De Vera Sapientia.

De Remediis utriusque fortunae.

Psalmi poenitentiales (with various prayers).

De Rebus Memorandis (Anecdotes, legends, to illustrate moral and philosophical arguments).

Itinerarium Syriacum (Genoa to Palestine).

De Viris Illustribus (famous Romans).

Epistolae (four series). These are: familiar letters to friends, etc., to illustrious people, and others without title to indicate to whom addressed; one letter, addressed to posterity, forms a kind of autobiography. Ital. Trans., ed., F. Corazzine, 1897.

Other minor writings.

Poetry.

Africa, in nine books, 1339–1442. On Scipio Africanus. *Ed.*, Corradini, 1874.

Carmen bucolicum (12 eclogues), and sixty-four metrical epistles.

MSS. of Works, Florence, Bibl. Med. Laur. ; Bibl. Naz. (Palat., Magliab., S. M. Novella, SS. Annunziata). Bibl. Riccardiana ; Bibl. Marucelliana. Lucca, Mantua, Milan (Brera), Modena (Estense), Naples (Naz. ; Gerolamini), Padua, Parma, Pavia, Rome (Casanatense, Angelica), Turin, Venice (Marc). *See* " I codici Petrarch. delle Bibl. Governative, etc." The British Museum has MSS. in Harleian and Addit. Collections.

Splendid collections of Petrarch's works are in—
The Rossetti Coll., Bibl. Civica, Trieste. Cat. Ed., A. Hortis, 1874. Palesa Coll., Padua. Left by Agostino Palesa together with his Dante collection. The collection of Prof. Marsand, bought in 1821 by Charles x. of France, and preserved in the Louvre, was destroyed during the siege of 1870.

For bibliographies, *see* Marsand (1826) ; Hortis (*op. cit.*), and Ferrazzi, 1887.

86 Even during his lifetime Petrarch began to have imitators ; the style known as *Petrarchismo* prevailed from the middle of the 14th century. The influence of Petrarch did not entirely supersede that of the older poets, it may rather be stated to have flourished side by side with that of Dante and others ; his influence is general, however, over the form of the later 14th century verse, which became more studied, not always to the increase of its flexibility, and developed in the hands of the inferior poets of the Renaissance, into a pedantic classicism. *See* Gröber, "Grundrisz der Rom. Phil.," Bd. ii. Abth. iii. p. 116.

Among Petrarch's followers were Fazio degli Uberti, a lyric and didactic poet, in whose writings the earlier influence of Dante as well as that of Petrarch is traceable; Franco Sacchetti, a prolific writer, who left works in verse and prose; and Coluccio Salutati, one of the chief promoters of humanistic culture, and a writer of Latin poems.

Lyrical Verse.

Fazio (Bonifazio) degli Uberti, b. cir. 1305–10; d. cir. 1370. (§ 40.)

Fazio degli Uberti belonged to one of the chief Ghibelline families who were banished in 1268. His lyrics deal both with love and politics; in the latter he shows himself genuinely patriotic; love he writes of with feeling and grace of expression, which earn for his lyrics a place among the best of the period. His verse comprises Canzoni and Sonetti. The latter are chiefly occupied with abstract subjects, Pride, Envy, etc. *Ed.*, "Liriche edite ed inedite de F. degli Uberti," R. Renier, 1883. *MSS.* in all the chief libraries of Florence; Rome (Chigi.); Vatican (Barber.); Venice (Marc.); Milan (Ambros.), etc.

Franco Sacchetti, b. cir. 1330; d., probably of plague, cir. 1400. (*See* § 37.)

Canzoni, Sonetti, Madrigale, Ballate, Frottole, Cacce.

Franco Sacchetti held several public appointments, and in 1383 was one of the Priorate. Ballate and Madrigale were the best of Sacchetti's lyrics; one of his finest Ballate was the one beginning, "O vaghe montanine pastorelle." To him is due one of the earliest comic-heroic poems, "La Battaglia delle Giovani belle con le vecchie" (Battle of the Young and Old). Sacchetti is best known by his "Novelle." *Ed.*, G. Carducci, "Rime di Cino da Pistoia ed altri." By same editor, "Cantilene e Ballate"; "Cacce in rime dei sec. xiv. e xv.," 1896; "Batt. d. Giovani, etc."; Rigoli, "Rime di diversi buoni Autori," 1825. *MSS.*, Auto. MS. of Canzoniere, Laurenz., Ashburnham, 574; copies, Florence, Bibl. Naz.; Palatina, 205; Magliabech. vii. 4, 852; Rome (Chigi. Corsi.); Vatican, Paris, etc.

N.B.—The "Frottola" was a poem of a varying number of lines of a variety of measure; the most usual form had three lines linked with the same rhyme. The "Caccia" was a popular form of verse, describing some passing event. *See* G. Carducci, "Cacce in Rima, etc.," *op. cit.*

Coluccio Salutati, b. 1331; d. 1406. Elected Chancellor of the Florentine Republic in 1375. Only a few sonnets are extant by this poet. He wrote chiefly in Latin, being one of the supporters of the classical revival. He made a considerable collection of manuscripts. *MSS.*, Florence (Bibl. Naz.; Riccard., Marucell.; Laurenz); Milan, Vatican, Parma, Moück.

For names of other lyric writers, *see* "Propugnatore," N.S., vols. i. and following. In these, P. Bilancioni has given a list of the MSS. and of the edition of works by the poets of the first three centuries of Italian literature.

Among the writers of didactic lyrics were Antonio Pucci and Antonio Beccari.

Antonio Pucci, b. cir. 1310; d. cir. 1380. (*See* §§ 41, 42.) A Florentine belonging to the lower classes. "The earliest Italian satirist." His verse is popular, realistic, and satirical. Among the subjects of his verse are the horrors of the pestilence in 1348, and he accompanies his account of them with directions as to how to live and eat at such times (ed. 1884); the description of the most beautiful woman in Florence in 1335; the necessity of marriage for a man; the indispensability of women, to which conclusion two men finally come after a dispute concerning the opposite sex (*see* Wesselofsky, "Propugnatore," ii. 397; iii. 35); a good recipe for a sauce, etc. Politically, he reflects the feelings of the townspeople of his native city. *Ed.*, San Luigi, "Delizie degli eruditi," vols. iii.–vi.

Antonio Beccari, b. 1315; d. previous to 1364. A physician and friend of Petrarch. Author of a large number of poems, many of scholastic tone. "Less plebeian as a writer than Pucci, although a popular versifier, he lacks the spontaneity and adroitness of versification which mark Pucci's work." *Ed.*, Bottoni, "Saggio di Rime inedite di etc.," 1878 ; *see* "Giorn. Stor. Lett.," xiii. 1–36 ("Una Canzone di etc."). *MSS.*, Bilancioni, "Propugnatore," N.S., vol. ii. pt. i. 69 ff.

87   Prose.

Narrative and Didactic, etc.

Jacopo Passavanti, b. cir. 1300; d. 1357. A Dominican, and Teacher of Theology.

Specchio di vera penitenza. The work is in five divisions or *distinzioni* ; it demonstrates what penitence really is ; and then deals with things which induce, things which are impediments to, the same ; with contrition and confession, the latter subject forming a second part. " The whole is rendered impressive by the tales that are introduced." Following on the " Specchio " are treatises on Pride, Humility, Vain-glory, etc. Translations of Latin works attributed to Passavanti are added in the edition by Polidori. " The language and treatment are admirably clear." *Ed.*, F. L. Polidori, 1856. *MSS.*, Polidori ed. based on early eds. of 1495, 1585, 1725, and on MS. Magliabechiano, iv. 59.

Giovanni Sercambi, b. 1347 ; d. 1424. (*See* § 38.) Occupied the highest post in his native city (Gonfaloniere di Giustizia).

155 *Novelle* have come down to us. The tales are interspersed with moral interludes and descriptions, in prose and verse. Some of the tales are also found in Sercambi's "Chronicle." *Ed.*, A. d'Ancona, 1871 ; 2nd set, 1886. Others ed. by Renier, 1889. *MS.*, Milan, Trivulziano, 193.

Note.—Another MS. (Baroni), differing in some respects from the " Trivulziano," is thought by Renier to be an earlier draft of the tales, used afterwards for the " Chronicle," and later on enlarged and improved, some of the tales being suppressed for the collection as we have it in the Milan MS.

Franco Sacchetti. (§ 36.)

Trecento Novelle, of which only two hundred and twenty-three have come down to us. Each tale is followed by moral reflections. "The collection is a delightful record of the manners of the time." The tales are written in an easy and familiar style, often taking the form of dialogue. *Ed.,* O. Gigli, 1860–61. *MSS.,* ed., O. Gigli, according to MS. Borghiniano; Magliabechiano, vi. 112 (to Novello, 140); Laurenziano, 42, 12 (beginning at Novello, 140).

Giovanni da Firenze. A notary of Florence, banished in 1378.

Il Pecorone, a collection of fifty, in some MSS. of fifty-three tales. The tales are told by a young Florentine who turns monk, and who has fallen in love with the nun Saturnina, and by the latter; the two meet at a certain hour every day, and each tells a tale. A ballata closes each day's recital. The tales are taken from different sources, many from Villani's "Chronicle." *Ed.,* G. Poggiali, 1793; earliest printed edition, 1558. Trans., Eng., W. G. Waters, 1897. "Tale of Giannetto" (from "Pecorone"), Ital. and Eng., Shakespeare Libr., vol. ii., 1843; "The Merchant of Venice, with the adventures of Giannetto," Cassell's Nat. Libr., 1886. Trans. of Giannetto, and trans. of Novel from Boccaccio, 1755. *MSS.,* best MS. Magliabechiano.

Filippo della Gazzaio, b. probably 1339; d. 1422. A Monk of Siena, and Prior of his convent from 1398.

Assempri (Examples). Edifying tales founded on legends of saints and similar materials. The author is reported to have been an indefatigable writer, but the only authenticated work that has come down to us is the collection contained in an autograph MS. at Siena. Sixty-two Assempri are given by Carpellini, one being omitted. *Ed.,* F. C. Carpellini, 1864. *MSS.,* Siena, Bibl. Communale, Cod. i. v. 10; Cod. i. iv. 9. The first named has only the Assempro of the *Donna lisciata dal diavolo.*

Among the religious prose writers of this century was **S. Catherine of Siena (Caterina Benincasa)**, b. 1347; d. 1380. Born of poor parents, she was driven by her religious zeal, when still almost a child, to enter the Dominican order. The extreme severity which she exercised towards herself was equalled by her pity and charity to the poor and suffering; during the terrible time when the plague was ravaging the country she devoted herself to the afflicted. Later on, she went about preaching a general crusade; she urged Church reform, and her piety and enthusiasm won the ear of those in power, and from the people the love and reverence "in which legend has its birth." "Her writings are the chief interpreters of the religious ideal of her age." We have letters of hers addressed to ecclesiastical and secular potentates, princes, popes, etc. *See* V. D. Scudder, "S. Catherine of Siena as seen in her letters," 1905.

Epistole utile e divote (thirty-one letters).

Epistole devotissime. Containing more letters.   *Printed ed.*, 1492, 1500 (Aldine).
Ed. (Letters), N. Tommaseo, 1860.

Dialogo della Divina Providenza; or *libro della Divina Dottrina*, being a dialogue between the Saint and God. *Printed ed.*, 1472; several other eds. during 15th century.
Ed., Works, G. Gigli, 1707–54.

N.B.—Other religious letters are extant by Colombini, and dalle Celle.

An Italian version of the *Vision of Tundalus* has been ed. by Corazzini.   *MSS.*, Riccard. 2404; Magliabech. 71, Pal. ii.; Magliabech. 158, cl. xxiv.

La Navigatio Sancti Brendani.   Ed., F. Novati, "Bibl. Stor. Lett. Ital.," i., 1896. From the MS. Ambrosiano D. 158. With introduction on the prose Italian versions, which he thinks must "take rank among the earliest of the two groups into which modern criticism has distributed the vernacular texts of the legend."

38 *Historical.*

Matteo Villani, Philippo Villani. A continuation of Giovanni Villani's "Cronica" (§ 33). Matteo, Giovanni's brother, carried it on to 1363; his son Filippo, the author of the lives of famous Florentines, written in Latin, and a public lecturer on Dante, continued it to 1364.

Baldassarre, known as **Marchionne Stefani,** b. cir. 1320; d. 1385.

Istoria fiorentina. A long work in twelve books. Starting with the beginning of the world and carried up to 1386; he enters very fully into matters concerning his own city, giving a valuable list of the priors, etc. *Ed.,* I di San Luigi, "Delizie degli eruditi," vii.–xvii., 1776. *MSS.,* used by Luigi, Florence, Libreria di S. Paolino; Magliabech. 590; Magliab. Gaddiano; Libreria Strozzi (late copy).

Donato Velluti, b. 1313; d. 1370. Velluti held high positions in his native town of Florence.

The *Cronica domestica,* 1330–1370, is a history of the historian's family which belonged to the rich merchant class, including his own life and that of his children; written when he was an older man, and breaking off at his death. "It is excellently written and of great interest as a description of the life of the rich citizen of that time." *Ed.,* D. M. Manni, 1731. *MSS.,* Magliabechiana, xxv. 461 (the best MS.).

Lapo da Castiglionchio, a famous Jurisconsult of the 14th century; born early 14th; d. 1381.

Epistola o sia Ragionamente di Messer Lapo da C. The "Epistola" is in three parts, addressed to Bernardo his son; the latter's answer, and another of Francesco di Alberto his nephew, are given in the edition by L. Mehus, 1753. Lapo gives account of his own life and that of his family, in fine language. He belonged to an ancient family, and had to escape in 1378 as the chief of the Guelph party, and the remainder of his life was spent in exile. *MS.*, Mehus uses one from Libreria Medicea di S. Lorenzo.[1]

Other cities, among them Pisa, Siena, Bologna, and Venezia, also had their chroniclers.

Giovanni Sercambi, b. 1348; d. 1424. Commentator of Dante's "Paradiso." (*See* § 37.)

Cronaca, of his native city of Lucca. The oldest and fullest historical monument of this city. *Ed.*, S. Bongi, 1892–93. *MSS.*, Lucca, Archiv di Stato, 1st part, finished April 1400 (illustrated); Domestic Arch. dei signori Guinigi, 2nd part. Copies also extant.

MISCELLANEOUS.

Some familiar letters belonging to this century have been edited by Pietro Dazzi, "Alcune Lettere familiari," 1868.

89 Descriptions of travels became more numerous in this century.

Fra Niccolò da Poggibonsi.

Libro d'Oltramare. An account of travels to Jerusalem, Egypt, and other parts of the East, undertaken between the years 1346–1349. *Ed.*, A. Bacchi della Lega, 1881. *MSS.*, Magliabech. (4); Palatina (3); Riccardiana (3), Paris, Bibl. Schefer; Siena; Jerusalem, Monastery of Zion.

Leonardo di Niccolò Frescobaldi and Simon Sigoli.

These two travellers with three other companions journey to Egypt and the East. Both wrote a description of their travels, of which that of Frescobaldi is the more noted, and a third was given by Dino Gucci. They started 10th August 1384, arriving in Alexandria on the 28th September, the long

---

[1] A later work by F. Novati, "Libro memoriale dei figliuoli di M. Lapo da C.," 1893, is mentioned by Casini (Grundr. Rom. Phil.).

description of Cairo being most interesting. *Ed.*, Frescobaldi, Manzi, 1845. *MSS.*, Frescobaldi (Manzi)
Barberina, 932; Gargiolli has used a Riccardiana (d. 818),
and a Ricasoliano. Other MSS.: Florence, Bibl. Naz.
Magliabech. (2); Milan (Ambros.); Ravenna.

Simon Sigoli.

Viaggio al Monte Sinai (*see* above). *Ed.*, B. Puote,
1831 (based on Poggi, 1829). Gargiolli has edited both
the above, with Gucci's, 1862. *MSS.*, Bibl. Naz.
Magliabech. (2); Palat. E. 5, 9, 10; Riccard. (2); Paris,
Bibl. Nat. fds. Ital. 897.

40 POETRY.

Didactic.

Fazio degli Uberti. (§ 36.)

Dittamondo (*Dicta Mundi* = *Ragguagli del Mondo*. (In
terza rima.) The form of this enormous work is in
imitation of Dante. Virtue having appeared to the poet and
exhorted him to return to the right way, he confesses himself,
and starts on a journey, led by Solino, who shows him in turn
all the countries there known. History, geography, and
moral instruction are combined in the course of this description,
which ends when the poet, after traversing the chief European
lands and Egypt, has arrived in the Holy Land, the work
remaining unfinished. *Ed.*, V. Monti e G. Perticari, 1826.
See "Giorn. di Fil. Rom.," iii. (for MSS.) *MSS.*,
Numerous: Laurenz. pl. (16); Laurenz. Strozzi. (1);
Riccard. (4); Magliabech. (1); Palatina (1); Chigi. L. vii.
(2); Corsiniana (1); Barberina (1); Marciana (2);
Milan, Ambros. (2); Paris, B.N., 7775, 7781, 8375; Ashburnham (1); Bodleian (fragment); Siena, Lucca, Bologna,
Naples, Turin, Modena, etc.

Frederigo Frezzi, b. cir. 1350; d. 1416. A member
of the Dominican order; elected Bishop of Foligno in 1403.

Quadriregio. A poem in four books, written in terza
rima. The four kingdoms through which the poet takes his

journey are those of Love, Satan, the Vices, and the Virtues. He has several guides in the course of his journey, among them Enoch and S. Paul; Charity finally mounts with him to the highest heaven. Figures of all classes from ancient and mediæval times, as well as those of contemporaries, are introduced. Theological and scientific questions are discussed by the poet. This poem is considered one of the best imitations of Dante. *Ed.*, 1725. First printed ed., 1481. *See* "Giorn. Stor. Lett.," ii. 31–49. *MSS.*, Ravenna; Ferrara; Milan (Estense); Rome (Angelica); Riccardiana O. ii. vii.; Magliabech. ii. ii. 34; ii. ii. 35; Berlin (Hamilton), 29, 265.

Further imitations of Dante, "with the fundamental motives of a dream and a journey," are:

Jacopo del Pecora da Montepulciano. During the earlier part of an imprisonment, which lasted from 1390 to 1407, the author wrote an allegorical poem in terza rima, entitled

Fimerodia (famous song of love), "poor in colour, and inferior to Frezzi's work." Thought by some to be an allegorical account of Luigi Dasanzati's love for Alessandra de' Bardi. It shows the influence of Petrarch's "Trionfi," and Boccaccio's "Amorosa Visione," and of the "Roman de la Rose." *See* Art. by R. Renier, "Il Propugnatore," xv. pt. i. *MSS.*, Florence, Bibl. Naz., Magliabech. ii. ii. 128 (imperfect); copy, Magliabech. vii. 963; Palch. 8; Vatican 3216 (one chapter only).

N.B.—J. del Pecora's poems, *ed.*, Gentile and Tennerone, "Giorn. Stor. L. Ital.," iii. and xi.

Ristoro Canigiani, d. 1380; leader of the Guelph party and at one time Ambassador at Naples.

Il Ristorato (terza rima), a version of *Fiore di Virtù* (§ 23), written at Bologna in 1364, whither the poet had escaped from the plague. *Ed.*, L. Razzolini, 1848; G. Galvani, "Propugnatore," iv. 2, 3–52. *MS.*, Ricasoliano.

Giovanni Gherardi, or **Aquettino** (for identity with
G. da Prato, *see* Ed.), b. 1367 ; d. cir. 1445.

Paradiso degli Alberti, 1389. The poet journeys through
the celebrated cities of antiquity, visits certain sacred spots,
and the third book relates the learned conversations held by
well-known men at Paradiso, the residence of Alberti,
enlivened by the presence of women, music, etc. It shows
the influence of the "Decameron," and is of no literary value,
merely interesting as representative of the thought and manners
of the times. Many tales are introduced. *Ed.*, A.
Wesselofsky, 1867. *MSS.*, Ed. from Auto. and Anonymous MS., Riccardiana, N., 1280.

N.B.—Giovanni da Prato was a writer of love poems,
and of didactic verse, and of an allegorical poem, *Filomena* ;
and a public lecturer on Dante.

Certain didactic works were written in cycles of sonnets.
Among them is

Il Bel Pome (the Forbidden Fruit). *Ed.*, L. Frati,
"Giorn. Stor. Lett. Ital.," vi. *MS.*, Magliebech. xxiii.
4, 140.

Another of this class was *Cinque Sonetti Antichi.*, *ed.*,
Mussafia, 1874. *MS.*, Vienna (Palatina).

41 *Historical.*

Antonio Pucci. (§§ 36, 42.)

Della Guerra di Pisa Confortando Lucca. A poem in seven
cantos of ottava rima, beginning—

> "O Lucchesi pregiati
> Rinfrancator della vostra cittade,
> Amate Libertade
> Ricordivi de' ma' tempi passati."

Ed. with "Centiloquio," *see* below. *MS.*, Florence,
Seymour Kircoup.

Centiloquio. An abridged and versified edition of Villani's Chronicle. Written in terza rima. *Ed.,* I. di San Luigi, "Delizie degli erudite Toscani," 3–6, 1772. *MSS.,* used by Luigi, Strozziana, 740; Magliabech. 131; Libr. Marchesi Tempi.

Gorello d'Arezzo.

Cronaca Aretina. Recording events from 1310–1384 (in terza rima). *Ed.,* Muratori, "Rer. Ital.," 15.

42 *Narrative.*

N.B.—Among other narrative poems were versions of the older epics, such as "Buovo d'Antona," "Rinaldo da Montalbano," "Spagna" (the latter tells the tale of Roncesvalles), all of which belonged to the Charlemagne cycle. There is also extant a rhymed version of *Fiorio e Biancifiore,* dating from the early century, taken from the same source as Boccaccio's *Filocolo.*

Antonio Pucci. (§§ 36, 41.) Pucci's tales are written in ottava rima.

Istoria della Reina d'Oriente. This Queen of the East desiring an heir, and having only a daughter, dresses the latter in male costume and has her brought up as a man. When it becomes necessary for the heir to marry, a miraculous transformation of sex takes place. *Ed.,* 1862; A. Bonucci, 1867. *MSS.,* 1862 ed., MSS., Bologna; and Lanci (Sig. Cav. Fortunato Lanci); 1867, MS. Marucelliano. Early printed ed., Florence, 1483.

Istoria di Apollonia di Tiro (see England, § 16). Early printed ed., Venice, 1486.

Gismirante. The hero, Gismirante, has for some reason or other to kill a pig; inside this wonderful animal is found a hare, and inside the hare a sparrow. *Ed.,* Corazzini, 1853.

Madonna Lionessa. Similar in motive to the "Merchant of Venice." A prose tale by Sercambi, which corresponds to "Madonna Lionessa," is given in Gargiolli's edition. *Ed.,* C. Gargiolli, 1866. *MS.,* Riccardiana, N. 2873 (same MS. as contains "La Lusignacca").

Pucci is also thought to be the probable author of *Cantare de lo Bel Gherardino,* which is one of the "thoroughly good old mediæval tales, with tournaments, transformations, etc." The chief motive of the tale is familiar. G. after living at ease for some time with Fata Bianca, leaves her to go to his own country, promising to return within the year; he discloses the secret of a magic glove which she gives him at parting, and trouble follows. Bianca, not seeing him, proclaims a tourney, the victor at which is to be her husband; G. arrives and carries off the palm. *Ed.,* F. Zambrini, 1867. *MS.,* Magliabech. vii., 1272, dated 1383; the poem is thought to be of earlier date than this.

Anonymous. "Perhaps by Pucci" (Casini).

La Lusignacca (ottava rima). A similar tale is No. 44 of Boccaccio; others of the latter's collection were also put into rhyme. *Ed.,* G. Romagnoli, 1863. *MS., see Lionessa.*

N.B.—Other short tales have been edited by Zambrini, "Novelle d'incerti autori," "Scelta di curiosità Letteraria," 93.

43 XVth CENTURY.

The influence of Petrarch, the first of the "Humanists," who prepared the way for the "Renaissance," and of Boccaccio, strengthened by the teaching of Greek by Chrysoloras at Florence, to which city he was invited in 1396, prevailed in the 15th century. The Humanists, chief among whom was Leonardo Bruni (1369–1444), devoted themselves to the study, the translation, the imitation, and the collecting of ancient works.   Latin was used in preference to Italian by the more cultivated writers.   The native tongue however, was not silenced, for before the close of the century were published Pulci's "Morgante Maggiore," Boiardo's "Orlando innamorato," and Andrea da Barberino's "Reali di Francia." *See* G. Voigt, "Die Wiederbelebung des classischen Alterthums," 1888–1901.

SPAIN

LIST OF GENERAL AUTHORITIES.

Ticknor, "History of Spanish literature," 3 vols., 1888 ; J. Fitzmaurice Kelly, "History of Spanish Literature," 1898 ; Gröber, "Grundrisz der Romanischen Philologie" (Spanish section by Baist), Bd. ii. Abth. 2, 1894 ; E. Gorra, "Lingua e Letteratura Spagnuola delle origine," 1898 ; Amador de los Rios, "Historia Critica de la Literatura Española," 7 vols., 1861–5 ; Wolf, "Studien zur Geschichte der Spanischen u. Portugiesischen Nationalliteratur," 1859 ; Boudet de Puymaigre, "Les Vieux Auteurs Castillans," 1888; Dozy, "Recherches sur l'histoire politique et littéraire de 'Espagne pendant le moyen Âge," 3rd ed., 1881 ; Puibusque, "Histoire Comparée des Littératures espagnole et française," 1843 ; Morel Fatio, "Etudes sur l'Espagne," 1890, 1895 ; Menendez y Pelayo, "Origenes de la Novela," 1905 ; J. Fernandez-Espino, "Curso historico-critico de Literatura Española," 1871 ; H. B. Clarke, "Spanish Literature Handbook," 1893.

TEXTS.—Aribau, "Biblioteca de autores Española" (generally known under the name of "Rivadeneyra"), 72 volumes. The series includes the works referred to under Janer ("Poetas Castellanos anteriores al Siglo xv."), vol. lvii. ; and under Gayangos ("Escritores en Prosa anteriores al Siglo xv."), vol. li. ; and Duran's, "Romancero General," vols. x. and xvi. ; Additions to this series are in progress. Selections are given in Menendez y Pelayo, "Antologia de Poetas liricos Castellanos," vols. i., ii. ; "Romances," vol. viii., 1890, etc.

N.B.—The above works are referred to as *op. cit.*

BIBLIOGRAPHY.—Gröber, Kelly.

SPAIN

THE vernacular idioms of Spain, in common with the other romance languages, were developed from the vulgar Latin which continued to be the spoken language of the country for many centuries after it had thrown off the Roman dominion.

Of the three chief early dialects of Spain, Catalan, the language of the ancient kingdom of Aragon, was allied to the Provençal, and the Galician of the north-west to the Portuguese; Castilian, the first to assume a literary form, shared the pre-eminence finally obtained over the other states by that portion of the peninsula from which it derived its name, and became the dominant idiom of the country.

The Goths, who ruled in Spain from the second half of the 5th to the beginning of the 8th century, left comparatively little trace of their influence on the language of Spain (*see* Puymaigre, " Les Vieux auteurs Castillans," p. 25, for some of the words derived from the Gothic), and, notwithstanding the many centuries of close contact between the natives and the Arabs, who subsequently became their masters, the words borrowed from the latter are chiefly confined to technical and scientific terms (*see* Kelly, *op. cit.*, p. 19), or to such as represented things unknown before the advent of these conquerors.[1]

The Arab power was crushed at the great battle of Tolosa, in 1212, when this common enemy was defeated by the combined forces of Leon and Castile, Navarre, and Aragon,

---

[1] *See* G. Diercks, " Die schöne Literatur der Spanien," 1881, who says, " ten per cent. of words in the Spanish speech are Arabic." " It is unthinkable," he also writes, " that the eight hundred years' dominion of the Moors in Spain should not have left considerable traces of its influence. . . . Chivalry, among other characteristics of the Middle Ages, arose from the mingling of Spanish and Moorish elements on Spanish soil."

the three Christian kingdoms which had been founded during the period of the Arab domination and had gradually risen into importance. It only remained for Granada to become a vassal of Castile (close 15th century) and the history of Spain henceforth was that of her Christian rulers. The union of Spain under one head was finally effected by the conquest of Navarre at the beginning of the 16th century, under Ferdinand II. of Aragon and Isabella of Castile.

LITERATURE.

Several of the most noted Latin writers of the first centuries A.D., among them Lucan, Seneca, and Martial, were Spaniards by birth.

The Arabs were essentially patrons of letters, and a large body of Arabic and Jewish writings is extant, dating from the period of the Moorish dominion. The earliest public library was that at Cordova, founded in the 10th century by Al-Hakem; and other libraries, as well as colleges, were founded at Madrid, Malaga, Granada, Seville, etc., amounting in number to over seventy, the enlightenment of the Arabs appearing in striking contrast to the contemporary state of learning in the neighbouring countries of Christendom. (*See* Schack, "Poesie u. Kunst der Araber," 1877.)

Catalan had its literature, which underwent a revival in the last century, and numbered among its early writers the famous philosopher, poet, and novelist, Ramón Lull (13th century). There was a school of Portuguese-Galician troubadours in the 13th century, and for some time this dialect was the chosen one of the lyric poets of Spain, among them Alfonso x. A collection of the lyrics written in this idiom is preserved in the Vatican MS. 4803; but Spanish literature proper is confined to the works written in the Castilian dialect. The first beginnings of this literature consist in verse, of which the earliest extant monument dates from the 12th century.

Berceo in his "Alexander" mentions the "joglar" and the "trovador," the latter a maker and singer of songs, and this and other references of the kind in ancient chronicles are

taken as decisive evidence of the existence of popular song in
the 11th and 12th centuries, and of its having been on the
lips of the people for many previous centuries. Nothing,
however, remains of this ancient poetry, but something of its
character has been gathered from the Spanish romances
collected later on ("Cancionera de Baena," compiled 1440–
1454 (*ed.*, P. J. Pidal, 1851), and the "Cancionera General,"
1511 (*ed.*, Soc. Bibliofil. Españ., 1882); and the "Romancero
General," 1600 (reprint (N. Y.), 1904), although the
original poems contained in them are works of more
recent poets, and there are only a few versions of old popular
song. From these it has been concluded that the basis of the
measure used for these ancient compositions was the "versus
redondillas"—strophes of four octosyllabic lines.[1]

The favourite heroes of ancient popular song[2] were Rodrigo
Diaz de Bivar, the Campeador or Cid; Bernard del Carpio,
the victor of Roncesvalles; and the seven sons of Lara, whose
deeds were commemorated in a considerable number of
romances. (R. Menéndez Pidal, "La Leyenda de los
Infantes de Lara," 1896; W. L. Holland, 1860.)

Notwithstanding the social intimacy which existed for
centuries between the Arabs and their Christian subjects,
known as Mozarabians, early Castilian literature shows no
trace of Oriental influence. An explanation of what seems
inexplicable is given by Puymaigre ("Les Vieux auteurs
Castillans"); the Arabs, he writes, when they first took possession of Spain were only a little way removed from barbar-
ism; they found the remains of a civilisation superior to their
own, and adopted it as the Goths had accepted that of the
Romans. Arab literature, consequently, had too much in
common with Spanish to exercise any marked influence upon
it. The literature of the Mussulmans in Spain differed also
from the Arab literature of Bagdad and Damascus; the influence of the East was felt by the more learned, the philosophers and the Court poets, but did not filter through to the
masses, and the popular Arab poetry of Spain does not reflect

[1] Grimm thought originally two long lines. He edited a small collection of Spanish ballads in 1815. English translations of some are given
in Lockhart's "Ancient Spanish Ballads, etc.," 1870.

[2] *See* Milá y Fontanals, "De la Poesia Heroica-popular Castellana,"
1874.

it at all. It was not until the scientific branches of literature had received fresh impulse from the encouragement given to learning by Alfonso x., that Arab influence, imparted through the medium of the schools and courts, became a factor to any considerable extent in Spanish literature. (*See* also Kelly, *op. cit.*, pp. 14–16.)

Provençal influence, again, did not take early root in Castile. The troubadours were as familiar there as elsewhere in Spain and Italy, but, as the same authority quoted above explains, poetry in Castile appears to have sprung up among the lower classes, to whom narrative verse is more acceptable and intelligible than the artistic lyric, especially when the vehicle of such amorous subtleties as the troubadours delighted in, and, as literature had to be lifted to a certain level to make use of Arab learning, so had it to become elevated to a certain pitch to profit by Provençal models, the work in this case as in the former being due to Alfonso x. (*See* Mila y Fontanals, " Trovadores in Espagna," 1861.)

On the other hand, French influence is unmistakably present in early Castilian works, for we find themes borrowed from French originals, and in one old fragment of verse there is a distinct translation from the French, while the expression Cantar de Gesta, and the introduction of Roland's name on occasions points to a familiarity with the songs of the trouvères. It may be noted, however, that notwithstanding the occurrence of a Gallicised idiom in certain poems, there are no works which are considered to be written in an intermediate tongue, as was the case in Italy.

To whatever outside influence the Spaniards were subjected, their early poetry retained an essentially national character, " breathing the spirit of men who were for centuries under arms in close touch with a powerful enemy." Although the "Cid" and the " Cronica rimada" belong to the more cultured style of poetry, they have a basis of popular romance.

2   Traces of a vernacular are found as far back as in the writings of Isidor of Seville, but the oldest existing document in the vulgar tongue was generally considered to be the confirmation of a charter of Avilès, dated 1155, until its authenticity was questioned by the Spanish scholar, A. Fernandez-Guerra, who assigns it to a date more than a hundred years later. G. Baist, on the contrary ("Grundrisz Phil. Rom."), states that the MS. is of the 12th century, and considers therefore that even if not genuine, the document belongs to the earlier century. *Ed.*, "El Fuero de Avilès," A. Fernandez-Guerra, 1865, (facsimile of document).

The two oldest extant specimens of Castilian verse are the "Cid" and the "Misterio de los Reyes Magos," as to the relative antiquity of which there has been much discussion.

3 Anonymous.

Poema del Cid (Cantares del Cid, or Gesta de myo Cid).

The references to Cantares de Gesta in the "Cronica general," and the fragments of old romances found in the prose "Chronicle of the Cid," have led to the conclusion that this poem is one of several of the same class of which it is the only survivor. There has been considerable discussion as to the date, and as to the composition of this poem. The last two lines run:

> " Per abbat le escribió en el mes de mayo
> En era de mill e cc...xlv años.

Per Abbat is now universally acknowledged to be merely the copyist; but the question arose whether a third *c* has been erased or only an *e* (and) in the space above indicated in the date. The MS. has finally been ascribed to the 14th century, the original text to a date about fifty years after the death of the Cid, *i.e.*, cir. middle 12th century.

There has been further discussion as to whether the poem is composed of several distinct ballads, or a work complete in itself. Mr. Kelly (*op. cit.*) considers that " there is an unity of conception and of language which forbids our accepting the "Poema" as the work of several hands, and the division of the poem into separate Cantares is managed with a discretion which argues a single artistic intelligence."

The poem, if not wholly popular in character, is entirely national in tone, and although recalling the French Chanson de Geste " it is not to be assumed," to quote again from the same English authority, " that similarity of incident implies direct imitation." The rhythm is very irregular, the number of syllables in a line varying greatly; it has evidently been considerably maltreated, but the long line which, divided into hemistichs, constitutes the typical romance metre, is thought to have been the one employed for this old poem, in support of which theory, M. Cornu, "Études Romanes dédieés à G. Paris," 1891, gives a considerable number of lines which have come down intact.

The hero of the poem is Rodrigo, or Ruy Diaz de Bivar, known as the Cid (Lord), and the Campeador (Champion, the word, however, has been variously interpreted), who took part in the wars between Sancho and his brother Alfonso, the sons of Ferdinand 1.; Sancho was assassinated, and Ruy Diaz, for some reason which has remained obscure, was banished from Alfonso's court. An oath, declaring his innocence of his brother's death, which Ruy Diaz compelled Alfonso to take before he would swear allegiance to him, is thought possibly to be the cause of the hatred which Alfonso, according to some accounts, bore towards his vassal. In the poem, however, we never find the Cid wanting in loyalty to his sovereign, to whom he sends magnificent presents from the rich booties which he captured from time to time. The Cid, banished, carried on the brilliant warfare with the Arabs with which his name is associated, the final achievement being the capture of Valencia in 1094, in which town, five years later, 1099, he died. The sources of the Cid's history, beyond a contract of marriage between him and Chimène, daughter of Diego, Count of Orviedo, are short notices in old Latin chronicles, and further accounts in those of Lúcas de Tuy and Rodrigo of Toledo; the life of him given in the "Cronica General" and the corresponding one in the prose chronicle of the Cid (MS. Madrid, Bibl. Acad. Hist.), founded probably on the older chronicles; the "Gesta Roderici Campedocti," found in the library of the convent of Saint Isidor at Léon (and published by the finder Risco in 1792, in "La Castilla y el mas famoso Castellano)," a biography which it is decided must have been written in 1238, before Valencia was taken by the King of Aragon, according to the statement concerning the then masters of the town, which fell again into the Saracens' hands after the Cid's death; a Latin poem, which seems to be a contemporary account of the Cid, and is thought to be an adaptation from some popular work of Castilian origin (*MS.*, Paris Bibl. Nat. 5132; *ed.*, E du Méril, in his work on popular Latin poetry of the Middle Ages); Arab historians; and traditional romance. All the sources do not agree in their view of the Cid's character; a letter in the "Gesta" accuses him of attacking Christians and pillaging churches; in the two Spanish chronicles we hear of treachery and cruelty towards the famine-stricken inhabitants of Valencia during his siege of the town. In the "Poema," it need hardly be said, he appears in a far more chivalric light, although there is an incident told in that which is hardly to his credit. The poem opens, as now preserved, on the eve of the Cid's departure for exile, as he stands mourning over the ruins of his home, weeping, gazing on the open doors, the gates without locks; furs and mantles are gone; falcons and hawks have disappeared.

> " De los sos oios tan fuerte mientre lorando
> Tornava la cabeça e estava los catando.
> Vio puertas abiertas e vços sin cañados,
> Alcandaras uazias sin pielles e sin mantos,
> E sin falcones e sin adtores mudados."

The first part is taken up with the doings of the Cid; the second part deals almost exclusively with the marriage of his two daughters to the Infanta of Carrion; the cowardice, and unchivalric behaviour of the latter towards their wives; the appeal of the Cid to Alfonso who summons the Cortes to meet at Madrid; the compensation which the Infanta are forced to make, among other things returning the Cid's two famous swords, Tizon and Colada, etc.; finally, the remarriage of the daughters to the Infant of Navarre and the Infant of Aragon. The Cid is continually referred to, or addressed in the " Poema," as " the man born in a good hour."

"Written with extreme simplicity of style, the 'Poema' is a curious picture of the Middle Ages, without the introduction of magic, or knight-errants, its hero being unpolished, energetic, a fervent Christian, a tender father, a loyal vassal, who fights for his living" (*see* Puymaigre, "Les Vieux auteurs Castillans," p. 202). *Ed.*, R. Menéndez Pidal, 1900. Reproduction of original MS. and English version (illus-

trated), by Archer M. Huntington, 1897; earlier translation
by J. Ormsby, 1879.   *See* also for specimens of early Spanish
literature, and notes, etc., Gorra, *op. cit.*   *MS.*, Unique MS.
found at Bivar, in possession of the Marques de Pidal. Some
pages in the beginning of the MS. and in the middle are missing.

Anonymous.

El Misterio de los Reyes Magos.   This is a fragment, found
written on the blank leaves of a Latin MS., consisting of the
first part of the only extant specimen of old Spanish liturgical
drama.   Lidforss and Amador de los Rios place it respectively as a work of the close of 11th century, and first
half of 12th; a later editor, K. A. Martin Hartmann, ascribes
it to the end 12th or beginning of 13th century.   According
to the latter, the names of Caspar, Melchior, and Balthasar,
which are given to the Magi in the Spanish mystery, were
not in general use before the sixties of the 12th century;
he further demonstrates, by tracing the development of the
dramatic element through the Latin offices of Limoges, Rouen,
Nevers, Compiègne, Freisingen, and Orleans, of which the
three earliest belong to the 11th century, that the Spanish
fragment, a late offshoot of the Benedictine liturgy, which
reached Spain by way of Cluny, shows considerable advance.
Again the absence of diphthongs, usual in Castilian, considered
by former editors as further proofs of an earlier date, are by
Hartmann put down to the scribe, the MS. itself being no
older than the 13th century (*see* below, G. Baist, who
argues against the correctness of Hartmann's premises).
The metre varies from six to twelve syllables in a line.   The
speakers are the three kings, Herod, and Rabbis, Herod
calling for the learned in all branches of science to search in
their mystic books that he may know the truth, having just
heard the Magi's tale.   The MS. begins with one of the
Magi speaking—

> "Dios criador qual maravila
> no se qual es achesta strela
> agora primas la e veida
> poco tempo a que es nacida.
> Nacido es el criador,
> que es de la gentes senior."

Ed., "Ueber das Altspanische Dreikönigspiel, etc.," K. A. Martin Hartmann, 1879. *See* Gorra, *op. cit.*; "Romania," vol. ix., 1880 (Morel Fatio); "Zeitschrift fur Romanische Philologie," vol. iv., 1880 (G. Baist).   *MS.*, Toledo, Bibl. del Cabildo, vi., No. 8.

4   XIITH TO XIIITH CENTURY.

Anonymous.

Cronica Rimada del Cid, or *Cantar de Rodrigo*. "Put together in the last decade of the twelfth century, or the first half of the thirteenth, retouched in the fourteenth by Spanish *iuglares*" (Kelly). This chronicle is also known as "Leyenda de las Mocedades de Rodrigo," as part of it contains an account of the Cid's youth. In this rhymed chronicle, which is preceded by an introduction in prose, are the earliest elements of the apocryphal history of the Cid; it is apparently composed of old romances. The Cid is here simply known as Rodrigue, and "the work has in general a more feudal tone about it than the poem." It begins with a description of the quiet of the country and absence of war everywhere, and how the Conde don Gomes de Gomas did great injury to Diego Laynes, striking his shepherds and carrying off his sheep—

" El Conde don Gomes de Gomas à Diego Laynes fiso daño : Fferióle los pastores, e robóle el ganado " (vers. 280, 281).

Ed., F. Wolf, "Jahrbücher der Literatur," cxvi.   *MS.*, Paris, Bibl. Nat. Espagñ. 12 (Anc. fds. 9988).

5 Anonymous.

Vida de Santa Maria Egipçiaca (*aci comença la vida de Madona Santa Maria Egipciaqua*). "The first example in Castilian poetry of nine-syllabled verse" (Kelly). An early life of this saint had been written in the 7th century by

Sophronius. The Spanish version is taken from a French original. Santa Maria, having spent many years in sinful pleasures, was converted by a strange incident which occurred on the occasion of a religious festival at Jerusalem. Wishing to enter the church with other worshippers, she was confronted by angelic powers that held her back. She was so affected by this that she vowed herself to a life of penitence, and, retiring into the desert, where she was miraculously fed, she there spent the remaining forty-seven years of her life. Her body was discovered by a wonderful light emitted by it, and, as a crowning marvel, a lion came to the assistance of the Brother who had found her, and helped to dig her grave. *Ed.*, Janer, "Poetas anteriores al siglo xv.," 1864; Gorra, *op. cit.* See "Ueber die Quelle der altspanischen Vida de S. M. E.," A. Mussafia, 1863. *MS.*, Escurial, iii. K. 4. This MS. also contains "Libro de los Reyes de Oriente" and "Libre de Appollonia."

Anonymous.

Libro de los Reyes de Oriente. This title is somewhat mis-leading, as the poem chiefly tells the tale of the attack by robbers on the Holy Family, as they were fleeing into Egypt. One of the robbers takes them into the shelter of his cave; there they find the wife in trouble, owing to her little son being leprous; Mary takes the child and dips him in the water in which she has bathed the infant Christ, and he is immediately cured. This child reappears in after-life as the good thief on the Cross.

Poem begins—

> "Pues muchas vezes oyestes contar
> De los tres Reyes que vinieron buscar
> A Jhesuchristo, que era nado,
> Una estrella los guiando."

Ed., Janer, *op. cit.*; Gorra, *op. cit.* *MS.*, Escurial iii. K. 4.

Disputa del alma y del Cuerpo. The well-known dialogue, of which the oldest version is the Anglo-Saxon of the 10th century (*see* England, § 8). The Spanish is modelled on the six-syllabled poem in Anglo-Norman (*see* France, § 12).

The following specimen is taken from the edition given below—

"Un Sabado (o ex)ient,
dom(i)ngo amanecient,
ví una grant vision
en mio leio dormient."

The lines run on in the MS. without the divisions into verses. *Ed.*, Octavio de Toledo, "Zeits. f. Rom. Phil.," p. 60, 1878; R. Menéndez Pidal, 1900. *MS.*, Madrid, Archiv. Historia Nacional. oña. iv. 380.

Lupus me fecit de Moros is written at the close of the two poems which follow one another in the MS. given below. The poems have seemingly a connection with one another, but differ entirely in subject. The first is a love-poem "on the model of the French Pastourelle." A student, being in a beautiful garden, sees a damsel lamenting; the two recognise each other by the gifts which they had formerly exchanged, and a love-scene follows. In the garden stand two vessels, one of wine, one of water: into the latter a dove descends, interrupting the interview. This incident links the first poem to the second, which is a "Débat" between "Agua y el Vino." Gorra suggests that the poet had two separate poems at hand (Provençal or French), and thought it convenient to unite them in one composition. *Ed.*, A. Morel Fatio, "Romania," xvi. p. 364 ff. *MS.*, Paris, Bibl. Nat. Latin, 3576.

N.B.—In this same MS. are found the Ten Commandments in prose, which, according to Gorra, are perhaps the earliest specimen of didactic prose in Spanish. They are given by Morel Fatio, *op. cit.*

6 Gonzalvo de Berceo.

Berceo is the first Spanish poet of whom any authenticated details are known. He was born at Berceo, and educated,

31

as he tells us in the course of his poems, at San Millan. He is thought to have been born, at the latest, towards the close of the 12th century. Berceo's works, which are many in number, are all, with the exception of the "Alexander," of a religious nature; his legends of the Virgin have won for him the name of the Spanish Gautier de Coinci; Berceo did not rise to any great height of poetic inspiration; his aim was to reach the people, and to write as one neighbour might speak to another. His poems were written in the "cuaderna via" (stanzas, "coplas" of four monorhymed lines of fourteen syllables), which became the general metre for didactic verse throughout the remaining 13th and the 14th century. French influence is marked in Berceo's writings, and his "Alexander" was founded on French models.

Works—

1. *Vida de Sancto Domingo de Silos*, 777 coplas (stanzas of four lines).

2. *Vida di San Millan*, 489 coplas.

3. *Del Sacrificio de la Missa*, 297 coplas.

4. *Martyrio de Sant Laurençio*, 105 coplas.

5. *Loores de nuestra Sennora* (*Praises of Our Lady*), 233 coplas.

6. *De los Signos que aparesceran aute del Juico* (*Of the signs which will precede the Last Judgment*), 77 coplas.

7. *Milagros de nuestra Sennora* (*Miracles of Our Lady*), 901 coplas. (The greater number of these miracles are to be found in Gautier de Coinci, *see* France, § 48.)

8. *Duelo que fizo la virgen Maria el dia de la pasion de ser Fijo Jesuchristo* (*The Virgin's Lament over her Son*), 210 coplas. A canticle is introduced into this poem (lines 178–190) with the refrain of "eya velar."

9. *Vida de Sancta Oria, Virgen*, 205 coplas.

10 *Libro de Alexandre*, *see* below.

11. Three *Hymns*.

Mr. Kelly, "Hist. Span. Lit.," when comparing Berceo to Gautier de Coinci, writes: "Beside him (G. de C.) Berceo shines by his power of selection, by his finer instinct for the essential, by his relative sobriety of tone, by his realistic eye, by his variety of resource in pure Castilian expression, by his richer melody, and by the fleeter movement of his action."

Libro de Alexandre. Berceo took Gautier de Lille's (or
de Châtillon) "Alexandreis" as the basis of his poem, the
"Roman d'Alexandre" (*see* France, § 27) being also brought
into service; the result was a poem of nearly 10,000 lines.
As long as only the Osuna MS. was known, doubt was cast
on Berceo's authorship of this work, the name given at the
close of this being, as was generally thought, only that of the
copyist, and the dialect having a Leonese colouring; latterly,
however, a second MS. has been discovered (Paris) in which
we have the original end lines, which leave no doubt as to
Berceo being the author of the poem.

Concluding lines of Paris MS.

"Sy queredes saber quien fizo este ditado,
 Gonçalo de Berceo es por nombre clamado,
 Natural de Madrid, en Sant Mylian criado,
 Del abat Johan Sanchez Notario por nombrado."

Ed., Janer, *op. cit.*, from Osuna MS.; "Romania," iv. p.
790 (Morel Fatio). *See* "Romanische Forschungen," vi.
290 (Baist). *MSS.*, Osuna; Paris, Bible Nat. Espagñ.,
488.

The *Voeux du Paon*, by Jacques de Longuyon (*see* France,
§ 27), was another poem belonging to the Alexander cycle,
mentioned as existing in a Spanish version by the Marques de
Santillana, but now lost.

Libre de Apollonia (monorhymed quatrains of fourteen-
syllabled lines). There is discussion still as to where exactly
to place this poem, it remains undetermined whether it is
older or younger than Berceo's "Alexandre," with which it
has points in common. A. de los Rios places it at the end
of the first third, or the beginning of second third of 13th
century; De Puymaigre gives it a date anterior to Berceo's
poems, and only a little later than the *Cid*; Pidal places it
middle 13th century. (For the history of King Apollonius
of Tyre, *see* England, § 16.)

The "nueva maestria" mentioned in the following lines
has been thought to refer to the use of this new rhythm which

is different to that of the *Cid*, and the one used by G. de
Berceo and other poets up to the time of Hita.

> " En el nombre de Dios e de Santa Maria
> Si ellos me { guiassen   { querria
>   { guiasen estudiar { queria
> Co { n   { hun
>   { mponer { un romance de nueva maestria
> Del buen rey Apolonio e de su cortesia."

Ed., Janer, *op. cit.*; Pidal, " Revista de Madrid," 1840.
MS., Escurial, iii. k. 4.

Poema del Conde Fernan Gonzalez.[1] Written in " cuaderna
via," probably by a monk of San Pedro de Arlanza, who
imitated and borrowed from Berceo. The work has been
variously ascribed to the 12th, 13th, and 14th century. The
history of Fernan is preceded by account of Gothic invasion,
and fight at Roncesvalles. Fernan, who has been stolen as
a child and brought up among the mountains, comes at last
to a knowledge of his origin, and, in defence of his country,
takes up arms against the infidels. He is made prisoner by
the King of Navarre, escapes with the help of the latter's
daughter, and flees with her. The poem ends three years
previous to the death of the hero, who has meanwhile been
engaged in victorious combat with the enemy. Gonzalez,
who is celebrated in many poems and romances, was born
890–895, and died 970; the battle of Osma, which occurred
in 934, was the subject of the first division of the poem.
" He was to the North of Spain what the 'Cid' became
somewhat later to Aragon and Valencia " (Ticknor). The
poem corresponds in parts to the " Cronica General," the
latter supplying the link where the poem is defective : which
of the two is the earlier composition has been matter of
question, but the latest editor of the poem has decided that
it dates from 1250, or very little later. The poem on the
whole is prosaic in style, and, although ostensibly in the
" cuaderna via," strophes occur of three, five, and even a

---

[1] A prose chronicle of this hero is a later work written by Arredondo,
Abbot of San Pedro de Arlanza.

greater number of lines.   *Ed.*, C. Carroll Marden, 1904;
Janer, *op. cit.*   *See* R. Menéndez Pidal, "Estudios de Eru-
dicion Española," vol. i. p. 429 ff., 1899; and "Modern
Language Notes," xii. 196 ff.   *MS.*, Escurial, iv. B. 21;
a MS. formerly at San Pedro de Arlanza, and another in the
Bibl. Columbina at Seville have been lost sight of.

7 Two less important works of late 13th or early 14th
century were :

Las palabras que dixo Salamon.   These proverbs of Solomon,
written in the "cuaderna via," are ranked among the first
specimens of didactic Castilian verse.   A shorter version of
the same, known as *Proverbios en rimo del sabio Salomon,
rey de Israel*, was given by Fernan Martinez de Burgos in
his "Cancionero."   The oldest MS. copy assigns them to
one Pero Gomez, and A. de los Rios ascribes them to the
Pero Gomez who collaborated in the translation of Brunetto
Latini's "Tesoro," but Baist ("Grundrisz Phil. Rom."),
refutes the idea that this Gomez had anything to do with
them.   *See* Amador de los Rios, "Hist. Crit. Lit. Esp.,"
iv. pp. 52–57; "Romania," x. 300.   *MSS.*, Toledo, Caj.
17, No. 6 (oldest and most complete).   Escurial, f. iiij. 1
(only four strophes).   Madrid, Acad. Hist., the shorter
version from this MS. is given in the Spanish translation of
Ticknor's "History."

Vida de S. Ildefonso (cuaderna via), cir. 1313 (Kelly).
Written by a priest, a prebend of Ubeda, who tells us that
he had previously written the history of the Magdalene, a
work now lost.   The "Ildefonso," which takes Berceo as
model, is of slight literary merit, but is held in value as
indicating the growing taste for didactic writing, and therefore as being of interest in connection with the development
of Castilian literature.   *Ed.*, Janer, *op. cit.*   *MS.*, A late
MS., written as prose, was found in the Bibl. de San Martin
at Madrid.

8 Early Prose Writings.

An exposition of the Ten Commandments has already been mentioned as a specimen of early Spanish. Of the many annals extant, written in the vernacular, the three following are among the earliest—

Anales Toledanos, I. and II. These are merely short annalistic notices, skipping over several years at times, and often recording only one event in the course of a year. Some of the notices are longer, where possibly the writer had more personal knowledge of the event he describes.

Anales I. extend from the birth of Christ to 1219.

Anales II., after preliminary computation of dates from Adam, begins with Mahomet, and ends 1250.

(Specimen, 1118 : El rey de Aragon, con ayuda de Dios, è de sus Christianos, en el mes de mayo priso a Zarogoza de Maros, era MCLVII.")

A third division of the annals is of later date. *Ed.,* P. H. Florez, " Espana Sagrada," vol. xxiii. *See also* Gorra, "Lingua e Lett. Spanuola." *MS.,* Toledo; Madrid, Acad. Hist. Salagar. M. 35 (Anales III.).

Anales de Aragon y Navarra. From the Augustan period to 1196. Written in similar style to the above, "en era de mill cxxx. aynos morió mio Cid en Vallencia." *MS.,* Madrid, Bibl. Nac. D. 56.

Anales de Los Reyes Godos de Asturia, Leon, Castilla, Aragon e Navarra. A summarised translation of the Latin "Historia Gothica" by Rodrigo Ximenes, Archbishop of Toledo (1170-1247), who finished his work in 1243. These annals, written in a more advanced style from the above, start with the Deluge, and many popular traditions find a place in the course of the narrative. *Ed.,* Lidforss, "Sund. Universitets Arsskrift," vols. viii. and ix., 1871-2. *MSS.,* Toledo, Bibl. Cabildo, Caj. 26, No. 23. Several Spanish versions of this history are extant; the one contained in the MS. given is thought by de los Rios (iii. 419, 420) to be by Rodrigo himself, as the original text has been manipulated in a way which he thinks only the writer himself would have ventured upon.

9 To this period belongs also

Fuero Juzgo (*Forum Judicum*). A Castilian version of the "Lex Visigotorum," given to his Spanish subjects at Cordova in 1241, and later on to those of Seville and Murcia, by King Ferdinand. These laws are partly Roman and partly Gothic, translated from the Latin. "The primitive history of the Spanish idiom may be traced in this Castilian version. It will be seen how the degenerate Latin was transformed into the other idiom at the beginning of the 13th century." *Ed.* (Latin and Castilian), "La Real Acad. Española," 1815. A specimen of the Murcian Codex is given with one of the old illustrations. *MSS.*, Paris, Bibl. Nat., 256; Murcia; Toledo; Madrid, Bibl. Real.; Escurial (several); Lisbon, and Munich.

10 Alfonso X. of Castille, el Sabio (the Wise, or Learned), the son of Ferdinand iii., was born 1221 (1226 and 1230 are also given as birth dates), and died 1284. It has been noticed with astonishment that during a reign of such constant warfare, and with the cares of government on his shoulders, Alfonso x. was able to find time for study and for the production of literary works which have justly won him fame. He gave encouragement to every branch of literature, he himself being poet, astronomer, historian, and legislator. He called Arabic and other scholars to his assistance for the compilation of large works and for translations carried out under his auspices, he himself, we are told, overlooking what was prepared for him, improving the style, taking out what was superfluous, and adding prologues. According to the historian Mariana, he was the first to enforce the use of Castilian for all public documents; his own prose "was rich and expressive, and under him the language became a polished literary medium." "He was the soul of that admirable society of science and letters which sprang up in the midst of the obscurity of that age like a phenomenon." In the first year of his reign, 1252, were drawn up

Las Tablas Astronomicas (*Libro de las Tablas Alfonsies*), with the help of Arabic and Hebrew scholars. These astronomical tables were written to replace those of Ptolemy, and were held in high repute; although they display no great advance in astronomical science they give many corrections of the Ptolemaic tables. The learned collaborators were summoned by Alfonso to Toledo, where they carried on their work of correcting and compiling from 1258 to 1262, receiving forty thousand "escudos" from the King in payment. Other astronomical works were also undertaken under Alfonso's auspices, and these, "Libros del Saber de Astronomia" ("Books on the Science of Astronomy"), have been edited with the "Tablas" by the Real. Acad., 1863. The names of Christian, Hebrew, Arabic and Greek scholars who helped in preparing these works are given in this edition, together with an account of fifty-nine MSS. of astronomical works of real or spurious Alfonsine origin. *MSS.*, MSS. used for Real. Acad. ed.: Madrid, Bibl. de la Central. This is the Codice Alfonsi, thought to be the original MS. of Alfonso, beautifully illuminated with ornamental capital letters, and otherwise illustrated; Bibl. Nac. L. 3, L. 97; Real. Acad. Hist. Est. 26, grada 4a, D. No. 97; Escurial (copy of Bibl. Central); MSS. given by de los Rios (iii. 634); Bibl. Nac. L. 184, T. 273, K. 196; Escurial, iii. Q. 26.

In the same year appeared the

Espejo de todos los derechos (*a Mirror of all Laws*), in which is given an interesting insight into the uses and customs of the times, as of those of the Castilian Court, and further details concerning regulations in connection with the royal household. This work and the "Fuero Real" were introductory to his chief compilation, the "Siete Partidas." *Ed.*, "Real. Acad. Hist.," 1836 ("Opusculos Legales del Rey Alfonso el Sabio). *MSS.*, MSS. given in this edition: Escurial (several); Toledo; Madrid, Bibl. Real.; Real. Acad. Esp.; Monastery San Millan; Exemo Sr. Duque del Infantado (text taken from the last-named MS.).

Siete Partidas (seven parts). Alfonso's crowning work.

This body of laws was prepared under his supervision, his desire being to make a digest of the codes belonging to different territories, as discrepancies in these had given rise to grievances. It is thought that the moulding of the whole work, and the language, which is a model of style, are due to the King. The seven divisions treat respectively of Religion; the Relation between King, State, and Subjects; Administration of Justice; Matrimony; Contracts; Wills; Crimes and Punishments. *Ed.*, "Hist. Acad.," 1807. *MSS.*, The MSS. given in this edition are numerous. One at Madrid, in the Bibl. Nac., is a valuable codex, formerly belonging to the Catholic Kings. The greater number of MSS. are in the Bibliotheca Real and at the Escurial; others at Toledo, S. Yglesia; Silos, S. Domingo; Salamanca, S. Bartolomé; Madrid, Academia.

The other prose works, of which Alfonso expressly states that he was author, are the two "Chronicles" and "Septennario."

Historia, or *Cronica de España*, also known as *Cronica General*. In four parts. This is the first historical work of importance in Spanish. First part: From the Creation; Histories of Greece, Troy, and Rome. Second: The Goths in Spain. Third: Arab Invasion of France; Charles Martel; Charlemagne; Roncesvalles; Bernard del Carpio; Fernan Gonzalez; seven Infantas of Lara; the Cid; Princes of Spain to death of Ferdinand III. Fourth: Contemporary history.[1] *Ed.*, F. de Ocampo, 1604. (Notice of forthcoming edition by Menéndez Pidal.) *MSS.*, These are numerous, and show considerable variations; Escurial, X. 1, 4 (most correct); X. 1, 11; Y. 1, 2; X. 1, 7; Y. ij. 11; Bibl. Nac. Est. Ii.; X. 61; F. 42; Bibl. Real. 2, H. 3, 2, E. 4; Paris, Bibl. Nat., Spagn., 326, 12; B.M. Egerton, 289, etc.[2]

---

[1] The *Cronica General* of 1344 was a version of Alfonso's, with additional matter carrying the chronicle to Alfonso XI. In it was incorporated the *Cronica del Moro Razio* (§ 14).

[2] Thirty-one MSS. are mentioned by J. Facund Riano in his valuable address given before the Real. Acad. Hist. in Madrid, 1869; this "Discursos," however, has not been accessible in the London Libraries.

N.B.—The *Cronica particular del Cid*, which gives some of the earliest versions of the tales in connection with the Cid, is a more popular work, which is now generally thought to be based on Alfonso's "Chronicle." *Ed.*, Huber, 1844; Eng. trans. by R. Southey, 1808; First printed ed., 1512.

Grande y General Historia. In this work Alfonso desired to set forth all the great events that had happened since the beginning of the world to his own time, and the deeds of God, the prophets and saints, as well as those of kings and other men of note, of knights, and of ordinary people; in short, the whole history of humanity as it demonstrated the unity of the human race, not hiding the truth about anything. For this purpose the king had recourse to Greek, Latin, Hebrew, and Arabic works, both ancient and contemporary, among the latter being Viterbo's "Pantheon," the extent of his reading being enormous (*see* for a list of some other works used by him, de los Rios, vol. iii. p. 593). The translation of the sacred books form a nucleus of this history, added to, and amplified, from the vast sources of profane history mentioned above. The work is incomplete; as extant it consists of the following parts—

1st part. From Genesis to the end of the Pentateuch.
2nd ,, From Joshua to death of King David.
3rd ,, Other books of the Bible, including Psalms and Minor Prophets.
4th ,, Captivity, to Antiochus the Great.
5th ,, To Christ and the Apostles.

The work remains inedited (*see* J. Rodriguez de Castro, "Biblioteca Española," vol. i. p. 411). A few chapters are given by Menéndez Pidal ("Revista d. Archivos," 1902), in his edition of "Poema de Yusuf." *MSS.*, Escurial, J. Y. 4, 6, 7, 8, 9; j. Z. 11; iij. J. 12; j. x. 1, 2; iij. Y. 13; ij. Y. 22. Madrid, Bibl. Nac., 816; F. 1, contemporary with Alfonso (Rios).

N.B.—The earliest known translation of the whole *Bible* into Spanish, was made from the Latin of the Vulgate for King Alfonso.

First psalm as translated for Alfonso x.—

" Bien aventurado es el varon
Que non andudo en el consejo de los malos syn ley.
Nin estudo en la carrera de los pecadores
Nin en la sylla de nusimiento se assento."

See Böhmer, " Spanish Reformers," ii. 321, 1874, etc.

Septennario. A work at one time attributed to Alfonso's
father, but now thought to have been begun by the latter with
the help of his son, who completed it. A portion only
remains, sufficient however to show the encyclopædic scheme
which was intended to be carried out. The liberal arts,
pagan and Christian beliefs, are severally dealt with, the
accounts of these being prefaced by a eulogy of Ferdinand III.
and a description of Seville. *Ed.*, First nine chapters
(Toledo MS.), Burriel, " Memorias para la vida de San
Fernando." *See* J. R. de Castro, " Biblioteca Española,"
vol. ii., for the titles of the chapters as they appear in the
Escurial MS. *MSS.*, Escurial, P. ij. 20; Toledo, caj.
27, No. 14, the latter MS. contemporary with Alfonso.

Many works have been ascribed to Alfonso x. on no
sufficient foundation,[1] others again have been lost : it is thought
that the books on hunting and fishing may have been incorporated in the " Septennario." A book on chess, games of dice,
and draughts is still extant, written at his command, to
which it is thought that he probably contributed a considerable share.

Libro de los juegos, de dudos, y de tablas, 1321. *See* part ii.
chapter v., in " El Ajedrez " (general work on chess) José
Brunet y Bellet, 1891. *MS.*, Escurial, j. T. 6, with
miniatures.

We have also—

Libro de las Peidras. *Ed.*, 1881, " Lapidario del rey
D. Alfonse x.," being a facsimile of the Escurial MS., richly
illuminated, with coloured miniatures of birds, animals, and

---

[1] For one of these, " Las Querellas," *see* E. Cotarelo y Mori, 1898.

figures, ships, etc.; plates of the Zodiac with initial letters enclosing coloured scenes. *See* Castro, "Bibl. Españ.," vol. i. 104; de los Rios, vol. i. 104. *MSS.*, Escurial, I. h. 15 and 16, 13th century.

Alfonso takes no mean rank among the poets of his time, but his poetical works do not rightly belong to Spanish literature, as they were written in the Gallician tongue; *Cantigas de Santa Maria,* for which he also composed the melodies, are his chief compositions in verse. *Ed.,* "Real. Acad. Españ.," 1889; *see* L. A. Cueto, "Sobre las Cantigas," 1897. *MSS.*, Escurial, T. j. i., j. b. 2, the most complete; Florence, Magliabechiana; Toledo, Cabildo (the oldest MS.).

A work translated by Alfonso's commission, in which it is thought if he had a share at all, it was only a slight one, was

Calila é Dimna, cir. middle 13th century, better known under the title of the "Fables of Pilpay," or "Bidpay," the name of the narrator. The personages in it have the form of animals. The fables are of Indian origin, and were translated in the 6th century into old Persian, and later in Arabic; they then passed into several languages, finally reaching the West. The old Sanscrit version is lost, but there are traces of its origin in the Panchatantra, a collection of tales which authorities date from about the end of the 5th century A.D. compiled for the sons of a king of the Deccan. *Ed.,* P. de Gayangos, "Autores Españoles," vol. li. *MSS.*, Escurial iii. h. 9; iii. X. 4.

11 Anonymous.

Libro de los engannos é assayamientos de las mugeres (On the Cunning and Wiles of Women). MS. in possession of S. Conde de Puñonrostro, 15th century. Translated by order of the Infanta Don Frederigo, 1253, two years after his brother Alfonso had had the "Calila é Dimna" put into Castilian. *Ed.,* A. Bonilla y San Martin, 1904. The Arabic from which this was translated was a version of the old "Sindibad, or Tale of the Seven Sages" (Sindibad was the name of the prince's tutor). Researches concerning the old Book of Sindibad have been made by Domenico Comparetti (1869), from whose work the following account is taken. The family of popular works which have the "Seven Sages" as a common base may be divided into two groups: the Eastern and the Western. To the former belong all the MSS. in Oriental languages, and those in the European which are more or less free translations of the Oriental text. To the Western group belong: "Dolopathos," "Historia Septem Sapientum," "Erasto," and other various European texts of the Middle Ages. These two groups represent two widely divergent forms of the old Indian book from which they all derive. The Oriental texts have so many elements in common, in spite of their differences, that the original form is recognisable, and often the words of the old book, which is the common base, may be detected. With the Western group it is otherwise, for although the parentage, and the derivation of the narrative material, is evidently the same as that of the Eastern, all trace is lost of the actual book or of the narrative as originally written. The Oriental texts do not differ from one another as the Western differ from the Oriental, either in the form of the fundamental tale, or in the tales which are inserted, of which hardly four are common to the two groups. Oral tradition, the intermediary between Eastern and Western, probably accounts for this, as also for later divergences in the Western texts themselves.

The oldest mention of a "Libro di Sindibad" is in an Arabic writing of the 10th century.

Of the five oriental versions, the oldest is "Syntipas," a Greek translation, from the Syriac, end 11th century, by Michele Andreopalo. This version best represents the original. The Spanish version agrees the most closely in text with the "Syntipas." An English translation of Comparetti's researches, together with that of the *Libro de los Engannos* was published by the Folklore Society, 1882.

Several didactic works, of which the precise date is uncertain, but which are generally placed in the period immediately following Alfonso's reign, are among the earlier prose writings, the following being two of the oldest specimens in Castilian of this class.

Libro de los doce Sabios, published under the title of " Libro de la Nobleza y Lealtad," in Burriel, " Las Memorias para la vida del Santo Rey Fernando III." This work deals with the education of princes. *MSS.,* Escurial. B. ij. 7 ; Bibl. Nac. B.B. 52 ; C.C. 88.

Flores de Philosophia. A collection of maxims taken from Arabic and other works, which became as popular in Spain as similar compilations elsewhere. Intended as a guide to conduct for all classes, it is interesting from the insight it gives of social conditions of the age, being of greater linguistic than literary value. Both the above works are *ed.,* Knust, " Dos Obras Didacticas y dos Leyendas," pp. 1–83, 1878. *MSS.,* Escurial, & ij. 8 ; X. ij. 12 ; h. iij. 1 ; Madrid Bibl. Nac. BB. 33, and two fragments.

Libro de los buenos Proverbios, translated from the Arabic of Honein ben Ishak (cir. 809–873), who was born in Chaldea, studied medicine in Bagdad, and Arabic in Bassora. He was appointed physician to the Caliph, and held in high honour. He wrote original works on medicine, natural science, and philosophy, among them being the work of which the above is a translation. He also translated works by Hippocrates, Galen, and others (*see* Knust, 524, 525). *Ed.,* Knust, " Mittheilungen aus dem Escurial," 1899. *MSS.,* Escurial, L. iii. 2 (14th century) ; h. iii. 1 (15th century).

Bocados de Oro, " El qual conpuso el rrey Bonium rrey de Persia," translated from the Arabic of Abu'l-Wefa Mobeschir Jbn Fatik (11th–12th) century, who was born in Damascus, and lived in Cairo. He was a philosopher and physician, wrote philosophical and medical works, and formed a library ; his studies appear to have caused a separation between him and his wife, who, after his death, ran in with her female slaves and threw the books into a water tank in the courtyard (*see* Knust). *Ed.,* Knust, *op. cit. MSS.,* Escurial, e. iii. 10 (15th century) ; Madrid, Bibl. Nac. BB. 59 bis ; Bibl. Real, 2, F. 5 ; 1st edit. 1495.

A French version from a Latin text of these proverbs was written by Guillaume de Tignonville, one of Charles iv.'s counsellors (late 14th century). In 1450, Stephen Scrope, Squire, translated the French version for his father-in-law, John Fostalf, Knight (Harleian, 2266), and twenty-five years later Tignonville's text was again translated by Lord Rivers, and became part of the first book printed in England, Caxton's " Dittes and Sayings of the Philosophers," 1477, which was published in 1877, in facsimile, by Blades, in celebration of the fourth centenary of printing. A Latin version of these proverbs is in B.M. Add. 16906 and Arundel, 123.

The Pseudo-Cato *Disticha* were known at this time, and are referred to in the *Doze Sabios*. *See* " Two old Spanish Versions, etc." *Ed.*, R. Pietsch, 1902.

12 *Donzella Theodor.* At the close of the MS. (h. iij. 6) containing the " Bocados de Oro," is the tale of " Teodor, la Donsella," translated from the Arabic. The first edition was printed in 1540, and the tale continues to be read in Spain. The MS. of which the title runs "Capitulo que fabla de los enxenplos e castigos de Teodor, la donsella," differs somewhat from the printed editions, but the main tale is as follows : A merchant of Babylon buys a slave girl for a high price ; he teaches her, and she becomes learned in the arts and sciences ; being forced by circumstances to sell her, he offers her for a large sum to King Almançor. Being examined by three wise men, she answers with skill and far-reaching knowledge ; the King gives the money, and she returns to her old master. *See* Gayangos, Rivadeneyra, vol. xl. *MSS.*, Escurial, h. iii. 6.

13 END OF XIIIth CENTURY.

Sancho iv., son of Alfonso x., d. 1295. Sancho closes the list of writers of the 13th century.

Lucidario. An encyclopædic work which starts from the beginning of all things : " What was the first thing in heaven and earth ? " (" Qual es la primera cosa que ha en el cielo e en la tierra ? "), and the comprehensiveness of its instruction will be illustrated by stating that the whiteness of negros' teeth and guardian angels are both subjects dealt with by the author. *See* Gayangos, *op. cit.* (A table of contents of work and specimens.) *MSS.*, Madrid, Bibl. Nac. L. 131, T. viii. ; Private Royal Libr. (two MSS.); Private poss., Count Puñonrostro (Rios).

Castigos y documentos (*advice and instructions*) *para bien vivir*, written by the King for the benefit of his son, and, as one MS. states, in the year that the town of Tarifa was taken. At the close of the Escurial MS. is written, " E Nos el Rey don Sancho que fezemos este libro lo acabamos aqui en este logar en la era de mill et trezjentos et treynta et un años. Deo gracias." " This production, disfigured by the ostentatious erudition of the Middle Ages, is saved from death by its shrewd common sense, by its practical counsel, and by the admirable purity and lucidity of style that formed the most valuable asset in Sancho's heritage." (Kelly, *op. cit.*) *Ed.*, Gayangos, *op. cit.*; de los Rios, iv. 570 (extracts). *MSS.*, Escurial, iij. Z. 4 ; Madrid, Bibl. Nac., P. 23 ; S. 23 ; S. 1.

Sancho also commissioned the translation of Brunetto Latini's " Tesoro."

14 *Gran Conquista de Utramar* (*History of the Crusades*). This history is based on that of William of Tyre's (12th century) " Historia rerum in partibus trans marinis Gestarum," translated, as it is stated in MSS. and first edition from a French version of the same, the French original, however, not being known. Incorporated with the historical facts of the old work are the tales of Berta, and Mainet, and the legend of the Knight of the Swan, and portions of a Provençal poem on the taking of Antioch have been shown to be transferred to this Spanish history. (*See* G. Paris, " Romania," xvii., xix., xxii.) The introduction of many romantic elements has transfigured the intended history into a different style of work altogether. The oldest of the three MSS. assigns the work to Sancho iv.

as patron, and it is thought to have been probably undertaken under his auspices and finished about the beginning of the 14th century. *Ed.*, Gayangos, Rivadenenyra, 44. *See* Puymaigre, "Les Vieux auteurs Castillans," vol. i. *MSS.*, Madrid, Bibl. Nac. (2). One of these (J. I.) de los Rios speaks of as magnificent. Royal Private Library. First ed., 1503.

No other historical work of any considerable extent belongs to this period. A translation of a Latin history of the Holy Land is extant, and a *Cronica del Moro Razis*, translated from the Arabic.[1] *See* Gayangos, "Memorias leidas en la Acad. Hist.," t. viii., and R. Menéndez Pidal, "Cronicas Generales, etc.," 1898, p. 15, and 25 ff. *MSS.*, Toledo, Cabildo ; Escurial (Morales) ; Bibl. Real. 2 J. 6 (which supplies a gap in the two former MSS.) ; Bibl. Gayangos ; copy in Paris, Bibl. Nat., Esp. 213.

Alfonso xi. (1312–1350), another King to whom Spain owed the encouragement of national literature, commissioned several works to be carried out, among others a history to fill the gap between the *Cronica de España* and his own time. This was the beginning of a series of official chronicles.

15   XIVth CENTURY.

Prose underwent a quicker development in Spanish than in the other Romance languages. "Alfonso x. created Castilian prose. To a member of his family (*see* below) is due the honour of having brought it to perfection, of having employed it for genuinely literary works, and of having done for it what Boccaccio was later to do for Italian prose" (Puymaigre). Didactic works were much in favour during this century.

Don Juan Manuel, a nephew of Alphonso the Wise, b. 1282 ; d. 1348. As gifted, as indefatigable, and as fond of literary study as his uncle, Don Juan, like him, combined

---

[1] *See* note, *Cronica General* (§ 10.)

32

intellectual pursuits with a political life which his own disposition helped to make one of constant turmoil. Don Juan
is one of the chief among Spanish writers; his works come
under such different headings as philosophy, history, poetry,
and fiction. "Don Juan and the Archpriest Hita, unlike as
they are, both represent fresh beginnings, and should be read
side by side, if the age they lived in and the one that followed
are to be known and understood" (Baist). Some of this
writer's works are lost: *Libro de la Caballeria; de los
Engeños* (military machines); *de los Cantares; libro de las
Reglas del Trobar; libro de los Sabios.*

Don Juan's works are given in " Rivadeneyra," vol. li.

The extant works which are unquestionably authentic are—

Cronica abreviada. An abridged version of "Cronica de
España." *MS.*, Madrid, Bibl. Nac. F. 81.

N.B.—Most of the extant works are in Bibl. Nac. S. 34.

Libro del Caballero y del Escudero. A hermit, formerly a
knight, instructs a young squire in the arts of chivalry.
Occasion is taken to introduce encyclopædic matter of all
kinds, from God and the angels to non-animate creations;
astronomy, morals, and philosophy all finding a place. The
work is partly based on Ramón Lull's "Libro del orde
de Cavayleria." *Ed.*, S. Gräfenberg, "Romanische
Forschungen," vol. vii.

Libro de la Caza. A book on the Chace, recommended
by its Editor to those who take an interest in the subject, the
only one, as he states elsewhere, in which the Middle Ages
showed exactness of knowledge gathered from actual observation; Don Juan's book is in this respect still of value.
Ed., G. Baist, 1880, with notes, and appendix dealing with
the chronology of Don Juan's works.

Libro del Infante, or *de los Estades, de los Leyes.* Civil and
ecclesiastical laws, with reference to the different estates of
man. Of greater value than the previous work. *Ed.*, G.

de la Vega, "Bibl. Venatoria." *See* Benavides, "Memorias
del Rey Fernando iv. de Castilla," 1860, 444 ff.

Libro de los Castigos et de los Consejos, or *Libro Infinido*. His
own personal experience inspired this book of wise counsels,
addressed to his son.

Tractado sobre los Armas, that is, the arms that had been
conferred on his father, the Infant Don Manuel; a memoir of
his house, at the close of which he gives King Sancho's
speech before his death. *MS.*, An Escurial MS. L. ij. 6;
Rios mentions it as having of late years disappeared.

The best known and most widely read work by Don Juan
is *Conde Lucanor*, or, *Libro de Patronio*, or, *Libro de los
Exemplos*; the last title indicates the didactic intention of the
work.[1] Finished 1335. The framework is a dialogue
between Count Lucanor and his wise counsellor, Patronio.
There are fifty or fifty-one tales in all, each ending with
a moral or proverbial saying, such as, "If you are well
seated, do not rise," "If you do a thing in too great haste
it is only right you should live to repent it." "If you
must have enemies, have them as far away as possible."
Puymaigre, "Les Vieux auteurs Castillans," in summing up
Don Juan's style, writes, that it has conciseness and strength,
and a "naïveté sérieuse" which it is difficult to reproduce in
another tongue. "One recognises in his writings a remarkable
spirit of observation, an acuteness of observation which might
easily become satirical if a knowledge of mankind and the
experiences of a long life had not lent to it something of indulgence." "He tells his tales well, although at times there is
perhaps a monotony of tone." The work itself, he considers,
holds a peculiar and distinguished place in the annals of mediæval
literature, as one of the finest monuments of the age. One
marked feature of the work is the absence of coarseness, and
the delicacy with which difficult situations are handled, in
contrast to the usual indulgence of contemporary writers; "if,"
writes Puymaigre, "Juan Manuel does not enjoy the same
celebrity as Boccaccio, it is because he does not offer forbidden

[1] *See* Menéndez y Pelayo, "Origenes de la Novela," p. xc.

fruit to his readers." *Ed.*, Gayangos, 1860; H. Knust, 1900; E. Krapf, from the Puñonrostro MS., 1902. First done into English by J. Y. York, 1868. *See* also "The Moorish Marriage," a tale, given with Spanish original, by F. W. Cosens, 1867, similar to Shakespeare's "Taming of the Shrew." *MSS.*, Madrid, Bibl. Nac. S. 34: M. 100. Real Acad. Hist., Est. 27 gr. 3; E. no. 78; Counts of Puñonrostro. Earliest printed edition 1575.

The *Cronica Complida* is not universally considered to be the work of Juan Manuel. It is not in the Madrid MS. S. 34, but has been identified by some authorities with MS. B.M. Add. 30057. *See* Baist, "Romanische Forschungen," vii. p. 531 ff.

Juan Manuel, who had seen how often corruptions arose in the copying of MSS., had his works written out in a single MS., which he confided to the care of the Monastery of Peñafiel; this MS. is unfortunately lost; and some of the author's works, as already stated, have not been recovered.

16 Climente Sanchez de Vercial.

Libro de los Gatos (*Cats*), translation of Odo of Cheriton's "Narrationes." Book of short prose fables, which afford no sufficient explanation of the title, unless, as Baist suggests, it arises from the fact that one illustrated MS. of the work gives prominence to the Cat tales, which are comparatively few. The work is a satire on the highest classes of society and on the clergy, "it is better written than any other work of this class with the exception of Don Juan's writings." *Ed.*, "Aut. Esp.," *op. cit.*, li.
Kelly ("Tercentenary of Don Quixote") dates this early 15th century, and adds that "Speculum Laicorum," an adaptation of Cheriton's work, generally ascribed to John Hoveden, was translated about the same time.

Libro de los Exemplos, or, *Suma de Exemplos por A. B. C.*, end 14th or more probably 15th century (Menéndez y

Pelayo). *See* Morel Fatio, "Romania," vii. 481. *MSS.*, Madrid, Bibl. Nat.; Paris, Bibl. Nat. fds. Espagñ., 432.

N.B.—C. Sanchez de Vercial was also known as the author of "a kind of liturgical Manual," entitled "Sacramental," in great vogue till put on the Index by the Inquisition (Menéndez y Pelayo).

17   CYCLES OF ROMANCE.

Several romances were translated into Castilian from the French or Latin. To the Carolingian Cycle belong *El Cuento del Emperador Carlos Maynes de Roma, é de la buena enperatriz Sevilla, ser Mujer* (*see* de los Rios, v. p. 344); *Cuento muy fermoso del Emperador Otta's et de la Infanta Florence su fija* (*ibid.*, p. 391), from the French *Florence de Rome* (*see* France, § 54). Another variant of this tale of the virtuous and persecuted wife is given by Mussafia, "Wien. Akad. Wissensch." (Phil. Hist.), liii. To this cycle also belongs, *Historia de Enrrique fi de Oliva, rey de Jherusalem Emperador de Constantinopla*, corresponding in part with the tale of Sibilla (*ed.*, Soc. Bibliofil. Españ., 1871); *Flores y Blanca Flor* (*see* Giorn. Fil. Rom., iv. 159). An account of Charlemagne in the "Cronica General," which retains assonances, points to an early Spanish version of *Mainet*. (For further tales of this Cycle, *see* under *Gran Conquista de ultramar*.)

The Breton legends did not find so much favour on Spanish soil. The earliest mention of King Arthur is in *Anales Toledonus I* (Menéndez y Pelayo). Fragments of a primitive version of *Tristan* are preserved in the Vatican Library, and in the Madrid Bibl. Nac. The first complete text was the printed edition of 1501. The Bibl. Nac. also possesses a *Lançarote* (*see* A. Bonilla y San Martin, "Anales de la Literatura Española," 1904). Baist mentions a *Libro de Josep ab Arimatia* in a MS. of the 14th century.

Of the Troy Cycle there are extant two translations of Benoit de St[e] More, of which many MSS. exist (Escurial, H. 1, 6, etc.; and a Gallician version, Bibl. Nac. (Osuna).

See Mussafia, Wien. Akad. Wissensch. (Phil. Hist.), lxix. p. 39 ff.

Of independent romance there was a version of the Eustace legend (*S. Eustaquio*), and a translation of *Guillaume d'Angleterre* (*see* France, § 15), both of which are given by Knust, "Dos Obras didacticas, etc.," *op. cit.*

The chivalric romance was fully established in Spain in the 15th century. The *Amadis* was known to Ayala, but the only literary form in which it has come down is the Castilian text of Garci Ordóñez de Montalvo, of which the earliest edition dates from 1508. There is nothing to enable the language in which it was first written to be positively settled (*see* Menéndez y Pelayo, *op. cit.*, p. ccxxii.).

18   TRANSLATIONS.

Among these were Spanish versions of Plutarch's "Lives"; of G. delle Colonne's, "Historia Troiana" (Lopez de Ayala); Boethius; Isidor of Seville's "De Summo Bono."

19   POETRY.

Juan Ruiz, Archpriest of Hita. Little is known of the personal history of Juan Ruiz. He seems to have been born in the early 14th century, and his poems were written during an imprisonment of thirteen years (cir. 1337–1350), to which he was condemned by Cardinal Albornoz, Archbishop of Toledo. According to the Salamanca MS., the book was composed in 1343; in one poem, in which he complains of the hardship imposed on the clergy of Talavera by certain regulations of the Archbishop, he speaks of himself as an old man, and it is thought that he may have died not long after, as in 1351 another name appears as Archpriest of Hita (Clarus).

This poet has been compared to Rabelais, Cervantes, to Regnier, and to Chaucer. "It would be impossible to be more Spanish than Juan Ruiz, or more French than Rabelais, or to express in a more lively manner than these two writers, the national character of the *raillerie* of France and Spain"

(Puibusque). A profound and irresistible irony, peculiar, Wolf says, to the Spaniard, which spares not even himself, a drastic wit, an admirable description of character, gay sallies, happy combinations, animation and ease of language, and general poetical worth, have placed Juan Ruiz high in the rank of poets and story-tellers.

Libro de Buen Amor. J. Ruiz took his tales in great part from northern French sources. The variety of metre used by him "makes his book a veritable patter-book of rhythms in use before the 15th century"; the greater number, however, are in four-lined strophes. There is an indication in his work in "a kind of twelve-syllabled line" of the "Versus de Arte Mayor," which became a usual form later on. The mixture of devotion and immorality in the poet's writings was, as Puymaigre remarks, common at that time. Juan Ruiz hopes not to be misunderstood by his reader; and, to demonstrate the different ways in which the same words may be interpreted, gives a most amusing anecdote of two men, a Greek and a Roman, who converse together with signs (*see* Puibusque, *op. cit.*, p. 85). Personal adventures are mingled with the stories. *Ed.*, Jean Ducamin, 1901; "Aut. Esp.," *op. cit.*, lvii. *MSS.*, Madrid, Bibl. Real, 2. 1. 4 (known as Salamanca MS.), page facsimile given in last edition. Bibl. Acad. Esp. (Gayoso MS.), page facsimile given. Bibl. Nac. (Toledo MS.), page facsimile given. Fragments in Royal Private Library. Copies. First ed. 1790, by Sanchez.

20 Lopez de Ayala, b. 1332; d. 1407. Prose writer and poet. "L. de Ayala and J. Manuel were learned writers, brave soldiers, wise philosophers, and consummate moralists." L. de Ayala was born of an illustrious family. Serving at first under Pedro the Cruel, he finally enlisted on the side of Enrique de Trastamare, and fought for him with the French allies under du Guesclin against the English, who were led by the Black Prince. Taken prisoner, he remained in captivity in England for some time. Later on he was again taken prisoner by the Portuguese, at the battle of

Aljubarrota, but was not for so long in confinement. He died under Juan II. In prose he wrote the

Cronica de los reyes de Castilla (Pedro the Cruel, Enrique II., Juan I., and Enrique III.). "The analysis of Pedro's character was a new feature in historical work." *Ed.*, Rosell, Rivadeneyra, lxvi., lxviii., 1875, etc. *MSS.*, Paris, Bibl. Nat. Espagñ., 143 (Enrique III.). B.M. Add. 17906, Egerton, 294, 295; Add. 8684 (part only).

El Libro de las Aves de Caça. Finished in the Castle of Oviedes, in Portugal, June 1386, while a prisoner. All details are given of the birds of chace, plumage, diseases, etc. *Ed.*, Soc. de Bibliofilos, 1869. *MSS.*, Many MSS., Madrid, Royal Private Libr. (3); Bibl. Nac. L. 188, etc.; Bibl. Real Acad.; Paris, Bibl. Nat. fds. Espagñ. 292.

Rimado de Palacio (Court rhymes) (meaning of title uncertain, as use of word Rimado at that time doubtful—Baist). A didactic and satirical work written almost entirely in "cuarderna via," Ayala being "one of the last poets to use this metre with the Alexandrine." A prologue in verse is followed by paraphrase of ten commandments ("Luego en lo primero, Sennor, tu nos mandaste Adorar a ty solo, e por él tu nos vedaste," etc.). Then follow the seven deadly sins, seven works of mercy, seven works of the Spirit. Government, Court life, merchants, etc., are all dealt with in turn. The work dates from different periods of the author's life, "it is a lively protest against the morals of the 14th century."

21 *Poema de Yusuf.* Three hundred and twelve strophes in "cuarderna via," written in Castilian or Aragonese (Pidal says the latter) language and Arabic characters (reproduced in facsimile by H. Morf, 1883). The work is a specimen of the literature known as "Aljamiado" or "Aljamia"; Arabic words are occasionally introduced. Ticknor places the poem in the middle of the 14th century, after which time the strophe of four lines began to disappear; later scholars place it considerably less early.

"There is a marked similarity of tone between the "Historia de Yusuf" and its predecessors, the "clerkly poems." An oriental subject handled by an Arab gave the best possible opportunity for introducing Orientalism in the treatment; the occasion is eschewed and the lettered Arab studiously follows in the wake of Berceo and the other Castilian models known to him. There could scarcely be more striking evidence of the irresistible progress of Castilian modes of thought and expression. The Arabic influence, if it ever existed, was already dead."—Kelly.

Ed., R. Menéndez Pidal, " Revista de archivos, etc.," August, October, November, 1902 (with poem in Arabic, and Latin characters); Ticknor, " Hist. Span. Lit.," vol. iv. ; Janer, xv. p. 413, *op. cit.*   *MS.*, Madrid Bibl. Nac. Gg. 101. Acad. Hist. (Gayangos MS.).

Historia del Cavallero Cifar. First half 14th century. First independent specimen of Castilian fiction (Baist). It is not merely a knightly romance but a transition work, in which are mingled romance, didactic teaching, and hagiography (Menéndez y Pelayo). The title tells us that Cifar was for his virtuous deeds finally made King of Menton. It is a knightly romance, such as had come into being with the archpriest's narrative verse and Juan Manuel's tales. The work is in three parts, the first part alone being the tale proper. The tale is that of separation from wife and children, of child being carried off by wild beast, of happy reunion, etc., a Spanish version of the old Eustace legend (cf. Guillaume d'Engleterre, Octavian, Die Gute Frau). The author made use of a French original. The second book is composed of "Castigos" moral instructions given to his son, taken from old sources, the "Flores de Philosophia," being literally copied. The third gives an account of the wanderings—through imaginary countries—of the son, who became Emperor of Tigris.   *Ed.*, H. Michelant, " Bibl. Litt. Verein. cxii.," 1872.   *See* C. P. Wagner, " The sources of ' El Cavallero Cifar,' " " Revue Hispanique," x. *MSS.*, Paris Bibl. Nat. fds. Esp. 36; Madrid, Bibl. Nac. B.B., 136; Osuna, 140. Printed 1512, by Cronberger.

22   *Poema de Alfonso Onceno.* Based on a Chronicle of Alfonso xi. Written in " coplas redondillas." Baist says Castilian version of a Portuguese or Gallician original, by one whose name was perhaps Rodrigo Eannes, as the name Rodrigo Yanes occurs in the poem, but it is uncertain whether it signifies or not the author of the whole epic. The author gives his name in the course of the poem as Rodrigo (or Ruy) Yannez. The composition is better in its details than as a whole structure. The descriptions of battles are thought to bear indication of the work of a contemporary. "The last expression of the old Castilian epic" (Kelly). *Ed.*, Janer, "Autores Esp.," vol. lvii. ; Gorra, *op. cit.* *MS.*, Escurial, Y. iii. 9.

23 *La Danza de la Muerte.* Some lines in prose precede the seventy-nine strophes of twelve-syllabled lines (a b, a b b c, c b) of the Danza ; these are headed "Prologo en la trasledacion," which shows that the Spanish is a translation, or rather a version, of the original French. Beginning with an address by Death, a preacher then appears upon the scene, who exhorts all to good works, seeing that death is inevitable ; then death invites men and women of all ages and standing, in turn, to dance with him, beginning with two young girls. This poem is assigned to the 14th century (1360) by A. de los Rios and Wolf, but Seelman, and Baist ("Die Totentänze des Mittelalters," 1892) consider it a work of late, or middle, 15th century. It is unknown where or when the first "Dance of Death" was written, or painted, probably, it is thought, during the 14th century. The oldest known version is the earliest French text of the "Dance Macabre," which accompanied the painted "Dance" on the· churchyard walls of the Monastery "Aux Innocents," at Paris (1424 or 1425). Lydgate's free translation of this text for Old St. Paul's is the only complete English version extant ; some lines of verse are still to be seen in Salisbury Cathedral, remains of an old "Dance." Basle has the third oldest text, all others belonging to 15th or 16th century. The Spanish version was not accompanied with pictorial representation ; it points to an old French original, the "Dance" being known in France in the 14th century. The strophe of the Danza, not being found in other monuments of Spanish poetry, is assumed to have been faithfully copied from the French model (Seelman). *Ed.*, Menéndez y Pelayo, "Antologia, etc.," vol. ii. ; C. Appel,

"Beiträge z. Rom. u. Eng. Phil.," 1902. *See* W. Seelman, "Jahrbuch des Vereins für Niederdeutsche Sprachforschung," 1891. *MS.*, Escurial iv. 6, 21.

Rabbi Don Sem Tob (Santob de Carrion).

Proverbios Morales, in "redondillas." *Ed.*, L. Stein, 1900; Ticknor, "Hist. Span. Litt.," vol. iii. app.; "Autores Esp.," lvii. *MSS.*, Escurial, iv. 6. 21; Madrid, Bibl. Nac. Bb. 82. (The Escurial MS. is given as h. iii. 21, in "Revue. Hispan.," vii. 512).

24 Among the chief names of the 15th century are:

Enrique de Villena, grandson of Enrique ii. Poet and Prose Writer, b. 1384; d. 1434.

Lopez de Mendoza, Marques de Santillana, Poet, b. 1398; d. 1458.

Juan de Mena, spoken of as the "Prince of Castilian Poets," b. 1411; d. 1456.

Fernán Pérez de Guzman, a nephew of Ayala. Poet and Historian, b. 1378; d. 1460.

ADDENDA

P. 78.—*Floriz and Blauncheflur.* See under G. Huet, "Romania," xxviii. and xxxv., as regards an Arabic, rather than a Byzantine origin for this tale.

P. 112.—*Handlyng Synne.* Add. MSS., Harl. 1701; Bodl. 415; Dulwich, 24.

P. 161.—*Disciplina Clericalis.* The only known Middle English version of this work has lately been discovered by Mr. W. H. Hulme in Worcester Cathedral (see *Athenæum*, November 3, 1906). *N.B.*—The French version should have been put under the heading of Anonymous.

P. 180.—*Tristan.* The second volume of M. J. Bédier's edition of Thomas' work contains a splendid study on the formation of the Tristan legend from its Pictish origin, and a detailed comparison of the extant versions, showing their relationship to the primitive poem. That such existed seems now established; G. Paris finally gave his adherence to the belief in this archetypal work, which he, however, thought was an English poem. M. Bédier (p. 309) gives following dates: Thomas, 1160–70; Béroul, cir. 1180; Continuator, cir. 1209; Eilhart, 1190–1200; Gottfried, early 13th century.

P. 192.—*Gui de Warwick.* Add to MSS., Marske Hall, Yorkshire; Camb. Univ. Libr. (fragment). See also J. A. Herbert, "An early MS. of G. De W., sold in 1901 at Sir Hope Edwardes's sale," "Romania," xxxv.

P. 198. — Add to bibliography of Fableaux: J. Bédier, "Les Fabliaux; Étude de litt. populaire, etc.," 2nd ed., 1895.

P. 232.—*Poème Moral.*—This should be under "Anonymous."

P. 251. — *Boron de Hanstone.* Add : Stimming derives all the French versions from the Anglo-Norman, the latter representing a separate type, to which the Welsh is more closely allied than the Old Northern.

P. 269.—*Tombeur de Notre Dame.* Add : English translation by P. H. Wicksteed, 1894, 1900.

P. 325.—*Der Arme Heinrich.* Add : Paraphrase by D. G. Rossetti, 1905.

INDEX

511

33